After thirty-five years, the regime based on the Antarctic Treaty is more vigorous than ever. Here leading scholars of international law and international relations examine the effectiveness and legitimacy of this regime by asking two questions: are current changes affecting the ability of this regime to cope with major problems in the region, and how do those changes affect its standing among parties to the Treaty and in the wider international community? Individual chapters deal with Antarctic regimes for marine living resources, mineral activities, environmental protection and tourism. Throughout, a keen eye is kept on how these components interact and reinforce each other. This analysis is supported by in-depth studies of compatibility and tension between the Antarctic Treaty System and the international community at large. It also draws upon case studies of how domestic concerns and decision-making in four selected countries affect international cooperation in the Antarctic.

Governing the Antarctic

Governing the Antarctic

The effectiveness and legitimacy of the Antarctic Treaty System

edited by

OLAV SCHRAM STOKKE & DAVOR VIDAS

The Fridtjof Nansen Institute, Norway

CAMBRIDGE
UNIVERSITY PRESS

Published by the Press Syndicate of the University of Cambridge
The Pitt Building, Trumpington Street, Cambridge CB2 1RP
40 West 20th Street, New York, NY 10011-4211, USA
10 Stamford Road, Oakleigh, Melbourne 3166, Australia

© Cambridge University Press 1996

First published 1996

Printed in Great Britain at the University Press, Cambridge

A catalogue record for this book is available from the British Library

Library of Congress cataloguing in publication data

Governing the Antarctic: the effectiveness and legitmacy of the
Antarctic Treaty system / edited by Olav Schram Stokke and Davor
Vidas.
p.   cm.
Includes index.
ISBN 0 521 57237 1 (hc)
1. Antarctic Treaty system.   2. Antarctica–International status.
I. Stokke, Olav Schram, 1961–   . II. Vidas, Davor.
KWX70.G69 1997   341.2'9–dc20   96–26083   CIP

ISBN 0 521 57237 1 hardback

Contents

Concluding remarks   150

6   The effectiveness of CRAMRA   152
    CHRISTOPHER C. JOYNER
    Introduction   152
    The evolution of CRAMRA   153
    CRAMRA and the sovereignty problem   158
    CRAMRA and the proper-use problem   161
    The frailties of CRAMRA's effectiveness   167
    The legal status of CRAMRA today   171
    Concluding remarks   172

7   The effectiveness of the Protocol on Environmental
    Protection to the Antarctic Treaty   174
    FRANCISCO ORREGO VICUÑA
    Introduction: growing concern about the Protocol's
        effectiveness   174
    The emergence of the Protocol   175
    Protecting the environment?   189
    Removing the minerals issue?   197
    Completing or depleting accommodations?   199
    Concluding remarks: a positive but limited contribution   201

8   The regulation of Antarctic tourism: a study in
    regime effectiveness   203
    RICHARD A. HERR
    Introduction   203
    The problem of Antarctic tourism   204
    The actors in Antarctic tourism   208
    Toward regime responsibility for Antarctic tourism   211
    Sub-regime or *status quo*?   216
    Regime effectiveness and Antarctic tourism: an assessment   222

    PART IV: THE LEGITIMACY OF ATS REGIMES

    The legitimacy of ATS regimes: introduction   227
    DAVOR VIDAS AND WILLY ØSTRENG
    The shaping of normative and structural elements in the ATS
        regimes   228
    Legitimacy questions pursued in the case studies   231

Figures

Notes on contributors

BRUCE W. DAVIS is Deputy Director of the Institute of Antarctic and Southern Ocean Studies and leader of the Oceans Policy Program, Antarctic Cooperative Research Center, University of Tasmania. He is a former member of the Australian Antarctic Science Advisory Committee, and has a number of consultancy and advisory roles within government. He is co-editor with R. A. Herr of *Asia in Antarctica* (Canberra and Hobart: CRES and Antarctic CRC), published in 1994.

RICHARD A. HERR is a Reader in the Department of Political Science at the University of Tasmania. A political scientist from Duke University, he serves on the Antarctic Research Evaluation Group's sub-committee on Human Impact, and is author and editor of a number of monographs on international treaties, regional integration and ocean policy questions, with a focus on Antarctic and South Pacific affairs. Among his most recent books are *Asia in Antarctica* (co-edited with B. Davis), published in 1994, and *Antarctica's Future: Continuity or Change?* (co-edited with H. R. Hall and M. G. Haward), published in 1990. Dr Herr has been a consultant on Antarctic tourism and is currently an advisor to the regional governments of the South Pacific on institutional reform.

MARIA TERESA INFANTE is Professor of International Law at the Institute of International Studies and the Law School of the University of Chile, and Professor of International Law at the Diplomatic Academy of Chile. She has been a member of Chilean delegations to the Third UN Conference on the Law of the Sea and the Antarctic Treaty Consultative Meetings, and took part in legal expert groups on Antarctic affairs. Currently, she is President of the Chilean Society for International Law. Her publications address various aspects of Antarctic law and politics, including a study on maritime conventions in Antarctica published in the *German Yearbook of International Law* in 1992.

CHRISTOPHER C. JOYNER is Professor of Government at George-town University in Washington, DC. He has also taught at George Washington University, Dartmouth College and the University of Virginia, and served as Senior Research Fellow at the Marine Policy Center, Woods Hole Oceanographic Institution, and the Institute of Antarctic and Southern Ocean Studies at the University of Tasmania. He has published extensively on Antarctic law and politics, including *Antarctica and the Law of the Sea*, 1992, and *The Antarctic Legal Regime* (co-edited with Sudhir Chopra), 1988, both published by Martinus Nijhoff Publishers. His most recent books in this field are *Managing the Antarctic Commons* (University of South Carolina Press) and, co-authored with Ethel Theis, *Eagle Over the Ice: US Foreign Policy and Antarctica* (University Press of New England), both forthcoming in 1996.

FRANCISCO ORREGO VICUÑA is Professor of International Law at the Institute of International Studies and the Law School of the University of Chile since 1970, *associé de l'Institut de Droit International*, and President of the Chilean Branch of the International Law Association. He was Vice-President and President of Chile's delegation to the Third UN Conference on the Law of the Sea, Chilean Ambassador to the United Kingdom (1983–5) and lecturer at The Hague Academy of International Law. He has written numerous works on Antarctic law. He is author of *Antarctic Mineral Exploitation: The Emerging Legal Framework*, 1988, and editor of *Antarctic Resources Policy*, 1983, both published by the Cambridge University Press. His most recent book in this field is *El Derecho Internacional de la Antártida* (International Law of the Antarctic) published by Editorial Dolmen in 1994.

WILLY ØSTRENG is Director of the Fridtjof Nansen Institute, Norway, and Professor, Department of Sociology and Political Science, University of Trondheim. A political scientist from the University of Oslo, Østreng has been affiliated as Research Associate at the Institute of International Studies, University of California, Berkeley, and as Research Fellow at the Center for International Affairs, Harvard University. He is author and editor of numerous books and journal articles on northern security, resource management, and polar and ocean politics, including *The Antarctic Treaty System in World Politics* (co-edited with A.

Jørgensen-Dahl), published by Macmillan in 1991, and *International Resource Management: The Role of Science and Politics* (co-edited with S. Andresen), published by Belhaven Press in 1989.

OLAV SCHRAM STOKKE is Senior Research Fellow at the Fridtjof Nansen Institute, Norway, and Director of the International Antarctic Regime Project (1992–4). A political scientist from the University of Oslo, he has taught international relations at that University since 1983 and still gives graduate courses in fields such as transnational politics, resource management and polar affairs. Before joining the Fridtjof Nansen Institute in 1987, he had also been affiliated with the Norwegian College of Fisheries Science at the University of Tromsø. His research interest is international political economy, with special emphasis on regime theory applied to regional cooperation and joint management of natural resources and the environment. He has published numerous monographs and journal articles in these fields, the most recent book being *The Barents Region: Cooperation in Arctic Europe* (co-edited with O. Tunander), published by SAGE in 1994.

DAVOR VIDAS is Senior Research Fellow at the Fridtjof Nansen Institute, Norway, where he was Coordinator of the International Antarctic Regime Project (1992–4). He has taught public international law, as well as the law of the sea at the Faculty of Law of the University of Zagreb since 1984. He was a member of the Norwegian delegation to the XVII and XVIII Antarctic Treaty Consultative Meetings, and participated in informal meetings of the Treaty parties. His works on Antarctic law and politics are published in law journals in several countries, including the *German Yearbook of International Law* and the *Netherlands International Law Review*. His most recent book in this field is *Antarktik u medjunarodnom pravu i medjunarodnim odnosima* (The Antarctic in International Law and International Relations), forthcoming in 1996.

Preface

This book on international governance of the Antarctic is itself the outcome of a three-year collaborative venture – the International Antarctic Regime Project (IARP, 1992–4), involving eight authors from four different continents. Along with the Fridtjof Nansen Institute in Norway, which initiated and coordinated it, IARP has involved scholars in political science and international law from the George Washington University in the United States, the Institute of International Studies at the University of Chile and the Institute of Antarctic and Southern Ocean Studies/ Cooperative Research Centre at the University of Tasmania, Australia.

In this project, we have addressed the interplay of political and legal challenges and adaptations in Antarctic affairs in a series of carefully designed case studies. Importantly, the project allowed the research team to meet at regular intervals in a series of *workshops* over the project period, gradually and jointly hammering out the various components of an integrated line of argument. A very useful vehicle in this regard was a set of cooperatively developed *analytical templates*, which ensured that the four clusters of case studies on external pressures, regime effectiveness, regime legitimacy and the impact of domestic policy processes in certain Antarctic Treaty states were approached in closely compatible ways by the various authors.

Another notable feature of how this book came about is the continuous interaction, at separate sessions of each workshop, between the IARP research team and a large number of *practitioners* in Antarctic affairs. In this context, we are very grateful to a number of individuals who contributed views and insights in the course of the project workshops: at the *Washington*, DC, session, in October 1994, R. Tucker Scully and Raymond Arnaudo (the United States Department of State); at the *Charlottesville* (Virginia) session the same month, John Norton Moore (the Center for Oceans Law and Policy at the University of Virginia); at the *Hobart*

(Tasmania) session in April 1994, Andrew Jackson and Patrick Quilty (the Australian Antarctic Division) and Esteban de Salas and David J. Agnew (the Commission for the Conservation of Antarctic Marine Living Resources); at the *Santiago* session in November 1993, Jorge Berguño (Chilean Ministry of Foreign Affairs), Marìa Luisa Carvallo and Patricio Eberhard (Chilean Antarctic Institute), José Valencia, Luz O'Shea, Margarita Préndez and Mario Palestini (the University of Chile), Carlos de Toro (Joint Chief of Staff, Chilean Ministry of Defence), Juan Bastías (Chilean Air Force), Christián Jara and Guillermo Schiess (Chilean business community); at the *Punta Arenas* session the same month, Mateo Martinić and Sergio Laušić-Glasinović (University of Magallanes) and Pedro Barrueto (Chilean Air Force); and at the *Oslo* session in May 1992, Stein P. Rosenberg (Norwegian Ministry of Justice), May Britt Brofoss (Norwegian Ministry of Foreign Affairs) and Olav Orheim (Norwegian Polar Institute).

We are highly appreciative of two anonymous reviewers who provided lucid and very constructive suggestions on an earlier version of the manuscript; and also of the large number of others, scholars and practitioners alike, who in the course of the preparation of this book have generously offered comments and advice on various parts of the book. In addition, we should like to thank Susan Høivik and Ann Skarstad for language assistance, and Bente Ekeberg, Ivar M. Liseter, Stian Reklev and Anne-Christine Thestrup for the technical assistance they have provided.

The Chilean Air Force generously provided air services for our session on King George Island in November 1993. We are especially grateful to the Tinker Foundation, the Norwegian Ministry of Foreign Affairs, the Norwegian Ministry of Environment and the Norwegian Ministry of Justice, as well as the participating institutions, for providing the financial basis for the IARP project – thus making the appearance of this book possible.

Olav Schram Stokke and Davor Vidas

Abbreviations

AAT	Australian Antarctic Territory
ACAP	(Australian) Advisory Committee on Antarctic Programmes
ACF	Australian Conservation Foundation
ALP	Australian Labor Party
ANARE	Australian National Antarctic Research Expedition
APG	(United States) Antarctic Policy Group
APWG	(United States) Antarctic Policy Working Group
AREG	(Australian) Antarctic Research Evaluation Group
ARPAC	(Australian) Antarctic Research Policy Advisory Committee
ASAC	(Australian) Antarctic Science Advisory Committee
ASOC	Antarctic and Southern Ocean Coalition
ATCM	Antarctic Treaty Consultative Meeting
ATCP	Antarctic Treaty Consultative Party
ATS	Antarctic Treaty System
ATSCM	Antarctic Treaty Special Consultative Meeting
BIOMASS	Biological Investigation of Marine Antarctic Systems and Stocks
Budsj.innst.	Budsjettinnstilling (Budgetary Proposition to the Norwegian Storting)
CCAMLR	Convention on the Conservation of Antarctic Marine Living Resources
CEMP	CCAMLR Ecosystem Monitoring Program
CEP	Committee for Environmental Protection
CODEFF	(Chilean) Committee for the Defence of Flora and Fauna
COMNAP	Council of Managers of National Antarctic Programs
CRAMRA	Convention on the Regulation of Antarctic Mineral Resource Activities

DEST   (Australian) Department of the Environment, Sport and
                Territories
DFAT   (Australian) Department of Foreign Affairs and Trade
DOD   (United States) Department of Defence
ECOSOC   United Nations Economic and Social Council
EEZ   Exclusive Economic Zone
Environmental   Protocol on Environmental Protection to the Antarctic
  Protocol   Treaty
EPA   (United States) Environmental Protection Agency
FAO   Food and Agricultural Organisation
FIDE XII   Fundación para el Desarrollo de la XII Región de
                Magallanes (Foundation for the Development of the
                XII Magallanes Region)
GOSEAC   Group of Specialists on Environmental Affairs and
                Conservation
IAATO   International Association of Antarctic Tour Operators
IARP   International Antarctic Regime Project
ICAO   International Civil Aviation Organisation
ICJ   International Court of Justice
ICRW   International Convention for the Regulation of
                Whaling
ICSU   International Council of Scientific Unions
IDC   (Australian Antarctic) Inter-Departmental Committee
IEI   Instituto de Estudios Internacionales (Institute of
                International Studies, University of Chile)
IGO   Inter-Governmental Organisation
IGY   International Geophysical Year
IHO   International Hydrographic Organisation
ILET   Instituto Latinoamericano de Estudios Transnacionales
                (Latin American Institute of Transnational Studies)
IMO   International Maritime Organisation
INACH   Instituto Antartico Chileno (Chilean Antarctic Institute)
Innst.   Innstilling (Recommendation of a Standing Committee
                of the Norwegian Storting)
IOC   Intergovernmental Oceanographic Commission
IPCC   International Panel on Climate Change
IUCN   International Union for the Conservation of Nature
                and Natural Resources (now: World Conservation
                Union)
IWC   International Whaling Commission

LOS Convention	United Nations Convention on the Law of the Sea
Madrid Protocol	Protocol on Environmental Protection to the Antarctic Treaty
MARPOL	International Convention for the Prevention of Pollution from Ships 1973, as modified by the Protocol of 1978
MMC	(United States) Marine Mammal Commission
NEPA	(United States) National Environmental Policy Act
NGO	Non-Governmental Organisation
NOAA	(United States) National Ocean and Atmospheric Administration
NPI	Norsk Polarinstitutt (The Norwegian Polar Institute)
NSF	(United States) National Science Foundation
OAU	Organisation of African Unity
OES	(United States Department of State) Bureau for Oceans and International Environment and Scientific Affairs
OPEC	Organisation of Petroleum Exporting Countries
Ot.prp.	Odelstingsproposisjon (Norwegian Government Proposition to the Odelsting)
PATA	Pacific Asia Travel Association
PCC	(United States) Policy Coordinating Committee
PM&C	(Australian) Prime Minister and Cabinet
Protocol	Protocol on Environmental Protection to the Antarctic Treaty
SCALOP	Standing Committee on Antarctic Logistics and Operations
SCAR	Scientific Committee on Antarctic Research
SCOR	Scientific Committee on Oceanic Research
Seals Convention	Convention for the Conservation of Antarctic Seals
St.meld	Stortingsmelding (Norwegian Government Report to the Storting)
St.prp.	Stortingsproposisjon (Norwegian Government Proposition to the Storting)
TAC	Total Allowable Catch
UN	United Nations
UNCED	United Nations Conference on Environment and Development

UNCLOS III   Third United Nations Conference on the Law of
             the Sea
UNCTAD   United Nations Conference on Trade and
             Development
UNEP   United Nations Environment Programme
UNGA   United Nations General Assembly
US   United States
WMO   World Meteorological Organisation
WTO   World Tourism Organisation
WWF   World Wildlife Fund (now: Worldwide Fund
             for Nature)

Introduction

OLAV SCHRAM STOKKE AND DAVOR VIDAS

In the span of less than a decade, profound and rapid changes have occurred in the governance system arising from the Antarctic Treaty.[1] This book examines those changes, envisaged in Consultative Meetings by an expanding group of Consultative Parties to the Treaty,[2] against the backdrop of two basic questions: have those changes affected the ability of this governance system to cope with major problems in the region? And, what have the results been on its position among parties to the Treaty and in the larger international community? Thus, current developments in the Antarctic Treaty System are explained and evaluated by examining the *effectiveness* and the *legitimacy* of this international regime.

A SYSTEM UNDER PRESSURE

The Antarctic is a desolate, cold and stormy place; more so than anywhere else on earth. While in the past it was a region for exploration, sealing and whaling, currently the primary target of extraction is not natural resources but scientific knowledge. The frozen continent commands the curiosity and at times the fervent interest of millions of people around the world, most of whom will never in their lifetime come anywhere near it. Such wide interest has made its mark on the Antarctic Treaty System (ATS): especially in the past decade, developments in Treaty cooperation have been substantially affected by relations to non-members.

---

[1] The Washington Conference, at which the Antarctic Treaty was negotiated, was held from 15 October to 1 December 1959. The Antarctic Treaty was signed by Argentina, Australia, Belgium, Chile, France, Japan, New Zealand, Norway, South Africa, the Soviet Union, the United Kingdom and the United States, in Washington, DC, on 1 December 1959, and entered into force on 23 June 1961; text in *United Nations Treaty Series*, vol. 402, pp. 71ff.

[2] The various components of the ATS, including the role of Consultative Parties and Consultative Meetings, are presented in Chapter 2.

1

To a large extent, the three principal values of the ATS – peace, science and environmental protection – have served to uphold the external standing of the ATS in the international community. Let us take a closer look at those values, which are codified in the three fundamental principles of the Antarctic Treaty and its associated instruments.

First, the Antarctic Treaty of 1959 provides for *peaceful use* of the Antarctic by otherwise competing states:

Antarctica shall be used for peaceful purposes only. There shall be prohibited, *inter alia*, any measure of military nature, such as the establishment of military bases and fortifications, the carrying out of military manoeuvres, as well as testing of any type of weapon.[3]

In the same vein, the parties to the Treaty in Article IV agreed to put aside their competing positions on territorial claims to the continent, thus achieving an 'agreement to disagree' on the sovereignty issue.[4] And the prohibition of nuclear explosions and disposal of radioactive waste material in Antarctica was the first of its kind,[5] later emulated in treaties pertaining to other areas, including outer space and the deep seabed. Throughout the Cold War period, the Antarctic stood out as a notable breather in the East–West rivalry: international collaboration continued there despite dramatic fluctuations in overall relations between the two global power blocs. By the same token, in the early 1980s, the United Kingdom and Argentina maintained their cooperative Antarctic relations even while engaged in a direct military confrontation over the nearby Falkland/Malvinas Islands.

Science is the second principal value of the ATS. The Antarctic Treaty provides that:

Freedom of scientific investigation in Antarctica and co-operation toward that end, as applied during the International Geophysical Year, shall continue.[6]

Thus, the region has been dedicated to a joint quest for knowledge for the benefit of mankind.[7] The non-governmental Scientific Committee on Antarctic Research (SCAR) has played an important advisory role in the

---

[3] Antarctic Treaty, Art. I.
[4] Seven states have forwarded territorial claims in the Antarctic Treaty Area, i.e. south of 60°S: Argentina, Australia, Chile, France, New Zealand, Norway and the United Kingdom. Some of these claims overlap; and none of them has been recognised by non-claimants.
[5] Antarctic Treaty, Art. V, para. 1.
[6] *Ibid.*, Art. II.
[7] *Ibid.*, Preamble, paras. 3 and 4.

ATS since the late 1950s. Unique geomagnetic conditions, a location far from great centres of population and production, and the opportunities for analysing Antarctic ice, are only a few of the features which render the region particularly well suited for the study of phenomena in the upper atmosphere or geospace, as well as such global environmental issues as sea-level variations or climate change. It was a world sensation when, in 1981, scientists working in Antarctica could present persuasive evidence of a dramatic depletion of the protective layer of stratospheric ozone over the continent – later to be discovered elsewhere as well.[8]

The third principal value of the ATS, *environmental protection*, emerged gradually up to its codification in the 1991 Environmental Protocol to the Treaty:[9]

The Parties commit themselves to the comprehensive protection of the Antarctic environment and dependent and associated ecosystems and hereby designate Antarctica as a natural reserve, devoted to peace and science.[10]

Hence, the Protocol assembled the three principal values of the Treaty cooperation in a single provision.

Like peaceful use and scientific freedom, the rising prominence of environmental protection has been decisive for the reputation of Treaty cooperation. In the early 1980s, a group of third parties, comprising mainly developing countries and led by Malaysia, initiated discussions on the 'Question of Antarctica' in the UN General Assembly. When this matter was raised in the UN for the third consecutive time in 1985, a fragile consensus was broken.[11] In the years following, the Consultative Parties and most other Antarctic Treaty states limited their participation to a joint statement, made by one Consultative Party on behalf of all.[12] Beyond this, the arena was left to the Malaysia group and the General Assembly adopted a series of resolutions on the Antarctic, calling for broader involvement in the management of the region, especially a greater role for the UN.

---

[8] See J. May, *The Greenpeace Book of Antarctica* (London: Dorling Kindersley, 1988), pp. 60–1.
[9] The Protocol on Environmental Protection to the Antarctic Treaty was signed in Madrid, on 4 October 1991, and has not yet entered into force; text reprinted in *International Legal Materials*, vol. XXX, 1991, pp. 1,416*ff*.
[10] *Ibid.*, Art. 2.
[11] See UN doc. A/C.1/40/PV.48–54 (from 25 November to 3 December 1985).
[12] See a joint statement of states parties to the Antarctic Treaty, presented by Australia, in UN doc. A/C.1/41/PV.51, of 19 November 1986, pp. 11–21. This practice has since been followed by the Treaty parties.

This mobilisation must be seen in the light of more general calls for a new international economic and political order, including greater influence of developing countries in international institutions. But the interest of these countries had also been stimulated by a decade-long optimism regarding the abundance and availability of Antarctic natural resources. Indeed, speculations about the possible riches of a *Terra Australis Incognita* have marked the Antarctic discourse ever since accounts of Gonneville's and later Bouvet's journeys were issued in the seventeenth and eighteenth centuries.[13] Such speculations were revived when in 1973 the US scientific research vessel *Glomar Challenger* discovered gaseous hydrocarbons – methane, ethane and ethylene – in three of four exploratory holes drilled in the Ross Sea. Influential newspapers cited estimates of a US Geological Survey study, commissioned by the National Security Council, that in the seabed of the Ross, Weddell and Bellingshausen Seas alone, as much as 45 billion barrels of petroleum and 115 trillion cubic feet of natural gas may be found.[14] The impact of this news was magnified by the first 'oil crisis', which occurred the same year. Thus, minerals became a prominent item on the ATS agenda and gradually fuelled external interest in Antarctic affairs.

A decade and a half later, another Antarctic journey gave rise to headlines worldwide, but now the slant was very different. The Argentinian supply vessel *Bahia Paraiso* sank just off the Antarctic Peninsula, causing the first oil spill in Antarctic waters and demonstrating the vulnerability of seals, penguins and sea birds to accidents affecting the marine environment, especially in the breeding season. By that time, the scramble for Antarctic resources had largely yielded to environmental concerns. In the United States, a Congressional report had estimated that at current costs, profitable mining could not take place for at least three decades, and that no known mineral deposits of commercial interest existed in the Antarctic.[15] Equally, the second environmental wave in global politics had hit

---

[13] In a search for 'Gonneville's Eden', abundant in all kinds of riches, there is a measure of irony in Bouvet's discovery of a desolate island situated at 54°22'S and 40°15'E and named after him. This tiny island (57 km²) proved later to be the remotest island on earth, the closest land being over 1,600 km away. See 'An Elusive Paradies', in *Antarctica: Great Stories From the Frozen Continent* (Sydney: Reader's Digest, 1985), pp. 70–1.

[14] J. Spivak, 'Frozen Assets?', *Wall Street Journal*, 21 February 1974.

[15] See US Congress, Office of Technology Assessment, *Polar Prospects: A Minerals Treaty for Antarctica*, OTA-O-428 (Washington, DC: US Government Printing Office, 1989), pp. 17 and 20, which substantially toned down speculations about minerals riches in the Antarctic.

the ATS with particular force:[16] during the 1980s, Treaty cooperation became vital to a cluster of expanding and transnationalising green organisations, eager to link up environmental values with salient political processes. This interest may seem somewhat surprising, since, by normal standards, Antarctica is in fact remarkably clean. Locally produced pollution is minuscule: fewer than fifty stations are inhabited on a year-round basis by human beings;[17] and no more than 10–15,000 scientists, station personnel and tourists arrive on this vast continent in the course of a year, very few of them outstaying the short Austral summer.[18] True, visitors tend to seek out the narrow ice-free areas, poor in terms of biological diversity, competition as well as capacity to absorb pressure. But on the whole, the Antarctic is fairly resilient to current levels of human pressure: the icecap is already largely devoid of life, and the ocean space is a high-energy, fertile system with great buffering capacity.

Significantly, the environmental debate on Antarctica transcends local impacts. In addition to the practical role of the region in providing natural resources and knowledge about the global environment, the Antarctic is also a salient *symbol* of surviving wilderness. The remoteness of the continent is one reason for this, but even more the fact that the Antarctic is widely seen as a pristine area – a virgin still, in a global brothel.[19] Accordingly, many tend to see Antarctic developments as a litmus test of whether state leaders are prepared to halt the global spread of environmental decay. That perception can explain the intensity of negative reactions to incidents which, had they occurred elsewhere, probably would have passed without notice. One example is the controversy over the reported unauthorised killing of a number of penguins and pigeons in 1983 and 1984 during the construction of an airstrip near the French Dumont d'Urville base.[20] Because of this symbolic role, human activities in the

---

[16] An important catalyst for this wave was the *Report of the World Commission on Environment and Development 'Our Common Future'*, adopted in 1987 by the UN General Assembly (see UN doc. A/42/427 of 4 August 1987) and followed up by the 1992 UN Conference on Environment and Development, held in Rio de Janeiro.

[17] For details see J. C. M. Beltramino, *The Structure and Dynamics of Antarctic Population* (New York: Vantage Press, 1993).

[18] *Ibid.*

[19] The inaccuracy of this notion, given the long Antarctic history of overexploitation of seals, whales and fish, does not detract from its political force.

[20] See May, *The Greenpeace Book*, p. 136; the occurrence is also discussed in C. C. Joyner, 'Protection of the Antarctic Environment: Rethinking the Problems and Prospects', *Cornell International Law Journal*, vol. 19, no. 2, 1986.

Antarctic are evaluated not only by the actual pressure exerted on the environment but also by the attitude demonstrated.

As discussed further in Chapter 2, the elevation of environmental values in the ATS, along with other changes within the ATS (especially regarding participation and information flow), has served to weaken the basis for criticism against the ATS in the UN General Assembly. For the first time in ten years, a consensus resolution was adopted at the 1994 General Assembly session.[21] It expressly acknowledged the merits of the ATS in the governance of Antarctic affairs.

QUESTIONS PURSUED IN THIS BOOK

We have a two-fold ambition with this volume. One is to provide an in-depth analysis of major contemporary changes in the *Antarctic Treaty System in particular*, by narrowing in on forces shaping the effectiveness and legitimacy of that particular regime.[22] A second and equally important ambition has been to structure the study so as to nurture the wider debate on the effectiveness and legitimacy of *international regimes in general*. Those two goals have shaped the design of the book.

The sole chapter in Part I, *Analytical Framework*, provides an overview of how the core notions of 'international regime', 'effectiveness' and 'legitimacy' are understood in international relations and international law theory. Here the conceptual and theoretical basis for the rest of the book is laid by inquiring into how those phenomena can be assessed in empirical analysis.

Characteristic of most international regime studies is an issue-specific approach to governance.[23] In this book also, component parts of the ATS focusing on particular activities, like the arrangements established by the Convention on the Conservation of Antarctic Marine Living Resources (CCAMLR)[24] and the Environmental Protocol, are drawn out for particular scrutiny. While this permits deeper examination of those particular governance systems, it may also obscure how the effectiveness and legitimacy of a given regime depends on its placement in the broader system of international law. In this book, we try to avoid that trap by keeping a keen eye on the systemic nature of the ATS, or how its component parts

[21] UN General Assembly resolution 49/80, of 15 December 1994.
[22] See Chapter 1.
[23] See Chapter 1.
[24] The Convention was signed in Canberra, on 20 May 1980, and entered into force on 7 April 1982; text reprinted in *International Legal Materials*, vol. XIX, 1980, pp. 837*ff*.

interact and support each other, and by bringing out the way the ATS itself relates to the larger system of international law.[25] This is the purpose of Part II, *The Antarctic Treaty System in the international community*. Chapter 2 reviews the gradual development of the ATS as a system and its distinctive features in the international community. Particular attention is paid to the legal and political position of the ATS in that broader context, distinguishing two spheres where external pressure has been considerable: the normative one, related to principles and rules of ATS instruments, and the structural one, related to participation and access.[26] That overview is elaborated in the subsequent chapters. Chapter 3 provides a case study of *normative* pressure by examining how changes in the law of the sea, as compared with ATS developments, have affected the compatibility of the two; whereas Chapter 4 deals in greater depth with pressures in the *structural* sphere by analysing the changing role of non-governmental organisations in the ATS.

This wider international setting of ATS processes is important for the effectiveness and legitimacy studies comprised in the next two parts of the book. Four salient Antarctic issue areas are singled out for scrutiny – fisheries, minerals activities, environmental protection and tourism. In the four chapters of Part III, *The effectiveness of ATS regimes*, the impact of regimes existing or emerging within the ATS is assessed in terms of problem-solving in those four issue areas, focusing on CCAMLR, the Convention on the Regulation of Antarctic Mineral Resource Activities (CRAMRA),[27] the Environmental Protocol and the provisions pertaining to Antarctic tourism activities. In Part IV, *The legitimacy of ATS regimes*, the same regimes are assessed in terms of applicability and acceptance, which form the core of the regime legitimacy concept.[28]

An important observation emerging from the case studies of individual ATS regimes, is that their effectiveness and legitimacy result from a carefully restrained *adaptation* on the part of the Consultative Parties to

---

[25] For a review of international conventions adopted outside of the ATS and applicable to the Antarctic, see S. A Hajost, 'International Agreements Applicable to Antarctica: A Survey', in R. Wolfrum (ed.), *Antarctic Challenge III: Conflicting Interests, Cooperation, Environmental Protection, Economic Development* (Berlin: Duncker & Humblot, 1988), pp. 79–104.

[26] On the distinction between normative and structural components of a regime, see Chapter 1; for its application to the ATS case, see Chapter 2.

[27] The Convention was adopted at Wellington, on 2 June 1988, but has not entered into force; text reprinted in *International Legal Materials*, vol. XXVII, 1988, pp. 868*ff.*

[28] Like impact and problem-solving, applicability and acceptance are elaborated further in Chapter 1.

accommodate tensions among themselves or with external actors in a balanced way. In Part V of the book, *Domestic politics and ATS change*, we try to bring out whether this ability to reach agreement among themselves and adapt the ATS to new challenges is related not only to external pressure, as discussed in Part II, or issue-area politics, dealt with in Parts III and IV, but also to certain features of *domestic* decision-making processes in the states shaping this governance system. This aspect of Antarctic politics has not been given much attention in the literature. In four chapters we try to clarify the distinctive features of the Antarctic policy arenas of four selected countries – Australia, Chile, Norway and the United States – and examine whether those features affect the ability of the Consultative Parties as a group to cope with differences among themselves as well as external strains.[29]

There are important differences between the four ATS regimes discussed in this book. The regime for marine living resources, based in *CCAMLR*, is clearly coming of age: the Convention has been legally in force for more than a decade and the institutions envisaged by it are in place; scientific investigations are on the increase, and a steady flow of authoritative regulations are being produced. *CRAMRA*, on the other hand, is a coherent minerals convention which was put aside by the Consultative Parties soon after its adoption. CRAMRA was superseded by the third instrument carefully analysed in this book, the *Environmental Protocol* with its fifty-year ban on minerals activities in the Antarctic, save for scientific research. For its part, and more than the others, the ATS *tourism* regime is in a process of evolution. There is no certainty that it will ever emerge as a separate regime: today it is defined by several specific recommendations adopted by the Consultative Parties on the subject, along with the more general regulation set forth in the Protocol. The implications of these differences for our analysis of effectiveness and legitimacy are addressed in the Introduction to Parts III and IV respectively: among other things, they allow us to shed some light on the significance of coherence and legal force.

Also, the focus on those four issue areas permits us to follow the major transition in Antarctic politics from the 1970s up to today. The negotiation of CCAMLR was the first comprehensive attempt of the Consultative Parties – anxious not to aggravate the disputed sovereignty question – to

---

[29] For a discussion of the appropriateness of this selection of countries, see Introduction to Part V, pp. 323–30.

deal with *resource management* within the ATS framework.[30] With CRAMRA, the negotiation of which dominated the ATS agenda for most of the 1980s, that effort was extended to mineral resources. This spurred external interest in the ATS, and was important in bringing environmental matters to the forefront of Antarctic politics – a process which culminated with the adoption of the Protocol. The current deliberations on a more specific ATS regime on tourism imply that the Consultative Parties are again addressing the regulation of, rather than prohibiting, economic use of the Antarctic continent.

The four regimes discussed in this book are closely interrelated. To some extent, they have been conditioned by similar underlying circumstances, especially the sovereignty issue and the external criticism of the ATS; and to some extent, they reflect changes in those circumstances. With the exception of the Protocol regarding mineral activities, all four regimes refer to and support each other, and quite often norms or procedures from one regime may spill over into the design of another. Together, in their respective issue areas, they embody the three principal values of Antarctic Treaty cooperation.

---

[30] The 1972 Convention for the Conservation of Antarctic Seals was limited to seals; that Convention was adopted in London on 1 June 1972, and entered into force on 11 March 1978; see *United Nations Treaty Series*, vol. 1,080, pp. 175*ff*; text also reprinted in *International Legal Materials*, vol. XI, 1972, pp. 251*ff*.

PART I

Analytical framework

1

Effectiveness and legitimacy of international regimes

OLAV SCHRAM STOKKE AND DAVOR VIDAS

INTRODUCTION

Originating in French law, the term *regime* generally refers to 'a system of rules or regulations'.[1] It is often used when rules pertaining to a particular phenomenon have reached an adequate level of coherence. In international law, the term is used for concepts as different as the 'navigational regime', the 'continental shelf regime', or the 'Antarctic Treaty regime'. Traditionally, however, it implies two categories: the first distinguishes various spatial *objects* of international law.[2] In the law of the sea, for instance, the maritime and submarine space is divided into high seas, continental shelf, territorial sea, etc.; regimes pertaining to these objects include certain norms and differentiate between subjects of international law in terms of legal position – or their freedoms, rights, obligations and duties. A second category comprises special regimes for various types of *activities*, like fishing, navigation, or scientific research; and normative contents and the positions of actors vary depending on the object where the activity is performed. For both categories, the legal source of rights and obligations is not limited to international treaties, but comprises all relevant sources of international law.[3]

In international relations theory, the most widely used definition conceives of regimes as 'sets of implicit or explicit principles, norms, rules, and decision-making procedures around which actors' expectations con-

---

[1] *Black's Law Dictionary*, 6th ed. (St Paul, MN: West, 1990), p. 1,283.

[2] The usage of the term 'object' in this chapter should not be confused with the ancient *theory of (state) territory as object*. Rather, the term 'object of international law' is used here in accordance with Ibler's formulation, to denote all spaces accessible to humankind (both within and outside states' sovereignty), which international law differentiates by their respective legal statuses: see V. Ibler, *Rječnik medjunarodnog javnog prava* (Dictionary of International Public Law), 2nd ed. (Zagreb: Informator, 1987), pp. 201–2.

[3] I.e. also customary law, general principles of law and sometimes even unilateral acts.

verge in a given area of international relations'.[4] Since the early 1980s, this definition has been subject to considerable debate,[5] especially as to 'whether regimes are to be identified on the basis of *explicit rules and procedures*, or on the basis of *observed behaviour*, from which rules, norms, principles, and procedures can be inferred'.[6] The tendency today is to emphasise explicit rules; beyond this, regimes are differentiated as to whether they also achieve prescriptive status, in that actors regularly refer to these rules when commenting on behaviour, and whether in addition they give rise to a measure of rule-consistent behaviour.[7]

Hence, while they have evolved rather independently, the 'international regime' concepts used in international law and international relations theory are very close. Within specific *issue areas*, defined spatially and in terms of activity, regimes comprise a *normative* component of principles and rules, and a *structural* component assigning states and other subjects roles within the regime; sometimes also instituting procedures for collective decision-making. This book is concerned with the extent to which behaviour is conditioned by the normative and structural components of international regimes, and why this is so. We will approach these questions by turning to the concepts of effectiveness and legitimacy of international regimes.

EFFECTIVENESS OF INTERNATIONAL REGIMES

In economics, 'effectiveness' is usually defined by a relationship between the benefits of a given outcome and the costs associated with reaching it. In international law, 'effectiveness' may refer to the legal status of a rule, meaning that it is binding upon those addressed by it; or, when linked to implementation of rules, to their impact on the relevant factual situation. The latter understanding is close to the core of the effectiveness debate among scholars of international relations: while there is no consensus on a single definition, there is wide agreement that the effectiveness

---

[4] See S. D. Krasner, 'Structural Causes and Regime Consequences: Regimes as Intervening Variables', *International Organization*, vol. 36, no. 2, 1982, p. 186.

[5] For a recent overview, see M. A. Levy, O. R. Young and M. Zürn, 'The Study of International Regimes', *European Journal of International Relations*, vol. I, no. 3, 1995, pp. 267–330.

[6] R. O. Keohane, 'The Analysis of International Regimes: Toward A European–American Research Programme', in V. Rittberger (ed.), *Regime Theory and International Relations* (Oxford University Press, 1993), pp. 26–7.

[7] See O. R. Young, *Report on the 'Regime Summit'*, held at *Dartmouth College in November 1991* (Hanover, NH: Institute of Arctic Studies, 1991).

of international regimes must be related to their results or consequences.[8] Our understanding of regime effectiveness draws upon both international law and international relations theory.

Defining regime effectiveness

In this book, the effectiveness of a regime is understood as the impact it has on certain basic *problems* which it addresses – whether these problems are conceived of in economic, environmental or any other terms.[9] As regimes are social institutions and work through social agents, to state that a regime has had an *impact* implies that it has affected the *behaviour* of actors.[10]

The notion that international regimes have substantial independent effects is a contested one. Indeed, the literature on the subject has been met with constant criticism from political realists, some of whom argue that international regimes are merely epiphenomena reflecting predominant patterns of interest and power.[11] As we shall see, however, while considerations of power are by no means absent from an analysis of regime impact, the analysis will often benefit from including other facets of the situation as well. Nevertheless, the challenge from the realist tradition has clarified the need to establish plausible *causal* links between the regime and behavioural adaptation.

In addition to causation, there is an element of *evaluation* in the effec-

[8] For a discussion of various components of the regime effectiveness concept, see O. R. Young, *International Governance: Protecting the Environment in a Stateless Society* (Ithaca, NY: Cornell University Press, 1994); also A. Underdal, 'The Concept of Regime "Effectiveness" ', *Cooperation and Conflict*, vol. 27, no. 3, 1992, pp. 227–40.

[9] See also O. R. Young and M. A. Levy (with G. Osherenko), 'The Effectiveness of International Regimes', in M. A. Levy and O. R. Young (eds.), *The Effectiveness of International Regimes* (Ithaca, NY: Cornell University Press, forthcoming), which reports results from a collaborative project on regime effectiveness. One of the authors of the present chapter participated in that project.

[10] This is not necessarily borne out by *changes* in behaviour. The purpose of the voluntary moratorium on mining in the Antarctic in the period of negotiations for CRAMRA was precisely to keep actors from changing their behaviour and initiating mining activities. When discussing the impact of regimes, therefore, behavioural *adaptation* is the preferred notion, because it includes cases when the impact of the regime has been to impede undesired changes in behaviour.

[11] See, for instance, S. Strange, 'Cave! Hic Dragones: A Critique of Regime Analysis', *International Organization*, vol. 36, no. 2, 1982, pp. 479–97. The classical text in modern political realism is K. N. Waltz, *Theory of International Relations* (Reading, MA: Addison-Wesley, 1979).

tiveness concept. The key questions to ask are what kind of behavioural adaptation should qualify as relevant to effectiveness; and how much adaptation should be required before the regime can be judged effective. For both questions, it might be tempting to resort to goals expressed in basic documents, or by actors who took part in their negotiation or are subject to the regime. Formal goal attainment, however, can be an unreliable yardstick of effectiveness. Frequently, the objectives and purposes explicitly defined in international agreements are too ambiguous or incomplete to offer much guidance. And even when goals are operationalised in specific behavioural prescriptions, it could be misleading to confine effectiveness to a matter of compliance. Where these prescriptions are based on poor understanding of the issue area addressed, adherence to them may even generate consequences which counter the purpose of the regime.[12] There is also the issue of hidden agendas. For instance, although this is nowhere stated explicitly in the Convention's text, it is widely accepted that among the major problems addressed by CCAMLR was the perceived challenge from outside actors to the prominent decision-making position of the Consultative Parties in matters related to the Antarctic.[13]

That is why in this volume, it is not formal but real goal attainment – deduced from the major *problems* addressed by the regime – which forms the basis for assessing effectiveness. The key question is whether the behavioural adaptation caused by the regime has contributed significantly to solving those major problems. This does not remove any of the difficulties of specifying the contents and origins of a standard of evaluation. Rather, it acknowledges the fact that formal goal attainment is insufficient and urges the analyst to proceed with a broader and more in-depth assessment of the socially defined purpose of the regime. Such a specification of the basic problems addressed is not always a straightforward matter: *priority* may be required; there can be *divergences* between various actors in how they understand the problem; and *changes* may occur over time in that understanding. These dimensions should be incorporated in the evaluative standard, hence allowing judgments also on the adaptability of the regime to a changing social environment.

---

[12] See, for instance, A. Weale, 'Implementation Failure: A Suitable Case For Review?', in E. Lykke (ed.), *Achieving Environmental Goals: The Concept and Practice of Environmental Performance Review* (London: Belhaven Press, 1992), pp. 43–66. See also Art. 32 of the 1969 Vienna Convention on the Law of Treaties, *United Nations Treaty Series*, vol. 1,155, pp. 331*ff.*

[13] See Chapter 5.

To this it might be objected that such an effectiveness concept, unlike a ready comparison with formal goals, may produce arbitrary results, in the sense that different analysts might employ different definitions of the problem and subsequently reach different substantial conclusions about effectiveness. However, even traditional means of treaty interpretation, as codified in Articles 31 and 32 of the Vienna Convention on the Law of Treaties, are not limited to the treaty text itself, but require that account be taken of the context and circumstances of a treaty's conclusion, other relevant agreements between parties, their subsequent practice, etc. In general, it is crucial to have a well-grounded basis for evaluation out in the open in order to sharpen the effectiveness claim, by stating clearly the underlying understanding of the problem. In the following, we shall show how this effectiveness concept can be applied in the analysis of international regimes.

Assessing regime effectiveness

Since effectiveness implies causal impact, it cannot be observed directly. What we may discern is the formation of, or changes within, a regime and certain behavioural adaptation. But while international regimes may be important features of world affairs, actor behaviour is undoubtedly conditioned by several other factors as well. For instance, in the realm of environmental protection, decisions to install purification equipment may depend in part upon the financial ability of the firms in question or the availability of technological solutions at acceptable prices. They may even reflect adherence to another set of regimes than the one under scrutiny. Such other relevant processes must be taken into consideration when assessing the effectiveness of a particular international regime.[14]

In stating that a regime has had an impact, we imply that in a counterfactual situation without the regime, behaviour would have been different. The conventional way to render this statement plausible is to *compare outcomes* before and after the formation of or change in a regime, or across policy areas which are similar in important ways but vary in terms of regime endowment.[15] This approach is less helpful when there are many other ways, apart from regime impact, to explain differences in outcome –

[14] See in general A. L. George, 'Case Studies and Theory Development: The Method of Structured, Focused Comparison', in P. G. Lauren (ed.), *Diplomacy: New Approaches in History, Theory, and Policy* (New York: The Free Press, 1979), pp. 43–68.
[15] See for instance G. King, R. O. Keohane and S. Verba, *Designing Social Inquiry: Scientific Inference in Qualitative Research* (Princeton University Press, 1994), chapters 5 and 6.

and when there are few comparable units of analysis. Unfortunately, this situation is common in the study of international regimes: because such regimes are rather few in number and tend to operate in highly complex and usually changing circumstances, it can be difficult to isolate the impact of the regime.

Another, complementary approach to the control problem focuses on *process* rather than ultimate outcomes, and is often taken in single-case studies.[16] Here evidence for a particular causal account is built by bringing out the fine details of how an outcome came about through a sequence of events, each of which has a causal history less complex than the ultimate outcome and hence is easier to control.[17] Different mechanisms can be invoked when spelling out this process, accounting for how international regimes may affect behaviour. The mechanism most frequently resorted to is *reward* or punishment. For instance, when the effectiveness of resource management regimes is discussed, attention is usually drawn to the adequacy of monitoring or sanctioning provisions. The underlying idea is that for a regime to have an impact, it must render non-compliance more costly or adherence more beneficial than would otherwise have been the case. The indirect version of this mechanism may be just as relevant, since regimes can make it easier for members to enter into or adhere to regimes, by rendering negotiations a regular rather than an *ad hoc* exercise and by enhancing the flow of information and thus the confidence that others too are behaving cooperatively. Quite often, also, international regimes involve scientific activities which may generate *learning* regarding the consequences of current behaviour. This way, activities within the regime may affect perceptions about the conduciveness of that behaviour. Regimes can also, as in the case of the ecosystemic objective of CCAMLR, help states to specify new goals which are different from established ones though not necessarily incompatible. Learning may even refer to processes where regime members are gradually enabled to come to terms with differences in approaches and identify common ground. Other mechanisms can be elaborated as well:[18] while they will not be

[16] See R. K. Yin, *Case Study Research: Design and Methods* (London: Sage, 1989).
[17] See A. L. George and T. J. McKeown, 'Case Studies and Theories of Organizational Decision Making', *Advances in Information Processing in Organizations*, vol. 2, 1985, pp. 21–58.
[18] See Young and Levy, 'The Effectiveness of International Regimes', which elaborates a number of general mechanisms, including the above. These mechanisms imply different causal pathways between an international regime and the solution of the problem addressed. A similar but less stringent attempt is made in P. M. Haas, R. O. Keohane and

equally relevant in each given case, such a broader range of mechanisms can be useful for substantiating the impacts of international regimes on behaviour.

A mechanism given particular attention in this book is *authority*, to be dealt with in greater detail below when we discuss the legitimacy of a regime. Likewise, considerable attention will be paid to how international regimes can affect the *domestic politics* of states, by enhancing the ability of certain domestic groups to shape foreign policy at the expense of others. For instance, it is often argued that one reason for scientists to favour international environmental regimes is that regimes tend to include commitments to improved environmental monitoring and hence increased funding for scientific investigations.[19]

In many instances, several mechanisms may be at work at the same time, or subsequent to each other. Indeed, the effectiveness principle of international law suggests that once adhered to by relevant subjects – e.g., for reasons of reward or punishment – the authoritative force of a regime is enhanced. Similarly, there is much to suggest that for social learning to take place as a consequence of a regime, the regime must have been in operation for a certain period, so that activities within it may accumulate a track record and domestic agencies have a chance to change their routines.

Moreover, the mechanisms mentioned above are quite general in nature, and there is no one-way street between their operation and the effectiveness of the regime. On the contrary, in some cases, any new incentives introduced by a regime may impede rather than promote the solution of the problem addressed. For instance, if the regime leads to widening attention to an issue area, some actors may be tempted to emphasise more than before the symbolic aspect of their participation, focusing on the values signalled by their positions rather than the instrumental effects; and this may not always be conducive to collective problem-solving. Furthermore, a regime may encourage forceful domestic alliances not only among groups concerned about the problem addressed by the regime, but also among those oriented towards the potential costs of regulation. Hence, when activated, such mechanisms suggest possible causal processes mediating between the regime and behaviour; whether

M. A. Levy (eds.), *Institutions for the Earth: Sources of Effective International Environmental Protection* (Cambridge, MA: MIT Press, 1993).

[19] However – especially in the Antarctic context – environmental monitoring is not always a popular task among scientific organisations: see Introduction to Part III.

or not that behaviour is conducive to the solution of the problem must be assessed separately.[20]

Part III of this book employs both outcome- and process-oriented approaches when substantiating the impact of the ATS regimes. In assessing the effectiveness of these regimes, it is also necessary to decide whether those impacts are adequate contributions to solving the problem. This is ultimately a matter of judgment, but it is important to elucidate the basis for such a judgment by explicitly discussing what would constitute an adequate improvement in the status of the problem addressed by the regime. These specific requirements must be elaborated in the context of each case; in this volume, this is conducted in Part III. However, for the regimes discussed here, there are reasons to assume considerable similarities regarding the definition of the problem. First, certain political conflicts, like those between claimants and non-claimants, are present in all areas of Antarctic politics. Second, the regimes discussed in this book share an important feature in that they are all related to the management of natural resources and the environment, which tends to generate distinct controversies in the Antarctic context. And third, as emphasised in Chapter 2, the ATS is a coherent system, so that legal or political proposals in one issue area will always be considered in light of possible consequences in other areas.

LEGITIMACY OF INTERNATIONAL REGIMES

Legitimacy is a complex and multifaceted phenomenon, with different features in the domestic and the international spheres. The inquiry in this book concentrates on one of its facets only: the legitimacy of international regimes. Essentially depending on the persuasiveness of argument, legitimacy can easily be contrasted to power arrogance with its ultimate basis in sheer force. But it can sometimes be difficult to distinguish legitimacy from several closely related phenomena, like legality or justice.

The main questions of *legality* concern the legal validity of a rule and how the behaviour of those addressed shall be brought into conformity with it. At the outset, a legitimacy assessment too may be concerned with the question of legal validity, but more central is the question *why* subjects addressed by law choose to respect it and adapt their behaviour accordingly. Legitimacy depends on whether and to what extent those addressed

---

[20] In the Conclusions, we will focus on five specific ATS mechanisms which appear to *enhance* the effectiveness and legitimacy of ATS regimes.

by a rule see themselves as obliged by it. Crucial here is the measure to which such an attitude is conditioned by the quality of rules, and not by the power which created and supports them. Thus, while the legality of a rule relies on its legally binding force, the legitimacy of a rule depends on its *persuasive* force.

Nor is the legitimacy question identical with that of *justice*; legitimacy may clearly exist even in the absence of justice.[21] As observed by Koskenniemi, legitimacy 'is an intermediate concept whose very imprecision makes it available to avoid the attacks routinely mounted against the formal, but too abstract, idea of legal validity and the substantive, but too controversial, notion of justness'.[22]

Legitimacy in the international arena?

There is no agreed definition of international legitimacy; indeed, as Wight has noted, in the literature on diplomatic theory and international law, it is difficult to find broad discussions of the theory of legitimacy.[23] Even major reference books on international law lack any explanation of the notion of international legitimacy.[24] In attempting to explain why this matter is so seldom a focus of inquiry in international law, some question the appropriateness of exploring legitimacy in the international context, arguing that legitimacy conveys ideas of constitutional rather than international law.[25] On the other hand, the lack of a centralised legislator and

---

[21] For an extensive elaboration of this distinction see T. M. Franck, *The Power of Legitimacy Among Nations* (Oxford University Press, 1990), pp. 208–46; see also Koskenniemi's discussion with Franck in M. Koskenniemi, 'The Power of Legitimacy Among Nations. By Thomas M. Franck' (book review), *American Journal of International Law*, vol. 86, no. 1, 1992, pp. 177–8.

[22] Koskenniemi, *ibid.*, p. 175.

[23] M. Wight, 'International Legitimacy', in M. Wight, *Systems of States*, edited with an introduction by H. Bull (Leicester University Press, 1977), p. 153. In this connection, Jørgensen-Dahl more recently noted that 'the situation has not changed much in the intervening years'; A. Jørgensen-Dahl, 'The Legitimacy of the ATS', in A. Jørgensen-Dahl and W. Østreng (eds.), *The Antarctic Treaty System in World Politics* (London: Macmillan, 1991), p. 287. However, the process of change has been initiated: see especially Franck, *The Power of Legitimacy*.

[24] See major encyclopedias and dictionaries of international law such as Max Planck Institute's twelve-instalment *Encyclopedia of Public International Law* (Amsterdam: Elsevier, 1981–90), and *Parry and Grant Encyclopaedic Dictionary of International Law* (New York: Oceana, 1988).

[25] See V. Golitsyn, 'Reflections on the Legality of the ATS', in Jørgensen-Dahl and Østreng (eds.), *The Antarctic Treaty System in World Politics*, p. 343.

legal hierarchy suggests that, in the international arena, particular attention should be paid to reasons for compliance other than legal force. Hans
Morgenthau has noted that 'the great majority of the rules of international law are generally observed by all nations'.[26] A basic question,
therefore, is: 'Why do powerful nations obey powerless rules?'[27] As indicated in the effectiveness discussion above, distribution of capabilities and
calculation of self-interest are not the only answers to this question: *inter
alia*, certain rules are complied with because of obligation. But to induce
such obligation, international law tends to avoid extreme solutions,
because it has to rely on the harmonisation of interests. Therefore, the
adoption of rules in international law requires particular attention to the
quality of the rules and the *attitudes* towards them among subjects.

The qualitative and attitudinal aspects of rules are precisely the ones
emphasised by Thomas Franck, whose conceptual elaboration of legitimacy is the most advanced in contemporary international law.[28] According to Franck's definition, legitimacy comprises, first, 'a property of a rule
or rule-making institution which itself exerts a pull towards compliance
on those addressed normatively'; and, second, a 'perception of those
addressed by a rule or a rule-making institution that the rule or institution
has come into being and operates in accordance with generally accepted
principles of right process'.[29] We shall now turn to a specific aspect of
legitimacy in the international arena: the behaviour conditioned by the
legitimacy of international regimes.

Defining the legitimacy of international regimes

If one is ever to demonstrate the existence of the legitimacy factor in securing
obedience to norms, the global polis is where that elusive factor may be found,
isolated, and studied by the social scientist.[30]

Here lies the importance of international regimes to our understanding
of international legitimacy: by singling out specific issue areas within the

[26] H. J. Morgenthau, *Politics Among Nations: The Struggle for Power and Peace*, 5th ed. (New York: Alfred A. Knopf, 1978), p. 267.
[27] Franck, *The Power of Legitimacy*, p. 3.
[28] See in particular his seminal work, *The Power of Legitimacy*, as well as a more recent study: T. M. Franck, 'The Emerging Right to Democratic Governance', *American Journal of International Law*, vol. 86, no. 1, 1992, pp. 46–91.
[29] Franck, *The Power of Legitimacy*, pp. 16 and 19.
[30] *Ibid.*, p. 21.

'global polis', regimes *isolate* areas of potential or actual conflict and cooperation among states. Thus, they offer opportunities to identify and observe the operation of the 'elusive factor' of legitimacy, as well as other causal links between a regime and behaviour pursuant to its rules.

Legitimacy of an international regime can be defined as the *persuasive force* of its norms, procedures and role assignments. As such, legitimacy is *manifested* in a degree of positive attitude to the regime: a regime is legitimate when specific rules are accepted by various actors because they recognise the normative basis, the procedure through which they are adopted and implemented, and the positions of actors in terms of rights and obligations.

Two characteristics of regime legitimacy deserve special mention. First, unlike legality, the legitimacy of international regimes is a matter of *degree*. This ranking of legitimacy in degrees should be kept in mind when contrasting 'legitimate' to 'illegitimate': 'Legitimacy runs the scale from complete acclaim to complete rejection.'[31] Second, the legitimacy of international regimes is a highly *relative* phenomenon: it may vary considerably between and within groups of subjects and third parties, depending on their attitude towards the regime. It may also vary over time, due to changes in the nature of the problem, or subject matter, addressed by a regime.

It follows from this definition that the legitimacy of international regimes comprises both the quality of regime rules and the way they are perceived by relevant actors. Hence, the criteria for legitimacy of international regimes cannot be related exclusively either to the various components of the regime or exclusively to the sphere of attitudes. For analytical purposes, two broad categories of legitimacy criteria can be formulated as, first, the extent of applicability of the rules of the regime and, second, the level of acceptance of a regime by relevant subjects.

Applicability

As an objective category, applicability refers to certain qualities of the rules, procedures and roles set up by the regime. For international regimes, applicability has both an internal and external aspect. The *internal* aspect involves whether its rules are conducive to the solution of the problem addressed and internally consistent. Consistency of a rule in

---

[31] J. Hertz, 'Legitimacy, Can We Retrieve It?', *Comparative Politics*, vol. 10, no. 3, 1978, p. 320.

the ATS context may be understood as comprising two elements: determinacy and adherence to the normative principles of the regime.[32] However, sometimes each of these elements can be fully realised only at the expense of another. For instance, the sovereignty provisions in various ATS regimes are based on Article IV of the Antarctic Treaty, which is essentially an 'agreement to disagree' on the status of sovereignty claims in the region. Hence, a rule pertaining to the sovereignty situation in the Antarctic can adhere to the normative hierarchy of the ATS only by a low degree of determinacy. The most obvious illustration of this is the so-called *bifocal approach* contained in CCAMLR which helps to legitimise this regime not by adding determinacy but by reducing it, through a 'productive unclarity' on sovereignty which preserves the legal positions of both claimants and non-claimants within the CCAMLR regime.[33] Consistency sometimes requires such a cautious balance between clarity and adherence to a normative hierarchy. And in turn, this balance is likely to affect the other side of internal applicability: the conduciveness of provisions to the subject matter addressed by the regime.

To be *externally* applicable, the normative and structural components of a regime must be consistent with major developments in the international community. This involves placing a particular regime in the wider normative order of the international community, and seeing whether there is discord or harmony in their relationship. Equally, it involves a study of whether changes in decision-making structures in the wider international community are reflected in that particular regime.

Acceptance

The second criterion for regime legitimacy is acceptance. International regimes operate not in a vacuum, but within the broader international community. Therefore, account should be taken not only of parties to the regime, but also of third parties: like applicability, acceptance has both an internal and an external aspect. Among *parties* to a regime, acceptance is manifested by acknowledging, implementing and adhering to regime

---

[32] See Franck, *The Power of Legitimacy*, pp. 50–194; Franck, 'The Emerging Right', pp. 51–90. Franck explains determinacy as 'the literary property of a rule: that which makes its message clear'; for its influence on legitimacy, he argues that: 'The determinacy of a rule directly affects its legitimacy because it increases the rule's transparency and thus its capacity to pull members of the international community toward voluntary compliance . . . the more opaque and elastic the rule text, the less compliance pull it is likely to exert': Franck, 'The Emerging Right', p. 56.

[33] See Chapters 5 and 9 for more detail here.

provisions. It may also be demonstrated by parties' presentation and support of the regime in wider international fora or in interactions with other actors.

Third parties can be *addressed* by the regime – either in general terms, as in formulations about the 'interest of all mankind',[34] or more directly, when regimes differentiate between potential rights of third state.[35] Also, their rights or interests may be *affected* by the regime: Article X of the Antarctic Treaty, for instance, obliges parties to the Treaty to 'exert appropriate efforts' to ensure that no one engages in any activity in Antarctica contrary to the principles and purposes of the Treaty. With similar effect, Article 7 of the Protocol prohibits any activity relating to Antarctic mineral resources, except scientific research.[36] The level of regime acceptance by these external actors will be manifested through the strength and persistence of their attitudes, on a scale ranging from open criticism, implied opposition, indifference, acquiescence, acknowledgment or recognition, and, finally, accession to the regime.[37]

Awareness of these two dimensions of acceptance goes far towards explaining why the legitimacy of a regime may be lost even without any external challenge to it; likewise, that it may be retained or even strengthened in spite of strong external criticism.

An ideal picture of regime legitimacy, studied in isolation, would be composed of optimal applicability and overall acceptance. Often, however, one of them can be strengthened only at the expense of the other. This brings us to the question of how to balance applicability and acceptance when legitimising a regime under changing circumstances.

Assessing the legitimacy of international regimes

The evolution of regimes is conditioned by changes in a variety of social, economic, technological and other aspects of international life. From the first indications that a regime may be needed, a particular regime may

[34] Preamble, para. 1, of the Antarctic Treaty states that 'it is in the interest of all mankind that Antarctica shall continue forever to be used exclusively for peaceful purposes'.

[35] Art. XIII, para. 1, of the Antarctic Treaty introduces such differentiation, by stipulating that the Treaty shall be open for accession by any state which is a member of the UN, while other states may accede only if invited to do so, with the consent of all the Consultative Parties.

[36] On the latter example, and how this provision of the Protocol may affect rights of third states, see Chapter 3.

[37] In the last case the circle between external and internal aspects of acceptance becomes closed, due to the strength of external acceptance leading a previously external actor to join the regime.

pass through several stages: initiative, negotiation and adoption, then entry into force, and – in some cases – the loss of legal validity and derogation. However, a *de facto* decline of a regime in political terms does not necessarily imply the loss of legal force; a failed regime may remain, for a shorter or longer time, legally in force – thus properly dubbed a 'paper tiger'.

This only partial overlap of *de facto* and *de jure* is a promising field for exploring legitimacy, since the latter tends to vary over time and situations. The practical question, to be posed at each stage of a regime's 'life cycle', is: what regime features serve to enhance its legitimacy? In other words, how does legitimisation occur? This brings us beyond attention to 'static' qualities of rules and their impact on acceptance, and introduces the element of change in the assessment of a regime's legitimacy.

A process of change may be initiated by *challenges* to the regime, posed either by changes in the nature of the problem or by parties to the regime or third parties. Such challenges will put to the test the ability of a regime to *adapt* to a new situation. This ability is an important feature of regime legitimation. However, if a regime adapts to any challenge whatsoever, fully complying with the demands posed by that challenge, its legitimacy may actually be jeopardised: there are limits to how far adaptation will serve to legitimise a regime. These *limits to adaptation* will be different for each concrete regime.[38] In the ATS, for instance, the retention of decision-making authority within the Consultative Meetings, which require consensus, is important for maintaining the fine balance between claimants and non-claimants in Treaty cooperation. Any adaptation of the ATS which removed this equally shared veto would run the risk of jeopardising internal acceptance.

INTERLINKAGES BETWEEN EFFECTIVENESS AND LEGITIMACY

There is often a tendency to equate legitimacy with effectiveness of international regimes, arguing either that they are interchangeable or that one will automatically result in the other. The reason may be that, empirically, the two phenomena are often tied together in that greater effectiveness tends to enhance the legitimacy of a regime, and *vice versa*. Such co-determinacy is different from conceptual identity, however, and while plausible, it is essentially a matter of empirical research. While declining effectiveness may threaten the legitimacy of a regime in the long run,

---

[38] See Chapter 2, for distinct systemic features as limits to adaptation within the ATS.

there are often considerable time lags involved: legitimacy tends to imply a reservoir of goodwill which can be drawn upon in periods of poor effectiveness.[39] The opposite is true as well. A regime seen as declining in terms of external legitimacy may still have substantial impact on the behaviour of relevant subjects – paradoxically, sometimes even due to that perceived decline. For instance, there are clear indications that the external questioning of the legitimacy of the ATS in the 1980s actually galvanised cohesion among the Consultative Parties and enhanced their determination to tackle contentious problems among themselves.[40]

Indeed, there are two lines of thought regarding the interlinkages of legitimacy and effectiveness. First, in a *trade-off* perspective, some worry that the attempt to accommodate external challenges to the legitimacy of the ATS, especially by permitting wider participation and attendance at Consultative Meetings, would reduce the decision-making strength of the latter. Underlying this view is that actors less experienced and less committed to Treaty cooperation may be less flexible and adaptive than the group of original signatories of the Treaty. In other words, the trade-off perspective suggests that the Consultative Parties may be too adaptive to external challenges, selling off one of the main virtues of the ATS.

A second perspective, the *cumulation* thesis, emphasises instead the beneficial effects of a gradual inclusion of critics in the political deliberation. In this reading, wider involvement in Antarctic politics serves to transform critics of the ATS into loyal cooperating partners. As discussed further in Chapter 2, both the successful inclusion of India and China into the group of Consultative Parties, and the granting of observer status to the Antarctic and Southern Ocean Coalition of green NGOs and later tourism associations, tend to support the cumulation thesis. There is little doubt that this openness has reduced criticism, and so far it has not deprived Treaty cooperation of its decision-making ability.

Regarding the *distinction* between effectiveness and legitimacy of international regimes, we have seen that the former is essentially focused on the impact of a regime. The key question is the extent to which the regime matters in solving the problem for which it was created. Hence, attention is geared primarily at features of the factual situation addressed by the regime; we are interested in the ability of the regime to produce

---

[39] M. Dogan, 'Conceptions of Legitimacy', in M. Hawkesworth and M. Kogan (eds.), *Encyclopedia of Government and Politics* (London: Routledge, 1992), vol. I, p. 123.

[40] S. Harris, 'The Influence of the United Nations on the Antarctic System: A Source of Erosion or Cohesion?', in Jørgensen-Dahl and Østreng (eds.), *The Antarctic Treaty System in World Politics*, pp. 309–28.

particular consequences. Regime provisions and changes in them are interesting only to the extent that they allow us to reach conclusions about the impacts of regimes, either by comparing outcomes or tracing processes: they do not in themselves constitute effectiveness.

Legitimacy, on the other hand, is essentially focused on certain features of the regime itself, particularly whether it provides means which are conducive for realising regime objectives, internally consistent and not seriously challenged by competing regimes – and at the same time accepted by parties to the regime and third parties.

We note that conduciveness to the subject matter of the regime is essential to both effectiveness and legitimacy. Indeed, for effectiveness and legitimacy, the specific definition of the problem addressed by the regime provides a common basis for measurement. With effectiveness, this definition is juxtaposed with regime *impacts*; while in legitimacy studies, it is juxtaposed with the applicability and acceptance of its *norms and structures*.

DOMESTIC POLITICS AND INTERNATIONAL REGIMES

It is an ambition of this volume to relate the effectiveness and legitimacy of international regimes to legal and political processes in states participating in them. The specific studies involve the domestic Antarctic processes of Australia, Chile, Norway and the United States. Apart from the descriptive one, the purpose of these comparatively structured country studies is two-fold. First, they are meant to address a weak spot in the conventional analysis of international relations, namely the interaction between international and domestic processes. We want to describe such interactions in order to understand better changes in the ATS. Second, we will be drawing on information presented in those country studies when substantiating effectiveness and legitimacy arguments in this book.

It is not self-evident that domestic politics and law need to be taken into consideration when accounting for international affairs. In general, the public plays a far more modest role in foreign than in domestic affairs: unfamiliarity is pervasive, the level of awareness moderate, and the degree of inclusion of societal groups in the development of policy usually lower. Dealing with the security of the state, foreign affairs tends to be seen as requiring a highly stable and consistent policy which can be ensured only by centralisation: thus the tendency is to give the executive branch of government a privileged position in the foreign policy area. While this

is still the case in many states, societal actors have increasingly come to
see themselves as having high stakes in foreign policy decisions and,
hence, seek some influence over them. As discussed in Part V, this is true
for both interest groups and promotional organisations like those targeting environmental matters.[41]

For some, an additional reason to downplay domestic processes is the
belief that they are rendered unimportant by the anarchical nature of
international relations. According to this view, the foreign policy of a
state is so determined by its position in the international system that we
do not lose much insight by ignoring differences at the domestic level.[42]
And if foreign policy or international politics can be analysed without
reference to complex and meticulously documented domestic processes
in a large number of states, so much the better.

With these notes of caution, let us now see how domestic politics and
law may influence the effectiveness and legitimacy of the ATS. It may be
useful to visualise such an influence in two steps. First, domestic processes
may affect the specific foreign policy of the state in question, by limiting
the range of normative or structural arrangements which are acceptable
to that state. In turn, the compatibility and rigidity of these positions
will determine the collective ability of the Consultative Parties to reach
agreement on changes in the ATS.[43]

Two approaches may be distinguished in the analysis of domestic origins of foreign policy.[44] A society-centred *sectional-interest* approach

---

[41] See also the discussion in Chapter 4.

[42] For a discussion of this assumption, often made by political realists, see K. Goldmann,
'The Concept of "Realism" as a Source of Confusion', *Cooperation and Conflict*, vol. 23,
no. 1, especially pp. 5–7. Anarchy denotes a lack of central authority, which, according
to this line of thought, makes the international realm fundamentally insecure.

[43] For an early discussion of hjow those two steps may provide a basis for assessment of
the relative bargaining strength of actors and·the likelihood of agreement, see R. Putnam,
'Diplomacy and Domestic Politics: The Logic of Two-Level Games', *International Organ-
ization*, vol. 42, no. 3, 1988, pp. 427–60; see also P. B. Evans, 'Building an Integrative
Approach to International and Domestic Politics: Reflections and Projections', in P. B.
Evans, H. K. Jacobson and R. D. Putnam (eds.), *Double-Edged Diplomacy: International
Bargaining and Domestic Politics* (Berkeley, CA: University of California Press, 1993),
pp. 397–430.

[44] See also G. J. Ikenberry, D. A. Lake and M. Mastanduno, 'Introduction: Approaches to
Explaining American Foreign Economic Policy', *International Organization*, vol. 42, no. 1,
1988, pp. 1–14; and A. Moravcsik, 'Introduction: Integrating International and Domestic
Theories of International Bargaining', in Evans *et al.* (eds.), *Double-Edged Diplomacy*,
pp. 3–42.

focuses on efforts of sub-national actors to influence state attitudes to, e.g., proposed regime standards.[45] Here, attention rests on societal alignment patterns, and it is a feature of many contemporary political issues that this kind of activity takes place not only domestically but transnationally and internationally as well. As discussed in Chapter 4, governments tend to be interested in including non-state actors in the political process, in order to channel their expertise into the decision-making process or to impute in a manageable way relevant societal views, especially among those most strongly affected by a foreign policy decision. Instrumentally, this may heighten the sensitivity of the decision to societal opposition and support; and because such inclusion may also build commitment and loyalty, this may facilitate subsequent implementation.[46]

For its part, a state-centred, *institutionalist* approach focuses on formal or informal aspects of the state apparatus when accounting for the domestic origins of foreign policy. Particular attention is given to the level of centralisation, decision-making rules and procedures, as well as norms regarding inclusion of societal groups in the formulation of foreign policy. These features may vary over time and between issues, and there are interesting interactions involved here. In Part V, we will see that certain groups, such as scientists or some non-governmental organisations, enhance their domestic influence in the Antarctic policy arena by virtue of expertise acquired through following deliberations at the international level. And the other way around: the fact that environmental organisations were permitted to take part in domestic preparations for ATS meetings in a few key countries, like the United States and Australia was instrumental for their subsequent inclusion as observers in the consultative process. The study of domestic politics and law given in Part V of this book relies on both of these approaches, by relating sectional interests and decision-making patterns with the positions and roles of various states in Antarctic politics. In the Conclusions, we return to the second step of the analysis, by asking how those domestic patterns affect the ability of the Consulta-

---

[45] A recent illustrative example is the refusal of the US National Science Foundation (NSF) to relinquish total control over the US Antarctic Program, with the effect of impeding domestic implementing legislation for the Environmental Protocol. In turn, this stand of the NSF – if unchanged – has the effect of blocking domestic legislation, and thereby preventing US ratification of the Protocol: see 'National Science Foundation Stalls US Protocol Legislation', *The Antarctica Project Newsletter*, vol. 3, no. 4, 1994, p. 1.

[46] The more critical perspective on the latter function terms it cooptation: societal opposition is pacified by the state system and tied up to a given policy by their participation in its formulation.

tive Parties, striving to enhance the effectiveness and legitimacy of Treaty cooperation, to adapt ATS regimes.

SUMMARY

While regime effectiveness concerns how a regime has contributed to solving the problem addressed, regime legitimacy refers to its persuasive force, as manifested in the level of applicability and acceptance. Conduciveness is a common thread of these two concepts, as measured in the effectiveness case by comparing the impacts of a regime with certain standards of adequacy and in the legitimacy case by examining the quality of its provisions under changing circumstances. Effectiveness and legitimacy may support each other, but this cannot be taken for granted.

As to the dynamics of international regimes, an often neglected set of factors can be found at the level of domestic law and politics. In this book, we seek to bring out how deliberations in international regimes can be influenced by patterns of sectional interests and decision-making processes also at the national level. While the effectiveness and legitimacy of ATS regimes are discussed in Parts III and IV, Part V offers case studies of the domestic side of Antarctic policy-making in four selected countries.

PART II

——

*The Antarctic Treaty System in the
international community*

2

The Antarctic Treaty System in the international community: an overview

DAVOR VIDAS

INTRODUCTION

The Antarctic Treaty System (ATS) fits into the broad spectrum of institutions and mechanisms that exist within the international community. Moreover, the majority of the population of that international community – more than two-thirds of it – live in states which are parties to the Antarctic Treaty.[1] In view of these facts, it has been rightly noted that the dichotomy sometimes drawn between the ATS and the international community is a false one.[2] The fact of the Antarctic Treaty, however, justifies another view as well: the ATS, evolved on this basis, embodies its own *special* political characteristics. And from the legal point of view there is a division: some states have become parties to the Treaty, others have remained third parties. The special position of the Consultative Parties, and the method of operation of the entire consultative machinery, bear witness to the peculiarity of the ATS in the wider international community. Hence, what we actually have in the case of the ATS is a special, separate system, but nevertheless one anchored in the wider international community. The consequences of this situation shall be viewed through the prism of mutual impact.

This chapter analyses that problematic through an inquiry into two broad sets of questions. First, in relation to the notion of the ATS, we inquire whether the ATS really is a 'system', as its name implies, and, if

---

[1] The Antarctic Treaty was signed in Washington, DC, on 1 December 1959 by twelve states, and entered into force on 23 June 1961; text in *United Nations Treaty Series*, vol. 402, pp. 71*ff*. To date (7 May 1995), the number of states parties to the Treaty has increased significantly, numbering altogether forty-two states.

[2] R. T. Scully, 'The Antarctic Treaty as a System', in R. A. Herr, M. R. Hall and M. G. Haward (eds.), *Antarctica's Future: Continuity or Change?* (Hobart: Tasmanian Government Printer, 1991), pp. 96–7.

so, in what sense is the notion of system used in the ATS context. Second, in relation to the standing of the ATS in the international community, an exploration of the reasons for the relative isolation of the ATS from the wider international community in the ATS' early phase of development is made. The key questions posed are: how and why did the situation of relative isolation begin to change; and how and why did this development eventually change the mode of relationship between the ATS and the wider international community? The discussion leads to the concluding part of this chapter, demonstrating the influence of the systemic nature of the ATS on its component parts as well as on the System as a whole, and on its standing in the wider international community.

THE ANTARCTIC TREATY SYSTEM

What is this phenomenon called *the Antarctic Treaty System*? Does the systemic nature of the ATS influence the effectiveness and legitimacy of its components as well as of the System as a whole?

Let us commence with a brief inquiry into the bases and procedures which explain the evolution of the ATS, from the adoption of the 1959 Antarctic Treaty to its present level of development. The components of the ATS will be analysed, and thus the systemic nature of the ATS evaluated. Based on this, we will see that the ATS, being a system, embodies certain special characteristics which make it a distinct one in the international community.

From the Antarctic Treaty to the System

Claims to territorial sovereignty over parts of Antarctica, forwarded by several states in the first half of the century,[3] gave rise to disputes over sovereignty on the one hand,[4] and non-recognition of these claims on

---

[3] The United Kingdom (1908), New Zealand (1923), France (1924), Australia (1933), Norway (1939), Chile (1940) and Argentina (1942).

[4] Disputes over sovereignty have been especially acute between the United Kingdom, Chile and Argentina, whose claims partly overlap in the Antarctic Peninsula. In 1949, following a series of incidents in the Southern Ocean, the three countries exchanged the Tripartite Naval Declaration, agreeing to refrain from sending warships south of 60°S latitude during the 1948–9 season. All three countries renewed the declaration annually, until the entry into force of the Antarctic Treaty.

the other.[5] The success of the International Geophysical Year (1957–8) stimulated the idea of continuous international cooperation in scientific research in the Antarctic, as a mode of shelving the controversies that persisted in that region. The 1959 Washington Conference laid down two basic principles of the Antarctic Treaty: the dedication of Antarctica for peaceful purposes only (Article I) and the continuance of freedom of scientific investigation and cooperation (Article II). To make this possible, the Antarctic Treaty codified an 'agreement to disagree' on sovereignty claims (Article IV), safeguarding the *status quo* on the legal positions taken by claimant and non-claimant parties to the Treaty.

Built on this foundation, a unique, continuous cooperation among a group of states was established for the Antarctic. While avoiding the formation of an international organisation, Article IX of the Antarctic Treaty provided for periodic meetings of the representatives of the *Consultative Parties* to the Treaty, for the purpose of exchanging information, consulting and recommending to their governments various measures (known as *recommendations*)[6] to further the principles and objectives of the Treaty. In effect, by giving to a group of states the competence to commence a process of continuous formulation of Antarctic law and politics through the Antarctic Treaty *Consultative Meetings*, this provision contained the nucleus of what later came to be termed as 'the Antarctic system'.[7]

The growing complexity of the procedures, practices and instruments adopted accordingly on various matters has been reflected in the common vocabulary of Antarctic policy-makers; gradually, the term 'system' has become an adjunct to the name of the Antarctic Treaty. The term *Antarctic Treaty system* was thereupon codified by the Consultative Parties in 1979, in an international instrument, Recommendation X-1[8] of the Washington Consultative Meeting. Since this meeting was held on the twentieth anniversary of the conclusion of the Antarctic Treaty, the Consulta-

---

[5] The United States and the Soviet Union, while reserving their own rights, have expressly refused to recognise claims. No other country gave recognition to claims.

[6] Recommendations are directed at regulation of several areas of cooperation enumerated in the Treaty: see Art. IX, para. 1(a)–(f), of the Antarctic Treaty.

[7] This term was first used by an Argentine scholar and diplomat, Roberto Guyer, in his 1973 lectures at The Hague Academy of International Law: see R. Guyer, 'The Antarctic System', in *Hague Recueil des Cours*, vol. 139-II, 1973, pp. 149–226, at p. 156.

[8] See para. 2 of the Preamble of Recommendation X-1, on Antarctic mineral resources, employing the formulation of 'the principles and purposes of the Antarctic Treaty system'; text reprinted in W. M. Bush (ed.), *Antarctica and International Law: A Collection of Inter-State and National Documents* (London: Oceana, 1982), vol. I, p. 365.

tive Parties felt it appropriate to stress 'important achievements of the Antarctic Treaty system during its first two decades' as well as to underline the difference between 'the Treaty and the Treaty system'.[9] As of 1981, when an agenda item for the XI Consultative Meeting contained in its title 'operation of the Antarctic Treaty system',[10] a review of the operation of the ATS became a regular agenda item for each successive Consultative Meeting. The term 'Antarctic Treaty system' was soon after acknowledged by the United Nations, in the 1983 resolution of the General Assembly on the 'Question of Antarctica',[11] and thereupon used in the 1984 Report of the Secretary-General on the 'Question of Antarctica'.[12]

Eventually, in 1988, with the adoption of CRAMRA, the ATS defined itself as a 'system' for the first time in a treaty provision.[13] Soon after, in 1991, the Consultative Parties modified that definition in another international treaty, the 1991 Protocol on Environmental Protection to the Antarctic Treaty.[14]

While some authors have written that the 'Consultative Parties use the not entirely apt term "Antarctic Treaty system" or "Antarctic system" ',[15] others, on the contrary, considered it to be the apt term.[16] That dilemma will be addressed in this section in two steps: first, by an analysis of the components comprising the ATS; and, second, by an evaluation of how these components constitute the systemic nature of the ATS. The task is limited to shedding light on those elements

[9] See para. 17 of the Final Report of the X Antarctic Treaty Consultative Meeting, held in Washington, 17 September–5 October 1979; text reprinted in Bush (ed.), *Antarctica and International Law*, vol. I, p. 364.

[10] Agenda item 5, the full title of which reads: 'Twentieth anniversary of the entry into force of the Antarctic Treaty and examination of the operation of the Antarctic Treaty system': see Final Report of the XI ATCM, in Bush (ed.), *Antarctica and International Law*, vol. I, p. 435. A discussion on the operation of the ATS has since become a regular agenda item of each Consultative Meeting.

[11] See UN General Assembly resolution 38/77 of 15 December 1983, para. 3 of the Preamble and para. 1 of the text.

[12] See 'Questions of Antarctica', *Study Requested under General Assembly Resolution 38/77, Report of the Secretary-General*, UN doc. A/39/583 (Part I), of 31 October 1984, especially section III, on 'The Antarctic Treaty System in Practice', pp. 44ff.

[13] CRAMRA, Art. 2, para. 1.

[14] Protocol. Art. I(e), contains the definition of the ATS; see below, pp. 42–3.

[15] F. M. Auburn, *Antarctic Law and Politics* (London: Hurst & Co., 1982), p. 147. However, some more recent works of Auburn suggest a change of his criticism directed to the usage of the term 'Antarctic Treaty System': see, e.g. F. M. Auburn, 'Aspects of the Antarctic Treaty System', *Archiv des Völkerrechts*, vol. 26, no. 2, 1988, pp. 203–15.

[16] F. Orrego Vicuña, *Antarctic Mineral Exploitation: The Emerging Legal Framework* (Cambridge University Press, 1988), p. 22.

which justify regarding the ATS as a system in the wider international community. This should open the way for discussions in subsequent sections of this chapter.

The notion of system in the ATS context

First, a brief explanation is due in respect of the understanding of *system* in the ATS context. This word is used so widely and in such a variety of contexts that it is important to determine precisely what is understood as a 'system' for the purpose of our analysis.[17]

In the ATS, the term 'system' does not refer to the distinction often made between 'international system' and related concepts like the 'international society' or the 'international community'.[18] Nor is it associated with the specific conceptual apparatus applied in system analysis.[19] Rather, the usage is similar to that conceptualising international law as a system. As a systemic discipline, international law: (a) embodies certain *special characteristics* by which it may be contrasted with other branches of law;[20] and (b) its components are *mutually related* and coherent rather than merely a collection of loosely related norms.[21]

The first systemic property leads us to the question of the contents of international law as a system: what are the categories comprising the system? A direct answer is not easily found in the international law literature, but must be derived from a definition of international law itself: 'a structure of norms regulating relations among recognised subjects within

---

[17] As demonstrated by Buzan and Little, 'system' as a concept is curiously underdeveloped in the discipline of international relations: B. Buzan and R. Little, 'The Idea of "International System": Theory Meets History', *International Political Science Review*, vol. 15, no. 3, 1994, pp. 232–6. Nor is the situation much better in the theory of international law.

[18] See in general M. Hollis and S. Smith, *Explaining and Understanding International Relations* (Oxford: Clarendon Press, 1990), pp. 93–118.

[19] See especially D. Easton, 'An Approach to the Analysis of Political Systems', *World Politics*, vol. 9, 1957, pp. 383–400; D. Easton, *A System Analysis of Political LIfe* (New York: John Wiley, 1965); D. Easton, *A Framework for Political Analysis*, 2nd ed. (The University of Chicago Press, 1979).

[20] Note that Parry uses the term 'system' to draw a distinction between, on the one hand, international law and domestic law (as two different systems of law), and on the other, between international law and international relations: see C. Parry, 'The Function of Law in the International Community', in M. Sørensen (ed.), *Manual of Public International Law* (London: Macmillan, 1968), pp. 1–54.

[21] See J. Andrassy, *Medjunarodno pravo* (International Law), 7th ed. (Zagreb: Školska knjiga, 1978), p. 2.

the international community'.[22] This definition – *prima facie* a normative one exclusively – actually indicates a causal relationship among the two component categories: (a) *normative* components, comprising the norms by which the relations between subjects of international law are being regulated in a certain way; and (b) *structural* components, comprising subjects (actors) whose relations are being regulated and the procedures through which those relations are being performed.

The second systemic property shows how these components operate: the systemic nature of international law implies that it is able to provide at least general directions on how to solve problems which may arise *ad hoc*.[23] In other words, two characteristics of international law which bear witness to its systemic nature are: the strong interrelationship of its components, and an obvious intention towards comprehensiveness.[24]

Apparently with such an understanding of a 'system' in mind, Watts undertook an overall review of the provisions of the ATS, with the purpose of establishing:

whether they are to be regarded as simply a collection of individual and separate provisions, or whether (and if so to what extent) they together constitute a comprehensive regime for the area with a collective value greater than the sum of its various parts.[25]

The operation of the ATS as a system, accordingly, cannot be explained solely by interpreting its norms. These norms are being implemented as well as adapted, changed or amended through certain procedures. And, finally, these norms are produced by certain subjects, to which – in turn – they are applied.

Normative components of the ATS

The components of the ATS can be grouped into the normative and structural categories. Their interplay is important, since, on their own,

---

[22] *Ibid.*, p. 1. The choice of this definition of international law, among many others, is due to its two extraordinary qualities; it is the most condensed one which, despite its brevity, does not fail to capture the essence of the subject.

[23] *Ibid.*, p. 3.

[24] See on the same line V. Ibler, 'Sistem mirnog rješavanja sporova' (The System of the Peaceful Settlement of Disputes), in B. Vukas (ed.), *Novo pravo mora* (The New Law of the Sea) (Zagreb: Sveučilišna naklada Liber, 1982), p. 262.

[25] Sir Arthur Watts, *International Law and the Antarctic Treaty System* (Cambridge University Press, 1992), p. 291. Note that Watts uses the terms 'regime' and 'system' interchangeably: see especially *ibid.*, p. 292.

neither of these categories can fully explain the systemic nature of the ATS.[26]

A number of studies are based on definitions of the ATS which *enumerate* its normative components. While some among such definitions of the ATS are limited to the Antarctic Treaty and several international conventions adopted by the Consultative Parties,[27] others add the recommendations of the Consultative Meetings,[28] sometimes also the 1964 Agreed Measures for the Conservation of Antarctic Fauna and Flora (approved as Recommendation III-8),[29] results of Meetings of Experts and the decisions of Special Consultative Meetings,[30] effects of the work of the Scientific Committee on Antarctic Research[31] (or even SCAR itself)[32] and – finally – sometimes also drafts of international instruments evolving through negotiations among the Consultative Parties.[33] Others have instead used shorter formulations, defining the ATS as 'comprising a range of multilateral arrangements centred upon the 1959 Antarctic Treaty',[34] or

[26] This is actually the main deficiency of definitions of the ATS relying on one category of components only: see some examples below, pp. 41–2.
[27] E.g., L. A. Kimball, 'The Role of Non-Governmental Organizations in Antarctic Affairs', in C. C. Joyner and S. K. Chopra (eds.), *The Antarctic Legal Regime* (Dordrecht: Martinus Nijhoff, 1988), p. 33 and note at p. 57; also C. C. Joyner, *Antarctica and the Law of the Sea* (Dordrecht: Martinus Nijhoff, 1992), p. 94 (Joyner lists the Antarctic Treaty, the Seals Convention, CCAMLR, CRAMRA and the Protocol as the main components comprising the ATS).
[28] E.g., J. A. Heap (ed.), *Handbook of the Antarctic Treaty System*, 8th ed. (Washington, DC: US Department of State, 1994), p. 8; also J. Rowland, 'The Treaty Regime and the Politics of the Consultative Parties', in Joyner and Chopra (eds.), *The Antarctic Legal regime*, p. 11; R. T. Scully, 'The Evolution of the Antarctic Treaty System – The Institutional Perspective, in *Antarctic Treaty System: An Assessment* (Washington, DC: National Academy Press, 1986), p. 391.
[29] C. C. Joyner, 'The Antarctic Legal Regime: An Introduction', in Joyner and Chopra (eds.), *The Antarctic Legal Regime*, p. 3; L. Migliorino, 'The New Law of the Sea and the Deep Seabed of the Antarctic Region', in F. Francioni and T. Scovazzi (eds.), *International Law for Antarctica* (Milano: Giuffrè Editore, 1987), p. 384.
[30] Heap (ed.), *Handbook*, p. 8.
[31] *Ibid.*
[32] Joyner, 'An Introduction', p. 3; Kimball notes that 'many Antarctic experts also include . . . SCAR as an integral component of the ATS'; Kimball, 'The Role of NGOs', p. 57, note 1; also L. A. Kimball, 'The Antarctic Treaty System', *Oceanus*, vol. 31, no. 2, 1988, pp. 15–16.
[33] E.g., in a study written in 1986, Migliorino listed 'the 1984 Draft Articles for the Antarctic Mineral Resources Regime' as a component of the ATS; Migliorino, 'The New Law', p. 384; similarly Joyner, 'An Introduction', p. 3 and note 13 at p. 7.
[34] P. J. Beck, 'A New Polar Factor in International Relations', *The World Today*, vol. 45, no. 4, 1989, p. 65.

'the Antarctic Treaty and its supporting agreements and arrangements'.[35]

Those definitions demonstrate a wide theoretical agreement on the existence of the ATS as a (normative) 'system'. Common to all of them is the approach that the ATS is composed of several separate normative parts, i.e. international instruments. This approach is useful in defining the subject because it indicates the strong *interrelationship* of the instruments enumerated. On the other hand, the choice of normative elements portrayed as constituting component parts of the ATS is somewhat voluntarily left to individual authors. Moreover, the failure to specify the categories into which these instruments fall makes their interrelationship blurred. Importantly, such definitions are necessarily short-lived, soon overcome by the ongoing evolution of the ATS, including the introduction of new instruments and the changes in the legal nature of existing ones.

By establishing itself as a self-determining system, the ATS has also simplified the search for its normative parts. According to the Protocol, the 'Antarctic Treaty system' means:

> the Antarctic Treaty, the measures in effect under that Treaty, its associated separate international instruments in force and the measures in effect under those instruments.[36]

Indeed, this provision shall acquire a legal nature with the entry into force of the Protocol. Were the Protocol already in force, the ATS would accordingly be composed of the following four normative categories:

1   the Antarctic Treaty, constituting *the basis* for the evolution of other normative parts of the ATS;
2   those among more than 200 *recommendations* adopted at the Consultative Meetings which are *in effect*;[37]
3   *treaties in force*, adopted on the basis of the Antarctic Treaty: the 1972

---

[35] J. D. Myhre, *The Antarctic Treaty System: Politics, Law, and Diplomacy* (Boulder, CO: Westview Press, 1986), p. 1.

[36] Art. 1(e) of the Protocol. For an analysis of differences between this definition of the ATS and the earlier definition contained in Art. 2, para. 1 of CRAMRA, see Watts, *International Law and the Antarctic Treaty System*, pp. 292–3.

[37] Thus, recommendations not yet in effect are excluded from this category, pending their entry into effect. Definitely excluded are various other measures, such as the decisions of Special Consultative Meetings.

Convention for the Conservation of Antarctic Seals,[38] the 1980
CCAMLR[39] and the 1991 Protocol, with Annexes;[40] and
4 measures in effect under those treaties.

This definition might be said to be too restrictive, especially since it does
not include the 1988 Convention on the Regulation of Antarctic Mineral
Resource Activities. On the other hand, it would be difficult to reconcile
in a consistent system the Protocol's *prohibition* of mineral activities[41] with
the *regulation* of such activities as offered by CRAMRA. However, the
criterion of legal force (or effect) might obscure the *evolutionary trend* of
the ATS' normative parts. Although CRAMRA may not constitute part
of the same system with the Protocol and its ban on mineral activities, it
was nevertheless significant in paving the way towards the Protocol and
substantially influenced the content of several provisions in the Protocol.[42]

In addition, this definition does not explicate a separate Antarctic tourism regime; however, in its present stage of evolution, such a regime is
based partly in recommendations in effect and partly in the Protocol.[43]

Taking the Protocol's definition of the normative components of the
ATS as our point of departure, let us see how these are interrelated to
constitute the ATS as a (normative) system. Though the normative components of the ATS are separate legal instruments in terms of legal technique, all of them are closely linked to the Antarctic Treaty and mutually
interrelated.

Indeed, it might be asked whether the above 'separate international
instruments in force'[44] complement the Antarctic Treaty, the recommendations and each other, thus forming a single legal system; or whether
they stand as independent international treaties without a mutual interrelationship to substantiate the claim of their integration in a system.

---

[38] The Convention entered into force on 11 March 1978; published in *United Nations Treaty
Series*, vol. 1,080, pp. 175*ff*, reprinted in *International Legal Materials*, vol. XI, 1972,
pp. 251*ff*.

[39] The Convention entered into force on 7 April 1982.

[40] The Annexes form an integral part of the Protocol. Annexes additional to Annexes I–IV
may be adopted; thus, Annex V, on Area Protection and Management, was adopted as an
Annex to Recommendation XVI-10, at the 1991 Consultative Meeting held in Bonn.

[41] Protocol, Art. 7.

[42] This is why CRAMRA is included in the analysis in this volume (see especially Chapters
6 and 10). At the same time, this may serve as an illustration of the argument maintained
in this chapter, that any purely normative definition of the ATS may clarify only one
aspect of its systemic nature.

[43] See Chapters 8 and 12.

[44] Protocol, Art. 1(e).

Those treaties have significant mutual differences in several respects: their lists of parties overlap only partially;[45] they were not negotiated and concluded at the same fora; nor are their respective areas of application entirely identical.[46]

However, the *Antarctic Treaty*, as the 'constitutive instrument' of the ATS, is the ultimate source of all the instruments constituting the normative components of the System. Moreover, their norms rest on the three principles of the ATS: use of the Antarctic for peaceful purposes only; freedom of scientific research in the Antarctic; and the protection of the Antarctic environment. Further, all of these separate international treaties have in common the preservation of the 'freeze' in Article IV regarding the sovereignty issue.

Since the initiative for each respective regulation has originated, either formally or actually, in the consultative mechanism,[47] all of the instruments adopted have an ultimate common source: Article IX of the Antarctic Treaty.[48] This is also clear from the role given to the Consultative Parties in all of the ATS instruments.

[45] As of 7 May 1995, out of forty-two states parties to the Antarctic Treaty, only sixteen are also parties to the Seals Convention, while twenty-eight are simultaneously parties to CCAMLR (plus the European Community). However, fifteen out of sixteen parties to the Seals Convention are Consultative Parties (among these sixteen, only Canada is not a Consultative Party), while twenty-four out of twenty-eight states which are parties to CCAMLR are also Consultative Parties (i.e. all except China and Ecuador). Not all the parties to the Antarctic Treaty need to be parties to the Protocol in order for it to enter into force, only those twenty-six among them which were the Consultative Parties at the date of the adoption of the Protocol, 4 October 1991. Hence, *consultative status* is a prominent feature in the composition of parties to these international treaties, either as a formal requirement or as a fact.

[46] See Art. VI of the Antarctic Treaty (applies to the area south of 60°S); Art. 1, para. 1 of the Seals Convention (applies to the seas south of 60°S only); Art. I, paras. 1 and 4 of CCAMLR (applies to the Antarctic marine living resources both south of 60°S and north of 60°S, between that latitude and the Antarctic Convergence). The Protocol lacks a specific provision on the scope of its territorial application; however, it stems from the fact that the Protocol is meant to supplement the Antarctic Treaty so, in lacking any provision to the contrary, its area of application is identical with that of the Antarctic Treaty: see in more details Chapters 3, 7 and 11.

[47] See C. D. Beeby, 'The Antarctic Treaty System: Goals, Performance and Impact', in A. Jørgensen-Dahl and W. Østreng (eds.), *The Antarctic Treaty System in World Politics* (London: Macmillan, 1991), p. 11; Scully, 'The Evolution', p. 404.

[48] Art. IX, which provides for the consultative machinery, also establishes the crucial linkage between the normative and the structural components of the ATS. It has often been argued that the norm-producing competencies of the Consultative Parties are limited to several areas of cooperation enumerated in Art. IX, para. 1(a)–(f). However, a closer look reveals that this enumeration refers to the subject matter of *recommendations*, while other-

Indeed, since the adoption of the Seals Convention in 1972, the ever-closer integration of each subsequent instrument into the ATS has become an increasing trend, culminating with the 1991 Protocol to the Antarctic Treaty. This also bears witness to the consistent intentions of the negotiating states to aim at firmer integration of the System. Several specific provisions of those treaties have to date created an elaborate network of mutual interrelationships, implying that while not yet coalesced into a single unit, these components fully justify their being treated as together constituting a single system with its own internal integrity.[49]

The normative interrelationship of the ATS instruments is found in their reliance on the three principles of the ATS and in the preservation of the *modus vivendi* on the sovereignty issue, based in Article IV of the Antarctic Treaty. This is also what makes the normative components of the ATS a distinct category of the System.

Structural components of the ATS

Actors within the ATS

The line of delimitation between states as actors within and outside the ATS essentially corresponds to the international law differentiation between the (forty-two)[50] states parties to the Antarctic Treaty and those states, as well as other actors, not parties to the Treaty.[51] The Antarctic Treaty, in its Article IX, introduced a further categorisation of states parties to it, by dividing them into two main groups, later designated as Consultative and Non-Consultative Parties.[52] Neither is the group of Consultative Parties formally homogeneous; those twelve Consultative Parties comprising the original signatories of the Antarctic Treaty retain their consultative status unconditionally, while the remaining (fourteen)[53] Consultative Parties – who have subsequently acceded to the Antarctic Treaty and whose consultative status has been recognised on the basis of

---

wise Art. IX provides that the Consultative Parties shall meet 'for the purpose of ... consulting together on matters of common interest pertaining to Antarctica', which is an all-embracing formulation of their competencies.

[49] See Watts, *International Law and the Antarctic Treaty System*, p. 86.

[50] As of 7 May 1995.

[51] In accordance with Art. XII of the Antarctic Treaty, only states may become parties to it.

[52] See Rule 1 of the revised Rules of Procedure for the Consultative Meetings, 1983; reprinted in Heap (ed.), *Handbook*, pp. 272–5.

[53] As of 7 May 1995.

their demonstrated interest in Antarctica – retain that status conditionally: as long as they continue to demonstrate such interest.[54]

Recently, various international and non-governmental organisations have gradually become actors present *within* the ATS, thereby influencing changes in its processes and norms. All the same, the main difference between the Consultative Parties and other actors within the ATS remains: only the Consultative Parties have full rights in the ATS decision-making process, while others may exert varying degrees of influence. Actors in the ATS are neither formally nor in substance in an equal position.

Procedures within the ATS

Actors' roles in the ATS are activated through the procedural components of the System, which appear in a variety of interconnected ATS procedures, both formal and informal.

As noted, the Antarctic Treaty provided the initial procedural device for the creation and the evolution of the System: the *Consultative Meetings*, with recommendations as their main normative product. In the course of the past three and a half decades of ATS operation, an entire complex of decision-making procedures has been developed, whenever the need has arisen. The regular practice of biannual Consultative Meetings[55] was followed by a period during which it was found necessary to introduce several other procedural components as well – Meetings of Experts, Special Consultative Meetings[56] and Informal Meetings – ultimately resulting in additional sorts of international instruments pertaining to the Antarctic.[57] These various sorts of meetings have had a common source in the consultative practice, i.e. in Article IX of the Antarctic Treaty.

The steadily firmer institutionalisation of the ATS is another aspect of

---

[54] Antarctic Treaty, Art. IX, paras. 1 and 2.

[55] At the XVI Consultative Meeting, held in Bonn, 7–18 October 1991, it was decided that regular Consultative Meetings should be held annually; see para. 134 of the Final Report of the XVI Consultative Meeting, reprinted in Heap (ed.), *Handbook*, p. 31. This decision was directly related to the adoption of the 1991 Protocol, and thus illustrates the interlinkage between the procedural and normative components of the ATS.

[56] For a brief explanation of the main differences between these two sorts of meetings as well as between them and regular Consultative Meetings see Heap (ed.), *Handbook*, p. 21.

[57] When appropriate, separate diplomatic conferences were convened for the adoption of the texts of new international conventions, as in the cases of the Seals Convention and CCAMLR.

the procedural component of the ATS provided for not directly in Article IX of the Antarctic Treaty but in provisions of other international treaties that make up the ATS' normative components. However, the need for these treaties has been defined within the consultative mechanism;[58] in this sense, the institutionalisation of the ATS ultimately originates in Article IX of the Treaty. Initially, this new trend in the ATS was marked by the creation and operation of the institutions established under CCAMLR. More recently, pending the entry into force of the Protocol, arrangements were made at the 1992 and 1994 Consultative Meetings[59] for entry into operation of the main functions of the Committee for Environmental Protection (CEP). The Consultative Parties decided that the 1995 Consultative Meeting[60] would include a Transitional Environmental Working Group to deal with those questions which, under the Protocol, would be dealt with by the CEP. The inclusion of this Transitional Working Group within a Consultative Meeting illustrates the interlinkage among the procedural components of the ATS, as well as the central role of Article IX of the Antarctic Treaty.

And finally, the emerging Antarctic Treaty Secretariat, once established, will add to the institutionalisation of ATS decision-making procedures, by coordinating administratively the operation of the System.

Additional important procedural components of the ATS are found in relations with SCAR. And, significant for the success of the ATS along with its formal procedures, it owes much to the *informal practice* of consultations among the Consultative Parties through diplomatic channels.[61]

This focus on the procedural aspect of the ATS has frequently been found both in theory and in state practice.[62] There is wide agreement

---

[58] Scully, 'The Antarctic Treaty as a System', p. 96.
[59] The XVII Consultative Meeting, held in Venice, 11–20 November 1992; and the XVIII Consultative Meeting, held in Kyoto, 11–22 April 1994.
[60] To be held in Seoul, 8–19 May 1995.
[61] As pointed out by Argentina: 'Ever since it [the Antarctic Treaty] took effect, procedures have been distinguished by two essential characteristics: a relative informality and a direct communication among Parties': see ATCM XIV, doc. ANT/XIV/WP.2, of 5 October 1987, in Bush (ed.), *Antarctica and International Law* (New York: Oceana, 1991), Booklet AT 3, February 1991, pp. 27–8.
[62] It has been dealt with especially by R. Tucker Scully in several articles: see Scully, 'The Evolution', pp. 391–411; R. T. Scully, 'The Antarctic Treaty System: Overview and Analysis', in L. M. Alexander and L. C. Hanson (eds.), *Antarctic Politics and Marine Resources: Critical Choices for the 1980s* (Kingston, RI: Center for Ocean Management Studies, 1985), pp. 3–11; Scully, 'The Antarctic Treaty as a System', pp. 95–102. See also Beeby, 'The ATS: Goals', pp. 4–21.

that it is precisely this evolutionary nature which strongly characterises the process of the ATS.[63]

Hence, the distinct characteristics of actors as components of the ATS lie in the special status and the role of the Consultative Parties. The procedural component of the ATS is, hence, distinguished by the operation of a complex consultative machinery which is in part directly based on Article IX of the Antarctic Treaty, and which in part ultimately originates from it. The central role of the Consultative Meeting is obvious, since all other procedural elements of the ATS are closely tied to it.

THE ANTARCTIC TREATY SYSTEM IN THE INTERNATIONAL COMMUNITY

Half a century ago, when the first proposals for creating an international Antarctic regime were initiated among a limited group of states, interactions with the wider international community, such as those of the present-day kind, scarcely existed. From the post-World War II period to the present, the position of the Antarctic in international politics and law evolved under the influence of a broad spectrum of factors. Some of those factors are nowadays commonly shared with the evolution of the wider international community, while others are closely linked to the peculiarities of the Antarctic. While placing the general international politics towards the Antarctic in a historical perspective, it has been observed that:

In the world of international political affairs ... Antarctica's dominant international characteristic was its obscurity. That obscurity is disappearing.[64]

This sweeping yet accurate illustration of the evolutionary trend of the position of the ATS in the wider international community raises crucial questions. What were the reasons for the obscurity, or relative isolation, of the ATS from the wider international community in its early phase – apart from the fact that Antarctica is, geographically, an isolated continent? How and why did that obscurity begin to disappear, and how did this affect the mode of relationship between the ATS and the wider international community?

---

[63] See Auburn, *Antarctic Law and Politics*, p. 147; G. D. Triggs, 'The Antarctic Treaty Regime: Legal Issues – Introduction', in G. D. Triggs (ed.), *The Antarctic Treaty Regime* (Cambridge University Press, 1987), p. 54; Watts, *International Law and the Antarctic Treaty System*, p. 12; Orrego, *Antarctic Mineral Exploitation*, p. viii.

[64] *Antarctica: The Next Decade*, Report of a Study Group Chaired by Sir Anthony Parsons (Cambridge University Press, 1987), p. 3.

The Antarctic and the ATS in the time of
obscurity: peace and science

It is, indeed, neither solely nor primarily the geographical status of Antarctica as a 'pole apart' which explains why Antarctica remained outside the broader international debate in the post-World War II period. In the late 1940s and early 1950s, conflict rather than cooperation dominated the Antarctic scene, with conflicts ranging from localised disputes about claims or boundaries, to major rivalries between superpowers,[65] with an inherent potential to spread to other areas. Only gradually did the first signs of *détente* appear in Antarctica, initially in the Tripartite Naval Declaration of 1949 exchanged between Argentina, Chile and the United Kingdom[66] and then more obviously during the International Geophysical Year of 1957-8. These roots of the 1959 Antarctic Treaty, codified in the Treaty's principles of peace and science in Antarctica and coupled with a pragmatic *modus vivendi* on the sovereignty issue, provide part of the explanation as to why the Antarctic Treaty has effectively prevented a broader debate on the Antarctic issue in the international community.

We should not, however, lose sight of certain other significant aspects of that Treaty at the time of its conclusion. The strategic problems then connected with Antarctica were largely a reflection of the rivalry between the two political blocs elsewhere in the world.[67] In that situation, the achievements of the Antarctic Treaty came close to being revolutionary. This was the first international agreement to be concluded in the Cold War period which introduced a complex system of mutual unilateral inspection of parties' activities (Article VII) – including inspections between the United States and the Soviet Union. Furthermore, the Antarctic Treaty progressed even beyond preserving Antarctica for peaceful purposes only (Article I); in global relations, it established Antarctica as the first internationally agreed area where nuclear explosions and disposal of radioactive waste material were banned (Article V). Already these

[65] See in more detail F. Orrego Vicuña, 'Antarctic Conflict and International Cooperation', in *Antarctic Treaty System: An Assessment*, pp. 55-61; on categories of conflicts in Antarctica in the post-World War II period see W. Østreng, 'The Conflict and Alignment Pattern of Antarctic Politics: Is a New Order Needed?', in Jørgensen-Dahl and Østreng (eds.), *The Antarctic Treaty System in World Politics*, pp. 434-6.
[66] On this declaration, which was renewed annually up to 1960, see note 4 above in this chapter.
[67] See H. J. Taubenfeld, 'A Treaty for Antarctica', *International Conciliation*, no. 531, 1961, p. 261.

accomplishments were clearly seen as a convincing argument for third parties to let Antarctic issues remain within the Antarctic Treaty framework.

Moreover, any potential gains of disrupting this framework would be very moderate. With the lapse of successful sealing in the Southern Ocean, and with whaling already regulated at the international level, human activity in the Antarctic had been dominated by scientific research. Any question of other uses of Antarctica, raised at a broader international level, was seen as entailing a potential for opening the Pandora's box of the sovereignty problem, left untouched in Article IV of the Treaty.

This is not to say that questions of the global significance as well as the resource potential of Antarctica were not then raised at all at the wider international level. Even prior to the conclusion of the Antarctic Treaty, India attempted, first in February 1956, to take up these questions in the UN, but withdrew its initiative in the face of diplomatic opposition from several among the countries which were later to become original signatories of the Antarctic Treaty.[68] In this connection, Orrego has observed that the proposals raised in the early 1980s, in the UN debate on the 'Question of Antarctica', were far from new.[69] But, the *circumstances* surrounding the Malaysian initiative were new, compared to the Indian initiative of some three decades earlier. These changing circumstances explain why, unlike the earlier Indian initiative, the Malaysian one (perhaps the strongest external attack on the legitimacy of the ATS to date) had several consequences in the relationship between the ATS and the wider international community as well as in substantial changes within the System. Let us now look more closely at these changing circumstances.

Obscurity disappearing: the ATS enters the era of new resource uses

The early and middle of the 1970s brought questions connected with utilisation of natural resources in the Antarctic to the forefront of the Consultative Parties' consideration, and soon after to the attention of the wider international community. This is the time when the ATS 'emerged from obscurity'. The period was characterised by such dominant global features as relaxation of the superpower Cold War tension and by the

---

[68] See India's Explanatory Memorandum of 16 October 1956, with commentary, in Bush (ed.), *Antarctica and International Law*, vol. I, pp. 505–6.
[69] Orrego, 'Antarctic Conflict', p. 62.

emergence of a number of new states onto the international scene, through the process of decolonisation. These developing states also introduced a new ideology to the international arena, demanding a restructuring of existing relations in the international community, now to be fully based on the sovereign equality of states, including the equitable sharing of natural resources. This so-called New International Economic Order ideology soon found expression in demands for a restructuring of the global order for the oceans, by introducing the concept of a common heritage of mankind in the law of the sea. Little did the Maltese representative in the UN General Assembly realise that as early as 1967, when he had argued that the seabed and its resources beyond the limits of national jurisdiction should be proclaimed the common heritage of mankind, that the seed was sown for a later initiative on the 'Question of Antarctica' in the UN. Eventually, some fifteen years later, the results of the Third UN Conference on the Law of the Sea (UNCLOS III) served as a stimulus for certain developing countries to link the common heritage of mankind concept to the legal and political status of the Antarctic. Dissatisfied with the outcome of UNCLOS III,[70] a group of developing countries, led by Malaysia, launched in the early 1980s a critique of the ATS in the UN.[71]

That critique initially targeted the specificity of the ATS consultative process, characterising it as an *exclusive club* of rich and powerful states. It went on to argue that the issue of Antarctica is a global one, and that it is a matter of the sovereign equality of states to have an equal say in any such global issues. This was a powerful legitimising argument employed by critics of the ATS. At that time, when the consultative mechanism had been in operation for over two decades, the group of the Consultative Parties had been joined by only two among the acceding states

[70] The main thrust of this dissatisfaction concerned the considerable extension of the continental shelf regime, on the one hand, and the refusal of major industrialised countries to agree with Part XI of the 1982 UN Convention on the Law of the Sea (LOS Convention), on the other: see in more detail Chapter 3.

[71] The idea for this major external challenge to the ATS was directly linked with the finalisation of UNCLOS III; it was announced by the Malaysian Prime Minister in a speech in the UN General Assembly, drawing consequences from closure of the UNCLOS III and pointing out the need for a new UN conference on uninhabited lands, in particular the Antarctic (see UN doc. A/37/PV. 10, pp. 17–20); this idea, now addressing the Antarctic more directly, was reiterated by Malaysia on the occasion of signing the LOS Convention, in Montego Bay, on 10 December 1982 (see UN doc. A/CONF. 62/PV. 189, pp. 81–2).

to the Treaty (Poland in 1977 and the Federal Republic of Germany in 1981), thus comprising fourteen countries altogether.

Hence, the external critique of the ATS, launched in the early 1980s, involved two main strands of criticism, closely interrelated. One was a demand for *normative* changes which would allow the application of the common heritage of mankind concept, as formulated in Part XI of the LOS Convention, to the Antarctic. Another strand of criticism was directed at the *structure* of the ATS – i.e. its *procedural* aspects and the *roles of actors* within the ATS, demanding substantial transformation of the width of participation[72] and the decision-making process in Antarctic affairs. The development of the external critique of the ATS along these two lines gradually served to introduce the 'time of transparency' into ATS affairs.

Demands for normative changes: from regulation of resource use to environmental protection

Demands for *normative* changes were directly linked with the perceived existence of rich natural resources in the Antarctic and the belief that they might soon prove economically exploitable. It has often been noted that the ATS critics in the UN, while advocating the application of the common heritage of mankind principle in connection with Antarctic *mineral resources*, consider gains from a purely economic perspective: namely, to achieve economic redistribution of benefits derived from any future exploitation.[73] Hence, the critique of the ATS, in targeting its feature of exclusive participation in decision-making, has had – along with an ideological background – an economic one as well. Indeed, until 1988 ATS critics in the UN put forward demands for wider participation in the Antarctic minerals negotiations, arguing that a moratorium on ATS negotiations to establish a minerals regime should be imposed until such time as all members of the international

---

[72] This demand was directed not only at wider participation, but also argued for the exclusion of a certain actor from the ATS, namely South Africa. However, this situation changed when the African National Congress came into power in South Africa, thus solving one of the trickiest issues for the Consultative Parties in responding adequately to the UN critique.

[73] See E. J. Sahurie, *The International Law of Antarctica* (New Haven Press, 1991), pp. 441 and 579; R. E. Money, Jr, 'The Protocol on Environmental Protection to the Antarctic Treaty: Maintaining a Legal Regime', *Emory International Law Journal*, vol. 7, 1993, p. 163.

community could participate fully in such negotiations.[74] However, the adoption of CRAMRA in June 1988 created a new situation, prompting the developing countries – critics of the ATS – to adjust their arguments. Gradually, the importance of *environmental* issues in connection with the Antarctic, including Antarctica's relevance to global processes (climatic, atmospheric, oceanic and geological), came into the focus of the critique along with the dangers for the vulnerable Antarctic environment implied in any minerals exploitation. Signalled in 1988, this new focus became quite obvious in the UN discussions in 1989, a development on which Beck has aptly commented that 'the UN goes green on Antarctica'.[75] Analysing the 1989 UN session, Beck observed:

Perhaps the key innovation was the strong focus on the environment, including Antarctica's role in global environmental systems. The common heritage notion, treated traditionally as connoting an exploitative intent, was interpreted increasingly from a world park perspective.[76]

Malaysia, initiator of the 'Question of Antarctica' in the UN and traditionally the fiercest critic of the ATS, gave firm support to Australia, France, Belgium and Italy for their decision to abandon CRAMRA.[77] In 1989, this situation of 'cross-alliance'[78] might have been interpreted as adding fuel to the flames of crisis within the ATS, so evident at the XV Consultative Meeting, held in Paris in October 1989. From a contemporary perspective, however, the Malaysian view was mainly a vigorous support of the mining ban adopted two years later through the Protocol. It marked the shift from what can been called 'resourcism'[79] in the UN's

---

[74] See 1987 UN General Assembly resolution 42/46 on the 'Question of Antarctica'; also statement issued on 8 June 1988 by Antigua and Barbuda, Bangladesh, Brunei Darussalam, Cameroon, the Congo (*sic*), Ghana, Indonesia, Kenya, Malaysia, Nepal, Nigeria, Oman, Pakistan, Rwanda, Sri Lanka, the Sudan, Uganda, Zambia and Zimbabwe, on the Antarctic minerals regime negotiations held at Wellington, New Zealand, from 2 May to 2 June 1988, UN doc. A/43/396, of 9 June 1988, p. 2.

[75] P. J. Beck, 'The UN Goes Green on Antarctica: The 1989 Session', *Polar Record*, vol. 26, no. 159, 1990, pp. 323–5; see also V. S. Safronchuk, 'The Relationship between the ATS and the Law of the Sea Convention of 1982', in Jørgensen-Dahl and Østreng, *The Antarctic Treaty System in World Politics*, pp. 330–1.

[76] Beck, 'The UN Goes Green', p. 325 (emphasis added).

[77] Statement of Malaysia, UN doc. A/C.1/44/PV.44, p. 19.

[78] Østreng, 'The Conflict and Alignment', especially p. 434 and figure at p. 440.

[79] In Evenden's words, 'Resourcism is a kind of modern religion which casts all of creation into categories of utility': N. Evenden, *The Natural Alien: Humankind and Environment* (Toronto University Press, 1985).

view on Antarctic mineral resources, to 'Earth-patriotism'.[80] This environmental focus characterised UN discussions on the 'Question of Antarctica' in 1989 and received further emphasis in 1990, when ATS critics overwhelmingly supported the initiative for a mining ban in the Antarctic.[81] The trend gained further in intensity during the 1991 UN discussion, when the newly adopted Protocol was criticised for not establishing a permanent mining ban.[82] Moreover, this is reiterated in the 1992 and 1993 General Assembly resolutions which welcome the ban on prospecting and mining in and around Antarctica for the next fifty years by the Consultative Parties in accordance with the Protocol, and reiterate the call for the ban to be made permanent.[83]

In summing up the line of reasoning of the UN critique over the past decade, we may note a serious conceptual contradiction. The critique of the ATS in the UN has actually enhanced the legitimacy of the Protocol's ban on any mineral activity (other than scientific research), by arguing for an even more rigorous permanent ban. However, it is difficult to reconcile a ban on mineral activities, which applies also to the Antarctic maritime area and its seabed, with the common heritage of mankind concept as formulated in Part XI of the LOS Convention. Indeed, at the core of the latter concept are elements of utilisation of minerals and redistribution of benefits acquired from minerals exploitation.[84] Chapter 3 deals with various aspects of this problematic.

[80] The concept of Earth-patriotism is formulated in the UN Secretary-General's Report on the Work of the Organisation in 1989 as 'looking at the planet and its atmosphere as an object for protection and not for aggression and pillage': see UN doc. A/44/1, p. 21.

[81] For discussions on this item in the First Committee of the UN General Assembly in 1989 see UN docs. A/C.1/44/PV.42–6; for discussions in 1990 see UN docs. A/C.1/45/PV.40–5 and 47. This was reflected in UN General Assembly resolutions on the 'Question of Antarctica' in 1989 and 1990: see resolution 44/124B of 15 December 1989 (especially para. 13 of Preamble, and para. 5 of the text) and resolution 45/78A of 12 December 1990 (especially paras. 8, 11 and 12 of Preamble, and para. 4 of the text).

[82] See especially statements by Malaysia (UN doc. A/C.1/46/PV.38, p. 9), Antigua and Barbuda (*ibid.*, p. 16), Pakistan (UN doc. A/C.1/46/PV.39, p. 17) and Bangladesh (*ibid.*, p. 21). See also UN General Assembly resolution 46/41 of 6 December 1991, para. 6.

[83] See UN General Assembly resolutions 47/57 of 9 December 1992, paras. 8 and 9; and 48/80 of 16 December 1993, paras. 7 and 8.

[84] Here it should be noted that the idea of common heritage of mankind can acquire different forms for actual concretisation, and therefore it ought to be interpreted depending on the context in which it is applied. In this case, however, it was the concept of the common heritage of mankind as formulated in Part XI of the LOS Convention.

Demands for changes in structure: widening participation and evolving institutionalisation

Let us now inquire into the other strand of the relationship between the ATS and the wider international community, *in procedural changes* and the *changing roles of actors* within the ATS. Here we shall trace the impact of changes in structure of the international community, and the resulting demands for analogous changes within the ATS.

In 1983, the ATS was criticised for being an 'exclusive club' of rich and powerful states, veiled by secrecy of their work and resulting instruments. This was, in terms of the ATS' international legitimacy, a powerful accusation – directed primarily at the privileged status of the Consultative Parties. The latter defended their position, and thus the ATS, by selectively co-opting potential additional critics within their lines. It was a significant feature of that period that between the small group of fourteen Consultative Parties, on the one hand, and the Malaysian group, on the other, stood a large body of grumbling but still-undecided opinion. Such states were found both within and outside the ATS;[85] thus, the strategy of co-optation was directed simultaneously at both camps.

Within the ATS, two major changes occurred in the consultative process. Since 1983, Non-Consultative Parties had been eligible to attend the Consultative Meetings, albeit without any formal decision-making power. In the same year, India[86] and Brazil became Consultative Parties, while China[87]and Uruguay gained consultative status two years later. This split the otherwise often firm camp of developing states, as some of them were now Consultative Parties while others criticised that privileged status from outside. This prevented the rich North versus the poor South

---

[85] On the eve of the UN critique, the Antarctic Treaty numbered twenty-four states parties, of which altogether fourteen had the status of Consultative Parties. Hence, over twenty years after its entry into force, the number of states parties had doubled, but only two of them were recognised as fulfilling the requirements for becoming a Consultative Party.

[86] Incidentally, India acceded to the Antarctic Treaty on 19 August 1983, and became a Consultative Party on 12 September 1983, less than one month later. In comparison for Poland that same process took sixteen years, from its accession to the Treaty in 1961 to becoming a Consultative Party in 1977. Both India and Brazil were recognised as having fulfilled the requirements for consultative status not by the fact of establishment of a scientific base in Antarctica, but on the basis of their 'firm plans' to do so in the following season, which sufficed at the time: see *Final Report of the Fifth Special Antarctic Treaty Consultative Meeting*, Canberra, 12 September 1983.

[87] With China, the group of Consultative Parties had secured the fifth permanent member of the UN Security Council for their ranks.

parallel from being convincingly employed in the relationship between the ATS and the wider international community, thus weakening the ideological strength of the UN critique. It also scaled down the number of votes that the Malaysia-led critique was able to collect in the UN General Assembly.

Moreover, this stimulated several states then still outside the ATS to join it: the middle of the 1980s saw a wave of accessions to the Antarctic Treaty.[88] The changes within the ATS' structure were both quantitative and qualitative.

Apart from states, international and non-governmental organisations also gradually became admitted to the consultative process, some as observers[89] while others were invited to designate experts to attend the Consultative Meetings. This development occurred partly as a by-product of the UN critique, and partly resulted from the demands of the environ-mental lobby in the late 1980s. The Antarctic and Southern Ocean Coalition (ASOC) first appeared at the XI Special Consultative Meeting, and thereafter at regular annual Consultative Meetings. The most recent development in this direction, in the early 1990s, was connected with the Antarctic tourism issue. The World Tourism Organization, the International Organization of Antarctic Tour Operators, and the Pacific Asia Travel Organization got their seats at the Consultative Meetings in the period from 1991 to 1994.

Hence, several potential and indeed actual critics of the ATS have, over the past decade, become participants or cooperative partners, in various roles: some states as Consultative Parties, others as acceding states to the Treaty, while some international and non-governmental organisations have been included in the consultative process as observers. Even without formally being granted equal status with the Consultative Parties, these actors regularly demonstrate loyalty to the System. The consultative prac-tice can offer examples of coalitions between some Consultative Parties and non-governmental organisations – notably the one in the late 1980s between Australia. and France on the one hand, and environmental non-governmental organisations on the other, in the case of the mining ban,

---

[88] As of 7 May 1995, the Antarctic Treaty numbers forty-two states parties, of which twenty-six have the consultative status. In other words, the dynamics of both accession to the Treaty and expansion of the Consultative Parties group was significantly increased over the past decade, when compared with the period from 1961 to 1983.

[89] The Scientific Committee on Antarctic Research, the Commission on the Conservation of Antarctic Marine Living Resources, and the Council of Managers of National Antarctic Programs.

and the dismissal of CRAMRA. A more recent example is that of the United States and ASOC in the issue of the Antarctic tourism regime. This witnesses in favour of the legitimacy of the contemporary ATS structure. Changes in the ATS are now more influenced by factors within than outside the System, as exemplified by the position of Non-Consultative Parties. On the one hand, some Non-Consultative Parties perform an active role at the Consultative Meetings, thus influencing the consultative process in which they have no formal decision-making power.[90] Others, like the Netherlands, have opted instead to attempt to redefine the criteria for consultative status, arguing that the proliferation of scientific bases in some areas of Antarctica now threatens the environment.[91] Apparently, it is the environmental aspect which is coming to the fore in today's criteria for consultative status, and is reflected in the requirement of accession to the Environmental Protocol as a pre-condition for consultative status.[92] In short, the ATS is becoming less of an 'exclusive club' of rich and powerful Consultative Parties.

Another significant feature is the *diminishing secrecy* of the work and results of the consultative process. The flow of information from the ATS to the wider international community has become far smoother than a decade ago. This is partly a by-product of the wider participation in the process itself; but other mechanisms also are important, like the regular practice of submitting reports from the Consultative Meetings and some of the ATS instruments to the UN Secretary-General, as well as the introduction and publication of national contact points of Treaty parties,[93] providing the opportunity for inquiry about information.

This transparency, in turn, enables third parties to exert influence on developments within the ATS, by providing them with an easily accessible update on the consultative process. The diminution of ATS secrecy has

---

[90] Examples are Canada and Switzerland, as well as Austria, Denmark and Greece.

[91] See A. Bos, 'Consultative Status under the Antarctic Treaty: Redefining the Criteria?', in Jørgensen-Dahl and Østreng, *The Antarctic Treaty System in World Politics*, pp. 335–42.

[92] After the date of entry into force of the Protocol, as stipulated in its Art. 22, para. 4, the Consultative Parties 'shall not act upon a notification regarding the entitlement of a Contracting Party to the Antarctic Treaty to appoint representatives to participate in Antarctic Treaty Consultative Meetings in accordance with Article IX(2) of the Antarctic Treaty *unless* that Contracting Party has first ratified, accepted, approved or acceded to this Protocol' (emphasis added).

[93] Publication of a list of national contact points, for the purposes described in Recommendation XIII-1, appeared first in the Final Report of the XIV Consultative Meeting, held in Rio de Janeiro in 1987, and has been included in the final reports from the Consultative Meetings since. It is also published in Heap (ed.), *Handbook*, pp. 291–5.

thus paved the way to growing interaction between the ATS and other actors – as demonstrated in the role of environmental NGOs in the ATS, and more recently in the inclusion of tourism industry organisations in discussions on an ATS tourism regime.[94] This growing transparency also facilitates the early involvement of interested third actors in a normative regulation of issue areas handled within the ATS.

All this also goes a long way in explaining how the *institutionalisation* of the ATS ceased to be a taboo theme for the Consultative Parties. The establishment of institutional bodies within the ATS is a natural consequence of the wider participation in the consultative process and its diminishing secrecy, on the one hand, and of the normative expansion of the System, on the other. The fears of some Consultative Parties – claimants in particular – that the establishment of permanent institutions within the ATS might disturb the balance of positions on the sovereignty issue, have gradually become secondary to the actual implementation needs of the new ATS regimes. This has also been stimulated by the pressure from external actors, such as environmental NGOs, for better availability of data and the insight into the operation of the ATS regimes. Establishment of permanent institutional forms within the ATS became a less sensitive issue in the middle of the 1970s, and was obviously manifested in institutions established under CCAMLR: Commission, Scientific Committee and the Secretariat.[95] CRAMRA introduced the most complex institutional structure in the ATS,[96] while a new institution – the Committee for Environmental Protection – is to be established under the Protocol.[97] Requirements for broader participation have had their implications in provisions on the composition and decision-making in these institutions.[98] Thus, in the context of the growing transparency of the ATS, institutionalisation introduces a further significant political aspect in the relationship between the ATS and the wider international community. In addition, the establishment of an ATS Secretariat in the foreseeable future will mean that the ATS will become adequately represented outside. In relation to third parties, it will also get a contact point of its own, along with the national contact points of parties to the Antarctic Treaty.

[94] See Chapter 4.
[95] See Chapters 5 and 9.
[96] See Chapters 6 and 10.
[97] See Chapters 7 and 11.
[98] For an overview, see Conclusions of this book.

CONCLUDING REMARKS

We have seen in the second section of this chapter that the ATS possesses two crucial *systemic properties* around which the others are centred.

First, the ATS embodies certain *distinctive characteristics* in the international community. This we saw when analysing the ATS through its two categories of components, normative and structural. Both are centred around special ATS features. All of the ATS instruments, comprising its normative component, distinctly rely on the three principles of the ATS, and on the preservation of the pragmatic 'agreement to disagree', or the balance of positions, on the sovereignty issue in the Antarctic. Within the structural component, the actors are distinguished by the special status and role of the Consultative Parties within the ATS. And finally, procedures of the ATS are marked by the operation of a complex consultative machinery in which the Consultative Meeting has the central role.

Second, the ATS is characterised by the coherent *interrelationship* among all of its components, aptly termed the 'systemic integrity'[99] of the ATS. This enables a constant evolution through the procedures of the System, demonstrating the intention towards comprehensiveness in regulating its subject matter.

The *interplay* of these properties is what gives the ATS its systemic nature. Along with the special characteristics which persist in any ATS regulatory solution, the ATS also demonstrates a high degree of flexibility. While maintaining its constant, systemic features, the ATS is very much able to adapt to both internal and external challenges. Moreover, when faced with difficult and complex issues, the System employs innovative regulatory solutions. Hence, the ATS demonstrates flexibility, on the one hand, and persistent preservation of its core systemic features, on the other.

Let us now turn to the findings in the third section of this chapter: what were the *main areas of interaction*, or of compatibility and tensions between the ATS and the wider international community? First, the ideological background and the initiative for the UN critique of the ATS had its roots in UNCLOS III, and in one part of its outcome, namely Part XI of the LOS Convention.[100] Second, along with states and international organisations, the environmental NGOs have become influential actors

---

[99] Watts, *International Law and the Antarctic Treaty System*, p. 75.
[100] Indeed, in conjunction with Part VI of the LOS Convention, on the continental shelf.

on the Antarctic scene; their demands have been directed both to comprehensive environmental protection in the Antarctic and to wider participation in the System.

In the remaining two chapters comprising this Part, our attention will be concentrated on these two *contemporary* and *relevant* global issue areas of mutual interaction of the ATS with the wider international community. The *normative* side of the relationship between the ATS and the international community will be examined in Chapter 3, through the juxtaposition of the ATS and the general law of the sea, especially as resulting from UNCLOS III.[101] Changes in *structure* in the relationship between the ATS and the international community will be explored in Chapter 4, through the study of the changing roles of NGOs in Antarctic politics.

The growing environmental focus is apparent in both areas under closer scrutiny in those two chapters. In dealing with the juxtaposition of the ATS with the new law of the sea, and with the role of NGOs, our inquiry will focus on three points of interaction between the ATS and the wider international community: the uses of resources; environmental protection; and participation in decision-making. Those focal points will also serve as useful devices for observing changes within individual regimes of the ATS, to be studied in Parts III and IV of this volume.

[101] As demonstrated above, the critique of the ATS in the UN had its source and inspiration in the experience and results of UNCLOS III.

3

The Antarctic Treaty System and the law of the sea:
a new dimension introduced by the Protocol

DAVOR VIDAS

INTRODUCTION

Discussions on the relationship between the 1982 United Nations Convention on the Law of the Sea[1] (hereinafter LOS Convention) and the Antarctic Treaty System (ATS) are becoming more urgent due to recent developments within both regimes. The LOS Convention entered into force on 16 November 1994,[2] supplemented by the 1994 Agreement relating to the implementation of Part XI of the United Nations Convention on the Law of the Sea of 10 December 1982[3] (hereinafter Implementation Agreement). The 1991 Protocol on Environmental Protection to the Antarctic Treaty,[4] which – as we shall see in this chapter – introduced a change in the *normative* relationship between the ATS and the law of the sea, also has good prospects of entry into force in the near future.[5]

---

[1] UN doc. A/CONF.62/122; reprinted in *International Legal Materials*, vol. XXI, 1982, pp. 1,261*ff*.

[2] The sixtieth instrument of ratification of the LOS Convention was deposited by Guyana on 16 November 1993. In accordance with Art. 308, para. 1 of the LOS Convention, it entered into force twelve months after the date of deposit of the sixtieth instrument of ratification or accession. As of 16 November 1994, when it entered into force, the LOS Convention had sixty-eight states parties: see the list in *Law of the Sea Bulletin: Special Issue IV*, 16 November 1994, pp. 29–39. The dynamics of ratification of and accession (as well as succession) to the LOS Convention has been significantly enhanced: as of 7 May 1995, there were seventy-five states parties to the Convention.

[3] The Implementation Agreement is adopted as an annex to the UN General Assembly resolution 48/263, of 28 July 1994: reproduced in *Law of the Sea Bulletin: Special Issue IV*, 16 November 1994, pp. 8–25. The Implementation Agreement gained the acceptance of a large majority of countries, both developed and developing: for a list see *ibid.*, pp. 26–8.

[4] Reprinted in *International Legal Materials*, vol. XXX, 1991, pp. 1,461*ff*.

[5] In accordance with its Art. 23, para. 1, the Protocol shall enter into force on the thirtieth day following the date of deposit of instruments of ratification, acceptance, approval or accession by all states which were Antarctic Treaty Consultative Parties at the date on which the Protocol was adopted. As of the adoption of the Protocol (on 4 October 1991)

62   *The ATS in the international community*

The relationship between the ATS and the law of the sea in general, and the LOS Convention in particular, has considerable legal and policy implications, and thus has been the subject of exploration in the literature over the past decades. When we observe the development of this normative relationship from a contemporary perspective, we see that it has gone through several phases. Each of these phases has taken its own approach and has chosen its own focus, responding to the state of affairs of its period. This chapter asserts that there are three main phases in the relationship between the ATS and the law of the sea. The first phase dates from the adoption of the 1959 Antarctic Treaty[6] to the early 1970s; at this time it was possible to claim that the Treaty left in ambiguity the status of the Antarctic maritime area, which accordingly would have to be resolved by the application of the general law of the sea. During the second phase, commencing in the early 1970s, it was gradually recognised that the status of the Antarctic maritime area is actually regulated not only by one but by two normative systems (the law of the sea *and* the ATS), largely due to the development of the ATS through its resource regimes.[7] This chapter will suggest that a *third* phase has commenced, marked by the adoption of the 1991 Protocol, which introduced a new dimension in the relationship between the ATS and the law of the sea. This Protocol, within its area of application, challenges some basic law of the sea concepts related to the submarine areas, including both the continental shelf and the seabed beyond the limits of national jurisdiction, as far as these are connected with mineral resource activities.

This chapter aims at portraying the development of the *normative* relationship between the ATS and the law of the sea. We begin with an overview of the development of this relationship since the adoption of the 1959 Antarctic Treaty. Then we go on to concentrate on the most recent phase introduced by the Protocol, arguing that it has introduced a substantially new dimension with respect to the status of the Antarctic

there were twenty-six Consultative Parties; as of 7 May 1995, sixteen of these ratified the Protocol.

[6] *United Nations Treaty Series*, vol. 402, pp. 71*ff.*

[7] Most notably the 1972 Convention for the Conservation of Antarctic Seals (published in *United Nations Treaty Series*, vol. 1,080, pp. 175*ff*; reprinted in *International Legal Materials*, vol. XI, 1972, pp. 251*ff*); the 1980 Convention on the Conservation of Antarctic Marine Living Resources (reprinted in *International Legal Materials*, vol. XIX, 1980, pp. 837*ff*); the 1988 Convention on the Regulation of Antarctic Mineral Resource Activities (reprinted in *International Legal Materials*, vol. XXVII, 1988, pp. 868*ff*).

submarine areas. This might serve as a stimulus for rethinking some LOS Convention concepts, such as the common heritage of mankind, in a new light.

THE ANTARCTIC TREATY AND THE STATUS OF THE
ANTARCTIC MARITIME AREA

The question of the legal status of the Antarctic maritime area poses a problem at the outset: what is actually meant by 'the Antarctic maritime area'? Any determination of its internal boundary is complicated by different ice structures and a choice of a proper criterion for their assimilation either to the land or to the sea. Furthermore, if the Antarctic maritime area were defined as correspondent to the area of the Southern Ocean, its external boundary would, both in oceanographic and ecosystemic terms, be marked by the Antarctic Convergence, being the zone of delimitation between the Southern Ocean and the three major oceans – the Pacific, Atlantic and Indian.[8] Within this area, however, a difference exists both in legal and political terms between the major part of the Southern Ocean which is within the Antarctic Treaty area,[9] and the remaining part situated outside of this area, i.e., north of 60°S latitude and extending to the Antarctic Convergence.[10]

Is there a uniform or a dual law of the sea applicable to the Southern Ocean? The Antarctic Treaty offers two provisions directly relevant to this question. By stipulating in Article VI that its provisions shall apply to the area south of 60°S latitude, including all ice shelves, the Antarctic Treaty provides the legal boundary for the Antarctic maritime area within the wider Southern Ocean area. However, though mentioning high seas, Article VI fails to determine which part of the area in question is actually high seas.[11] The status of the coastal area of Antarctica does

---

[8] See Sir George Deacon, *The Antarctic Circumpolar Ocean* (Cambridge University Press, 1984).

[9] The Antarctic Treaty area is determined by the Antarctic Treaty, Art. VI, which provides: The provisions of the present Treaty shall apply to the area south of 60° South Latitude, including all ice shelves, but nothing in the present Treaty shall prejudice or in any way affect the rights, or the exercise of rights, of any State under international law with regard to the high seas within that area.

[10] On areas of application of other conventions adopted in the ambit of the ATS, see Chapter 2. Regarding the area of application of CCAMLR see in particular Chapters 5 and 9.

[11] In this connection, van der Essen has pointed out that the original intention of the drafters of Art. VI of the Antarctic Treaty was not for it to deal with the problem of economic

not offer a firm criterion for determining various regimes at sea; by 'freezing' the problem of sovereignty claims in Article IV, the Antarctic Treaty offers no more than an 'agreement to disagree' on the sovereignty issue.

The well-known problem of sovereignty claims creates a difficulty in itself, as it leads to the ambivalent interpretations with respect to the legal status of the Antarctic maritime area. Moreover, the fact of overlapping claims as well as the existence of an unclaimed part of Antarctica both contribute to the ambivalence of such interpretations.[12]

When the Antarctic Treaty was adopted in 1959, its scope was rather restricted, and – presumably due to the issue of sovereignty claims – it left in ambiguity the legal status of the Southern Ocean area within the Antarctic Treaty area.[13] This left ample room for arguing for the application of general norms of the law of the sea to this part of the Southern Ocean.

THE ANTARCTIC MARITIME AREA AND THE LAW OF THE SEA

Views seem to have diverged not only in connection with the question *how* to apply the law of the sea in general, and the LOS Convention in particular, to the Antarctic maritime area, but – prior to this – *whether* the LOS Convention is indeed applicable to that area at all. Several authors have pointed out that the Third United Nations Conference on the Law of the Sea (1973–82; hereinafter UNCLOS III) has intentionally failed to deal with this area: i.e., that the wording of the LOS Convention was no product of chance, but that the Antarctic was excluded deliberately

---

uses and of jurisdiction, but to apply the broad principles of the Antarctic Treaty (such as non-militarisation, the ban on weapons-testing, a freeze of claims to sovereignty, freedom of scientific research, as well as access to the results for all parties) to the Antarctic maritime area; in van der Essen's view, the contradictory text of Art. VI is a result of changes which were made during its drafting: see A. van der Essen, 'The Application of the Law of the Sea to the Antarctic Continent', in F. Orrego Vicuña (ed.), *Antarctic Resources Policy: Scientific, Legal and Political Issues* (Cambridge University Press, 1983), p. 233.

[12] The claims of Argentina, Chile and the United Kingdom partially overlap; the area situated within 90°W to 150°W longitude, and south of 60°S latitude is unclaimed.

[13] It should be stressed already here that this limited scope has been significantly widened in the course of the development of the ATS, primarily through the resource regimes and, more recently, through the Protocol: see below, especially at pp. 69–70.

from UNCLOS III negotiations.[14] In contrast to this, the 1986 Report of the UN Secretary-General stressed:

It is a global convention applicable to all ocean space. No area of ocean space is excluded. It follows that the Convention must be of significance to the Southern Ocean in the sense that its provisions also apply to that ocean.[15]

Similarly, Orrego has argued:

the exclusion of Antarctica from the ambit of the 1982 Convention's application would have required an express provision to that effect, which certainly is not the case.[16]

Moreover, the same author has pointed out that the basic concepts of the law of the sea – such as the territorial sea, the continental shelf, the exclusive economic zone and the regime of the high seas – have all become part of customary international law and can thus be applied to Antarctica independently of any conventional regime.[17] The view that the general law of the sea is of significance for the Antarctic maritime area has prevailed in the doctrine.[18]

If the law of the sea in general, and the LOS Convention in particular, is made applicable to the Antarctic maritime area, the question remains: *how* to apply it? In connection with this, Vukas has stressed that:

---

[14] See S. Müller, 'The Impact of UNCLOS III on the Antarctic Regime', in R. Wolfrum (ed.), *Antarctic Challenge: Conflicting Interests, Cooperation, Environmental Protection, Economic Development* (Berlin: Duncker & Humblot, 1984), p. 174; G. D. Triggs, 'The Antarctic Treaty System: Some Jurisdictional Problems', in G. D. Triggs (ed.), *The Antarctic Treaty Regime: Law, Environment and Resources* (Cambridge University Press, 1987), p. 92; E. J. Sahurie, *The International Law of Antarctica* (New Haven Press and Dordrecht: Martinus Nijhoff, 1991), p. 442. Sahurie points out examples of the subsequent state practice as indications in support of such a view.

[15] UN doc. A/41/722, of 17 November 1986, p. 29.

[16] F. Orrego Vicuña, 'The Law of the Sea and the Antarctic Treaty System: New Approaches to Offshore Jurisdiction', in C. C. Joyner and S. K. Chopra (eds.), *The Antarctic Legal Regime* (Dordrecht: Martinus Nijhoff, 1988), p. 101.

[17] *Ibid.*

[18] See C. C. Joyner, *Antarctica and the Law of the Sea* (Dordrecht: Martinus Nijhoff, 1992); van der Essen, 'The Application'; B. Vukas, 'Commentary', in T. A. Clingan, Jr (ed.), *The Law of the Sea: What Lies Ahead?, Proceedings of the 20th Annual Conference of the Law of the Sea Institute* (Honolulu, HA: The Law of the Sea Institute, University of Hawaii, 1988), pp. 404–7; B. H. Oxman, 'Antarctica and the New Law of the Sea', *Cornell International Law Journal*, vol. 19, no. 2, 1986, pp. 211–47; P. Gautier, 'The Maritime Area of the Antarctic and the New Law of the Sea', in J. Verhoeven, P. Sands and M. Bruce (eds.), *The Antarctic Environment and International Law* (London: Graham & Trotman, 1992), pp. 121–37.

the regimes of the seas adjacent to the coast have been developed on different physical and legal realities than those existing in Antarctica.[19]

First, the existing rules of the law of the sea have been conceived for waters adjacent to coasts not possessing such specific properties as those caused by the Antarctic ice structures.[20] Second, the law of the sea, as embodied both in customary and in conventional rules, relies on two basic concepts: the concept of the *coastal state* and the concept of the *baselines of the territorial sea*, derived from the first concept. It was due to the different approaches of the states concerned with respect to the issue of sovereignty claims to Antarctica that the law of the sea was initially approached from divergent 'positions of principle'.[21] These positions of principle were based on the view of either the existence or the non-existence of state sovereignty in Antarctica. They led to a purely legal logical exposition of the two essentially different lines of reasoning.

Both of them have taken a common point of departure – the notion of the coastal state. This notion is among the key concepts of the law of the sea, as it provides the basis for delimitation of different legal regimes for the marine and submarine areas, with their respective disparate statuses. While the coastal state possesses a certain degree of legal power over the marine and submarine areas situated relatively close to its coast (the internal waters, the territorial sea, the contiguous zone, the exclusive economic zone and the continental shelf), such legal power is not recognised by the law of the sea rules for the marine and submarine areas situated relatively distant from its coast (the high seas, and the seabed outside the limits of national jurisdiction).[22] This legal order is based on the general customary law of the sea, which is embodied partly in the provisions of the four conventions adopted at the First UN Conference on the Law of the Sea (Geneva, 1958)[23] and entirely in the provisions of the 1982 LOS Convention.

[19] Vukas, 'Commentary', p. 405.
[20] *Ibid.*; see also Sir Arthur Watts, *International Law and the Antarctic Treaty System* (Cambridge University Press, 1992), p. 163; Joyner, *Antarctica and the Law of the Sea*, pp. 81–4 and 195–205.
[21] Term introduced by Orrego, 'New Approaches', p. 97.
[22] Saying this, one should keep in kind the phenomenon of the so-called 'creeping jurisdiction' of coastal states, which has been (and remains) an obvious trend in the evolution of the law of the sea.
[23] The four 1958 Geneva Conventions are: Convention on the Territorial Sea and the Contiguous Zone (*United Nations Treaty Series*, vol. 516, pp. 205*ff*); Convention on the High Seas (*United Nations Treaty Series*, vol. 450, pp. 82*ff*); Convention on the Continental Shelf (*United Nations Treaty Series*, vol. 499, pp. 311*ff*); and Convention on Fishing and Conservation of the Living Resources of the High Seas (*United Nations Treaty Series*, vol. 599, pp. 285*ff*).

Furthermore, states which are not coastal do not possess legal power over the marine and submarine areas (sovereignty, sovereign rights and territorial jurisdiction). Moreover, an area that is 'coastal' in a geographical sense but without the recognised legal elements of statehood accordingly may not possess the power of the coastal state over the adjacent marine and submarine areas.

Thus, the fact of the existence of the coastal state is the backbone of all legal regimes in the law of the sea where the state exercises some degree of legal power based on its territory as well as the relevant fact for determining the limits of the law of the sea regimes characterised by the absence of a state's territorial jurisdiction. Indeed, the starting question has been formulated: does a coastal state exist in Antarctica? For the claimant states, the answer is in the affirmative, with all the consequences resulting from the rules of the law of the sea, as already summarised above. For the non-claimant states, the answer is in the negative, again with all the consequences resulting from the rules of the law of the sea.

Regarding the latter view, the law of the sea determines that all parts of the sea not included in the exclusive economic zone, in the territorial sea or in the internal waters of a state, or in the archipelagic waters of an archipelagic state, are the high seas.[24] Applying this rule to the status of the Antarctic marine area along with the hypothesis of the non-existence of the coastal state, the conclusion is, clearly, that *all* the sea south of 60°S latitude is high seas. And if the entire sea surrounding the Antarctic is high seas, then there is no sovereignty or sovereign rights of individual states over the seabed and its subsoil as well. In lacking the continental shelf regime, the entire submarine area under the Antarctic high seas, together with its natural resources, is outside the limits of national jurisdiction. However, there have been two lines of reasoning available when it comes to the legal interpretation of the regime of the submarine areas situated beneath the high seas, but beyond the outer limits of the continental shelf. According to one, advocated by the technologically most developed states, the regime of the high seas shall be applied analogously to such submarine areas, indeed including all the analogous high seas freedoms with regard to the natural resources of such submarine areas.[25] According to another view, advocated by a large group of developing states, the seabed outside the limits of national jurisdiction

---

[24] See the LOS Convention, Art. 86.

[25] This position is expressed in the US Deep Seabed Hard Mineral Resources act, of 28 June 1980, sec. 2(a)(12); reprinted in *International Legal Materials*, vol. XIX, 1980, pp. 1,003*ff.*

and its natural resources are considered in international law a common heritage of mankind.[26]

In summing up, when cumulatively applied to the Antarctic maritime area, the above views based on the 'positions of principle' may lead only to deadlock. If they were consequently put into practice, this would lead to irreconcilable legal solutions.

THE LAW OF THE SEA AND THE ANTARCTIC TREATY SYSTEM

The above interpretation of the law of the sea rules – and their application to the Antarctic maritime area based on the positions of principle – fails to take into consideration the *substance* of the regimes at the sea adjacent to the coast, whose *raison d'être* does not lie solely in the existence of the coastal state. As emphasised by Vukas:

> there are some interests, activities, and relations, non-existent in the high seas, that have to be regulated in the coastal waters independently of the existence of coastal sovereignty: for example, the prevention of land-based pollution, the prevention of infringement of sanitary regulations applied on land, the protection of coastal species, the regulation of discharging or embarking, etc.[27]

Moreover, the logical constructions based on the positions of principle may be maintained as long as one claims that the proper way to determine the legal status of the Antarctic maritime area is solely by applying the rules of the general law of the sea to that area. Such a line of reasoning, however, fails to take into consideration the *complexity of the normative situation*: the problem lies not in the application of one legal system (the law of the sea) to the factual situation (the Antarctic maritime area) but in the combined application of the two legal systems (the law of the sea *and* the ATS) to the same factual situation. The 1958 Geneva Conference on the Law of the Sea codified the then-existing customary law of the sea, pre-dating the adoption of the Antarctic Treaty by only one year. Since then, these two legal systems have had a parallel development, the former resulting in the 1982 LOS Convention and the latter in today's ATS. The system which has grown up on the basis of the Antarctic Treaty has clearly established a special body of rules tailored to the special circumstances of

---

[26] See the 1970 Declaration on the Principles Governing the Sea-Bed and the Ocean Floor, and the Subsoil Thereof, Beyond the Limits of National Jurisdiction (UN General Assembly resolution 2749 (XXV) of 17 December 1970); see also Part XI of the LOS Convention.

[27] Vukas, 'Commentary', p. 406.

the Antarctic.[28] Hence, the present legal status of the Antarctic maritime area may be properly determined by *two* international systems of rules in conjunction: the ATS and the general international law of the sea.

One important factor is the unique geophysical circumstances in the Antarctic, especially various ice structures.[29] However, other factors have led the ATS into the regulation of the specific issues otherwise regulated by the law of the sea: according to what is known today, significant natural resources in the Antarctic Treaty area may be found predominantly in its maritime area, which is characterised by its unique ecosystem. Thus, the initially restricted scope of the Antarctic Treaty[30] has been widened through the ATS' developing rules relevant to the management of the Antarctic marine resources. As observed by Orrego, it is for this reason that solutions to the pertinent legal problems have begun to emerge within the context of various resource regimes.[31] Hence, the vital need for an Antarctic resources policy has led to a gradual revision of the initial 'positions of principle'.[32] This, in turn, has had implications for the applicability of the general law of the sea to the Antarctic maritime area. At this point, Orrego links resource regimes with Article VI of the Antarctic Treaty (with implications for the extent of applicability of the law of the sea in general), by concluding that:

questions of jurisdiction and economic utilization related to offshore maritime areas and the high seas have been dealt with through practice within the system and the development of its special regimes.[33]

While analysing the relationship between the ATS and the law of the sea from another perspective, Vukas arrives at a similar conclusion:

Although Article 6 of the Antarctic Treaty is drafted in a somewhat ambiguous manner, it is obvious that south of 60° South latitude the high seas regime, subject to the principles of the Antarctic Treaty, applies. In respect of the living resources, the 1980 Conservation Convention is an important addition to the applicable general rules.[34]

---

[28] See Watts, *International Law and the Antarctic Treaty System*, p. 291.
[29] See Joyner, *Antarctica and the Law of the Sea*, p. 79; Watts, *International Law and the Antarctic Treaty System*, p. 291.
[30] This scope, in normative terms, may have been reduced to the Treaty's two main principles, i.e. peaceful uses and scientific research, as well as to the establishment of a *status quo* with respect to the issue of sovereignty claims.
[31] Orrego, 'New Approaches', pp. 97–8.
[32] *Ibid.*, p. 98.
[33] *Ibid.*, p. 101.
[34] Vukas, 'Commentary', p. 405.

To sum it up, this line of reasoning leads us to the conclusion that the proper approach lies not in the direct application of the general law of the sea to the Antarctic maritime area but in the concurrence of the two existing systems of legal norms, that is, the law of the sea (mainly as codified in the 1982 LOS Convention) and the ATS. At that stage, it might be asserted, these two normative systems, when combined in a complex legal mosaic, offer the most acceptable basis for building the legal regime for the Antarctic maritime area.

Although this approach delves considerably deeper into the essence of the specific situation of the Antarctic maritime area, it still leaves several fundamental questions open. As it obviously takes its point of departure in the general law of the sea, this approach seeks primarily to determine which aspects of the law of the sea are relevant and applicable to the Antarctic maritime area.[35] In doing so from the perspective of general law, it still has to cope with the core problem: territorial claims in Antarctica. Thus, even in the conjunctive treatment of the two legal systems applicable to the Antarctic maritime area, the law of the sea perspective nevertheless relies upon the coastal state concept. Perhaps the best solution one may invent in such a situation is the ambivalent phrase 'bifocal approach'.

THE ANTARCTIC TREATY SYSTEM PERSPECTIVE ON THE LAW OF THE SEA QUESTIONS

The ATS has introduced and gradually developed its own perspective to the law of the sea questions, which made it possible to bridge the difficulties connected with the traditional concepts of the general law of the sea. Under the ATS, the concept of the coastal state has in fact acquired its 'functional equivalent',[36] conceptualised by van der Essen as the joint jurisdiction of the Consultative Parties over the Antarctic area.[37] Joyner has observed that the legal basis for the ATS' self-designed resource management and jurisdictional functions in waters offshore Antarctica is derived in large part from its political authority, which might attain per-

---

[35] In this connection, Joyner has pointed out that 'the 1982 United Nations Convention on the Law of the Sea did little to resolve these issues. In fact, certain aspects of the new law of the sea may have actually produced greater ambiguity concerning jurisdictional responsibilities and uses of Antarctic waters': Joyner, *Antarctica and the Law of the Sea*, pp. 75–6.

[36] See *ibid.*, p. 98.

[37] See van der Essen, 'The Application', pp. 235 and 242.

suasiveness owing to the acknowledged success of the ATS over the past thirty years.[38]

The common policy adopted by the Consultative Parties in establishing the resource regimes has led to the reconciliation of otherwise irreconcilable positions of principle. Significantly, the resource regimes do not differentiate between claimed and unclaimed sectors in the Antarctic. Here, one could argue that the ATS breaks with the fixity of legal concepts, in going beyond the freedom–sovereignty–commons trichotomy of ordering systems, which had proven itself unsuited for allocating authority in Antarctica.[39]

Although largely innovative and suited for the special circumstances of the Antarctic, the ATS resource regimes have still implied the necessity of compromising between the Antarctic regional peculiarities and the requirements stemming from the already established general legal rules as well as policy considerations. However, it is maintained in the remaining part of this chapter that the Protocol has introduced a qualitatively new dimension in the ATS in this respect. The shift from the mineral resource regime to the environmental protection regime has had significant consequences with regard to the regulation of the status of the Antarctic submarine areas. Let us have a look at the evolution of this regulation from the Convention on the Regulation of Antarctic Mineral Resource Activities (CRAMRA) to the Protocol, on the one hand, and its relationship with the concepts of the general law of the sea, on the other hand, in order to explain the argument concerning the introduction of a new dimension in the ATS perspective on the law of the sea.

A NEW DIMENSION INTRODUCED BY THE PROTOCOL

Recent developments within the ATS have added to the controversy of the relationship between the ATS and the law of the sea, in particular with respect to the status of the Antarctic submarine areas. The law of the sea order has created two separate regimes for the submarine areas beyond the outer limits of the territorial sea: the continental shelf, and the regime for the seabed beyond the limits of national jurisdiction (the latter being, according to the LOS Convention, together with its resources the common heritage of mankind). Both regimes are largely

---

[38] Joyner, *Antarctica and the Law of the Sea*, pp. 89 and 98–9.
[39] See Sahurie, *The International Law of Antarctica*, pp. 574–5.

concerned with the exploration and exploitation of minerals.[40] While the coastal state exercises sovereign rights over the continental shelf for the purpose of exploring it and exploiting its natural resources,[41] the minerals recovered from the Area[42] may only be alienated in accordance with Part XI of the LOS Convention and the rules, regulations and procedures of the International Seabed Authority.[43] True, Part XI of the LOS Convention has been substantially reformed by the 1994 Implementation Agreement; however, the *redistributive element* of the common heritage of mankind concept persisted in this thorough revision of Part XI.[44] Thus, if applicable, both the continental shelf and the Area regimes of the LOS Convention would allow for mineral resources activities in the seabed offshore Antarctica. In contrast, the Protocol has introduced the prohibition of any activity relating to mineral resources, other than scientific research,[45] in the Antarctic Treaty area. This may indicate that compatibility between the ATS and the general law of the sea is reduced.

The genesis and evolution of norms of both the law of the sea and the ATS, regulating the status of submarine areas (implying the regulation of the mineral resource activities), may be traced back to the middle of the 1940s and early 1970s, respectively. This may add to the clarification of the present relationship between the LOS Convention and the Protocol.

THE LAW OF THE SEA AND CRAMRA

The problem of the Antarctic minerals regime dominated the ATS' focus for nearly two decades.[46] Although not expected to enter into force in the

---

[40] In addition, Art. 56, para. 1(a) of the LOS Convention provides that: 'In the exclusive economic zone, the coastal State has: (a) sovereign rights for the purpose of exploring and exploiting, conserving and managing the natural resources, whether living or non-living, of . . . the sea-bed and its subsoil.' However, it is provided in Art. 56, para. 3 that these rights shall be exercised in accordance with Part VI of the LOS Convention, which concerns the continental shelf regime.

[41] LOS Convention, Art. 77, para. 1.

[42] In the LOS Convention terminology, 'Area' means the seabed and ocean floor and subsoil thereof, beyond the limits of national jurisdiction: see LOS Convention, Art. 1, para. 1(1).

[43] LOS Convention, Art. 137, para. 2.

[44] See also UN General Assembly resolution 49/28, on the 'Law of the Sea', of 19 December 1994, Preamble, para. 3.

[45] Protocol, Art. 7.

[46] It is beyond the scope of this chapter to elaborate on the variety of reasons and factors underlying the Antarctic minerals regime: Chapters 6 and 10 deal with this in more

foreseeable future, CRAMRA may for several reasons serve as a useful object of analysis for clarifying the relationship between the ATS and the law of the sea. As one illustration of the ATS' law of the sea perspective in the 1980s, we may note that certain provisions of CRAMRA, to be examined below, stand in contrast to the relevant provisions of the Protocol.

The necessity for CRAMRA to concern itself with law of the sea issues has been associated with the nature of the Antarctic minerals issue; however speculative and hypothetical, if any minerals-related activities were to occur in Antarctica in the foreseeable future, their field would be prevailingly in the Antarctic offshore submarine areas. In this connection, the 'core issue' which remained unsettled during the negotiations for CRAMRA until the last session of the IV Special Consultative Meeting, actually concerned one of its central provisions: the area of application of CRAMRA.[47] Eventually agreed upon in Article 5 of CRAMRA, this area of application is fixed by a complicated formula, reflecting the need for both internal (ATS) and external accommodations and compromises in its adoption. Article 5 reads:

1   This Convention shall, subject to paragraphs 2, 3 and 4 below, apply to the Antarctic Treaty area.

2   Without prejudice to the responsibilities of the Antarctic Treaty Consultative Parties under the Antarctic Treaty and measures pursuant to it, the Parties agree that this Convention shall regulate Antarctic mineral resource activities which take place on the continent of Antarctica and all Antarctic islands, including all ice shelves, south of 60° south latitude and in the seabed and subsoil of adjacent offshore areas *up to* the deep seabed.[48]

3   For the purposes of this Convention 'deep seabed' means the seabed and subsoil beyond the geographic extent of the continental shelf as the term continental shelf is defined in accordance with international law.[49]

---

depth; also, ample literature is available on this issue: see especially F. Orrego Vicuña, *Antarctic Mineral Exploitation: The Emerging Legal Framework* (Cambridge University Press, 1988), and the bibliography listed there.

[47] See R. Wolfrum, *The Convention on the Regulation of Antarctic Mineral Resource Activities: An Attempt to Break New Ground* (Berlin: Springer-Verlag, 1991), pp. 7, 9 and 31–4.

[48] Emphasis added. In this connection, para. 7(iv) of the 1981 Recommendation XI-1, which gave the mandate to the Consultative Parties to commence the negotiations for CRAMRA, provided that the future regime should: 'Apply to all mineral resource activities taking place on the Antarctic Continent and its adjacent offshore areas *but without encroachment* on the deep seabed' (emphasis added). In the Preamble of Recommendation XI-1, the Consultative Parties stressed that they are: '*Mindful* of the negotiations that are taking place in the Third United Nations Conference on the Law of the Sea'.

[49] The Final Act of the IV Special Consultative Meeting made it clear that the 'geographic extent of the continental shelf', as referred to in this provision, would be determined by

4   Nothing in this Article shall be construed as limiting the application of other Articles of this Convention in so far as they relate to possible impacts outside the area referred to in paragraphs 1 and 2 above, including impacts on dependent or on associated ecosystems.

At the level of *internal* ATS accommodations, the negotiations which led to the adoption of CRAMRA have confirmed the argument that a consequent adherence to the 'positions of principle' is actually a dead end: consensus could be reached neither for a regime which would amount to the recognition of the claims to sovereignty in substance nor for a regime which would in fact extinguish such claims.[50] Again, the issue of sovereignty (and thus of the coastal state) has changed its perspective through the agreement that the minerals activities can be undertaken only pursuant to the provisions of the minerals resource regime.

With respect to *external* accommodations, Wolfrum has aptly formulated it:

The complicated formula found in Article 5 represents a compromise between those arguing that the whole of the deep seabed falls under the jurisdiction of the International Seabed Authority and those according to which the Antarctic Treaty consists of a special regime and thus exempts the seabed south of 60° south latitude from the jurisdiction of the International Seabed Authority.[51]

At this point, we must stress that the Antarctic minerals issue served as a stimulus for the initiation of the 'Question of Antarctica' in the UN in 1983, which was – in turn – directly linked to the outcome of UNCLOS III, or, more precisely, to the interconnection between the provisions of the LOS Convention on the continental shelf (Part VI, especially Article 76) and on the Area (Part XI). The interest of developing states in Antarctic mineral resources has presumably been enhanced by the provision of Article 76 of the LOS Convention, which extended the continental shelf across the entire continental margin and, in many areas where the width of the continental margin does not exceed 200 nautical miles, to the deep seabed as well. Thus, the continental shelf regime has comprised the commercially most import-

reference to all the criteria and the rules embodied in Art. 76 of the LOS Convention, which contains the definition of the continental shelf.

[50]   Wolfrum, *CRAMRA: An Attempt*, p. 14. For the way CRAMRA attempted to balance sovereignty positions in its provisions, see especially Chapters 6, 10 and Conclusions of this book.

[51]   Wolfrum, *CRAMRA: An Attempt*, p. 33.

ant part of the submarine areas.[52] It should be remembered that many states had more optimistic expectations during the preparations for UNCLOS III. In 1967 Malta suggested the cessation of further expansion of the continental shelf regime at the boundary which was *then* technologically accessible, in order to leave as much space as possible for the application of the then proposed common heritage of mankind regime. However, UNCLOS III did not fully fulfil such expectations of developing countries.

After the adoption of the 1982 LOS Convention, the Antarctic attracted the attention of developing countries as an area open for the new initiative; this coincided with the commencement of the negotiations for CRAMRA at the IV Special Consultative Meeting.[53] As pointed out in Chapter 2, immediately upon the close of UNCLOS III, Malaysia, joined by Antigua and Barbuda, launched an initiative to have the 'Question of Antarctica' included in the agenda of the UN General Assembly. Discussions of the 'Question of Antarctica' in the UN reached a peak in November 1985,[54] when, following the forty-second ordinary session of the Council of Ministers of the Organization of African Unity,[55] the ATS' negotiations for the Antarctic minerals regime were highlighted, along with the question of the relevance of the LOS Convention,[56] in particular its Part XI, for the Antarctic submarine areas.[57]

---

[52] It is estimated that about 87 per cent of total oil and gas reserves are to be found in the area between the coast and the boundary line 200 miles distant from the territorial sea baselines; the percentage is actually even higher, because the geo-criterion for the continental shelf comprises the continental margin as well.

[53] See J. A. Heap, 'Meeting on Antarctic Mineral Resources, Wellington, New Zealand, 17–28 January 1983', *Polar Record*, vol. 21, no. 134, 1983, pp. 500–2; J. A. Heap, 'The Political Case for the Minerals Convention', in G. Cook (ed.), *The Future of Antarctica: Exploitation versus Preservation* (Manchester University Press, 1990), pp. 44–52.

[54] For further comments see P. J. Beck, 'Antarctica at the United Nations, 1985: The End of Consensus?', *Polar Record*, vol. 23, no. 143, 1986, pp. 159–66; C. Maquieira, 'The Question of Antarctica at the United Nations: The End of Consensus?', in R. Wolfrum (ed.), *Antarctic Challenge III: Conflicting Interests, Cooperation, Environmental Protection, Economic Development* (Berlin: Duncker & Humblot, 1988), pp. 253–70.

[55] In the resolution on Antarctica adopted at that session, held in Addis Ababa, 10–17 July 1985, the OAU declared Antarctica to be the common heritage of mankind: UN doc. A/40/666, annex II, resolution CM/Res. 988 (XLII).

[56] See further T. Treves, 'The United Nations General Assembly, Antarctica and the Law of the Sea Convention', in F. Francioni and T. Scovazzi (eds.), *International Law for Antarctica* (Milano: Giuffrè Editore, 1987), pp. 281–9.

[57] Pursuant to the UN General Assembly resolution 40/156 A, of 16 December 1985, the UN Secretary-General has updated and expanded the 1984 Study on the 'Question of

The ATS solution found several years later in Article 5 of CRAMRA was obviously not an easy one. It tried to keep a balance between the LOS Convention's concepts of the continental shelf and the Area, recognising both to some extent. Article 5 of CRAMRA makes a concession with respect to the Antarctic deep seabed, which it attempts to define by using a mixture of the geographic and the legal concepts of the continental shelf, later interpreted in the Final Act of the IV Special Consultative Meeting to be in harmony with the continental shelf concept of the LOS Convention.[58] As such, CRAMRA may serve as a prominent example of difficulties in attempts at reconciling the concepts introduced by the two normative systems – the law of the sea and the ATS – when cumulatively applied to the Antarctic maritime area.

THE PROTOCOL AND CRAMRA

Several commentators have pointed out the comprehensiveness and stringency of CRAMRA's provisions on the protection of the Antarctic environment;[59] accordingly, CRAMRA has been viewed as representing a decisive step in the conceptual evolution of environmental protection regimes in the Antarctic.[60] Moreover, CRAMRA has been praised for its progressiveness in setting new standards in international law on the protection of the environment for areas beyond indisputable national jurisdiction,[61] since some of its provisions were used as a model by the Preparatory Commission for the International Seabed Authority and the

Antarctica' (UN doc. A/39/583, Part I) by addressing, *inter alia*, the question of the significance of the LOS Convention in the Southern Ocean as well as the associated issues of sovereignty and jurisdiction: see *Question of Antarctica, Report of the Secretary-General*, UN doc. A/41/722, of 17 November 1986, pp. 29–37; in the final section of the Report, by way of conclusion, it is stated that 'the question of the applicability of the international regime for the sea-bed and ocean floor beyond national jurisdiction to the sea-bed in the Antarctica region, and hence the significance thereto, *remains unclear*' (emphasis added).

[58] In the opinion of Gautier, 'the concept of the continental shelf is only used in the Convention of Wellington to explain the phrase "deep sea-bed", which shows the concern of the authors of the text to safeguard the particularities of the Antarctic system': Gautier, 'The Maritime Area', p. 132.

[59] See especially Watts, *International Law and the Antarctic Treaty System*, p. 276; Wolfrum, *CRAMRA: An Attempt*. See also Chapter 6.

[60] F. Orrego Vicuña, 'The Protection of the Antarctic Environment', *IARP Publication Series* (Lysaker: Fridtjof Nansen Institute, 1992), no. 5, p. 18.

[61] Watts, *International Law and the Antarctic Treaty System*, p. 276; Wolfrum, *CRAMRA: An Attempt*, pp. 30–1 and 89.

International Tribunal for the Law of the Sea (hereinafter PrepCom) in preparing the Draft Regulations on the Protection and Preservation of the Marine Environment from Activities in the Area.[62] Finally, comparison of the provisions of CRAMRA and of the Protocol indicates that several of the Protocol's provisions have built on those previously agreed in CRAMRA.[63]

Without denying the similarities between certain provisions of CRAMRA and of the Protocol as well as the fact that the former instrument has contributed a great deal in the formulation of the latter, we should note that the differences between CRAMRA and the Protocol are considerably more significant for the subject of this chapter. When it comes to mineral resource activities in the Antarctic submarine area, two principal differences between CRAMRA and the Protocol should be highlighted.

First, while the main purpose of CRAMRA was to protect the Antarctic environment through a *regulation* of mineral resource activities, the Protocol (Article 7) aims at preservation of the Antarctic environment by *prohibiting* any activity relating to mineral resources, other than scientific research. This provision has been termed an 'innovative principle',[64] a 'drastic clause'[65] or an 'entirely novel basis'[66] for the protection and preservation of the Antarctic environment. It marks an abrupt change of direction – the Protocol effectively undermines the leading principle of CRAMRA.[67] Moreover, closer examination of Articles 7 and 25 of the Protocol in conjunction reveals that the Protocol

---

[62] UN doc. LOS/PCN/SCN.3/WP.6/Add.5; however, already at first glance it is noticeable that the PrepCom's Draft Regulations are less stringent in respect of mining activities than the corresponding provisions of CRAMRA; see also V. S. Safronchuk, 'The Relationship between the ATS and the Law of the Sea Convention of 1982', in A. Jørgensen-Dahl and W. Østreng (eds.), *The Antarctic Treaty System in World Politics* (London: Macmillan, 1991), p. 332.

[63] See Chapter 10; also Watts, *International Law and the Antarctic Treaty System*, p. 276; for an extensive comparison between provisions of CRAMRA and of the Protocol see Wolfrum, *CRAMRA: An Attempt*, pp. 84–94.

[64] F. Francioni, 'The Madrid Protocol on the Protection of the Antarctic Environment', *Texas International Law Journal*, vol. 28, no. 1, 1993, pp. 60–1.

[65] Orrego, 'The Protection', p. 28.

[66] K. R. Simmonds, 'The Antarctic Protocol', *Oil and Gas Law and Taxation Review*, vol. 9, no. 12, 1991, p. 384.

[67] See Watts, *International Law and the Antarctic Treaty System*, p. 287; Wolfrum, *CRAMRA: An Attempt*, pp. 28 and 88.

in fact imposes a conditionally *indefinite* ban on Antarctic mineral resource activities.[68]

The second major difference arises from the fact that the Protocol, unlike CRAMRA, eliminates any differentiation of legal regimes applicable to the Antarctic submarine area by simply prohibiting any mineral resources activity other than scientific research. In contrast to this, Article 5 of CRAMRA has provided for a differentiation of legal regimes in the Antarctic submarine area by introducing a distinction between one legal regime applicable in the area of the continental shelf (to which CRAMRA would have applied), and another applicable in the deep seabed (excluded from the application of CRAMRA provisions).

Indeed, we might well conclude from this differentiation that the area of application of CRAMRA and that of the Protocol are essentially different. However, an unambiguous determination of the Protocol's area of application is made difficult by the absence of any specific provision on the territorial scope in the Protocol itself. On the one hand, it would stem from the fact that the Protocol is meant to supplement the Antarctic Treaty that – in lacking any provision to the contrary – its area of application should be identical with that of the Antarctic Treaty.[69] Moreover, the heart of the Protocol lies in its Article 3, which comprises 'all activities in the *Antarctic Treaty area*' (emphasis added).[70] The Protocol uses the formulation 'Antarctic Treaty area' throughout the text of its provisions. On the other hand, it appears environmentally inadequate to confine the Protocol to a geographic limit which would seem insufficient in the context of the Protocol's provisions.[71]

---

[68] In support of such interpretation see Orrego, 'The Protection', p. 29; Simmonds, 'The Antarctic Protocol', p. 384; S. K. N. Blay, 'New Trends in the Protection of the Antarctic Environment: The 1991 Madrid Protocol', *American Journal of International Law*, vol. 86, no. 2, 1992, pp. 395–7; P. Gautier, *Belgium and the Antarctic* (Brussels: Ministry of Foreign Affairs, External Trade and Development Cooperation, 1992), p. 22; for the negotiating history of Art. 25 of the Protocol see Francioni, 'The Madrid Protocol', pp. 68–70.

[69] See comment by W. M. Bush (ed.), *Antarctica and International Law: A Collection of Inter-State and National Documents* (New York: Oceana, 1992), Booklet AT91C, p. 2; see the Protocol, Art. 4; the Antarctic Treaty, Art. VI; at another place Bush comments: 'the area south of 60 degrees south latitude . . . is the same as the area of operation of the protocol'; *ibid.*, Booklet AT91D, p. 11. In line with such comment, see Orrego, 'The Protection', p. 22.

[70] See also comment by Bush (ed.), *Antarctica and International Law*, Booklet AT91C, p. 2.

[71] *Ibid.*, pp. 2–3.

In this connection, Chile made an interpretative declaration[72] on the adoption of the Protocol, which in its relevant part reads:

In Article 7, the Protocol forbids mineral activities in all their phases. We understand that the prohibition of Antarctic mineral activities shall apply to the whole territory to which we claim sovereign rights in the Antarctic, and to the respective continental platform, even in the event that it stretches north of the 60 degrees southern latitude.[73]

This declaration seems to rely on the geographic rather than on the legal criterion for determining the outer limit of the continental shelf. Its content might imply an intention toward specific interpretation of legal implications of the Protocol regarding the continental shelf regime in the application area of the Protocol.

THE PROTOCOL AND THE LOS CONVENTION

The mere fact that the Protocol has introduced a prohibition on any activity relating to mineral resources, other than scientific research, implies a contradiction of the concepts for submarine areas as embodied in the Protocol and in the LOS Convention. Both the continental shelf regime and the Area regime of the LOS Convention are concerned with the exploration and exploitation of submarine mineral resources. The difference between these two regimes lies not in *whether* mineral resource activities are permitted or prohibited, but in *who* is entitled to claim, acquire or exercise rights with respect to minerals recovered from the respective areas covered by these two regimes. In prohibiting such activities, the Protocol adopts an entirely different approach.

The solution to such a contradiction between approaches is to be found neither in Article 311 of the LOS Convention[74] nor in Article 4 of the

---

[72] While reservations to the Protocol are not permitted (see Art. 24 of the Protocol), in the Final Act of the XI Special Consultative Meeting, para. 12 (reprinted in *International Legal Materials*, vol. XXX, 1991, pp. 1,460–1) it is stated that: 'this did not preclude a State, when signing, ratifying, accepting or approving the Protocol, or when acceding to it, from making declarations or statements . . . provided that such declarations or statements do not purport to exclude or to modify the legal effect of the Protocol in its application to that State'.

[73] Text of the Chilean declaration, para. 3, of 4 October 1991, as reprinted in Bush (ed.), *Antarctica and International Law*, Booklet AT91D, p. 10; note the term used in the declaration: the 'continental platform', not the 'continental shelf'.

[74] LOS Convention, Art. 311, on relation to other conventions and international agreements, the application of which is limited to states parties to the LOS Convention.

Protocol.[75] Rather, it ought to be sought in the *ratio*[76] of the regimes in question and contemporary tendencies regarding the approaches in conflict.

The prohibition of mineral resource activities and the continental shelf concept

The *ratio* of the continental shelf concept, when introduced in the law of the sea in the age of an early development of submarine mining technology,[77] was the desire of coastal states to acquire exclusive rights for utilisation of oil and gas from offshore areas adjacent to their coasts but still beyond the *then* established limits of territorial jurisdiction (which at that time was the outer limit of the territorial sea). Such claims were based upon the argument that since the continental shelf is merely a continuation of the land mass, it is only natural that the coastal state controlling the land mass should also control its extension beneath the sea.[78] By the time the First Conference on the Law of the Sea was held in Geneva in 1958, the concept of the continental shelf had become a part of customary international law. It was codified in the 1958 Convention on the Continental Shelf, which recognised that all coastal states have sovereign rights over the continental shelf for precisely two purposes: for *exploring* it and *exploiting* its natural resources.[79] The corresponding provisions are contained in the LOS Convention (Article 77, paragraphs

---

[75] Protocol, Art. 4, which is limited to the relationship of the Protocol with other components of the ATS.

[76] *Ratio est legis anima; mutata legis ratione mutatur et lex* (reason is the soul of law; the reason of law being changed the law is also changed': see *Black's Law Dictionary*, 6th ed. (St Paul, MN: West, 1990), p. 1,262.

[77] The first claim was advanced by the United States in a proclamation of 28 September 1945 (text reprinted in *American Journal of International Law*, vol. 40, 1946, Supp., pp. 45–6); soon after it was followed by similar claims by a number of states, mainly Latin American and Near Eastern states.

[78] See J. Andrassy, *International Law and the Resources of the Sea* (New York: Columbia University Press, 1970), p. 51.

[79] Convention on the Continental Shelf, Art. 2, para. 1: 'natural resources' of the continental shelf were defined as the mineral and other non-living resources of the seabed and subsoil together with living organisms belonging to sedentary species: see Convention on the Continental Shelf, Art. 2, para. 4. Sedentary species are defined as 'organisms which, at the harvestable stage, either are immobile on or under the sea-bed or are unable to move except in constant physical contact with the sea-bed or the subsoil' (*ibid.*). On the question of living organisms in the Antarctic maritime area see G. A. Knox, 'The Living Resources of the Southern Ocean: A Scientific Overview', in Orrego (ed.), *Antarctic Resources Policy*, pp. 21–60.

1 and 4). Indeed, oil and gas are, from the commercial point of view, the most attractive natural resources found in the continental shelf.

By stipulating that any activity relating to mineral resources, other than scientific research, shall be prohibited, the Protocol substantially diminishes the privilege of 'bifocalism' regarding the legal status of the Antarctic continental shelf. The most important continental shelf rights – the exploration and exploitation of its mineral resources – are now prevented by the Protocol.[80] The concept of the continental shelf has thus lost its *ratio* in the Antarctic submarine area. To illustrate the scope of Article 7 of the Protocol, let us imagine that Article IV of the Antarctic Treaty is revised to acknowledge sovereignty of claimant states in Antarctica: even if these states are recognised as coastal sovereigns, their continental shelf rights would still remain prevented by Article 7 of the Protocol. In this context, the Protocol seriously questions the appropriateness of the coastal state concept as a relevant factor for determination of the legal status of the Antarctic continental shelf.

The prohibition of mineral resource activities and the concept of the Area

The concept of the Area was initially introduced in the law of the sea during the middle and late 1960s, opposing the trend of extension of coastal states' authority over enlarged submarine areas on the basis of a formal interpretation of the definition of the continental shelf as set forth in the 1958 Convention on the Continental Shelf.[81] The 1967 Maltese initiative to prevent such development even further contained a proposal to declare the seabed and the ocean floor beyond the limits of national jurisdiction a common heritage of mankind. The main components of this concept were formulated in the principles of the Maltese explanatory memorandum of 17 August 1967,[82] which may be summarised around two major points: (a) the reservation exclusively for peaceful purposes of

---

[80] Protocol, Art. 7, exerts the same effect on a part of the concept of the exclusive economic zone, as provided for in Art. 56, para. 1 of the LOS Convention; see also note 40 above.

[81] Convention on the Continental Shelf, Art. 1, defines the continental shelf as the seabed and subsoil of submarine areas adjacent to the coast but outside the area of the territorial sea, to a depth of 200 metres, or beyond that limit, to where the depth of the superjacent waters permits the exploitation of the natural resources of the said areas; problems connected with the criterion of *exploitability* contained in this definition ultimately led to UNCLOS III.

[82] UN doc. A/6695.

the seabed and its subsoil; and (b) the use of the resources of these sub-marine areas in the interest of mankind, through an economic redistri-bution of the net financial benefits accumulated from their *exploitation*. With the adoption of the LOS Convention in 1982, these general prin-ciples found their elaboration and legal expression.[83]

The Protocol and Part XI of the LOS Convention are in the same line of reasoning with regard to use of the submarine areas exclusively for peaceful purposes. The contradiction occurs regarding another element of the concept of the Area, i.e., the provision stipulating that the minerals recovered from the Area may only be alienated in accordance with Part XI of the LOS Convention – now as supplemented by the Implemen-tation Agreement – and the rules, regulations and procedures of the Authority.[84] Alienation of minerals presupposes, of course, the pros-pecting, exploration and exploitation of mineral resources.[85] It is precisely these activities that fall under the prohibition of Article 7 of the Protocol. This means that the application of perhaps the most important element of the common heritage of mankind principle as elaborated in the LOS Convention concept of the Area is prevented in the Antarctic submarine areas. In this context, one may start to wonder what, in substance, remains of the common heritage of mankind principle of sharing the benefits from mineral resource activities in the Antarctic submarine area, if those same activities are prohibited in the Antarctic submarine areas. Regarding the relationship of the Protocol's mining ban with the LOS Convention's concept of the Area, as far as the *redistributive* element of the common heritage of mankind principle is concerned, Money's obser-vation holds true:

by banning mineral exploitation and thus foreclosing the possibility of accruing benefits from such exploitation, the common heritage of mankind principle, orig-inally based on economic redistribution, simply fails to apply meaningfully to Antarctica.[86]

Various lines of reasoning might be expected, arguing against the above

---

[83] See the LOS Convention, Arts. 136–49.
[84] The LOS Convention, Art. 137, para. 2; pursuant to the LOS Convention, Art. 1, para. 1(2) 'Authority' means the International Sea-Bed Authority.
[85] As defined by the LOS Convention, Art. 133, for the purposes of its Part XI:
  (a) 'resources' means all solid, liquid or gaseous mineral resources *in situ* in the Area at or beneath the sea-bed, including polymetallic nodules;
  (b) resources, when recovered from the Area, are referred to as 'minerals'.
[86] R. E. Money, Jr, 'The Protocol on Environmental Protection to the Antarctic Treaty: Maintaining a Legal Regime', *Emory International Law Review*, vol. 7, 1993, p. 192.

thesis on the normative collision between the Protocol's mining ban and the LOS Convention's common heritage of mankind concept. First, one can argue that the common heritage of mankind concept can take different forms; for example, that it can be interpreted as embodying elements of environmental protection and non-appropriation of resources, instead of their exploitation and redistribution of benefits. Indeed, various interpretations of the common heritage of mankind are possible, but the result will depend on the *context* in which an interpretation is employed – and in this case, the context is provided by the LOS Convention. And the letter of the LOS Convention, especially its Part XI, does *not* allow for such an extensive interpretation of the common heritage of mankind concept.[87] Neither does the Implementation Agreement eliminate the redistributive element regarding benefits of exploitation of minerals from the Area: on the contrary, among the main motives for the adoption of the Implementation Agreement was the circumstance that industrialised states had criticised Part XI of the LOS Convention for not being responsive enough to *market* forces.[88] The exploitative element thus persists in the Area, under the LOS Convention, as supplemented by the Implementation Agreement.

It can be argued, moreover, that the mineral resources in the Area, even if they should be subject to the exploitative element of the common heritage of mankind, do not necessarily need to be exploited in each and every part of the Area. This might suggest that, in the seabed area south of 60°S latitude, the Authority will consider that no need exists for the exploitation of minerals. However, this should be a free decision to be taken by the Authority itself, not prejudiced by a previous decision made by any other forum or laid down in any other international treaty, unrelated to the LOS Convention.

And finally, one can approach the entire problematic rather cynically, by arguing that the entire question is purely theoretical, since the Southern Ocean seabed minerals are of no practical interest: the polymetallic nodules found there are poor in valuable metal content, while the existence of deposits of offshore oil and gas is still only speculative. However, following this line of reasoning, the ultimate question would be:

---

[87] See, e.g., S. Mahmoudi, *The Law of Deep Sea-Bed Mining* (Stockholm: Almqvist & Wiksell International, 1987), especially Part 3, on the constituent elements of the legal regime for the deep seabed (chapter 5: 'Utilization System', pp. 171–253; and chapter 6: 'Utilization Machinery', pp. 255–305). Mahmoudi considers the *utilisation* element as the main constituent element of the legal regime for the deep sea-bed under the LOS Convention.

[88] See, e.g., B. H. Oxman, 'The Law of the Sea Convention', *ASIL Newsletter*, November 1994, Annex, pp. 1–4.

why does the mining ban feature in the Protocol at all, and why is such significance attributed to it by both the Consultative Parties and third states?

Let us thus take a brief look at the positions and legal situation of these two groups of states.

The prohibition of Antarctic mineral resource activities: the position of third states

In order to explore the position of third states, this section will focus on the evolution of the 'Question of Antarctica' in the UN. This has been the major forum[89] where third states have, since 1983, had the opportunity on an annual basis to present their views, relevant also for the subject under discussion here.[90]

As noted in Chapter 2, third states criticised the Consultative Parties, up to 1988, for negotiating and creating an Antarctic minerals regime which would not allow for an equitable distribution of benefits accrued from the exploitation of minerals, as provided for in Part XI of the LOS Convention. When CRAMRA was adopted, however, this external critique of the ATS changed its major argument, adapting it to the newly created situation.

Malaysia, the initiator of the 'Question of Antarctica' in the UN and main critic of the ATS, gave support to Australia, France, Belgium and Italy for their decision to abandon CRAMRA, by stating:

The case against the exploitation of Antarctic mineral resources is a compelling one indeed. It would be to the benefit and in the interest of mankind to ban all prospecting and mining activities in Antarctica.[91]

The Malaysian statement went on:

We therefore commend the efforts against mineral activities and call on the inter-

---

[89] This said, it should be borne in mind that the questions concerning a ban on Antarctic mineral activities as well as the strengthening of the environmental protection measures have been approached in other fora as well: see, for example, a resolution of the European Parliament, of 16 February 1989, opting for the banning of mineral activities in the Antarctic and granting the 'world natural reserve status' to the Antarctic: doc. B.2-1347/88.

[90] As pointed out by the UN Under-Secretary-General Vasiliy Safronchuk: 'It would be fitting to trace genesis and development of the Question of Antarctica within the UN to find out what is the relationship between the Antarctic Treaty System (ATS) and the Convention on the Law of the Sea': Safronchuk, 'The Relationship', p. 328.

[91] Statement of Malaysia, UN doc. A/C.1/44/PV.44, p. 19.

national community to support the banning of all prospecting and mining activities in Antarctica[92]

and concluded:

it is self-evident that . . . any regime or framework designed to give effective protection must be acceptable to the international community.[93]

This was strong support for a mining ban in the Antarctic, actually adopted two years later through the Protocol.

This new aspect characterised UN discussions on the 'Question of Antarctica' from 1989 onwards. It gained in strength in 1990, when ATS critics came out overwhelmingly in support of the initiative to introduce a mining ban in the Antarctic.[94] UN General Assembly resolutions on the 'Question of Antarctica', adopted from 1989 on, even demanded that the minerals ban be made permanent. The voting pattern is interesting: the list of states voting in favour of these UN General Assembly resolutions on the 'Question of Antarctica' overlaps to a considerable extent with the list of parties to the LOS Convention.

At this point one starts to wonder: has the critique of the ATS in the UN actually enhanced the legitimacy of the Protocol's ban on all mineral activity other than scientific research, arguing for an even more rigorous permanent ban? Indeed, one important difference from a *structural* point of view has remained, as these countries have demanded that such a regime be negotiated with the full participation of all members of the international community. Nevertheless, the *normative* aspect remains unchanged: in the Antarctic context this would, essentially, amount to an interpretation of the common heritage of mankind principle which would omit the element of the exploration and exploitation of resources coupled with economic redistribution, introducing instead the element of the prohibition of resource activities in order to protect the Antarctic environment for mankind.[95] However, as already noted, the letter of the LOS Convention, especially its Part XI, does not permit such wide interpret-

---

[92] *Ibid.*, p. 20.
[93] *Ibid.*
[94] For discussions on this item in the First Committee of the UN General Assembly in 1989 see UN docs. A/C.1/44/PV.42–6; for discussions in 1990 see UN docs. A/C.1/45/PV.40–5 and 47.
[95] In this connection, it may be appropriate to note that the participants in the discussions within the Preparatory Commission 'came to the conclusion that inevitably they would have to prepare the ground for changing the LOS Convention to make it 100 per cent proof from the environmental point of view': Safronchuk, 'The Relationship', p. 332.

ation. In substance, on the other hand, such a shift from economic utilisation to environmental protection through the prohibition of resource
activities is exactly in line with developments within the ATS, which have
gone from CRAMRA to the Protocol. Worthwhile highlighting, the
essence of Article 7 of the Protocol (embodying the minerals ban) is found
expressed already earlier in paragraph 5 of the 1989 UN General
Assembly resolution on the 'Question of Antarctica'[96] (urging the establishment of a ban on prospecting and mining in and around Antarctica).

Regardless of formal acceptance or rejection of the Protocol as a legal
instrument adopted by the Consultative Parties, the statements of states
which are not parties to the Antarctic Treaty as well as the texts of UN
General Assembly resolutions since 1989 provide evidence of the *emergence* of a new *opinio juris*, one which demands the prohibition of any
activity relating to Antarctic mineral resources, other than scientific
research. This alone – it may be argued – does not suffice for the creation
of a new customary norm, since that would require a certain consistency
and uniformity of state practice[97] in this respect. On the other hand, such
an argument also implies that there are no longer any grounds for claiming that the principle of the common heritage of mankind, as contained
in Part XI of the LOS Convention, can be applied to the seabed area
beyond the limits of national jurisdiction, and south of 60°S latitude,
based on customary law, since the requirement of the consistency and
uniformity of state practice is now clearly not met.[98]

Consequently, this would imply exempting the mineral deposits found
in the Antarctic submarine areas from the application of the conflicting
provisions of Part XI of the LOS Convention: after all, if mining is prohibited, then there is nothing left for economic redistribution pursuant
to the common heritage of mankind principle.

The legal situation for states parties to the Protocol and to the LOS Convention

There is another aspect of this contemporary relationship between the
ATS and the law of the sea, as introduced by the Protocol's minerals ban,

---

[96] See UN General Assembly resolution 44/124 B of 15 December 1989, para. 5.
[97] On these requirements see, e.g., K. Wolfke, *Custom in Present International Law*, 2nd ed.
(Dordrecht: Martinus Nijhoff, 1993); also R. Bernhardt, 'Customary International Law',
in R. Bernhardt (ed.), *Encyclopedia of Public International Law* (Amsterdam: Elsevier, 1992),
vol. I, pp. 898–905.
[98] A contrary view, indeed prior to the adoption of the Protocol, has been held by F. Orrego
Vicuña: see Orrego, 'New Approaches', p. 102.

which has the potential to reflect on the LOS Convention: the issue of states which are parties to both the Protocol and the LOS Convention. Of the total of forty-two parties to the Antarctic Treaty, only six states are (as of 7 May 1995) also parties to the LOS Convention. However, five of them (Australia, Brazil, Germany, Italy and Uruguay) are simultaneously Consultative Parties and parties to the LOS Convention. It might be rather difficult in legal terms to reconcile the requirements of Article 311, paragraph 6 of the LOS Convention[99] with the prohibition embodied in Article 7 of the Protocol. A legal problem is likely to arise, since the Protocol requires ratification of all twenty-six states which were Consultative Parties at the time of its adoption – Australia, Brazil, Germany, Italy and Uruguay being among them.[100]

In the context of the global law of the sea, both the third parties participating in the UN discussions on the 'Question of Antarctica' and the parties to the Antarctic Treaty were largely in agreement when voting in favour of the 1993 UN General Assembly resolution on the 'Law of the Sea'.[101] This resolution, in taking into account developments over the past decade since the adoption of the LOS Convention:

Recognizes that political and economic changes . . . underscore the need to re-evaluate, in the light of the issues of concern to some States, matters in the regime to be applied to the Area and its resources.[102]

Furthermore, a majority of Consultative Parties and a number of third parties, including developing countries actively involved in the 'Question of Antarctica' in the UN, gave their support to the Implementation Agreement.

This harmony in positions of both groups of states might lead to a practical solution for the normative clash between the Protocol's mining ban and the exploitative element of the LOS Convention's common heritage of mankind concept. Even if no consensus is reached between the

---

[99] Art. 311, para. 6 of the LOS Convention reads: 'States Parties agree that there shall be no amendments to the basic principle relating to the common heritage of mankind set forth in article 136 and that they shall not be party to any agreement in derogation thereof.'

[100] All five countries have already ratified the Protocol. Moreover, all the twenty-six Consultative Parties have repeatedly made statements on voluntary implementation of basic principles of the Protocol (the minerals ban being *par excellence* a basic principle of the Protocol) even prior to its entry into force.

[101] Resolution 48/28 of 9 December 1993, adopted with 144 votes in favour, 1 against (Turkey) and 11 abstaining (among the latter, Ecuador, Germany, Peru, the United Kingdom and the United States are parties to the Antarctic Treaty).

[102] *Ibid.*, para. 6.

Consultative Parties and third states, the Implementation Agreement provides these very countries which are among Consultative Parties with crucial decision-making rights in the Authority.[103] This could be used for adopting a decision by the Authority to exempt the seabed area south of 60°S latitude from mineral resource activities.[104] Special treatment for the area south of 60°S latitude, in view of the particular need for its environmental protection, would not be without precedent. Several other recent international regimes contain provisions to that effect. In 1990, for example, the IMO designated the Antarctic, i.e. the area of the Southern Ocean south of 60°S latitude, as a special area deserving greater environmental protection under Annexes I and V of the 1973/78 International Convention for the Prevention of Pollution from Ships.[105] Also, the Convention on the Control of Transboundary Movements of Hazardous Wastes and Their Disposal[106] contains an explicit provision for the area south of 60°S latitude.[107]

CONCLUDING REMARKS

Let us now return to the thesis formulated in the title of this chapter: what does it mean that the Protocol has introduced 'a new dimension' into the relationship between the ATS and the law of the sea?

Initially, the Antarctic Treaty left ambiguous the status of the Antarctic maritime area, thus allowing the argument on the need to apply general law of the sea to gain strength. Over time, however, solutions to the problems pertinent to the status of the Antarctic maritime area have begun to emerge within the ATS, through the development of its

[103] On changes introduced by the Implementation Agreement in decision-making by the Authority, see B. H. Oxman, 'The 1994 Agreement and the Convention', *American Journal of International Law*, vol. 88, no. 4, 1994, pp. 689–91.
[104] As long as there is no commercial interest, such a decision would most probably hold without a serious demand for its change.
[105] MARPOL Convention, done in London, on 2 November 1973, as modified by the Protocol of 17 February 1978; entered into force on 2 October 1983; text reprinted in *International Legal Materials*, vol. XVII, 1978, pp. 546*ff*. The designation of the area south of 60°S latitude as a special area was adopted as a resolution of the Marine Environment Protection Committee of the International Maritime Organisation, IMO doc. A1/U/ 3.16 (N.V.1): see Joyner, *Antarctica and the Law of the Sea*, p. 155; R. B. Mitchell, *International Oil Pollution at Sea: Environmental Policy and Treaty Compliance* (Cambridge, MA: MIT Press, 1994), p. 104.
[106] The Convention was done in Basle, on 22 March 1989, entered into force on 5 May 1992; text reprinted in *International Legal Materials*, vol. XXVIII, 1989, pp. 657*ff*.
[107] *Ibid.*, Art. 4, para. 6.

resource regimes. This has led to the recognition of the normative complexity regarding the status of the Antarctic maritime area. The solutions
to this do not lie in the direct application of the general law of the sea,
but in the concurrence of the two existing systems of legal norms – the
law of the sea *and* the ATS.

Regarding the status of the Antarctic submarine area, the Protocol has
significantly changed the overall balance between the ATS and the law
of the sea. We should recall that the introduction of the continental shelf,
which embodied the concept of the seabed as an area for the exploitation
of non-living resources, represented a revolutionary change in the law of
the sea.[108] Over a period of years, this concept stimulated another change
of format – the concept of the seabed beyond the limits of national jurisdiction, together with its resources, as being the common heritage of
mankind. Both regimes are concerned with the exploitation of minerals,
with the basic difference between them lying in the distribution of benefits acquired by such activity. If made applicable, however, both regimes
would in fact allow for mineral resource activities in the Antarctic submarine area.

That stage of the development of the law of the sea has been reflected
in the provisions of CRAMRA. Although a main objective of the
CRAMRA regime was claimed to be the protection of the Antarctic
environment,[109] CRAMRA would nonetheless allow for the exploitation
of minerals in the seabed offshore Antarctica. In this sense, there was no
essential departure from the general law of the sea found in CRAMRA;
rather, the question concerned the careful delimitation of the area of
application of CRAMRA from that of the LOS Convention regime for
the Area. The issue remained at the level of the concurrence of the
regimes which 'speak the same language', in the sense that both allow for
exploitation of seabed minerals.

In contrast, the Protocol has introduced prohibition on any activity
relating to mineral resources, other than scientific research. This excludes
the aspect of utilisation found in the regimes of the continental shelf and
the Area, and characteristic for CRAMRA as well. In this context, it is
not only that the Protocol has superseded CRAMRA: it also implies that
the *ratio* of both the continental shelf and the Area concepts no longer

---

[108] On the same line see C. Rozakis, 'Continental Shelf', in Bernhardt (ed.), *Encyclopedia of
Public International Law*, vol. I, p. 791.
[109] See C. D. Beeby, 'An Overview of the Problems Which Should be Addressed in the
Preparation of a Regime Governing the Mineral Resources of Antarctica', in Orrego
(ed.), *Antarctic Resources Policy*, p. 192.

exists for the Antarctic submarine area. The most important continental shelf rights involve the exploration and exploitation of its mineral resources: and they are now banned by the Protocol. Regarding the concept of the Area, as embodied in Part XI of the LOS Convention, it is obvious that, if mining is prohibited, there is nothing left for economic distribution pursuant to the common heritage of mankind principle. The prohibition of mineral resource activities in the Antarctic, apart from being embodied in the Protocol, has since 1989 been consistently demanded by the states which are not parties to the Antarctic Treaty, as well as recurring in the texts of UN General Assembly resolutions.

It is in this sense, then, that this chapter claims that the Protocol has introduced a new dimension into the relationship between the ATS and the law of the sea. We may now arrive at two theses as to the ATS' law of the sea dimension: first, the concept of the coastal state has lost considerable weight in the Antarctic maritime area;[110] when needed, its functions are performed by the ATS rather than by individual states. And second, the specific legal concept introduced in the ATS through the adoption of the Protocol offers a prism through which to view the law of the sea for the Antarctic maritime area as well as the need for rethinking some general law of the sea concepts from the perspective of the Antarctic Treaty System.

---

[110] CRAMRA, which might have been said to contain significant exceptions to this thesis, has been abandoned, partly also on the background of its threatening to disturb the balance on the sovereignty positions: see especially Chapters 6, 10 and Conclusions of this book.

4

The changing roles of non-governmental organisations in the Antarctic Treaty System

RICHARD A. HERR

INTRODUCTION

Antarctica is a region justifiably characterised by superlatives.[1] It is the coldest, driest, highest and most remote of the continents. Its ecosystem, including an abundant biota, is unique. And for many, these qualities of uniqueness extend to the remarkable international regime which claims control over human activities in and around the frozen continent. The demilitarisation of Antarctica, the banning of nuclear weapons and preservation of an entire continent for its environmental and scientific values are quite fairly perceived to mark Antarctica as a special case in the political history of this planet. Underlying the admiration some feel for these aspects of the Antarctic Treaty System (ATS), however, is sometimes a mistaken belief that the Treaty has suspended the operation of sovereignty in this corner of the world. Distrust of sovereignty (and the state system it sustains) is scarcely novel, but pursuit of the ideal of a stateless society in which to demonstrate the cooperative rather than the competitive in human nature has probably never enjoyed such a grand laboratory or been perceived so widely to have succeeded as in Antarctica.[2] Indeed, the Antarctic experience has been so captivating that, regardless of philosophical orientation, it is widely used by scholars to make theoretical points about the creation and maintenance of regimes at the international level.[3]

---

[1] The author expresses his gratitude to Mr Andrew Darby, MA, of the Institute of Antarctic and Southern Ocean Studies at the University of Tasmania, for his assistance with aspects of this chapter based on his research into the influence of environmental NGOs on the Madrid Protocol.
[2] See for examples chapters by Sir Vivian Fuchs, 'Evolution of a Venture in Antarctic Science' and F. Sollie, 'The Political Experiment in Antarctica' in R. S. Lewis and P. M. Smith (eds.), *Frozen Futures* (New York: Quadrangle, 1973).
[3] See for an example O. R. Young, *International Cooperation: Building Regimes for Natural Resources and the Environment* (Ithaca, NY: Cornell University Press, 1989).

One test of how unusual the politics of Antarctica are in reality would be to consider the role of the mundane, the commonplace, in this system. Are the 'ordinary' politics of the international system relevant or irrelevant to the Antarctic Treaty System? In order to answer this question, the present chapter reviews the role of non-governmental organisations (NGOs) in Antarctica in terms of their contribution to the effectiveness and legitimacy of the ATS. Popular myths about the operation of the state system in Antarctica, if accepted at face value, could be used to construct an argument for a large NGO role in Antarctic affairs. In essence, such an argument would draw on the specific circumstances of the ATS to show that the normal mechanisms (and thus the predictability) of the state system do not apply to Antarctica. Thus, if state-based mechanisms are inadequate, then non-state mechanisms such as NGOs should come into their own. And, in theoretical terms, some schools of thought predict this is precisely what should happen. Where the legitimate authority of the state is unclear, disputed or impractical, some other source of legitimacy will be found or created. On the other hand, it has also been argued that the state system is not being challenged by the ATS; that, in fact, the rhetoric of the suspension of sovereignty is largely a myth invented by those who have misunderstood the origins of the Antarctic Treaty and the regime(s) it has spawned.[4]

There is an tendency in some schools of international relations theory to view NGOs as competitive with states, which has implied an adversarial relationship between states and non-state actors. This is not a necessary part of the interaction, however. Even at the highest level of the current international system, the United Nations, advantages have long been found in engaging cooperatively with the NGO system. In reality, it can be argued, the special threat attributed to NGOs by their critics is an attempt to give the state system a special status by protecting it from the influence of NGOs. It will be argued in this chapter that the broader interaction between the state system and NGOs applies with equal force in Antarctica. The Antarctic NGOs have played much the same role in the ATS as they do at the domestic level in state politics. They help to legitimate processes and outcomes; to provide information; to contribute to regime maintenance; to represent interests and to advocate reform. This is not to say that the unusual characteristics of the arena within which they must operate

[4] R. A. Herr and H. R. Hall, 'Science as Currency and the Currency of Science' in J. Handmer (ed.), *Antarctica: Policies and Policy Developments* (Canberra: Centre for Resource and Environmental Studies, Australian National University, 1989), pp. 15–24.

have not affected these roles. They have. Nevertheless, the novelty of the ATS does not outweigh its conformity with the practices and experience of other regimes, other policy arenas, other aspects of international order. Indeed, the very fact of the emergence and constructive participation of the Antarctic NGOs has demonstrated the capacity of the ATS to adapt and develop over time in ways that have contributed significantly to its legitimacy and effectiveness in the larger international arena.

NGOs AND THE STATE SYSTEM

Assessing the role of NGOs in the international arena (including Antarctica) poses significant methodological questions. Simply identifying an international NGO can be problematical, since a group does not itself have to have an international membership to enjoy international influence. Time is also an issue. How long must a group express a common identity or purpose before it becomes an 'organisation'? The difficulties of creating, developing and maintaining an international organisation are real both for the NGOs and for those who would deal with them. To what extent is recognition or acceptance by the state system a genuine consideration? It is clear that the purposes of an NGO are a factor in its recognition and acceptance by other international actors including states. Generally, special-interest NGOs (also known as sectional NGOs) have found organising effectively across national boundaries rather easier than have social-advocacy (promotional NGOs) groups.[5] This arises, in part, because the particular interest or expertise of sectional groups is already accepted at the state level as either being technically relevant or giving the NGO a 'stakeholder' status; and, in part, because there is no commonly accepted definition of the public interest claimed by promotional groups to ease opposition to their operation internationally.

International acceptance has been a key issue for NGOs in the contemporary global order. Because the state remains the basic unit of the modern international order, the international acceptability of NGOs has depended less on the perceptions of various peoples in particular regions or around the globe than on the attitudes of states and state-based organs such as inter-governmental organisations.[6] The state's dominance of

---

[5] P. Willetts, *Pressure Groups in the Global System: The Transnational Relations of Issue-Oriented Non-Governmental Organizations* (London: Frances Pinter, 1982), pp. 2–8, develops more fully the distinctions between sectional and promotional NGOs.

[6] Young, *International Cooperation*, p. 14.

international decision-making processes has been changing during the course of the twentieth century, however.[7] The pace of this change has proceeded at an almost exponential rate in what can best be described as a positive feedback loop between social contract theories of the state and the technology of communication. The process appears to be operating rather like this: the adoption domestically of such democratic political principles as majority rule and human rights by an ever larger number of states has encouraged greater international openness. As interaction among states (and especially among their citizens) has increased, technology has advanced to make more interaction possible. Indeed, in this regard the avenues of influence for international NGOs are very like those of state NGOs – control of physical (including financial) resources, mobilisation of political support, informing public opinion and providing access to expert knowledge.[8]

For some such as David Mitrany,[9] the logic of this process (coupled with an abhorrence of the devastation of war in this century) led to the prospect of eroding the state system itself in the long run. The flavour of his argument ran roughly thus: the state is an impractical or inappropriate mechanism for promoting common interests across national boundaries because no state alone can meet the functional and technical needs of its citizens. Since people want their needs met, they will seek other sources of authority to promote the cooperative interaction which can meet their needs. By investing non-governmental associations with their trust, people create an alternative source of influence which, at the minimum, will inhibit the capacity of states to make war.

The attempt to address the failure of competitive, national interest-based mechanisms through voluntary, non-coercive, non-governmental associations has been identified with a form of Idealism in international relations theorising known as 'Functionalism'. This school enjoyed its greatest influence at the end of World War II when it significantly influ-

---

[7] J. Lador-Lederer, *International Non-Governmental Organizations* (Leyden: A. W. Sythoff, 1962), pp. 61–2.

[8] For specific examples of the mechanisms used by NGOs to achieve influence see J. M. Berry, *Lobbying for the People: The Political Behavior of Public Interest Groups* (Princeton University Press, 1977); A. Hurrell and B. Kingsbury (eds.), *The International Politics of the Environment: Actors, Interests, and Institutions* (Oxford: Clarendon Press, 1992); and Willetts, *Pressure Groups*.

[9] For a review of Mitrany's contribution to the development of international functionalism see J. E. Dougherty and R. L. Pfaltzgraff, Jr (eds.), *Contending Theories of International Relations: A Comprehensive Survey*, 2nd ed. (New York: Harper and Row, 1981), pp. 418–21.

enced the development of the United Nations.[10] The UN's member states found an institutional *locus* of influence for non-governmental organisations within its structure. Although never as influential as the Idealists had hoped, the incorporation of NGOs into the UN process through the Economic and Social Council (ECOSOC) was a watershed in the state system. It provided for the formal acceptance of non-state actors by states, thus conferring a legitimacy which the former have since been able to utilise routinely with states in a variety of arenas.

This is not to suggest that NGOs won complete and universal acceptance from the state system which gave them recognition. What they achieved was scarcely co-equal international status with sovereign states. The UN's formal acceptance of NGOs was tightly circumscribed. Indeed, even today the UN's limited acceptance of NGOs imposes fairly strict procedural criteria on groups seeking 'consultative status' under Article 71 of the United Nations Charter. They must:

1 be international (defined as having branches in two or more countries);
2 pursue activities within the competence of the Economic and Social Council – the one principal organ mentioned in Article 71;
3 have an established headquarters and secretariat; and
4 have a representative policy-making body for their members.[11]

The fourth criterion is particularly significant in that it is intended to ensure that those NGOs operating internationally have demonstrable legitimacy in terms of their authorising constituencies in a manner not dissimilar to the contractarian view of legal authority which validates states.

Although not universally followed, the UN approach to NGOs has set a precedent which has been widely accepted.[12] Broadly this orientation confers a conditional legitimacy on NGOs limited to the extent that these associations support (and operate within) the state system and are representative of their memberships. In addition to these formal qualifications, there has been a further practical constraint on the operation of

---

[10] It should be noted that offsetting gains were also made by the Realists, who also enjoyed success in the UN Charter through the entrenchment of Great Power responsibility for international security with the device of permanent membership including the power of veto in the Security Council.
[11] Union of International Associations, *Yearbook of International Organisations – Volume 1 1992/93*, 29th ed. (Munich: K. G. Saur, 1992), p. 1,649.
[12] Willetts, *Pressure Groups*, pp. 11–17.

NGOs at the international level. Although this is disputed by some scholars,[13] ECOSOC does not appear to have played as prominent a role in the UN system as many had hoped; therefore the NGOs have not had the opportunity to exert the sort of influence that early Functionalism predicted. The state system has conceded, in effect, a begrudging acceptance where NGOs can be 'helpful' as defined in terms of system-supporting, utilitarian values such as expertise, efficiency or mobilising public support for specific issues. Legitimacy, on the other hand, has generally been withheld from NGOs by the state system for continuing formal roles such as agenda-setting or the representation of peoples or interests.

NGOs AND ANTARCTICA: THE EPISTEMIC PERIOD

The activities and role of NGOs must be included among the many unique features of contemporary political Antarctica. The extraordinary ambivalence toward sovereignty which has applied in Antarctica from the middle to the late 1950s might have been expected to offer fertile ground for experimentation with non-state instruments such as NGOs. Yet, in the event, any such expectation would have proved unfounded. The state system has demonstrated a considerable degree of resilience in Antarctica even though it has been forced to operate without the substantial prop of national sovereignty. Nonetheless, NGOs have emerged to play a role in Antarctic affairs, although this development has been slow and uneven – as indeed, it has been in the rest of the international order. The evolution of NGO activity within the Treaty System can be grouped into three periods – from 1959 to the middle of the 1970s; from the middle of the 1970s to the Protocol on Environmental Protection to the Antarctic Treaty; and the current period from the Protocol. This evolution illustrates not only the increasing acceptance of NGOs in the ATS but also a diversification of interests expressed, and roles played, by NGOs.

During the first period – unlike in the second and third, to be dealt with below – there was but a single influential NGO.[14] The Special (later Scientific) Committee on Antarctic Research (SCAR) was established by the International Council of Scientific Unions (ICSU) to assist in coordi-

---

[13] L. S. Finkelstein, 'The Politics of Value Allocation in the UN System', in L. S. Finkelstein (ed.), *Politics in the United Nations System* (Durham, NC: Duke University Press, 1988).

[14] It is noteworthy that the involvement of an NGO in the ATS made its activities 'transnational' (that is, a mixed system of state and non-state actors) *ab initio*.

nating Antarctic research in the years after the 1957–8 International Geophysical Year. Naturally the ICSU operated its committee along the lines of its own practice, so that the membership of SCAR was made up of representatives of national academies of science. After the signing of the Treaty in 1959, SCAR was to enjoy significant responsibilities[15] but it also was to remain unique. Not only did the members of the Antarctic Treaty fail to institutionalise themselves formally for more than a score of years, the relative policy vacuum did not attract non-state actors beyond SCAR into the Antarctic region nor did it encourage the establishment of additional Antarctic-focused NGOs.

To dwell unduly on the novelty of SCAR as an Antarctic NGO is to minimise the incorporation of SCAR into the core of the Antarctic Treaty's scientific processes, however. Under the 1959 Treaty, science enjoyed co-equal status with security as one of the Antarctic Treaty's twin key objectives. And, for many years subsequently, SCAR was not only the sole NGO of significance in Antarctic affairs, it served as a central organ of the Treaty system capable of mobilising considerable resources to achieve cooperative scientific objectives.[16]

Whether SCAR did achieve the full degree of multilateral cooperation desired initially may be debated. Even today the vast weight of research remains nationally based, with the results alone subject to international cooperation. Nevertheless, SCAR was perceived to be vital to the *raison d'être* of the Treaty. This perception has continued over the years. SCAR has been accorded roles in the Agreed Measures for the Conservation of Antarctic Fauna and Flora (1964); the Convention for the Conservation of Antarctic Seals (1972); the ill-fated Convention on the Regulation of Antarctic Mineral Resource Activities (CRAMRA) and the Protocol on Environmental Protection (1991).[17]

SCAR, an NGO despite the quasi-governmental aspects of its membership,[18] has enjoyed this highly visible and influential role in the ATS over the past thirty-five years not because it purports to represent unexpressed public opinion but because it serves as a principal mechanism of the Antarctic epistemic community; that is, it is recognised as authoritative both

---

[15] P. J. Beck, *The International Politics of Antarctica* (London: Croom Helm, 1986), p. 41.
[16] *Ibid.*
[17] It is a noteworthy feature of the CCAMLR that it established a Scientific Committee to advise the Commission and therefore seems to have had less institutional need to provide a specific role for SCAR.
[18] J. H. Zumberge in 'Introduction' to R. Fifield, *International Research in the Antarctic* (Oxford University Press, 1987), p. 1.

by the scientific community from which its membership is drawn and by the state members of the ATS for its control of professional knowledge. SCAR's role as an expert sectional NGO is underscored by its self-imposed embargo on political advocacy.[19] While commitment to the highest scientific professionalism has undoubtedly enhanced SCAR's role of promoting international cooperation through the Antarctic Treaty System, the fact that its central activities are supportive of the state-based Treaty system has occasionally provoked external doubts as to its real value among other NGOs critical of the priorities of the ATS.[20]

NGOs AND ANTARCTICA: THE PUBLIC INTEREST PERIOD

The cause of environmental protection became a significant issue in the middle of the 1970s largely due to geological research which suggested that the mineral wealth of the continent, both onshore and offshore, was potentially exploitable. Further, although the traditional living resources of Antarctica (seals and whales) were not seen as growth areas, the new marine resources of krill and finfish were perceived to be potentially lucrative. The Third United Nations Conference on the Law of the Sea (UNCLOS III) was then in progress, and the attention it focused on marine resources added an element of urgency to developing regulatory regimes within the ATS to avoid possible conflicts with the UN regime. The prospect of substantial resource development in Antarctica – especially of offshore oil – set off alarm bells in the minds of an increasingly outspoken environmental movement.

The 'decision' of the environmental movement (broadly defined) in the 1970s to embrace Antarctica as a cause brought the politics of promotional NGOs to the ATS. The various groups which eventually became involved relied less on elite expertise to justify their claim for influence (although some groups could claim such expertise) than on the ultimate rectitude of their values, especially as these benefited the interests of the mass of unrepresented and underrepresented humanity.[21] Perhaps the two most significant groups to become active in the Antarctic arena during this period were the International Union for the Conservation of Nature and Natural Resources (IUCN) and the Antarctic and

---

[19] *Ibid.*, p. 2.

[20] G. Mosley, 'The Natural Option: The Case for an Antarctic World Park', in S. Harris (ed.), *Australia's Antarctic Policy Options* (Canberra: Centre for Resource and Environmental Studies, Australian National University, 1984), p. 323.

[21] K. Suter, *Antarctica: Private Property or Public Heritage?* (London: Zed, 1991).

Southern Ocean Coalition (ASOC). Greenpeace, Friends of the Earth and other environmentally oriented groups were to follow in later years. Of course, not all NGO effort was expended in the ATS arena. Significant impacts in national arenas were achieved during the campaign against CRAMRA by national NGOs such as the Sierra Club in the USA.

It is a singular feature of this period of the evolution of NGO interest in Antarctica that, although the environmental groups tended to regard themselves as countervailing the pressure for economic development, no industry groups organised to promote their putative interests.[22] There may be several reasons for this apparent anomaly. Perhaps the critical factor was the absence of a substantial private industry to organise. Except for Japan, the primary fishing interest in the Southern Ocean was from countries with centrally planned economies, such as the USSR and Poland.[23] Thus NGOs organised to advocate an industry position on issues such as harvesting, processing or marketing were never a likely prospect. A second significant consideration was the timing of the CCAMLR negotiations. The krill and Antarctic finfish fisheries were in a very early stage of their development, so that the economic activity was quite small. (By global standards, these fisheries are still relatively modest despite the long-term promise of the krill resources.) Arguably, even had the Antarctic fishing interests been more private in character, the scale of the industry would have militated against a large industry influence through some form of organised international lobbying.

There is an element of irony in the fact that it was the fisheries regime that emerged first from the resource scramble of the 1970s. The non-living resources of Antarctica, especially hydrocarbons, were probably the larger attraction from the early 1970s, but foreseeable difficulties with developing a minerals regime delayed consideration of this convention

---

[22] While it is true that there were no international industry groups created to pursue a representational role in the negotiation of either CCAMLR or CRAMRA, this is not to say that national industry bodies were also absent. At least one national industry association, the Deep Sea Trawler's Association, was regarded as having had a critical influence on the position of Japan, a key state in the negotiation of CCAMLR. Environmental NGOs have been formally included in national delegations since the USA began the practice in 1977. For the latter, see L. A. Kimball, 'The Role of Non-Governmental Organizations in Antarctic Affairs', in C. C. Joyner and S. K. Chopra (eds.), *The Antarctic Legal Regime* (Dordrecht: Martinus Nijhoff, 1988), pp. 46–7.

[23] Given the state interest of Soviet fishing in the Antarctic, it is arguable that there was no substantial difference between the position of the Soviet state and that which might have been pursued by a Soviet fishing industry sectional NGO in negotiating the CCAMLR agreement.

until after the questions of living resources had been addressed.[24] Nevertheless, the longer time which this delay afforded the potentially more significant minerals industry to mobilise had no effect as far as Antarctic NGOs were concerned. As with the fisheries industry, no mining associations formed to contest the terms of the emerging international agreement on the regulation of minerals activities or to counter the advice and arguments of the organised environmental groups.[25] One important effect of the lopsidedness of this development of Antarctic NGOs was a juxtaposition of state and non-governmental interests in the development of the region's resources. Rather than environmental NGOs confronting industry NGOs, environmental activists challenged the member states of the ATS.

While the activities of NGOs during this second phase tended to be aimed at raising mass awareness of the threats to the Antarctic, it would be incorrect to treat them all as clearly promotional rather than sectional groups. IUCN is organised along lines somewhat reminiscent of SCAR although it does have a global, rather than regional, scope and it does admit countries in their own right. Its primary membership is drawn from associations with science-based ethos. The legitimacy of the IUCN as an NGO with a strong science base has stood it in good stead in its dealings with the ATS despite its promotional stance on Antarctic issues. Not only has the IUCN worked with SCAR on joint projects, it was the first 'outside' NGO to gain formal access to the ATS. The CCAMLR agreement involved the IUCN in its preparation, and this opportunity appears to have been utilised to promote NGO interests.[26] The CCAMLR agreement provides for the Commission and its Scientific Committee to consult with NGOs.[27] CCAMLR's formal acceptance of NGOs in its basic charter proved to be something of a threshold in the ATS, opening the

---

[24] H. R. Hall, *Antarctica and World Politics: The Significance of Political Factors in Antarctic Affairs during the Twentieth Century* (MA thesis) (Hobart: University of Tasmania, December 1986).

[25] For one apparent industry attempt to exert influence on the emerging minerals convention, see Chapter 13.

[26] Kimball, 'The Role of NGOs', p. 40; and J. N. Barnes, 'Environmental Protection and the Future of the Antarctic: New Approaches and Perspectives are Necessary', in G. D. Triggs (ed.), *The Antarctic Treaty Regime: Law, Environment and Resources* (Cambridge University Press, 1987), p. 153.

[27] See Chapters 5 and 9; also W. M. Bush, 'The Antarctic Treaty System: A Framework for Evolution', in R. A. Herr, H. R. Hall and M. G. Haward (eds.), *Antarctica's Future: Continuity or Change?* (Hobart: Tasmanian Government Printer, 1990), p. 143.

door of acceptance within the system to the new Antarctic NGOs.[28] The IUCN obtained 'invited expert' status at the XIV Consultative Meeting, in 1987, and has maintained this access at every subsequent Consultative Meeting and CCAMLR meeting.[29]

Other environmental NGOs involved with Antarctic issues have also tended to blur the distinction between promoting broad community interests and advancing particular sectional interests. While the initial strategy of the Antarctic and Southern Ocean Coalition (ASOC) was to bring together a large number of environmental protection groups under a single umbrella to mobilise more effectively public opinion, it has increasingly been able to utilise this network as a source of expertise to gain acceptance within the ATS. Governmental perceptions that ASOC would operate negatively, essentially as a veto group, on their activities in the Antarctic have gradually yielded to appreciation that ASOC resources can add constructively to Antarctic decision-making processes. By the middle of the 1980s, ASOC had won individual positions on national delegations, but it remained unable to secure a formal role in its own right for several years more. ASOC achieved observer status with the plenary of CCAMLR in 1988 and with CCAMLR's scientific committee in 1991. In each case, ASOC's admission was contested by at least one CCAMLR member state, but the NGO's persistence in pursuing CCAMLR recognition paid dividends for ASOC elsewhere in the ATS. It was included in the 1990 session of the XI Special Consultative Meeting as an invited expert – a status it has continued to enjoy at all subsequent Consultative Meetings.

Greenpeace, a constituent member of ASOC, entered the Antarctic arena in its own right rather late. It was only during 1983 that the direct action body, reacting to pressure for involvement in the nascent CRAMRA convention, embraced Antarctica as a campaign issue.[30] Although a late starter, Greenpeace accepted its self-assigned challenge with extraordinary energy and flair. It also devoted an uncommon amount of resources to the task. The Greenpeace ethos of 'direct action' distinguished it from other NGOs intent on challenging the existing values

---

[28] *Ibid.*
[29] Observer status in the ATCMs is restricted to SCAR, CCAMLR and COMNAP, while all other inter-governmental organisations or NGOs can be invited to designate experts to attend ATCMs. The key to this distinction is access to the Meeting's agenda. Observers may contribute working papers; invited experts may only offer information papers. Additionally, observers rank above invited experts in order of precedence.
[30] J. May, *The Greenpeace Book of Antarctica* (London: Dorling Kindersley, 1988), p. 172.

of the ATS. Because direct action gave Greenpeace the appearance of being more of a gadfly than a serious reformer in the eyes of many actors within the ATS, formal acceptance of Greenpeace as a player in the ATS was always problematical. Yet more than any other NGO except SCAR, Greenpeace pursued tactics which, at the minimum, paralleled those of the ATS.

Intriguingly, although its philosophy of direct action depended upon mass support for legitimacy, Greenpeace proved unwilling to rely solely on popular acceptance to achieve its objective of making the entire continent a world park as part of the common heritage of mankind. Even while attacking the basis of the state system (muted though sovereignty is in Antarctica), Greenpeace pursued a tactic of acting as though it were eligible to become a formal member of the inner circle of decision-makers within the ATS – the Consultative Parties. It set up a scientific station, World Park Base, in the Ross Sea near Robert Scott's historic base. From this station, Greenpeace sought to engage in reciprocal inspections and attempted to perform the duties expected of sovereign states operating within the Antarctic Treaty. While some Consultative Parties appear to have regarded these activities as a parody of the ATS, Greenpeace seems to have genuinely intended its attempt to operate in a Consultative Party fashion to give it status in the ATS.[31] Insofar as this was the objective, the attempt failed, however; after five years of operation World Park Base was dismantled in 1992. Greenpeace continues to devote significant resources to Antarctic issues, but the antagonism of some Consultative Parties has denied it a formal involvement in its own right in the ATS at any level.[32]

One of the features of this period of NGO activity in Antarctica was an alliance of interests between some of the NGOs opposed to the proposed minerals convention and state interests opposed to the ATS. The arena for this alliance was the UN.[33] The opportunity was created by the Malay-

---

[31] *Ibid.*, p. 174.

[32] The practical (as opposed to symbolic) significance of this exclusion may be questioned given the extensive involvement of Greenpeace in ASOC and in some national delegations to various ATS meetings.

[33] Lee Kimball uses the emergence of the UN as an arena for the Antarctic to separate the second period identified in this chapter into two by distinguishing between the dominance of resource issues from the middle of the 1970s and the emergence of a United Nations interest from 1983: see Kimball, 'The Role of NGOs', pp. 36–42. While accepting that there is a substantial change in Antarctic affairs from 1983 due to the UN involvement, the critical influence of the United Nations was not in the NGO arena but in the state system arena where the Consultative Parties appear to have responded to the Malaysian

sian decision in late 1982 to bring Antarctica under the control of United Nations processes as the common heritage of mankind; a decision pursued during 1983 through the device of inscribing the 'Question of Antarctica' on the annual agenda of the General Assembly.[34] ASOC and Greenpeace initially were attracted to the idea of the United Nations authority replacing the ATS with its limited membership and less open attitude toward NGOs.[35] Subsequently, a split emerged in ASOC over whether to continue to use the UN to challenge the ATS or to seek to work with the ATS, but Greenpeace made a policy decision in 1984 to support the ATS.[36] While apparently concluding that more effective change was likely to be achieved by operating within the ATS than outside it, Jim Barnes indicated several years later that both NGOs saw significant benefits in a substantial UN involvement with Antarctica.[37]

If the first phase of NGO activity in Antarctica was characterised by a high degree of internal and external consensus on the need for non-state scientific input into the nascent ATS in order to achieve central regime objectives, the same cannot be said of the second phase. Many new actors emerged and came into the Antarctic arena to challenge the prevailing orthodoxies. These NGOs brought with them a new agenda with new preferences and priorities. As this period is defined by the interest in resource exploitation which gave rise to CCAMLR and CRAMRA, predictably a major consideration in the resulting conflicts was the opposition of pro- and anti-development interests. The novelty in Antarctica was that the interests representing resource development were all located in the governmental sector, while the conservation interests were substantially located in the non-governmental sector. Consequently, the tensions generated by the resources issues of the 1970s and 1980s typically revolved around conflicting state and NGO priorities. Inter-NGO rivalries were rare. Indeed, if there was one, it was the subterranean contest for influence between the environmental NGOs and SCAR. Acceptance of the expertise of groups such as ASOC, the IUCN and the World Wildlife Fund (WWF) was attributed by some as diminishing the role of SCAR in the ATS relative to earlier years.[38]

gambit by opening the doors to expanded state membership in the hitherto exclusive 'Antarctic Club'.

[34] See Chapter 2; see also Suter, *Antarctica: Private Property*, pp. 75–6.
[35] Kimball, 'The Role of NGOs', p. 39.
[36] *Ibid.*
[37] May, *The Greenpeace Book*, p. 175.
[38] *Final Report of the XVI Consultative Meeting*, Bonn, 1991, p. 236.

NGOs AND ANTARCTICA: A PERIOD OF PRIVATE INTERESTS?

While the third period of NGO activity in Antarctica has only just begun, its inauguration is more clearly marked than the second. It dates from the 1991 Protocol, which added the new core value of environmental protection to the original two – security and science – in the Antarctic Treaty. In another of the several ironies attached to the story of NGOs in Antarctica, the elaboration of NGO activity since the signing of the Protocol has witnessed the emergence of industry-based associations. Indeed, superficially the third phase is almost a mirror image of the second with regard to conservation and industry. The critical resource decisions made during the fifteen years prior to the Protocol failed to engender international associations of industry to project and protect industry interests in the development of the fisheries and minerals regulatory regimes; by contrast, the Protocol, rather than encouraging a further flowering of environmental groups, has instead generated new industry activity.

In recent years, the emphasis has reverted from promotional to sectional NGOs largely because new proposals for regulation under the Protocol – especially suggestions for a 'Tourism Annex' – would challenge an industry which is already in operation and is substantially private in character. Unlike fisheries and minerals, tourism has been an established (albeit limited) industry in Antarctica for decades, having been inaugurated even before the advent of the Treaty itself. Tourism has also had a significant private enterprise base and thus been capable of responding in much more conventional ways to proposals that its regulatory arrangements be changed. This is not to say that the Antarctic tourism industry has sought to contest the logic or purpose of the Protocol in the way in which a mining NGO might have been expected to do, had one existed during the negotiation of CRAMRA. The issues of industry legitimacy within the ATS have been rather more subtle in the present period.

Discussion of the need to deal with tourism during the talks which ultimately produced the Protocol clearly galvanised the industry to act. The mainly American travel operators providing commercial tour access to Antarctica had been in contact with each other for some years. Generally they were concerned to maintain standards of appropriate behaviour and codes of conduct that would accord with the expectations of the Consultative Parties. Most appear to have taken some pride in being environmentally sensitive to the special circumstances of Antarctica. Yet there was also some suspicion among some Treaty members that the tourist industry could not be trusted to police itself adequately. Indeed, it was precisely this concern which had raised the desire to further environmental protection by regulating more closely tourist activities in the South.

The formation of the International Association of Antarctic Tour Operators (IAATO) in August 1991 represented as much an attempt by the majority of tour operators to improve their capacity at self-regulation as to influence the regulations likely to be pursued by the Consultative Parties.[39] IAATO was supported by an existing industry NGO, the Pacific Asia Travel Association (PATA). PATA complemented the tour operators to a real extent since its membership is composed of the travel agents who sell the tour packages to Antarctica. Until early 1991, PATA did not have an Antarctic interest but rather was drawn into the issue of Antarctic tourism by members who believed that the long-term interests of tourism generally depended on environmental sensitivity. The resistance of the Consultative Parties to industry NGOs frustrated the attempt by both IAATO and PATA to obtain invited expert status at the XVI Consultative Meeting, held in Bonn in 1991, but both earned places at the table of the informal meeting on tourism prior to the XVII Consultative Meeting in Venice; and, by an *ad hoc* decision of that Meeting, IAATO was invited to contribute to the discussion of tourism during its formal meeting. As can be seen in Chapters 8 and 12, the industry (sectoral) has consolidated its formal relationship with the ATS in the years since Venice.

Several factors can be said to have contributed to the acceptance of the industry NGOs into the ATS. As with other successful sectional NGOs, the recognised expertise of the two tourism bodies has helped to confer legitimacy on their involvement. Also important was the legitimacy of the issue area they represent. The Consultative Parties have formally acknowledged the validity of Antarctic tourism as an activity at least since 1971. The two industry NGOs in turn have acknowledged the primacy of the ATS and clearly signalled their intention to operate within this system. Arguably, it has been much easier for the new industrial NGOs to find a place at the ATS table because they have been prepared from the outset to support the regime and work within it on the regime's terms. The industry's willingness to assume this role of regime supporter was perhaps particularly important given its timing. The tourism NGOs were

[39] Many of these observations on the development of an organised industry body have been reported in R. A. Herr, 'Antarctic Tourism and its Likely Development', in J. Handmer and M. Wilder (eds.), *Towards a Conservation Strategy for the Australian Antarctic Territory* (Canberra: Centre for Resource and Environmental Studies, 1993), pp. 91–107.

enthusiastic enlistees to the bandwagon rolling toward indorsement of the Protocol and for the environmental values entrenched in it.

AN ASSESSMENT OF THE ROLES OF NGOs

The changing preoccupations and numbers of states with Antarctic interests have transformed the Antarctic Treaty System over the years since 1959. With each extension of the System's ambit of interests, new opportunities for non-state involvement were created, although not always utilised. The initial phase began with the creation of the Treaty, but there was so little non-governmental interest that only the government-supported SCAR found a niche for itself as a sectional NGO. The circumstances surrounding the Treaty's origins ensured that SCAR helped to sustain and legitimate the regime's commitment to science, which in turn was regarded by its members as a major legitimating factor in their management of the region. The role played by SCAR went well beyond a passive legitimating influence. SCAR helped to make the ATS work in terms of effectiveness by acting as a facilitator for regime objectives, providing a clearing house for scientific information. Moreover, its constituent organs at the national level served in many countries as a lobby group for both resources and support for the ATS regime.

The second phase of NGO involvement began in the second half of the 1970s with a growing awareness that resource exploitation was likely to become a significant factor in Antarctica. In a more developed policy arena, the prospect of economic gain might have promoted the formation of interest associations on all sides of the development debate. That this did not occur demonstrates the unevenness of Antarctic interests. In the event, both actual fisheries exploitation and potential minerals development were closely identified with state interests, so the new interests raised in the creation of CCAMLR and CRAMRA focused on the risks to the environment from resource exploitation. Because the development side of this debate rested in the state arena, a new style of relationship emerged between NGOs and the ATS. This style was adversarial as the regime objectives themselves became the contentious issue for these newly active Antarctic NGOs.

Initially, the major role adopted by the new NGO players was that of alternative agenda-setter. Seeking to challenge the ATS agenda – as they perceived it – the environmental NGOs offered another agenda, the world park concept. This challenge contained two elements. The first was leadership. The leadership of these NGOs encompassed both intellectual initiative (in proposing the world park concept) and interest aggregation (in terms of building transnational support to oppose CRAMRA). The second element concerned the core values of the ATS. The environmental NGOs believed the ATS was defective as long as it did not accord a central place to nature conservation. In the event, a compromise of sorts was reached. Although only grudgingly conceded, the regime accepted these 'outside' interests largely on the grounds of their environmental expertise, and these NGOs more or less accepted the legitimacy of the ATS. If this was cooptation, it could be argued that it came at a high price. Insofar as the environmental NGOs were able to get environmental concerns incorporated formally into the ATS through the Protocol, they had to pay for this gain by surrendering the world park concept.

The third phase, dating from the reversal of the agreement on CRAMRA which led to the Protocol, has consolidated the gains of the 1970s and 1980s for NGOs within the ATS by extending these gains to include industry NGOs. Unlike in the previous period, however, the new NGOs did not pursue a strategy of challenging the ATS. Rather these new players adopted the roles of supporter and facilitator. IAATO and PATA have acknowledged the legitimacy of the ATS and have offered to cooperate with the regime in achieving regime objectives. Moreover, they have indicated that they are willing to help facilitate the success or effectiveness of the regime in their areas of interest by assisting with information collection, education and compliance, in exchange for their participation in regime policy-making. Of course, the gains made by the environmental NGOs were further entrenched by their relationship with the ATS during this third period with their active participation in emerging issues. These have included the debate over the proposed Tourism Annex, and environmental NGO attempts to influence the continuing institutionalisation of the ATS in such matters as the establishment of a permanent secretariat and the development of a liability regime.

While formal acceptance and incorporation of NGOs into the ATS may be the more dramatic development in the changing relationships between the two, the process was scarcely a one-way street. Each of these non-state actors incurred costs for their respective gains. SCAR's acceptance as a substantial player was purchased, in the eyes of its critics, at the cost of cooptation by the system. While ASOC could not be said to have been similarly coopted, its acceptance did serve as a pretext to isolate and exclude Greenpeace from the ATS. Moreover, it is arguable that the environmental movement has had to abandon its favoured world park solution to the management of Antarctica in favour of the Protocol to maintain acceptance within the ATS. IAATO now has a place at the table as an industry NGO also by fitting within the ATS framework and assisting the current regime to meet its objectives. On the other hand, the ATS also has adapted in order to accommodate the NGOs. SCAR apart, the NGOs gained significant but very limited access through changes in the 1987 Rules of Procedure for Consultative Meetings. Revisions to the Rules of Procedure adopted in 1992 gave all NGOs much more liberal access to the Consultative Meetings' agenda items so that, at the XVIII Consultative Meeting, held in Kyoto in 1994, NGOs were barred only from discussions on organisational arrangements at the opening and closing of Consultative Meetings and from the debates on the proposed ATS secretariat.[40] Nonetheless, and perhaps significantly, NGOs have been denied direct involvement in the deliberations of the Working Group of Legal Experts on Liability.

CONCLUDING REMARKS

The experience of NGOs in the Antarctic policy arena has become more sophisticated and mature over the years by the ever-increasing diversification of interests included within it. It is difficult to imagine that Antarctic policy-making will ever again be as narrowly focused as in the early 1960s. The extension of acceptance to a wider variety of groups within the ATS has necessarily extended legitimacy to the broader range of interests these groups represent. In reciprocation, the willing participation of this broader range of NGOs has helped to legitimate the ATS. The roles played by the NGOs also include substantive support for the achievement of regime objectives. The differing expertise of the Antarctic NGOs is helping to mobilise resources and support for the ATS in ways that contribute directly to its effectiveness.

At the broader theoretical level, the experience of NGOs in the ATS regime tells us something about the way the international order as a whole is changing. While the operation of sovereignty has appeared relatively problematic for the state system in Antarctica at a theoretical level, in practice the experience of Antarctic NGOs has demonstrated how thoroughly the state system has remained unaffected by the 'freezing' of sovereignty in Antarctica. If the Antarctic Treaty was to have been an important litmus test for the use of international regimes to reform the state

---

[40] *Draft Final Report of the XVIII Antarctic Treaty Consultative Meeting*, Doc. XVIII ATCM/ WP 37, Kyoto, 22 April 1994, para. 125.

system, the results to date suggest that reform may take much longer than the Idealists hope. Nonetheless, a review of the óne aspect of the role of non-state actors in Antarctica shows change, even if glacial, is taking place.

In terms of broader scholarly concerns, while the experience of the interaction between states and NGOs in Antarctica can be used to support the argument that NGOs play a significant role in the international order, arguably the alternative interpretation is supported by the stronger evidence. The state system has clearly remained paramount within Antarctica despite the limitations of the partial suspension of sovereignty in Article IV of the Antarctic Treaty. This has been demonstrated rather convincingly at both levels of legitimacy. At the external level, two significant tests of will have shown the effectiveness of the Consultative Parties in countering the attempts by dissenting NGOs to challenge the international validity of the ATS. Inscription of the 'Question of Antarctica' on the UN agenda has succeeded only as a procedural device. A decade of debate has not transferred control of the frozen continent from the Consultative Parties to the UN. Nor has Antarctica been alienated from the Consultative Parties by a successful campaign for declaration of a world park. The internal aspect of legitimacy is rather more complex. The growth of NGOs with Antarctic interests from the middle of the 1970s has revealed the depth of public acceptance of promotional activities in defence of these interests. Yet at the Antarctic policy level, the Consultative Parties have appeared to enjoy substantial success as gatekeepers to the system. For example, they have been able to withhold legitimacy within the ATS from Greenpeace, despite its strong internal support and external acceptance elsewhere.[41]

While such evidence serves to demonstrate the resilience and strength of the state system, it is nevertheless clear that this evidence is qualified. The ATS has also had to be adaptive. The Consultative Parties have been able to exercise some discretion as to which NGOs they will admit to their club, but, over the years these governments have also increasingly had to yield ground to NGOs. Long-term pressure on the member governments, individually and collectively, to acknowledge and work with an increasing number and range of NGOs has succeeded despite the

---

[41] There is a fascinating case study to be pursued here in identifying precisely the line of demarcation which separated Greenpeace from ASOC in the minds of the ATCPs so that one, ASOC, ultimately has been accorded the legitimacy of invited expert status while the other, Greenpeace, has been refused such acceptance.

resistance of at least some Consultative Parties. Paralleling the development of a more open style for conducting its business as demanded by Third World states in the 1970s and by the UN in the 1980s, the ATS' engagement with NGOs during the 1980s has promoted greater transparency between the ATS and the rest of the world. Moreover, the Consultative Parties' concessions to the NGOs have not just affected procedural values. Even the core values of the ATS have been influenced by the activities of Antarctic NGOs. It is clear that the success of those NGOs which opposed CRAMRA in reversing the support of the Consultative Parties for the minerals convention contributed significantly toward making the ATS more acceptable to the membership of these NGOs. The Consultative Parties managed to coopt these groups only by changing the core values of the Treaty itself.

The Protocol thus owes much to a reciprocal interaction between the ATS and interested NGOs. It can be said fairly that the negotiation of the Protocol engendered much of the debate that might have been expected from a thirty-year review of the Treaty. Where these changes will lead is not yet certain. The closure and removal of World Park Base by Greenpeace suggests strongly that, *inter alia*, the Protocol has so changed the political landscape within which some promotional NGOs were operating that new tactics and objectives now appear warranted. On the other hand, the Protocol also appears to be creating a new demand for acceptance and legitimacy from new sectional NGOs. IAATO seems likely to be a significant new player among NGOs in the ATS. The heightened saliency of NGOs under the Protocol will continue to give currency to the issue of transnationalism within the ATS, in terms of both regime legitimacy and effectiveness. The continuing interaction among state and non-state actors appears certain, then, to maintain the impetus for institutional change and adaptation in the ATS well into the next century.

PART III

The effectiveness of ATS regimes

The effectiveness of ATS regimes: introduction

OLAV SCHRAM STOKKE AND WILLY ØSTRENG

A regime is effective if it contributes significantly to the solution of the major problems addressed by it. Those problems must be specified in each given case, with reference both to objectives set forth in basic documents and views expressed by regime participants or external analysts. As argued in Chapter 1, such problem definition should always be an explicit part of assertions of regime effectiveness, because different specifications may yield different assertions. In the next four chapters, various ATS regimes are assessed: in the areas of fisheries, minerals activities, environmental protection and tourism. As we shall see, four types of problems are shared by the ATS regimes addressing those issue areas: external acceptance, accommodation of the sovereignty issue, protection of science, and striking a balance between economic use and environmental protection.

THE SAMPLE OF REGIMES

The regimes reviewed in this book differ substantially in terms of maturity, or stage in their life cycle. An intriguing question is whether such differences are decisive for effectiveness. The *CCAMLR* regime, dealt with in Chapter 5, lends itself rather straightforwardly to a discussion of effectiveness. It is based in a coherent, self-contained international convention, has an elaborate institutional structure, and produces a steady flow of data and regulations. At first glance, discussing the effectiveness of the ATS minerals regime would seem far more problematic, since the negotiated treaty, *CRAMRA*, was put aside shortly after its adoption by the Consultative Parties. Intuitively, we would expect a regime based in a treaty which is not only legally pending but even superseded by another one not to have any substantial impact on either its subjects or third parties. Here it is important to recall, however, that legal obligation is only one of the ways in which an international regime may affect behaviour.[1] Hence, Chapter 6 shows that the adoption of CRAMRA had a significant impact on the political tug-of-war on Antarctic minerals, both within certain key countries and at the ATS level.

Another set of objections may seem relevant when evaluating the effectiveness of the regime based in the *Environmental Protocol*, with its ban on minerals activities. Because this is a very recent regime, any analysis of its effectiveness will necessarily differ from that of CCAMLR or CRAMRA. It is still too early to inquire into the behavioural impacts of the Protocol regime, so Chapter 7 focuses largely on the degree of changes inherent in the Protocol provisions, and the conduciveness of these changes to solving the problems addressed. As such, the effectiveness and the legitimacy analyses are more similar in the case of the Protocol than for the other regimes in this volume.[2]

And finally, the ATS *tourism* regime is an emerging one, and its form is still unsettled.[3] On the other hand, the fact that there is no separate convention, or annex to existing ones, devoted to tourism, does not imply that the ATS has been without notable impact on the main problems raised by this activity. Hence, in Chapter 8, the effectiveness question takes its point of departure in the evolving set of ATS norms and decision-making structures pertaining to tourism activities, including the ongoing deliberations on whether to elaborate a more detailed and specific tourism regime.

FOUR MAJOR PROBLEMS ADDRESSED BY ATS REGIMES

Because certain conflicts in Antarctic politics, like the sovereignty dispute, transcend issue boundaries, and since the ATS is a closely integrated legal system, we assumed in Chapter 1 that a careful analysis of the main problems dealt with by each of the various ATS components would yield fairly congruent definitions. The following chapters confirm this, although the manifestation and relative weight of the major problems differ from case

---

[1] Chapter 1 suggests several causal pathways between international regimes and actor behaviour.

[2] As shown in Chapter 1, regime legitimacy is assessed in terms of the evolving applicability and acceptance of its provisions. Regarding the legitimacy of the Protocol, Chapter 11 focuses in particular on how these provisions have evolved over time in response to challenges and changing circumstances.

[3] See also Chapter 2.

to case. Four major problems emerge, and let us briefly consider their substance and relative significance in the issue areas covered in this volume.

External acceptance

We saw in Chapter 2 that there is a clear connection between the focus of outside criticism of the Treaty cooperation and the relative significance attributed to each of the three principal values of the ATS. While the shift of emphasis from peaceful use and scientific freedom to environmental protection largely reflects changing priorities among the Consultative Parties themselves, it was also spurred by the fact that external criticism was increasingly targeting environmental matters: in some measure, the Consultative Parties seem to have sought to adapt the ATS to the substance of the external pressure. This observation is supported by the case studies discussed in the following chapters: they all emphasise the concern of the Consultative Parties to gain external approval for their Antarctic arrangements. Hence, when judging whether an ATS regime is effective, a salient factor is whether it supports the external acceptance of Treaty cooperation in the pertinent issue area, or of the ATS as a whole. Since external acceptance also forms part of the general criterion for legitimacy of international regimes, the success of an ATS regime in this respect will also have a bearing on its legitimacy. Note that this common thread between effectiveness and legitimacy is not a conceptual one: it is specifically in the ATS context that external acceptance is perceived by regime members as a major requirement.[4]

The advent of resource management on the ATS agenda increased external pressure on Treaty cooperation, because it raised the issue of who should benefit from the natural resources of the region and attracted the attention of the global environmental movement. In the following chapters, we will see that, although never spelt out explicitly in regime objectives, enhancement of external acceptance has been a salient concern of the Consultative Parties when drawing up ATS regimes for fisheries, minerals, environmental protection and tourism. In their efforts to solve this problem, they have been prepared to adapt these regimes in terms of both normative contents and decision-making structure.

---

[4] Reasons for this are discussed in Chapter 2 and in the Conclusions of this book. Conceptual relationships between effectiveness and legitimacy are addressed in Chapter 1.

The sovereignty problem

A second major ATS problem, emphasised in all the effectiveness studies in this book, is to ensure that activities conducted in the Antarctic do not affect the status of the various positions on the disputed sovereignty claims in the region. This problem is related to the firm determination of the Consultative Parties to prevent the sovereignty issue from turning into open conflict, either among themselves or in their relations with the wider international community. As shown in Chapter 2, Article IV of the Antarctic Treaty freezes seven contested sovereignty claims in Antarctica by stipulating that neither the Treaty, nor activities taking place while it is in force, shall add to or detract from those claims. However, this Article does not put the matter entirely at rest: there is a linkage in international law between actual exercise of regulative authority and the strengthening of claims to sovereignty, implying that the sovereignty problem will resurface whenever management of economic activity is concerned.

As we will see, in the regimes set forth in CCAMLR and CRAMRA, this problem was especially salient in discussions on the geographic extent of the conventions, on which decision-rule to choose in the various institutions, and on the balance of powers between institutions. By postponing the minerals issue, the Environmental Protocol is much less affected by the sovereignty problem than are the resource regimes: preservation is less sensitive than resource management in this respect because it does not involve allocative and distributive decisions. In the tourism regime, however, sovereignty is again becoming a problem, because adequate governance of this activity may require explicit rules regarding liability and insurance, and this is difficult to establish without touching on the question of jurisdiction.

The protection of Antarctic science

The most prolific activity in the Antarctic is science, and we have seen that freedom of scientific operations is one of the principal values of Treaty cooperation. Just like preservation of the sovereignty *status quo*, protection of Antarctic science from various types of disturbances reappears as a salient policy problem in all the four cases discussed in this volume. We may distinguish a financial, a regulative and a physical aspect to this problem.

As to the *financial* side, some complain that funds previously allocated to basic science are increasingly being rechannelled to meet requirements for applied research in the new management regimes in the ATS, and require compensation for this.[5] It should be noted that this is not a threat to Antarctic science *per se*, but to the general orientation this activity had during the first two decades of the ATS.

A second part of the science problem, addressed in Chapter 7, is to prevent *regulative* provisions in the evolving ATS from resulting in severe impediments or prohibitive additional costs for the scientific operations in the Antarctic.[6] This matter surfaced first in the CRAMRA negotiations, when there was some concern that the definition of prospecting, subject to elaborate regulations and notification rules, could imply the preclosure of geological investigations of a type conducted in the Antarctic for decades. Later, as discussed in Chapter 7, certain features of the Environmental Protocol, especially the waste management rules and possibly the requirements for environmental impact assessment, have been seen by some as levying unacceptable and unnecessary additional costs on Antarctic scientific operations.

The issue of *physical* interference has been particularly salient in the elaboration of rules to manage the rising tide of tourism to certain locations on the continent. As discussed in Chapter 8, this is not only a matter of scientists being disturbed during their intensive Antarctic summer activities by sociable travellers who sometimes even interfere with ongoing measurements,[7] but also that possible accidents associated with tourism may swamp logistical capabilities already fully employed with scientific assignments.

Balancing use and protection

All the regimes discussed in this book have evolved in response to the growing need for the ATS to deal explicitly with economic activity in the region. Therefore, a fourth major problem addressed by these regimes is how to balance economic use of the Antarctic with the need to conserve, even preserve, its resources and related environments over time. In

[5] See for instance the report from a US National Science Foundation symposium on Antarctic science in *Antarctic Journal of the United States*, vol. 25, no. 4, 1990, p. 6.

[6] Such concerns have, *inter alia*, been voiced by R. T. Scully, 'Resource Management and the Changing Profile of Science in Antarctica: A Growing Pressure for Relevance?' *International Challenges*, vol. 10, no. 1, 1990, p. 41.

[7] See A. Karlquist, 'The Changing Role of Antarctic Science', in A. Jørgensen-Dahl and W. Østreng (eds.), *The Antarctic Treaty System in World Politics* (London: Macmillan, 1991), pp. 277–86.

assessing whether this balance has been struck successfully, the following chapters tend to focus on whether the regimes affect practices in the domains of science, regulation and enforcement.

Thus, a first part of this requirement is that the regime should help to generate adequate scientific *knowledge* to permit informed judgments about whether and how a specific activity should be carried out in the Antarctic. In CCAMLR, as shown in Chapter 5, this issue appeared, *inter alia*, in the controversial question of which procedures and scales to use when reporting catches, and in the protracted emergence of a system of scientific observers. In CRAMRA, discussed in Chapter 6, it became relevant when deciding on the status and role of the Technical and Environmental Advisory Committee envisaged by that convention, and on the information requirements before an operator may proceed from prospecting to exploration and development of minerals resources. As addressed in Chapters 7 and 8, this was taken further in the environmental evaluation rules in the Protocol, which are also pertinent for tourism activities.

Another important factor when evaluating whether a regime helps in solving the dilemma of use and protection, is its impact on the production of appropriate *regulative measures* to govern activities in the Antarctic. To what extent are regulative efforts of the Consultative Parties enhanced by the fact that they occur within the normative and structural framework of an established regime, rather than *ad hoc*? In CCAMLR, the regulative question has revolved around two points: first, how to give substance to the ecosystem principle; and second, whether or not to take precautionary measures in the face of scientific uncertainty. The latter question was also central in the regime envisaged by CRAMRA and in the decision to establish a ban on minerals activities through the Environmental Protocol. Beyond this, as noted above, the Protocol is assessed in Chapter 7 on the basis of whether it strengthens existing regulations in areas such as marine pollution, waste management and area protection. In the case of tourism, one of the most difficult issues has been whether the distinctive features of this phenomenon warrant a separate set of regulations.

The final requirement for these regimes to be deemed conducive to solving the dilemma of utilisation and conservation is that they stimulate adequate *enforcement* of adopted measures. In fisheries management, this becomes pertinent when discussing the impact of CCAMLR on the reporting and monitoring practices of its members. Similarly, key enforcement issues in the CRAMRA negotiations were inspection, linked to procedures for suspension of activities, and liability. And as shown in

Chapters 7 and 8 respectively, both of these issues resurfaced in connection with the Environmental Protocol and in the deliberations on an enhanced tourism regime.

SUMMARY

All the regimes analysed in the following chapters relate to four major problems, although the relative severity of each differs from case to case. The first of these problems is defined in terms of origin rather than substance: while external criticism may vary in contents, a major requirement of ATS regimes is that they should support external acceptance of Treaty cooperation. The second shared requirement of ATS regimes is that they preserve the pragmatic *modus vivendi* on the sovereignty issue as set forth in the Antarctic Treaty. The third requirement of the regimes discussed in this book is that they protect Antarctic science from serious disturbances; and the fourth that they should be conducive to the basic tasks of resource management: knowledge-building, regulations and enforcement practices.

In assessing the effectiveness of these regimes, the focus rests on whether and how they contribute to solving these problems. As noted in Chapter 1, such an analysis should be sensitive to the possible impacts of a regime on processes like learning, obligation and domestic alignment patterns in member states.

5

The effectiveness of CCAMLR

OLAV SCHRAM STOKKE

INTRODUCTION

Some twenty years ago, long-distance fishing nations held high hopes that Antarctic waters could make up for the reduced catches entailed by extended fisheries zones elsewhere. Today, these dreams have proved futile. Unable to sustain the intensive exploitation in the early 1970s, harvest of Antarctic finfish stocks have varied between 50,000 and 100,000 tons a year. Also catches of krill, the shrimp-like hub of the Antarctic marine ecosystem, fall far below earlier expectations: until the radical decline in Russian activity in the 1992–3 season, annual harvest would average between 300,000 and 400,000 tons.[1] The unusual dependence of this ecosystem upon this one species has been the source of considerable concern.

Regarding resource management, the Antarctic Treaty suggests no more than a whispering regime. On the illustrative list of areas to be addressed by the Consultative Meetings,[2] preservation and conservation of Antarctic living resources is the only item not couched in the explicit objectives and principles of the Treaty. However, as shown in Chapter 2, the Consultative Parties soon moved to tackle environmental issues. The 1964 Agreed Measures, preparations for which started at the first Consultative Meeting, prohibit the taking of native birds, animals or flora without a special permit; and while stating that this may change, the 1972 Seals Convention establishes a temporary ban on commercial sealing.[3]

---

[1] *CCAMLR Statistical Bulletin* (Hobart: Commission for the Conservation of Antarctic Marine Living Resources, 1994), vol. 7, Table 1.

[2] Antarctic Treaty, Art. IX, para. 1.

[3] Just like the Convention discussed in this chapter, the Seals Convention was set up as an international convention, open for accession also by states not parties to the Antarctic Treaty.

The reluctance to actually manage, rather than preserve, Antarctic resources was finally overcome with the adoption of the 1980 Convention on the Conservation of Antarctic Marine Living Resources (CCAMLR).[4]

In this chapter, the effectiveness of CCAMLR is assessed along the lines set out in Chapter 1. First, the main features of the regime are outlined. Then follows an analysis of the specific problems which prompted the Consultative Parties to negotiate CCAMLR. Finally, there is an assessment of how CCAMLR affects the solution of these problems, paying particular attention to *how* that impact occurs.

CCAMLR IN A NUTSHELL

CCAMLR is explicitly embedded in the more comprehensive legal structure of the ATS. The primary function of these legal linkages is to bind those current and future CCAMLR Parties which are not Parties to the Antarctic Treaty to the basic principles of that Treaty as well as certain other components of the ATS. This embeddedness is expressed in the Preamble of CCAMLR, in which Parties recognise the prime responsibilities of the Antarctic Treaty Consultative Parties for the protection and preservation of the Antarctic environment, particularly living resources. And six of the thirty-three Articles of CCAMLR serve to link the Convention firmly to the rest of the ATS.[5] It also differs from the Treaty in important ways, however, as its geographic area of application extends also north of 60°S and by allowing the accession of regional economic organisations.[6]

A second salient feature of CCAMLR is its objective, which is to 'conserve' the living resources in the Southern Ocean and at the same time

---

[4] Signed at Canberra, on 20 May 1980, the Convention entered into force on 7 April 1982; the text is reprinted in *International Legal Materials*, vol. XIX, 1980, pp. 837*ff.*

[5] In Art. III, Contracting Parties pledge loyalty to the principles of the Antarctic Treaty; Art. IV reiterates in the new context the freeze on sovereignty claims; Art. V repeats the special responsibilities of the Consultative Parties mentioned in the Preamble and emphasises the relevance of the Agreed Measures for the management of marine living resources; Art. VII ensures for those states which had consultative status at the time, all of whom took part in the negotiations of CCAMLR, non-conditional membership in the decision-making body of CCAMLR; Art. IX obliges the decision-making body to take full account of any relevant measures or regulations established or recommended by the Consultative Meetings; and Art. XXIII makes it clear that the institutions set up by CCAMLR shall cooperate with the Consultative parties on all matters falling within the competence of the latter.

[6] See, respectively, CCAMLR, Art. I, para. 1 and Art. XXIX, para. 2.

permit '*rational use*'.[7] The tension between these two components indicates the competing priorities of those who negotiated the regime. Moreover, operationalising them is necessary to really come to grips with the
regime objective, and this is where CCAMLR spells out its much-revered
three-stranded ecosystem standard:

1 stocks shall be kept at levels close to the one which permits their
   maximum net recruitment;
2 ecological relationships between the various species shall be maintained; and
3 non-reversible reductions of any species shall be avoided.[8]

What the harvesting nations had favoured was a single-stock standard
corresponding to the first of the three strands finally agreed to.[9]

The third major feature of CCAMLR is that, unlike previous components of the ATS, it set up a new, two-tiered institutional structure.
While the *Commission* is not independent of the Consultative Parties,
it is nevertheless a new decision-making body within the ATS, meeting
annually, with a very broad repertoire of management techniques,
including competence to set levels of total allowable catches (TAC).[10]
After intensive debate during the negotiations, it was decided that the
Commission was to operate on the basis of *consensual* decision-making.[11]
However well this procedure may have functioned in the Antarctic
Treaty context, it is vulnerable to what may be termed the law of the
least ambitious programme.[12] While in practice it is somewhat more
complex,[13] the consensus rule in principle gives to each member the
power of veto. Indeed, the opting-out clause harboured in Article IX,
which allows members to reserve themselves against given regulative

---

[7] *Ibid.*, Art. II, paras. 1 and 2.
[8] *Ibid.*, Art. II, para. 3.
[9] See W. M. Bush (ed.), *Antarctic and International Law: A Collection of Inter-State and National Documents* (London: Oceana, 1982), vol. I, p. 402.
[10] *Ibid.*, Art. IX. Whether or not it may also allocate national quotas is a disputed matter, but most observers believe that it cannot. See Bush, *Antarctica and International Law*, vol. I, p. 411.
[11] CCAMLR, Art. XII, para. 1.
[12] See A. Underdal, *The Politics of International Fisheries Management: The Case of the Northeast Atlantic* (Oslo: Universitetsforlaget, 1980).
[13] See F. Zegers, 'The Canberra Convention: Objectives and Political Aspects of its Nego-tiation', in F. Orrego Vicuña (ed.), *Antarctic Resources Policy: Scientific, Legal and Political Issues* (Cambridge University Press, 1983), pp. 149–58.

measures, implies a double veto, which is not uncommon in international fisheries regimes.

The Commission has at its disposal a *Scientific Committee*, which also meets annually, and is composed of representatives from the states which are members of the Commission.[14] It has been argued that while the Scientific Committee definitely needs to conduct research on its own, especially fishery-independent data collection, in order to provide sound management advice, it can in fact do so only if prompted by the Commission.[15] However, there is nothing in the Convention to prevent the Scientific Committee from taking initiatives to the Commission; and over time, it has proved increasingly active in this respect.[16] In addition to the two key institutions, and unlike the Antarctic Treaty to date, CCAMLR provides for a *Secretariat*.

THE NATURE OF THE PROBLEM

The objective stipulated by CCAMLR, then, is the conservation of Antarctic marine living resources. As shown in Chapter 1, however, to restrict the effectiveness analysis to such a goal is to risk engaging in a purely formalistic exercise. There is little doubt that CCAMLR was designed to address a broader set of problems than the distributive and allocative ones associated with resource exploitation. As noted by Orrego, this convention is more than a fisheries arrangement: it is a fisheries arrangement within the ATS.[17] Accordingly, the politics of CCAMLR cannot be understood without an awareness of how resource management is embedded in the classical conflict lines in the ATS.

[14] CCAMLR, Art. XIV, paras. 1 and 2; functions and procedure are detailed in *ibid.*, Arts. IV and XVI.

[15] See for instance M. Howard, 'The Convention on the Conservation of Antarctic Marine Living Resources: A Five Year Review', *International and Comparative Law Quarterly*, vol. 38, no. 1, 1989, p. 128.

[16] For instance, it has been very active in encouraging the Commission to strengthen the reporting procedures so vital for its work. Also, its somewhat leading question to the Commission about which management strategy to pursue in producing quantitative advice, triggered the most consequential management decision in CCAMLR to date: that as a general rule fishing mortality should be held at $F_{0,1}$. See *Report of the VIth Meeting of the Scientific Committee* (Hobart: Commission for the Conservation of Antarctic Marine Living Resources, 1987), p. 38; for more detail, see pp. 134–48 below.

[17] See F. Orrego Vicuña, 'The Effectiveness of the Decision-Making Machinery of CCAMLR: An Assessment', in Jørgensen-Dahl and Østreng (eds.), *The Antarctic Treaty System in World Politics*, pp. 25–43.

Rainer Lagoni has argued that the Consultative Parties had in mind three major concerns when drawing up CCAMLR:[18] the conservation of krill, in case ongoing harvesting should explode as many observers believed it would; avoidance of conflict over sovereignty claims between claimants and non-claimants; and retention of authority over Antarctic affairs in the face of increasing interest among certain external actors, notably the FAO. This three-faceted account of the problem corresponds closely to the most significant conflict lines in Antarctic politics. While only the first of them is explicitly reflected in its formal objective, it is not difficult to find evidence of the other two in the Convention text as well as in statements of those who negotiatiated it. Article IV is largely devoted to the sovereignty issue and is generally seen as an effort to uphold the fragile compromise of the Antarctic Treaty between claimants and non-claimants in an era when collaboration is moving from science and nature protection to more active management of resources. A representative of a non-governmental organisation, who was also a member of the US delegation during the negotiations, notes that partly because CCAMLR was seen as a guinea pig for a future minerals convention, several states considered it crucial to avoid compromising their legal position on the sovereignty claims, and that this issue was among the most difficult ones to agree on.[19] Regarding the eagerness among the Consultative Parties to retain or even enhance external acceptance for their governance role, it has been noted above that the Preamble as well as six Articles in the Convention seek to bind Contracting Parties to the larger ATS structure. At the same time, Article XXIII is devoted to the external relations of CCAMLR, *inter alia*, obliging the Commission and the Scientific Committee to cooperate, as appropriate, with FAO and other specialised agencies.

Let us have a closer look at the substantive content of the three basic problems addressed by CCAMLR, in order to assess the extent to which the Convention has contributed to solving them. The *sovereignty problem*

---

[18] See R. Lagoni, 'Convention on the Conservation of Antarctic Marine Living Resources: A Model for the Use of a Common Good?', in R. Wolfrum (ed.), *Antarctic Challenge: Conflicting Interests, Cooperation, Environmental Protection, Economic Development* (Berlin: Duncker & Humblot, 1984), pp. 96–7.

[19] See J. N. Barnes, 'The Emerging Convention on the Conservation of Antarctic Marine Living Resources: An Attempt to Meet the New Realities of Resource Exploitation in the Southern Ocean', in J. I. Charney (ed.), *The New Nationalism and the Use of Common Spaces: Issues in Marine Pollution and the Exploitation of Antarctica* (Totowa, NJ: Allanheld, Osmun and Co., 1982), pp. 239–86.

follows the classical Antarctic conflict line separating seven claimant states from the non-claimants.[20] Regarding the marine areas adjacent to Antarctica, there is legal disagreement on whether claims to the subsequently extended marine zones are implied in the original territorial claims, or whether this should be seen as an enlargement of existing claims and hence in violation of the freeze in Article IV of the Antarctic Treaty.[21] The sovereignty question arises in resource management questions because of the linkage in international law between the accepted exercise of regulative authority and a strengthening of claims to sovereignty. This is why, despite the freeze Article in the Antarctic Treaty, claimants have been especially eager to introduce safeguards whenever natural resources are concerned, so as to avoid compromising their legal position on the sovereignty issue: hence the so-called bifocal components in the Agreed Measures on flora and fauna, i.e. legal formulas that can be interpreted differently by claimants and non-claimants. In implementing these regulations on their nationals, the former can invoke the jurisdictional principle of territoriality, and the latter that of nationality.[22]

The Agreed Measures do not involve decisions about the allocation or distribution of resources, however, and thus do not require a decision-making arena or agency in order to function. This way, the productive unclarity of the legal formulations does not have to be exposed or put to a test. Marine living resource management is different in this respect – both because states disagree on the need for regulations, and because of the distributive implications of regulative measures. Most important, because they differentiate more, management measures typically generate a greater need for a system of inspection and enforcement than does a moratorium. Resource management requires the exercise of authority and thus runs a greater risk of activating the highly contested sovereignty issue than do measures for environmental preservation.

Hence, in order to address effectively the sovereignty problem, the regime must ensure that fisheries management does not compromise the legal position of either claimants or non-claimants as to the status of claims to Antarctica. This problem was especially acute in the formative stages of CCAMLR, but has also lingered on as the Commission moved to tackle the controversial inspection issue.

[20] See the Introduction to Part III.
[21] See Lagoni, 'Convention on the Conservation', p. 101.
[22] See P. J. Beck, 'The Antarctic Resource Conventions Implemented: Consequences for the Sovereignty Issue', in Jørgensen-Dahl and Østreng (eds.), *The Antarctic Treaty System in World Politics*, p. 242.

A second problem relevant in assessing CCAMLR effectiveness, the *external acceptance* of ATS arrangements in the fisheries area, stems from the conflict line between 'insiders' and 'outsiders' in Antarctic politics, in terms of access to decision-making processes in the Treaty cooperation. 'Outsiders' refers to non-parties to the Treaty, and one of the motives of the Consultative Parties in drawing up CCAMLR was to pre-empt regulative action by precisely such actors. The UN Environment Programme had toyed with the idea of encouraging the UN to establish guidelines for the conduct of marine resource exploitation in the Southern Ocean.[23] However, because one of FAO's functions is to facilitate the negotiation of international agreements on the conservation and exploitation of world resources, it was especially the interest shown by this organisation which caused worry on the part of the Consultative Parties.[24] Acutely aware that resource management could rekindle the controversial sovereignty issue, the latter were definitely not enthusiastic about the prospect of the Southern Ocean being regulated by fora other than those controlled by themselves. It is quite possible, therefore, that more was at stake in the negotiation of CCAMLR than just the authority to regulate harvesting in the Southern Ocean. If the Consultative Parties failed to deal with this issue in a manner acceptable to external actors, their entire self-imposed role as stewards of the Seventh Continent could be questioned, disrupting the fine balance between claimants and non-claimants.

Thus, the external acceptance problem is adequately addressed only if CCAMLR helps to discourage competing management arrangements in the Southern Ocean or substantial harvesting by non-parties to the Convention. Like the sovereignty problem, the question of external acceptance was particularly acute in the early stages where challenges to the regime were the most credible. However, the Consultative Parties have been well aware that sustained support for CCAMLR will depend on its conservation performance.

Regarding the third problem addressed by CCAMLR, *fisheries conservation*, two dilemmas are involved: the choice between present and future use, since the amount taken today will affect future harvesting opportunities; and that between various present users.[25] Both harbour the seeds of

---

[23] See P. J. Beck, *The International Politics of Antarctica* (London: Croom Helm, 1986), p. 276.

[24] See R. H. Wyndham, 'Comment', in Wolfrum (ed.), *Antarctic Challenge*, pp. 114–19.

[25] Of course, this is a simplification: it is not only the amount taken which matters but also the fishing pattern, i.e. the segment of the stock biomass targeted. Indeed, this is the very rationale for management measures such as mesh-size requirements or area closures.

disaster, because marine living resources are a scarce, common property. While the individual harvester hauls on board the full benefit of heavy exploitation, the cost of overfishing in the form of stock depletion will be shared by many – including, in some cases, generations unborn. Of the two, the dilemma between present and future use has predominated in Antarctic politics. Even though they feed on the same resources and hence view each other as competitors, the fishing nations have formed a quite firm alliance in management matters. One reason is that none of the major fishing nations in the area are among the claimants to sovereignty in the Antarctic; thus, none of them can argue for privileged access to the marine resources.

The fishing companies operating in Antarctic waters are global in reach, which means they may be able to escape the costs of overexploitation by simply leaving for other fishing grounds. In consequence, they may favour safe profits today rather than an uncertain profit in the future. This is why a number of non-harvesting actors in Antarctic politics were not convinced that the harvesters, if left to themselves, would resolve that dilemma in a manner compatible with ecosystemic stability in the Southern Ocean. CCAMLR differs from most fishery management regimes in that the harvesting nations are outnumbered two to one by non-harvesters. To the latter, the management dilemma is far less problematic; especially since several of them, such as the United States, the United Kingdom and Australia, have a number of quite vociferous non-governmental green organisations actively pressuring their governments to take a firm stand in the protection of Antarctic marine living resources.

So one part of the conservation problem addressed by CCAMLR is to resolve, in a consensus-based system, the conflict between, on the one hand, a quite small group of fishing nations highly sceptical towards restrictions, and, on the other, a large majority of states considerably more oriented towards future availability of resources, as well as a green image, than present use. The second part of the problem involves giving substance to the formidable ecosystem principle underlying CCAMLR. Here we should note a few significant barriers to the implementation of the three-stranded ecosystem principle.[26] Maximum net recruitment of any species in a system can only be estimated at given abundance levels of related species; the definition of such levels is politically controversial and

---

[26] See M. Basson and J. R. Beddington, 'CCAMLR: The Practical Implications of an Eco-System Approach', in Jørgensen-Dahl and Østreng (eds.), *The Antarctic Treaty System in World Politics*, pp. 54–70.

not always under the authority of CCAMLR – as in the case of whales.[27] Also, ecological relations vary considerably in strength and are difficult to establish due to long time scales, varying spatial scales of interaction, and substantial natural variations. These factors also render difficult the assessment of the third component of the ecosystem principle, concerning the reversibility of stock decline.

In general, conservation can be split up into three closely related behavioural tasks.[28] The first is to generate adequate *knowledge* about the health of the stocks and the impact of harvesting on the realisation of the regime objective of ecosystem management in the Southern Ocean. The second task is to ensure that the scientific knowledge available is applied in the negotiation of *regulations* which give effect to that objective. And the third requirement is *compliance* control, including monitoring in order to assess adherence to regulations, and the imposition of sanctions when rules are found to be violated.

In summary, the problem addressed by CCAMLR is adequately solved if three requirements are met:

1   regime members must be able to tackle living resource management in the Southern Ocean without compromising the legal position of either claimants or non-claimants;
2   external acceptance of the ATS as the natural forum to address Antarctic matters must be retained; and
3   to realise ecosystemic conservation, the members must be able to generate sufficient knowledge about species dynamics and interrelationships to make an informed choice between present and future use, a choice which must be translated into collectively agreed-upon regulations and supported by a satisfactory compliance control system.

CCAMLR AND SOVEREIGNTY

We have seen that, when the Consultative Parties move on from measures to preserve areas and species to actual resource management, it is harder

---

[27] While CCAMLR does not regulate whale harvesting, the ecosystem principle implies that the conditions and needs of Antarctic whale stocks are important premises for decisions on other marine species. Bush, *Antarctica and International Law*, vol. I, pp. 401–8, points out that marine mammals are not explicitly excluded from the management domain of CCAMLR, but that international law gives pre-eminence to earlier conventions, in this case, the International Convention for the Regulation of Whaling and the Convention for the Conservation of Antarctic Seals.
[28] See also the Introduction to Part III.

to avoid affecting the legal status of the sovereignty claims. In the absence of a regime, claimants would be obliged by the emerging law of the sea to introduce measures to protect endangered stocks in the marine areas claimed to lie within their jurisdiction;[29] failure to move in this direction could even be interpreted as a renouncement of claims. Having proclaimed management zones outside their claimed territory, these states could hardly ignore major fishery activities taking place within it.[30] On the other hand, unilateral regulations on the part of claimants would not be acceptable to states which do not recognise those claims and regard the Southern Ocean, except the waters off undisputed territories, as high seas.

The *bifocal* cover-up used in CCAMLR is based on the fact that the CCAMLR Area largely follows the oceanographic boundary of the region, i.e. the Antarctic Convergence, and thus, unlike the Antarctic Treaty, embraces also areas north of 60°S. Accordingly, the CCAMLR Area includes islands where sovereignty is not disputed, such as Kerguelen, Prince Edward Islands and Bouvetøya. By referring alternately to the 'Antarctic Treaty area' and 'the area to which this Convention applies', a productive ambiguity is introduced as to exactly which marine areas are intended when Article IV states that neither CCAMLR nor activities taking place under it shall detract from any rights or claims to exercise coastal state jurisdiction; nor prejudice any position regarding these claims.[31] While claimants are free to interpret this as confirming the existence of (albeit suspended) coastal state rights related to all territory claimed in Antarctica, non-recognisers of claims can equally argue that coastal state jurisdiction refers to non-disputed territories north of 60°S.[32] Orrego adds that this unclarity had to be supported by the decision-making procedure in the Commission for the claimants to be satisfied:[33] with the consensus rule in place, they would never end up in a position where authoritative decisions had been made without their consent.

Thus, CCAMLR generally makes conservation a more attractive option for claimants and non-claimants than it would have been otherwise. Its bifocal component reduces the potential *costs*, in terms of compromising

[29] Several states, including Australia, Argentina, Chile and New Zealand, have proclaimed 200-mile resource zones adjacent to disputed territorial claims in Antarctica.
[30] See F. M. Auburn, *Antarctic Law and Politics* (London: C. Hurst & Co., 1982), p. 218.
[31] Art. IV, paras. 2(b) and (c) respectively.
[32] See Bush, *Antarctica and International Law*, vol. I, p. 406.
[33] Orrego, 'The Effectiveness', p. 27.

one's position in the claims issue, associated with both the launching and the acceptance of various conservation measures – especially regulation and inspection, so close to the core of sovereignty. Without a regime in place, the traditional Antarctic conflict avoidance would have been difficult to uphold because, as shown above, failure to regulate endangered stocks would have been costly for claimants whereas non-recognisers would have paid a significant price if they were to adhere to unilaterally imposed rules.

There is little doubt, moreover, that the interested states have been greatly helped in their efforts to cope with this dilemma by a measure of *learning* from the experiences and solutions already developed within the ATS. Both the freeze Article and the idea of productive unclarity spring easily to mind. The Seals Convention too was vital for the realisation of CCAMLR: through it, the Consultative Parties acquired experience in including high seas areas in their regulative domain.[34]

In summary, the sovereignty problem appears to have been dealt with quite satisfactorily in the regime. Features enabling this outcome are the embeddedness of CCAMLR in the larger ATS framework, which has facilitated adaptive learning regarding how to circumscribe the sovereignty issue, and even more, the bifocalism inherent in Article IV, which has reduced the cost of compliance control.

EXTERNAL ACCEPTANCE

The second major problem addressed by CCAMLR is to achieve acceptance of an ATS arrangement in the fisheries area among non-Treaty parties and international organisations, and to avoid considerable fishing activity by non-parties in the waters off Antarctica. Two regime effects are particularly relevant here: the withdrawal of challenges from the FAO to the special role of the Consultative Parties in the Southern Ocean; and the accession to the Convention of the most significant harvesting nation in the region not already a party to the Antarctic Treaty.

Withdrawal of challenges

The year after CCAMLR entered into force, a group of Third World states raised the issue of Antarctica for the first time in the UN General

---

[34] See J. A. Heap, 'Has CCAMLR Worked? Management Politics and Ecological Needs', in Jørgensen-Dahl and Østreng (eds.), *The Antarctic Treaty System in World Politics*, p. 46.

Assembly; and there it has remained each year since then.[35] If there were ever expectations that CCAMLR would assuage the general concern among outsiders as to the prominent position of the Consultative Parties in the ATS, events proved them wrong. However, regarding the more fisheries-specific challenge to the Consultative Parties, CCAMLR has played a role in deterring the promotion of competing regimes – especially by the FAO, which was seen as a credible challenger. The latter's plan to put US$45 million into a ten-year Southern Ocean programme was dropped in 1979; pressure from the Consultative Parties being generally held as a significant reason.[36] By that time, it will be recalled, CCAMLR negotiations were already at an advanced stage. Two acts on the part of the FAO's Governing Council were particularly significant for the external acceptance of the Consultative Parties as caretakers of Antarctic affairs:[37] at its eighteenth meeting, the Council explicitly recognised the lead role of the Consultative Parties regarding the preparation of conservation measures in the Southern Ocean; and once CCAMLR had been negotiated, the FAO refrained from trying to establish rules of its own.

The considerable opposition from the Consultative Parties to an initiative from the FAO rendered it difficult indeed for that organisation to assume the activist role in Antarctic affairs some of its most diligent members wanted it to: the Consultative Parties include the wealthiest nations in the world and contribute the bulk of the FAO's budget. Through CCAMLR, the Consultative Parties could point out that they were taking the problem of resource management seriously, and this made it easier to stop the FAO initiative. The Parties' environmental record as stewards of Antarctica was quite favourable, especially through the Agreed Measures and the Seals Convention, and it could be argued that what the FAO criticised was the legal vacuum in the area rather than the position of the Consultative Parties. There are limits to this interpretation: certain representatives in the FAO Fisheries Committee made it very clear in the formative years of CCAMLR that if the latter were made into an exclusive regime, these states would refuse to acknowledge its standing.[38]

Bush notes that after the adoption of the Seals Convention, the Consultative Parties were no longer as careful as in the past in excluding the high seas from the effects of consultations and recommendations: see Bush, *Antarctica and International Law*, vol. I, p. 69.

[35] See Chapter 2.

[36] See Beck, *The International Politics of Antarctica*, p. 276.

[37] See Zegers, 'The Canberra Convention', p. 152.

[38] J. A. Heap, cited in 'Discussion', in Wolfrum (ed.), *Antarctic Challenge*, p. 130.

In fact, the FAO is among the very few external organisations explicitly listed in the CCAMLR text as natural cooperation partners.[39] This has been followed up in practice by the regime members, first by granting the FAO observer status to Commission meetings and inviting it to take part in the work of the Scientific Committee; and then by the recognition of the FAO's previous statistical work through the compilation and adaptation of its Statlant data base. This recognition of the FAO can be seen as accommodation on the part of the Consultative Parties to the organisational interests of the FAO; a *reward* offered by the regime. Another regime feature relevant in this respect was the explicit emphasis on the ecosystem principle. While this concept had been much discussed, it had not been introduced in prior international management arrangements. The International Union for the Conservation of Nature commended CCAMLR negotiators for hammering out this principle;[40] and according to Zegers, the FAO saw the ecosystem principle as a major reason for acknowledging the authority of CCAMLR.[41] Thus, while the regime primarily confirmed the centrality of the Consultative Parties, there was 'something in it' for the FAO as well.

Other fishing nations acceding to the Convention

It was noted above that CCAMLR is designed to tie up contracting parties which have not acceded to the Antarctic Treaty to the principles of that Treaty, including the privileged position in Antarctic decision-making of the Consultative Parties. This implies that every new accession to CCAMLR serves to enhance the external acceptance of the ATS as a whole. And indeed, the Convention appears to have had this effect. After the Convention entered into force, South Korea has acceded to it and gained membership in the Commission; later this country acceded to the Antarctic Treaty as well.

When explaining the role of CCAMLR in inciting non-parties like South Korea, and later the Ukraine, to accede to the Convention, it should be remembered that long-distance fishing nations are generally acutely concerned about avoiding acts which may restrict their rights to operate in high seas areas. Thus, acknowledgment of regimes set up without their participation and influence is no matter of routine for such

---

[39] See Art. XXIII, paras. 1–3.
[40] See Bush, *Antarctica and International Law*, vol. I, p. 403.
[41] See Zegers, 'The Canberra Convention', p. 151.

countries. The role allotted to them under the new regime was probably received with some ambiguity. On the one hand, they were relegated to a position slightly below that of the original signatories: while they could become full members of the Commission enjoying all the rights of the latter, they would remain so only as long as they were actively engaged in either harvesting or research in the Southern Ocean.[42] On the other hand, upon reflection such a membership requirement was not necessarily detrimental to their interests: experience from the International Whaling Commission (IWC), where the rapid rise of non-harvesting members was leading to an increasingly preservationist policy, had convinced many harvesting states that they would be better served by some form of restricted membership.

Thus, while non-party fishing nations may have preferred to have been included in its formation, CCAMLR did offer clear *rewards* for those who chose to join, i.e. full membership in the decision-making body of a convention which explicitly included rational use among its objectives. Such membership was particularly attractive because of the decision-rule adopted: the consensus and reservation procedures provided each member with a double veto regarding restrictions on the harvesting operations of its vessels. Moreover, while CCAMLR encourages a high degree of openness regarding the reports of the Scientific Committee, there is little doubt that active participation in the working groups implies greater access to information about stock size and behaviour, information which might be highly relevant for fishing vessels. Indeed, the fact of coordinated research in the framework of CCAMLR, in which all participating scientists can benefit from the work of the others, might produce a widening knowledge gap between those participating in the regime and those who do not.

Moreover, although it is highly unlikely that CCAMLR can be termed an objective regime, binding for non-parties as well, the latter cannot rule out the possibility of various forms of sanctions by the generally quite powerful members of CCAMLR if they disregard the measures established by the Commission. The regime obliges its members to exert appropriate efforts to ensure that no one engages in activity contrary to the objectives of the Convention.[43] The precise contents of the formulation 'appropriate efforts' is somewhat unclear: the case of whaling dem-

---

[42] See CCAMLR, Art. VII, para. 2(b). Accession to the Convention is open to any state interested in research and harvesting in the Southern Ocean; see *ibid.*, Art. XXIX, para. 1.

[43] CCAMLR, Art. XXII, para. 1.

onstrates that at least one leading proponent of conservationist measures in CCAMLR – the United States – has domestic legislation which allows the introduction of economic sanctions on states which diminish the effects of internationally agreed regulations.[44] To a country like South Korea, the United States is an important market, also in the seafood sector, and a desire to influence the contents of such regulations must have served as an incentive to join the Convention, especially in the period when blocking proposed conservation measures was the rule of the day in CCAMLR.

In summary, like that of not compromising sovereignty positions, the external acceptance problem of CCAMLR appears to be largely solved. Notions of establishing a management regime outside the ATS have been abandoned, and the most significant non-parties have now joined the Convention. To some extent, this is caused by factors external to the regime – like the financial and political muscle of the Consultative Parties – but certain features of CCAMLR have also facilitated the outcome. Regarding the deterrence of competing regimes, there has been noted above the external accommodation inherent in CCAMLR's non-exclusiveness, the ecosystem standard and the cooptation of the FAO as a key cooperation partner – all of which serve to remove reasons for challenging the regime. As to the accession of third states, the conditional inclusiveness of CCAMLR, combined with the consensus procedure, implies that new members are offered a regime less likely to develop into a preservation organisation than a global one would be. Also, the consensus procedure involves some degree of protection from unilateral enforcement practices on the part of some Consultative Parties, such as those relevant for whaling. A final feature that also affects the costs of cooperation is the free access for parties to the accumulated results of the Scientific Committee.

CCAMLR AND ECOSYSTEMIC CONSERVATION

Today, the biomass of the key Southern Ocean finfish species is less than 10 per cent of pre-harvesting levels.[45] It would hardly be fair to blame CCAMLR for this – apart from noting sardonically, as some do, that this regime is too little too late – as shown in Figure 5.1, for most of the

---

[44] The Pelly Amendment (*International Legal Materials*, vol. XXV, 1986, pp. 1,587*ff*) to the 1967 Fishermen's Protective Act (*International Legal Materials*, vol. VII, 1968, pp. 1,391*ff*).
[45] See Basson and Beddington, 'CCAMLR: The Practical Implications', p. 61.

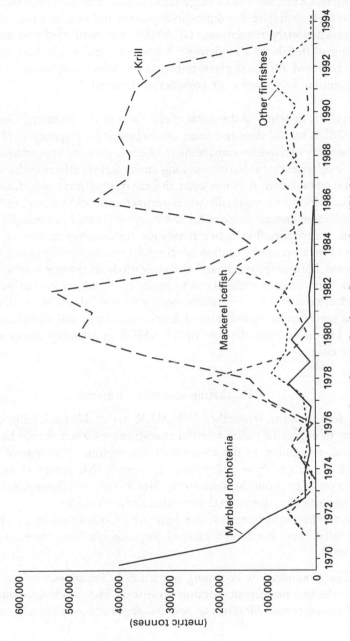

Figure 5.1. Catches of major Southern Ocean species, 1970–94

Southern Ocean fish stocks, large-scale exploitation preceded the regime. Nevertheless, despite this dramatic depletion and despite strong demands for precautionary regulations, CCAMLR has permitted continual harvesting of finfish on a moderately high level; and stocks have definitely not recovered. Of the thirteen finfish stocks which can be assessed in the Convention Area, twelve are considered depleted.[46]

Therefore, in terms of the *status of the stocks* in the Southern Ocean, the CCAMLR record does not seem overwhelmingly impressive. However, in the study of fisheries management, there is growing appreciation of the fact that harvesting is but one among many factors affecting the status of stocks; quite often, it is not even the most significant one. Changes in natural conditions, especially water temperature and salinity, can have a considerable impact; likewise for the much-discussed but scarcely understood interrelationship between various components in marine ecosystems. Therefore, some caution is called for when drawing causal linkages between human behaviour and the conditions of marine stocks. On the other hand, it does make sense to study the kinds of human behaviour which are relevant for the current stock situation. Above, we distinguished three major conservation tasks: science, regulation and compliance control. Let us examine the role of CCAMLR in affecting the conduct of those tasks.

Facilitating scientific research?

The first question is whether CCAMLR has enabled scientific organisations to engage in policy-relevant investigations which would have been difficult to achieve in the absence of the regime. The type of science which would qualify as policy-relevant here is that geared at increasing our knowledge about the abundance, distribution and dynamics of stocks; and in particular, the interrelationships between stocks.

As to the performance of the Scientific Committee, most observers agree that there has been a marked improvement over time, in at least five ways.

1   The Committee is becoming more firmly *institutionalised*, as evident in the two permanent working groups on Fish Stock Assessment and Environmental Monitoring and Management respectively, ensuring

[46] See K.-H. Kock, *Antarctic Fish and Fisheries* (Cambridge University Press, 1992), p. 255.

more focused and sustained research programmes in these key areas.[47]

2 Scientific *results* have improved in terms of preciseness and comprehensiveness, as shown especially by the publication since 1989 of statistical summaries of the most significant fish stocks in the Southern Ocean. In 1990, fine-scaled catch and effort reports since 1987 enabled the Scientific Committee to assert that krill fishery occurred in highly concentrated areas, some of which were close to important growth areas for major predators, thus providing at least some scientific basis for precautionary measures on krill.[48]

3 The evolution of the CCAMLR Ecosystem Monitoring Program (CEMP) is yet another promising development. A special CEMP Working Group was set up in 1984, to detect significant changes in key components of the ecosystem, trying to distinguish those due to commercial harvesting from natural fluctuations.[49] CEMP monitors main predators close to the areas where fishing takes place, in three so-called Integrated Study Areas.[50] This programme may help to improve the level of coordination with scientific activities conducted by the IWC or under the Seals Convention, which has to date been very moderate.[51] At the meetings of the Scientific Committee, a representative from the scientific committee of IWC regularly attends as an observer; and the SCAR Antarctic pack-ice seals programme is coordinated with the needs of the CEMP programme, in which crabeater seals are used as an indicator species.[52]

4 After a very slow and dissensual start, the *flow of input* from the Scientific Committee to the Commission has improved dramatically since 1987. The watershed was the decision made during the sixth Commission meeting to fix a conservative fishing mortality rate and to

---

[47] The Environmental Monitoring and Management group is a result of a 1994 merger of the working groups on krill and on the CCAMLR Ecosystem Monitoring Program: see *Report of the XIIIth Meeting of the Scientific Committee*, 1994, p. 182.

[48] See J. P. Croxall, I. Everson and D. G. M. Miller, 'Management of the Antarctic Krill Fishery', *Polar Record*, vol. 28, no. 164, 1992, p. 65. See also pp. 142–8.

[49] See *CCAMLR Ecosystem Monitoring Program* (Hobart: Commission for the Conservation of Antarctic Marine Living Resources, 1991).

[50] See Croxall *et al.*, 'Management of the Antarctic'; these areas are found in South Georgia, on the Antarctic Peninsula and in Prydz Bay.

[51] See K.-H. Kock, *Fishing and Conservation in Southern Waters* (Hobart: Commission for the Conservation of Antarctic Marine Living Resources, 1993), SC-CAMLR-XII/BG/11, p. 28.

[52] See *Report of the XIIth Meeting of the Scientific Committee*, 1993, p. 60.

instruct the Committee to provide concrete management advice, preferably in option form – finally enabling the latter to play a significant role in the decision-making process.[53]

5   And finally, a Scheme of International *Scientific Observation* was adopted in 1992, setting up clear procedures for dispatching and accepting scientific observers.[54] Their main task is to help to improve the quality and reliability of catch and effort data which forms part of the basis for the Committee's work. This scheme was slow in getting established because fishing nations feared that such observers, remaining onboard for an extended period of time, would become *de facto* inspectors.

Concerning the role of CCAMLR in producing this steadily improving performance, it is natural to point out that its commitment to ecosystemic management *obliges*, indeed urges, the conduct of applied scientific investigations in the Southern Ocean, because multispecies considerations are more demanding in terms of scientific knowledge than a single-stock approach. This is further enhanced by the fact that scientists can refer to new obligations associated with their central, advisory role in the preparatory phase of decision-making. When the Scientific Committee complains about poor data availability because of inadequate contributions to CEMP, it is hard for the Commission not to echo this concern.[55] This means putting some pressure on non-participant states and, perhaps more importantly, providing a channel for states with ongoing or planned projects and an eagerness to demonstrate their constructive role in the cooperation. Following the designation of Bouvetøya as a CEMP site, Norway has initiated a pilot monitoring programme on this island;[56] likewise, CEMP is becoming increasingly important in shaping Australia's research priorities in marine biology.[57]

Its advisory role was also invoked by the Scientific Committee in requesting complementary data from the fishing nations when updating and adapting the historical catch and effort statistics compiled within the

[53] See *Report of the VIth Meeting of the Commission* (Hobart: Commission for the Conservation of Antarctic Marine Living Resources, 1987), p. 19.
[54] See *Report of the XIth Meeting of the Commission*, 1992, p. 19.
[55] See *Report of the IXth Meeting of the Commission*, 1990, pp. 11–13.
[56] See the Report to the Storting, *St.meld. 42 (1992–93)*, *Norsk Polarforskning* (Norwegian Polar Research) (Oslo: Norwegian Ministry of Environment), p. 66.
[57] See P. G. Quilty, 'The Sharing of Scientific Knowledge in Regime Management' (unpublished paper) (Hobart: Antarctic Division, 1994).

FAO.[58] And for the same reason, the SCAR Group of Specialists on the Southern Ocean Ecosystem and Living Resources, who had launched the large-scale basic research programme BIOMASS[59] in the late 1970s, declared their willingness both to make their results available to CCAMLR and, if so desired, update the data from the first experiment.[60] The same is true for the Scientific Committee's own compilation of catch, effort and biological data,[61] where the major problems concerned the reporting practices of the biggest harvester, the Soviet Union.[62] These problems were greatly relieved when the Commission in 1987 agreed on clear criteria for the timely and systematic collection and submission of such data by member states.[63]

However, this advisory role is not necessarily an advantage for scientists oriented towards applied research. Few would argue that the Scientific Committee was a resounding success in its early years; and the major reason for the early squabbles over procedural matters was precisely the fact that this work was embedded in a management regime, implying that its activity might produce political action on the part of the Commission. The Soviet Union in particular, acutely aware of the potential authority of scientific advice offered by the Committee, was eager to ensure that forwarding of scientific advice would require consensus among Scientific Committee members rather than a simple majority.

Dynamic modelling of multispecies relationships requires a very high level of coordination between various types of investigation, including stomach studies and simultaneous sampling of different stocks. In general, this is a quite *costly* activity, which serves to make it less attractive to decision-makers, especially if material gains are uncertain or distant in time. It has been a frequent complaint in CCAMLR circles that the level

---

[58] See Howard,'The Convention on the Conservation', pp. 124–5.

[59] Biological Investigation of Marine Antarctic Systems and Stocks.

[60] See T. Nagata, 'The Implementation of the Convention on the Conservation of Marine Living Resources in Antarctica', in Orrego (ed.), *Antarctic Resources Policy*, pp. 130–1.

[61] Biological data originate not only from commercial activities but also from research vessels, compilation of historical statistics, etc.

[62] Former Chairman of the Scientific Committee, Dieter Sahrhage, cited in 'General Discussion', in R. Wolfrum (ed.), *Antarctic Challenge II: Conflicting Interests, Cooperation, Environmental Protection, Economic Development* (Berlin: Duncker & Humblot, 1986), p. 138.

[63] This provision was made in the Conservation Measure 8/VI related to mackerel icefish around South Georgia, which in 1987 accounted for almost three-quarters of the finfish catch. See Figure 1.

of coordination between various national surveys has been too low.[64] After
the CEMP programme got underway, the data input even from states
with active programmes in the Southern Ocean has varied much from
one year to another.[65] Here too, the embeddedness of applied science in
a management regime may have an ambiguous effect on the cost–benefit
balance of scientific investigations. On the one hand, it serves to involve
a larger number of actors in the funding and conduct of science relevant
for the harvesting fleets. On the other hand, as lack of adequate knowledge can often be cited as a reason for not establishing new regulations,
harvesting nations may be wary about changing this situation. There can
also be incentives to safeguard scientific findings, which might be of considerable commercial value.[66] Conversely, the Scientific Committee has
been criticised for failing to launch scientific projects on species not promising immediate commercial reward, such as squid.[67] While not yet
reflected in budget cuts, the sharp decline in the East European harvest
in the Southern Ocean is likely to increase even more the importance of
cost concerns in the years to come.

The gradual emergence of cooperation within the Scientific Committee, in the absence of dramatic changes on other accounts, suggests
that CCAMLR, by placing the scientists in a forum for regular interaction
on increasingly policy-relevant issues, has stimulated adaptive *learning*
among its members. According to John Gulland, who participated in this
process for a number of years, the general consensus-drive of the ATS
has been a major condition for this to take place:[68] at the outset, there
was a strained atmosphere of mutual distrust among marine scientists
operating in the Southern Ocean, largely because most of them were also
engaged in the conflicts of the IWC. Without the larger ATS and
CCAMLR framework, he argues, accommodation within the Scientific
Committee would have been unlikely. Moreover, quite aside from these
conflicts, the tasks assumed by the Committee were innovative enough
to require some time before they could be dealt with properly. Not until

[64] See for instance *Report of the IVth Meeting of the Commission*, 1985, p. 9. At its next meeting, the Commission was able to praise the informal consultation which preceded the
surveys of seven states that year, noting that more comprehensive coordination should
be developed in the future: see *Report of the Vth Meeting of the Commission*, 1986, p. 21.
[65] See *Report of the XIIth Meeting of the Commission*, 1993, p. 11.
[66] See also Auburn, *Antarctic Law and Politics*, p. 214.
[67] See Howard, 'The Convention on the Conservation', pp. 129–30.
[68] See J. A. Gulland, 'The Antarctic Treaty System as a Resource Management Mechanism –
Living Resources', in *Antarctic Treaty System: An Assessment* (Washington, DC: National
Academy Press, 1986), pp. 229–30.

1985 was the Committee able to identify with some accuracy the scales of information necessary to fulfill its task.[69] The Committee needed several years before it could begin to function as a real forum for coordination of research; but since then, it has given the scientists an opportunity to generate experience and develop practices, especially regarding interaction with the Commission, acceptable to all.

What would have happened in the area of management-relevant research had it not been for CCAMLR? One indicator is that while the Scientific Committee in the early 1980s was fighting over procedure, SCAR was busy organising the ambitious, multispecies-relevant BIOMASS programme on the abundance, distribution and dynamics of krill in the Southern Ocean.[70] While this programme was definitely oriented towards basic research, one of its motives involved the scientific requirements of managing the Southern Ocean resources. This is not to say that in the absence of CCAMLR, SCAR could have filled the scientific needs for management decisions equally well. But the ability of SCAR to organise the largest and most ambitious ecosystem programme ever launched in the Southern Ocean, suggests that an already established institution might have managed to perform some of the knowledge-generating functions now executed by the Committee.

In summary, the regime has failed as yet to produce the knowledge necessary for fine-tuned ecosystemic management in the Southern Ocean; so far, the impediments to such a goal are far better known than the solution. On the other hand, scientific coordination under the Convention has improved markedly in recent years in terms of both process and output, and the relationship between the Scientific Committee and the Commission is far more productive today. While there are probably other factors as well, such as the general improvement in East–West relations, this improvement is partly explained by certain features of CCAMLR. By its very demanding management standards and by institutionalising scientific coordination in a Committee allowing gradual familiarisation and conflict reduction, CCAMLR has stimulated the generation of management-oriented knowledge on the Southern Ocean. The advisory role of the Committee has been helpful when it has requested more detailed data submission or accumulated information from already established

[69] See J. A. Gulland, 'The Management Regime for Living Resources', in C. C. Joyner and S. K. Chopra (eds.), *The Antarctic Legal Regime* (Dordrecht: Martinus Nijhoff, 1988), p. 235.
[70] See Nagata, 'The Implementation', p. 120.

ventures such as BIOMASS and the FAO's statistical production. And the fact that scientists from a greater number of states than the harvesters participate in management-oriented research may tip the cost–benefit balance for certain investigations.

Facilitating ecosystemic regulation?

While Howard[71] in a five-year review of CCAMLR operations concludes that the regime has failed to meet the requirements of its ambitious objective, a close study of the *decisions* of the Commission up to the present reveals that increasingly sophisticated conservation measures have been taken. These measures include area closures for a growing number of species, mesh size regulations and, since 1987, total allowable catches for most commercially relevant fish stocks. Contrary to Howard's earlier assessment, this would suggest a pattern similar to that sketched for scientific investigations.

After a slow start, the Commission has improved its decision-making capacity and reached agreement on a steadily *growing number* of restrictive conservation measures. It is indicative that more than 80 per cent of the ninety-one conservation measures adopted by May 1995 by the Commission have been made after 1990.[72] However, the number of regulative measures is hardly a satisfactory indicator of effectiveness, although many authors do use it. One can easily conceive of situations where having no restrictions on harvesting would be an excellent way of balancing the concerns for ecosystemic stability and present use. Similarly, there will be cases where even very stringent restrictions on fishing activity are totally inadequate. Hence, such trends must at least be juxtaposed with a qualified, scientific view on what is required.[73]

Here it should be recalled that according to the rules of procedure of the Scientific Committee, advice must be reached by consensus: at times, there has been a pattern of scientists from harvesting nations acting to prevent the Committee from reaching consensual decisions on regulatory advice. However, it is evidence of the Committee's growing integrity that

---

[71] Howard, 'The Convention on the Conservation' (1987), pp. 135–6.
[72] See Commission Meeting reports from 1982 to 1994: the latest of those is Conservation Measure 87, but several earlier measures have been readopted in amended form.
[73] For a discussion of this point, see S. Andresen, 'The Convention on the Conservation of Antarctic Marine Living Resources (CCAMLR)', in J. Wettestad and S. Andresen, *The Effectiveness of International Resource Cooperation: Some Preliminary Findings* (Lysaker: Fridtjof Nansen Institute, 1991), p. 32.

in recent years it has provided management advice which has subsequently been turned down by the Commission.

Therefore, two components need to be analysed when assessing the regulation practices of CCAMLR – both the ability of the Scientific Committee to identify and agree on what it deems as appropriate *advice* to the Commission; and the regulative *response* of the latter.

When it comes to *information* measures, like the establishment of working groups under the Scientific Committee and reporting procedures on catch and effort, the Commission has indorsed most measures proposed by the Committee. In particular, the fine-scaled reporting procedures which became effective in 1987 were highly significant for the development of a credible argument in favour of stronger regulations.

As for *regulatory* measures, let us inspect the three historically most significant commercial stocks in the Southern Ocean: marbled nothotenia, mackerel icefish and krill. Here we shall focus on the waters off South Georgia. In the Convention Area as a whole, these three species account for nearly 90 per cent of the historical catch.[74]

Marbled nothotenia

Marbled nothotenia around South Georgia was the first target when the Scientific Commission finally began considering regulative matters.[75] The protective recommendation of the scientists was immediately followed up by the Commission, which introduced mesh-size regulations and an area closure within twelve miles from the island.[76] The following year, while unable to agree on additional measures to protect juveniles, the Scientific Committee suggested a ban on directed fishing of this species in the entire area around South Georgia, and this too was followed up immediately by the Commission.[77] In 1986, again prompted by the Committee, the Commission extended this ban to the waters off the Antarctic Peninsula and South Orkney Islands.[78] Since then, the taking of marbled nothotenia around South Georgia has been allowed only as bycatch.

---

[74] *CCAMLR Statistical Bulletin*, vol. 1-7, Tables 2, 4 and 6. Even when counting only the South Georgia stocks, their cumulative share of the entire harvest in the Southern Ocean is above 30 per cent. The waters around South Georgia are referred to in CCAMLR statistics as sub-area 48.3.

[75] See *Report of the IIIrd Meeting of the Scientific Committee*, 1984, p. 18.

[76] Conservation Measures 1/III and 2/III.

[77] Conservation Measure 3/IV; see *Report of the IVth Meeting of the Scientific Committee*, 1985, p. 22.

[78] I.e. sub-areas 48.1 and 48.2 respectively: Conservation Measure 5/V and 6/V.

Mackerel icefish

Since 1975, mackerel icefish has been the main finfish target in the Southern Ocean. The Scientific Committee did not voice serious concern about this species until 1986, when it suggested several regulative options for conserving the stock around South Georgia.[79] The exchange which followed on this matter led the Commission to make the crucial 1987 decision on a conservative general management strategy, thus enabling the provision of TAC advice as well as quota regulations.[80] Since then, with the exception of the 1990–1 season,[81] the Commission has consistently opted for the lower end of the ranges suggested by the Scientific Committee.

   In 1989 a more principled debate evolved in the Scientific Committee and the Commission on how to regulate stocks when available data are insufficient to assess their status. The proponents of a *precautionary* approach gradually carried the day in this debate. At its tenth meeting, in 1991, the Scientific Committee gave a range of quota options from 8,000 to 62,000 tons, but the Commission deemed the data basis insufficient and decided to prohibit directed harvesting operations for mackerel icefish around South Georgia.[82]

Krill

As to the third species, krill, the emergence of a precautionary approach is closely linked to the ecosystem principle of CCAMLR. The sustainability of krill stocks is not threatened by current harvesting, but not enough is known about the impact of krill fishing upon the abundance of its major predators. Figure 5.1 shows that krill is by far the biggest target in the Southern Ocean; until the recent decline in Russian activity,

---

[79] See *Report of the Vth Meeting of the Scientific Commission*, 1986, pp. 16–17.

[80] See *Report of the VIth Meeting of the Commission*, 1987, p. 19. The TAC for mackerel icefish, based on $F_{0,1}$, was made in Conservation Measure 8/VI. $F_{0,1}$ is defined as the fishing mortality at which a marginal yield per recruit is equal to one-tenth of the original catch per recruit per unit effort in the very lightly exploited fishery: see S. Cunningham *et al.*, *Fisheries Economics: An Introduction* (London: Mansell, 1985), p. 230. In 1990, the Commission noted that even this low level would not be appropriate for depleted stocks: see Kock, *Antarctic Fish and Fisheries*, p. 217.

[81] That year the Committee was unable to settle on a recommendation, and the quota was subsequently set several times higher than catches the year before (Conservation Measure 20/IX).

[82] Conservation Measure 33/X.

it fed the biggest crustacean fishery in the world.[83] Except for the advice in 1986 that the Commission should require fine-scaled reports in the Integrated Study Areas of CEMP, which was followed up the year after,[84] and later specified further to haul-by-haul reporting,[85] the Scientific Committee did not present specific advice on krill until 1991. That year, a precautionary TAC for the Atlantic sector, admittedly set four times higher than the harvest in previous years, was recommended and subsequently acted upon by the Commission.[86] During the two previous years there had been extensive discussions between scientists from harvesting nations and other parties about the basis for a krill quota, but they had been unable to reach agreement. In 1993, another precautionary TAC was set for an area in the Indian Ocean sector.

The precautionary approach is also shown in the notification procedure now in place regarding *new fisheries*. Following a decision in 1991, nations wishing to engage in any new fishery in the Convention Area must notify the Commission three months prior to its next meeting, in order to give the latter sufficient time to consider the matter.[87] This procedure has proved useful in the case of the US exploratory fishery for crab and Chilean longline operations around the South Shetland Islands.[88]

In summary, for the main commercial species in the Southern Ocean, we note a clear development towards more specific regulations over time, and the measures adopted by the Commission have to a large extent been in line with scientific recommendations. Moreover, when given several options, the Commission has tended to choose from the lower, more conservative end.

CCAMLR has facilitated this development, partly by strengthening the conservationist side in the debate over *controversial* restrictions, or measures on which harvesters and conservationists disagree. Let us look more

---

[83] See S. Nicol, 'CCAMLR and its Approaches to Management of the Krill Fishery', *Polar Record*, vol. 27, no. 162, 1991, p. 230.

[84] *Report of the VIth Meeting of the Commission*, 1987, p. 22.

[85] This was decided in 1989: see *Report of the VIIIth Meeting of the Commission*, 1989, p. 10. Three years later, the provision was extended to the entire Convention Area: see *Report of the XIth Meeting of the Commission*, 1992, p. 8.

[86] Conservation Measure 32/X: see *Report of the Xth Meeting of the Scientific Committee*, 1991, p. 22.

[87] Conservation Measure 31/X.

[88] See, respectively, *Report of the Xth Meeting of the Commission*, 1991, p. 16, and *Report of the XIth Meeting of the Commission*, 1992, p. 20.

closely at the role of the regime regarding the solution of the conservation problem.

We cannot rule out that the objective of the regime, particularly its ecosystem standard, has served to strengthen the views of those who would give priority to future health over present use, even to the extent of advocating precautionary measures. If anything, the considerable opposition to this standard from the harvesting nations seems to suggest a fear that this would be a consequence.[89] Nevertheless, calculations of self-interest are often more persuasive than reference to vague and even ambiguous norms: and as noted, the CCAMLR objective explicitly includes rational use as well.

Hence, another factor is probably even more significant for the ability of the regime members to set up relevant regulative measures for harvesting in the Southern Ocean. Because deliberations are quite open, due to the participation of a number of observers from international organisations and the inclusion of private organisations' representatives in several delegations, CCAMLR introduces new *rewards* for taking regulative initiatives as well as new costs of opposing them. First, states not active in Antarctic fisheries, like Australia, the United States and Norway, can take a firm stand against excessive harvesting, thus enhancing their green image without any significant costs to themselves. Second, there are certain limits to the kind of measures that can be blocked by harvesting nations without ensuing political costs. During the conflict-ridden first years of CCAMLR operation, members of a US environmental NGO suggested that US authorities consider trade sanctions on recalcitrants in CCAMLR deliberations through the application of the Pelly Amendment to the Fishermen's Protective Act.[90]

Given the Antarctic tradition of non-confrontation, however, political embarrassment is a more relevant version of the cost mechanism. While regulations can sometimes be reasonably opposed on grounds of inadequate scientific information, it is far more difficult to argue against decisions oriented towards improving the knowledge base – such as the reporting procedures referred to above which were resisted for a while by the major fishing nations; or the establishment of scientific working

[89] On the positions of harvesting nations during the CCAMLR negotiations, see Barnes, 'The Emerging Convention', p. 250.
[90] See W. Y. Brown and B. S. Manheim, 'Conservation of Antarctic Marine Living Resources: The Environmental Perspective', in L. M. Alexander and L. C. Hanson (eds.), *Antarctic Politics and Marine Resources: Critical Choices for the 1980s* (Kingston, RI: Center for Ocean Management Studies, 1984), p. 127.

groups in areas central to the objective of the Convention. This is precisely the way CCAMLR regulative measures have evolved. Apart from the early area closure around South Georgia, which was quite uncontroversial because the poor state of the nothotenia stock rendered its impact on harvesting minimal,[91] the major activity on the part of the Commission in the early years concerned information measures. But the more detailed the information, the more difficult it is to argue reasonably against regulative measures when that information, albeit uncertain, suggests that stocks are in jeopardy.

Two features of the regime are particularly salient for this 'embarrassment mechanism' to work well. First, the Commission is to a significant extent restricted by the advice of the Scientific Committee: according to Article IX, the Commission must take 'full account' of Committee recommendations. The Commission must also make publicly available all the data presented to it by the Committee. Second, the public embarrassment mechanism is not altogether blocked by the consensus rule in the Scientific Committee: in the absence of consensus, the Committee Report to the Commission shall reflect 'all the views expressed' during the deliberations.[92] If a Committee member expresses concern or offers advice which is more restrictive than that agreed to by all, this must go into the report. While less authoritative than consensual advice, reference to such views – especially, as is quite common in CCAMLR, if these are advanced by a majority – will add force to the arguments of the conservationist side in Commission deliberations.

Information measures may also be significant to the regulative ability in another way: if improved knowledge convinces harvesting nations that long-term profit will be best served by a certain restraint, a process of *learning* has been achieved in which these states, on the basis of new information, will reassess the cost–benefit balance of continuing operations.

CCAMLR has facilitated regulation in the Southern Ocean also by enhancing the ability of various fishing nations to make and keep credible commitments, rendering collectively wise restraint more attractive to each. This is particularly relevant for *uncontroversial* regulations – meas-

---

[91] See K.-H. Kock, 'Present Knowledge of Antarctic Marine Living Resources and Means of Ensuring the Compliance with Protection Measures', in Wolfrum (ed.), *Antarctic Challenge II*, p. 61.

[92] Rule 3 in the Rules of Procedure of the CCAMLR Scientific Committee: see *Basic Documents*, 3rd ed. (Hobart: Commission for the Conservation of Antarctic Marine Living Resources, 1988), p. 100.

ures which harvesting states would have preferred had they been in exclusive charge of the fishery. The area closures around South Georgia definitely fall into this category, as do the simultaneous mesh-size restrictions which simply echoed an already established unilateral Soviet measure. Were it not for the opportunity of coordinating this restraint with others, the fear that others might take advantage of their restraint could easily have rendered such measures unstable: it is of course disturbing to have the gains from moderation cancelled out by the continued operations of others.

The mechanism referred to here can be expected to work particularly well if a credible monitoring and inspection routine is in place. As shown below, the CCAMLR compliance-control system has been gradually strengthened since the middle of the 1980s, and this may be one explanation for the increasing number and stringency of regulative measures made by the Commission in the period under discussion.

In summary, CCAMLR is producing a growing number of increasingly detailed information and regulative measures, largely in line with recommendations from the Scientific Committee and, to some extent, based in ecosystemic considerations. A precautionary approach to management is evolving in CCAMLR, as shown both in the explicit pledge to set low quotas when the data situation is poor and in the notification procedures regarding new fisheries. The ecosystem management principle has probably served as an authoritative argumentative arsenal for those in favour of precautionary measures. More tangibly, the relative openness of the Commission meeting introduces new costs and benefits from promoting or opposing information and regulative measures. This occurs partly directly, in the form of green credit, political embarrassment or even fear of sanctions; and partly indirectly, in that the regime enhances transparency about fishing operations and facilitates reciprocity among harvesting nations. As information measures are more difficult to oppose on grounds of scientific uncertainty, there is in the process a momentum which serves to support both a shift of the cost–benefit calculus and a process of learning among harvesting states.

Enhancing compliance?

The compliance-control system of CCAMLR has three components. In 1987 its *reporting procedures* were explicated and strengthened, greatly enhancing the flow of information on fishing practices both to the Scientific Committee and to the Commission. A joint *inspection* system within

CCAMLR was adopted in 1988, supervised by a Standing Committee on Observation and Inspection.[93] Finally, the major *enforcement* mechanism is that the Commission will make the flag state, whether or not a party to the Convention, aware of whatever violation has been exposed.[94] This system has been criticised as deficient on several accounts. Fishing vessels do not report catch and effort directly to the Commission, but via their relevant government. The same is true of inspectors.[95] And whenever violations are identified, enforcement is left to the flag state, without any guidelines regarding sanctions. Moreover, with the growing occurrence of reflagging of fishing vessels into open registries, the flag state may not always be the politically relevant state.

It should be noted here that verification is generally a weak spot of international environmental regimes, both because legal enforcement is close to the core of sovereignty and because wide differences between states in terms of sanctioning practices render common guidelines difficult.[96] While there is little doubt that CCAMLR is considerably closer to a satisfactory system today than only five years ago, the fact that the United Kingdom in 1992 decided to enforce unilaterally a 200-mile maritime zone around South Georgia and the South Sandwich Islands suggests the limits of this achievement. Since 1978, France has conducted unilateral enforcement within the other major finfish area, the Kerguelen Islands.[97]

As discussed above, CCAMLR's major achievement in facilitating the evolution of a compliance system in the Southern Ocean has been to *decouple* inspection and enforcement from the difficult sovereignty question, thus allowing conservation measures to be handled without significant harm to any position regarding the status of sovereignty claims.

But CCAMLR affects compliance control in other ways as well. Just as for regulation, the gradual emergence of a compliance system under

---

[93] See *Report of the VIIth Meeting of the Commission*, 1988, pp. 29–35.

[94] CCAMLR, Art. X.

[95] *Ibid.*, Art. XXIV (2)(b).

[96] See S. Andresen, 'International Verification in Practice: A Brief Account of Experiences from Relevant International Cooperative Measures', in E. Lykke (ed.), *Achieving Environmental Goals: The Concept and Practice of Environmental Performance Review* (London: Belhaven Press, 1992), pp. 101–21.

[97] Kerguelen, South Georgia, and the South Sandwich Islands are located north of 60°S and hence beyond the Antarctic Treaty area. While France's claim over Kerguelen is undisputed, the South Georgia and South Sandwich Islands are claimed by both the United Kingdom and Argentina: see Bush, *Antarctica and International Law*, vol. I, pp. 405–6.

CCAMLR suggests that the regime enabled *familiarisation* with the idea of inspections in the Southern Ocean. When the United Kingdom raised this issue in 1984, only observance was suggested, geared not at exposing violations but at improving scientific information;[98] and even this was problematic to Japan and the Soviet Union. However, when the first inspections were launched in the 1989–90 season, their mandate was not restricted to compilation of scientific data. A learning process appears to have taken place in which the conflict lines between the fishing and the conservationist side have softened. It may also have become clearer, as shown above, that an inspection system may be beneficial to harvesting nations as well, by enhancing their ability to make credible commitments regarding less controversial measures. This argument needs to be tempered, however, by the fact that while twenty-six inspectors had been nominated in 1993, only a single inspection was actually carried out; in 1994, the number of inspections was three.[99] As pointed out by a former chairman of the Scientific Committee, the costs of operating an inspection infrastructure are prohibitive unless, as in the case of France in the economic zone around Kerguelen, backed by strong national interests.[100]

In summary, the compliance system of CCAMLR was slow to emerge and remains only moderately intrusive. However, this feature it shares with most other environmental regimes, especially those involving unsettled sovereignty issues. The role of CCAMLR appears to have been quite productive, both in offering an arena where various models could be discussed over a protracted period of time, and in lowering the sovereignty costs of the arrangements finally agreed to.

CONCLUDING REMARKS

This chapter has approached the question of regime effectiveness by asking what problem the CCAMLR regime was designed to solve. Not only formal goals of regime documents were taken into account but also other features of the regime, as well as views of actors involved in its negotiation and scientists observing it. Thus we reached a three-dimensional formulation of the problem, emphasising in addition to con-

---

[98] See Howard, 'The Convention on the Conservation', pp. 141–2.
[99] See, respectively, *Report of the XIIth Meeting of the Commission*, 1993, p. 20, and *Report of the XIIIth Meeting of the Commission*, 1994, p. 15.
[100] See also Kock, *Fishing and Conservation in Southern Waters*, p. 23.

servation the protection of actor positions on the sovereignty issue and the external acceptance of the Consultative Parties in Antarctic affairs.

While the sovereignty and external acceptance parts of this problem have been solved almost impeccably, much remains to be done regarding ecosystemic conservation. This holds for all three strands: generating knowledge, making regulations and establishing a compliance-control system in the Southern Ocean. That said, however, the performance of CCAMLR has improved quite dramatically also in terms of conservation, with the emergence of cooperative multispecies stock surveys, precautionary regulations based on ecosystemic considerations, and the formal structure at least of a credible inspection system.

As to the role of the regime, we have seen that certain features of it appear to have contributed substantially to solving those problems, in the sense that they would have been difficult indeed to tackle in the absence of CCAMLR. By decoupling fisheries management from the strengthening of territorial claims, the bifocal component and the consensus rule helped solve the sovereignty problem. And by removing incentives to form competing regulative arrangements – and also making accession more attractive to potential harvesting nations – the conditionally open nature of CCAMLR ensured external acceptance. The ecosystem principle served the same purpose. Moreover, that ambitious principle, supported by the institutional centrality of scientific investigations, has served to support the financial basis for research activities in the Southern Ocean, as well as to enhance the argumentative standing of the conservationist side in tugs-of-war over regulation and compliance-control measures. The political force of the ecosystem principle has been considerably strengthened in recent years, partly due to improved data availability – but also because growing transparency of decision-making implies new rewards for environmental champions and greater embarrassment for environmental laggards – in CCAMLR as in other parts of the Antarctic Treaty System.

6

The effectiveness of CRAMRA

CHRISTOPHER C. JOYNER

INTRODUCTION

Throughout the 1980s, the Antarctic Treaty Consultative Parties (ATCPs) convened in a series of Special Consultative Meetings to negotiate a regime that could regulate the future development of mineral resources in the Antarctic.[1] The consensus-derived product of those long-drawn negotiations came in 1988 in Wellington, New Zealand, in the form of a unique multinational minerals treaty, the Convention on the Regulation of Antarctic Mineral Resource Activities (CRAMRA).[2] Yet, within two years, the legal attraction to and political support for that instrument among most Consultative Parties had substantially been lost. By 1990 the status of CRAMRA had fallen from a recognised legal instrument establishing a new international regime to that of an ill-conceived notion abandoned on grounds of being politically undesirable and practically ineffective.

As discussed more thoroughly in Chapter 1, regime effectiveness refers to how well a regime can attain desired results: the degree to which the

---

[1] The twenty ATCP states which attended these meetings and participated in the final session of the Fourth Special Consultative Meeting on Mineral Resources were: Argentina, Australia, Belgium, Brazil, Chile, China, France, the German Democratic Republic, the Federal Republic of Germany, India, Italy, Japan, New Zealand, Norway, Poland, South Africa, the Soviet Union, the United Kingdom, the United States and Uruguay; representatives from thirteen Non-Consultative Parties to the Antarctic Treaty also attended and participated in this final session: Bulgaria, Canada, Czechoslovakia, Denmark, Ecuador, Finland, Greece, the Republic of Korea, the Netherlands, Papua New Guinea, Peru, Romania and Sweden: Final Act of the Fourth Special Antarctic Treaty Consultative Meeting on Antarctic Mineral Resources, reprinted in *International Legal Materials*, vol. XXVII, 1988, pp. 859ff.
[2] Convention on the Regulation of Antarctic Mineral Resource Activities, done at Wellington, 2 June 1988, opened for signature 25 November 1988. Doc. AMR/SCM/88/78 (2 June 1988), reprinted in *International Legal Materials*, vol. XXVII, 1988, pp. 868–900.

regime can solve those problems that it was created to address. Effectiveness concerns the impact that a regime has upon its environment; put tersely, it implies causation. To be effective means to get results, to cause desirable or intended reactions toward achieving some desired end or articulated objective. If the actions resulting from a regime produce intended results that have desired impacts, then the presence of the regime matters and we can say that it exerts a certain effective influence in attaining those ambitions. Should the regime falter in solving relevant problems, then its effectiveness can be said to diminish. Similarly, if the situation or problem for which the regime was created should change or disappear, then the regime's effectiveness may also change or become irrelevant.

For CRAMRA, the nature of the problem came down to devising a regime that could ensure *proper use* of Antarctic mineral resources, in a way which provides adequate protection of the regional environment; and in the process, accommodate the *sovereignty* issue between claimant and non-claimant states.

What factors contributed to the severe erosion of ATCP support and the devaluation of CRAMRA as a worthy legal instrument? How had the sophisticated product of nearly eight years of complex, tedious multilateral negotiations unravelled so quickly and become discarded as a legal effort? And to what extent did this development affect the solution of the proper use and sovereignty problems addressed by the regime? This chapter examines these queries with a view toward assessing the ways and means taken by the Consultative Parties to make CRAMRA into an effective international regime, as set against the reversal in perceptions that led to CRAMRA's demise – to its being considered not only an ineffective regime, but also one inappropriate for the tasks at hand.

THE EVOLUTION OF CRAMRA

Interest in Antarctic minerals was first expressed at the Sixth Antarctic Treaty Consultative Meeting in Tokyo in 1970. Concern arose at that time over the need to develop a minerals regime that would preclude Antarctica from becoming an object of international discord. At the Seventh Consultative Meeting two years later in Oslo, the issue was re-examined. The upshot was to place the subject of Antarctic mineral resources and the effects of exploration formally on the agenda for the Eighth Consultative Meeting in 1975.

In the interim, two events thrust Antarctic minerals into international prominence. First, in 1971–2 the *Glomar Challenger* expedition to the Ross Sea discovered traces of methane and ethane during the Deep Sea Drilling Project. These discoveries fuelled speculation that hydrocarbons might exist on Antarctica's continental shelf. The second factor was the Arab oil embargo during 1973–4, which heightened anxieties about the reduced availability of world petroleum resources. Taken in tandem, these developments contributed to making the resource potential of Antarctica appear more interesting as a commercial opportunity.

A special preparatory meeting on minerals was held by the Consultative Parties in Paris in 1976 to address the emerging resource potential of Antarctica. The next year, at the Ninth Consultative Meeting in London, fundamental principles concerning Antarctic mineral resources were adopted as Recommendation IX-1. In 1981 at the Eleventh Consultative Meeting in Buenos Aires, Recommendation XI-1 set out the framework for mineral negotiations and provided that a minerals regime should be predicated on the following principles:

1 The Consultative Parties should continue to play an active and responsible role in dealing with the question of Antarctic mineral resources.
2 The Antarctic Treaty must be maintained in its entirety.
3 Protection of the unique Antarctic environment and of its dependent ecosystems should be a basic consideration;
4 The Consultative Parties, in dealing with the question of mineral resources in Antarctica, should not prejudice the interests of all mankind in Antarctica.
5 The provisions of Article IV of the Antarctic Treaty should not be affected by the regime. It should ensure that principles embodied in Article IV are safeguarded in application to the area covered by the Antarctic Treaty.[3]

The design of institutions to implement these principles began to take shape in June 1982 at the Fourth Special Consultative Meeting on Antarctic Minerals in Wellington, New Zealand. By early 1983 a draft text for a minerals regime had been prepared by the Chairman of the negotiations, Christopher Beeby. Following six iterations of this so-called 'Beeby text',

---

[3] Recommendation XI-1, 'Antarctic Mineral Resources', adopted at the XI ATCM, Buenos Aires, paras. 4 and 5.

by June 1988 the Consultative Parties had agreed through consensus to an Antarctic minerals treaty in the form of CRAMRA.[4]

Institutions

In order to make the Antarctic minerals regime effective, four new institutions, to be served by a Secretariat, were created by CRAMRA. First, there was to be an Antarctic Mineral Resources Commission, comprised of all states which were then Consultative Parties.[5] The Commission would play an executive role to facilitate exchange of scientific information for assessing environmental impacts of mineral resources activities, designate areas prohibited from minerals development, adopt measures to protect the Antarctic ecosystem, and, most importantly, determine whether to identify an area for possible exploration and development.[6] Voting in the Commission on substantive decisions would be by three-quarters majority vote, but consensus was required to pass decisions relating to budgetary matters, principles of non-discrimination and identification of an area for possible mineral exploration and development. Procedural matters would be decided by simple majority vote.[7]

Second, a Special Meeting of States Parties, open to all parties of CRAMRA, would be established. Having largely a symbolic role, the Special Meeting convenes only to advise the Commission on decisions concerning identification of an area for possible minerals activities.[8]

The third institution was the Scientific, Technical and Environmental Advisory Committee. Composed of all parties to the Convention, this Committee, as its name implies, has as its main function to advise the Commission and special Regulatory Committees on matters requiring scientific, technical, or environmental expertise about mineral resource activities. The Advisory Committee is not a decision-making organ, nor are its findings binding. It is intended merely to operate as a 'forum for

---

[4] For discussion of the negotiations that produced this agreement, see C. C. Joyner, 'The Antarctic Minerals Negotiating Process', *American Journal of International Law*, vol. 81, no. 4, 1987, pp. 888–905; F. Orrego Vicuña, *Antarctic Mineral Exploitation: The Emerging Legal Framework* (Cambridge University Press, 1988); and R. Wolfrum, *The Convention on the Regulation of Antarctic Mineral Resource Activities: An Attempt to Break New Ground* (Berlin: Springer-Verlag, 1991), pp. 3–11.

[5] CRAMRA, Art. 18.

[6] *Ibid.*, Art. 21.

[7] *Ibid.*, Art. 22.

[8] *Ibid.*, Art. 28.

consultation and cooperation' in gathering scientific information about Antarctic mineral resource activities.[9]

For each specific geographic area designated by the Commission for possible minerals exploration and development, a fourth institution, the Regulatory Committee, would be established.[10] Such Regulatory Committees were designed to play critical roles in the process for overseeing mineral resource activities in Antarctica and were accordingly entrusted with broad powers. Among the responsibilities elaborated for them in CRAMRA were: undertaking preparatory work prior to identifying an area for exploration; examination and approval of applications for exploration and development permits; consideration and approval of management schemes (i.e., contracts between operators and the Convention's regulatory authority); issuing exploration and development permits; monitoring exploration and development activities; and carrying out certain inspection and dispute-settlement functions.[11] The Regulatory Committee for an area also was given the authority to suspend mineral resource activities if these resulted in 'impacts on the Antarctic environment or dependent or associated ecosystems beyond those judged acceptable' pursuant to CRAMRA.[12]

Membership of each Regulatory Committee followed a detailed, complex formula, owing to the particularly sensitive role assigned to these bodies in accommodating claimant and non-claimant positions in Antarctica. Each such committee normally would be composed of ten original members to the Commission: four members that assert rights or claims to Antarctica, inclusive of the state(s) asserting a claim to the area identified by the Commission; and six non-claimant states, inclusive of the 'two members . . . which assert a basis of claim in Antarctica' (i.e., the United States and the then Soviet Union).[13] Decisions taken on substantive matters by a Regulatory Committee would proceed by two-thirds majority vote. Importantly, decisions concerning approval of exploration and development proposals by two-thirds majority must include a simple majority from both the four claimants as a group and the six non-claimants as a group. A simple majority vote would suffice for procedural matters.[14]

[9] *Ibid.*, Arts. 23 and 26.
[10] *Ibid.*, Art. 29.
[11] *Ibid.*, Arts. 42–54.
[12] *Ibid.*, Art. 51.
[13] *Ibid.*, Art. 29.
[14] *Ibid.*, Art. 32.

Finally, as noted, CRAMRA provided for the establishment of a Secretariat that would perform staff functions and facilitate work in and between the other four institutions.[15]

Regulation of mineral activities

To fix CRAMRA's effectiveness as a regulatory instrument, the area of its application covered the Antarctic continent, all Antarctic islands and their associated ice shelves south of 60°S latitude, as well as the seabed and subsoil of adjacent offshore areas.[16] CRAMRA specifically did not purport to regulate mineral resource activities on the deep seabed, beyond the geographic extent of Antarctica's continental shelf, to avoid conflict with relevant provisions in the 1982 UN Convention on the Law of the Sea.[17]

Mineral resource activities would be divided into three phases. The first stage, 'prospecting', concerned geological and geophysical activities aimed at identifying areas with resource potential and would not be restricted by the need to obtain prior authorisation from the CRAMRA regime.[18] 'Exploration', the second stage, consisted of activities aimed at identifying and evaluating specific mineral occurrences or deposits.[19] Exploratory drilling, dredging or excavations would be used to determine the size, nature and potential of mineral deposits and the feasibility of their development. Of critical import, the decision to proceed with the exploration stage would be taken only by consensus among the Commission members.[20]

Should the Commission go forward with a decision to identify an area for exploration, a special Regulatory Committee would be constituted for that area and would set requirements for exploration activities. Pending approval of a management scheme, the Regulatory Committee would issue a permit to the applicant by two-thirds majority vote.[21]

The third stage, 'development', pertained to activities associated with the exploitation of specific mineral resource deposits.[22] Application for a

---

[15] *Ibid.*, Art. 33.
[16] *Ibid.*, Art. 5, para. 2.
[17] *Ibid.*, Art. 5, para. 3.
[18] *Ibid.*, Art. 1, para. 8.
[19] *Ibid.*, Art. 1, para. 9.
[20] *Ibid.*, Art. 22, para. 2(c) and Art. 41, para. 2.
[21] *Ibid.*, Art. 29.
[22] *Ibid.*, Art. 1, para. 10.

development permit (with modified management scheme) would be made to and decided upon by the appropriate Regulatory Committee by two-thirds majority vote, with simple majority vote qualifications required among the four claimant and six non-claimant states.[23]

CRAMRA AND THE SOVEREIGNTY PROBLEM

For an Antarctic minerals regime to be effective, it had to accommodate concerns over the status of sovereignty on the continent. That is, the effectiveness of CRAMRA depended on the willingness of the Consultative Parties to compromise on rights to regulate mineral activities within the context of sovereignty in the region. The seven claimant states presumably could argue in the extreme that their claims to sovereignty in Antarctica endowed them with exclusive lawful rights to regulate minerals activities by all persons within their respective territorial sectors. Implicit in those rights is the sovereign authority to permit, restrict, or prohibit prospecting, exploration and development activities. Such sovereign control would ostensibly also convey rights to license mineral activities, to impose taxes and royalties and to enforce national law in those territories. Other states – the non-claimants – explicitly refused to recognise the lawfulness of such claims. Viewed from the extreme non-claimant vantage point, Antarctica represents a continent absent sovereignty. Accordingly, any rights accrued for permitting, licensing, or regulating minerals activities should therefore derive from the sponsoring state of the operator.

The effective operation of CRAMRA as a minerals regime hinged on accommodation of sovereignty concerns in the Antarctic. The fundamental dilemma confronting Antarctic minerals treaty negotiators early on was how to address alleged attributes of sovereignty in a manner acceptable to both claimants and non-claimants. Could attributes of sovereignty in Antarctica be integrated and dispersed to all Antarctic states? Could claimant states be assigned presumed rights to grant permission for undertaking and overseeing mineral activities on the continent, without formally acknowledging that rights to license and tax activities would be allocated to all sponsoring states? Ultimately, this dilemma over sovereignty attributes was addressed through the institutional framework established in CRAMRA.

The balance of national interests in Antarctica was reflected in the bal-

[23] *Ibid.*, Art. 32, para. 2.

ance of institutional powers in the new regime. The manner in which the regulatory institutions were constructed, their relative authority and functions, and the voting schemes for taking decisions – these were the means used to reconcile the impasse over sovereign authority and regime rights between claimant and non-claimant states. Critical here was the creation of roles assigned to Regulatory Committees within the Convention framework. The effectiveness of CRAMRA as a viable regime was instigated through effective accommodation of national interests in CRAMRA's decision-making structures.

Claimant states advocated that, because of their special territorial status on the continent, they should receive guaranteed seats on every Regulatory Committee. The claimants also desired the right individually to veto any undesirable activities within 'their' sectors. Both of these positions were untenable to non-claimant states, who favoured a qualified high majority system, preferably a two-thirds vote rule. The claimants' position was further challenged by the non-claimants, who refused to consent to any provisions that acknowledged validity to claimants' assertions to title on the continent.[24]

Complications were also evident over how potential profits derived from mineral activities in Antarctica might be apportioned within the regime. Claimant states advocated their rights to receive an automatic share of revenues derived from minerals activities on the continent. They contended that these royalties were essential to the process of internal accommodation in the Antarctic Treaty System. Claimants proposed that such revenues might be generated by their presumed right to tax development activities within their respective sectors. Another justification for these payments was the claimants' purported capacity (associated with the doctrine of permanent sovereignty over natural resources) to set some kind of compensatory fee for relaxing mining rights.

Non-claimants rejected these suggestions straightaway. Even to enter into discussions on royalty payments matters would give unwarranted credibility to claimant assertions that they possessed legitimate claim to valid title. The extenuating legal implications of this situation were such that non-claimants flatly opposed any consideration of royalties or tax payments to be made to claimant states. Effectiveness of a futuristic regu-

[24] See C. C. Joyner, 'The Evolving Antarctic Minerals Regime', *Ocean Development and International Law*, vol. 19, no. 1, 1988, pp. 73 and 83.

latory mining regime would not be won with implicit recognition of special claimant sovereign rights.[25]

This all led to a clear need for policy compromise and diplomatic accommodation. Political interests of claimant states clearly were protected by guaranteeing their membership on any Regulatory Committee whose area of competence lay within their claimed territory. The disparity of interests between claimant and non-claimant states was reflected in the bipartite composition of the Regulatory Committees – the four-state claimant group and a six-state non-claimant group, inclusive of the United States and the former Soviet Union. Internal accommodation was also evidenced in the special voting procedures mandated for adopting general requirements and particular decisions affecting exploration and development.[26]

The role of Non-Consultative Parties in the new regime also became contentious. It had been decided early in the negotiations that the Consultative Parties would automatically gain full membership on the Commission. But what part should Non-Consultative Party states (and non-parties to the Antarctic Treaty as well) play in developing minerals on the continent? Should the Non-Consultative Parties be given a vote in decisions relating to minerals activities, or should these governments merely be given observer status? As provided for in CRAMRA, Non-Consultative Parties will sit on the Commission and Regulatory Committees as observers, and they would be full members of the Advisory Committee and Special Meeting of States Parties. The latter two bodies, however, have no decision-making powers.

Another troublesome issue concerned the procedure to follow for voting in the Commission. Specifically there was the question of how far consensus should extend in the new regime. Pro-development states opposed a consensus requirement for opening an area, since that would mean that any one state could block minerals activities in an area. Environmentalists adamantly favoured consensus, particularly for taking any critical, threshold decision for beginning the exploration or exploitation stages of mineral activities. Eventually, agreement was mustered for consensus, largely because of the signal import the act of opening an area for minerals activities would pose for the Antarctic environment.

The minerals convention was broadly arranged to protect the interests

[25] See 'Status of Antarctic Minerals Negotiations', *Antarctic Briefing*, no. 13, 30 June 1987, p. 9.
[26] See CRAMRA, Arts. 29 and 32.

of all states parties. These protections are contained in specific functions of the plenary bodies – the Commission and the Advisory Committee – as they relate to Regulatory Committees. The Commission may issue directives to review actions by the Regulatory Committees. The Commission has the authority to check a Regulatory Committee's actions in order to determine if they are consistent with standards and principles in the Convention. No claimant or sponsoring state, nor any Regulatory Committee as a whole, possesses absolute power to negotiate its own contracts. Negotiations must proceed in line with the Commission's functions and authority, subject to the Advisory Committee's technical evaluation and assessment of relevant environmental factors and any potential repercussions. Every management scheme must be approved by the entire ten-member Regulatory Committee to ensure that a proposal is consistent with the purposes and principles of the Convention. Hence, effectiveness of the minerals regime came to depend on accommodation of sovereign interests between claimants and non-claimants, as well as on an operational balance between CRAMRA's functional institutions. Upon its adoption, CRAMRA was seen as having successfully accommodated the sovereignty problem among the Consultative Parties, while furnishing an acceptable institutional equilibrium. As we shall see, subsequent events proved this perception wrong.

CRAMRA AND THE PROPER-USE PROBLEM

CRAMRA created a mechanism to regulate mineral activities in Antarctica, thus making it possible to put a brake on any impending mineral development. By doing so CRAMRA sought to stabilise the political and legal situation should minerals development ever go forward in Antarctica. The treaty regime also filled a legal vacuum by purposefully allocating rights to resources that might be discovered. This situation clearly reduced chances for legal uncertainty and economic rivalry over mineral resources that might produce conflict and competition in Antarctica, at the expense of the regional environment.

Certain specific features suggest CRAMRA's inherent potential for effectiveness. The precautionary approach in CRAMRA was bolstered by several elements designed to secure implementation of its regulations, such as: monitoring by Regulatory Committees (under Article 52); a system for institutional and national inspections (as provided by Article 12); provision for suspension, modification or cancellation of activities when it was demonstrated that they had unacceptable environmental impacts (in Article

51); provision for liability and response actions (under Article 8); and a notably rigorous dispute settlement provision (in Chapter VI, as well as the Annex for an Arbitral Tribunal). Importantly, all these provisions were explicitly intended to promote compliance with the regime.

CRAMRA furnished much that was innovative and laudable in environmental regulation. It also entailed an agreed-upon system for dealing with a volatile problem that could erupt into confrontation in the Antarctic. Convention supporters argued that it did so in an environmentally responsible manner: CRAMRA was intended to ensure that uncertainties over resource exploitation did not disrupt the stability of the Antarctic Treaty System. By providing a potential regulatory regime, CRAMRA permitted continuation of the Antarctic as a peaceful preserve and sustained the integrity of the Antarctic Treaty System. In sum, it created new institutions, set new standards and fixed new responsibilities for the Consultative Parties to follow, should mineral activities go forward in the Antarctic. It was intended to be a preclusive agreement, not a reactive one. That intent was admirable, but it was not sufficient for international acceptance of CRAMRA.

Impacts on the domestic level

CRAMRA established a viable mechanism for administering and regulating mineral activities in the Antarctic. Even so, conservationists had raised considerable doubts about the perceived inability of the regime to deal effectively with protecting Antarctica's environment, in the event of mineral resource activities. The crunch came in the spring of 1989, when two of the claimant states, Australia and France, decided not to sign, much less ratify, the Convention. This act proved to be the catalyst that moved the Antarctic Treaty System away from policies of resource exploitation and toward a firm commitment to regional environmental protection and conservation.

On 22 May 1989, Prime Minister Robert Hawke of Australia announced that his government would not sign CRAMRA. The Hawke government instead declared its intention to negotiate a comprehensive environmental protection convention and establish Antarctica as an international wilderness preserve wherein all mining and oil-drilling activities would be prohibited.[27] This decision effectively torpedoed the Conven-

---

[27] Press release from the Prime Minister for Australia: Joint Statement with the Minister for Foreign Affairs and Trade, Senator Gareth Evans QC and the Minister for Arts,

tion, since Article 62 in that instrument required that all claimant states must be parties for it to enter into force. Australia, of course, is a claimant state and actually asserts the largest territorial claim in Antarctica.

It is important to appreciate why Australia abruptly decided to reverse course in its Antarctic minerals policy. Firstly, the Australian cabinet was influenced by four reported environmental disasters that had occurred in polar waters in 1989. On 28 January 1989, the Argentine supply ship *Bahia Paraiso* hit rocks offshore the US Palmer station on the Antarctic Peninsula. Some 250,000 barrels of diesel fuel spilled into the sea, killing thousands of krill, scores of penguins and other marine birds, and ruining several scientific projects along the coast.[28] On 7 February 1989, news of another Antarctic accident was reported. The British resupply ship *HMS Endurance* hit an iceberg four feet below its water line near Deception Island. Photographic evidence by Argentine scientists of the vessel in Esperanza Bay shortly after the accident suggests that a spill probably occurred, although this was vehemently denied by the British Antarctic Survey. On 28 February 1989, the Peruvian research vessel *BIC Humboldt* ran aground and began leaking oil in Fildes Bay off King George Island. While only a minor oil spill resulted, the *Humboldt* incident became the third ecological threat to the region in less than a month.[29] These three episodes in the Antarctic were vastly overshadowed on 24 March 1989 by the Arctic disaster which resulted when the tanker *Exxon Valdez* struck a reef off Prince William Sound, Alaska. Some 11 million gallons of crude oil spilled into the frigid waters and killed thousands of otters, birds and fish as it washed ashore along a 45-mile-long pollution zone. Paradoxically, the *Exxon Valdez* tragedy may be the best thing ever to happen for Antarctic environmentalists. It graphically demonstrated the high costs and real liabilities of transporting crude oil in frigid waters. Clearly, the pervasive international publicity generated by this eco-catastrophe figured in Australia's decision to oppose the minerals treaty.[30]

The Hawke government was also motivated by the increasing domestic awareness about environmental issues among the general public. Of spe-

---

Sport, the Environment, Tourism and Territories, Senator the Hon. Graham Richardson, 22 May 1989 (mimeograph). See D. Scott, 'Australia Advocates "Wilderness" Status for Antarctica', *Christian Scientist Monitor*, 24 May 1989, and R. Cockburn and A. Morgan, 'Australia Blocks Antarctic Mining Operation', *The Times*, 23 May 1989.
[28] J. N. Wilford, 'Sunken Ship's Oil Spill Held a Peril to Antarctic Wildlife', *New York Times*, 9 February 1989, p. 7A.
[29] 'New Shipwreck Causes Oil Slick in Antarctic', *New York Times*, 1 March 1989.
[30] See *New York Times*, 25 March 1989, p. 1; *ibid.*, 4 April 1989, section III, p. 1.

cial concern in Australia was publicity about the widening ozone hole over Antarctica and reported increases in skin cancer for Australians.

Policy perceptions by the Hawke government were obviously influenced by the ascendant political power of the environmental movement in local Australian elections. Earlier in May, 'Green' Independents had won five legislative seats in the Australian state of Tasmania, a number sufficient to control the balance of power in that local parliament. Realisation that twenty environmental groups had formed a political coalition to make environment issues prominent in the March 1990 federal election also weighed in Australia's anti-minerals treaty position.

Thirdly, and perhaps the most critical consideration influencing the Australian government hinged on the negative implications that CRAMRA would pose for the status of Australia's territorial claim to Antarctica. Establishment of a multinational minerals regime was perceived by some as undermining the legal validity of Australia's claim to sovereign title to the continent. By agreeing that a treaty-based minerals arrangement on the continent was necessary and proper, Australia would be admitting that its claim to sovereignty was soft and compromisable. No less important for Paul Keating, then the Hawke government's Exchequer, was that CRAMRA failed to provide any royalties to claimant states for other states' exploration or exploitation activities in claimed sectors. This premeditated failure to compensate claimant states with privileged payments for mining operations in claimed sectors could be read as a tacit admission that claimant states were willing to give up full administrative control over *their* territory. Notwithstanding the popular appeal of environmental motivations, the sacrifice of sovereignty argument apparently carried enough compelling sway to push the Australian government's decision not to sign the Convention.

France, another claimant, declared in June 1989 that it would join Australia in not signing CRAMRA. The impetus for the French action stemmed largely from the pervasive rise of green politics in France, as well as from public pressure produced by a massive popular petition movement generated by the famous ocean explorer Jacques Cousteau. In August, the Prime Ministers of Australia and France announced a joint initiative to promote the protection of the Antarctic environment.[31]

International commitment to CRAMRA began to unravel rapidly as

---

[31] Joint Statement on International Environment Issues Agreed by Prime Ministers Hawke and Rocard, Canberra, 18 August 1988. See M. W. Browne, 'France and Australia Kill Pact on Limited Antarctic Mining and Oil Drilling', *New York Times*, 25 September 1989, p. A10.

other Consultative Parties indicated that they, too, were having second thoughts about the purposes and implications of putting a minerals treaty in place. By December 1989, Belgium, Italy, India and the People's Republic of China had all signalled doubts about going forward with the Convention. By March of 1990 reports from New Zealand suggested that government's possible shift away from the minerals treaty as well. CRAMRA had been stopped dead in its diplomatic waters. Negotiations began later in 1990 on a comprehensive environmental agreement, and by the middle of 1991 successful negotiation among the Consultative Parties of the Environmental Protocol had sealed CRAMRA's fate for the foreseeable future as an unwanted convention.

The demise of CRAMRA came about precipitously. This was surprising, considering the extraordinary investment of time, energy and intellectual effort made by ATCP governments in the minerals negotiations during the 1980s. Why had CRAMRA, a painstakingly negotiated, highly sophisticated legal instrument containing environmental protection provisions that ranked among the strongest, most comprehensive of any international agreement ever concluded, been summarily dumped by the Consultative Parties? The answer lies in perceptions of CRAMRA's ineffectiveness, together with a new-found conviction by the Consultative Parties that the mineral treaty's purpose was neither appropriate nor desirable for the Antarctic.

Impacts on the international level

The Consultative Parties realised in October 1989 at the Fifteenth Consultative Meeting in Paris that the Antarctic Treaty System was lacking in its protection of the Antarctic environment. At this meeting, formal consideration of negotiating a special agreement on comprehensive protection of the Antarctic environment was launched with the adoption of Recommendation XV-1. This measure recommended to ATCP governments that:

They undertake as a priority objective the further elaboration, maintenance and effective implementation of a comprehensive system for the protection of the Antarctic environment and its dependent and associated ecosystems aimed at ensuring that human activity does not have adverse impacts on the Antarctic environment or its dependent or associated ecosystems or compromise the scientific, aesthetic or wilderness values of Antarctica.[32]

---

[32] Recommendation XV-1, of the XV ATCM, Paris, October 1989, reprinted in J. A. Heap (ed.), *Handbook of the Antarctic Treaty System*, 7th ed. (Cambridge: Scott Polar Research Institute, 1990), pp. 2,103–4.

To discuss the ways and means for effecting this objective, an Eleventh Special Consultative Meeting was convened in Viña del Mar, Chile, from 19 November to 6 December 1990. Out of these discussions emerged agreement on the need for a legally binding instrument for the protection of the Antarctic environment and its dependent and associated ecosystems, in the form of a protocol to the Antarctic Treaty.[33] The draft text produced from these discussions formed the basis for an informal working document that was refined by the Consultative Parties in their follow-up meeting in Madrid, during April and May 1991. That meeting produced the draft Protocol to the Antarctic Treaty on Environmental Protection,[34] which was again refined during a second meeting in Madrid in June 1991.[35]

The culmination of these negotiations came in Madrid on 4 October 1991 when the Consultative Parties adopted the Protocol on Environmental Protection.[36] This instrument, built on the core environmental protection principles contained in CRAMRA, was made an integral part of the Antarctic Treaty.[37] It establishes a relatively comprehensive, legally binding regime for ensuring that all activities undertaken in Antarctica are consistent with protection of that environment and the continent's dependent and associated ecosystems. Perhaps most significantly, adoption of the Protocol marked a turning point for the Consultative Parties in their protracted efforts to preserve and protect the Antarctic environment. The Protocol and its annexes demonstrated a shift away from possible resource exploitation under the proposed Antarctic minerals treaty,

---

[33] Considerable debate arose over whether such an instrument should be an independent convention or assume a protocol format. In the closing hours of the discussions, agreement on the instrument's general structure coalesced around a protocol format, thanks largely to the introduction of a draft text personally presented by Rolf Trolle Andersen of Norway. See Antarctic Treaty, Protocol to the Antarctic Treaty on Environmental Protection, Doc. XI ATSCM/8, 5 December 1990.

[34] Antarctic Treaty, Protocol to the Antarctic Treaty on Environmental Protection, Antarctic Treaty Doc. XI ATSCM/2/30, 29 April 1991. In addition, four draft annexes attached to the Protocol were agreed to in Madrid: an Annex on Conservation of Antarctic Fauna and Flora; an Annex on Environmental Impact Assessment Procedures; an Annex on Marine Pollution; and an Annex on Waste Disposal and Waste Management. A fifth Annex, on Area Protection and Management, was adopted by the ATCPs in October 1991 at the XVI ATCM in Bonn.

[35] Protocol to the Antarctic Treaty on Environmental Protection, Antarctic Treaty, the XI ATSCM, Madrid, 17–23 June 1991, ATCP Doc. XI ATSCM/2, 21 June 1991. See 'Pact Would Ban Antarctic Mining', *New York Times*, 1 May 1991, p. A9.

[36] Protocol to the Antarctic Treaty on Environmental Protection, opened for signature in Madrid on 4 October 1991, Antarctic Treaty Doc. XI ATSCM/2, 21 June 1991.

[37] For discussion of this point, see Chapter 10.

and a move toward pronounced preservation of the Antarctic region as a 'natural reserve, devoted to peace and science'.[38] The 1991 Madrid Protocol consolidates environmental measures into a single agreement under the Antarctic Treaty and provides a mechanism to enact improved measures as environmental circumstances evolve. In large part, the weaknesses and deficiencies that had made CRAMRA perceived internationally as an ineffective regulatory instrument had been satisfactorily remedied by the Protocol.

THE FRAILTIES OF CRAMRA'S EFFECTIVENESS

The fatal flaw with CRAMRA came not to rest on its inability to regulate Antarctic mineral resource activities. Rather, it turned on CRAMRA's perceived lack of efficacy and a widespread belief that the regime could not effectively prevent environmental degradation of the pristine Antarctic.

Antarctic law, like international law in general, remains predicated upon the principle of efficacy: only those claims and conditions producing demonstrable results become law with international effect. A situation is considered effective if it becomes activated in real life. Thus, for international norms to become law governing the conduct of activities in the Antarctic, they must be perceived by states as real and durable, as well as authoritative and controlling. To remain effective, such norms must engender confidence and support among affected states. For CRAMRA, that sense of confident effectiveness was never realised.

Imprecise language

Several serious questions were raised about CRAMRA's actual intent and perceived capability to limit environmental degradation. Environmentalists saw the CRAMRA instrument as containing inadequate and, indeed, ineffective provisions for safeguarding the Antarctic environment. This depiction of ineffectiveness evolved into a self-fulfilling reality and precipitated disintegration of support for the regime.

Intense criticism over CRAMRA's wanting effectiveness came principally from the environmental community. Environmentalists voiced sharp concern over the lack of specificity and definition for threshold terms used in environmentally related provisions in the Convention. For

[38] Protocol, Art. 2.

example, what were the non-'negligible impacts' used to define 'damage' in Article 1, paragraph 15? What standards constituted 'significant damage' or 'substantial risk' in Article 4, paragraph 2? By what scientific measures could these be accurately set and determined? How much information was 'adequate' or 'sufficient' for gauging environmental impacts? The Convention did not provide the necessary answers.[39]

Environmentalists also contended that CRAMRA contained language that was ambiguous and allowed for too broad and varied interpretations. There was scepticism over how the consensus requirement in CRAMRA would operate. The concern was that these voting provisions in the Convention could be construed in many ways, and that decisions to open areas might be taken on the basis of political considerations, rather than stipulated scientific criteria. Only one step in the Convention separated decision-making between the phases of exploration and development. Critics alleged that an exploration state might automatically receive approval for development.

Insufficient information

Questions were further raised about the extent and accuracy of information necessary to make prudent, environmentally sound decisions. Would sufficient information about the Antarctic environment be available to both the Commission and the Regulatory Committees for them to make informed, prudent decisions on mineral resource activities? Conservation organisations also contended that insufficient opportunities existed for outside, more impartial, non-governmental observers to contribute to the environmental assessment process. This situation, they argued, exacerbated the lack-of-accountability problem between the regime and the general public and could lead to decision-makers being shortchanged of relevant environmental information that might be helpful in their deliberations.[40]

Institutional weaknesses

Additional concern surfaced over the weak role of the Scientific, Technical and Environmental Advisory Committee in the decision-making pro-

---

[39] See generally Annex A, 'Illustrative Improvement to Remedy Defects in the Antarctic Minerals Convention', in Antarctic and Southern Ocean Coalition (ASOC), 'Analysis of the Convention on the Regulation of Antarctic Mineral Resource Activities', *ASOC Information Paper*, no. 4, 29 October 1988.

[40] See ASOC, 'Analysis of the Convention', pp. 4–5.

cess. The Advisory Committee would have been critical for supplying the appropriate scientific and technical information to the Commission and Regulatory Committees for appraising local environmental conditions. But its role was only hortatory. The Advisory Committee was without binding power. As a consequence, concern arose that decisions might be taken by the Commission or by Regulatory Committees irrespective or in spite of the Advisory Committee's recommendations.

Critics also noted that the review functions of the Commission over the Regulatory Committees were weak and wanting. The Commission lacked the authority to overrule a Regulatory Committee decision, thus creating a situation where accountability was lacking between a critical decision-making body, the Regulatory Committee, and the principal political body in the regime, the Commission. Environmentalists contended that a thorough review of standards, regulations and activities had to take place, both periodically and in response to new information as it became available to the regime. Most important, there had to exist genuine opportunities to modify rules and tighten limitations on activities if local environmental conditions warranted.[41]

Strong doubts were also voiced about the liability provisions in CRAMRA. Critics asserted that even stricter liability and full responsibility for all damage done to the environment must be placed on the operator conducting activities in the area. In this way, those at fault would be made fully responsible for environmental restoration. Such a costly scenario would, it was thought, act as a stronger deterrent to environmental abuse and presumably would furnish greater incentives for operators to exercise caution and prudence in conducting mineral resource activities.

Another criticism concerned compliance. CRAMRA did provide for inspection, monitoring, reporting, compulsory dispute settlement, access to courts and suspension of activities causing unacceptable damage to the environment. Enforcement, however, remained in the hands of individual governments. The degree of environmental integrity was left to be elaborated and fixed by each state, according to its own rules and regulations. The problem here was that each state differed in gauging what should constitute environmental protection, and in allocating amounts of financial and scientific resources, as well as levels of expertise.[42]

---

[41] See ASOC, 'Analysis of the Convention', pp. 5–6.
[42] See ASOC, 'Analysis of the Convention', pp. 6–7.

Other perceived deficiencies

CRAMRA could never guarantee that accidents might not occur if minerals development went forward in the Antarctic. The isolation of Antarctica, aggravated by severe storms, high winds, frigid temperatures and iceberg infested waters – all these exacerbated the likelihood of accidents in the Antarctic. These same conditions would also impede the ability of operators to respond to oil spills and well blowouts in a timely and efficient manner, thus making well capping attempts and clean-up efforts even more difficult.[43]

Moreover, environmentalists suggested that the new minerals regime could present difficulties for promoting international scientific cooperation in Antarctica. Increased emphasis by Consultative Parties on resource issues, plainly evidenced by the adoption of the 1980 Convention on the Conservation of Antarctic Marine Living Resources (CCAMLR), as well as CRAMRA, could detract from international scientific cooperation by encouraging applied research for national programmes. One can easily imagine this to be the case for geological or geodesic research, where scientific activities might be labelled 'prospecting', thus preserving the confidentiality of commercially valuable data. Non-publication of scientific data was already a problem, seen during the 1980s as some states withheld mandated CCAMLR reports of fish catches in the Southern Ocean and as certain governments were reluctant to supply information regarding drilling activities in the Ross Sea.

Finally, opponents suggested that if minerals exploitation were eventually permitted through CRAMRA, this situation might lead to disputes over resources and possibly even to hostilities between claimant states and sponsoring states operating within some claimed sector. Ironically, this development would upset the chief purpose of the Antarctic Treaty System: namely to prevent Antarctica from becoming the scene or object of international discord.

---

[43] See Annex A, 'Illustrative Improvements', in ASOC, 'Analysis of the Convention', pp. 12–13. See also J. N. Barnes, 'Protection of the Environment in Antarctica: Are Present Regimes Enough?', in A. Jørgensen-Dahl and W. Østreng (eds.), *The Antarctic Treaty System in World Politics* (London: Macmillan, 1991), pp. 186–228. For a contemporary assessment of threats to the Antarctic environment, see C. C. Joyner, 'Protection of the Antarctic Environment: Rethinking the Problems and Prospects', *Cornell International Law Journal*, vol. 19, no. 2, 1986, pp. 259–74; and C. C. Joyner, 'The Southern Ocean and Marine Pollution: Problems and Prospects', *Case Western Reserve Journal of International Law*, vol. 17, no. 2, 1985, pp. 165 and 173–7.

The need to protect the Antarctic environment from the impact of minerals development came to be viewed as overriding any system that sought to regulate those activities. Minerals activities could not be regulated – they had to be prohibited. CRAMRA did not and could not assure this. Hence, CRAMRA was deemed not to be adequately effective for the purpose at hand.

The demise of CRAMRA brought to a close preoccupation by the Consultative Parties with a minerals regime for the Antarctic. But in doing so a legal vacuum had been created. Without CRAMRA, no legal mechanism was available to deal with minerals activities in Antarctica. This need gave rise to the opportunity to negotiate a new set of far-reaching measures that could elaborate and strengthen international law for environmental protection in the Antarctic.

THE LEGAL STATUS OF CRAMRA TODAY

It is important to recognise that CRAMRA is not dead legally. The Convention may be politically bankrupt at the present time, but its status as a legal instrument technically remains that of an active Convention caught up in the process of ratification. Granted, its purpose has been overtaken by the ban on mining and environmental provisions in the Madrid Protocol. Granted, too, that it is unlikely that any state will now seek to accede to or ratify CRAMRA in the foreseeable future. The fact is, however, that while politically inert, CRAMRA is not legally defunct. It remains open for accession by any state that is a Contracting Party to the Antarctic Treaty.[44] There is no expiration date for ATCP accession to or ratification of that instrument. Hence, the status of CRAMRA remains stuck in a static condition of legal limbo. Should the time ever come when a minerals regime might be desirable or necessary, the procedural process for CRAMRA's entry into force would be legally available. Even so, if the Madrid Protocol should fail in national ratification efforts or collapse some time in the future, the greater likelihood appears that governments will opt to borrow the best features of CRAMRA and incorporate them into a new regulatory regime. The perceived ineffectiveness of CRAMRA may well have tarnished even its future acceptability among some Consultative Parties.

---

[44] See CRAMRA, Art. 61.

CONCLUDING REMARKS

CRAMRA's ability to regulate could be only as effective as its regime was able to relate to those activities targeted for regulation. But environmental regulation implies establishment of standards that can realistically be met and enforced. Regulation implies the existence of procedures to ascertain under what circumstances standards should be applied, when and to whom. Such circumstances should also be capable of determining whether and when prohibition is more appropriate than regulation. Critical here was the need to set the degree of environmental harm that would be tolerated, and to fix the ways and means for determining whether the threshold of unacceptable degradation to the environment had been breached.

CRAMRA left such pivotal needs unrealised. Problems of uncertainty thus came to undermine the potential effectiveness of CRAMRA, particularly as viewed by conservationists. The fact that provisions for environmental restoration or rehabilitation had been omitted from CRAMRA only served to heighten suspicions about the regime's effective worth.

But the ineffectiveness of the Convention should not obscure the genuine contributions it made toward creation of a more effective environmental protection arrangement for the Antarctic region. Had there been no CRAMRA, the question remains when, or even whether, a comprehensive environmental protocol might have been negotiated. Aspects of CRAMRA that had been deemed inappropriate and undesirable – hence making the instrument ineffective as an acceptable regulatory mechanism – were improved upon and renegotiated in the form of the Protocol. What had been procedural deficiencies in the minerals treaty were transformed into substantive strengths in the Protocol.

CRAMRA's legacy of effectiveness is clear: The successful negotiation of the Convention revealed the Antarctic Treaty Consultative Party governments' willingness to compromise in order to secure consensus on a regulatory regime. Had the regulation of potential minerals development been acceptable, then CRAMRA could have proven its effectiveness in meeting that task. But when comprehensive environmental protection arose as the standard, CRAMRA's efficacy could not pass the test. The demand for such a comprehensive environmental protection system rendered the purpose of a minerals treaty less than sufficiently effective to that end. As a result, that demand undid CRAMRA as an acceptable legal regime.

In the end CRAMRA was deemed insufficiently effective as a mechanism for protecting the Antarctic environment from possible degradation caused by minerals development. More damning, CRAMRA was seen as lacking neutrality on the mining issue. In fact the purpose of the minerals treaty came to be viewed as encouragement for that activity and as actually paving the way so that purported 'safe' mining might go forward. That perception was to prove the fatal flaw undercutting the opportunity for CRAMRA to be effective as part of the Antarctic Treaty System.

7

The effectiveness of the Protocol on Environmental Protection to the Antarctic Treaty

FRANCISCO ORREGO VICUÑA

INTRODUCTION: GROWING CONCERN ABOUT THE PROTOCOL'S EFFECTIVENESS

Since the Protocol on Environmental Protection to the Antarctic Treaty was signed in 1991[1] a number of important questions have been raised concerning its effectiveness. Many of these questions are indeed pertinent in that they point up the issue of whether this Protocol can meet the expectations created when it was negotiated.[2]

The genuine objective of all governments participating in these negotiations was of course the enhanced protection of the fragile Antarctic environment.[3] However, this shared objective must be qualified in the light of different perceptions through which additional concerns were introduced in the negotiating process. While for some governments the main purpose lay in the updating and development of the various recommendations approved over the years by the Antarctic Treaty Consultative Parties so as to provide for a new comprehensive system of environ-

---

[1] Protocol on Environmental Protection to the Antarctic Treaty, 4 October 1991, reprinted in *International Legal Materials*, vol. XXX, pp. 1,455*ff.*

[2] On the negotiations of the Protocol see generally F. Francioni, 'The Madrid Protocol on the Protection of the Antarctic Environment', *Texas International Law Journal*, vol. 28, no. 1, 1993, pp. 47–72; also published as 'Il Protocollo di Madrid sulla protezione dell'ambiente antartico', *Revista di Diritto Internazionale*, vo. 74, 1991, pp. 797–820. See also S. K. N. Blay, 'New Trends in the Protection of the Antarctic Environment: the 1991 Madrid Protocol', *American Journal of International Law*, vol. 86, no. 2, 1992, pp. 377–99; F. Orrego Vicuña, 'The Protection of the Antarctic Environment, *IARP Publication Series* (Lysaker: Fridtjof Nansen Institute, 1992), no. 5; J. Verhoeven, P. Sands and M. Bruce (eds.), *The Antarctic Environment and International Law* (London: Graham & Trotman, 1992); C. Redgwell, 'Current Developments: Antarctica', *International and Comparative Law Quarterly*, vol. 40, no. 4, 1991, pp. 976–81.

[3] Protocol, Art. 3, on 'Environmental Principles'; and comments by Francioni, 'The Madrid Protocol', pp. 59–61.

mental protection,[4] others held that environmental protection could be achieved only through prohibiting Antarctic mineral activities and dismissing the 1988 Convention on the matter – thereby meeting the demands of domestic public opinion in some instances.[5] For other participants the question of potential resource needs – and the fact that the appropriate technology is not yet readily available – did not seem so pressing as to oppose postponement of basic decisions in this matter for five decades.

It follows from the above that discussion about the Protocol's effectiveness will have to be measured in relation to five separate points.

1 Has the Protocol provided for an effective and comprehensive approach to the protection of the Antarctic environment as compared with the situation prior to its adoption?
2 Has the Protocol effectively disposed of CRAMRA and, more generally, of the issue of mineral activities in Antarctica, or is this issue likely to re-emerge as soon as a mineral deposit is found?
3 How effective could the Antarctic Treaty System generally be in case the Protocol does not enter into force or, having done so, it collapses in fifty years' time because one or several states have chosen to opt out under its clauses?
4 Has the Protocol contributed to the enhancement of internal accommodation among the Antarctic Treaty parties, or has it rather evidenced a first major departure from this accomplishment of the System?
5 Has external accommodation on environmental management been achieved or will the Protocol lead to growing demands in this area by international public and private organisations?

THE EMERGENCE OF THE PROTOCOL

As discussed in Chapter 6, the environmental debate in the framework of the Antarctic Treaty System peaked in intensity because of a series of regrettable accidents that caused damage to the sensitive environment.

---

[4] On the comprehensive system of environmental protection and the earlier work of the Antarctic Treaty Consultative Meetings on the environment and related measures, see Orrego, 'The Protection', pp. 1–11 and 19–21.
[5] On the debate following the adoption of the Convention on the Regulation of Antarctic Mineral Resource Activities, see R. T. Scully and L. A. Kimball, 'Antarctica: Is There Life After Minerals?', *Marine Policy*, vol. 13, no. 2, 1989, pp. 87–98.

Among these were the accidents of the Argentine ship *Bahia Paraiso*, and the Peruvian ship *Humboldt*, the oil spill at the US station at the South Pole, and, even though it took place in another ice-bound area, the accident of the *Exxon Valdez* oil tanker in Alaska. All of this provoked a justified reaction of alarm in public opinion which led the government of Chile to formally raise the subject of comprehensive environmental protection of the Antarctic in 1988.

The negotiations

Complex negotiations were initiated within the System directed to the preparation of a Protocol or a Convention on Comprehensive Measures of Environmental Protection. Initial drafts were presented by Australia,[6] Australia and France jointly,[7] Chile,[8] New Zealand,[9] the United States[10] and Sweden,[11] as well as opinions or studies from different specialised entities,[12] all of which led in 1989 to the approval of Recommendation XV-1[13] on the concept of the Comprehensive Measures. All these drafts shared the common purpose of elaborating a complete system of environmental protection, strengthening existing measures, and filling in the lacunae and additional necessities that could be detected, but they differed in the degree of intensity proposed as well as in whether or not they

---

[6] Australia: 'Antarctic Environment Protection Convention: Australian Proposals', 1989, mimeograph.

[7] Australia and France: 'Non-Paper on a Possible Approach to Components of a Comprehensive Convention for the Preservation and Protection of the Antarctic', 9 August 1989. Australia and France: 'Draft Working Paper on Possible Components for a Comprehensive Convention for the Preservation and Protection of Antarctica', 22 August 1989. See also 'Nuevo Documento Franco-Australiano sobre los elementos de un régimen global de protección del medio ambiente de la Antártida y de sus ecosistemas dependientes y relacionados', 16 March 1990. See also doc. XV ATCM/WP.2 and 3, 1989.

[8] Chile: 'Working Paper', doc. XV ATCM/WP.7, 1989.

[9] New Zealand: 'White Paper on Antarctic Environment', August 1989 and doc. XV ATCM/WP.4, 1989.

[10] United States: 'Medidas globales para la protección del medio ambiente antártico y sus ecosistemas dependientes y relacionados', doc. XV ATCM/WP.8, 1989.

[11] Sweden: 'Working Paper', doc. XV ATCM/WP.14, 1989.

[12] International Union for the Conservation of Nature, *A Strategy for Antarctic Conservation*, November 1989; ASOC, 'Protección Permanente para Antártida: se requierecon carácter urgente una convención para su conservación', Information Paper no. 2, 11 May 1989.

[13] Recommendation XV-1, J. A. Heap (ed.), *Handbook of the Antarctic Treaty System*, 7th ed. (Cambridge: Scott Polar Research Institute, 1990), section 2.1.1.

intended to follow CRAMRA.[14] Whereas Australia and France sponsored the concept of the Antarctic as 'natural reserve, land of science', which would make the idea of any mineral exploitation impossible, the United States proposed a scheme based on all the components of the Antarctic Treaty System which included CRAMRA, and Chile sought an intermediate position through the development of the concept of the Antarctic as a Special Conservation Area.

Recommendation XV-1 was an especially important step in this respect. Along with referring to the main measures, recommendations and conventions of the Antarctic Treaty System, thereby indicating the juridical unity among all its components, it pointed out the essence of all the proposals formulated; on this basis, important actions were recommended. The central recommendation is, naturally, to elaborate, maintain and apply effectively a comprehensive system of environmental protection in the Antarctic, seeking to ensure that human activity neither causes adverse effects nor affects the scientific, aesthetic, or natural values of the region. For this purpose existing principles should be considered as well as those principles that should be broadened, reviewing the measures in effect so as to identify aspects that should be updated, providing greater juridical precision and promoting research related to the environment, as well as appropriate procedures for assessment, monitoring and information. The related institutional necessities should also be considered.

It is in these orientations that the crucial aspects of environmental policy are found, which consist of achieving protective measures that respond to specific realities, over and above ideological connotations. For this reason, such measures must be based on a policy of scientific research and on the procedures of assessment, monitoring and collection of information. Equally essential was that all this be compatible with the scientific research carried out in the Antarctic: otherwise, the research could be harmed, thus affecting the fundamental purpose of the Antarctic Treaty.[15]

---

[14] Report from the XV ATCM, Paris 1989, paras. 40–67; see Heap (ed.), *Handbook*, pp. 2,105–7.

[15] For the discussion on environmental policies and its regimes see L. A. Kimball, 'The Antarctic Conservation Agenda', in R. A. Herr, H. R. Hall and M. G. Haward (eds.), *Antarctica's Future: Continuity or Change?* (Hobart: Tasmanian Government Printer, 1990), pp. 81–90. See also P. J. Beck, 'The UN Goes Green on Antarctica: The 1989 Session', *Polar Record*, vol. 26, no. 159, 1990, pp. 323–5; P. J. Beck, 'Antarctica Enters the 1990's: An Overview', *Applied Geography*, vol. 10, 1990, pp. 247–63; J. R. Burgess, 'Comprehensive Environmental Protection of the Antarctic: New Approaches for New Times', Conference on 'Antarctica: An Exploitable Resource or Too Important to

The XI Special Consultative Meeting of the Antarctic Treaty, which began its work in November 1990, was called to consider all these initiatives. On the occasion of its first meeting, the meeting about the Protocol on Liability of the Convention on Mineral Resources, called by Recommendation XV-2,[16] also took place.

At the XV Consultative Meeting, the President of Working Group I had proposed some basic principles that served as the foundation for the new environmental protection scheme.[17] The idea of minimising and avoiding adverse effects on the Antarctic environment featured in them, with special reference to the global or regional climate, the quality of air and water, the atmospheric, terrestrial or marine environment, the distribution, abundance or productivity of the species of fauna and flora, or the degradation of areas of special biological, scientific, historic, aesthetic or natural significance. The need for appropriate information,

---

Develop' (Centre for Australian Studies, University of London, 21 February 1990); W. M. Bush, 'Australia and Antarctica: Recent Developments. A New Look at the Minerals Convention and Environmental Protection', in R. Falk and S. K. Chopra, *The Future of the Antarctic Regime: A World Order Perspective*, 1990; *Australia and the Antarctic Environment* (Canberra: Department of Foreign Affairs and Trade, February 1990); S. K. N. Blay and B. M. Tsamenyi, 'Australia and the Convention for the Regulation of Antarctic Mineral Resource Activities (CRAMRA)', *Polar Record*, vol. 26, no. 158, 1990, pp. 195–202. R. J. L. Hawke, 'Australia's Policy in Antarctica', in Herr *et al.* (eds.), *Antarctica's Future*, pp. 17–20; R. Woolcott, 'Challenges and Changes', in Herr *et al.* (eds.), pp. 21–8; P. G. Quilty, 'Antarctica as a Continent for Science', in Herr *et al.* (eds.), pp. 29–37; B. W. Davis, 'Science and Politics in Antarctica and Southern Oceans Policy: A Critical Assessment', in Herr *et al.* (eds.), pp. 39–45; P. Law, 'The Antarctic Wilderness – A Wild Idea!', in Herr *et al.* (eds.), pp. 71–80; L. Goldsworthy, 'World Park Antarctica: An Environmentalist's Vision', in Herr *et al.* (eds.), pp. 90–3; G. D. Triggs, 'A Comprehensive Environmental Regime for Antarctica: A New Way Forward', in Herr *et al.* (eds.), pp. 103–18; W. M. Bush, 'The Antarctic Treaty System: Toward a Comprehensive Environmental Regime', in Herr *et al.* (eds.), pp. 119–79; Fundación para el Desarrollo de Magallanes, 'Segundas Jornadas Antárticas y Primeras Jornadas del Medio Ambiente', Punta Arenas, Chile, 20–5 August 1990; Comité Nacional Pro Defensa de la Fauna y Flora, 'Primer Taller Latinoamericano de organizaciones no gubernamentales sobre Conservación Antártica', 24–8 September 1990, Santiago, Chile.

[16] The first session of the XI Special Consultative Meeting was held in Viña del Mar, from 19 November to 6 December 1990; the second session in Madrid, from 22 April to 30 April 1991; and the final session likewise in Madrid, from 2 October to 4 October 1991. See generally J. Schmied, 'XI Reunión Consultiva Especial del Tratado Antártico', *Boletín Antártico Chileno*, vol. 10, no. 2, Octubre 1990–Mayo 1991, pp. 5–9; M. L. Carvallo: 'Las X y XI Reuniones Consultivas Especiales del Tratado Antártico', *ibid.*, pp. 9–12.

[17] 'Comprehensive Measures for the Protection of the Antarctic Environment and Dependent and Associate Ecosystems: Draft Principles put forward by the Chairman of Working Group I': see Heap (ed.), *Handbook*, p. 2,107.

monitoring procedures, and effective procedures to respond to accidents
was pointed out, as well as the contribution of scientific research.

Several drafts prepared by interested governments sought to translate
this concern into an organised environmental protection system. A draft
Convention presented by Australia, Belgium, France and Italy,[18] based on
the concept of the Antarctic as a 'natural reserve, land of science', anticipated strict environmental control of activities on that continent, some
of which would be prohibited while others would require prior authorisation. An institutional system was proposed, with a Permanent Committee for the Protection of the Antarctic Environment, a Scientific and
Technical Committee and a Permanent Secretariat.

Another draft presented by the United States[19] gathered together as
main principles those proposed at the end of the XV Consultative Meeting, incorporating in annexes detailed provisions on subjects such as waste
disposal, protection of fauna and flora, and other high-priority aspects.
In the institutional field, a more restricted approach was adopted than in
the proposal mentioned above, confined to an Advisory Committee for
Environmental Protection and a Secretariat, all within the framework of
the Consultative Meetings. There was also an elaborate system for settling disputes, based on the option of a recourse to the International
Court of Justice or an arbitral procedure. A similar approach was followed
in the draft proposed by the United Kingdom,[20] the basic principles of
which also had the support of Argentina, Norway, the United States and
Uruguay.[21]

New Zealand also presented a detailed draft[22] where the substantive
provisions were included in the body of the proposed convention and not

---

[18] Australia, Belgium, France and Italy: 'Indicative Draft of a Convention for the Comprehensive Protection of the Antarctic Environment', doc. XI/ATSCM/1, 18 November
1990. Also see Australia and France: 'The Conduct of Antarctic Scientific Research under
a Comprehensive Environment Protection Convention', doc. XI/ATSCM/INFO 3, of 19
November 1990. Australia: 'Manejo de combustible', doc. XI/ATSCM/W.G II/4 1990.

[19] US: 'Protocol Supplementing the Antarctic Treaty', doc. XI/ATSCM/4, of 18 November
1990; Add. 1, Annex: Assessment of the Impact on the Environment; Add. 2, Annex:
Agreed Measures for the Conservation of Antarctic Fauna and Flora; Add. 3, Annex:
Specially Protected Areas.

[20] United Kingdom: 'Provisions for a Protocol Supplementing the Antarctic Treaty', doc.
XI/ATSCM/3, of 18 November 1990.

[21] Argentina, Norway, the United Kingdom, the United States and Uruguay: 'Outline of
a Protocol Supplementing the Antarctic Treaty', doc. XI/ATSCM/5, of 20 November
1990.

[22] New Zealand: 'Draft Protocol to the Antarctic Treaty on Environmental Protection',
doc. XI/ATSCM/2, of 18 November 1990.

in annexes, but the content of which followed criteria similar to the drafts of the United States and the United Kingdom. The fundamental difference lay in the fact that the New Zealand initiative would prohibit mining in the Antarctic. Other general or partial initiatives were presented by India, Sweden, the Netherlands and other countries,[23] as well as by non-governmental organisations.[24]

Despite the difference in points of view contained in these initiatives, they were gradually harmonised on the basis of the negotiations carried out, a process which led to the approval of the Protocol on Environmental Protection to the Antarctic Treaty. The first draft of this Protocol, prepared in December 1990,[25] contained a very important decision: that the instrument would adopt the form of a Protocol to the Treaty of 1959 and not the form of a supplementary convention, as some initiatives had proposed. This indicated the special rank accorded to the subject of environmental protection.

---

[23] India: 'Medidas Comprensivas para la Protección del Medio Ambiente Antártico y Ecosistemas Dependientes y Asociados', doc. XI/ATSCM/7, 1990; Norway, 'Evaluación del Impacto Ambiental'; United States: 'Propuesta sobre Disponibilidad de Información referente a la Geociencia', doc. XI/ATSCM/WP.4, 1990; United Kingdom: 'El sistema de áreas antárticas protegidas', 1990; Sweden: 'Cooperación en la Antártida', doc. XI/ATSCM/WG II/6, 1990; The Netherlands: 'Preparación de Una Evaluación del Impacto sobre el Medio Ambiente del Turismo sobre toda la Antártida', doc. XI/ATSCM/WG II/INFO.1, 1990; Chile: 'Código de Conducta para las Actividades Turísticas y no Gubernamentales en la Antártida', doc. XI/ATSCM/WG II/INFO.2, 1990; Italy: 'Usos de energías alternativas para reducir el impacto en el Medio Ambiente Antártico', doc. XI/ATSCM/WG II/5; Chile: 'Antarctic Natural Hazards', doc. XI/ATSCM/INFO.54, 4 December 1990. For other documents submitted to the negotiation see the Interim Report of the Second Session of the XI Special Consultative Meeting, Madrid, 22–30 April 1991, doc. XI/ATSCM/2/31 of 30 April 1991.

[24] ASOC, 'The Convention on Antarctic Conservation', *ASOC Information Paper*, 7 November 1990.

[25] 'Protocolo al Tratado Antártico sobre Protección del Medio Ambiente', Interim Report of the XI Antarctic Treaty Special Consultative Meeting, Viña del Mar, 19 November to 6 December 1990, pp. 111–55. For an analysis, see L. A. Kimball, *Report on Antarctica* (Washington, DC: World Resources Institute, 1991). See also the Reports of Working Groups I and II of the Second Session of the XI Special Consultative Meeting, Madrid, 22–30 April 1991, doc. XI/ATSCM/2/32, of 30 April 1991 and doc. XI ATSCM/WG II/33, of 30 April 1991. The second revision of the Protocol appears in doc. XI ATSCM/ 2/30, 29 April 1991. See also the Interim Report of the Second Session, as referred to in note 23 above in this chapter. The final text of the Protocol was signed in Madrid on 4 October 1991, and is reproduced in doc. XI ATSCM/2/3/2, of 3 October 1991. See also the Final Report of the Eleventh Special Antarctic Treaty Consultative Meeting, 4 October 1991. See also 'ASOC Statement on the Environmental Protocol', 3 October 1991.

The Protocol on Environmental Protection

The main purpose of the new instrument is to supplement the Antarctic Treaty and the legislative action developed under the latter, ensuring ample protection of the environment. The appropriate environmental principles are defined for this purpose; the scope of the basic provisions of the 1959 Treaty regarding scientific research is broadened; and a series of juridical and institutional measures are adopted. The latter includes *consultation* and cooperation among all parties in the different Antarctic instruments; the assignment of functions to the *Consultative Meetings* to enact and enforce general environmental policies; the creation of the *Committee for Environmental Protection*; and the incorporation of provisions to facilitate compliance by contracting parties, carry out inspections, respond efficiently in the face of accidents, and ensure the compulsory settlement of disputes.

In regard to the general *objectives* of environmental protection, no great differences between the various national drafts and positions were noted. Nevertheless, discrepancies were clearly expressed regarding specific mechanisms to implement such principles, especially whether Antarctic activities should be submitted to environmental assessment, review, or approval prior to conduct; whether new decision-making organs should be established; whether independent, institutionalised inspection should be created; the extent of liability for environmental damage; and, especially, whether mineral activities should be prohibited and what the future role of CRAMRA should be.[26]

From the moment the system aspires to provide comprehensive environmental protection, it *applies* to all human activities in the Antarctic. Initially it was proposed that activities developed under other conventions of the System, like fishing, should also be submitted to the new Protocol. However, this approach did not prevail. Although the Protocol supplements the Antarctic Treaty, it does not modify or amend the Treaty. On the other hand, none of the provisions of the Protocol derogates from the rights and obligations derived from other instruments of the Antarctic System already in force. The Preamble of the Protocol also reaffirms the principles of conservation underlying CCAMLR. Also, the need for consultation and cooperation with the parties in those other instruments and their respective institutions is anticipated in order to avoid interference and ensure the compatibility of the respective measures. The

---

[26] Kimball, *Report on Antarctica*, p. 4.

Final Act of the XI Special Consultative Meeting specifies that the Protocol will not include activities developed under CCAMLR, the Convention for the Conservation of Seals or the International Convention for the Regulation of Whaling. The ice also will not be included in the prohibition against mineral activities.

Another expression of the amplitude of the system established is found in the criteria regarding *participation*. The Protocol is open to signature by all parties to the Antarctic Treaty, but it is also provided that the designation of new Consultative Parties will not be approved if that Contracting Party is not previously a party to the Protocol. The doubt that remains is that activities a party to the Antarctic Treaty carries out before becoming a party to the Protocol, including those necessary to become a Consultative Party, might not be subject to strict environmental protection criteria.[27] It should also be noted that this Protocol does not admit reservations.

The area of application of the Protocol was also discussed in regard to the *geographic* extent of the system. There were proposals directed to extend its application farther north than the 60°S latitude, to cover especially the Antarctic Convergence, but finally the Protocol will be restricted to the geographic area of application of the Antarctic Treaty. Nevertheless, cooperation with the parties that exercise jurisdiction over those other adjacent areas is provided for, in order to avoid adverse environmental effects. The ambit of application so defined poses potential problems regarding the seabed and areas of the continental shelf. A declaration of the Chilean delegation, made on the occasion of the signing of the Protocol, specifies that the prohibition of mineral activities will be applied to the whole territory claimed by this country, including the continental shelf, also north of the 60°S latitude.[28]

The central concept of this comprehensive protection lies in the designation of the Antarctic as a *'natural reserve, devoted to peace and science'* an expression that comes from the above-mentioned Franco-Australian initiative. For this purpose applicable environmental principles are elaborated which are closely related to those which emanated from the works of the XV Consultative Meeting. The values of nature, aesthetics and an area for the development of scientific research are especially emphasised,

---

[27] *Ibid.*, pp. 4–5.
[28] Text of that Chilean declaration reprinted in W. M. Bush (ed.), *Antarctica and International Law: A Collection of Inter-State and National Documents* (New York: Oceana, 1992), Booklet AT91C, November 1992, p. 3.

seeking the planning and development of human activity with a view to avoiding adverse effects. Emphasis is also put on the information necessary to evaluate these problems and the existence of an adequate monitoring system.

The original proposal of France, Australia and other countries involved a system of prior collective authorisation for the development of high-risk activities, establishing a consensus system to exempt activities from this rigorous procedure, while it directly prohibited other activities permanently. This naturally caused great concern in the scientific community, as any research would be subject to these difficult conditions, even though its environmental effects were minimal or localised. Such a system clearly was not in harmony either with the freedom of the scientific research characteristic of the Antarctic Treaty.

For these reasons the Protocol has adopted a different approach. First, it emphasises the value of the Antarctic as an area for carrying out *scientific research*, while it grants these objectives priority. Next, it requires not collective authorisation but the application of an environmental assessment procedure which is a matter of regulation in a special Annex of the Protocol. This environmental assessment is applied basically on a national level, even though the institutions have some participation in the general policy and other aspects. In any case, a distinction is made between activities that have no impact or small impact, those of minor or transitory impact, and those where the impact exceeds the latter level. Thus consideration is given to different potential situations, and an effort is made to ensure the normal development of scientific research so that it is compatible with the objective of environmental protection.

The application of environmental principles is based to an important extent on the development of plans for cooperation among the parties, with special emphasis on joint programmes for environmental protection, assistance in preparing environmental impact assessments, joint expeditions and selection of sites to establish stations so as to avoid their excessive concentration. Special priority is also given to the availability, exchange and circulation of the appropriate information, especially concerning environmental assessments, disposal, emergencies and statistics. Every party is also to prepare an annual report on how it has put the provisions of the Protocol into practice. These national and institutional reports will be available to the public.

The provisions regarding *compliance* with this Protocol strengthen in some aspects the rules that characterise the tradition of the Antarctic Treaty System. Every party is to adopt the measures within its competence to assure compliance with this instrument, including those of legislative, regulatory and administrative character. It can be seen that these are obligations of greater legal precision than the earlier ones. These obligations of compliance that fall on the parties refer to both their own activities and the non-governmental or private expeditions over which they have jurisdiction, such as tourist operators and other programmes of their nationals. It is also interesting to note that there are provisions in the Annexes that directly bind individuals regarding compliance. In the event of incompatibility with environmental principles, such activities should be modified, suspended or cancelled. The obligations established in the Annexes, but not those in the Protocol itself, are also related to the procedures for compulsory settlement of disputes as far as compliance is concerned.

As in the Antarctic Treaty itself, the parties are to adopt measures compatible with the Charter of the United Nations so that no one carries out activities contrary to the Protocol; and parties are to bring to the attention of other parties or even third parties, activities that affect the application of the objectives and principles of the instrument.

The system is completed with measures regarding *inspection, response to emergencies, and liability*. Regarding the first two, a system of individual or collective inspection is provided for, which will rely on national inspectors but potentially also on inspectors appointed by the Consultative Meetings. The proposals directed to establish an independent inspectorate were not well received – partly because of their higher cost and partly because they could affect the existing system under the Antarctic Treaty and other instruments. Regarding response to emergencies, the parties are under obligation to establish an adequate response system and necessary contingency plans, all of which should also be subject to prior assessment.

The rules on responsibility, as is now customary in this kind of instrument, have proven more complex than might be thought at first. On the one hand, the view has been set forth that they should be as strict as the rules in CRAMRA. On the other hand, it has been pointed out that activities like tourism and others that will be submitted to this Protocol do not pose as many environmental risks as mineral activities, for which reason they require simpler norms. The Franco-Australian draft, for example, was based on the most classic rules on liability, requiring the proof of fault, which contrasted with other more advanced proposals. Due to these difficulties, the Protocol is limited to establishing the commitment to develop rules and procedures on this matter through the negotiation of an additional annex; meanwhile, it should be guaranteed that there will be juridical recourses available under domestic law for claims regarding environmental damage. The pending negotiations should take into account the most recent trends in international law on the subject of environmental liability, including the liability of the state and the operators, assessment of damage, entitlement to claim, and subsidiary liability, as well as other aspects.

The Annexes to the Protocol

The obligations established by the Protocol are specified in detail regarding some important matters in its various Annexes, which form an integral part of the same instrument. The Consultative Parties will be able to approve additional Annexes under the terms of Article IX of the Antarctic Treaty. It is established that all the Annexes contain provisions regarding the rapid entry into force of measures adopted within its framework, and that they include the compulsory mechanisms for the settlement of disputes established under the Protocol. These Annexes, on their respective subjects, unite and develop the rules enacted to date by the Consultative Meetings, providing a series of more structured and coherent environmental provisions. Four Annexes were adopted at the time of signing the Protocol: on Environmental Impact Assessment (Annex I), on the Conservation of the Antarctic Fauna and Flora (Annex II), on Waste Disposal and Waste Management (Annex III) and on the Prevention of Marine Pollution (Annex IV). Through Recommendation XVI-10 of 1991 a fifth Annex was incorporated into the Protocol, regarding the Protection and Management of Areas in the Antarctic (Annex V).

The Annex on *Environmental Impact Assessment* specifies the criteria and procedures to be followed to fulfill this requirement. All Antarctic activities must be submitted to this assessment, except those that will have no impact or where the impact will be minor. This obligation extends to non-governmental expeditions and activities, but it avoids making each individual scientist or tourist apply the procedure: responsibility is assigned to the governments and the organisers of these activities. The comprehensive environmental assessments that the parties must make are presented for the consideration of the institutions; there was intense debate over whether the Committee for Environmental Protection should make a collective review of the projects and even withhold approval in the event of questions about a project being compatible with the Protocol. These comprehensive assessments are also to be made available to the

public. Some exceptions are also established regarding activities undertaken in emergency situations.

Waste disposal is also part of an Annex that basically follows the criteria
established in Recommendation XV-3. Some interesting additional
aspects are the obligation to incorporate measures on this subject in the
planning and implementation of Antarctic activities, as well as the principle that whoever generates waste is responsible for its disposal.

A third Annex deals with the *Conservation of Antarctic Fauna and Flora*,
developing the criteria contained in the Agreed Measures of Recommendation III-8. Here again those obligations are specified and perfected,
applying also the environmental impact assessment to certain government
authorisations or measures.

The provisions regarding *marine pollution*, contained in a fourth Annex,
are of special interest due to their relationship to the International Convention for the Prevention of Pollution from Ships of 1973 (MARPOL).
The Committee for the Protection of the Marine Environment of the
International Maritime Organisation designated the Antarctic as a 'special
area' under MARPOL on 15 November 1990, thereby creating obligations for all parties to this last Convention, whether or not they are
parties to the Antarctic Treaty or the Protocol.[29] This matter, the principal points of Recommendation XV-4, are also followed in general, with
some interesting innovations. Among the latter the obligation to apply
rules of control not only to ships flying the flag of a state party but also
to ships of other flags that support their Antarctic activities stands out.
At one point in the negotiations, various international conventions were
indicated in the Annex so as to ensure compliance by the parties to the
Protocol, but the final Annex refers specifically only to MARPOL.[30] The
problem of legal immunity should also be dealt with in relation to the
claims of liability for damages, a field where clear justification of immunity is no longer found.

The Annex dealing with Protected Areas in the Antarctic has simplified

[29] Kimball, *Report on Antarctica*, p. 14.
[30] The following conventions were mentioned in the draft Annex during its early negotiation: Convention on the Prevention of Marine Pollution by Dumping of Wastes and
Other Matter (1972); the International Convention for the Prevention of Pollution from
Ships (1973) and the Protocol of 1978 (MARPOL 73/78); the International Convention
on Standards of Training, Certification and Watchkeeping for Seafarers with Annex
(1978); the International Convention for the Safety of Life at Sea (1978) and the Protocol
of 1978; the International Convention on Load Lines (1966); and the Convention on the
International Regulations for Preventing Collisions at Sea (1972).

the various types of designation enacted by the Consultative Meetings over the years. Antarctic Specially Protected Areas and Antarctic Specially Managed Areas are to be the two designations applicable in this matter. Environmental monitoring, tourism and non-governmental activities were at one time considered as additional subjects to be included in Annexes,[31] but this did not materialise.

Institutional framework

Although some of the initial drafts provided for an elaborate institutional framework for environmental protection, the Protocol opted for a simpler, more functional system. As noted, within this system it is the responsibility of Consultative Meetings to define the general policy on environmental protection and adopt the necessary measures to apply the Protocol. For this purpose the Meeting will review the work of the Committee for Environmental Protection, guided by the Committee's opinions and recommendations as well as by the recommendations contributed by SCAR. In this manner, a balance is achieved between environmental and scientific criteria. On the other hand, the Consultative Meetings have specific functions in such aspects as inspection, annual reports of the parties and amendment of the Protocol.

These new duties, like others that the Consultative Meetings have undertaken within the Antarctic Treaty System, have made evident the necessity of a permanent Secretariat responsible for coordination, information and similar technical aspects. Some of the Protocol drafts also provided for the creation of such a Secretariat, but as it would also have functions under other instruments of the system it was decided that its creation should be decided by an ordinary Consultative Meeting.[32]

The *Committee for Environmental Protection* was the organ that prompted most debate during the negotiations leading to the Protocol, because the various proposals were based on very different perspectives. In the view of Australia and France, this organ should have main decision-making power and be responsible for authorising collectively the Antarctic activities of the parties in terms of environmental criteria – which would in fact mean subordinating national decisions to an international

---

[31] Kimball, *Report on Antarctica*, pp. 17–18, and Reports as referred to in note 25 above in this chapter.
[32] On this and other institutional aspects see F. Orrego Vicuña, *Antarctic Mineral Exploitation: The Emerging Legal Framework* (Cambridge University Press, 1988), chapter VIII.

organisation. Also the proposal of New Zealand included the power to postpone a national activity in the event of incompatibility with environmental policies. Other countries, however, felt that this organ should be mainly of a technical character and not become involved in decision-making. Instead it should advise the Consultative Meetings, which would have the central powers.

The Protocol has adopted an intermediate path, but one generally closer to the latter position. Its functions are to give opinions and make recommendations to the parties concerning the application of the Protocol and its Annexes; but it is also provided that this will be considered by the Consultative Meetings. There is, then, an opinion that is expressed regarding the parties but which is also submitted to the consideration of the Consultative Meetings which maintain the basic decision-making power. Notwithstanding the above, the latter may delegate functions to the Committee, particularly concerning the effectiveness and the strengthening of measures adopted, the need for additional measures, and procedures relating to environmental impact assessment, emergency actions, inspection, information and scientific research. The fact that the Committee itself is empowered to make recommendations poses, however, a potential problem of conflict of competence with the Consultative Meetings.

The *structure* of this organ is simple: it is made up of representatives of the Contracting Parties, together with observers from other parties to the Antarctic Treaty that are not parties to the Protocol. The President of SCAR, the President of the Scientific Committee of CCAMLR, and occasionally other scientific, environmental, or technical institutions authorised by the Consultative Meetings will also participate as observers. The Committee is also to consult all these entities in performing its functions. Every session of the Committee must be the subject of a report that will include all matters dealt with and opinions expressed; the reports will be presented to the Consultative Meetings. Such reports will also be circulated to the parties and observers and then will be made available to the public. The Committee adopts its rules of procedure, which must be approved by the Consultative Meetings.

The *dispute-settlement* procedures are of special interest, from both the institutional and substantive point of view. The general rule is that when a dispute arises over the interpretation or application of the provisions of the Protocol or its Annexes, the parties to the dispute should consult one another about the procedure of choice – whether it be negotiation, investigation, mediation, conciliation, arbitration, or judicial settlement –

a procedure which follows the traditional perspective of the Antarctic Treaty System. Nevertheless, regarding the Annexes and the provisions of the Protocol on the prohibition of mineral activities, environmental impact assessment and emergency actions, an entirely different compulsory procedure is envisaged.

In point of fact, the Protocol provides that the parties should opt to settle a dispute by recourse to the International Court of Justice or before an Arbitral Tribunal, the constitution and procedures of which are established in the Protocol itself. This is to be done by means of a declaration; in the event that no choice is made, it is understood that the Arbitral Tribunal is chosen. This procedure may be initiated at the request of just one party to the dispute if, within the period of twelve months from the beginning of the general consultations indicated above, no agreement has been reached on the appropriate procedure. Neither the Arbitral Tribunal nor the International Court of Justice will have jurisdiction to decide about any matter that falls within the scope of Article IV of the Antarctic Treaty, whereby problems regarding territorial sovereignty are safeguarded.

Two aspects that are an innovation within the Antarctic Treaty System are counted among the powers of the Arbitral Tribunal. The first is that any party to the dispute may request that provisional measures be prescribed, and the Tribunal can also prescribe such measures to prevent serious damage to the environment. The second aspect is that provisional emergency measures can also be requested at any time by a party to a dispute.

PROTECTING THE ENVIRONMENT?

The Protocol can be generally considered a step forward in terms of providing for a comprehensive approach to the protection of the Antarctic environment. This is certainly true from a formal point of view, since the governing regime will be embodied in a comprehensive instrument composed of the Protocol and its various Annexes. This provides for a coherent framework in a field previously characterised by various *ad hoc* arrangements adopted at different times and not always following a similar approach, a situation which has been rightly criticised.[33]

---

[33] D. H. Overholt, 'Environmental Protection in the Antarctic: Past, Present, and Future', *Canadian Yearbook of International Law*, vol. 28, 1990, pp. 227–62, at pp. 248–54.

The Protocol: formal legal quality versus substantive improvement

The legal nature of the regime for environmental protection has also been perfected by transforming a broad body of 'soft law' developed since the 1960s into a modern 'hard law' treaty arrangement, following very closely current trends.[34] Indeed, the Protocol is the equivalent of a framework convention providing for the basic features of the regime; and the more detailed measures and requirements are laid down in the Annexes, the latter having a more expeditious system of amendment and updating.

This type of enhancement of the legal quality of the regime is clearly relevant for the questions of enforcement and compliance, which have also been a matter of concern. However, it should be noted that recommendations adopted under the Antarctic Treaty System have generally been more effective than similar measures of several other international organisations,[35] for which reason the Protocol will not necessarily mean an important difference in this regard. On the other hand, as will be examined further below, the Protocol itself is increasingly being criticised on the issue of enforcement capabilities.

Beyond the formal structure of the regime, the question of whether the Protocol has made a substantive contribution to the environmental protection of Antarctica requires more detailed consideration. In view of the importance of the environmental measures approved by the Antarctic Treaty Consultative Parties up to 1991, it was not easy to achieve the objective of substantively improving this *corpus juris*. Moreover, it soon became evident that the Protocol was being negotiated in a rush so as to respond to public opinion concerns in some countries and also to assuage the pressures and demands of active environmental organisations. This could not but affect the capability of the Protocol to consider and introduce substantive improvements in environmental protection, as can be seen from the examination of its key Annexes and other provisions.

Annex I: Environmental Impact Assessment – the unfinished task

Environmental Impact Assessment under the Protocol, with its Annex I, has been criticised for falling short of what was expected in terms of

---

[34] On current trends in the making of international environmental law see generally P. C. Szasz, 'International Norm-Making', in E. Brown Weiss (ed.), *Environmental Change and International Law: New Challenges and Dimensions* (Tokyo: The United Nations University Press, 1992), pp. 41–80.

[35] Orrego, *Antarctic Mineral Exploration*, pp. 57–67.

strongly protective measures for the Antarctic environment.[36] The deliberate ambiguity of several of its provisions, as well as the fact that interpretation has been left open in regard to key questions, such as what is to be considered a minor or transitory impact and what might be below or above this measurement, have been pointed out as particularly unreliable approaches to environmental protection.[37]

Valid as this criticism may be, in many cases there is an underlying mistrust as to the ability of the Antarctic Treaty Consultative Parties to manage the environmental protection system. In several instances, such views have been coupled with a call for strong institutional machinery and even for intervention by the United Nations and other international organisations.[38] But this is a separate issue altogether, involving institutional options and questions of legitimacy.

The historical record of the Antarctic Treaty System clearly supports the role of Consultative Parties in managing the area in a competent manner.[39] Thus, there is every reason to expect that improvements in environmental protection measures will be introduced as warranted by periodic evaluations and practical experience.[40]

In some respects, the requirements for Environmental Impact Assessment in Antarctica go beyond what is normally the situation at the domestic level. While the latter generally apply only to major developments, in Antarctica these requirements are made applicable to almost any activity, including minor activities, which are subject to some form of scrutiny.[41] This very stringent approach has raised serious concerns in the scientific community[42] for it could interfere with the development of Antarctic science. That would contradict the very purpose of 'a natural reserve, devoted to peace and science', in addition to the effect it might have on the cost of conducting activities in Antarctica.

In light of the Antarctic tradition it does not appear that the role of national authorities in deciding which activities should be notified and

---

[36] D. Lyons, 'Environmental Impact Assessment in Antarctica under the Protocol on Environmental Protection', *Polar Record*, vol. 29, no. 169, 1993, pp. 111–20.

[37] *Ibid.*, at pp. 114–15.

[38] E. F. Foreman, 'Protecting the Antarctic Environment: Will a Protocol be Enough?', *American Journal of International Law and Policy*, vol. 7, 1992, pp. 843–79, at pp. 878–9.

[39] F. Orrego Vicuña, *El Derecho Internacional de la Antártida* (Santiago: Editorial Dolmen, 1994), chapter VI.

[40] L. Pineschi, *La Protezione dell'Ambiente in Antartide* (Padova: CEDAM, 1993), pp. 291–2.

[41] Lyons, 'Environmental Impact Assessment', p. 114.

[42] R. Laws, 'Science as an Antarctic Resource', in G. Cook (ed.), *The Future of Antarctica: Exploitation versus Preservation* (Manchester University Press, 1990), pp. 20–1.

which activities can proceed because of being judged environmentally harmless is entirely unwarranted. While there is here an important degree of discretionality this does not mean that any party can do as it pleases. First, the practical guidelines prepared by the Council of Managers of National Antarctic Programs on Environmental Assessment provide a common frame of reference.[43] Second, both the Consultative Meetings and the Committee for Environmental Protection have a role to play in the overseeing and evaluation of the process as a whole.[44] And third, there are national assessment procedures which in some instances are more elaborate than those mandated under the Protocol.[45] While independent review would be indeed an important safeguard, at the time of negotiations this view was equated with the proposal for an all-powerful Environmental Committee, which in turn meant a paralysing structure alien to the Antarctic traditions.[46] Independent review should not be ruled out in the future but only in the context of a streamlined and functional approach.[47]

These very considerations help to explain the fact that implementation of the Protocol is largely left to domestic action as opposed to international enforcement mechanisms. Because the latter alternative was again identified with the all-powerful Environmental Committee it came to be questioned from the outset. But here again the parties are not entirely on their own, and restraints similar to those mentioned above operate in terms of implementation and enforcement. Although theoretically a party could refuse to suspend or cancel an environmentally unsafe activity in the absence of enforcement procedures, in practice this is not likely to happen since the restraints in place will amount to a significant international and domestic pressure. Ironically, these shortcomings are to a large extent the result of the outright attack on CRAMRA – a Conven-

---

[43] *The Antarctic Environmental Assessment Process: Practical Guidelines* (Washington, DC: Council of Managers of National Antarctic programs, 1992).

[44] Protocol, Arts. 10 and 12.

[45] See, for example, *Environmental Defense Fund Inc. v Massey*, 986 F. 2d 528 (DC Cir. 1993), a case in which it was held that the requirements of the US National Environmental Policy Act on environmental impact statement apply to the activities of certain federal agencies in Antarctica. See further W. J. Holmes, 'A Comparison of the United States and Russian Federation Regimes for Protection of the Antarctic by the Use of Environmental Impact Assessments', *Georgetown International Environmental Law Review*, vol. 6, no. 1, 1993, pp. 73–98, at pp. 83–5; and see also J. M. Bondareff, 'The Congress Acts to Protect Antarctica', *Territorial Sea Journal*, vol. 1, 1991, pp. 223–44.

[46] Orrego, 'The Protection', p. 20.

[47] Lyons, 'Environmental Impact Assessment', pp. 115–16.

tion that provided for an extremely interesting enforcement model from which a number of Consultative Parties were more than happy to be relieved.[48] Wording from CRAMRA has been adapted[49] but not its enforcement capability, a situation which prompts the thought that much might be improved by returning to CRAMRA's standards and procedures.

Annex II: updating the Agreed Measures

The protection of fauna and flora embodied in Annex II of the Protocol is basically an updating of the Agreed Measures and subsequent measures adopted by the Consultative Meetings.[50] However useful this exercise might be, it has resulted in the introduction of very few new obligations of substance; moreover, it has broadened some exceptions relating to emergency. The jurisdictional questions involved in the issue of permits have also remained unchanged. Most of the updating is therefore rather formal, although new references to habitats and biological diversity seem to reveal a broader approach to conservation.[51]

One aspect in which the contribution of Annex II is very explicit is the extension of this protection of fauna and flora to the marine environment, a subject much debated in the work of Consultative Meetings.[52] Although the issue had been settled prior to the adoption of the Protocol, its indorsement under this instrument is significant. The exclusion of activities undertaken under CCAMLR and the Seals and Whaling Conventions referred to above is somewhat inconsistent with the purpose of providing for a comprehensive coverage and integrated system of environmental protection.

Annex III: a limited waste disposal and management regime

The approach of Annex III to the Protocol, on waste disposal and management, can generally be considered an improvement on the situation existing before, in that it tightens to some extent the obligations of the

---

[48] National self-interest, including territorial and economic aims, couched in environmental terms, was not alien to some negotiating strategies: for this see Redgwell, 'Current Developments: Antarctica', p. 981.

[49] Blay, 'New Trends', p. 389.

[50] *Ibid.*, p. 392.

[51] Pineschi, *La Protezione*, pp. 161–2.

[52] Orrego, *Antarctic Mineral Exploitation*, pp. 137–41.

Treaty parties.[53] This is particularly so insofar as it introduces the duty of waste management planning and training, prohibits the disposal of certain types of wastes, and requires the removal of other substances. A mild requirement of reporting is also provided for in the context of this regime.

However, several important limitations have been noted.[54] The Annex applies only to wastes produced after the Protocol enters into force, which could take a considerable time; in the meanwhile it can only be expected that signatories will comply voluntarily with these provisions, and in any event prior recommendations on the matter are still in force. More serious is that a number of provisions are excessively vague, relying on the very soft language of compliance 'to the maximum extent possible' or simply being entirely imprecise as to scope and extent.[55] Furthermore, many exceptions have been accepted, and enforcement again is mostly discretionary. National regulations will in some cases perform a useful supplementary role.

The effectiveness of this particular regime has also to be measured in relation to other relevant conventions. A very positive development is that the export of hazardous waste to Antarctica or its disposal has been prohibited under both the Basle[56] and the Bamako Conventions.[57] The London Dumping Convention, however, has not been mentioned at all in the context of the Antarctic regime, and some of the exceptions allowed under the latter do not appear to be quite compatible with the sense of the former.[58] If recent developments under these various conventions are taken into account, the Protocol appears to fall short of such evolving standards.

Annex IV: the contradictions of the regime on marine pollution

The shortcomings of the Protocol are still more evident in the field of marine pollution. The contribution is not so much related to substance

[53] Pineschi, *La Protezione*, pp. 309–17.
[54] *Ibid.*, pp. 319–25; Blay, 'New Trends', pp. 393–4.
[55] Blay, 'New Trends', p. 393.
[56] Basle Convention on the Control of Transboundary Movements of Hazardous Wastes and their Disposal, 22 March 1989, Art. 4, para. 6; reprinted in *International Legal Materials*, vol. XXVIII, 1989, pp. 657*ff*.
[57] Bamako Convention on the Ban of the Import into Africa and the Control of Transboundary Movement and Management of Hazardous Wastes within Africa; Organization of African Unity, 29 January 1991; see Art. 4, para. 3(1); reprinted in *International Legal Materials*, vol. XXX, 1991, pp. 773*ff*.
[58] On the discussion of exceptions see T. Scovazzi, 'The Application of the Antarctic System to the Protection of the Antarctic Marine Environment', in F. Francioni (ed.), *Inter-*

as to the cross-reference to one specific relevant treaty, namely MARPOL.[59] This in itself is not a negative approach, since it is more reasonable to build on existing rules than to develop an entirely separate regime which of necessity would be quite repetitive.[60] The problem lies in the fact that a Protocol is not at all necessary for this; recommendations of Consultative Meetings would be sufficient, as has already been the case in the past.

Several sources of pollution from ships are brought under the scope of the Protocol and Annex IV. To this extent there is indeed an effort to provide for a more comprehensive regime. It should also be noted that the MARPOL amendments relating to Antarctica point in a similar direction by providing that they shall apply to 'any' ship, thus being stricter than elsewhere; furthermore that facilities for the reception of sludge and other substances are to be available in ports used for departure to or arrival from Antarctica – steps of obvious importance in the effort to attain a comprehensive regime for environmental protection of maritime areas.[61] These improvements, however, had already been made by the Consultative Parties, quite independently of the negotiation of the Protocol.[62]

These comprehensive aims are contradicted by various other provisions of the Protocol.[63] In keeping with the sovereign immunity clause, warships and all government ships are excluded from the operation of the Protocol, even though most activities in Antarctica are carried out by ships of this kind. Silence is kept on the issue of liability and reparation of damage, and the 1969 Civil Liability Convention is totally ignored. Current negotiations on liability do not seem to point in an encouraging direction, either.

It should also be noted that various conventions of relevance for Antarctic marine areas are excluded from the scope of the Protocol, even in terms of environmental impact assessment. CCAMLR, the Seals Convention and the International Convention for the Regulation of Whaling fall

national Environmental Law for Antarctica (Milano: Guiffrè Editore, 1992), pp. 113–34, at p. 125.
[59] See generally *ibid.*, pp. 113–34.
[60] For a discussion on the application of maritime conventions to Antarctica see M. T. Infante, 'Maritime Conventions in Antarctica', *German Yearbook of International Law*, vol. 35, 1992, pp. 249–63.
[61] Scovazzi, 'The Application of the Antarctic System', pp. 127–8.
[62] The MARPOL amendments were promoted by a number of Antarctic Treaty Consultative Parties and adopted by the Marine Environment Protection Committee in resolution MEPC.42(30), on 16 November 1990. See Infante, 'Maritime Conventions', pp. 256–7.
[63] Blay, 'New Trends', p. 394.

within this exclusion. More serious is the fact that of the six conventions originally listed in Recommendation XV-4 and the Draft Protocol as to be complied with in view of their relevance for the protection of the marine environment, only MARPOL remained in the final text.[64] This is indeed a step backwards as compared with the regime existing before the adoption of the Protocol.

Since Annex IV does not in any way derogate from the specific rights and obligations of the parties to MARPOL under this treaty, it has been appropriately commented that the practical significance of Annex IV is to provide for minimal standards for non-parties to MARPOL operating in Antarctica or parties to MARPOL which have not accepted optional Annex V to it.[65]

Enforcement in relation to marine pollution has again been seen as weak, particularly in terms of existing restrictions on inspection.[66] A mechanism similar to that of the Paris Memorandum of Understanding on Port State Control might be advantageously introduced in the Antarctic context, so as to facilitate inspection by States whose ports are used for departure to or arrival from that continent.[67]

Annex V: Antarctic protected areas – the continuing evolution

The adoption of Annex V to the Protocol in 1991 has led to a reorganised, simplified and strengthened system of Antarctic protected areas, thus reaching a new stage in the evolution experienced under the Antarctic Treaty and specialised conventions.[68] Some problems of coordination remain in relation to prior designated areas or to the operation of special areas under other treaties, but these can be solved without great difficulty by the Consultative Meetings.

Specific obligations relating to the regulation of activities in these areas are combined with the jurisdictional authority of the parties over their nationals in Antarctica, thereby restricting to some extent the dis-

---

[64] Scovazzi, 'The Application of the Antarctic System', p. 127.
[65] *Ibid.*, p. 128.
[66] Infante, 'Maritime Conventions', pp. 256–7.
[67] Orrego, *Antarctic Mineral Exploitation*, pp. 282–3. On pollution accidents in the Antarctic marine environment see M. L. Canmann, 'Antarctic Oil Spills of 1989: A Review of the Application of the Antarctic Treaty and the New Law of the Sea to the Antarctic Environment', *Colorado Journal of International Environmental Law and Policy*, vol. 1, 1990, pp. 211–21.
[68] Recommendation XVI-10.

cretionality of such parties and providing for a common framework of control.[69] This is indeed a positive development. On the other hand, this approach was already evident in earlier recommendations of Consultative Meetings.[70]

The adoption of Annex V has also evidenced the advantages and flexibility of developing international environmental law by means of annexes or other such instruments attached to broadly conceived framework conventions.

REMOVING THE MINERALS ISSUE?

If the objective of providing for environmental protection by developing specific regimes has been attained only in part, it is not difficult to realise that the central question underlying the negotiations of the Protocol was the minerals issue. Such negotiations and the interplay of Articles 7 and 25 of this Protocol have been explained in detail elsewhere,[71] but the question that remains is whether the issue of mineral activities has been effectively dealt with.[72]

Protocol negotiations in this matter were characterised by a rather negative attitude. In the view of a number of Consultative Parties and environmental organisations, the question of mineral activities *per se* was tantamount to an unacceptable assault on the Antarctic environment, irrespective of the safeguards established under CRAMRA, the only legitimate alternative being that of a world park or similar concepts.[73] However legitimate this view might be, it assumed that any party interested in the regulation of prospective mining was opposed to environmental protection. But this was certainly not the case: first, CRAMRA was very

[69] Pineschi, *La Protezione*, pp. 191–3.
[70] Heap (ed.), *Handbook*, Part 3: 'The Antarctic Protected Area System', with particular reference to Recommendations XV-10 and XV-11, at pp. 3,501 and 3,601 respectively.
[71] Francioni, 'The Madrid Protocol', pp. 66–70; D. R. Rothwell, 'The Madrid Protocol and its Relationship with the Antarctic Treaty System', *Antarctic and Southern Ocean Law and Policy Occasional Papers*, no. 9, 1992, pp. 27–8; Orrego, 'The Protection', pp. 27–9.
[72] Rothwell, 'The Madrid Protocol and its Relationship', pp. 25–6.
[73] On the world park option see the discussion by B. P. Hebrer, 'Mining or World Park? A Politico-Economic Analysis of Alternative Land Use Regimes in Antarctica', *Natural Resources Journal*, vol. 31, no. 4, 1991, pp. 839–57. On the 'natural park' option and the related criticism of CRAMRA see A. Brown: 'New Proposal: The Natural Park', in Verhoeven *et al.* (eds.), *The Antarctic Environment*, pp. 97–101; and J. Berguño, 'The Antarctic Park: The Issue of Environmental Protection', in *ibid.*, pp. 103–7.

much on top of environmental concerns;[74] and next, following a well-established tradition in Antarctic affairs, there was the objective need of providing for a regulatory framework of potential activities in that continent before they actually began.

That negative attitude led to an artificial division between pro-mining states and environmentally concerned parties. Accordingly, the prohibition of Article 7 has been heralded as a 'significant coup for the anti-mining lobby in particular'[75] or as a 'victory for the environmentalist states and organizations'.[76] But it is precisely in adopting this attitude that the whole exercise became flawed. The objective merits of CRAMRA were ignored, even though it is one of the very few treaties to deal very stringently with environmental issues, including substantive standards, enforcement mechanisms and liability,[77] and it would not be entirely surprising that some states took advantage of the Protocol to do away with such a significant body of obligations and controls.

The most serious problem lies in the fact that the Protocol has created a legal vacuum that can provoke a dangerous situation for the Antarctic environment and the ATS as a whole. There can be little doubt that minerals are available in Antarctica, so it is entirely artificial to try to bury a question which can spring to life the very minute a deposit is found. Should this be the case, the Protocol would prove itself fundamentally unrealistic and its chances of survival would be virtually nil. Worse yet, with CRAMRA dismissed, there would be no regulatory framework whatsoever to deal with the matter; the environment would be basically unprotected and the ATS would face the greatest crisis of its lifetime.

In practice, of course, things may not be that dramatic, but such a scenario helps to illustrate the point that the minerals issue is not dead and that even CRAMRA might be revived once passions have abated. Furthermore, the need for the latter convention or some similar arrangement could very well arise in the eventuality that the Protocol might not come into force, or in any event once the fifty-year ban comes to an end, particularly if any state chooses to opt out under its clauses.[78] In all these

---

[74] W. M. Bush: 'The 1988 Wellington Convention: How Much Environmental Protection?', in Verhoeven *et al.* (eds.), *The Antarctic Environment*, pp. 69–83, p. 81.

[75] Blay, 'New Trends', p. 395.

[76] Francioni, 'The Madrid Protocol', p. 68.

[77] M. Poole, 'Liability for Environmental Damage in Antarctica', *Journal of Energy and Natural Resources Law*, vol. 10, 1992, pp. 246–66.

[78] W. M. Welch, 'The Antarctic Treaty System: Is it Adequate to Regulate or Eliminate the Environmental Exploitation of the Globe's Last Wilderness?', *Houston Journal of International Law*, vol. 14, 1992, pp. 597–657; R. E. Money, Jr, 'The Protocol on Environ-

circumstances the normative structure of the ATS would not be effective to deal appropriately with the problem in the absence of CRAMRA-type specific rules.

Thus it does not seem entirely unwarranted to suggest that the whole matter should be considered all over again – not to the detriment of those aspects of the Protocol which are useful and necessary but in particular to bring the minerals issue in line with both realism and the traditions of the Antarctic Treaty System.[79] However paradoxical it may seem, the end result would certainly be to the advantage of the Antarctic environment, since only then would the Protocol and related regulations become truly effective.

To that extent the Antarctic Treaty System will gain in added legitimacy in terms of its authority both to manage Antarctic affairs generally and to deal with environmental protection in particular. Nothing could be more harmful to the System's legitimacy than a failure on any of these counts.[80] Here it should be borne in mind that the Protocol has not put to rest international pressures nor the United Nations debate, where unfavourable attitudes towards the ATS have not disappeared but have only been reoriented. Neither has the Protocol abolished the potential interests of third parties to carry out activities in Antarctica.[81] For all such purposes legitimacy has to be kept intact, and this can be done only if solidly founded on effectiveness.

COMPLETING OR DEPLETING ACCOMMODATIONS?

The negotiation of the Protocol and its subsequent debate have prompted the question of whether this instrument has contributed to perfect the internal and external accommodation so characteristic of the Antarctic Treaty System, or whether it has sparked a process of disagreement and criticism which could lead to the deterioration of this important achievement.

---

mental Protection to the Antarctic Treaty: Maintaining a Legal Regime', *Emory International Law Review*, vol. 7, 1993, pp. 163–95.

[79] On the view that the problem of Antarctic mineral resource activities has not been resolved but merely postponed, see Redgwell, 'Current Developments: Antarctica', p. 981.

[80] On the question of the Antarctic Treaty System's authority and legitimacy, see D. R. Rothwell, 'The Antarctic Treaty: 1961–1991 and Beyond', *Sydney Law Review*, vol. 14, no. 62, 1992, pp. 62–85.

[81] S. T. Madsen, 'A Certain False Security: The Madrid Protocol to the Antarctic Treaty', *Colorado Journal of International Environmental Law and Policy*, vol. 4, 1993, pp. 458–83.

Internal accommodations

The successful completion of the negotiation process of the Protocol is in itself a pertinent expression of accommodation within the System. However, there are two fundamental issues which came to the fore during or as a result of these negotiations.

The first concerns who will manage the Antarctic and the Protocol itself from now on. The traditional and fundamental role of scientists in Antarctic management had been well integrated with that of the Consultative Parties and more recently with the role of Antarctic managers. But as a result of the Protocol this role of scientists, and even that of political or bureaucratic managers, has been challenged by environmentalists. On occasions the latter may be a respected part of the scientific community, but more often than not this will not be the case. Opposing views on this became quite evident during the negotiations, but it will be during the process of implementation and monitoring that these tensions are most likely to become serious. This scenario is not at all helpful for internal accommodation, and might lead to its deterioration. Consultative Parties should make quite clear that science is Antarctica's most fundamental value.

The second issue concerning internal accommodation is more troublesome and could have fundamental implications for the future of the System. It has become quite apparent that for a few Consultative Parties the issue of the demise of CRAMRA was founded not so much on environmental concerns but on the purpose of preventing a regulatory and institutional model which could erode traditional views about territorial sovereignty in the area.[82] To this extent the environment became a useful pretext. This means that for those countries the question of implementation of the Protocol will be of secondary importance; in any event it will be done in such a manner as to strengthen sovereignty. In turn, such an attitude will contrast with that of other Consultative Parties interested in genuine implementation, who would seek solutions based more on international approaches than on sovereignty. This dual-track frame of intentions and policies is not helpful either for the purposes of the internal accommodation.

---

[82] C. Redgwell, 'Environmental Protection in Antarctica: The 1991 Protocol', *International and Comparative Law Quarterly*, vol. 43, 1994, pp. 599–634, p. 634.

External accommodations

As mentioned above, the Protocol has not done away with external pressures but only ensured their reorientation for a limited period of time. External accommodation on this point does not appear entirely genuine since it is dependent on two basic questions: the effectiveness of its implementation and the possibility of continuously meeting the expectations it created in international organisations and other pressure groups.

Effectiveness is so far subject to an important question mark which can be answered satisfactorily only if an important effort is carried out by the parties to solve the many problems still pending. Meeting the expectations of pressure groups will be extremely difficult for three reasons: first, because the Protocol as an environmental-protection model falls short of what has already been achieved in comparable fields under international law; second, because it is unlikely that environmentalists will take control of the management of Antarctica as one was to an extent led to believe; and third, and most importantly, because if sovereignty proves to be the value underlying this scheme, international acceptance will quickly come to an end.

The external accommodation of the System has been in essence based on its ability to avert conflict and anticipate solutions. This is what the Protocol will need to prove, not excluding its ability to deal with the minerals issue.

CONCLUDING REMARKS: A POSITIVE BUT LIMITED CONTRIBUTION

Has the Protocol provided for an effective and comprehensive regime of environmental protection as compared with the situation existing prior to its adoption? This we can answer in the affirmative, albeit with a considerable degree of caution. Beyond the formal aspects of making available a better organised set of rules, which contrasts of course with the earlier dispersion, there is a contribution of substance of a rather limited nature. Several provisions relating to such contribution can be traced back to various recommendations, and in a few instances there has been a step backwards in terms of the extent of obligations. On the other hand, it is also fair to conclude that most, if not all, of the new developments would have equally taken place under the evolving action of the Consultative Meetings, independent of the adoption of a Protocol. This is not to say that the Protocol is not a useful instrument, for indeed it is, but simply to put its contribution in the correct perspective, which falls much shorter than its proclaimed virtues.

Accordingly, the Consultative Parties will have to undertake the task of completing this regime in order to make it truly effective and bring it into line with current developments in international environmental law. Although doubts have been expressed about their ability to do so, the record certainly shows otherwise, particularly in the recent past.

To this end the effectiveness of the regime will have to be perfected, particularly in terms of ensuring the proper internal accommodation. Moreover, the dimension of comprehensiveness will have at some point to undergo a serious reconsideration – first to achieve solutions which are already at hand in international environmental law; and above all to deal with the minerals issue, which has thus far been artificially ignored under the Protocol. On this basis, then, external accommodation can also be properly safeguarded for the future.

8

The regulation of Antarctic tourism: a study in regime effectiveness

RICHARD A. HERR

INTRODUCTION

Contrasts are among the most commonly used and powerful of mechanisms for making comparative judgments. Bob Dylan exploited this device ironically when he sang: 'There's no success like failure; and . . . failure's no success at all.' Often, however, we can know what success is only by contrasting it with failure. This logic of contrasts applies also to the assessment of regime effectiveness. In order for a regime to be deemed 'effective' it must be capable of being deemed ineffective. As argued in Chapter 1, when benchmarks of regime success are identified we also have the thresholds for measuring regime failure. Parenthetically, it is noteworthy that this understanding not only affects the assessment of regimes but also cuts to the core of defining regimes.[1] Thus, in assessing the effectiveness of the Antarctic regime's capacity to modify the behaviour of parties interested in Antarctic tourism, we necessarily must be able to contrast the effective modification of participant behaviour with the failure to modify behaviour or, even worse, produce outcomes away from the preferred direction.[2]

---

[1] Regime scholars such as Roger Tooze and Arild Underdal have recently canvassed the definitional difficulties which arise from both the empirical and the descriptive approaches to identifying regimes. See R. Tooze, 'Regimes and International Co-operation' in A. J. R. Groom and P. Taylor (eds.), *Frameworks for International Co-operation* (London: Pinter, 1990), pp. 227–40; and A. Underdal, 'The Concept of Regime "Effectiveness" ', *Cooperation and Conflict*, vol. 27, no. 3, 1992, p. 204. I have accepted the empirical approach since the descriptive approach tends to engender a tautological linkage between regimes and regime effectiveness. In essence, we see the relationship between regime definition and regime effectiveness in terms of the distinction between justification and vindication. To assess the effectiveness of a regime, it is necessary that regimes be defined in a way which allows them to be vindicated by their performance not merely justified by their definition.
[2] This nominal definition needs to be operationalised to be fully useful. However, given the high degree of contextual content inherent in any operationalisation of the phrase

203

This chapter is concerned with one specific area of regime effectiveness: that of the Antarctic Treaty regime with regard to the regulation of south polar tourism. After examining the perceived need for the regulation of Antarctic tourism, we survey the range of actors associated with this issue area. The interaction of these actors provides an understanding of the extent to which the increasing attention being paid to tourism can be regarded as a coherent attempt to create a sub-regime[3] within the context of the regime of the Antarctic Treaty System (ATS). Central to this assessment is the degree to which the parent regime has taken responsibility for south polar tourism as an issue area under its own processes. It is argued in this chapter that only latterly has the requisite degree of regime responsibility emerged to consider Antarctic tourism the subject of a coherent sub-regime. This development is being strengthened by the call for further regulation of tourism through an annex to the 1991 Protocol on Environmental Protection to the Antarctic Treaty (also known as the Madrid Protocol). Thus in assessing how effective the ATS has been in regulating international behaviour with regard to Antarctic tourism, we are necessarily drawn to a consideration of the broader issue of how regimes can limit their responsibilities as well as expand and strengthen the ambit of their coverage.

THE PROBLEM OF ANTARCTIC TOURISM

Commercial travel to Antarctica was proposed as early as 1910 (in the first blush of a public enthusiasm for the 'heroic age' of exploration) but was not to become a continuing feature of Antarctic affairs until and from 1956.[4] Nevertheless, the fact that commercial tourism began three years before the signing of the Antarctic Treaty may be an important legitimating factor within the ATS. Tourism enjoyed an existence prior to the Treaty, and yet was not made a subject of the Treaty. Moreover, this period of regulatory *laissez faire* or indifference was to last nearly a decade from the beginning of commercial tourism until the ATS turned its atten-

---

'modify the behaviour of parties interested in an issue in a direction desired by most participants', it is hoped that the development of these operational indicators throughout the remainder of this chapter will make its usage clear.

[3] A sub-regime is defined here as a semi-autonomous set of coherent rules for the management of a specific but subordinate issue area within the framework of a regime.

[4] R. J. Reich, 'The Development of Antarctic Tourism', *Polar Record*, vol. 20, no. 126, 1980, pp. 205–11.

tion formally to this activity in 1966.[5] The reasons why the ATS decided to turn its collective attention to the issue of tourism from 1966 is important in understanding what issues of responsibility the members of the regime saw as being raised by the question of commercial tourism in Antarctica. What was the problem which the regime sought to solve?

The most commonly asserted explanation for the perception of a problem is the growing number of visitors over the years since 1966 – particularly in the past decade. However, this measure is patently simplistic and methodologically inelegant as it assumes too much about the significance of raw numbers. Even interpretation of this indicator involves risks. For example, if the researcher wishes, commercial tourism can easily be made to loom as a larger and larger issue for the Antarctic regime (and thus justifying, perhaps, some form of regime response) on the basis of the growing tourist numbers. Recently, two such relational measures have been used to justify a policy concern. It has been noted that the total number of tourists has now grown to exceed the number of scientists working in Antarctica;[6] the rate of increase even appears to be continuing to accelerate over the past five or six years despite a global recession.[7] Second, in dollar terms, the value of the tourism industry makes it second only to fisheries as the most lucrative commercial use of Antarctic resources.[8]

Using indicators such as these tends to make a *prima facie* case for the relative importance of tourism within the Antarctic regime, although their intrinsic significance to the ATS regime is still open to interpretation. It is scarcely axiomatic that, as such, increasing numbers of tourists makes for a problem which demands Antarctic regime management. For example, while the absolute number of tourists visiting Antarctica in one year may now exceed the number of scientists, standardising this indicator by incorporating the hours, days or weeks per person spent in Antarctica dramatically shifts the total level of human impact firmly away from tourism and back into the category of science. Further, the economic value

[5] P. J. Beck, 'Regulating One of the Last Tourism Frontiers: Antarctica', *Applied Geography*, vol. 10, 1990, p. 344.
[6] D. J. Enzenbacher, 'Tourists in Antarctica: Numbers and Trends', *Polar Record*, vol. 28, no. 164, 1992, pp. 17–22.
[7] D. J. Enzenbacher, 'Antarctic Tourism: 1991/92 Season Activity', *Polar Record*, vol. 29, no. 170, 1993, pp. 240–2.
[8] Interestingly, there appears to be no agency able to provide precise figures for the annual value of tourism or fisheries in the Antarctic. The relative placement of the two activities here is based on the author's assessment following discussions with CCAMLR and IAATO officials.

of tourism as an enterprise is similarly deceptive. It would be almost impossible for tourism to rank other than first or second in a listing of the commercial exploitation of Antarctic resources. The exploitation of Antarctic resources for other uses such as weather forecasting and the like are not currently valued as commercial activities whatever their worth to the private sector and therefore cannot be incorporated easily into an economic assessment.[9]

Locating Antarctic tourism in the broader context of tourism as a global human activity further reduces the apparent significance of this activity even more. Antarctic tourism is not and never has been a commercially substantial industry. Indeed, the scale of the Antarctic industry can be made to look exceptionally modest. Using a Tasmanian example for comparison, the entire number of commercial tourists to Antarctica during the 1990–1 season (4,842)[10] was less than two-thirds the number (7,689)[11] to visit the tiny, historic site of Maria Island, the least-visited tourist destination in Tasmania, the smallest of the Australian states, during 1991. Given the modest size of the numbers involved and even allowing for the usually high costs per passenger (perhaps US$10–15,000 average per person), the total dollars generated by the industry makes it very much a small niche market for a few operators in terms of global tourism. On balance, the level of Antarctic commercial tourism makes it both absolutely and comparatively minuscule by virtually any industry standard for this activity, and thus scarcely an obvious candidate for detailed international regulation on commercial grounds.

Clearly the problem of Antarctic tourism is not primarily one of managing competitive commercial aspirations. Given the absence of a substantial economic interest in Antarctic tourism, it might be suspected that the problem of Antarctic tourism has fallen to the ATS by default; that south polar tourism is simply too small to be of interest to any actor other than those whose interests were touched tangentially by their involvement in the Antarctic Treaty. As attractive as this 'responsibility by default' explanation might appear, it is clearly inadequate. An Antarctic regime involvement, however marginal, requires that we locate some regime interests in dealing with tourism to explain utilising regime resources in

---

[9] For a cogent example of the difficulties in attributing dollar values to economic activities in Antarctica, see M. Wilder, *Antarctica: An Economic History of the Last Continent* (Department of Economic History, University of Sydney, 1992).

[10] Enzenbacher, 'Tourists in Antarctica', p. 17.

[11] Figure obtained through the kind assistance of the Tasmanian Department of Tourism, Sport and Recreation.

this issue area. This is all the more true when we recognise that the Antarctic Treaty operates intrinsically on the assumption that activities are permissible unless prohibited.

The members of the Antarctic Treaty System do have a general interest in preserving and enhancing the capacity of the regime to meet its primary objectives. This commitment tends to unite the ATS membership in maintaining the internal coherence of the regime and in deflecting external criticism. Both these considerations have played a role in the involvement of the ATS in the regulation of Antarctic tourism. Protection both of the central objectives of the regime and of the international image of the ATS does much to explain greater sensitivity to Antarctic tourism than might have been expected in terms of the activity's global significance. This also helps to explain, however, the low-key reaction of the ATS to the problem of Antarctic tourism until recently. A regime-centric line of inquiry therefore does not necessarily demonstrate that the issue has been brought within the ambit of the ATS; merely that the issue impacted on identifiable regime interests and thus was able to provoke a regime response.

The distinction between regime responsibility for an issue and a regime response to the issue is important to understanding the evolution of tourism as a policy area within the ATS. No system is perfectly static, so the perception of a problem will vary over time. If the matter is sufficiently long-lived and acquires sufficient gravity, the members of a regime will extend its coverage to new areas once regarded as marginal. Indeed, we would argue that this is precisely what has happened with regard to Antarctic tourism. The ATS perception of the problem of Antarctic tourism has been transformed since 1966. As will be developed further below, initially tourism was regarded as a minor inconvenience to be contained. Two lines of development then emerged which were substantially to alter ATS perceptions of the tourism issue. The ATS itself came under pressure from the late 1970s to broaden its membership and thus to extend the range of actors and interests represented within its decision-making processes. Not altogether unrelated to this development was a higher and broader policy profile which in turn so promoted the public's interest in things Antarctic that tourism became a substantial commercial activity in Antarctica during the 1980s. These two developments converged in the late 1980s to elevate the problem of Antarctic tourism to a level of sufficient magnitude to require more detailed regime attention and, possibly, even primary management through regime processes.

THE ACTORS IN ANTARCTIC TOURISM

Because tourism was not a central issue for the first quarter-century of the Antarctic Treaty regime, the relevant actors were few in number and limited in interest. For the first five years from 1956 to the Treaty's entry into force, these actors might be described fairly as the states involved in Antarctica, the tour providers (a category encompassing all elements of the commercial industry from the tour operators to the travel agents) and the tourists. From 1961, these actors were augmented by the Antarctic Treaty's constituent elements, particularly the Antarctic Treaty Consultative Parties (ATCPs), and associated bodies such as the Scientific Committee on Antarctic Research (SCAR). Much more latterly, inter-governmental organisations such as the World Tourism Organisation (WTO) and non-governmental organisations which encompassed both industry umbrella groups such as the International Association of Antarctic Tour Operators (IAATO) and the Pacific Asia Travel Association (PATA) and environmental bodies such as the Antarctic and Southern Ocean Coalition (ASOC) have been added to the roster of actors with a direct involvement in Antarctic tourism.

While the broad categories of interested parties may appear fairly clear, there can be no ready assumption that each category is easily defined or indeed even coherent. For example, if the category 'operators' is taken to mean those who offer travel services for a fee, then we must include not only national logistics organisations which opportunistically sell 'spare' berths and seats but also, increasingly, private yacht owners who provide fee-for-service access to Antarctica which can approximate a regular commercial charter arrangement.[12] Similarly, it is difficult to derive a precise definition of an Antarctic 'tourist'. The ATS has grouped tourists and non-governmental expeditioners together as a composite category even though the regime's language does indicate that the two are distinguishable.[13] A recent Australian parliamentary inquiry further extended the definitional morass when it focused on tourism as an activity rather than on the tourist as specific category. It identified the off-duty recreation of official expeditioners as tourism and so blurred even the in-principle distinction which the Treaty was prepared to make between scientific personnel and others.[14]

[12] Enzenbacher, 'Antarctic Tourism', p. 241.
[13] J. A. Heap (ed.), *Handbook of the Antarctic Treaty System*, 8th ed. (Washington, DC: US Department of State, 1994), pp. 2,287–300.
[14] Australia, House of Representatives, Standing Committee on Environment, Recreation and the Arts, *Tourism in Antarctica*, May 1989.

Whatever the definitional criteria, the range of interested actors has broadened over recent years, a fact significant as more than merely an indicator of the growing volume of Antarctic tourism. The increasing diversity of actors demonstrates both that tourism is impacting on a greater number of interests and that the regime reaction toward regulation is provoking a defensively pluralist response as new actors seek to influence the regime's policy-makers. The accumulation of active participants in the ATS policy processes for regulating tourism has probably made this policy area the most complete or well rounded of all the issue areas currently being addressed by the Antarctic regime.

As important as the diversification of actors has been in 'normalising' the policy process of tourism in the ATS, one effect of this process has been to accentuate the significant asymmetries in the capacity of the various actors to influence regime processes. Antarctic tourism was ignored by the regime for its first five years, in large part because the regime *qua* regime had no interest in challenging the dominance of member states with a stake in the issue. They were left to regulate the very minor airborne traffic, through traditional state-based mechanisms. The advent of commercial cruising in 1966 upset this balance albeit only slightly. A consensus was reached, despite the objections of Argentina and Chile that tourism was not an appropriate topic for the Consultative Parties' attention,[15] that some collective interests were raised which should not be left solely to the discretion of individual states. Yet, even in taking this decision, the regime's response was quite restrained. The appearance of tourism on the 1966 ATCM agenda did not immediately convert the issue into a regime responsibility leading to direct regulation.

Given the largely advisory nature of the ATS process, it would be difficult perhaps to suggest that any arrangement other than one centred on states could be utilised by this regime. However, as Beck reminds us, there were options available to the regime to elevate its level of responsibility on the question of Antarctic tourism.[16] It was a lack of political will at the regime level rather than a lack of opportunity which explains the modest role played by the ATS regime relative to individual states during this early period. The ATS thus abdicated to the state – and not necessarily *member* states, although the fact that major industry participants were based in ATS states undoubtedly reduced the pressure on the regime to take collective action. States with an interest in Antarctic tourism

[15] Beck, 'Regulating One of the Last Tourism Frontiers', p. 344.
[16] P. J. Beck, 'Managing Antarctic Tourism: A Front-Burner Issue', *Annals of Tourism Research*, vol. 21, no. 2, pp. 375–86.

remained the key actors as far as the regulation of Antarctic tourism was concerned, partially on the grounds of convenience for the regime – there was no consensus on a need for regime management of the issue – and partially on the grounds of prudence – the states involved appeared able to deal with the issue effectively.

From the operators' perspective, the dominance of states as actors in the regulation of Antarctic tourism seemed to pose no terrors for the nascent industry. On the contrary, the industry was undoubtedly advantaged by the relaxed regulatory environment and by its access to individual ATCP states. Indeed, the help of a number of ATCP states was vital to the emergent industry's early success. Access to stations, advice and information and the availability of emergency assistance or rescue were among the more important of the significant contributions ATCP states have made to the Antarctic tourism industry.[17] Nevertheless, while such assistance was made available within the guidelines of the ATS, it was not provided on the basis of a collective decision to assist or promote the growth of the industry. Rather, individual participating states offered support in response to individual requests. The intimate relationship between operators and national governments appears to have worked so well from the industry's vantage point that the operators found no reason to organise or seek to participate in regulatory processes beyond the state level until the *locus* of regulation began to move out of the state arena and into the regime arena at the turn of this decade.

Thus, for more than three decades from 1956, national policy and laws played the paramount role in, and were the most important influence on, the regulation of Antarctic tourism. The two principal gateway states – Chile and Argentina – occupied a critical position in the early years, as their generally sympathetic and supportive attitudes allowed commercial tourism to establish a niche for itself in Antarctica. The national and sub-national laws of other gateway states – particularly Australia, New Zealand and South Africa – similarly became significant influences favouring the growth and development of Antarctic tourism in subsequent years. A second basis for effective state control of Antarctic tourism centred on the supply of tourists. The United States, not a gateway state but the primary source of tourists, played this card from the passage of an Antarc-

---

[17] Parenthetically, it is worth noting for those who are sceptical of the industry's sensitivity to non-compulsory guidelines, these forms of assistance are indeed so valuable that threat of their withdrawal overhangs the industry as an exceedingly credible form of implied sanction against abuse of ATCPs' interests by tour operators. See Beck, 'Managing Antarctic Tourism'.

tic Conservation Act in 1978.[18] A third arrow in the states' quiver was the control of the tour operators providing the service. Again, US legislation has been particularly significant since, until very recently, virtually all the major tour operators have been based in North America.[19] The recent growth in Europe-based operators marks a change from the past in that previously non-American operators tended to carry American passengers but the European operators are carrying a majority of European passengers.[20]

TOWARD REGIME RESPONSIBILITY FOR ANTARCTIC TOURISM

Perhaps one of the first serious straws in the wind that regime attitudes to Antarctic tourism were changing appeared in 1985. Ian Nicholson, then an Assistant Secretary in the Australian Department of Foreign Affairs with responsibilities for Antarctic matters, examined the need for a comprehensive regime response to Antarctic tourism during a symposium held at the Institute of International Law in West Germany in September of that year.[21] Nicholson argued that increased numbers of visitors to Antarctica would eventually require the Antarctic Treaty system to take decisive action to establish a formal regulatory responsibility. Nicholson included speculation on the types of legal instruments and management procedures which might be required. In particular he recognised that safety aspects, as much as environmental management, would be key issues. Nicholson's foresight was perhaps ill-timed as the ATS was then fully preoccupied with the Convention on the Regulation of Antarctic Mineral Resource Activities Treaty (CRAMRA). Nonetheless, his assessment contained most of the elements which were to inform the later ATCP interests in pursuing the development of a more coherent regime-based approach to the regulation of Antarctic tourism.

Three specific factors explain the Antarctic regime's early reluctance to embrace tourism as a matter for direct regime regulation. The number of travellers involved in Antarctic tourism was modest, the number of actors limited and the regime's central interest was primarily that of maintaining the 1959 Treaty. It may well have been dysfunctional, in terms

---

[18] Beck, 'Managing Antarctic Tourism'; Enzenbacher, 'Antarctic Tourism', p. 241.
[19] Beck, 'Managing Antarctic Tourism'.
[20] Enzenbacher, 'Antarctic Tourism'.
[21] I. E. Nicholson, 'Antarctic Tourism: The Need for a Legal Regime?', in R. Wolfrum (ed.), *Antarctic Challenge II: Conflicting Interests, Cooperation, Environmental Protection, Economic Development* (Berlin: Duncker & Humblot, 1986), pp. 191–203.

of regime effectiveness, for the Antarctic regime to attempt to extend its regulatory responsibilities to tourism in the years prior to the middle of the 1980s. The availability of effective state-based alternative mechanisms congenial to the Antarctic regime made the gains from extended regulatory involvement too small and the risks of internal division too great. Thus, the initial ATS response to the development of Antarctic tourism was negative and containing: intended to limit the possible adverse effects of Antarctic tourism rather than to promote it for any recognised positive benefits. The primary concern of the ATS members was to ensure that their core regime interests in Antarctica were not put at risk by the activities of the tourists or the private operators providing the service.

Until the early 1980s, these interests were defined in terms of the Antarctic Treaty's two core values – security and science. No specific security concerns were identified in tourism, so this core value of the Treaty was not a factor in the early ATS perceptions of Antarctic tourism. The Consultative Parties recognised that with the advent of commercial seaborne tourism from 1966, however, substantial private travel into the region could threaten their science programmes in important ways. Unannounced visits could distract a station from its work at a vital time. Tourists unfamiliar with the needs of the scientists might make irresponsible demands which could have been avoided, had the visitors had clearer instructions on the terms of visitation. This could be more readily avoided also if the Consultative Parties shared knowledge among themselves on planned visits. Tours led by inexperienced operators or guides could involve dangerous situations which would require emergency rescue or assistance. Not only would such emergencies take personnel and equipment away from scientific projects, the costs would reduce already stretched budgets. Of course, to give weight to the Consultative Parties' concerns it was necessary that all non-governmental activity in the Antarctic accept and be familiar with the operation of the Antarctic Treaty and the decisions made under its authority.

Over the years, guidelines on each of these matters were developed to preserve the Consultative Parties' fundamental interests under the Treaty. In 1967, IV ATCM passed Recommendation IV-7 in three parts to deal with tourism, two of which were intended to protect the interests of the participating states' scientific stations in Antarctica and the third to provide a modest sanction for failure to accept the authority of the Antarctic Treaty. Over the next decade and a half, the range of separately identified concerns expanded to nine[22] but all were substantially concerned with

---

[22] Heap (ed.), *Handbook*.

measures to avoid disruption to ATCP science, to maintain the authority of the Treaty and to minimise the impact of tourism on the environment. These recommendations did not seek to regulate tourism but rather to assist members to establish and maintain guidelines in common. The sanctions, if any, would be applied by individual states through their own national processes or by the voluntary compliance of the tour operators and, through the operators, by the individual tourists.

Thus clearly, the regime's initial involvement was largely to provide guidance to member states on the regime's interests and advice on appropriate responses to protect these interests. The early recommendations to member governments by ATCMs from 1966 illustrate how limited were the regime's collective aspirations as an actor in the regulation of Antarctic tourism. According to Beck, the concerns of the ATS from 1966 to 1979 could be grouped under five categories:

1 promoting adherence to ATS measures;
2 safeguarding scientific research;
3 making available prior information;
4 avoiding adverse environmental impacts; and
5 encouraging responsible and organised tourism.[23]

While accepting Beck's typology, we would note that all the nineteen provisions of the five ATCM recommendations on tourism[24] were substantially concerned with protecting ATCP science and with maintaining the authority of the Treaty which promoted this science. Even the desire to minimise the impact of tourism on the environment appears more to safeguard scientific values than an intrinsic concern for the environment. Thus, the regime's early role was to advise member states of possible risks to their mutual interests, rather than to attempt to develop a collective responsibility for regulating this industry.

Although it could be argued that Consultative Parties accepted tourism as a legitimate use of Antarctica at least from the first reference to it in 1967,[25] tourism was not warmly embraced as an activity by the ATS. Indeed, given the formal aims of the Antarctic Treaty it was improbable that regime members would have seriously contemplated giving active encouragement to Antarctic tourism. There appears to have been no sus-

---

[23] Beck, 'Managing Antarctic Tourism', p. 378.
[24] Recommendations IV-27 (1966); VI-7 (1970); VII-4 (1972); VIII-9 (1975); and X-8 (1979).
[25] Recommendation IV-27 does not state explicitly that the ATCPs accepted tourism but, by providing for the more appropriate conduct of tourist visits, implied a recognition of the activity.

tained discussion of mobilising the infrastructure of organised tourism to assist the scientific objectives of the regime, or of the political benefits of a more informed and supportive domestic constituency which tourism might generate. Nor does it appear that regime member states considered going beyond hortatory guidelines to actually managing the industry by issuing licences, establishing visitor quotas, levying royalties or similar in order to ensure the success of a sustainable industry.

The 1980s brought two critical changes to the ATS. The first was a heightened sensitivity to external criticism for being too closed and exclusive a 'club'. It may seem unusual that a regional association should be willing to accept criticism for having a restrictive membership but the unusual character of the ATS as a regional regulatory regime and its membership of predominantly wealthy, industrialised states made it vulnerable to such criticism. The Third World quest for a New International Economic Order in the 1970s and the success of the Third United Nations Conference on the Law of the Sea (UNCLOS III) in inscribing the concept of 'common heritage' on the international agenda were telling factors. This sensitivity led to a dramatically rapid expansion of the regime's membership particularly among Third World states. The second substantive change in the regime concerned a significant amendment of the regime's core values with the installation of protection of the Antarctic environment as co-equal with security and science as objectives of the Treaty. This development centred on the rejection of CRAMRA and its replacement with the Madrid Protocol. Ironically, although the two processes of change began with antithetical objectives (one to gain wider access to the resources of Antarctica, the other to reduce the exploitation of Antarctic resources), by some international extension of Murphy's Law, the two came ultimately to be associated through the Madrid Protocol in a manner which approximated the thirty-year review which few Consultative Parties ever expected to be held.

These two critical shifts in the regime's established routine altered fundamentally both the course of Antarctic tourism (at least for the medium term) and ATS perceptions of its significance as a policy area. The controversy over the exclusiveness of the regime's membership not only brought in new state members but contributed to the diversification of participants by significantly broadening the category of observers, especially among the non-state actors.[26] While the new members certainly

---

[26] R. A. Herr and B. W. Davis, 'Antarctica and Non-State Actors: The Question of Legitimacy', *IARP Publication Series* (Lysaker: Fridtjof Nansen Institute, 1992), no. 4.

diversified the interests of the regime, there is no real evidence that this contributed directly to the upgrading of tourism as an issue. Indeed, the problem of Antarctic tourism has been most keenly debated among the 'old' membership rather than being an issue for post-1982 members. Nonetheless the controversy which arose in the wake of the 'exclusive club' charge did sensitise the regime to external criticism including that of the NGOs. And the NGO agenda in the early 1980s was driven by a desire to preserve the Antarctic environment.

The twin influences of a more diverse set of participating actors and the growing centrality of environmentalism to ATS priorities worked almost as a positive feedback loop in development of Antarctic tourism during the 1980s. Increasing numbers of people wanted to see the world's last great wilderness, and those who saw it advocated its protection. The regime itself became more of a public issue, and the intensifying controversy heightened the international saliency of Antarctica – thus deepening the popular demand for an opportunity to see Antarctica. Moreover, many tourists who saw national research facilities first-hand complained to policy-makers that the regime was not operating to protect the fragile polar environment as fully as they would wish. These sentiments tended to undermine faith in the state-based mechanism for regulating Antarctic matters but not always in favour of regime-based processes. The world park or United Nations alternatives appealed to many environmentalists.

Under such pressure, the ATS sought increasingly in the late 1980s to deflect criticism and to rebuild confidence in the regime. Whether it was necessary for CRAMRA to be sacrificed or whether the minerals convention could have been saved while restoring support for the ATS is now a moot point.[27] Something like the Madrid Protocol was as certain as 'death and taxes'; the extraordinary speed with which the Protocol was drafted and signed is ample evidence of the force of history at the end of the 1980s on providing a regime guarantee for environmental protection of Antarctica. And, in the gathering together of issues to ensure 'comprehensive' environmental protection, the ATS policy-makers turned serious attention to the development of a direct regulatory mechanism for Antarctic tourism as a sub-regime in its own right. The Madrid Protocol added five sub-regimes to the Treaty – through annexes dealing with: environmental impact assessment; the protection of fauna and flora; waste disposal and management; marine waste control; and maintenance

---

[27] For the flavour of this debate at a point when the issue was still perceived to be open, see Herr *et al.*, *Antarctica's Future: Continuity or Change?*

of protected areas – but failed to gain a consensus on an Antarctic tourism annex. This did not deter the proponents of such a sub-regime, and it has been discussed further at both subsequent ATCMs.

Chapter 12 in this volume surveys these post-Madrid proposals and counter-proposals for an Antarctic tourism sub-regime in some detail. Therefore this debate is not recapitulated here. Nonetheless, it is important to the present argument to note that the debate over the past two years has revolved substantially around the degree of responsibility that the regime was to take for tourism. ATS members such as the United States have argued against a specific sub-regime (through an annex to the Protocol) in part because they perceive the objectives of the Protocol to be primarily to give environmental protection co-equal status with the 1959 Treaty values. Thus, they have tended to regard the issue of tourism to be substantially one of human impact on Antarctica, and as such to be managed through the regime mechanisms in very much the same way that other human impacts are moderated by the Protocol. Others, however, such as France, Italy and Chile, appear to regard tourism as a suspect (or at least a marginal) activity which ought to be distinguished from all other activities and so subject to its own set of industry-specific regulations through a Protocol annex. This latter approach implies a much higher level of responsibility by the regime *qua* regime and might not be too far removed from the Seals Convention and CCAMLR if such an annex were to develop a sophisticated management structure.

Either of these two outcomes will extend significantly the responsibility overtly taken by the regime for the regulation of tourism. Even the minimalist position of relying on the environmental safeguards of the Protocol has become explicitly linked to regime responsibility by the debate of the past two to three years within the ATS. Were events to demonstrate that the present Protocol and its annexes (and likely annexes, in the case of the proposed liability annex) are deficient for protecting regime interests *vis-à-vis* Antarctic tourism, it is highly probable that in the current climate, regime members would take further steps to deal with tourism.

SUB-REGIME OR *STATUS QUO*?

Although debate on the need for a coherent sub-regime to deal with Antarctic tourism is very genuinely unfinished, there are reasons for suspecting that something less than a sub-regime will result. History is an important factor here. Today we can only speculate on what might have happened had the ATS embraced responsibility for the regulation of tourism before the industry blossomed fully. The delay of nearly thirty years, however, has had a number of effects which now appear to militate against the development of a sub-regime to regulate specifically this activity. Two of these may prove of overriding significance in the years ahead. First, the state interests and regulatory mechanisms entrenched since 1956 may not be easily dismantled or abandoned.[28] Second, the emergence of an internationally organised industry body to articulate and protect the operators' interests will tend to produce a more 'open' policy process, with the industry as capable of influencing regime regulations as being influenced by them.

The continuing importance of the state sector in the regulation of Antarctic tourism can be illustrated by reference to the Australian experience in recent years.[29] Although a gateway state, Australia has not been a substantial actor in Antarctic tourism. Nevertheless, by 1987 the public's imagination had been so captured by the beauty and significance of Antarctica that Australian entrepreneurs saw an opportunity to participate in the tourism generated by this global enthusiasm. Such aspirations were still speculative when the national Parliament, motivated by rumours of putative industry interest in the Australian Antarctic Territory (AAT), opened hearings into the need for regulating an Australian involvement in Antarctic tourism. With some historical irony, it was in May 1989 that the House of Representatives' Standing Committee on Environment, Recreation and the Arts tabled its report, entitled *Tourism in Antarctica*.[30]

This extensive review covered not only the existing and potential Australian involvement in Antarctic tourism but also the experience of Antarctic tourism elsewhere. The Committee made fourteen principal rec-

[28] The apparently anomalous support by Chile for the French position on a tourism annex may not be as contradictory to this proposition as may appear at first glance. Personalities rather than national interest have been suggested as an explanation for the apparent anomaly.

[29] While this case study is offered largely on the grounds of familiarity to the author, it is scarcely unusual among those states with a direct interest in Antarctic tourism. See, for examples from elsewhere, Beck, 'Managing Antarctic Tourism', pp. 379–80.

[30] Australia, House of Representatives, Standing Committee on Environment, Recreation and the Arts, *Tourism in Antarctica*, May 1989. The irony arises from the fact that this was the same month in which the Australian government decided to abandon its support for CRAMRA. Thus, on one hand, a part of the Australian state was moving to support collective regime responsibilities in one area, while on the other hand another organ appeared to be moving unilaterally to challenge a regime consensus.

ommendations, including three major policy proposals, bearing on Australian regulation of its own participation in the Antarctic tourism industry:

1 the Australian government should apply domestic legislation to regulate tourism in the AAT;
2 the Australian Antarctic Division should immediately develop management regimes for environmental protection and establish procedures for the planning, administration and monitoring of tourist activities within the AAT; and
3 until such time as a detailed conservation strategy for the AAT was developed, the Australian government should not approve tourism ventures which involved airstrip construction or onshore tourist accommodation.

The recommendations of *Tourism in Antarctica* have yet to be indorsed as official policy, but there are some illuminating aspects of this exercise in examining the balance between state and regime with regard to Antarctic tourism. While the orientation of this report did not preclude a multilateral solution to the regulation of Antarctic tourism, it did demonstrate that the Australian Parliament's strong environmental concerns for the AAT would influence its assessment of the impact of tourism on the AAT and this in turn would affect its willingness to rely on the processes of the ATS. The Australian parliamentary committee took the view that, given its strong feelings on the issue, the safest and most direct course of action was to rely on state-based legislation. Interestingly, this preference for national regulation was reinforced by Australia's efforts to resist the CRAMRA Treaty. Australia passed strong (and internationally controversial) national legislation to prevent mining by anyone in the AAT and by Australian nationals anywhere at all in Antarctica. Whether this attitude could be relaxed if an ATS sub-regime on tourism were to eventuate remains open.

Concerning the effects of national regulation, it is interesting to note that the mere tabling of the Committee's report appears to have dampened any private Australian interest in land-based tourism in the AAT. Seaborne tourism which was not so directly discouraged has continued to enjoy some commercial support, although the primary interest has been the sub-Antarctic islands rather than the AAT itself. Significantly, more than national regulation proved necessary in the case of Macquarie Island. Control of visitors to Macquarie Island also required Tasmanian state involvement, since Australia is a federation and the island is under

Tasmanian authority. This added layer of regulation complicated the national regulatory process rather more than was expected – at least from an industry perspective. In the event, actual visiting to Macquarie Island was less than that anticipated and there was some industry feeling that the fees charged for visits and the complexity of meeting permit requirements adversely impacted the industry.

Naturally, not all ATS states share the Australian perspective on the value and need of national legislation in regulating Antarctic tourism. Indeed, few could in precisely the same terms since much of the Australian position is grounded in its standing as a claimant state. Nonetheless, as noted previously, territorial responsibility (however disputed such claims might be) is not the only national basis for state regulation of the industry. Intervention can occur at the point of the tourist, the tour operator, the ship's charter – or any number of areas subject to national regulation. The American experience demonstrates that with sufficient political will virtually any aspect of the industry which falls within the ambit of national authority can be used to impose national priorities on the entire industry.

While the industry remained small and the regulatory restraints conventional, the entrepreneurs of the Antarctic tourist industry had little incentive to organise. There was no real arena in which to act collectively. (This fact in itself serves as a substantial indicator of the relatively low relevance of the ATS to the industry in the three decades from 1956.) The expansion of the industry, coupled with the emergence of an active and influential environmental lobby, helped to change the industry's perceptions of its stake in the Antarctic. As pressure for a sub-regime began to build within the ATS, the industry recognised two avenues of response: it could either press for the continuance of some form of self-regulation; or it could seek some form of effective participation in the formulation of the proposed sub-regime. Quite sensibly, the Antarctic tour operators sought to take out the insurance of keeping both options open. There was a clear preference for self-regulation but an acceptance of the need to work with the policy-makers of the regime in order to influence a tourism annex if necessary. In either case, the industry would have to be organised.

From an Australian perspective, there is a minor irony in the role that Australia unwittingly played in the emergence of an organised industry input into the ATS. Although Australia was not a significant participant in Antarctic tourism, the burst of enthusiasm at the prospect of Australian participation which led the Parliament to undertake an inquiry into tourism in the late 1980s also provoked the Pacific Asia Travel Association (PATA) to take an interest in Antarctica.[31] In 1990 at the instigation of its senior Australian officer, Ian Kennedy, this association of travel agents decided to examine the industry's position in Antarctica especially with regard to environmentally oriented tourism. Its 1991 Bali conference canvassed the issues and made several proposals for encouraging an environmentally sensitive industry, but it was the decision to meet again to establish a basis for involvement in the XVI ATCM (Bonn 1991) which probably had the most significant consequence.

PATA arranged for a smaller industry meeting in Honolulu in August 1991 to discuss the modalities of such participation. The PATA initiative had a catalytic effect on the various tour operators. The North American tour operators who had been meeting for some time together with American officials hastened to formalise their own inchoate organisation, IAATO, in order not to be overwhelmed by the larger, more diffuse and less experienced interests of the regional travel agents' association. Despite IAATO's reservations, however, the two travel groups did meet in the middle of 1991 and prepared some common positions for the Bonn ATCM.[32] The two bodies also cooperated the following year in preparation for the Venice meeting but much more loosely, as both were invited in their individual capacities to an informal meeting on tourism prior to the ATCM.

Organising as an industry was an important first step (one never taken by the fishing industry at any stage in the existence of CCAMLR) but the ATS appeared divided on whether to deal directly with industry interests. Both IAATO and PATA sought to secure recognition at the 1991 Bonn meeting but each was refused. Instead, an inter-governmental association, the World Tourism Organization (WTO), was invited to represent the issue of tourism in an advisory capacity, despite its lack of experience or familiarity with the Antarctic industry. This attempt to deny access to industry NGOs was rejected by the industry which recognised that it would have to represent itself if it was to protect its interests. To

---

[31] Many of these observations on the development of an organised industry body have been reported in R. A. Herr, 'Antarctic Tourism and Its Likely Development', in J. Handmer and M. Wilder (eds.), *Towards a Conservation Strategy for the Australian Antarctic Territory* (Canberra: Centre for Resource and Environmental Studies, Australian National University, 1993), pp. 91–107.

[32] The two associations raised but did not investigate seriously the possibility of forming a united body. Concern over the likely acronym 'PATATO' was only a minor inconvenience!

the credit of the ATS policy-makers, the experiment with WTO was recognised as inadequate and at the subsequent Consultative Meeting, in Venice 1992, both IAATO and PATA were included in the informal Special Meeting on Antarctic tourism which preceded the formal Meeting. Significantly but unexpectedly, IAATO was invited to remain after the informal Meeting to attend the formal session of the Consultative Parties. There is a real likelihood that this access will be continued and so some grounds for believing that the industry will be included directly in the ATS decision-making processes.

It still remains to be determined whether the industry would be better advantaged by a sub-regime or by the more traditional extra-regime mechanisms. The two industry associations adopted a common position at the Venice informal ATCM Meeting opposing the desirability of a specific (and additional) annex on tourism. They held instead that the existing Protocol with its existing annexes provides an adequate framework *for the present* for regulating human impacts in Antarctica. Indeed, there are grounds for concern that the existing provisions could be used to impose excessive regulation on Antarctic tourism. At the May 1992 Colmar meeting on Antarctic tourism, the suggestion was raised that Annex V could be used in a regulatory manner to bias access against tourism.[33] The land-use mechanisms of Annex V could be employed to designate protected areas and sites in such a way as to prejudice physical access uncritically in favour of science, regardless of the quality of the science.

Despite these reservations, the industry has recognised that there is much in the Protocol to favour its interests. The textual reference to aesthetic values is seen as giving something like formal acceptance to the legitimacy of tourism as an activity. Perhaps more significantly from a practical perspective, the Protocol's central purpose of maintaining the Antarctic environment helps to preserve the basic resource of the Antarctic tourism industry. After all, the unique environment of Antarctica is the key attraction drawing people to visit the region. The mainstream industry recognised this prudential self-interest long before the drafting of the Protocol; a recognition which led the industry generally to exceed voluntarily the ATS requirements for environmental protection. It has sought to establish that this record of voluntary compliance is so substan-

[33] R. Naveen, 'Recommendations for Managing Visitors and Tourists Under the Antarctic Treaty System', paper presented at the conference *Le Tourisme Dans Les Regions Polaires*, held in Colmar, France, 21–3 April 1992.

tial that it should not be singled out for 'special' (i.e. sub-regime) treatment. Rather, the legitimate interests of industry should be incorporated into an ATS regulatory process which acknowledges a substantial degree of self-regulation by the industry.

REGIME EFFECTIVENESS AND ANTARCTIC TOURISM:
AN ASSESSMENT

Has the Antarctic regime been effective with regard to tourism? On balance, the answer seems a rather unsatisfactory 'it depends'. Until very recently it was not an objective of the ATS regime to take direct responsibility for management of this issue area. In terms of what it wanted to achieve – containing the adverse impact of tourism on other regime priorities – the Antarctic regime was probably as effective as it could be. Thus it seems to have achieved its principal objectives. Only if one constructed other aspirations could the regime's involvement with Antarctic tourism be questioned. If, for example, the ATS had intended to discourage tourism, then the growth and development of the industry would have to be regarded as a sign of ineffectiveness. Similarly, if the regime members had hoped to manage Antarctic tourism as a sustainable industry (perhaps along the lines of the fisheries sub-regime), then clearly neither past nor present regulatory arrangements could be regarded as effective. Yet such aims were not set by the ATS; and the reality is that the regime's limited objectives for nearly thirty years scarcely could have failed to be met.

In recent years, however, the objectives of the regime have been significantly extended to include new areas of interests and to reconsider established interests. It is argued in this chapter that, as a result of the forces which have come to fruition in the Madrid Protocol, the regime has shown greater willingness to accept a more substantial responsibility for issues such as tourism. However, there are multiple means by which such increased responsibility can be expressed. For a variety of reasons – ranging from prudential concerns over the technical difficulties in adequately distinguishing tourism from other activities to philosophical qualms over relying on anything short of legally enforceable sanctions – the ATS has been unable to reach consensus on how to proceed, despite general support among the Treaty's members for greater direct regime responsibility over this issue. Given the indecision at Bonn and Venice on a Protocol annex to cover tourism (dealt with in Chapter 12 in this volume), it would be premature to assert that regime objectives have formally changed regarding tourism beyond those generalised alterations incorporated in the Madrid Protocol. And, thus, we are not yet free to join the critics of the ATS in concluding that the regime's effectiveness has declined in recent years due to its expanded ambit of responsibility.

There is a second basic indicator of regime effectiveness: the level of compliance with regime rules. Has the Antarctic regime achieved effectiveness under this rubric? Again, given the low expectations for outcomes until recently, it would be difficult to allege ineffectiveness. The regime relied primarily on state mechanisms for sanctions, and insofar as there were few flagrant breaches, the level of compliance would appear adequate, at least in formal terms. This is not to say there have not been breaches but rather, because the regime component of the attempted regulation of Antarctic consisted of non-compulsory guidelines, compliance was not strictly an issue for the regime. If, however, the Antarctic regime were to take on a more direct regulatory responsibility – perhaps through the proposed Protocol annex – compliance could become an important formal indicator of regime effectiveness. Nonetheless, it is noteworthy that to date informal compliance has been regarded by the industry as one of its strongest arguments for self-regulation.

Notwithstanding these observations, the growing energy and resources devoted to the question of regulating Antarctic tourism by the ATS in recent years have indicated fairly convincingly that the older *laissez faire* approach to tourism is raising qualms with an increasing number of ATS members. Whether or not this soul-searching produces an identifiable sub-regime through the mechanism of a Protocol annex, the current debate has worked towards a more coherent regulatory process. Indeed, the emergence of an organised industry lobby group which now enjoys participatory involvement with the ATS regulatory process is likely to encourage further policy coherence. The interests of established tour providers are generally supported by inclusion in the ATS regulatory process, especially with regard to mutual interests in maintaining the aims of the Madrid Protocol. Thus, the tour operators can be expected to cooperate with further regime-based regulation through this process, provided it does not impose too heavily on the industry. There can be little doubt that the ATS is accepting vastly more responsibility for tourism as a matter for regime regulation, and that this trend will continue for some time, whether or not this acceptance leads ultimately to a new sub-regime.

PART IV

The legitimacy of ATS regimes

The legitimacy of ATS regimes: introduction

DAVOR VIDAS AND WILLY ØSTRENG

This Part of the book goes beyond a discussion of the legal force of the regimes in question: the focus rests on their *persuasive* force. To what degree have these regimes succeeded in achieving such force, and how have the differences between them in this respect come about? In other words, which parameters have determined the legitimacy of the regimes under study here?

The four chapters which follow explore the question of legitimacy of the ATS regimes regarding marine living resources, mineral resources, comprehensive environmental protection and tourism. Consequently, they focus on four regimes in mutually varying stages: CCAMLR, legally in force and in operation for more than a decade; CRAMRA, adopted but subsequently superseded by another regime; the Protocol, still pending entry into force as treaty law, but already implemented in some instances;[1] and an Antarctic tourism regime, on which partial regulation does exist within the ATS, but is still in the formative stage as a more coherent regime.

The persuasive force of international regimes, as elaborated in Chapter 1, is manifested in the level of their applicability and acceptance. Hence, our inquiry in this Part will focus on those normative and structural features[2] of CCAMLR, CRAMRA, the Protocol and the tourism regime which affect their applicability and acceptance; and on factors which were crucial in shaping these features.

---

[1] The Consultative Parties have repeatedly, at the 1992 and the 1994 Consultative Meetings, given statements on voluntary implementation of the environmental principles codified in the Protocol, even prior to its entry into force as treaty law.

[2] As with international regimes in general, each of the ATS regimes comprises a normative component of principles and rules, and a structural component determining the roles of subjects and third parties as well as procedures within the regime: see Chapter 1.

THE SHAPING OF NORMATIVE AND STRUCTURAL
ELEMENTS IN THE ATS REGIMES

We have seen in Chapter 2, firstly, that certain normative and structural components are specific to the ATS as a system; and, secondly, how these components have evolved in interaction with the wider international community. Over the past two decades, the period in which the four ATS component regimes were built, the System evolved through a combination of *adaptation* and *persistence*: some of its components have been subject to change in response to challenges posed to it, while others have remained stable.

The following legitimacy case studies of the four ATS regimes examine how this pattern is reflected in the regimes under scrutiny, and indicate how this has affected their legitimacy. Let us therefore outline the way the legitimacy argument is pursued in the chapters of this Part, by tracing the genesis of the normative and structural elements in the regimes of the ATS.

Consistency within the ATS

To be *normatively* consistent within the ATS, component regimes must, first, uphold the three basic values of the Treaty cooperation: peace, science and environmental protection; and, second, preserve the balance between the various positions on the sovereignty issue in Antarctica.

Regarding the principles of the ATS, the regimes under consideration embody the shift of emphasis from the acuteness of actively upholding one principle (peaceful purposes and non-nuclearisation) to the emergence and gradually increasing priority of a subsequently introduced one (environmental protection) over another original principle of the Antarctic Treaty (science). This has occurred in a continuous regulatory process, in which recommendations adopted at Consultative Meetings preceded the creation of more coherent regimes in the form of international treaties – the Seals Convention, CCAMLR, CRAMRA and the Protocol[3] – through which the environmental principle has been built.

The crucial position of the sovereignty issue in the ATS, and the requirement of maintaining a *modus vivendi* as codified in Article IV of the Antarctic Treaty, is clearly evident in all the regimes under study

---

[3] The tourism regime follows this pattern, although at its present stage it is still based partly on recommendations and partly on the framework provided by the Protocol.

here. This imperative is especially difficult when a regime addresses either the use of natural resources or human activity like tourism in the Antarctic, because this would normally require unambiguous solutions on jurisdiction. The ATS regimes, however, have had to resort to ambiguity and to a variety of techniques in order to maintain the balance of positions on sovereignty. This normative imperative may also prove detrimental for the legitimacy of these regimes – as Chapter 10 sets out to discuss for the case of CRAMRA, and Chapter 12 for the tourism regime.

The consistency requirement also pertains to the *structural* elements of these regimes – as reflected especially in provisions for the institutions established within their ambit,[4] regarding the position and role of the Consultative Parties within each of the regimes, and the linkages with the Consultative Meetings. As the case studies will show, these structural features of the ATS not only persist in its regimes, but are in some instances even consolidated and strengthened – despite concessions introduced by the Consultative Parties for the limited participation and access of other actors in what remains largely *their* decision-making process.

Responsiveness to external demands

Two major types of *normative* demands were posed in the wider international community to the ATS regimes: the demand for equity in sharing benefits from resource exploitation; and the demand for comprehensive environmental protection of the Antarctic environment. Both demands affected CRAMRA with particular force, as elaborated in detail in Chapter 10: the former in the early stage of the negotiations, and the latter in the period immediately following the adoption of CRAMRA. This also led to the creation of the Protocol as an additional legal instrument in the ATS – although not necessarily to a basic novelty in the contents of its provisions, as Chapter 11 argues. While CCAMLR and the tourism regime were not exposed to the same level of mobilisation from third parties, responsiveness to external demands is a common feature in these regimes as well. In relation to CCAMLR, Chapter 9 points out that the interest in the middle of the 1970s of the UN Food and Agricultural Organization in mapping the living resources of the Southern Ocean was perceived by the Consultative Parties as a challenge

---

[4] The tourism regime is an exception here: decision-making in it is even more directly linked to the Consultative Parties, since it has not established any special institution and is confined to the Consultative Meetings.

to their regulatory competency. Regarding the tourism regime, Chapter 12 explains how the self-regulation of the tourism industry posed a threat – perhaps not a deliberate one – to the normative authority of the ATS to regulate any human activity in the Antarctic.

Closely related to the normative demands for external accommodations in the ATS regimes, third parties put forward demands for changes in the *structure* – especially wider participation in decision-making and access to information in these regimes. The evolving institutionalisation of the ATS regimes has proved instrumental in selectively accommodating these demands. A common feature of the institutions established by CCAMLR, CRAMRA and the Protocol is that they allow for observer status to certain international and non-governmental organisations and enhance the availability of information. Chapter 12 shows that with the Antarctic tourism regime, this has been done in a formally different manner, but that the pattern of inclusion of interested actors within the Consultative Meetings is analogous to that in the institutions of other ATS regimes.

Conduciveness to solving the problem

How conducive an ATS regime is to the regulation of its subject matter can be crucially affected by, on the one hand, the requirements for internal consistency within the ATS, and on the other hand, responsiveness to external demands. The legitimacy question is related here to the extent to which the regime can harmonise these considerations, without loss of conduciveness.

Since it is a common thread to the regime effectiveness and legitimacy concepts, this problematic has already been elaborated in general in Part III of this volume. Here it is touched upon from the aspect of legitimacy.[5]

Each of the case studies demonstrates how consistency and external accommodation may be achieved at the expense of the conduciveness to solving the problem. This is probably the least accentuated in CCAMLR. However, Chapter 9 also notes that in some instances – as with attempts to avoid conflicting jurisdiction with non-ATS regimes or in reaching agreement on a decision-making rule – external demands or the internal consistency requirement may have resulted in lower conduciveness to solving the problem in question.

Chapter 10 notes that, in the late 1980s, CRAMRA was widely seen as legally the strongest, most environmentally protective international

---

[5] See the general discussion in Chapter 1.

treaty ever negotiated. Hence, apparently it was highly conducive to the regulation of mineral activities in the Antarctic: it balanced use and protection, contained provisions to protect science, and also sought to maintain the *modus vivendi* on sovereignty.[6] However, mineral activities *as such* were eventually perceived as illegitimate in the Antarctic.

The conduciveness of one crucial part of the Protocol – the provisions related to the mining ban[7] – is questioned in Chapter 11, by arguing that it nullifies an important and complex work which the ATS has achieved in this field. As a result, a legal *vacuum* is created, especially in the longer term if a renewed interest in Antarctic minerals should arise.

Chapter 12 points out the need for a more comprehensive approach, if the ATS provisions on tourism are to be conducive to regulating this activity. However, such regulation would also require jurisdictional solutions, and rules on liability and insurance – and this might cause a disequilibrium in the sensitive *modus vivendi* on the sovereignty issue.

LEGITIMACY QUESTIONS PURSUED IN THE CASE STUDIES

On this background, each of the four case studies poses its own special legitimacy questions, related more specifically to the status of these regimes in the ATS and to the different subject matters regulated by them.

Chapter 9 has, at least at first glance, an easier job than the remaining three chapters: CCAMLR is today a regime implemented by its parties and widely acceptable to the international community. This case study inquires into how the timing of CCAMLR and the *evolution* of its normative and structural components have affected the legitimacy of the regime as a whole.

In the case study on the legitimacy of CRAMRA – a legally stillborn regime – the question of legitimacy becomes more difficult. In arguing that CRAMRA left a *'legacy* of legitimacy', or that there is a large measure of normative continuity between CRAMRA and the Protocol, Chapter 10 pursues two fundamental questions: what complex of factors during 1989 and 1990 prevailed over the perceived adequacy of CRAMRA? And, which elements can be found today for legitimising CRAMRA's legacy as evidenced in the Protocol? Chapter 11 portrays the Protocol as

---

[6] Chapter 10 demonstrates also that the fragility of the balance on the sovereignty issue was among reasons for CRAMRA's demise.

[7] Protocol, Arts. 7 and 25.

reflecting a gradual adaptation of the ATS to changing circumstances. Also, a fundamental thesis in this case study is that the legitimacy of the Protocol derives not so much from its actual provisions as from the fact that they are largely based on the *prior* work of the Consultative Meetings – the recommendations and conventions already adopted within the ATS.

And finally, the analysis of the legitimacy in Chapter 12 proceeds from the juxtaposition of two approaches on how to regulate Antarctic tourism: one, that a comprehensive regime is still needed; and another, that this regime already exists scattered within the ATS, and that all that needs to be done is to *present it* clearly. The latter approach was recently adopted by the Consultative Parties, and has been accepted by other interested actors.

9

The legitimacy of CCAMLR

BRUCE W. DAVIS

INTRODUCTION

Within the theory of international relations, there is often an assumption that diplomatic negotiations are carried out by representatives of sovereign states, meeting in formal and confidential circumstances.[1] While this may be true of many deliberations, it ignores the reality that diplomatic outcomes are often influenced by domestic political factors, and also that the policy community has now widened to include special interest groups such as scientific and environmental organisations, as well as other stakeholders.[2] In consequence, the diplomatic agenda and mode of international discourse have changed markedly in recent decades, and this must be taken into account when gauging the legitimacy of any given regime. This is particularly true in the case of the 1980 Convention on the Conservation of Antarctic Marine Living Resources (CCAMLR).[3] As elaborated in Chapter 1, in this book the legitimacy of international regimes is discussed in the light of a two-fold criterion: *applicability*, referring to the quality of regimes rules, and *acceptance*, related to the attitudes of subjects and third parties.

When negotiated, CCAMLR responded to the needs of both the Antarctic Treaty parties and of third parties for a management arrangement in the Southern Ocean. In the late 1970s, there was a desire to prevent a scramble for living resources of the Southern Ocean, especially krill, which was believed to sustain a considerably higher harvesting effort than

---

[1] See T. Knutson, *A History of International Relations Theory* (Manchester University Press, 1993).

[2] See L. Elliott, 'Continuity and Change in Cooperative International Regimes: The Politics of the Recent Environmental Debates on Antarctica', Working Paper 1991/3, Research School of Pacific Studies (Canberra: Australian National University, 1991).

[3] The Convention was signed at Canberra, on 20 May 1980, and entered into force on 7 April 1982; text reprinted in *International Legal Materials*, vol. XIX, 1980, pp. 837*ff.*

the level at that time. This concern was fuelled by environmentalist pressures to protect the krill as a foodbase for cetaceans and finfish. As discussed in Chapter 5, it was also spurred by the interest in Southern Ocean living resources shown by the UN's specialised agency, the Food and Agricultural Organisation (FAO).

This is why the *timing* of the CCAMLR negotiations was so essential for its internal and external acceptance. Indeed, the regime could be portrayed as anticipatory in two respects. First, institutions for collective regulation were negotiated before the most promising species, krill, had been depleted. With the Southern Ocean harvest of krill moderate in scale, vested interest proved less than many had anticipated, which affected the room for manoeuvre. In general, when the stakes in a set of negotiations are moderate, it is easier to reach agreement on conflictual matters – particularly when, as in the ATS, those negotiating have a tradition of cooperation. Second, this consensual inclination was probably galvanised further by the shared concern of the Consultative Parties, who negotiated the regime,[4] to establish some form of a regime within the ATS framework *before* the FAO had become too interested in the Southern Ocean.

Chapter 5 laid out the basic provisions of CCAMLR and portrayed its evolving effectiveness, focusing on the impact of this regime on resource use and management practices in the Southern Ocean. This chapter will try to identify those aspects of the regime which are the most significant for its *applicability* and *acceptance*. Legitimacy is not a static concept: as shown in Chapter 1, the degree of applicability and acceptance may change over time, depending on the willingness and ability of participating nations to *adapt* the regime to meet new needs or challenges. Therefore, this chapter will discuss the evolution of the major structural and normative components of CCAMLR in the light of how they affect the applicability and acceptance of the regime as a whole. As to *structural* features of the regime, the focus will rest on the evolving participation, access and decision-making rules of CCAMLR and the geographic and functional scope of the regime; whereas the discussion of its *normative* component will highlight the ecosystemic management principle of the CCAMLR regime.

---

[4] Two Non-Consultative Parties, and the European Economic Community, were invited to the final, signatory Conference in Canberra, 1980, but the negotiations had been conducted by the Consultative Parties alone.

PARTICIPATION, ACCESS AND DECISION-MAKING

In terms of participation and access, CCAMLR has been more inclusive than the Antarctic Treaty: the Convention expanded the criterion for membership in the decision-making body by mentioning not only demonstrated scientific interest in Southern Ocean living resources but harvesting as well. In anticipation of the Common Fisheries Policy in the European Community, it also allowed the participation of regional economic cooperation organisations. In recent years, following the dissolution of the Soviet Union, the members of the CCAMLR Commission have signalled their preparedness to give observer status to the Ukraine as well as to Bulgaria and Greece.

This inclusiveness has been demonstrated towards international organisations as well. CCAMLR gives explicit observer status to an international organisation like the FAO; and while somewhat reluctantly and without offering decision-making rights, the Commission as early as 1987 allowed a non-governmental environmental umbrella organisation, the Antarctic and Southern Ocean Coalition (ASOC), to take part in plenary discussions.[5] This wider participation and access to decision-making fora have resulted in more transparency regarding decision-making processes and the background to measures adopted within CCAMLR. Although Commission meetings remain closed to the public and to the media, the observer status of international and non-governmental organisations ensures that information is usually readily available.

These participation and access rules serve to enhance the *applicability* of CCAMLR. While the rules, as noted, tend to be more permissive than those set forth in other ATS regimes, they are nevertheless consistent with a general trend in Treaty cooperation. In 1983, Non-Consultative Parties to the Treaty were granted attendance at Consultative Meetings. And as demonstrated when the Netherlands was acknowledged as a Consultative Party in 1990, even the scientific activity criterion of the Antarctic Treaty is in the process of being broadened: establishment of a scientific station is no longer an absolute requirement for gaining consultative status. The granting of observer status to international and non-governmental organisations

---

[5] In comparison, ASOC was for the first time invited to appoint experts to attend at a regular Consultative Meeting in 1991, for the XVI ATCM, held in Bonn, from 7–18 October 1991. On the argument that ASOC is a representative of the non-governmental environmental organisations, Greenpeace has not been granted observer status in the CCAMLR Commission.

has been reflected in subsequent instruments as well, such as CRAMRA and the Environmental Protocol. The structural provisions of CCAMLR can be seen also as conducive to the subject matter of the regime. The openness of the Commission to any nation engaged in harvesting operations in the Convention Area reduces the risk of substantial activity by non-members of the regime. And the inclusion of the FAO as an observer enhances the flow of knowledge and experience from an organisation involved in a great number of regional management regimes around the world.

But these access and participation rules should also be seen as efforts to ensure *external acceptance* of the Convention. As noted, in the middle of the 1970s, the FAO's interest in mapping the living resources of the Southern Ocean was seen by the Consultative Parties as a challenge, or at least a sign that certain member states in that organisation would be less than satisfied if the Southern Ocean were to be managed by the Consultative Parties alone.[6] A new external factor, however, which the Consultative Parties were initially faced with in connection with the negotiations for CCAMLR, was a significant interest of environmental NGOs in shaping the Antarctic resource regimes. As discussed in Chapter 4, these organisations have become involved in CCAMLR in two ways. The International Union for the Conservation of Nature and Natural Resources (IUCN), and, since 1987, ASOC as well, have been formally invited to take part as observers in the plenary discussions of the Commission; but much earlier, particularly knowledgeable individuals from such organisations were included in the national delegations of some Commission members, like Australia and the United States. There is little doubt that this inclusion of external actors has served to increase the level of external acceptance of CCAMLR.

However, while providing for wider participation and more transparency than previously in the Treaty cooperation, CCAMLR simultaneously contains provisions aimed at protecting the privileged position of the Consultative Parties in the actual decision-making. While any state may accede to the Convention, the right to membership in the Commission is reserved to those satisfying the activity criterion mentioned above – engagement in research or harvesting activities in relation to Antarctic marine living resources.[7] Others may join as observers in the

---

[6] See J. A. Heap, cited in 'Discussion', in R. Wolfrum (ed.), *Antarctic Challenge: Conflicting Interests, Cooperation, Environmental Protection, Economic Development* (Berlin: Duncker & Humblot, 1984), pp. 119–31, especially p. 130.

[7] CCAMLR, Art. VII, Para. 2(b).

Commission, but have no decision-making rights. Moreover, the Convention links the institutions established by it closely to the Antarctic Treaty Consultative Meetings,[8] and acknowledges the special obligations and responsibilities of the Consultative Parties.[9] Indeed, only two states have ever been a member of the Commission without also being a Consultative Party, and both of them gained consultative status in the course of the 1980s;[10] out of twenty-eight states parties to CCAMLR as of 1 November 1994, only four are Non-Consultative Parties.[11] Therefore, the provisions in CCAMLR regarding participation and access serve to enhance the external standing of that regime while at the same time preserving internal consistency with the structural rules of the wider Treaty cooperation, particularly those emanating from Article IX of the Antarctic Treaty.

Consensus is required for all decisions taken by the Commission on matters of substance;[12] and, in addition, by their entitlement to object to a conservation measure, Commission members can avoid being bound by it.[13] On the one hand, there is little doubt that this double veto enhances the internal consistency of the Convention by supporting the pragmatic *modus vivendi* on the sovereignty issue in the Antarctic, originally formulated in Article IV of the Antarctic Treaty and echoed, as we shall see below, in CCAMLR. This consistency with the 'sovereignty freeze' of the Antarctic Treaty was essential to the internal acceptance of CCAMLR as well. To each of the claimants, this veto ensures that no regulative measure can be made pertaining to the claimed area without their consent. Moreover, the fact that the veto right is enjoyed also by non-claimants satisfies the need of the latter to avoid or minimise special treatment of those claiming sovereignty rights in the Antarctic. But on the other hand, consensus is a very demanding decision rule, since it enables one reluctant party to block any collective measure: a consensus rule favours *status quo*. And as shown in Chapter 5, especially in the early years this rendered the development of information and conservation measures

---

[8] *Ibid.*, Art. IX, para. 5.

[9] *Ibid.*, Art. V, para. 1; and Art. XXIII, para. 1.

[10] The German Democratic Republic, an original signatory to CCAMLR, joined the group of Consultative Parties in 1987; whereas the Republic of Korea acquired membership in the CCAMLR Commission in 1985 and consultative status four years later. In addition to states, the European Union is an original signatory to CCAMLR and hence represented in the Commission, without being a party to the Antarctic Treaty.

[11] Bulgaria, Canada, Greece and the Ukraine.

[12] CCAMLR, Art. XII, para. 1.

[13] *Ibid.*, Art. IX, para. 6(c) and (d).

in the Southern Ocean a protracted and cumbersome process. Hence, to some extent, the consensus rule implies that consistency and acceptance have prevailed over problem-solving conduciveness.

The adoption of CCAMLR was a significant move within the ATS towards wider participation and diminishing secrecy in decision-making. At the same time, the Convention reflects the awareness among its nego-tiators of a need to preserve certain distinct features of the ATS. In par-ticular, this goes for provisions securing the maintenance and furtherance of the ATS consultative mechanism, including the privileged position of the Consultative Parties in it, and the provisions aiming at preserving the balance between claimants and non-claimants in Treaty cooperation.

THE SCOPE OF THE CONVENTION

The CCAMLR Area extends northwards to the Antarctic Convergence[14] This is a logical limit in scientific and ecological terms, because the Con-vergence is a natural boundary for many Southern Ocean species, but it differs from the Antarctic Treaty boundary of 60°S latitude. This differ-ence proved highly instrumental in rendering the Convention acceptable to both claimants and non-claimants because it helped them formulate Article IV of CCAMLR. This Article expresses the relationship between this Convention and the competing positions on the sovereignty claims in a way which both sides could interpret as compatible with their own view.[15] This so-called *bifocal approach* contributes to legitimising CCAMLR not by determinacy but, on the contrary, by an ambiguity which preserves the legal positions of both claimants and non-claimants. Because this matter is so sensitive in the context of resource management in general and because CCAMLR was seen as a test case for the even more controversial minerals negotiations, this provision was vital for the internal acceptance of CCAMLR.

Another internal accommodation deemed necessary for the realisation of CCAMLR was that France received explicit recognition for the view that within the 200-mile zones this country had established around its undisputed sub-Antarctic islands, measures taken prior to the entry into force of CCAMLR would remain in force. The other contracting parties to the Convention also did not object to the statement that in these waters

---

[14] *Ibid.*, Art. I, paras. 1 and 4.
[15] *Ibid.*, Art. IV, para. 2(b) and (c).

France would retain the competence both to decide whether or not new CCAMLR measures apply and to establish and enforce even stricter rules than those agreed to within CCAMLR; moreover, the observation and inspection system envisaged by the Convention would not apply in these waters unless France agrees.[16] In this case, then, consistency within the regime had to be suppressed in order for CCAMLR to achieve the necessary level of acceptance by key actors within the regime.[17]

There is also the intriguing question of what implications arise from declarations of exclusive economic zones (EEZ) around Antarctica. Most recently, in August 1994, the Australian government established a 200-nautical-mile EEZ around the nation, and simultaneously declared a similar zone around all external territories, including sub-Antarctic Macquarie, Heard and McDonald Islands and the offshore zone of the Australian Antarctic Territory.[18] Although *prima facie* this might have been interpreted as an attempt to bolster territorial claims and hence sovereignty, it does not appear to have generated protest by other Antarctic nations, and it is not yet placed under test, unless disputes should arise in future about fishing or whaling activities.

But the provisions on the area of application of CCAMLR reflect not only internal accommodation among claimants and non-claimants: they also demonstrate how its negotiators sought to avoid jurisdictional *overlap* with other relevant international regimes pertaining to the Southern Ocean. Although marine mammals are not explicitly excluded from the management domain of CCAMLR, the 1969 Vienna Convention on the

---

[16] While not explicated in the Convention itself, this recognition took the form of a statement to this effect by the Chairman of the Conference on the Conservation of Antarctic Marine Living Resources, recorded in the Final Act, to which no state objected. The text of the statement is reproduced in W. M. Bush (ed.), *Antarctica and International Law: A Collection of Inter-State and National Documents* (London: Oceana, 1982), vol. I, pp. 391–2.

[17] On the controversy among Conservative Parties on this point during the negotiations, see J. B. Barnes, 'The Emerging Convention on the Conservation of Antarctic Marine Living Resources: An Attempt to Meet the New Realities of Resource Exploitation in the Southern Ocean', in J. I. Charney (ed.), *The New Nationalism and the Use of Common Spaces: Issues in Marine Pollution and the Exploitation of Antarctica* (Totowa, NJ: Allanheld, Osmun & Co., 1982), pp. 239–86, p. 257.

[18] Australia declared a Fisheries Protection Zone around its Antarctic claims in 1979, without implementing it. According to R. H. Wyndham, this zone was aimed not at parties to CCAMLR but at third parties. See R. H. Wyndham, 'Comment', in R. Wolfrum (ed.), *Antarctic Challenge: Conflicting Interests, Cooperation, Environmental Protection, Economic Development* (Berlin: Duncker & Humblot, 1984), pp. 114–19, p. 117.

Law of Treaties[19] gives pre-eminence to earlier conventions, in this case the 1946 International Convention for the Regulation of Whaling[20] and the 1972 Convention for the Conservation of Antarctic Seals.[21] CCAMLR specifically states that nothing in it shall derogate from the rights and obligations of contracting parties to the Whaling Convention; and in subsequent practice, the CCAMLR Commission has been very cautious not to act in a way which could be seen as challenging the centrality of the decision-making body of that Convention, the International Whaling Commission (IWC). For instance, when invited to comment upon the French proposal for a whaling sanctuary in parts of the Southern Ocean, the CCAMLR Scientific Committee responded that no advice could be offered which would not already be reflected in the advice of the Scientific Committee of IWC.[22] Given the high degree of politicisation of the whaling issue, this restraint on the part of CCAMLR regarding marine mammals may have been important for the positive attitude which third parties have formed towards CCAMLR.

On the other hand, while CCAMLR does not regulate whale harvesting, the ecosystem principle implies that the conditions and needs of Antarctic mammal stocks are important premises for decisions on other marine species. Yet, there has been rather limited scientific interaction between CCAMLR and the scientific bodies related to the Whaling and Antarctic Seals Conventions.[23] To some extent, therefore, a price may have to be paid for the limited functional jurisdiction of CCAMLR, in that knowledge-generating efforts are not as comprehensive as the ecosystem principle requires. If so, it is another incident of external acceptance being achieved at the cost of conduciveness to the solution of the problem addressed by the Convention.

What is a matter for conjecture, however, is just how stable this restraint on the part of the Commission members in interactions with other regimes will remain. A new global strategic, economic and political order is emerging, and it is still not entirely clear which nations will be the leading players in Southern Ocean affairs during the coming decade.

---

[19] *United Nations Treaty Series*, vol. 1,155, pp. 331ff.

[20] *United Nations Treaty Series*, vol. 161, pp. 74ff.

[21] See Bush, *Antarctica and International Law*, vol. I, pp. 401–8.

[22] See *Report of the XIth Meeting of the Commission* (Hobart: Commission for the Conservation of Antarctic Marine Living Resources, 1992), p. 47.

[23] See K.-H. Kock, *Fishing and Conservation in Southern Waters* (Hobart: Commission for the Conservation of Antarctic Marine Living Resources, 1993), doc. SC-CAMLR-XII/BG/11.

Rapidly increasing human population may place new demands on oceanic resources in the years ahead. In particular, the need might arise for some accommodation and realignment between CCAMLR, the Whaling Convention, and post-UN Conference on Environment and Development (UNCED) decisions about high seas fisheries, an area where the FAO may play an important role.

Indeed, this point can be generalised. The various attempts to delineate ocean boundaries, manage marine resources and protect ocean environments have generated a considerable number of multilateral international treaties – so many in fact that they are now beginning to impact and interdict one with another. There is now an emerging need to analyse both the positive and negative implications of overlapping ocean regimes. There is also likely to be a lively debate about the manner in which broadly agreed concepts, such as sustainable development, biodiversity retention, the precautionary principle, intergenerational equity and the right to fish, can be made operationally effective. As a major regulatory authority for the Southern Ocean marine living resources, CCAMLR cannot stand aloof from such deliberations.

THE NORMATIVE CORE: ECOSYSTEMIC MANAGEMENT

Ever since negotiation of the Convention commenced, the question has been raised as to whether CCAMLR should be seen as an innovative ecosystemic conservation regime or merely a regular fisheries agreement for the Southern Ocean. The Convention is designed to provide a comprehensive conservation regime, since it is based on the principle of rational use of resources (Article II) but also an ecosystems approach to management (Articles II and IX). As shown in Chapter 5, the adoption of an ecosystem approach to management contributed to the *external acceptance* of CCAMLR by explicating for the first time in a major international convention a principle which was highly topical and which enjoyed the support of highly active environmental organisations.

One way of testing the *applicability* of the regime established by CCAMLR is to examine whether the regime provides for the *means* to realise this ambitious ecosystemic management objective. Here we shall focus on institutions, information flows and conservation measures.

In terms of *institutions*, CCAMLR provides a two-tiered structure, involving a Commission as principal policy-making and regulatory body; with a Scientific Committee providing support and expert advice and a Secretariat providing administrative services and data circulation. This is

a superior arrangement to the Antarctic Treaty proper, which still lacks
formal secretariat services. Over time, the work of the Scientific Committee has become more firmly organised in permanent Working Groups
facilitating the advisory role of the scientific community; especially
important here are the Fish Stock Assessment Group and Environmental
Monitoring and Management Group. The only real debate to arise about
CCAMLR institutional arrangements relates to the question of whether
the Scientific Committee should be able to commission its own research,
rather than rely upon some measure of coordination of national ventures
and on data provided by member states. But to adopt such a measure
would necessitate budget supplementation within CCAMLR, and few
contracting parties appear willing to contemplate such a prospect. As discussed in Chapter 5, the functional relationship between the Commission
and its Scientific Committee appears to have improved over the years: a
mutual education process appears to have taken place in which the scientific advice has gradually become more tailored to the needs of the
decision-makers, and the dialogue between scientists and diplomats on
how to respond to scientific uncertainties has improved.

As to *information flow*, the reporting requirements for harvesters in the
Southern Ocean have become increasingly stringent and the scales of
information have gradually become finer. These developments have supported the generation of knowledge to complement and make even better
use of the historical data made available, *inter alia*, by the cooperation
with SCAR and the FAO. But it was only from 1986 onwards, when the
CCAMLR Ecosystem Monitoring Program (CEMP) was instituted, that
a comprehensive view of the relationship between commercial species,
other biota and environmental conditions was approached. Even this
proved problematical – initially because of a lack of appropriate scientific
information, but also because of debate about indicator species and how
to develop standardised procedures for recording data as well as environmental parameters.[24]

Concerning *conservation measures*, it has been argued that up to the
middle of the 1980s, the CCAMLR Commission failed to address management in a comprehensive manner, as its approach was largely confined
to a traditional species-by-species orientation.[25] Also, regulations were

---

[24] See Kock, *Fishing and Conservation*, 1993.
[25] See J. A. Gulland, 'The Antarctic Treaty System as a Resource Management Mechanism –
Living Resources', in *Antarctic Treaty System: An Assessment* (Washington, DC: National
Academy press, 1986), pp. 221–34.

often criticised as being too little and too late, when some oceanic areas had already suffered resource attrition.[26] To some extent, this reflected lack of data for decision-making: but it also reflected the reluctance of distant-water fishing nations to release information on catch data which they regarded as commercial intelligence. Chapter 5 demonstrates that, since 1987, considerable progress has been achieved in developing a more comprehensive database, improving the flow of scientific advice into the decision-making process, and putting adequate regulatory measures in place. Important achievements include the setting in 1991 of precautionary catch limits for icefish mackerel and krill, and instituting step-wise management procedures for new fisheries.

Although an *inspection* system has also been put in place, there are substantial difficulties in rendering this effective, given the hostile and vast environment of the Southern Ocean and the decrease in fishing effort in the region in recent years. Hence, it is clear there is great reliance upon voluntary compliance.

Overall, the ecosystem principle set forth in CCAMLR has enhanced its external acceptance, but it will still take considerable time before provisions for information gathering, regulation and enforcement are sufficient to put that principle into practice.

CONCLUDING REMARKS

This chapter has assessed the legitimacy of CCAMLR by analysing how its evolving structural and normative components have affected the applicability and acceptance of this regime over time and within changing situational contexts.

The *applicability* of CCAMLR has been tested against three main indicators: the normative consistency within the wider ATS; its conduciveness to the solution of the problem; and its relationship to competing regimes. As to normative consistency within the ATS, CCAMLR has broken new ground by preserving in a resource management regime the sensitive *modus vivendi* on the Antarctic sovereignty issue. Also, the Convention is in harmony with the two original principles of the ATS, the use of the Antarctic for peaceful purposes and the freedom of scientific research; in addition, it contributed significantly to the emergence of the third norma-

---

[26] See, e.g. M. Howard, 'The Convention on the Conservation of Antarctic Marine Living Resources: A Five Year Review', *International and Comparative Law Quarterly*, vol. 38, no. 1, 1989, pp. 104–50.

The legitimacy of ATS regimes

tive principle of the ATS, namely environmental protection. Sometimes, however, as when recognising the French right to establish and enforce its own measures within the 200-mile zones around its sub-Antarctic islands, consistency has had to give way to the requirements for internal acceptance.

Regarding *conduciveness* to the solution of the problem, the analysis has largely relied on the argument in Chapter 5. In particular, we have seen that the ecosystemic objective set forth in the Convention is supported by the institutional structure and the evolving information and conservation measures taken by the CCAMLR Commission. But in some instances, as with attempts to avoid conflicting jurisdiction with non-ATS regimes or when in establishing a consensus rule, conduciveness to solving the problem of conservation may have suffered in order for the Consultative Parties to ensure external and internal acceptance for their management arrangement in the Southern Ocean.

Despite the actual existence of *competing regimes*, the legitimacy of CCAMLR is validated in this aspect of applicability, and to a high degree. However, a few caveats about future prospects should be added, given the interdiction with the International Whaling Convention and the FAO deliberations about global aspects of high seas fisheries. In this regard, the future of CCAMLR may rest not so much on the capacity and willingness of Commission members to adjust to new circumstances, but rather on the manner in which CCAMLR is inadvertently drawn into the emergence of a new international environmental order, as well as a new global strategic and economic order.

The second aspect of regime legitimacy is the level of *acceptance*. Internally, i.e. among the parties to the Convention, there have been some tensions between fishing nations and non-fishing nations within CCAMLR deliberations, and fairly protracted debates about particular matters such as catch data, inspection systems, conservation measures and precautionary limits to exploitation. Despite occasional altercations, there is no evidence to suggest that the regime has ever experienced such a severe internal strain that its internal legitimacy might be seriously harmed.

Externally, the regime has proven widely acceptable to the international community: it appears to be perceived primarily as a useful resource management arrangement rather than an extension of Antarctic territorial claims. In general, external challenges to CCAMLR have been less severe than what the Consultative Parties have had to face in the United

Nations.[27] Nevertheless, a new type of external accommodation has been initiated within the ambit of CCAMLR, with the widening involvement of international and non-governmental organisations. Even though this involvement has never been allowed to interfere with the decisive role of the Consultative Parties, it has served to buttress the external standing of CCAMLR as a highly acceptable international regime for the marine living resources of the Southern Ocean.

[27] See S. Harris, 'The Influence of the United Nations on the Antarctic System: A Source of Erosion or Cohesion?', in A. Jørgensen-Dahl and W. Østreng (eds.), *The Antarctic Treaty System in World Politics* (London: Macmillan, 1991), pp. 309–28; see also Chapter 2 in this book.

10

The legitimacy of CRAMRA

CHRISTOPHER C. JOYNER

INTRODUCTION

It has become politically fashionable to assert that the Convention on the Regulation of Antarctic Mineral Resource Activities (CRAMRA)[1] is dead and functionally illegitimate – that the Antarctic minerals regime it provided for has been abandoned and cast aside in favour of more comprehensive environmental protection as set out in the 1991 Protocol.

CRAMRA was legally stillborn, a condition brought about by the refusal of key states in 1989 to sign the agreement. Even so, negotiation of that instrument marked a milestone in Antarctic environmental law. Despite intense criticism from the environmental community, CRAMRA was widely heralded in the late 1980s as legally being the strongest, most environmentally protective international treaty instrument ever negotiated. Moreover, CRAMRA, despite a tarnished reputation in the Antarctic Treaty System, still contributed substantially to the evolution of the Environmental Protocol. Normative qualities of environmental protectionism – in the form of provisions originally agreed to and adopted for CRAMRA – were picked up and substantially incorporated into the Protocol.

This chapter explores two fundamental questions concerning the legitimacy of CRAMRA. First, what complex of factors during 1989–90 prevailed over the perceived adequacy of CRAMRA, invalidated its immediate legitimacy as a multilateral agreement and perpetrated its ultimate legal demise? Second, and more important, which factors can be found for legitimising CRAMRA's legacy as evidenced in the Protocol? Put

---

[1] Done 2 June 1988 in Wellington, New Zealand, opened for signature 25 November 1988; see doc. AMR/SCM/88/78, of 2 June 1988, reprinted in *International Legal Materials*, vol. XXVII, 1988, pp. 859–900.

another way, what normative attributes did selected provisions in CRAMRA contribute to the composition of the Protocol that connotate some legacy of legitimacy? The analysis thus seeks to link these queries first by assessing why CRAMRA failed as an international agreement. It then explores what legitimising legacies it left behind for the Protocol.

Brief comment should first be made about the nature of legitimacy in international politics. As discussed in more depth in Chapter 1, legitimacy in international politics concerns the quality of something and how it is regarded by the global community. Legitimacy may be viewed in terms of that thing's applicability to the real world (i.e., its perceived credibility and relevance) and its acceptability of purpose and content (i.e., the degree to which that thing is regarded as appropriate for dealing with its intended purpose). Importantly, legitimacy does not strictly mean legality. The legitimacy of something does not turn only on its lawful character or whether it was lawfully created and performs in a lawful manner. Nor does legitimacy come down to justice, which hinges more on righteousness and fairness. Rather, the notion of legitimacy turns on its obligatory attraction, on the magnetic sway exerted among states in compelling conformity to the norms, rules and principles held by the members of a society. International legitimacy turns on why something is respected and behaviour is accordingly modified, on questions of consent, acceptance and obedience to norms and rules absent of coercive enforcement, and on how that thing is perceived and respected by states in the international community.

The CRAMRA instrument may be viewed as less than fully legitimate because it has been replaced by the Madrid Environmental Protocol. Still, that situation does not diminish the fact that core normative concepts in CRAMRA were deemed so compellingly appropriate and necessary that they were subsequently incorporated into the Protocol. This realisation underpins the thesis that CRAMRA left a legacy of legitimacy as regards those key concepts.

Integral here is the status of legitimacy. Legitimacy is not only a condition or state of being: it also reflects the result of a process. The point here is plain: the CRAMRA instrument today is legally static; it has been intentionally abandoned in favour of the Protocol. The minerals regime's legacy nevertheless persists, seen in the adoption of certain core normative concepts by the Protocol. In an ironic sense, then, CRAMRA became an unwitting procreator to the Protocol, as key principles and normative objectives were borrowed from the former and transplanted into the latter. Most important in this regard are the core normative principles mandating restraint in the conduct of activities and proactive protection of the environment.

DISINTEGRATION OF CRAMRA

Evolution of the Antarctic minerals regime

The issue of mineral resources exploitation was not new to the Antarctic Treaty Consultative Parties (ATCPs). It had been considered informally in 1970 at the Sixth Consultative Meeting, and was first raised formally in 1972 at the Seventh Consultative Meeting with the adoption of Recommendation VII-6.[2] At the Eighth Consultative Meeting in 1975 the Consultative Parties agreed to a policy of voluntary 'restraint while seeking timely agreed solutions' to questions pertaining to Antarctic mineral resources as contained in Recommendation VIII-14.[3] This policy was reaffirmed in 1977 at the Ninth Consultative Party Meeting, and a set of principles agreed upon at a Special Meeting on minerals in Paris in 1976 was formally adopted in Recommendation IX-1. Though a minerals regime was not envisioned by all Consultative Parties at that time, they did agree to urge their nationals and other states to 'refrain from all exploration and exploitation of Antarctic mineral resources while making progress towards the timely adoption of an agreed regime concerning Antarctic mineral resource activities'.[4] At the Tenth Consultative Meeting in 1979, the Consultative Parties decided that a minerals regime should specify what mineral resource activities could be acceptable and provide for appropriate means to assess their environmental impact.[5]

In 1981 at the Eleventh Consultative Meeting, the Consultative Parties established the basis for future minerals negotiations through the adoption of Recommendation XI-1. This recommendation set forth core principles to be incorporated into the regime, among them that 'protection

---

[2] Recommendation VII-6, adopted at the VII ATCM, Wellington, 1972; reprinted in W. M. Bush (ed.), *Antarctica and International Law: A Collection of Inter-State and National Documents* (London: Oceana, 1982), vol. I, pp. 275–6.

[3] Recommendation VIII-14, adopted at the VIII ATCM, Oslo, 1975; reprinted in Bush (ed.), *Antarctica and International Law*, vol. I, pp. 328–9.

[4] Recommendation IX-1, para. 8, adopted at the IX ATCM, London, 1977; reprinted in Bush (ed.), *Antarctica and International Law*, vol. I, pp. 343–5.

[5] Recommendation X-1, adopted at the X ATCM, Washington, DC; reprinted in Bush (ed.), *Antarctica and International Law*, vol. I, p. 365.

of the unique Antarctic environment and of its dependent ecosystems should be a basic consideration'.[6] From 1981 through to 1988, eleven formal negotiating sessions were convened by the Consultative Parties as Special Consultative Meetings on Antarctic Minerals aimed at producing a special regime to regulate the prospecting, exploration and exploitation of mineral resources in the Antarctic, if ever these activities should occur there.[7] Agreement came in June 1988 on the text for a new minerals treaty, and in November 1988 the Convention on the Regulation of Antarctic Mineral Resource Activities was opened for signature in Wellington, New Zealand.[8]

The Convention remains an impressive document, containing sixty-seven Articles and an Annex for an Arbitral Tribunal. The Treaty is not a detailed mining code. Rather, it creates a regulatory framework for mineral activities. As presented in greater detail in Chapter 6, four new institutions, supported by a Secretariat, would comprise the CRAMRA regime.

1   An Antarctic Minerals Commission would be the forum for making executive policy decisions. The Commission would set rules and designate, through consensus, any areas to be opened for exploration and development.

2   A Special Meeting of States Parties open to all parties to the Antarctic Treaty would give advice to the Commission on any decision to open an area.

3   An Advisory Committee would advise the Commission and Regulatory Committees on matters requiring scientific, technical and environmental expertise about Antarctic mineral activities. Although not a decision-making body with binding powers, the Advisory Committee was created to provide special opportunities for consultation and cooperation.

4   Regulatory Committees would be established for each geographic area

[6] Recommendation XI-1, para. 5(c), adopted at the XI ATCM, Buenos Aires, 1981; reprinted in Bush (ed.), *Antarctica and International Law*, vol. I, pp. 441–3.

[7] See C. C. Joyner, 'The Antarctic Minerals Negotiating Process', *American Journal of International Law*, vol. 81, no. 4, 1987, pp. 888–905; R. Wolfrum, *The Convention on the Regulation of Antarctic Mineral Resource Activities: An Attempt to Break New Ground* (Berlin: Springer-Verlag, 1991); and F. Orrego Vicuña, *Antarctic Mineral Exploitation: The Emerging Legal Framework* (Cambridge University Press, 1988).

[8] See note 1 above. For the progressive development of the minerals regime, see C. C. Joyner, 'The Evolving Antarctic Minerals Regime', *Ocean Development and International Law*, vol. 19, no. 1, 1988, pp. 73–95.

designated by the Commission for possible minerals exploration and development activities. These mechanisms were designed to play central roles in the regime. CRAMRA allocated broad powers to the Regulatory Committees, including approval of applications for exploration and development permits, approval of management schemes (that is, the contracts between operators and the Convention's regulatory authority), as well as inspection and the power to suspend minerals activities in an area. Establishment of a Secretariat for CRAMRA was also viewed as desirable for coordinating management of the regulation of minerals activities on the continent.[9]

International concerns about mining in Antarctica

Most telling in the demise of CRAMRA's perceived legitimacy was the sea change in world attitudes about the desirability of mining in the Antarctic. During the 1980s, creation of a regime to regulate mining and development of Antarctic mineral resources was seen as a positive virtue. If exploitation of minerals should ever go forward, CRAMRA would supply a suitable regime for overseeing those activities. It was with this intention that the Consultative Parties' mineral negotiations proceeded from 1981–8. The premise undergirding CRAMRA's creation was that a regime was necessary to regulate eventual mining and development of Antarctic mineral resources; hence, appropriate regime formation was seen by the Consultative Parties as legitimate. Outside the Antarctic Treaty System, many states viewed the CRAMRA regime with great suspicion, but still favoured development of Antarctic mineral resources, which could come under the guise of a common heritage of mankind regime to promote and finance a New International Economic Order for the benefit of developing countries.

By the end of the decade, however, the thrust of international opinion had shifted from acceptance of possible Antarctic mineral development in the future, to pervasive rejection of that possibility. The groundswell of world public opinion came to question the desirability of that premise, and in fact worked to reverse it. By 1990 the pre-eminent attitude within both the Consultative Parties and the wider international community

---

[9] For comparative assessments of CRAMRA's operation, see C. C. Joyner, '1988 Antarctic Minerals Convention', *Marine Policy Reports*, vol. 1, no. 1, 1989, pp. 69–85; and P. J. Beck, 'Convention on the Regulation of Antarctic Mineral Resource Activities: A Major Addition to the Antarctic Treaty System', *Polar Record*, vol. 25, no. 152, 1989, pp. 19–32.

advocated that Antarctic mineral resources should *not* be developed, and that a new regime should be created to ban mining in Antarctica indefi nitely and provide for comprehensive environmental protection in the region.

Serious concern had arisen that CRAMRA would actually create the legal framework to regulate mining activities. The inference here was that the security, stability and confidence engendered by this framework agreement might enhance confidence and provide a better investment climate for miners to give stronger, more favourable consideration of exploring Antarctica for minerals or hydrocarbon resources. Put another way, Antarctica's current shaky legal status served to deter potential miners from taking substantial investment risks to work in Antarctica. CRAMRA helped to remove this legal uncertainty. The greater the amount of prospecting and exploration done, the greater likelihood that deposits of resources might be found, if such deposits in fact existed. Furthermore, if an operator received permission to proceed with develop- ment under CRAMRA, that operator was accorded exclusive development rights. Without CRAMRA, Antarctica's ambiguous legal status would likely dissuade potential developers from taking substantial investment risks to work in the Antarctic. The reality of CRAMRA as a regulatory regime would make the possibility of mining in Antarctica distinctly more a reality.

The sea change in international opinion against mining in Antarctica stemmed from a number of concerns about the Antarctic minerals regime, voiced from several sectors of the international community. The scientific community was intensely concerned about preserving the Antarctic environment. Scientists generally are not eager to have their pristine lab- oratory transformed into open-pit mining operations, nor to have oppor- tunities for research constrained or displaced because of mineral develop- ment activities, both onshore and offshore. Most vehement in promoting wilderness values were international environment groups, led by Green- peace and the Antarctic and Southern Ocean Coalition. These organis- ations lobbied long and hard during the minerals negotiations to persuade national delegates that the Antarctic should be left as a world park. Failing that, and given that a minerals regime was becoming inevitable, they then pressed for the strongest possible standards and environmentally sensitive provisions to protect Antarctica's flora, fauna and natural habitat from the certain environmental degradation that would result from mining operations. Much to these organisations' credit, throughout the nego- tiations, environmental standards were clarified, strengthened and integrated into the regime's infrastructure – though less so than what these groups had hoped to obtain.[10]

Also noteworthy for spotlighting international environmental concern over Antarctica were annual debates between 1983–8 in the UN General Assembly. Admittedly, these discussions often assumed more the form of political rhetoric than legal reasoning. Even so, the fact that they took place underscored the global community's concern over Antarctica and the disposition of its resource wealth. In so doing, environmental preservation became salient in the debate.[11]

General deficiencies of CRAMRA

Important for international legitimacy is the quality of a regime's applicability to the changing international society of which it is a part.[12]

In this respect, CRAMRA's perceived applicability as a regime was viewed as deficient and inadequate on several counts. For one, CRAMRA did not resolve the claims conundrum on the continent, whether in terms of the lawfulness of title or the legal status of overlapping sectors. The claims remained frozen under Article IV of the Antarctic Treaty, which in essence was repeated in Article 9 of CRAMRA. Even so, the seven claimant states were given a certain special status by virtue of their claims in the voting qualifications set out for the Regulatory Committees in Article 32. That claimant states enjoyed such special voting consideration because they have claims to the continent – claims not recognised by any member of the international community except themselves – should not

[10] See, e.g., Antarctic and Southern Ocean Coalition, 'Some Solutions to Problems with the Draft Antarctic Minerals Convention (MR/17, Revision IV)', *ASOC Information Paper*, no. 1, 1988 of 26 January 1988; Antarctic and Southern Ocean Coalition, 'Some Solutions to Problems with the Draft Antarctic Minerals Convention (MR/17, Revision V)', *ASOC Information Paper*, no. 2, 1988, of 26 March 1988; J. Barnes, P. J. Lipperman and K. Rigg, 'Waste Management in Antarctica', in R. Wolfrum (ed.), *Antarctic Challenge III: Conflicting Interests, Cooperation, Environmental Protection, Economic Development* (Berlin: Duncker & Humblot, 1988), pp. 491–529; and the many articles in *ECO*, the occasional newsletter of the Antarctic and Southern Ocean Coalition during 1983–8.

[11] Compare R. Woolcott, 'The Legitimacy of the United Nations' Challenge to the Antarctic Treaty', in Wolfrum (ed.), *Antarctic Challenge III*, pp. 229–342; A. Koroma, 'Safeguarding the Interests of Mankind in the Use of Antarctica', in *ibid.*, pp. 243–52; C. Maquieira, 'The Question of Antarctica at the United Nations – The End of Consensus?', in *ibid.*, pp. 253–70; and C. C. Joyner, 'Is There An Asian Perspective on Antarctica?', in R. A. Herr and B. W. Davis (eds.), *Asia in Antarctica* (Canberra: Centre for Resource and Environmental Studies, Australian National University, 1994), pp. 41–72.

[12] See Chapter 1.

be lost in appraising the legal significance of this Treaty. Detractors pointed to this as an undesirable feature of CRAMRA because it conferred on claimants an undeserved status not legally acceptable to the international community.[13]

Second, the Convention did not temper international criticism, especially in the UN General Assembly, over inclusion of the then white minority regime of South Africa as a member of the Consultative Party group. The government of South Africa remained a Consultative Party and enjoyed automatic rights to participate as a principal decision-maker in the minerals regime.[14]

Third, the Convention failed to specify where profits, or revenues derived from mineral activities in Antarctica, would go. Nor did it furnish satisfactory answers for explaining how revenues derived from minerals development might be disposed so as not to prejudice, in the words of the Preamble to the Antarctic Treaty, 'the interest of all mankind', but yet would still contribute to ensuring that 'Antarctica shall continue forever to be used exclusively for peaceful purposes and shall not become the scene or object of international discord'.[15]

Nor could the Convention guarantee that the Antarctic environment would remain in pristine condition should mining operations go forward on and around the continent. True, environmental principles and safeguards were plainly written into the Convention; their efficacy, however, remained to be tested as policy in practice. In any case, some environmental degradation was bound to occur if mineral resource activities proceeded, although any measure of those impacts eluded estimation.

Criticisms by the environmental community

Central to the debate over CRAMRA's legitimacy was whether a minerals regime would be likely to encourage or discourage exploratory and developmental pursuits by private corporations in Antarctica. Treaty advocates,

---

[13] Claims are asserted to portions of Antarctica by seven states: Argentina, Australia, Chile, France, New Zealand, Norway and the United Kingdom. On the legal questions and problematic nature of Antarctic claims, see C. C. Joyner, *Antarctica and the Law of the Sea* (Dordrecht: Martinus Nijhoff, 1992), pp. 41–74.

[14] See, e.g., UN General Assembly, resolution on the 'Question of South Africa', A/Res/40/156C, of 27 November 1985.

[15] As stated in the Preamble to the 1959 Antarctic Treaty, done 1 December 1959, entered into force 23 June 1961; published in *United Nations Treaty Series*, vol. 71, pp. 402*ff.* See generally the discussion in A. Koroma, 'Safeguarding the Interests of Mankind'.

such as the United States, the United Kingdom, Japan and the Soviet Union, argued that the Convention supplied an on site regulatory regime negotiated to consider the possibility of undertaking, and, if agreed upon, to manage, minerals activities in Antarctica. The premise here was that if no rules were put in place to regulate minerals activities in the frozen south, an unregulated scramble for minerals resources might occur there. CRAMRA's regulations would place legal strictures on potential miners, impose an orderly process for decision-making, operate to ensure environmental protection, and preclude Antarctica from becoming the 'scene or object of international discord'.[16]

Environmentalists countered that CRAMRA was gravely flawed in its primary purpose. The agreement was not really designed to preserve and protect the environment. Rather, environmentalists argued, its principal rationale was to provide opportunities and guarantees for mining and minerals development and to facilitate political accommodation between various groups of Consultative Parties. By its very character mining could not take place without damaging the environment. If a genuine aspiration to protect the Antarctic environment existed, the Consultative Parties would not permit any areas to be opened for minerals exploitation. Furthermore, if minerals development went forward in the Antarctic, not only would the physical environment suffer, but so too would the quality of vital scientific research on the continent. Scientific research and international cooperation, the hallmarks and founding purposes of the Antarctic Treaty, were depicted as being victimised by priorities of commercial exploitation. Preoccupation with the search for commercial resources would diminish scientific cooperation and breed competition over prospecting activities, at the expense of pure scientific research.

The environmentalist argument opposing creation of a minerals regime pivoted on maintaining the *status quo* of the continent as provided for in the 1959 Antarctic Treaty: a peaceful, non-militarised area of the world reserved for scientific research only. Environmentalists contended that an unregulated free-for-all for Antarctic minerals was not likely to occur in the absence of investment security and acknowledged property rights. On the other hand, by stabilising such guarantees for security and property

---

[16] For elaboration of this view, see generally R. T. Scully, 'The Antarctic Treaty as a System', in R. A. Herr, H. R. Hall and M. G. Haward, *Antarctica's Future: Continuity or Change?* (Hobart: Tasmanian Government Printer, 1990), pp. 95–102; and J. A. Heap, 'Sovereignty as a Source of Stress', in *ibid.*, pp. 181–8.

rights, the Convention might actually encourage mining. Environmentalists also alleged that mining in Antarctica might inject rivalry over strategic resources. If so, this situation not only could put Antarctica's environment at risk, it could also provoke destabilisation of the Antarctic Treaty and undermine the non-militarised status of the region.

Extremely disturbing for environmentalists was that the Convention would be the slippery slope leading inevitably to exploitation and development of mineral resources in Antarctica. It was feared that the Treaty supplied incentives for commercial mineral activities. Its entry into force would lift the policy of voluntary restraint and effectively make commercial mining lawful. It was believed that these developments would increase the chances for discovering commercially exploitable deposits. Clearing the way to mine legally would lead to prospecting, which could lead to mineral discoveries, which could give rise to exploration and exploitation. That pattern inevitably would have produced environmental degradation.

The environmental community vowed to point out deficiencies and doubts about both the environmental purpose and integrity of the proposed regime.[17] To a large degree they succeeded, as demonstrated by the decisions in 1989 of Australia and France not to participate in the agreement.[18]

CRAMRA'S LEGACY OF LEGITIMACY

When sufficient state practice is demonstrated, applicability and acceptance – as qualities of a regime's legitimacy – can give rise to international legal obligations. Such obligations, or norms, arise when a valid legal requirement created by states is imposed by states upon themselves. International norms oblige or impose duties upon members of international society. Obligation has to do with the notion of bindingness. Norms imply that parties are obligated, not merely obliged, to conform with that particular directive. The critical consideration that emerges is whether a government ought to comply with that norm. Further, international law not only deals with values of world society. It also pertains directly to facts. Normative behaviour is learned and is culturally relative. As inter-

[17] See generally J. Barnes, 'Protection of the Environment in Antarctica: Are Present Regimes Enough?', in A. Jørgensen-Dahl and W. Østreng (eds.), *The Antarctic Treaty System in World Politics* (London: Macmillan, 1991), pp. 186–228.
[18] See the discussion in Chapter 6.

national guidelines, norms are supposed to indicate means of social restraint to preserve international order.[19]

The Antarctic Treaty System contains norms that embody directives according to which the Consultative Parties governments are bound to act. The proof of a norm's validity comes in the actual practice of those states. If a government acts in ways that reflect the effective operation of an espoused norm, then we can say the norm directive exists in fact, and also that that government's action is legitimate. However, if numerous governments operate contrary to the behaviour prescribed by an international norm – in an intentional, persistent and continuous manner – then the actual legitimacy of the purported norm may become questionable and suspect. Also, if a single government intentionally acts contrary to the directive of an acknowledged norm, then the action of that government may be said to be illegitimate.[20]

In the case of Antarctica, the Consultative Parties clearly agreed that the normative principles enshrined in Articles 2 and 4 of CRAMRA were of such importance that they should be preserved and enhanced in a more comprehensive environmental protection protocol. That supplies compelling evidence that the CRAMRA legacy continues as a viable reality, notwithstanding the static legal condition of that instrument.

The negotiation over eight years of an instrument designed to regulate minerals activities in the Antarctic produced a certain consensus on cardinal norms among the parties involved. Chief among these normative considerations was the need to undertake minerals activities only after certain criteria for ensuring environmental protection were met. The core thesis of this chapter maintains that these normative considerations negotiated for CRAMRA coalesced into three central norms of environmental law, which eventually were inserted into the Protocol:

---

[19] See generally J. Kunz, 'Revolutionary Creation of Norms of International Law', *American Journal of International Law*, vol. 41, no. 1, 1947, p. 119; and C. C. Joyner, 'UN General Assembly Resolutions and International Law: Rethinking the Contemporary Dynamics of Norm-Creation', *California Western International Law Journal*, vol. 11, no. 2, 1981, pp. 445–78.

[20] The normative basis for states involved in Antarctic affairs is, of course, the 1959 Antarctic Treaty, around which other components to the Antarctic Treaty System are appended. Among the norms prominent in this Treaty are peaceful uses only of the region, non-militarisation of Antarctica, non-nuclearisation of Antarctica, freedom of scientific research and open exchange of scientific information in the Antarctic. Inspections provided for in Article VII of the Treaty are intended to verify the lawfulness of states' activities in the area. More than 100 inspections have been conducted by national observers, and as of 1996, not one overt violation of the Antarctic Treaty has been publicly reported.

1　protection of the Antarctic environment and its dependent and associ-
　　ated ecosystems is the paramount consideration for conducting activi-
　　ties in the region;
2　sufficient information regarding environmental impacts must be avail-
　　able before making decisions about whether activities should go for-
　　ward in Antarctica; critical in this respect is the role of and need for
　　environmental impact assessments; and
3　persons who degrade or injure the Antarctic environment are liable
　　for the resultant damage.

To assist in enforcing this effort, monitoring of activities and inspections
of operations is permissible. Even though CRAMRA fell increasingly into
international disrepute, Consultative Party negotiators recognised the
value of retaining these norms. Each accordingly was purposefully integrated into the Protocol.

The normative legacy of CRAMRA

The Convention contributed notably to enhancing the normative foundation for environmental protection in the Antarctic Treaty System. The
agreement marked completion of the resource protection regime under
the ATS (the other aspects being for fauna and flora, seals, and living
marine resources) by providing regulation and environmental standards
affecting minerals activities. It provided a negotiated, agreed-upon consensus approach for dealing with the regulation of mineral activities that
impinge upon complex questions of national sovereignty and environmental protection in Antarctica. CRAMRA created formal institutions to
address those issues. It established substantive norms for environmental
protection, chief among them the principle that one may not proceed in
mineral activities unless sufficient information on exploration or development is available. Importantly, the sufficient information requirement
entailed a process checked by the need for consensus agreement by all
parties. Each of these contributions by CRAMRA was subsequently integrated into the Protocol.

　　The Convention affirmed a strong position on protecting the environment from damage caused by mineral activities. Article 4 set down principles for judging the acceptability of mineral activities, though in a general way possibly open to subjective interpretation. Decisions would be
taken on the basis of 'sufficient information'. That is, before proceeding
with minerals development, sufficient information had to be available for

decision-makers to ascertain whether unacceptable damage might be done to the environment.

The legitimacy of CRAMRA rests in its furnishing the normative core of the environmental protection system for the Protocol. For CRAMRA, the paramount normative considerations are found in Articles 2 and 4, which were substantially carried over as Article 3 of the Environmental Protocol. A comparative assessment of these provisions clearly substantiates the influence of the former upon the latter. This is true in terms of both authoritative wording and substantive content.

The need for environmental protection

The Convention evolved over eight years through a process of negotiations chaired by Christopher Beeby of New Zealand. The so-called Beeby texts, named for and personally drafted by the Chairman, underwent numerous revisions. Though they were neither officially indorsed nor authoritatively released, these draft texts evolved into the CRAMRA instrument. By 1988, the objectives of the minerals regime had been extensively elaborated into their eventual form. In full, Article 2 of CRAMRA provided that:

1 This Convention is an integral part of the Antarctic Treaty System, comprising the Antarctic Treaty, the measures in effect under that Treaty, and its associated separate legal instruments, the prime purpose of which is to ensure that Antarctica shall continue forever to be used exclusively for peaceful purposes and shall not become the scene or object of international discord. The Parties provide through this Convention, the principles it establishes, the rules it prescribes, the institutions it creates and the decisions adopted pursuant to it, a means for:
   (a) assessing the possible impact on the Antarctic environment of Antarctic mineral resource activities;
   (b) determining whether Antarctic mineral activities are acceptable;
   (c) governing the conduct of such Antarctic mineral resource activities as may be found acceptable; and
   (d) ensuring that any Antarctic mineral resource activities are undertaken in strict conformity with this Convention.
2 In implementing this Convention, the Parties shall ensure that Antarctic mineral resource activities, should they occur, take place in a manner consistent with all the components of the Antarctic Treaty system and the obligations flowing therefrom.
3 In relation to Antarctic mineral resource activities, should they occur, the par-

ties acknowledge the special responsibility of the Antarctic Treaty Consultative Parties for the protection of the environment and the need to:

(a) protect the Antarctic environment and its dependent and associated ecosystems;

(b) respect Antarctica's significance for, and influence on, the global environment;

(c) respect other legitimate uses of the Antarctic;

(d) respect Antarctica's scientific value and aesthetic and wilderness qualities;

(e) ensure the safety of operations in Antarctica;

(f) promote opportunities for fair and effective participation of all Parties; and

(g) take into account the interests of the international community as a whole.

Article 2 of CRAMRA thus set out objectives and principles of the minerals regime as regards other appendages of the Treaty system: namely, the preservation of Antarctica for peaceful purposes only, representation of world community interests, and protection of the Antarctic environment.

According to paragraph 1 of Article 2, CRAMRA would become an essential facet of the Antarctic Treaty System that has as its 'prime purpose' to ensure that Antarctica shall be used forever exclusively for peaceful purposes and never become the scene or object of international discord. The overt presumption is that CRAMRA, by its promulgation, is to contribute toward that desirable end. Article 2 goes on to designate the overall objective of the Antarctic minerals regime as supplying a means for accomplishing five goals:

1 The regime through its institutions would assess what possible impacts Antarctic mineral resource activities might have upon the Antarctic environment.

2 The regime aimed to ascertain whether such activities might be 'acceptable'.

3 The regime through its institutions aimed to govern environmental, technological, political, legal and economic aspects of minerals activities that are determined to be permissible.

4 The regime through its institutions would establish rules to protect the Antarctic environment.

5 The regime through its institutions would work to ensure that any Antarctic mineral resource activities that should proceed are in 'strict conformity' with the regulations of the regime, including principles established by it.

Several reasons suggest that provisions in Article 2 of CRAMRA contributed importantly to the Protocol. First, Article 2, paragraph 1 provides that the means to protect the Antarctic environment from unwanted impacts produced by minerals activities will come from the principles established, the rules prescribed and the institutions adopted by CRAMRA. Enforcement of such rules and principles is accomplished through prohibition of mineral activities unless deemed permissible and conducted in line with CRAMRA and all other regulations set down by the regime.

The objective of protecting the Antarctic environment against adverse impacts produced by mineral activities is to be accomplished in several different ways: by means of decision-making procedures that take into account environmental impact assessment, by setting substantive standards, by providing for the articulation of additional standards through institutions, and by institutionalising enforcement mechanisms. This stated criticality of broadly protecting the Antarctic environment asserted in paragraph 1 of Article 2 became a philosophical keystone underpinning the Protocol in general and its Article 3 in particular.

Article 2 of CRAMRA also clearly implies the need for an impact-assessment procedure. Such an assessment procedure would be done on two levels. First, on a general level, parties to CRAMRA would have to decide through the Commission whether mineral activities were generally acceptable, and whether an area should be opened for development of such activities. Second, the decision would bring into play provisions in Article 4 of CRAMRA requiring that certain preconditions must be met before an affirmative decision might be rendered about mineral resources activities.

The third paragraph of Article 2 of CRAMRA formally declares the 'special responsibility' of the Consultative Parties 'for the protection of the environment'. To this end, parties formally acknowledged several 'needs' as objectives, namely:

1 to protect the Antarctic environment and its dependent and associated ecosystems;
2 to respect Antarctica's significance for and its impact upon the earth's environment;
3 to respect other lawful uses of the Antarctic;
4 to respect Antarctica's scientific worth and aesthetic and wilderness values;
5 to ensure safe operations in Antarctica;
6 to promote opportunities for fair and effective participation by all parties; and

7   to take into account the interests of the international community. These are vital concerns that should not be disregarded.

These cardinal concerns of CRAMRA undergird the core principles of the Protocol as expressed in its Article 3. That provision affirms these essential 'needs' as it initially asserts the following:

The protection of the Antarctic environment and dependent and associated ecosystems and the intrinsic value of Antarctica, including its wilderness and aesthetic values and its value as an area for the conduct of scientific research, in particular research essential to understanding the global environment, shall be fundamental considerations in the planning and conduct of all activities in the Antarctic Treaty area.[21]

The point here is clear: the CRAMRA instrument assigned 'special responsibilities' in Article 2 for the Consultative Parties to perform certain 'needs' in protecting Antarctica's environment; the Protocol extrapolates and converts those 'needs' into the general commitment in its Article 3 as binding principles for environmental protection.

The requirement of sufficient information

The most salient substantive contribution made by CRAMRA to the Protocol is found in the former's Article 4, which designates 'Environmental Principles' for the minerals regime. The substance of this provision evolved substantially from its status as Article III in the early Beeby drafts into an eventual place as Article 4.

The final version of CRAMRA refines these principles into a more cogent, more inclusive, less subjective set of statements. Article III in the Beeby drafts was transformed into Article 4 in the final CRAMRA instrument and was made to contain the legally prescribed mandate for a 'sufficient information' requirement before any judgments could be made regarding minerals activities. That is, sufficient information about possible impacts of mineral resource activities had to be available to permit a well-founded determination of the likelihood of such impacts. Antarctic mineral resource activities would then not be allowed – i.e., would be prohibited – if such a determination found that those activities would produce significant adverse impacts upon the Antarctic environment or its dependent or associated ecosystems.[22] In addition, appropriate technology

---

[21] Protocol, Art. 3, para. 1.
[22] CRAMRA, Art. 4, para. 2.

must exist for carrying out safe operations[23] and for permitting monitoring of 'key environmental parameters and ecosystem components' in order to identify possible adverse effects and to enable effective and efficient response to accidents.[24]

The critical consideration here, which supplied the linchpin for CRAMRA's entire decision-making procedure, was contained in Article 4, paragraph 1. As mandated by this provision, no mineral activities could occur unless adequate information was available to permit informed judgments to be made about the potential impacts of mineral resource activities on the Antarctic environment:

Decisions about Antarctic mineral resource activities shall be based upon information adequate to enable informed judgements to be made about their possible impacts and no such activities shall take place unless this information is available for decisions relevant to those activities.[25]

As a consequence, mineral resource activities could go forward only if three criteria were met:

1 there had to be adequate information to evaluate possible impacts on the environment;
2 a premeditated judgment had to be made that such mineral activities would produce no adverse environmental effects; and
3 the conduct of such activities had to conform with CRAMRA and any regulatory measures taken pursuant to it.

Relatedly, the decision to identify an area to be opened for mineral activities had to be reached by consensus. Thus, any member of the Commission concerned over or dissatisfied about the identification of an area meeting environmental protection standards could block such identification – and hence exploration or development activity – with its single vote. Protection of Antarctica's environment had to be clearly confirmed by all, before any activity could be conducted to explore for or develop Antarctica's mineral resources.[26]

The adequate information requirement that had been incorporated into paragraph 4 of Article 4 of CRAMRA became neatly fitted into the Protocol as paragraph 2 of its Article 3. Article 4 of CRAMRA required that a judgment be made that the technology and procedures are available for

---

[23] *Ibid.*, Art. 4, para. 4(a).
[24] *Ibid.*, Art. 4, para. 4(c).
[25] *Ibid.*, Art. 4, para. 1.
[26] *Ibid.*, Art. 22, para. 2(c) and Art. 41, para. 2.

safe operations and compliance with environmental impact assessments.[27] Similarly, the Protocol's Article 3 maintains that judgments must take into account 'whether technology and procedures are available for environmentally safe operations'.[28] Article 4(4)(b) of CRAMRA required that there be present the 'capacity to monitor key environmental parameters and ecosystem components' as a precondition for judging whether Antarctic mineral activities might take place.[29] The Protocol borrows nearly verbatim from that provision. Article 3, paragraph 2(c)(v) of the Protocol asserts that activities in the Antarctic Treaty area shall be planned and conducted on the basis of sufficient information and informed judgments that take into full account:

whether there exists the capacity to monitor key environmental parameters and ecosystems so as to identify and provide early warning of any adverse effects of the activity and to provide for such modification of operating procedures as may be necessary in the light of the results of monitoring or increased knowledge of the Antarctic environment and dependent and associated ecosystems.[30]

This provision unmistakably owes its origin to the stipulation first negotiated for CRAMRA. Likewise, Article 4, paragraph 4(c) of CRAMRA would have required that no judgment be made until there existed 'the capacity to respond effectively to accidents, particularly those with potential environmental effects'.[31] The companion provision in the Protocol is its Article 3, paragraph 2. In nearly verbatim fashion, this paragraph mandates that judgments about the permissibility of conducting certain activities in the Antarctic Treaty area shall take full account of 'whether there exists the capacity to respond promptly and effectively to accidents, particularly those with potential environmental effects'.[32] Again, the progenitor of this provision is directly traceable to CRAMRA.

Environmental impact assessments

Paragraphs 2 and 3 of Article 4 in CRAMRA supplied precursors for the Protocol's application of environmental impact assessments as a protective precondition for activities in the Antarctic. The requirement for

---

[27] *Ibid.*, Art. 4, para. 4(a).
[28] Protocol, Art. 3, para. 2(c)(iv).
[29] CRAMRA, Art. 4, para. 4(b).
[30] Protocol, Art. 3, para. 2(c)(v).
[31] CRAMRA, Art. 4, para. 4(c).
[32] Protocol, Art. 3, para. 2(c)(vi).

environmental impact assessments in CRAMRA is set out in Article 4, paragraph 2, which in full provides that:

No Antarctic mineral resource activity shall take place until it is judged, based upon assessment of its possible impacts on the Antarctic environment and on dependent and associated ecosystems, that the activity in question would not cause:
(a) significant adverse effects on air and water quality;
(b) significant changes in atmospheric, terrestrial or marine environments;
(c) significant changes in the distribution, abundance or productivity of populations of species of fauna or flora;
(d) further jeopardy to endangered or threatened species or populations of such species;
(e) degradation of, or substantial risk to, areas of special biological, scientific, historic, aesthetic or wilderness significance.[33]

Paragraph 3 of Article 4 of CRAMRA goes on to assert that:

No Antarctic mineral resource activity shall take place until it is judged, based upon assessment of its possible impacts, that the activity in question would not cause significant adverse effects on global or regional climate or weather patterns.[34]

The Protocol melds these two paragraphs of CRAMRA neatly into paragraph 2(b) of its Article 3. In full, this provision in the Protocol provides that:

[A]ctivities in the Antarctic Treaty area shall be planned and conducted so as to avoid:
 (i) adverse effects on climate or weather patterns;
 (ii) significant adverse effects on air or water quality;
(iii) significant changes in atmospheric, terrestrial (including aquatic), glacial or marine environments;
(iv) detrimental changes in the distribution, abundance or productivity of species or populations of fauna or flora;
 (v) further jeopardy to endangered or threatened species or populations of such species;
(vi) degradation of, or substantial risk to, areas of special biological, scientific, historic, aesthetic or wilderness significance.[35]

The Protocol asserts as one of its cardinal principles the need for environmental impact statements. These statements are intended to facili-

---

[33] CRAMRA, Art. 4, para. 2.
[34] *Ibid.*, Art 4, para. 3(e).
[35] Protocol, Art. 3, para. 2(b).

tate the planning and conduct of activities and to assess what effects they might produce for Antarctica's air and water quality, as well as changes in the region's atmospheric, terrestrial, or marine environments. Such assessments are also intended to determine whether activities would constitute 'further jeopardy' to endangered species in the region, or result in degradation or 'substantial risk' to areas of special historical, biological, scientific and wilderness significance. Significantly, the progenitor for requisite environmental impact assessments stemmed directly from CRAMRA.

Enforcement through liability and inspection

Provisions in Article 8 of CRAMRA aimed at strengthening the environmental regulations in the regime. These provisions would make an operator strictly liable for damage to the Antarctic environment and associated ecosystems caused by its minerals activities.[36] The operator would be liable to pay for damage if restoration were not satisfactory, and the operator would be liable for clean-up costs incurred by another agent.[37] Significantly, the notion of liability is included in Article 16 of the Protocol, albeit the 'rules and procedures relating to liability for damage arising from activities taking place in the Antarctic Treaty area' are left to be elaborated in a special annex to that instrument.[38] That annex has yet to be completed.

Article 12 of CRAMRA provided for the inspection of mineral resource activities. Such inspections would be performed of all 'stations, installations, and equipment relating to Antarctic mineral resource activities in the area in which these activities are regulated by this Convention, as well as ships and aircraft supporting such activities at points of discharging or embarking cargoes or personnel'.[39] These inspections, including aerial inspections, could have been conducted by observers appointed by any member of the Commission, as well as by observers designated by the Commission or Regulatory Committees.[40] Presumably, violations of environmental standards were to have been reported back to the Commission and the relevant Regulatory Committee.

To facilitate enforcement of its provisions, the Protocol in Article 14 generally adopts the inspection procedure similarly set out in CRAMRA

---

[36] CRAMRA, Art. 8, para. 2.
[37] *Ibid.*, Art. 8, para. 2(d).
[38] Protocol, Art. 16.
[39] CRAMRA, Art. 12, para. 1.
[40] *Ibid.*, Art. 12, para. 1(4).

and authorised by Article VII of the 1959 Antarctic Treaty. Observers may be designated by any Consultative Party, and they are to be given 'access to all parts of stations, installations, equipment, ships and aircraft open to inspection under Article VII(3) of the Antarctic Treaty, as well as to all records maintained thereon'.[41] Importantly, inspection procedures are left to be established by a future Antarctic Consultative Party Meeting.[42]

Clearly, CRAMRA contains several provisions specifically designed to preserve, protect and conserve the Antarctic environment, inclusive of marine areas. It is also fair to posit that the environmental standards and safeguards in CRAMRA were among the strongest, most far reaching and authoritative ever negotiated for an international commons regime up to that time. That was not the equivalent of saying, however, that these provisions were capable of guaranteeing the prevention of environmental degradation, or insuring that incidents of regional pollution would not occur. No international legal instrument can ever be capable of accomplishing that, not even one as far-reaching as the Protocol.

CONCLUDING REMARKS

Antarctic Treaty law functions as a pragmatic legal system. It takes into account existing relationships among states and translates them into legal rules. In this manner, norms are derived from traditional sources of international law. As with norm creation in international law, actual demonstration through state conduct operates as the main indicator of international acceptability of norms for the Antarctic. In the case of Antarctic law, norms tend to evolve most directly out of negotiated principles formally agreed upon through consensus by the states most involved in Antarctic affairs.

Certain normative considerations in CRAMRA evolved for governments involved in Antarctic affairs. First, there is the need to plan for and assess the impact of conducting activities in the Antarctic so as to limit adverse impacts upon the environment. This is intended to meet the need to respect Antarctica's scientific value and protect its wilderness qualities. Second, there is the need to have available sufficient information before making decisions about activities that might have impacts upon the Antarctic environment. Third, some form of enforcement mechanism is

---

[41] Protocol, Art. 14, para. 3.
[42] *Ibid.*, Art. 14, para. 2(b).

necessary to ensure compliance with these mandates. The assignment of direct liability for damage and allowing for unannounced on-site inspectors anywhere on the continent can contribute substantively to this end. Each of these normative considerations, set down in the CRAMRA instrument, was subsequently preserved and strengthened in the Protocol.

The environmental-protection system in CRAMRA formally evolved through two provisions, Articles 2 and 4. The former deals with general principles and objectives of the regime, while the latter speaks to specific principles that should be considered in taking decisions on mineral resource activities. These principles and objectives were negotiated with normative intentions. They are accordingly reiterated in substantial part in the Protocol. Also important to realise in this regard is that CRAMRA relies on the same principles of conservation as does the Protocol. In fact, far from being contradicted, the legitimacy of CRAMRA is reinforced by the Protocol. The ban on mining aside, CRAMRA supplied exceedingly strong conservation measures aimed at environmental protection and resource preservation – measures which in effect were subsequently incorporated into the Protocol.

For CRAMRA proponents, the importance of CRAMRA was realised in its inherent contributions, in the novel regime and sophisticated institutions that were created to regulate the development of mineral resources in the Antarctic. For environmentalists, on the other hand, the importance of CRAMRA was seen in what was deleted from the regulatory system, in provisions absent in the regime that might more comprehensively safeguard the Antarctic environment. In either event, CRAMRA today remains in a condition of legal abeyance. It proceeds neither toward ratification and entry into force, nor toward withering away and total disintegration. CRAMRA remains a legally fertilised seed for a minerals regime lacking the necessary nutrients for germination.

In an Antarctic Treaty System of conventions run by states, legitimacy is determined by the willingness of national governments to translate normative concepts and principles into adherent policy actions. The fact is that norms negotiated for CRAMRA were subsequently incorporated into norms adopted for the Protocol. This realisation clearly confirms that CRAMRA left a notable legacy of legitimacy, even if that instrument is itself consigned to a static legal status. The ultimate demonstration of CRAMRA's legacy of legitimacy, however, will come only when the Protocol is fully ratified by the Consultative Parties and enters into force as environmental law binding upon the activities of those states throughout the Antarctic region.

11

The legitimacy of the Protocol on Environmental Protection to the Antarctic Treaty

FRANCISCO ORREGO VICUÑA

INTRODUCTION

The Antarctic Treaty provisions which refer to the environment have a rather general, or sometimes indirect, scope.[1] This has not prevented the Consultative Parties from undertaking intensive legislative action in this field.[2] From the simplicity of the first recommendations relating to the impact of man on the Antarctic environment, followed by the more specific measures on oil pollution, and arriving at the current complex regime for environmental protection, there has been a gradual expansion of protection systems and a noticeable development in the subject matter.

Chapter 7 discussed the Environmental Protocol and evaluated the adequacy of its main provisions. This chapter seeks to show how the evolvement of the Protocol reflects a gradual adaptation of the ATS to changing circumstances, focusing on the other three facets of the regime legitimacy concept: the internal coherence of the provisions; their relationship to other sources of regulation; and acceptance of the provisions among subjects and third parties.

ENVIRONMENTAL PROTECTION IN THE ANTARCTIC: EMERGENCE AND CHALLENGES

The legitimacy of the Protocol on Environmental Protection derives not so much from its very provisions as from the fact that it relies heavily on the prior work of the Consultative Meetings. The Protocol has in essence

---

[1] See especially Art. IX, para. 1(f) of the Antarctic Treaty in reference to the 'Preservation and conservation of living resources in Antarctica'.

[2] See F. Orrego Vicuña, *Antarctic Mineral Exploitation: The Emerging Legal Framework* (Cambridge University Press, 1988), chapter 2, section 2.

reordered and to some extent legally strengthened the aggregate of rules that were already available within the ATS, improving the internal coherence of this *corpus juris*.

The first measures for environmental protection to become the subject of Consultative Party legislative action addressed man's impact on the Antarctic environment.[3] The main concern at this level related to the identification and assessment of disturbances caused by human activity on the continent, the adoption of measures to minimise them, and the launching of pertinent scientific programmes to measure subsequent changes. For this purpose, a close association was established with the Scientific Committee on Antarctic Research (SCAR). Measures proposed by the latter organisation led, among other steps, to the adoption of the Code of Conduct for Antarctic Expeditions and Station Activities.[4]

Three equally important aspects of environmental policy were identified in the development of this line of action. First, no activity should be undertaken that could modify the environment of extensive Antarctic areas, without the necessary measures for protection and control. Second, all measures should be compatible with the interests of mankind. And third, the policy incorporated the notion of monitoring environmental changes and of appropriate public information in this particularly sensitive field.[5] The concept of protecting associated and dependent ecosystems also arose in this context.[6] It was these first steps which ultimately led to consideration of more comprehensive measures for environmental protection.

The aggregate of these measures came under increasing criticism with the rising concern for the environment throughout the world in the 1980s and 1990s. In particular, critics argued that there was no comprehensive protection system for the Antarctic and that many of the measures in force had arisen from isolated concerns, rendering the application and evolution erratic, and the environmental criteria lacking in precision.[7] Measures, it has been argued, are sectoral in their approach and without

---

[3] See especially Recommendations VI-4, VII-1, VIII-13, and IX-5, in J. A. Heap (ed.), *Handbook of the Antarctic Treaty System*, 7th ed. (Cambridge: Scott Polar Research Institute, 1990), section 2.1.1.

[4] Recommendation VIII-11; see Heap (ed.), *Handbook*, section 2.2.

[5] Recommendation VIII-13.

[6] Report of the IX ATCM, London 1977; see Heap (ed.), *Handbook*, p. 2,103.

[7] Australia: *Protection of the Antarctic Environment and its Dependent and Associated Ecosystems: A Review of Existing Measures*, doc. XI ATSCM/INFO.40, 23 November 1990, p. 2.

general rules and precise definitions; also, the procedures for adoption and application of measures tend to be overly time-consuming.[8] From the legal point of view, critics have complained that the measures lack binding effects or are too uncertain in this respect, often depending for their application on national jurisdiction.[9] All of this has allegedly resulted in unsatisfactory compliance, a certain weakness in the capacity to respond to incidents threatening the environment, and inadequate environmental impact assessment.[10] Other more extreme criticisms have been made with a view to justifying the establishment of a comprehensive environmental protection system for Antarctica.[11] The Protocol responded to this line of criticism but did not change the substance of the protection afforded under the ATS.

Undoubtedly, the current system for environmental protection in Antarctica is far from perfect, but there is also no doubt that it has shown a remarkable evolution and improvement over the years. If compared to an ideal model, its defects may stand out; but if the Antarctic protection system is compared to a model based on what is feasible and realistic, it will be clear that its contribution has been significant. Many aspects of the system may be improved, especially regarding its environmental assessment, collection and analysis of information, application and enforcement of measures, integration of the various protection systems and higher participation, among other measures;[12] but it would be a mistake to dispense with the results already achieved in the design of the approach followed by the Protocol. As will be demonstrated in this chapter, in practice the Antarctic Treaty System itself had already undertaken a good part of this improvement.

TOWARDS A COMPREHENSIVE PROTECTION SYSTEM

In the context of these challenges, six key components of the evolving Antarctic environmental protection system are of particular interest: environmental impact assessment, the protection of Antarctic fauna and

---

[8] *Ibid.*, pp. 6–9.
[9] *Ibid.*, pp. 9–11.
[10] *Ibid.*, pp. 11–13.
[11] Antarctic and Southern Ocean Coalition, 'Effective Legal Mechanisms for Protection of the Antarctic Environment', XI ATSCM, *ASOC Information Paper 1990-2*, 21 November 1990.
[12] L. A. Kimball, *Southern Exposure: Deciding Antarctica's Future* (Washington, DC: World Resources Institute, 1990), pp. 13*ff*.

flora, waste management, measures to protect the marine environment, the system of area protection, and the preservation of Antarctic resources. The issue of acceptance will be dealt with in the concluding section of this chapter, whereas this section discusses the internal coherence of Protocol provisions and their relationship to non-ATS legislation.

Environmental impact and risk assessment

As noted above, the Consultative Meetings gradually started to incorporate procedures relating to environmental impact assessment of Antarctic activities, both of a scientific and of a logistic nature. For this purpose, competent national organisations were repeatedly urged to carry out preliminary or detailed assessments, as required, to prevent, minimise and correct negative effects that could result from those activities.[13] Scientific guidelines to carry out this type of assessment have also been drawn up, based on work carried out by SCAR and the United Nations Environment Programme.[14] At the same time, ways to put them into practice have frequently been discussed – all of which, once again, has led to consideration of additional criteria in the context of comprehensive environmental protection measures.[15]

A very specific application of the evolving assessment criteria concerned the problem of the location of new stations built in Antarctica. Due to air transport services and other facilities offered by the Chilean Air Force between Punta Arenas and King George Island in the South Shetland Islands, a considerable number of stations have chosen to locate on that island, creating a problem of excessive concentration and its ensuing environmental effects and interference in the activities carried out there.[16] This matter was examined as from the XIII Consultative Meeting; it was recommended that the parties carry out a consulting, coordination and cooperation process before proceeding to locate new stations, seeking to minimise those harmful effects. Under all circumstances, a detailed environmental assessment of the plan in question should be prepared.[17]

---

[13] Recommendations XII-3 and XIV-2; see Heap (ed.), *Handbook*, section 2.1.2.
[14] Recommendation XIV-2.
[15] Reports of the XIV and XV Consultative Meetings, held in Rio de Janeiro 1987 and in Paris 1989, respectively; see Heap (ed.), *Handbook*, pp. 2,110–11.
[16] R. K. Headland and P. L. Keage, 'Activities on the King George Island Group, South Shetland Islands, Antarctica', *Polar Record*, vol. 22, no. 140, 1985, pp. 475–84.
[17] Recommendations XIII-6 and XV-17; see Heap (ed.), *Handbook*, section 2.1.3. See also Reports of the XIII ATCM, Brussels 1985, paras. 59–60; of the XIV ATCM, Rio de

On the basis of these recommendations, some countries have now built their installations in alternative locations.

Importantly, specific measures for environmental impact assessment were introduced in the *resource regimes* of the ATS. In 1988 the functioning of the *Seals Convention* was the subject of a thorough review in the light of its own mandate.[18] On that occasion the number of seals hunted between 1964 and 1985 under the permit system was examined specially; the average was 483 seals per year, which was estimated a low figure and could not be considered to have important harmful effects on any seal population.[19] However, the meeting considered the improvement of criteria for the issuance of special permits, exchange of information, development of research and other protection measures. No Contracting Party has notified that commercial exploitation of seals in Antarctica has been initiated, whereby it can be considered that the designed protection measures have proven reasonably efficient.

As to *CCAMLR*, the initial problems of proposed conservation measures being systematically blocked by a few important fishing nations were gradually overcome. Since 1987 the system has been marked by a relationship of greater trust among the institutions, government interests and scientific criteria, and this trust has paved the way for severe conservation measures. In addition to the establishment of total allowable catches for major species and the closing of some fishing areas, its expeditious information system should be emphasised.

During the first stage, relations between the Commission and the Scientific Committee were also difficult. This resulted in the former rejecting many of the latter's proposals as lacking in scientific evidence, while at the same time failing to make any effort to direct the work of the Committee towards activities of interest. But this was also to change. Consensus in the institutions has come to have a more technical than political perspective; the Commission and the Committee have worked together on designing a policy on conservation and management of fishing, and the collection and organisation of information has been facilitated beyond measure. This has led to a long-term programme for the

Janeiro 1987, paras. 106–12; and of the XV ATCM, Paris 1989, paras. 69 and 152–4, in *ibid.*, pp. 2,112–13.
[18] Meeting to Review the Operation of the Convention for the Conservation of Antarctic Seals, London, 12–16 September 1988; see Heap (ed.), *Handbook*, section 4.1.4.
[19] *Ibid.*, para. 12.

assessment and monitoring of the key components of the Antarctic marine ecosystem.[20]

The system of this Convention still has to be perfected in many aspects, but it is also evident that its evolution is moving in the right direction. As discussed in greater detail in Chapter 5, one interesting criterion evolving in this field is to reverse the burden of proof, shifting from those who call for conservation measures to those who carry out exploitation activities. This precautionary approach would mean that the latter should prove that their activities do not affect the conservation of the species, whereby conservation becomes the prevalent system.[21]

Several provisions of *CRAMRA* have a specific bearing on environmental policy: of these, the objectives and general principles in Article 2, the principles and environmental criteria in Article 4, the system of protected areas in Article 13, the respect for other uses of the Antarctic in Article 15 and the relationship established with the Antarctic Treaty System and international organisations as a whole in Articles 10 and 34[22] are especially important.

This environmental protection system is based on the fundamental principle that every decision must be adopted on the grounds of adequate information about the possible impact of the activity in question, and that none of these activities will take place until such information is available. Even in the case of prospecting, which is not subject to prior authorisation, the decision of a state may be objected to, which will result in the need to justify it with adequate information.

Another essential principle is that there will be no mineral activities,

---

[20] See in general, J. A. Heap, 'Has CCAMLR Worked? Management Policies and Ecological Needs', in A. Jørgensen-Dahl and W. Østreng (eds.), *The Antarctic Treaty System in World Politics* (London: Macmillan, 1991), pp. 43–53; M. Basson and J. R. Beddington, 'CCAMLR: The Practical Implications of an Eco-System Approach', in *ibid.*, pp. 54–69; C. Rinaldi, 'SCAR in the ATS: Conflict or Harmony?', *ibid.*, pp. 153–60. See also J.-P. Puissochet, 'CCAMLR – A Critical Assessment', *ibid.*, pp. 70–6; D. Powell, 'Antarctic Marine Living Resources and CCAMLR', in R. A. Herr, H. R. Hall and M. G. Haward (eds.), *Antarctica's Future: Continuity or Change?* (Hobart: Tasmanian Government Printer, 1990), pp. 61–70; S. Nicol, 'CCAMLR and Its Approaches to Management of the Krill Fishery', *Polar Record*, vol. 27, no. 162, 1991, pp. 229–36; Commission for the Conservation of Antarctic Marine Living Resources, *Schedule of Conservation Measures in Force 1991–1992*, 1992; Commission for the Conservation of Antarctic Marine Living Resources, *Reports of Members' Activities in the Convention Area 1989–1990*, 1991.

[21] Kimball, *Southern Exposure*, p. 15.

[22] L. A. Kimball, 'The Antarctic Minerals Convention', Special Report (Washington, DC: World Resources Institute, 1988), pp. 26–7.

including prospecting, without prior environmental assessment of the possible impact, and only if it can be judged that this will not cause any significant adverse effects on the quality of the air or water; significant changes in the atmospheric, terrestrial or marine environment; significant changes in the distribution, abundance or productivity of the flora or fauna; greater risk to endangered species or degradation of areas of special importance; or significant adverse effects on global or regional climatic or meteorological systems. Besides these strict, extensive criteria, there should also be positive judgment on the availability of appropriate technology[23] and procedures that will permit safe operations, as well as on the capacity to monitor the key parameters of the environment and other necessities.

Activities submitted for prior approval should be accompanied by a detailed assessment of their environmental impact, which is to be analysed by the Advisory Committee. This environmental analysis is applied also to the specific rules approved by the Regulatory Committees. It should also be kept in mind that mineral activities are forbidden in protected areas or others determined by the Commission, and that the Convention establishes the obligation to respect other uses of the Antarctic; close coordination between this regime and the other components of the Antarctic Treaty System has been foreseen for this purpose.

The consensus required to identify an area, a decision that initiates the complex process of control and institutional measures, the high majorities required in each organism for key authorisations, the specific functions of the Advisory Committee and the rules on liability – these are all indicative elements of the high priority given to the environmental theme within this regime.

The environmental principles and objectives did not warrant major objections as such, although a great deal of discussion certainly took place among the parties and interested organisations regarding the specific

---

[23] For an analysis on technology for exploitation of Antarctic mineral resources, see J. A. Dugger, 'Exploiting Antarctic Mineral Resources: Technology, Economics and the Environment', *University of Miami Law Review*, vol. 33, no. 2, 1978, pp. 315–39; J. F. Splettstoesser, 'Underground Technology for Offshore Hydrocarbon Development in Antarctica', *Fifth International Conference on Port and Ocean Engineering under Arctic Conditions* (Trondheim: Norwegian Institute of Technology, University of Trondheim, 1979), vol. III, pp. 233–45; E. F. Roots, 'Resource Development in Polar Regions: Comments on Technology', in F. Orrego Vicuña (ed.), *Antarctic Resources Policy: Scientific, Legal and Political Issues* (Cambridge University Press, 1983), pp. 297–315.

wording, extent, or requirements associated with each principle.[24] The greatest difficulty was raised on two other levels. The first concerns the specific rules of the exploration and exploitation system and the effect they will have on environmental aspects. The possibility that prospecting might take place without prior authorisation and might involve activities that are threatening or dangerous to the environment has been a cause of special concern. Another criticism is that the operator will be able to pass from the exploration phase to the exploitation phase by means of a simple procedure that does not include a thorough review of the original Management Plan.[25] Other criticisms of the system are based on similar considerations.[26]

The second level where difficulties arise concerns the institutional procedures to put into practice the objectives and principles mentioned above. The basic question is how to ensure that the legitimate environmental criterion that may emanate from specialised organs will be respected by the interests most closely linked to the objective of resource development.[27] This institutional relationship has already caused concern

---

[24] A publication of the non-governmental ecological organisations described the environmental principles and objectives of the regime as advocating 'strong feelings in favor of environmental protection', whereas it has also been expressed that these principles should be extended and precisely defined; see *ECO*, vol. 23, no. 1, 1983, p. 3. For a summary of opinions from the environmental organisations of the United States and the discussion of related subjects, see L. A. Kimball, 'Environmental Issues in the Antarctic Minerals Negotiations', in L. M. Alexander and L. C. Hanson (eds.), *Antarctic Politics and Marine Resources: Critical Choices for the 1980s* (Kingston, RI: Center for Ocean Management Studies, 1985), pp. 204–14. See also M. de Porter and S. Schmidt, 'Greenpeace Environmental and Scientific Programme in Antarctica', in J. E. Hay, A. D. Hemmings and N. G. Thom (eds.), *Antarctica 150, Scientific Perspectives, Policy Futures* (University of Auckland, 1990), pp. 39–42.

[25] A. Graham, 'Environment Hazards in the Antarctic', in *The Antarctic: Preferred Futures, Constraints and Choices* (Wellington: New Zealand Institute of International Affairs, 1983), pp. 25–30, particularly pp. 27–30.

[26] See the environmental considerations contained in *ECO*, vol. 23, no. 1, pp. 1 and 15–16; see also A. Machin, 'Preferred Futures: An Environmental View', in *The Antarctic: Preferred Futures*, pp. 69–74; see also the report from the Seminar of the New Zealand Institute of International Affairs on *The Antarctic: Preferred Futures, Constraints and Choices*, held at the Victoria University of Wellington, 17–18 June 1983, in *New Zealand International Review*, vol. 8, 1983, pp. 2–5; and L. A. Kimball, 'The Future of the Antarctic Treaty System: Environmental Community Suggestions', in Alexander and Hanson (eds.), *Critical Choices*, pp. 237–47.

[27] On the matter of regulated development and conservation see an article on this subject by M. W. Holdgate, 'Regulated Development and Conservation of Antarctic Resources', in G. D. Triggs (ed.), *The Antarctic Treaty Regime* (Cambridge University Press, 1987), pp. 128–42.

in the case of CCAMLR.[28] Furthermore, the fact that the regulatory authority will be broken up into several Regulatory Committees has been considered inappropriate for efficient management of the environment.[29] The procedures regarding the Regulatory Committee, the decision-making mechanisms and the Commission's powers of enforcement have also been criticised in this regard.[30] If the provisions of the Protocol on environmental impact assessment are evaluated in the light of the evolution and concerns explained, we can see that its contribution is basically of a procedural character, and again helpful in terms of laying down an orderly approach to the matter. However, the question of internal coherence of the provisions remains inseparable from the ATS as it has evolved.

The protection of fauna and flora

Legislative activity *within the ATS* is reflected intensively in the field of conservation of fauna and flora. Already the first Consultative Meeting considered this matter with a view towards adopting rules of conduct for expeditions.[31] This successively led to the adoption of the Agreed Measures for the Conservation of Antarctic Fauna and Flora,[32] identification of species and protection areas, the development of a more comprehensive system of protected areas and the Convention for the Conservation of Seals and CCAMLR.[33] All this represents a progressive sequence of environmental protection measures on specific matters.

Recommendation I-VIII, adopted on the basis of the scientific work of SCAR, started by acknowledging the pressing need for conservation measures relating to living resources, and that all persons entering the area should be informed about these measures. At the same time, necessary measures for coordination and cooperation were proposed. Of special interest were the general rules of conduct approved on that occasion, reiterated in Recommendation II-II.[34] It was recommended that their

---

[28] J. N. Barnes, 'The Emerging Convention on the Conservation of Antarctic Marine Living Resources: An Attempt to Meet the New Realities of Resource Exploitation in the Southern Ocean', J. I. Charney (ed.), *The New Nationalism and the Use of Common Spaces* (Totowa, NJ: Allanheld, Osmun and Co., 1982), pp. 239–86, at pp. 266–7.
[29] Graham, 'Environmental Hazards', pp. 28–9.
[30] *Ibid.*, pp. 28–30; see also Kimball, *Environmental Issues*.
[31] Recommendation I-VIII; see Heap (ed.), *Handbook*, section 2.4.1.
[32] Recommendation III-VIII; see Heap (ed.), *Handbook*, section 2.4.1.
[33] Heap (ed.), *Handbook*, section 2.4, Introductory Note.
[34] Recommendation II-II; see Heap (ed.), *Handbook*, section 2.4.1.

binding legal effect be ensured on the basis of their being incorporated into national legislation or international conventions.

It was Recommendation III-VIII which led this concern to be expressed in detail in the *Agreed Measures*. The legally binding nature of these Measures and their similarity with a treaty should not pass unnoticed. They seek to minimise human interference with normal living conditions of mammals and birds. Except in very special cases or situations of extreme emergency, the Agreed Measures prohibit activities that could cause disturbance – such as overflight or the presence of vehicles in areas where those species are concentrated, the discharge of firearms or the use of explosives, allowing dogs to run free, or other harmful activities.[35]

In accordance with these Measures, each government shall prohibit the killing, wounding or capturing of the said species, except in accordance with an explicit permit which shall be issued solely for scientific purposes, to provide specimens for museums, zoological gardens or other educational uses, or to provide food in limited quantities for expeditions or stations. In any case, the balance and normal reproduction of the species must be ensured. Moreover, *Specially Protected Areas* have been designated, for which the issuance of permits is even stricter, being justified only by compelling scientific purposes and only as long as the natural ecological balance is not jeopardised. Entry of non-authorised persons to such areas is also prohibited.[36] Other provisions prohibit the introduction into the Antarctic Treaty Area of non-indigenous species, parasites and diseases, with particular reference to the case of dogs.[37]

The fact that the Measures have also referred to the contamination of waters adjacent to the coast and ice shelf has been significant for the maritime projection of the Antarctic System. The appropriate way in which the various jurisdictional problems posed by these Measures have been solved, should also be borne in mind.

The approval of the Agreed Measures gave rise later to intensive work with a view to practical application and improvement. Some recommendations have referred to the standardisation of the exchange of information[38] or to cooperation between neighbouring stations,[39] whereas others have sought to improve the system of Specially Protected Areas.[40]

---

[35] Recommendation III-VIII, paras. VII and V.
[36] *Ibid.*, para. VIII.
[37] *Ibid.*, para. IX and Annexes C and D.
[38] Recommendations IV-19 and VI-9; see Heap (ed.), *Handbook*, section 2.4.2.
[39] Recommendation IV-18.
[40] Recommendations VII-2 and VIII-2; see Heap (ed.), *Handbook*, section 2.4.2.

On this subject, even stricter conditions regarding entry into these areas have been imposed;[41] some of these zones have been redefined[42] and, very significantly, the system of *Sites of Special Scientific Interest* has been established.[43] This set of provisions ultimately seeks to protect areas representative of the main ecological land and fresh-water systems of the Antarctic, areas where there are unique complexes of species or other phenomena, whose peculiarity requires them to remain unaltered.[44]

Rules on application have been directed to ensure that governments duly apply the Measures by means of *national legislation*, having first recommended that they be applied as guidelines for conduct until they become fully effective.[45] Some of this national legislation has played an important complementary part in the regime of Agreed Measures and other environmental aspects of the Antarctic Treaty System. Australian legislation, for example, provides for the necessary power to regulate or prohibit pollution of the Antarctic environment.[46] France[47] and Belgium,[48] with the purpose of putting the Agreed Measures into practice, have enacted provisions in their respective legislation that authorises the adoption of measures to avoid pollution of 'waters adjacent to the coast' and 'the ice shelves'. New Zealand legislation lists pollution in Antarctica as a crime when it has been carried out in a 'deliberate or negligent' manner.[49] British legislation, which considers oil disposal in territorial waters a crime, has been applied to the Falkland Islands Dependencies

---

[41] Recommendations VI-8 and VIII-5; see Heap (ed.), *Handbook*, section 2.4.2, Introductory Note.
[42] Recommendations VIII-2 and VIII-4; see Heap (ed.), *Handbook*, section 2.4.2, Introductory Note.
[43] Recommendation VII-3.
[44] See Recommendation VII-2, para. 1.
[45] Recommendations III-IX and IV-20; see Heap (ed.), *Handbook*, section 2.4.2.
[46] Australia, Antarctic Treaty (Environment Protection) Act 1980, Sec. 29(2)(c); text reprinted in W. M. Bush (ed.), *Antarctica and International Law: A Collection of Inter-State and National Documents* (London: Oceana, 1982), vol. II, pp. 212–25.
[47] France, Arret N.17 reglementant la protection de la faune et de la flore dans le district de Terre Adelie, 7 September 1966, Art. 10; text reprinted in Bush (ed.), *Antarctica and International Law*, vol. II, pp. 555–8.
[48] Belgium, Loi relative a la protection de la faune et de la flore dans l'Antarctique, 12 January 1978, Art. 7; text reprinted in Bush (ed.), *Antarctica and International Law*, vol. II, pp. 268–71.
[49] For a summary of New Zealand's legislation, see Bush (ed.), *Antarctica and International Law*, vol. III, pp. 89–95.

when these included the claimed British Antarctic Territory.[50] The United States has evidenced the same concern for pollution control in Antarctica.[51] In the case of claimant countries, general regulations referring to the environment could also be applicable by extension to the corresponding Antarctic territory; in some cases, such as the United Kingdom, this extension would have to be carried out by means of a specific legislative authority, whereas in other cases, such as Chile and France, this could occur automatically.

This important role of domestic law poses new needs regarding how to *harmonise* legislation within the Antarctic Treaty System.[52] When the British Parliament debated the approval of the Agreed Measures, one of the points of the debate was whether certain acts committed in the Antarctic could incur a higher penalty than if they had been committed in the United Kingdom, stressing that penalties for the same misdemeanour should be the same everywhere.[53] The opposite case has also been put forward: the possibility that national legislation should contain more stringent measures than those established in the Antarctic Treaty System. In the environmental sphere this situation should not be considered incompatible with the rules of that system – an aspect significant in the case of the mineral resources regime.[54]

Again in respect of the protection of fauna and flora the Protocol is limited to updating and slightly retouching the basic provisions enacted under the ATS, with particular reference to the Agreed Measures. While

---

[50] For a summary of British legislation, see Bush (ed.), *Antarctica and International Law*, vol. III, p. 379. See especially the Oil in Navigable Waters Act, 1955, as modified; text reprinted in United Nations Legislative Series, *National Legislation and Treaties Relating to the Territorial Sea* . . ., ST/LEG/SerB/15, 1970, pp. 520–40.

[51] For a summary of United States legislation, see Bush (ed.), *Antarctica and International Law*, vol. III, p. 379, as well as the US Antarctic Conservation Act of 1987. See also US Congress, Senate, Committee on Commerce, Science, and Transportation, Subcommittee on Science, Technology, and Space, *Hearing on Protecting Antarctica's Environment*, 1989, Senate Hearing 101–637. See also the 'Antarctic Protection Act of 1990', *Public Law*, 101–594, 16 November 1990; B. S. Manheim, Jr, *On Thin Ice: The Failure of the National Science Foundation to Protect Antarctica* (unpublished paper).

[52] See Orrego, *Antarctic Mineral Exploitation*, chapter III. Concerning the progress made on harmonisation of national regulations, see the Reports of the VII and VIII Consultative Meetings, in Heap (ed.), *Handbook*, pp. 2,409–10.

[53] United Kingdom, House of Commons, *Official Report*, Parliamentary Debates, Standing Committee C. Wednesday, 22 March 1967, declarations of Messrs Griffiths and Lever, pp. 12–13.

[54] See Orrego, *Antarctic Mineral Exploitation*, chapter V.

this may be helpful for improving coherence, it does not necessarily result in added effectiveness, as discussed in Chapter 7.

Waste disposal and management

Among the more detailed environmental measures developed in the ATS are those relating to the *Code of Conduct for Antarctic Expeditions and Station Activities*, an instrument attached to Recommendation VIII-11.[55] The main concern of these measures was to avoid the disposal of waste and the introduction of species alien to Antarctica, as well as other situations that could alter the delicate ecosystem of that continent. Successive recommendations and research[56] accentuated this concern, leading to approval of Recommendation XV-3, comprising very specific and legally binding provisions on the subject.[57] This recommendation contains the general obligation to reduce to a minimum waste production and disposal, the policy of planned management of this waste by means of plans and programmes and, above all, the indication of products that must be removed from Antarctica because of their polluting effect. It also contains provisions regarding disposal at sea and its relation to applicable international conventions. The concern about waste disposal has been more recent within the ATS, so here the Protocol could contribute to a greater internal coherence. However, this contribution has in fact fallen short of current undertakings under international environmental law.

Preservation of the marine environment

The first recommendations on oil pollution had a rather general scope,[58] but Recommendation XV-4 introduced specific obligations for the Antarctic Treaty System in this field.[59] Among these is the prohibition of all intentional discharges, disposal of plastic and other substances and disposal of waste water, specifying that some of these activities may not be carried out within a twelve-mile distance measured from the Antarctic

---

[55] See Heap (ed.), *Handbook*, section 2.2.
[56] Recommendations XII-4 and XIII-4; see Heap (ed.), *Handbook*, section 2.2.1. See also Antarctic and Southern Ocean Coalition, *A New Code of Conduct on Waste Disposal*, October 1989; P. Johnston and R. Stringer, 'Waste Disposal in the Antarctic: The Case Against Incineration', *Greenpeace Technical Note 10*, 20 September 1989.
[57] Recommendation XV-3; see Heap (ed.), *Handbook*, section 2.2.1.
[58] Recommendations IX-6 and X-7; see Heap (ed.), *Handbook*, section 2.2.3.
[59] Recommendation XV-4; see Heap (ed.), *Handbook*, section 2.2.2.

continent or the ice barriers. Especially interesting is the fact that a precise juridical link is established between the Antarctic Treaty System provisions and the international conventions on marine pollution, particularly those pertaining to the scope of the International Maritime Organisation.[60] In this last context, the Antarctic Treaty Area would be promoted for designation as a 'special area' in terms of MARPOL Annex II; additional restrictions would be considered within the framework of the London Dumping Convention, and reference has been made to the 1989 Convention on Transboundary Movements of Hazardous Wastes and their Disposal.[61] Many of these developments have in fact materialised, as discussed in Chapter 7.

Thus, Antarctic environmental law has started to integrate with *the international law of the global environment*. The application of treaties on marine pollution was an issue already raised in the deliberations of Consultative Meetings. Recommendation X-7 was based on the recognition that 'the presence of ice in Antarctic waters gives rise to particular hazards for the operation of ships'.[62] Regarding mineral resources, one author warned 'that perhaps the greatest risk of all to the Antarctic Oceanic ecosystem from oil exploration lay in the wreck amid icefields of a very large crude carrier'.[63] On the basis of these considerations, it had been recommended that the Consultative Parties review their obligations in the light of treaties on marine contamination by oil so as to 'consider whether their compliance with these obligations adequately minimises the risk of oil contamination of the Antarctic marine environment'.[64]

Interestingly, this recommendation already recognised the potential application of international conventions on prevention of marine pollution to the case of Antarctica, insofar as the Consultative Parties are parties to such conventions. To the extent that such conventions establish some link with the concept of coastal state or similar territorial elements, this could be an obstacle to its application in Antarctica by non-claimant countries, as it could contradict their basic legal approach to the issue of claims on that continent. On the other hand, although some claimants do not perceive themselves as facing that problem, a situation could arise

---

[60] *Ibid.*, para. 2.
[61] *Ibid.*, para. 5. See also Report of the XV ATCM, Paris 1989, para. 95; see Heap (ed.), *Handbook*, pp. 2,208–9.
[62] Recommendation X-7; see Heap (ed.), *Handbook*, section 2.2.3.
[63] M. W. Holdgate, 'Environmental Factors in the Development of Antarctica', in Orrego (ed.), *Antarctic Resources Policy*, pp. 77–101, at p. 85.
[64] Recommendation X-7; see Heap (ed.), *Handbook*, section 2.2.3.

wherein such conventions might clash with the freezing of claims under Article IV of the Antarctic Treaty.

However, such potential legal conflict has not materialised in the context of the environmental policy within the Antarctic Treaty System. On the contrary, on the basis of the previously mentioned review, the Consultative Parties at their XI Consultative Meeting decided that such conventions, in the light of current shipping operations in Antarctica, 'provide for the time being an adequate and sufficient basis for minimising risks of pollution'.[65] This conclusion, of course, left open the possibility that if the nature of these operations were to change – which would occur if supertankers were to operate in the region – stricter special regulations could be needed. Recommendation XV-4 itself harmonises the Antarctic case with the IMO conventions.

Also, on the occasion of the XI Consultative Meeting, Argentina introduced a proposal relating to this problem, suggesting that the 1954 International Convention for the Prevention of Pollution of the Sea by Oil, as amended in 1962 and 1969, should be complemented 'in order to adapt its application to the special characteristics of the Antarctic ecosystem'.[66] One author had pointed out that Antarctica did not appear among the 'special areas' referred to by the 1973 International Convention for the Prevention of Pollution from Ships, where stricter measures are required, implying that this need could arise if supertanker traffic should emerge in the area.[67] Recommendation XV-4 has anticipated this by foreseeing the designation of this special area, a step which has already materialised.

In addition to the conventions mentioned above, many other instruments adopted within the framework of the IMO are of interest to the Antarctic.[68] Special mention should be made of the 1969 International

---

[65] Final Report of the XI ATCM, Buenos Aires 1981, para. 15; see Heap (ed.), *Handbook*, p. 2,211.

[66] Argentina: *Draft Recommendation on Petroleum Contamination in the Antarctic Marine Enviroment*, doc. ANT/7XI/23, of 26 June 1981; reproduced as Annex 7 of the Report of the XI ATCM, Buenos Aires 1981, in Bush (ed.), *Antartica and International Law*, vol. I, pp. 448–9.

[67] B. A. Boczek, 'The Protection of the Antarctic Ecosystem: A Study of International Environmental Law', *Ocean Development and International Law*, vol. 13, no. 3, 1983, pp. 347–425.

[68] See in general International Maritime Organisation, *Status of Multilateral Conventions and Instruments in Respect of which the IMO or its Secretary General Performs Depository or Other Functions*, 31 December 1984. See also in general the following works: P. Birnie, 'Developments in the Law for Prevention of Marine Pollution from Petroleum during 1983–1984', in R. W. Bentham (ed.), *Recent Developments in United Kingdom Petroleum Law* (Dundee: Centre for Petroleum and Mineral Law Studies, University of Dundee, 1984)

Convention on Civil Liability for Oil Pollution Damage[69] and its subsequent amendments,[70] with particular reference to modifications made in 1984,[71] as well as of the International Convention on the Establishment of an International Fund for Compensation for Oil Pollution Damage signed in 1971,[72] and its subsequent amendments,[73] including those of 1984.[74] To the degree that they are applicable, these conventions could provide a supplementary mechanism for provisions on responsibility that have been drawn up regarding the mineral resources regime.[75]

Similarly, some of the norms agreed upon through regional conventions could be relevant to Antarctica for the parties to the Antarctic Treaty that participate in such conventions. One of these cases could be the inspection system established in the Paris Memorandum of Understanding of 1982, which could allow the parties to this instrument to inspect their ships leaving for Antarctica in European ports.[76] The agree-

---

pp. 72–127; C. C. Joyner, 'Oceanic Pollution and the Southern Ocean: Rethinking the International Legal Implications for Antarctica', *Natural Resources Journal*, vol. 24, no. 1, 1984, pp. 1–40; C. C. Joyner, 'The Southern Ocean and Marine Pollution: Problems and Prospects', *Case Western Reserve Journal of International Law*, vol. 17, no. 2, 1985, pp. 165–94; W. Y. Brown and B. S. Manheim, 'Conservation of Antarctic Marine Living Resources: The Environmental Perspective', in Alexander and Hanson (eds.), *Critical Choices*, pp. 123–9.

[69] International Convention on Civil Liability for Oil Pollution Damage, done in Brussels, 29 November 1969; for the state of signatures, ratification and others see IMO, *Status of Multilateral Conventions*, pp. 145–60.

[70] Protocol to the International Convention on Civil Liability for Oil Pollution Damage of 1969, done in London, 19 November 1976; for the state of signatures, ratification and others, see IMO, *Status of Multilateral Conventions*, pp. 161–8.

[71] IMO, Protocol of 1984 to the International Convention on Civil Liability for Oil Pollution Damage, doc. LEG/CONF.6/66, of 25 May 1984. For a commentary on this amendment, see C. E. Curtis, 'Recent Developments under Special Environmental Conventions', paper presented at Eighteenth Annual Conference of the Law of the Sea Institute, San Francisco, 24–7 September 1984, pp. 4–8.

[72] International Convention on the Establishment of an International Fund for Compensation for Oil Pollution Damage, done in Brussels, 18 December 1971; for the state of signature, ratification and others, see IMO, *Status of Multilateral Conventions*, pp. 187–94.

[73] Protocol of 1976 to the International Convention on the Establishment of an International Fund for Compensation for Oil Pollution Damage, done in London, 19 November 1976; for the state of signature, ratification and others, see IMO, *Status of Multilateral Conventions*, pp. 195–200.

[74] IMO, Protocol of 1984 amending the International Convention on the Establishment of an International Fund for Compensation for Oil Pollution Damage, doc. LEC/CONF.6/67, 25 May 1984; for a commentary see Curtis, 'Recent Developments', pp. 4–8.

[75] See Orrego, *Antarctic Mineral Exploitation*, chapter V, section 8.

[76] Memorandum of Understanding on Port State Control of Enforcement of Agreements on Maritime Safety and the Protection of the Marine Environment, done in Paris, 26

ment for the protection of the marine environment and coastal areas of the Southeast Pacific and related instruments, done under the sponsorship of the Permanent Commission of the South Pacific,[77] may be applied beyond the areas of national jurisdiction of the Contracting Parties and specifically to the high seas, up to a distance where its pollution could affect the areas under national jurisdiction. These provisions could eventually be of interest to the maritime areas claimed by Chile in Antarctica or to the high seas of Antarctica in the case there foreseen.

The Convention on the Law of the Sea contains another set of important rules on marine pollution equally interesting as far as Antarctica is concerned. These provisions have a wider scope as they gather basic principles and criteria applicable to this field, and at the same time are related to special conventions on marine pollution.[78] Some authors have been of the opinion that the relevant rules established in the 1982 Convention reflect existing customary international law, or that they determine the general application of rules established in the special conventions referred to above.[79] In any of these cases, obligations of a general nature that could affect the conduct of Consultative Parties in the framework of the Antarctic Treaty System would be implicit.

The only provision of this Convention relating specifically to floating ice fields is that of Article 234. Under this provision, coastal states have the right to adopt and enforce laws and regulations for the prevention,

---

January 1982. The following Consultative Parties of the Antarctic Treaty are parties to this agreement: Belgium, France, Germany, Norway and the United Kingdom; text in D. C. Jackson (ed.), *World Shipping Laws*, International Conventions, VIII-Marine Pollution, VIII/23/CONV, May 1984.

[77] Permanent Commission of the South Pacific, Agreement for the Protection of the Marine Environment and Coastal Areas of the Southeast Pacific, done in Lima, 12 November 1981; related agreements were signed on 12 November 1981 and 22 July 1983; United Nations, 1984.

[78] M. Valenzuela, 'IMO: Public International Law and Regulation', in D. M. Johnston and N. Q. Letalik (eds.), *The Law of the Sea and Ocean Industry: New Opportunities and Restraints* (Honolulu, HA: The Law of the Sea Institute, University of Hawaii, 1984), pp. 141–51.

[79] L. B. Sohn, 'Implications of the Law of the Sea Convention Regarding the Protection and Preservation of the Marine Environment', in R. B. Krueger and S. A. Reisenfeld (eds.), *The Developing Order of the Oceans* (Honolulu, HA: The Law of the Sea Institute, University of Hawaii, 1985), pp. 103–16. See also E. D. Brown, 'Pollution from Seabed Mining: Legal Safeguards', *Environmental Policy and Law*, vol. 10, 1983, pp. 122–34. For a schematic analysis of the responsibilities derived from the Convention on the Law of the Sea in relation to the environment, see *Conservation and Management of the Marine Environment: Responsibilities and Required Initiatives in Accordance with the 1982 UN Convention of the Law of the Sea* (Halifax: Dalhousie Ocean Studies Programme, 1984). The Convention on the Conservation of Antarctic Marine Living Resources regarding Art. 234 of the Convention on the Law of the Sea, is mentioned at p. 6.

reduction and control of marine pollution by ships in ice-covered areas within the limits of the exclusive economic zone, where especially severe climatic conditions and the presence of ice create exceptional danger or obstacles to navigation, and where pollution of the marine environment could cause significant damage or irreversible alterations in the ecological balance.[80] This provision originated in negotiations between Canada, the United States and the Soviet Union in their capacity as three important Arctic states,[81] and is related to the measures that Canada had introduced to control pollution caused by shipping operations in those areas.[82] The fact that this is a general provision of the Convention and that it is not restricted to a special geographical area such as the Arctic, makes it potentially applicable to Antarctica. Nevertheless, because this provision is restricted to the exclusive economic zone it could be argued that application of the rule presumes a recognised exclusive economic zone – which, of course, is not entirely the case in Antarctica. In any event, different opinions on the subject would have to be interpreted in the light of the safeguard of positions established in Article IV of the Antarctic Treaty.[83]

It is also worth noting that in the framework of environmental law the existence of some rules of customary international law has been suggested, especially regarding the obligation to avoid causing damage to the environment of other states in areas beyond the limits of national jurisdiction.[84] To the extent that such rules are identified, they would also be applicable to Antarctica.[85]

---

[80] See in general D. M. McRae and D. J. Goundrey, 'Environmental Jurisdiction in Arctic Waters: The Extent of Article 234', *University of British Columbia Law Review*, vol. 16, 1982, pp. 197–228; J. W. Kindt and T. J. Parriott, 'Ice-Covered Areas: The Competing Interests of Conservation and Resources Exploitation', *San Diego Law Review*, vol. 21, no. 4, 1984, pp. 941–83.

[81] D. A. Colson: 'Political and Boundary Issues Affecting Arctic Energy Resources', in Krueger and Reisenfeld (eds.), *The Developing Order*, pp. 513–23.

[82] J.-Y. Morin, 'Le progres technique, la pollution et l'evolution recent du droit de la mer au Canada, particulierement a l'egard de l'Arctique', *Canadian Yearbook of International Law*, vol. 8, 1970, pp. 158–248; L. Henkin, 'Arctic Anti-Pollution: Does Canada Make – or Break – International Law?', *American Journal of International Law*, vol. 65, no. 1, 1971, pp. 131–6.

[83] See in general Orrego, *Antarctic Mineral Exploitation*, chapter IV.

[84] For a commentary on the Principles of the Stockholm Declaration of the United Nations Conference on the Human Environment of 1972 and associated developments, and its relation to general international law, see Boczek, 'A Study', pp. 388–90.

[85] Other international agreements are also relevant to the protection of Antarctic fauna and flora. The following have been cited: (i) International Convention for the Regulation of Whaling, 2 December 1946; (ii) Convention on International Trade in Endangered Species of Wild Fauna and Flora, 3 March 1973; (iii) Convention for the Protection of the World Cultural and Natural Heritage, 23 November 1972; (iv) International Convention

Several of the Consultative Parties have specifically *applied* international conventions to their *claimed Antarctic territories*. Thus, for example, the previously mentioned 1954 Convention and some of its subsequent amendments have been applied by Australia to its external territories, which include the Antarctic territory, and by France to its southern and Antarctic territories.[86] These two countries[87] have also applied the 1969 Convention on Civil Liability and the International Convention relating to Intervention on the High Seas in cases of Oil Pollution Casualties,[88] also dated 1969, to their Antarctic territories. The 1972 Convention on Dumping of Wastes and other Matter[89] has been applied to the territories in question by Australia,[90] while France has other kinds of legislation for the same purposes.[91] The United Kingdom has applied some conventions to the Falkland Islands Dependencies, but not specifically to the claimed Antarctic territories.[92] In the case of other Consultative Parties, these conventions could be applicable to their Antarctic territories by extension, without the need for a specific mention. Nevertheless, the approach of Recommendation XV-4 which seeks a collective link with these Conventions will minimise the problem of individual national policies.

The Protocol has continued to facilitate the adaptation of the ATS to applicable international rules and standards, despite the shortcomings

for the Protection of Birds, 18 October 1950; (v) Convention on the Protection of Nature and the Preservation of Wildlife in the Western Hemisphere, 12 October 1940; (vi) Convention on the Conservation of the Migratory Species of Wild Animals, 23 June 1979. For references to these and other agreements on the subject, see Bush (ed.), *Antarctica and International Law*, vol. I, pp. 162–8. Certain special programmes of international organisations may also be relevant in this context: see, for example, United Nations Environment Programme: 'Prospects for Global Ocean Pollution Monitoring', Regional Seas Reports and Studies No. 47, UNEP 1984. On the general aspects of the Convention on the Law of the Sea regarding the marine environment, see also P. M. Dupuy and M. Remond-Gouilloud, 'La preservation du milieu marin', in R.-J. Dupuy and D. Vignes (eds.), *Traite du nouveau droit de la mer* (Paris: Economica, 1985), pp. 979–1,045.

[86] Bush, *Antarctica and International Law*, vol. I, pp. 379–80.
[87] *Ibid.*, pp. 380–1.
[88] International Convention relating to Intervention on the High Seas in Cases of Oil Pollution Casualties, done in Brussels, 29 November 1969; for the state of signature, ratification and others, see IMO, *Status of Multilateral Conventions*, pp. 127–38.
[89] Convention for the Prevention of Marine Pollution by Dumping of Wastes and other Matter, 29 December 1972; for the state of signature, ratification and others, see IMO, *Status of Multilateral Conventions*, pp. 275–81.
[90] Bush (ed.), *Antarctica and International Law*, vol. I, p. 381.
[91] *Ibid.*, p. 382.
[92] This is the case with the Convention on Civil Liability of 1969, and the Convention on Waste Disposal: see Bush (ed.), *Antarctica and International Law*, vol. I, pp. 381–2.

discussed in Chapter 7, being particularly severe in the field of marine pollution and related issues. Internal coherence and its ensuing legitimacy also have to be contrasted here with the pending questions about effectiveness.

Antarctic protected areas system

With the approval of the Agreed Measures, the development of a system of protected areas with environmental and scientific objectives was started in Antarctica. First was the Specially Protected Areas mechanism contemplated in Article VIII of the Measures, the main characteristics of which were examined above. To date, twenty areas of this kind have been approved, covering important ecosystems of the continent and its islands.[93] Initial rules have later been complemented by others that have incorporated the mechanism of management plans for such areas, also relating the issuance of permits to its compatibility with these plans.[94]

Due to some conflicts of interest between protection for environmental purposes and protection for scientific purposes in the ambit of the Specially Protected Areas mechanism, it was decided to establish a second separate protection mechanism for some scientific activities of particular interest. The latter was the mechanism of Sites of Special Scientific Interest for cases which required long-term protection from harmful interference, but which also had a fixed period of duration and a periodic revision to avoid it affecting the freedom of scientific research established in the Antarctic Treaty.[95] Thirty-two sites of this kind have been designated after a favourable opinion from SCAR.[96] Management plans are also applied in this mechanism. A development of particular interest at this level has been the creation of Marine Sites of Special Scientific Interest;[97] this new type of protected area was particularly relevant to the maritime projection of the Antarctic System.

Two new categories of protected areas were later incorporated. Recommendation XV-10 created the Specially Reserved Areas which are aimed at protecting areas of exceptional geological, glaciological, geomor-

---

[93] For the various recommendations and designations of Specially Protected Areas, see Heap (ed.), *Handbook*, section 3.2.

[94] Recommendations XV-8 and XV-9: see Heap (ed.), *Handbook*, pp. 3,220–1.

[95] Heap (ed.), *Handbook*, section 3.3, Introductory Note, p. 3,301.

[96] For the various recommendations and designations of Sites of Special Scientific Interest, see Heap (ed.), *Handbook*, section 3.3.

[97] Recommendation XIV-6: see Heap (ed.), *Handbook*, p. 3,337.

phological, aesthetic and scenic value or of natural life,[98] a mechanism that in substance follows the criteria of those examined above. Recommendation XV-11 provides for the establishment of Multiple-Use Planning Areas for those cases where human activity in the Antarctic, because of its combined and cumulative effect, could result in mutual interference or in harmful impacts on the environment.[99] Among the uses considered are: the construction and operation of stations; operations of ships, boats, airplanes, helicopters and vehicles; scientific research; visitors and others.[100]

In view of the proliferation of different kinds of Protected Areas, the XVI Consultative Meeting in 1991 decided to simplify the system by adopting two main kinds of areas: *Antarctic Specially Protected Areas* and *Antarctic Specially Managed Areas*. Recommendation XVI-10 approved this new system, which was incorporated as Annex V of the Protocol on Environmental Protection. On this point the Protocol has facilitated the framework for adding a specific Annex, but the substance of the matter and its coherence were already governed by the action of the Consultative Meetings.

Protection of historic sites and monuments is another lasting concern of the Antarctic Treaty System. It has periodically been recommended that they should be marked, reconstructed or preserved as a memorial of the heroic age of exploration of the continent.[101] As from Recommendation VII-9 a listing system was started for such sites and monuments, where fifty-five have been included.[102]

It should also be noted that in accordance with the Convention for the Conservation of Antarctic Seals, special areas have been established for sealing subject to periodic seasonal closure, as well as Seal Reserves where hunting is forbidden as these are reproduction and breeding areas or sites where long-term scientific research is carried out.[103] And as noted, certain conservation measures under CCAMLR also provide for the closure of excessively exploited fishing areas.

On the basis of SCAR recommendations[104] Consultative Meetings have

---

[98] Recommendation XV-10: see Heap (ed.), *Handbook*, section 3.5.

[99] Recommendation XV-11: see Heap (ed.), *Handbook*, section 3.6.

[100] *Ibid.*, para. 4(f).

[101] See, for example, Recommendations I-IX, V-4, VI-14, VII-9, XIV-8, XV-12 and XV-13: Heap (ed.), *Handbook*, section 3.4.

[102] Recommendation VII-9: see Heap (ed.), *Handbook*, section 3.4 and Preface to Part 3, p. 3,001.

[103] Heap (ed.), *Handbook*, section 3.7.

[104] *The Protected Area System in the Antarctic* (Cambridge: Scientific Committee on Antarctic Research, 1987).

considered varying initiatives and proposals regarding the aggregate of protected areas, especially in relation to their periodic assessment and the uniformity of information that should be collected.[105]

PRESERVATION OF ANTARCTIC RESOURCES

Three resource management regimes have been negotiated within the framework of the ATS. Unlike CCAMLR and CRAMRA, however, the principle set forth by the Environmental Protocol with regard to minerals resources is *preservation* rather than conservation management. In this it resembles the Seals Convention, which established a temporary ban on commercial sealing in the Antarctic.

The Protocol does not deal with the resource-management approaches of either the Seals Convention or CCAMLR, nor for that matter of other treaties relevant to Antarctica. This is important evidence that the prior work of the ATS has appropriately laid the ground for environmental protection and conservation in the area, with the Protocol being a further partial step in this process of adaptation. Again here internal coherence of the applicable rules is not found in the Protocol, except for some questions of coordination, but in those other components of the ATS. This situation furthermore poses a serious doubt about the decision of having raised this partial instrument to the legal category of a Protocol.

Commercial overexploitation of *Antarctic seals* is a classic example of a commercial activity leading to depletion and imminent danger of extinction of a resource. The Agreed Measures enabled this situation to be controlled on the continent, but the discussion on whether measures of this kind were applicable to pack ice and the marine environment implied a continual danger in the latter environment. Various recommendations introduced this concern to the ambit of the System,[106] which finally proceeded to adopt a separate Convention on the matter, the Convention for the Conservation of Antarctic Seals.[107]

This Convention is applicable to all seal species in the Antarctic seas, establishing limits for the exploitation of some of them and total prohib-

---

[105] See Recommendation XIII-5, and Reports from the XIII ATCM, Brussels 1985, paras. 50–5; XIV ATCM, Rio de Janeiro 1987, paras. 75–97; and XV ATCM, Paris 1989, paras. 122–5: see Heap (ed.), *Handbook*, section 3.1.

[106] Recommendations III-11, IV-21, V-7 and V-8: see Heap (ed.), *Handbook*, section 4.1.1. Recommendation IV-21 contained interim measures for voluntary regulation of pelagic sealing.

[107] Done in London, 1 June 1972; in force since 11 March 1978: see Heap (ed.), *Handbook*, section 4.1.3.

ition for hunting other species. The closure of all activities for a season, the existence of sealing areas and breeding areas for seals, together with a system for exchange of information and research activities have also been provided for. No permanent organs or measures for control and inspection have been established beforehand, however, and this has been subject to criticism.[108] It is foreseen that this will be done as soon as commercial exploitation activities are carried out.[109] The Convention operates on the basis of jurisdiction of each state over its nationals and ships flying its flag.[110] It also requires a special permit to hunt seals for scientific or educational purposes or to provide food.

The prohibition of mineral activities

As discussed in Chapters 6 and 7, France and Australia, after indicating that they would not sign the Convention on Mineral Resources, favoured its replacement by a comprehensive regime of environmental protection and a permanent prohibition of mineral activities. This position was later supported by Italy, Belgium, New Zealand and Sweden, as well as by Denmark, Greece and the Democratic Republic of Korea.[111] Nevertheless, at no point was the Convention on Mineral Resources completely rejected, among other reasons because the relevant Final Act contains an important moratorium on mineral activities until the Convention takes effect. The evidence that this last step would become impossible would have as a consequence the expiration of the said moratorium, and would open the door to unilateral actions. The Final Act of the XI Special Consultative Meeting contains a reiteration of this moratorium until the Environmental Protocol comes into effect.

In the first round of negotiations on the Protocol there was no agreement on this problem. However, in the second of these rounds it was agreed that the Protocol would contain a clause under which: 'All activity relating to mineral resources, other than scientific research, shall be prohibited.' In this way a prohibition was established regarding the prospecting, exploration and exploitation of mineral resources. To this extent the Protocol purports to undo an important and complex work which the

---

[108] ASOC, *Effective Legal Mechanisms*, p. 12.
[109] Seals Convention, Art. 6.
[110] *Ibid.*, Art. 2.
[111] L. A. Kimball, *Report on Antarctica* (Washington, DC: World Resources Institute, 1991), pp. 18–19. At the start of negotiations, Japan and the United Kingdom were in a more favourable position to safeguard the mineral activities option: *ibid.*, p. 19.

ATS had achieved in this field – a situation which, as noted in Chapter 7, creates a legal vacuum that is not helpful for the internal coherence of the System nor for the legitimacy of the Protocol, since it raises a serious problem about potential acceptance of this prohibition.

This drastic clause is closely related, however, to the rules on the entry into force and modification or amendment of the Protocol. According to the first, for the Protocol to enter into force, there must be ratification or accession by all the Consultative Parties that had this status at the time of adoption of the Protocol. If this unanimity is not achieved, the provisions of the Protocol, including the prohibition of mineral activities, will not be effective and the situation of the Convention on Mineral Resources and the associated moratorium will be maintained on the terms indicated.

If the Protocol enters into force, the rules relating to its modification or amendment should be kept in mind. First, the Protocol can be modified at any moment according to the provisions of the Antarctic Treaty which require the unanimous agreement of the Consultative Parties and provide for the automatic withdrawal of other Parties that do not ratify within a two-year period after the modification entered into force.[112] Second, the possibility of a conference to review the operation of the Protocol after a fifty-year period of being in force is also provided for; this conference will be convened upon the request of any Consultative Party. Any amendments will have to be adopted by the majority of the Parties, including three-quarters of the Consultative Parties that had this status at the time of adoption of the Protocol. But, in addition, it is provided that these amendments will enter into force only if ratified by three-quarters of the Consultative Parties, including all the states that were Consultative Parties when the Protocol was adopted. In practice, then, any of the current Consultative Parties can veto any amendment that would mean changing the prohibition on mineral activities or regarding any other matter, through the sole means of not ratifying it.

On the other hand, there is an additional requirement regarding the specific case of the said prohibition: it will continue to apply until a binding legal regime enters into force regarding Antarctic mineral resources, which shall include the rules and conditions to determine the acceptability of those activities. It follows that every proposal directed to amend this prohibition in a review conference should include such a binding legal

---

[112] Antarctic Treaty, Art. XII, para. 1(a) and (b).

regime. This regime may be that of CRAMRA or a different one, but it will be subject to this set of requirements.

This series of provisions makes it possible to conclude that this is a permanent prohibition on mineral activities that can be modified only by consensus before fifty years and by a majority in the ambit of a review conference called at the end of that period. Even so, such modification would require an alternative regime and all of it is subject to an even higher number of ratifications, including the veto of the current Consultative Parties. In addition, all disputes relating to this prohibition are subject to the compulsory settlement procedures indicated above.

Notwithstanding the above, the Protocol provides that if a modification or amendment has not entered into force within the three years following its adoption, any party may notify its withdrawal from the Protocol, which will take place two years later. In this manner the risk of an abusive veto that can paralyse necessary amendments supported by the majority is avoided.

As explained above, there always remains the doubt about whether a state that withdraws can undertake activities, including mineral activities, freely, or if it will remain subject to the environmental and other rules of the Antarctic Treaty System. One of them contemplated a prohibition for a specific period at the end of which its extension for additional shorter periods would be decided upon by consensus or by majority. Another associated idea was to prohibit mineral activities unless an alternative regime entered into force – with the dilemma once again of whether it should be adopted by consensus or by majority.

The solution finally adopted seeks to reconcile the environmental sensitivity existing at the time of the negotiations with the need to avoid the paralysation of activities that meet the necessary guarantees and support. However, only time will tell whether this was the right solution in terms of the evolution of the ATS, which in fact has been stopped in connection with one of its essential components.

CONCLUDING REMARKS

When the Protocol is evaluated from the perspective of the broad historical evolution of the ATS it can be seen that there are four main points of interconnection with the prior work undertaken by the Consultative Meetings:

1   *Perfecting* the evolution, particularly by means of strengthening the legal obligations and to that extent facilitating the implementation of

provisions. This contribution to the question of applicability is of course positive, but nonetheless rather marginal in the context of the broad substantive issue of environmental protection.

2 *Consolidating* the evolution, in terms of reordering the aggregate of provisions on the matter, but introducing little advancement in terms of substantive regulations, and in some few cases retreating from obligations already in place. Again this legal ordering facilitates application.

3 *Recognising* the evolution achieved in resource management regimes under separate conventions of the ATS, by deferring to such sources of regulation and by establishing some degree of coordination, a situation which again facilitates application by not unduly interfering with regimes in force.

4 *Stopping* the evolution in the specific case of mineral resources by introducing a temporary ban and paralysing the process which had culminated in CRAMRA. This is linked to the attempt by a few Consultative Parties to undo CRAMRA and its implications, a problem which has not yet been settled. The internal coherence of the ATS on this point has been damaged, albeit temporarily.

The level of acceptance of these solutions is of course varied. There is full acceptance of the functions relating to perfecting and recognising, since such positive contribution is helpful for the very objectives which the ATS had already defined and regulated. There is less than full acceptance concerning the issue of consolidating, to the extent that the Protocol could interfere with long-established Antarctic values such as unimpeded scientific research and the role of science in the management of the ATS. Acceptability will depend on the implementation of the Protocol in a manner compatible with such values.

The solution of stopping the evolution of mineral regulation is far from being accepted in the long term. Discrepancies have been temporarily bridged by the Protocol in terms of the fifty-year ban rule, but this issue can be reopened at any time and will certainly be discussed all over again in the future.

It follows from the above that the question of the Protocol's legitimacy is closely linked to its being capable of ensuring internal acceptability for the solutions envisaged, from where external acceptability will flow in turn. To date, this requirement has not been entirely met. It will be the task of the Consultative Parties to perfect the evolution of the ATS in the years ahead.

12

The legitimacy of the Antarctic tourism regime

DAVOR VIDAS[*]

INTRODUCTION

This chapter will apply the analytical approach to the legitimacy of international regimes as developed in Chapter 1 to elaborate various elements
of an evolving regime for Antarctic tourism within the Antarctic Treaty
System (ATS). The regulation of Antarctic tourism has been in the focus
of the Antarctic Treaty Consultative Parties' deliberations at several Consultative Meetings over the past few years. The position recently taken
by the Consultative Parties is that an Antarctic tourism regime already
exists within the ATS, and that it is merely a matter of its clear presentation to those addressed on how to implement such a regime. Another
view is that a tourism regime is still a part of an evolving process, which
should ultimately result in a comprehensive regime, suitable for regulating the peculiarities of this specific human activity in the Antarctic.

The question of legitimacy lies within the framework of such a wider
dilemma. In theory, the optimal approach to regulating Antarctic tourism
would be by clearly resolving the problem of jurisdiction in Antarctica.
This, however, would be at odds with the foundations of the ATS itself,
which contains several parameters for a tourism regime.[1]

This is the framework within which we shall approach the legitimacy of
the Antarctic tourism regime, assessing the acceptability of the proposed
solutions as well as their applicability. These elements have evolved
through a process of adaptation to challenges posed by the regulation of
Antarctic tourism within the ATS. The discussion in this chapter is
organised in the following way.

First, we shall look at the main challenges which Antarctic tourism

---

[*] The article upon which parts of this chapter are based was published in *German Yearbook
of International Law*, vol. 36, 1993.
[1] See Chapter 2 and Introduction to Part IV.

poses for the ATS. Second, we turn to the question of ATS adaptation to these challenges, and assess developments towards the regulation of Antarctic tourism. Here the emphasis will be on the procedural component as well as actors' roles in it. This in turn should provide us with conclusions regarding the ability of the ATS to adapt to challenges in this area. Finally, we will consider the level of acceptance by the relevant groups of subjects as well as the applicability to Antarctic tourism of the regulation which has been created within the ATS.

CHALLENGES FOR THE ATS FROM ANTARCTIC TOURISM

Such challenges may be divided into two main groups:

1   challenging *circumstances*: the nature of the challenge, illustrated by the identification of the main peculiarities of Antarctic tourism;
2   challenges exerted by *subjects*: external pressure on the ATS by third parties.

Let us look more closely at these challenges.

Challenging circumstances: main peculiarities of Antarctic tourism

Here we shall highlight the main peculiarities – or special features – of Antarctic tourism,[2] pointing out what makes Antarctic tourism different from tourism in other parts of the globe. This will focus attention on some of its aspects relevant for future regulation within the ATS.

Tourism without a clear recipient state

International tourism represents an important economic phenomenon which includes a notion of a *recipient* (or host) state. Yet, it is difficult to imagine a recipient state in Antarctica, even if we should accept that sovereignty claims evidence the real existence of sovereignty over the Antarctic. Which state would be a recipient on the Antarctic Peninsula?[3] And

---

[2] Accounts of the Development of Antarctic tourism may be found elsewhere: see in particular R. J. Reich, 'The Development of Antarctic Tourism', *Polar Record*, vol. 20, no. 126, 1980, pp. 203–14; P. D. Hart, 'The Growth of Antarctic Tourism', *Oceanus*, vol. 31, no. 2, 1988, pp. 93–100; N. Wace, 'Antarctica: A New Tourism Destination', *Applied Geography*, vol. 10, 1990, pp. 327–41; D. J. Enzenbacher, 'Tourists in Antarctica: Numbers and Trends', *Polar Record*, vol. 28, no. 164, 1992, pp. 17–22. See also Chapter 8.
[3] In this area, Argentina, Chile and the United Kingdom have forwarded sovereignty claims.

which in the unclaimed area? Only the notion of a *recipient base* could be applicable in Antarctica. When this is viewed in connection with problems of jurisdiction in Antarctica, the problem of enforcing the regulation of Antarctic tourism becomes more apparent.

Tourism restricted to certain areas in a short period of the year

As one of the globally fastest-growing industries, tourism is increasing in polar regions as well.[4] Antarctic tourism in particular has been experiencing substantial growth: while there were some 700 tourists visiting Antarctica in the season 1985–6, their number exceeded 2,500 in 1989–90, and doubled in the following season. In 1991–2, some 6,500 tourists visited Antarctica, but the increase has been somewhat more moderate since: over 7,000 people in 1992–3, and close to 8,000 visitors is a rough estimate for the 1993–4 season. In absolute terms, these numbers considerably exceed the number of scientists present in the Antarctic. However, such figures may be misleading: tourists stay in the Antarctic for a couple of days or weeks, while scientists are often there year-round. On the other hand, this very fact may give grounds for concern, since Antarctic tourism is restricted to a few parts of the continent, and tourist visits occur during a very limited period each year.

Antarctic tourism peaks during the brief polar summer in January and February. The danger of disturbing wildlife is especially high in the Antarctic summer during the breeding season. According to the United Nations Environment Programme (UNEP) Report, at the Cape Royds Adelie penguin rookery, a 50 per cent reduction in the birds' breeding population over a six-year period was attributable to stress from repeated visits by tourists (and the personnel of a nearby scientific station as well).[5] Here, an example is worth mentioning: the Chilean government formulated in 1984 an Antarctic tourism programme under which trips are scheduled so as not to interfere with scientific tasks, the best months being October, November, March and April each year.[6]

Besides, tourist visits tend to concentrate heavily on the Antarctic Pen-

---

[4] See in general Conference Communiqué from the Symposium on *Tourism in Polar Areas*, held in Colmar (France), 21–3 April 1991; also T. E. Armstrong, 'Tourists Visit the North Pole, 1990', *Polar Record*, vol. 27, no. 161, 1991, p. 130; T. Christensen, 'Greenland Wants Tourism', *Polar Record*, vol. 28, no. 164, 1992, pp. 62–3.

[5] Ocean and Coastal Areas Programme Activity Centre, UNEP, *Report on the State of the Environment in the Antarctic*, December 1989, p. 18 (quoted in *State of the Environment in Antarctica and its Impact on the Global System*, Report of the Secretary-General, UN doc. A/46/590, 25 October 1991, p. 8).

[6] *Chilean Antarctic Tourism Programme*, ATCM XIV doc. ANT/XIV/WP/19, October 1987.

insula, though a longer circumnavigation of the entire continent is available. Activities which would have a negligible impact in terms of the Antarctic as a whole may in fact be of more significance in particular regions and indeed of major significance in specific localities.[7] The Scientific Committee on Antarctic Research (SCAR) expressed in its report:

growing concern at the increasing frequency of visits by small boats and tourist ships, especially at the Peninsula area, and of flights by private or commercial aircraft.[8]

Moreover, the Consultative Parties recognised:

the necessity to restrict the number of places where large numbers of tourists may land so that the ecological effects may be monitored.[9]

Yet, the trend is toward an increase in landings at certain specific locations. During the 1989–90 season, ten landings were made at Almirante Brown Station, involving a total of 1,191 passengers; then in the 1990–1 season there were sixteen landings involving 1,471 passengers, and by the 1991–2 season, twenty-six landings and a total of 2,889 passengers.[10] *Areas of Interest*, an idea for channelling tourists to specifically designated areas, were mentioned in Recommendation VII-4; and *Areas of Special Tourist Interest* were to be listed or defined in Annex B to Recommendation VIII-9. However, no such areas have yet been designated at the ATS level. At the national level, the United Kingdom has declared areas of special tourist interest for the Falkland Islands Dependencies and has confined tourists to those areas.[11] Discussions at the XI Consultative Meeting, and more recently at the XVIII Consultative Meeting in Kyoto (in 1994) revealed serious reservations as to the advisability of designating such areas of special tourist interest.[12] Indeed, tourism is an activity within

[7] I. E. Nicholson, 'Antarctic Tourism – The Need for a Legal Regime?', in A. Jørgensen-Dahl and W. Østreng (eds.), *The Antarctic Treaty System in World Politics* (London: Macmillan, 1991), p. 416.
[8] SCAR, 'Report of the Working Group on Logistics (17th Meeting, Leningrad, July 1982)', *SCAR Bulletin*, no. 73, 1983.
[9] Recommendation VIII-9, Preamble, para. 4.
[10] Sources: *Compilation of Data on Tourist Visits to the Antarctic Peninsula* (submitted by the United States), ATCM XVI doc. ANT/XVI/INFO 68, 10 October 1991; and Data Compilation by the National Science Foundation, Washington, DC, 25 June 1992.
[11] Falkland Islands Dependencies Conservation Ordinance 1975, Art. 3(e), *Antarctica and International Law: A Collection of Inter-State and National Documents* (London: Oceana, 1988), vol. III, pp. 398–402.
[12] Final Report of the XI ATCM, Buenos Aires 1981, agenda item 12; see also p. 315 below regarding views on the concept of areas of special tourist interest at the XVIII ATCM, Kyoto 1994.

the framework of the comprehensive *Antarctic Protected Area System*, which comprises several elements applicable to Antarctic tourism.[13]

De luxe and adventure tourism

A further peculiarity of Antarctic tourism is its luxury. Cruises usually take from eleven days to three weeks, and some special programmes can even cost up to US$1,000 per day per person. It is therefore not surprising that most Antarctic cruise tourists come from wealthy countries – the great majority from the USA, but also some from Europe and Japan. Moreover, it would appear that Antarctic tourism is in itself not exotic enough. Adventure Network International has recently developed a substantially new programme including guided mountain climbs, ski safaris and flying visits to the South Pole (at substantial prices, indeed). Novel projects include a visit to an emperor penguin colony, and the 'Ellsworths Open', a golf tournament at the nine-hole course at Patriot Hills on New Year's Eve.[14]

Predominantly seaborne tourism

Antarctic tourism is necessarily either seaborne or airborne. Commercial cruise lines currently bring the great majority of tourists to Antarctica. One of the trickiest issues here is how to ensure that tour-company ships registered in countries not parties to the Antarctic Treaty meet safety and pollution-control standards. The so-called PAN-HO-LIB (Panama, Honduras, Liberia) registration is well known in Antarctic waters as well. These 'classical' *open registers* have been joined during the past decade by an increasing number of states (e.g. Vanuatu, the Bahamas, Gibraltar and the Isle of Man) to bring the total to approximately twenty-five to date. Since the early 1970s, the tonnage of ships flying traditional flags has fallen dramatically worldwide. However, the flag state not only possesses jurisdiction over vessels flying its flag, it must also effectively exercise control and jurisdiction in administrative, technical and social matters. Concurrent assertions of jurisdiction by other states on the basis of the

---

[13] See the Annex to the Recommendation XVI-10, forming Annex V to the Environmental Protocol, on 'Area Protection and Management'. In this connection see also draft Final Report of the XVIII ATCM, Kyoto 1994; ATCM XVIII doc. ANT/XVIII/WP 37, 22 April 1994, agenda item 7 (para. 57), in which the ATCPs noted that the application of Antarctic Specially Managed Areas concept on tourism would be beneficial in some cases.
[14] 'Tour Companies Opening Up Antarctic to Visitors', *Antarctic*, vol. 12, no. 5, p. 163.

nationality of the owner or charterer are, however, also possible. Increased jurisdiction of coastal and port states diminishes partially the traditional primacy of flag state jurisdiction. The present situation in the Antarctic waters appears even more complex as difficulties are created by the unclear situation regarding the actual existence of a coastal state in Antarctica. Moreover, there have been instances of *non-ice-strengthened ships* visiting Antarctica – and the significant risk of accidents associated with such vessels potentially affects all operators.

It has been recommended that vessels cruising the Antarctic should not exceed 300 berths capacity: 150 to 200 passengers is preferable, being an adequate number to control effectively in order to prevent disturbance of any kind.[15] However, the trend is towards increasing the tourist capacity of vessels.

Tourism in Antarctica as an inherently hazardous activity

A major problem for tour operators is Antarctica's unpredictable nature and harsh environment, where accidents may easily happen. Tourism in Antarctica, like any other human activity there, is inherently hazardous. Emergency preparedness in Antarctica has been mainly connected with the activities of non-governmental expeditions,[16] but numerous commercial tourist voyages have required emergency assistance as well.[17] As noted in a British draft recommendation of 1983, any need for emergency assistance from governmental facilities and resources in Antarctica would at best be disruptive for ongoing programmes. At worst, this could lead to loss of life or critical resources or both.[18] The Consultative Parties have noted at the XII Consultative Meeting that:

tour operators should be covered by adequate insurance and by some form of guarantee that would demonstrate their responsibility for their activities.[19]

However, since there was no agreement as to where responsibility for non-governmental operations should lie, the draft recommendation which

---

[15] *Australian Paper on Recommended Standards to be Met by Operators of Tourist Cruises in the Antarctic*, ATCM XII doc. ANT/XII/INFO 6, 12 September 1983.

[16] See, e.g., *US Policy on Private Expeditions to the Antarctic*, ATCM XIII doc. ANT/XIII/INFO 16, 10 October 1985.

[17] E.g., *Lindblad Explorer* has twice run aground in the Antarctic Peninsula, requiring expensive and disruptive rescue and repair operations to be mounted.

[18] *Revised Draft Recommendation Submitted by United Kingdom, Non-Governmental Expeditions*, ATCM XII doc. ANT/XII/4/Rev. 1, 22 September 1983, para. 3(iii).

[19] Final Report of the XII ATCM, Canberra 1983, para. 29.

had been tabled was withdrawn. Problems of liability and insurance were vaguely mentioned at the XIV Consultative Meeting, but with no solution reached.[20]

Challenges by subjects: external pressures exerted on the ATS

Tour companies

The title of an article published some years ago in the journal *Antarctic* illustrates developments from the late 1980s to the early 1990s: 'Tour Companies Opening Up Antarctic to Visitors'.[21] In July 1989 four Antarctic tour expedition leaders and naturalists indicated the need for an Antarctic Traveller's Code, explaining that:

at present the Antarctic Treaty parties have not fashioned sufficiently specific guidelines to govern tourism and other Antarctic visits.[22]

They have therefore introduced their own *Traveller's Code*, with 'readily understood and easily applied guidelines'.[23] This *Traveller's Code* has been criticised by Stonehouse[24] for not taking account of existing official guidance, including SCAR's *A Visitor's Introduction to the Antarctic and its Environment*. However, *A Visitor's Introduction* may hardly be termed 'official guidance': rather, as observed by SCAR's president himself,[25] it is a 'booklet', in need of revision. Although it has been translated into several languages and issued by various SCAR national committees, *A Visitor's Introduction* is still not available in many of SCAR's member countries. Moreover, *A Visitor's Introduction* hardly reaches people outside the scientific community. While neither SCAR nor documents from the Consultative Meetings[26] have been readily accessible to or phrased for

[20] Final Report of the XIV ATCM, Rio de Janeiro 1987, para. 121.
[21] *Antarctic*, vol. 12, no. 5, p. 162.
[22] R. Naveen, T. de Roy, M. Jones and C. Monteath, 'Antarctic Traveller's Code', *Antarctic Century*, vol. 4, 1989, p. 6.
[23] *Ibid.*
[24] B. Stonehouse, 'A Traveller's Code for Antarctic Visitors', *Polar Record*, vol. 26, no. 156, 1990, pp. 56–8.
[25] Presentation by the President of SCAR, Dr R. M. Laws, in *SCAR Report*, no. 5, 1991, p. 5.
[26] Statement of Accepted Practices and Relevant Provisions of the Antarctic Treaty (Annex A to Recommendation VIII-9), intended for the guidance of all those who visit the Antarctic, as well as the Guidance for Visitors to the Antarctic, formulated at the X ATCM in 1979.

the general public, the *Traveller's Code*, although perhaps not very informative, has been widely circulated.[27] At the 1990 Meeting of the Group of Specialists on Environmental Affairs and Conservation (GOSEAC II), it was noted that groups other than SCAR were providing instructions and guide books on commercial tourism in the Antarctic.[28] Major Antarctic tour operators have agreed on a voluntary code of conduct, based upon a 'composite of their experience'. The three US-based tour operators (Society Expeditions, Travel Dynamics and Mountain Travel) adopted in November 1989 their joint guidelines for both operators and tourists.[29]

More recent developments brought further 'legislation' by tour operators' to regulate Antarctic tourism. In August 1991 the major Antarctic tour operators founded the International Association of Antarctic Tour Operators (IAATO),[30] which soon gathered the majority of Antarctic tour operators.[31] In 1991, IAATO indorsed a set of guidelines for aircraft and land-based private-sector travel to and within the Antarctic interior.[32] Soon after, IAATO's self-regulatory framework expanded into three sets of guidelines: tour operator guidelines for shipborne operations, guidelines for operators of aircraft and land-based private-sector travel to and within the Antarctic interior and the IAATO Antarctica

---

[27] See also Stonehouse, 'A Traveller's Code', pp. 57–8.

[28] *SCAR Report*, no. 7, 1992, p. 10.

[29] For a concise review see P. J. Beck, 'Regulating One of the Last Tourism Frontiers: Antarctica', *Applied Geography*, vol. 10, 1990, p. 352.

[30] Society Expeditions, Ocean Cruise Lines, Salen Lindblad Cruises, Travel Dynamics, Adventure Network International, Mountain Travel Sobek and Zegrahm Expeditions. IAATO membership grew in 1992 to thirteen members, including the main cruise lines to be operating in Antarctica in the 1992–3 season: B. Stonehouse, 'IAATO: An Association of Antarctic Tour Operators', *Polar Record*, vol. 28, no. 167, 1992, p. 322. In 1994, IAATO membership included also Abercrombie & Kent/Explorer Shipping Corporation, Clipper Cruise Line, Hanseatic Cruises, Orient Lines, Quark Expeditions, Sea Quest Cruises, and Transocean Tours: see *IAATO Report of Activities for XVIII ATCM-Kyoto*, doc. XVIII ATCM/INFO 96, 20 April 1994, p. 6. Still, some tour operators sponsoring trips to Antarctica are not found in IAATO's membership.

[31] See in general 'International Association of Antarctic Tour Operators', *Polar Record*, vol. 27, no. 163, 1991, p. 372. It might be interesting to note that the SCAR Working Group on Logistics, at its meeting at Hobart, 5–9 September 1988, suggested that private operators should be encouraged to form an association through which they could receive information and assistance and in that way achieve self-regulation of the tourist industry in the Antarctic: see *SCAR Report*, no. 5, 1989, p. 44.

[32] Text in *Antarctica Tour Operators Form Association*, doc. XVI ATCM/INFO 20, 8 October 1991.

visitor guidelines.[33] More recently, IAATO's guidelines have been compiled into two sets of guidelines: Guidelines of Conduct for Antarctica Visitors, and Guidelines of Conduct for Antarctica Tour Operators.[34] Despite the legally non-binding nature of guidelines, any IAATO member failing to comply with them may find its membership revoked.

United Nations

The ATS' critics in the UN, most notably Malaysia, as well as Antigua and Barbuda, raised the issue of Antarctic tourism in the UN deliberations on the 'Question of Antarctica' in 1990. Antigua and Barbuda pointed out that 'there have been noticeable negative impacts, including the disruption of scientific programmes, and vandalism of historic sites'.[35] Malaysia accused tourists in Antarctica of 'often disturbing local breeding sites, trampling on vegetation or interfering with scientific research',[36] and warned that 'with a significant increase in the number of tourists, the fragile sites that are attractive to them will begin to show signs of irreparable damage'.[37]

The 1991 Report of the Secretary-General on the *State of the Environment in Antarctica and its Impact on the Global System*,[38] while assessing the types of negative environmental impact resulting from tourism, stated:

Thus far, tourism has had minimal adverse impact on the Antarctic environment since no significant tourist facilities have been constructed. Apart from the obvious problems that tourism may create for scientific programmes, it may also indirectly affect Antarctic ecosystems.[39]

Thus, the Secretary-General's Report did not provide any factual basis for alarming warnings on various negative impacts of Antarctic tourism. Yet, in the 1991 UN debate on the 'Question of Antarctica', critics of

---

[33] For a summary of these three sets of guidelines see Stonehouse, 'IAATO: An Association', pp. 322–3. According to Stonehouse, these guidelines are by far the most comprehensive and practical guides to visitor behaviour available for Antarctica: *ibid.*, p. 323.

[34] See *Tourism in Antarctica: Guidelines for a Low-Impact Presence*, submitted by IAATO, doc. XVII ATCM/INFO 65, 16 November 1992.

[35] UN doc. A/C.1/45/PV.40, p. 17.

[36] *Ibid.*, p. 27.

[37] *Ibid.*

[38] UN doc. A/46/590, 25 October 1991.

[39] *Ibid.*, p. 8.

the ATS regularly included a few words on Antarctic tourism when pointing out weaknesses of the ATS.[40]

ATS and 'thirds' in Antarctic tourism

During the period between the late 1980s and the early 1990s, individuals, companies, non-governmental organisations as well as international (intergovernmental) organisations were involved in addressing and – to some extent – even regulating Antarctic tourism. Is it imaginable that such a seemingly innocent and even exotic issue could carry the potential for doubts about the overall legitimacy of the ATS to regulate *all* activities in the Antarctic? Also, is it appropriate to consider these activities as third-party acts? The rules of the 1969 Vienna Convention on the Law of Treaties[41] limit the notion of *third* to relations between states with respect to treaties. Some authors have given a broader definition of *third* to include any subject of international law which is not a party to a given treaty,[42] but still it remains crucial to be *third* in relation to a certain treaty. However, no 'treaty' on Antarctic tourism has been adopted within the ATS.[43] Furthermore, the Antarctic Treaty made no specific provision for tourism. The only relevant provision may be found in Article X of the Antarctic Treaty, according to which:

Each of the Contracting Parties undertakes to exert appropriate efforts . . . to the end that no one engages in any activity in Antarctica contrary to the principles and purposes of the present Treaty.

'No one' can be interpreted to cover tour operators and tourists, while 'any activity' can be regarded as covering tourism. Is Antarctic tourism an activity contrary to the principles and purposes of the Antarctic Treaty?[44] No doubt, tourism must be regarded as a peaceful use of the

---

[40] See statements of Malaysia (UN doc. A/C.1/46/PV.38, pp. 9–10), Antigua and Barbuda (*ibid.*, p. 16), Guinea (*ibid.*, p. 27), Indonesia (UN doc. A/C.1/46/PV.39, p. 6) and Nepal (*ibid.*, p. 14).

[41] *United Nations Treaty Series*, vol. 1,155, p. 332.

[42] B. Vukas, *Relativno djelovanje medjunarodnih ugovora* (The Relativity of International Treaties) (Zagreb: Školska knjiga, 1975).

[43] In the period of substantial growth of Antarctic tourism and initial self-regulation of tourism industry, the Protocol was still a matter under negotiation within the XI Special Consultative Meeting (initiated in 1989, by Recommendation XV-1, and held from 1990 to 1991, in Viña del Mar and Madrid).

[44] Some tour operators have literally demonstrated their awareness of the 'principles and purposes' of the Antarctic Treaty: Adventure Network International planned a commemorative media event on 1 December 1991 with a live broadcast from Antarctica to mark

Antarctic. However, it might interfere with scientific research, freedom of which is *par excellence* the 'principle and purpose' of the Treaty. Tourists are often perceived as a threat to the cause of science, and this was a reason for the Consultative Parties to 'exert appropriate efforts', as provided for in Article X of the Antarctic Treaty, to ensure that this is not the case.

ATS ADAPTATION TO CHALLENGES: TOWARDS AN INTERNATIONAL LEGAL REGIME FOR ANTARCTIC TOURISM

An Antarctic tourism regime within the ATS *de lege ferenda*

As noted above, tourism in the Antarctic is indeed a peculiar phenomenon. It takes place not on the territory of a host country, but on a continent divided by disputed sovereignty claims. Since the Antarctic Peninsula area is the most easily accessible part of the Antarctic, tourism is mainly concentrated to the Peninsula area, where there are three overlapping sovereignty claims.[45] Since Antarctic tourism is predominantly seaborne, this means an even higher probability of jurisdictional problems, involving clashes of concurrent flag-state and coastal-state jurisdiction. Furthermore, Antarctic tourism may cause disturbances to both scientific research in Antarctica and Antarctic wildlife. Within the Antarctic Peninsula area, tourism is prevailingly concentrated to less than a dozen localities, mainly around larger and better equipped scientific bases. All this happens in a short period of the year, when Antarctic wildlife is also in its most vulnerable period. Moreover, while all human activities in the Antarctic are inherently hazardous, tourism often leads to adventurous projects, thereby increasing the likelihood of accidents, and of the need for emergency assistance. Its seaborne nature makes Antarctic tourism even more hazardous, particularly if not performed by special ice-strengthened ships with specially trained crew, etc. All these peculiarities bear witness to the need for a *special*, carefully shaped set of regulations to cope with them.

Comprehensive coverage of Antarctic tourism – to be elaborated in conformity with normative principles of the ATS, and simultaneously

---

the thirtieth anniversary of the entry into force of the Antarctic Treaty: see 'Tour Companies Opening Up', p. 163.

[45] Claims asserted by Argentina, Chile and the United Kingdom overlap between 53° and 74°W.

taking into consideration the peculiarities of Antarctic tourism – may be outlined as consisting of the following main elements:

1 Regulation of Antarctic tourism primarily connected with *science*:
    (a) prior notification system;
    (b) means for prevention of interference with scientific activities (e.g., 'no-go' areas);
    (c) means for avoidance of rescue operations and for preparation for cases of emergency: self-sufficiency, adequate training, avoidance of hazardous trips;
    (d) adequate insurance for compensation of costs connected with rescue operations.
2 Regulation of Antarctic tourism primarily connected with the *protection of the environment*:
    (a) means for *prevention*: information and licensing system; prior environmental impact assessment; prevention of marine pollution (and in this connection requirements for tour ships, like construction, facilities, etc.); requirements for crew and tourists (training, information, etc.); safety; contingency plans;
    (b) means for *regulation* of behaviour while in Antarctica: monitoring; waste-disposal regulation; protection of fauna and flora; protected area system; reporting system during and after visits; jurisdictional solutions (or responsibility for overseeing); control of third-party activities;
    (c) means for *reparation* of potential damage: liability rules; insurance.

A regulation to be elaborated on such lines would remain fully in compliance with the three normative principles of the ATS: peaceful purposes, freedom of scientific research and protection of the environment. It would also be conducive to the unambiguous regulation of that human activity in the Antarctic. However, some of its features – most notably jurisdictional solutions, liability rules and insurance – might lead to a disequilibrium in the sensitive *modus vivendi* on the sovereignty issue in the Antarctic. The issue is, hence, whether a comprehensive regulation of Antarctic tourism within the ATS is reconcilable with all the distinct features of that System.[46] A further question is whether a regulation which compromises between the peculiarities of Antarctic tourism on the one hand, and the

---

[46] See also Chapter 2.

distinct features of the ATS on the other, can be acceptable to the Antarctic Treaty parties and third interested actors alike.

The evolution of the entire problem of an Antarctic tourism regime within the ATS demonstrates the complexity of the dilemma pointed out above. It is not tourism as such which is difficult to regulate, but the *Pandora's box* that might be opened by this regulation.

Regulation of Antarctic tourism within the ATS prior to 1991

Antarctic tourism has regularly featured on the agendas of the Consultative Meetings since the IV Consultative Meeting in 1966.[47] However, extracts from the Final Reports of various Consultative Meetings can provide evidence of the obvious postponement of serious consideration of the matter:

owing to a lack of time for full discussion, the matter was referred to the Tenth Consultative Meeting;[48]

since there was insufficient time to give this matter adequate attention it was referred to the next Consultative Meeting.[49]

Prior to 1991, the Consultative Parties had adopted several recommendations on the effects of tourist and non-governmental expeditions in the Antarctic Treaty area (Recommendations IV-27, VI-7, VII-4, VIII-9 and X-8). However, in 1987 they also expressed concern that the existing measures were complex and that a simpler and more transparent set of measures should be adopted to assist operators in securing effective compliance.[50]

Adopting recommendations seemed, in terms of Article X of the Antarctic Treaty, the most 'appropriate effort' that the Consultative Parties may exert. However, recommendations formulated at the Consultative Meetings prior to the XVI Consultative Meeting (held in Bonn in 1991) date back to the 1960s and 1970s. As Beck notes in respect of those recommendations,[51] the regulation of tourism has 'never been approached systematically' by the Consultative Parties; moreover, Boczek has criti-

---

[47] See also the discussion in Chapter 8.
[48] Final Report of the IX ATCM, London 1977, para. 12.
[49] Final Report of the XIII ATCM, Brussels 1985, para. 68.
[50] Final Report of the XIV ATCM, Rio de Janeiro 1987, para. 124.
[51] Beck, 'Regulating One of the Last', p. 352.

cised the Consultative Parties' regulations pertaining to Antarctic visitors for a 'lack of conceptual rigor'.[52]

The contents of provisions of Recommendations IV-27, VI-7, VII-4, VIII-9 and X-8 have been well summarised by Heap[53] and Beck.[54] Also, the then Federal Republic of Germany summarised in a 1985 information circular its practices based on recommendations on Antarctic tourism.[55] Basically, these recommendations concern the need to be aware of ATS provisions, availability of prior information, protection of scientific research, prevention of adverse environmental impacts and promotion of self-sufficient tourism.

However, such a dispersed regulation, spread in various recommendations (and with an unclear legal nature) was both unsystematic and incomplete. Certainly, it was not the most appropriate solution which the ATS could have offered to regulate Antarctic tourism. The exact legal nature of ATS recommendations remains unclear, and their enforceability is, admittedly, a lasting dilemma for commentators on the ATS. We can assert that, prior to 1991, the issue of Antarctic tourism was granted only marginal attention from the Consultative Parties, and was fragmentarily addressed by several recommendations.

Activities of the Consultative Parties since 1991: towards the regulation of Antarctic tourism

The definitive change in the extent and intensity of the Consultative Parties' attention to Antarctic tourism was stimulated by the substantial rise in tourist visits combined with simultaneous activity of the tourism industry, organising itself and adopting its own regulation on Antarctic tourism. This process occurred in the period between 1989 and 1991: i.e. in the interim between the two regular Consultative Meetings.[56] This was also a period when the main focus of the Consultative Parties' regulatory

---

[52] B. A. Boczek, 'The Legal Status of Visitors, Including Tourists, and Non-Governmental Expeditions in Antarctica', in R. Wolfrum (ed.), *Antarctic Challenge III: Conflicting Interests, Cooperation, Environmental Protection, Economic Development* (Berlin: Duncker & Humblot, 1988), p. 465.

[53] J. A. Heap (ed.), *Handbook of the Antarctic Treaty System*, 8th ed. (Washington, DC: US Department of State, 1994), pp. 2,287–8.

[54] Beck, 'Regulating One of the Last', pp. 345–6.

[55] ATCM XIII doc. ANT/XIII/INFO 16, 10 October 1985.

[56] The XV ATCM was held in Paris, in October 1989, and the XVI ATCM in Bonn, in October 1991.

activity concerned negotiations for a comprehensive regime to protect the Antarctic environment.

From 1991 onwards, the Consultative Parties have paid increasing attention to the issue of Antarctic tourism. Initiated at the later stage of the XI Antarctic Treaty Special Consultative Meeting, discussions on Antarctic tourism were wide-ranging at the 1991 Bonn Consultative Meeting. Tourism became the major (and most controversial) agenda item at the 1992 Venice Consultative Meeting, and finally an agenda item characterised by greater consensus at the 1994 Kyoto Consultative Meeting. A condensed overview of developments during that period is presented below, aimed at demonstrating the modes and extent of ATS adaptation to the challenges posed by Antarctic tourism.

The XI Special Consultative Meeting, April 1991 session

Stimulated by the substantial growth of Antarctic tourism as well as by the approaching conclusion of negotiations to draft the Environmental Protocol, some Consultative Parties took the first steps towards bringing up the issue of a future Antarctic tourism regime. At the XI Special Meeting (first part of the second session, held in Madrid, 22–30 April 1991) two working papers on tourism were submitted, by Chile and France.[57] Many delegations participated in the discussion, thereupon agreeing to form an informal group on Antarctic tourism. This group accepted several principles which were, however, not a significant innovation in comparison to earlier recommendations on the subject (on the promotion of self-sufficient tourism, availability of prior information, prevention of adverse environmental impacts, etc.). However, greater awareness of the rising need for regulation of Antarctic tourism has been created.

The XVI Consultative Meeting, Bonn 1991

Tourism appeared as a busy agenda item at the XVI Consultative Meeting; several working papers as well as information papers were submitted,

---

[57] *Governmental and Non-Governmental Activities Concerning the Protection of the Antarctic Environment (Draft Annex to the Protocol)*, doc. XI ATSCM/2/WP.20, 23 April 1991 (submitted by Chile), text reprinted in W. M. Bush (ed.), *Antarctica and International Law: A Collection of Inter-State and National Documents*, Booklet AT91AA (New York: Oceana, 1993), pp. 62*ff*; *Tourist Activities in Antarctica and the Protection of the Environment*, doc. XI ATSCM/2/WP.3, 22 April 1991 (submitted by France), text reprinted in *ibid.*, pp. 16*ff*.

in particular by France, Chile, Japan, Italy and by Germany jointly with Japan, as well as by the United Kingdom and the United States (the latter two submitted information papers only).[58] Those countries were the ones most actively involved in discussions on the tourism agenda item. Worth noting is the fact that the Consultative Parties had invited the World Tourism Organization (WTO), the International Union for the Conservation of Nature and Natural Resources (IUCN) and the Antarctic and Southern Ocean Coalition (ASOC) to appoint experts to assist in the discussion of the agenda item on Antarctic tourism and non-governmental expeditions.

While some Consultative Parties – in particular France, strongly supported by Chile (as well as by Germany and Italy) – quite forcefully advocated the formulation of an annex on tourism to the Protocol, other views were also expressed at the XVI Consultative Meeting. Most notably, the United States opposed any regulation of tourism beyond the already existing provisions of the (then) newly adopted Environmental Protocol. Furthermore, in line with the US position, ASOC pointed out that – in order to be consistent with the comprehensive environmental regime established by the Protocol – an additional annex specifically confined to non-governmental activities is not required, since the Protocol and its annexes apply to all human activities in Antarctica.

The final outcome of these discussions was Recommendation XVI-13. This, however, indicated that one should not exclude that future development might lead towards an annex to the Environmental Protocol, on the comprehensive regulation of tourist and non-governmental activities in Antarctica.[59] Recommendation XVI-13 lists several environmental and operational issues to be taken into account by the informal Venice meeting of the Consultative Parties (see below). *Environmental* issues include: implementation of the Environmental Protocol and its Annexes; number of tourists and carrying capacity; harmonisation of standards relating to vessels; permanent infrastructure for tourists; concentration and dispersal of tourist activities; and access to unexplored areas. *Operational* issues

---

[58] France: *Tourism and Other Non-Governmental Activities in Antarctica and Environmental Protection*, doc. XVI ATCM/WP.2, 25 September 1991; Chile: *Tourism and Other Activities in Antarctica*, doc. XVI ATCM/WP.29, 8 October 1991; Japan: *Japanese Proposal on Tourism and Non-Governmental Expeditions*, doc. XVI ATCM/WP.34, 9 October 1991; Italy: *Tourist Activities in Antarctica*, doc. XVI ATCM/WP.37, 9 October 1991; Germany jointly with Japan: *Draft Recommendation: Tourism and Non-Governmental Activities in the Antarctic Treaty Area*, doc. XVI ATCM/WP.41, 10 October 1991.

[59] See Recommendation XVI-13, para. 1.

include: notification and expansion of information to be exchanged; a system for granting permission to visit stations; self-sufficiency; insurance, including search-and-rescue insurance; information obligation of Parties; preparation and training of tour guides and visitors' guides; examination of the need for specific kinds of control and monitoring; and requirements for organisational procedures.

An informal meeting of the Consultative Parties, to address these issues primarily, and to be convened with a view to making proposals to the XVII Consultative Meeting, was to begin its work in Venice on 9 November 1992.[60] The list of international and non-governmental organisations' representatives invited to attend the Venice informal meeting on tourism as observers was a lengthy one. Apart from SCAR (already with observer status at the Consultative Meetings) as well as those organisations whose experts attended the 1991 Bonn Consultative Meeting in respect of the agenda item on Antarctic tourism and non-governmental expeditions (ASOC, IUCN and WTO), the list also included the Council of Managers of National Antarctic Programs (COMNAP), the International Maritime Organisation (IMO) and – notably – representatives of the *tourism industry* from IAATO[61] and the Pacific Asia Travel Association (PATA).[62] Inviting these two organisations was a significant move, since it coupled their position of (formally) being third parties with that of (actually) becoming 'insiders'.[63]

The Informal Antarctic Treaty Meeting on Tourism, and the XVII Consultative Meeting, Venice 1992

High expectations for significant moves toward a regime for Antarctic tourism led the Consultative Parties to convene the Informal Meeting on

---

[60] *Ibid.*, paras. 1 and 3.

[61] In connection with this, Stonehouse observed that 'the Antarctic tourism industry, consistently maintaining its own standards of responsibility for three decades, has surely earned a hearing in the law making process. With well-considered policies based on extensive field experience, IAATO seems highly qualified to represent that industry's views': Stonehouse, 'IAATO: An Association', p. 324. The same author has suggested that IAATO should work in similar relation to the ATS as the Tourism Industry Association of Canada (TIAC) works closely with the government of Canada: *ibid.*, p. 323.

[62] PATA is a non-profit corporation composed of over 2,100 worldwide travel industry organisations, including 66 government, state and city tourism bodies and over 500 travel agencies. Nearly 17,000 individual volunteers are members of 74 PATA chapter organisations worldwide.

[63] Although, indeed, without any formal decision-making capacity. Here it is also worth noting that the United States included representatives of tourism industry on their

Tourism, held in Venice, 9–10 November 1992. The underlying reason was the need for the formulation of a Consultative Parties' *policy* with regard to Antarctic tourism. However, sharp polarisation among the Consultative Parties concerning the issue of a regime for Antarctic tourism became apparent in Venice even more than at earlier meetings. It soon became obvious that the approaches of various Consultative Parties were in deep conflict due to basic conceptual differences.

From the positions announced at the Informal Meeting, it would seem that the main polarisation was due to different views of two groups formed among the Consultative Parties: the so-called 'Group of Five' (Chile, France, Germany, Italy and Spain), on the one hand, and the United States and New Zealand, on the other. The United Kingdom maintained a special position, partially in disagreement with both groups (perhaps more in disagreement with the 'Group of Five'), while Australia tried to uphold a middle position – one which, eventually, the others were not willing to accept. Several other Consultative Parties were inclined to support one of the conflicting views, or were close to some of them: Belgium was close to the 'Group of Five', while the Netherlands seemed to give mild support to the same Group, emphasising, however, that its position was not yet fully defined. Norway gave, to a certain extent, support to the United Kingdom's approach, while Argentina and Japan expressed moderate views on the necessity of further clarification of the issue. Russia entered into discussion on several specific questions. Also Sweden announced its position, which appeared close to that of the United States. Some Non-Consultative Parties also took the floor: Austria supporting the Australian view, while Greece gave its support to the US position.[64] Other Consultative Parties remained silent, and in this connection Australia rightly noted that there was still a large body of undecided opinion among the Consultative Parties. On the other hand, there was also a small body of firmly decided opinion, whose polarised positions made it impossible for the Consultative Parties to reach any consensual solution.

Surrounded by the multiple division of the Consultative Parties, the tourist industry – represented by IAATO and PATA – offered its cooperation and the benefit of its thirty years of experience in Antarctic tourism. The IUCN was supportive of the proposal put forward by the 'Group of Five', while ASOC gave full support to the US position.

national delegations for the recent Consultative Meetings. Incidentally, the large majority of Antarctic tour operators are based in the United States.

[64] Incidentally, some cruise vessels owned by Greek ship owners (but sailing under a 'flag of convenience') are involved in Antarctic cruises each season.

Thus, the tourism issue was discussed at both Venice meetings among the narrow group of nine Consultative Parties, with the occasional involvement of the few additional Consultative Parties and several NGOs. Let us now try to condense the main positions.[65]

On behalf of the 'Group of Five', France introduced a preliminary draft Annex VI to the Protocol, on regulation concerning tourism and non-governmental activities. In support of this proposal, France put forward three basic arguments:

1 Antarctic tourism needs a specific policy;
2 this policy shall be contained in a single document, not scattered throughout a number of them; and
3 this document shall be legally binding.

Therefore, France suggested that a preliminary draft Annex, as proposed by the 'Group of Five', be taken as a basis for further discussion.

This proposal met with strong opposition. It was the United States' view that, since the Protocol applies to all human activities in Antarctica in a comprehensive manner, any new regulation specifically devoted to tourism would imply negligence of the Protocol. According to this view, any new regulation of tourism would be either a duplication of provisions already existing in the Protocol, or inconsistent with the Protocol. Instead, efforts should be directed to the overriding priority of the ATS: bringing into force the Protocol and not allowing the tourism issue to overshadow it. In support of this position, the United States highlighted relevant provisions of Recommendation XVI-13. New Zealand's position was close to that of the US. New Zealand suggested that the word 'activities' throughout the Protocol should be – for the purpose of Antarctic tourism – read as 'tourism', thus providing an adequate regulation.

The United Kingdom stated that there was no disagreement amongst

---

[65] The main positions were contained in several working papers: see Chile, France, Germany, Italy and Spain: *Preliminary Draft: Annex VI to the Protocol on Environmental Protection to the Antarctic Treaty; Regulation concerning Tourism and Non-Governmental Activities*, doc. XVII ATCM/WP 1, 9 November 1992; United States: *Antarctic Tourism and the Environmental Protocol*, doc. XVII ATCM/WP 6, 9 November 1992; United Kingdom: *The Regulation of Tourism and Non-Governmental Activities in the Antarctic Treaty Area*, doc. XVII ATCM/WP 2, 9 November 1992, together with the related information document: *The Regulation of Tourism and Non-Governmental Activities in the Antarctic Treaty Area (II)*, doc. XVII ATCM/INFO 6, 11 November 1992, as well as *A Revised Code of Guidance for Visitors to the Antarctic*, doc. XVII ATCM/WP 3, 9 November 1992; Australia: *Tourism and Non-Governmental Activities in the Antarctic Treaty Area*, doc. XVII ATCM/WP 14, 11 November 1992.

the Consultative Parties that tourism and non-governmental activities must be regulated: therefore, regulation would be not a question of *whether* but of *how*. Prior to deciding whether the existing regime, as embodied in recommendations, is adequate or not, an assessment should be made, first, of the nature and scale of the potential problems and impacts of tourism and non-governmental activities; and, second, of whether existing provisions adequately address those potential problems and impacts. The United Kingdom saw the task of the Venice Meeting as that of developing an explanation of how the Protocol addresses the issue of tourism, and – if there are shortcomings in the Protocol – how to solve these. However, responding to the French statement, the United Kingdom argued:

1   there is no need for a specific policy for Antarctic tourism;
2   the ATS already has one document: the Protocol;
3   the task of the Consultative Parties is to give the Protocol legally binding force, to implement it and to enforce it.

The position of Australia was that the need exists to develop a clear statement (or guidance) which can apply to tour organisers, but not a need for a new legal instrument. Hence, Australia maintained that significant new obligations were not needed: rather, the existing regulation shall be explained in a better, perhaps synthesised manner. Another important element in this view was a need to establish arrangements to determine which party should take responsibility for overseeing tourist and non-governmental activities.[66] However, Australia also warned of the risk in overregulating tourism activity from the Consultative Parties, stating that self-regulation was a necessary component of tourism. Intensifying consultations with the tourism industry would, in Australia's view, offer a more appropriate method of managing Antarctic tourism. However, any regulation would have to be applied equally to all forms of non-governmental activities, regardless of size. In this respect, Australia argued that the Protocol did provide a basic framework, but that the question of its implementation to tourist activities was rather complex.

Despite the abundance of proposals submitted, as well as the extensive discussions of the issue, the final outcome of the XVII Consultative Meeting with regard to Antarctic tourism was indeed poor: nothing

---

[66] This element made the Australian proposal unacceptable to several Consultative Parties, notably to the United States, the United Kingdom and New Zealand.

more than one page containing seven neutrally phrased paragraphs in the Final Report of the Meeting.[67]

The XVIII Consultative Meeting, Kyoto 1994

It became apparent from the beginning of the Kyoto Consultative Meeting that those Consultative Parties most actively involved in discussions on the tourism issue in Venice had now had ample time to contemplate and reconsider their positions. This was reflected in the proposals put forward[68] and the tone of discussions among the Consultative Parties on tourism at the Kyoto Meeting. The idea of a tourism annex to the Protocol was abandoned; instead, Chile and France forwarded a joint proposal for agreed measures on Antarctic tourism. Thus, the Venice 'Group of Five' which had so fiercely advocated the adoption of a tourism annex to the Protocol, became reduced to the 'Group of Two'. Their argument was now that, although IAATO disseminates its own guidelines on tourism, it is the responsibility of the Consultative Parties to manage the regulation of that activity in Antarctica. Chile stressed the need for the Consultative Parties to adopt a single document which would coordinate the existing ATS rules on tourism, so as to make them more visible to tourists and tour organisers. Australia again maintained a mediating role.[69] Linking up to Chilean and French views, Australia proposed that the entire problem of tourism be addressed at three levels: visitors, tour organisers and finally the role of the Consultative Parties. Both the United Kingdom and the United States supported this approach; the latter, however, pointing out that the third level of the Australian proposal was the one still to be dealt with in more detail at future

---

[67] Paras. 108–14 of the Final Report of the XVII ATCM, Venice 1992.
[68] See Australia: *Conduct of Tourism and Non-Governmental Activity in Antarctica*, doc. XVIII ATCM/WP 9, 10 April 1994; Chile and France: *Agreed Measures on Tourism in Antarctica*, doc. XVIII ATCM/WP 11, Rev. 1, 11 April 1994; United Kingdom: *The Regulation of Tourism and Non-Governmental Activities in the Antarctic Treaty Area*, doc. XVIII ATCM/ WP 18, 10 April 1994; United Kingdom: *A Revised Code of Guidance for Visitors to the Antarctic*, doc. XVIII ATCM/WP 19, 10 April 1994; United Kingdom: *Draft Recommendation (to Introduce Mandatory Provisions for Information Exchange and an Observation System)*, doc. XVIII ATCM/WP 20, 10 April 1994.
[69] The Australian proposal put forward at the Kyoto Meeting was actually a slightly modified version of Australia's position at the 1992 Venice ATCM, but now – importantly – omitting the concept of 'overseeing state', i.e. the idea of ascribing responsibility to an identified Contracting Party for tourist (and NGO) visits.

Consultative Meetings. There was a wide convergence of views concerning the issue, in that the objective of this Consultative Meeting was not to create new rules on Antarctic tourism, but merely to provide guidance to tourists and tour organisers. A small informal drafting group – composed of Australia, Chile, France and the United Kingdom – was thus given the task of drafting a single document with this agreed purpose. Albeit working in closed sessions, the group was occasionally enlarged by the United States, Germany, Italy, the Netherlands and New Zealand, whenever it was felt necessary underway. The United States maintained its position from Venice, that the Protocol already regulates all aspects of Antarctic tourism, but allowed that an interpretation of its rules might be needed. Germany, in particular, was keen to exempt issues of liability and insurance from such a document, in order not to interfere with subjects being dealt with by the group of legal experts on liability. The Netherlands put forward the idea of designating 'Areas of Special Tourist Interest', but agreed not to insist on this proposal, which met serious reservations by the majority of the Consultative Parties involved.

The result of the drafting group appeared in a two connected documents:

1 a text addressed to tourists, advising them in layman's language how to behave when visiting Antarctica; and
2 a text addressed to tour organisers, providing them with information on the relevant rules of the ATS on tourism, including the Protocol (when it enters into force). This text also set out procedures which might[70] be followed when planning and conducting a tour in Antarctica, and in the subsequent reporting on it.

At that stage, two questions remained for further discussion: first, the form such a document should have; and, second, the role of the Consultative Parties in respect of the document. Regarding the form, the proposals were put forward for a recommendation, agreed measures, guidelines, a 'decision', or simply an appendix to the Final Report of the Meeting. The solution eventually adopted was in the form of a recommendation,[71] with the guidance as an attachment to it. Regarding the role of the Consultative Parties, several of them were not willing to accept any legal obligation to be rec-

[70] 'Might' is the word used by the ATCPs in respect of a duty to follow these procedures: see para. 62 of the draft Final Report of the XVIII ATCM, Kyoto 1994.
[71] Recommendation XVIII-1.

ommended to their government (i.e., to legislate or to incorporate into internal legislation) in respect of tourism guidance.[72] Consequently, Recommendation XVIII-1 contained in its operative part that the governments of the Consultative Parties would be recommended to *circulate* the guidance as widely and as quickly as possible. Also, resulting from the intervention of Germany, the governments of the Consultative Parties were to be recommended to urge tourists and organisers to act in accordance with the guidance, consistent with the relevant provisions of their applicable *national* law.[73]

ACCEPTANCE AND APPLICABILITY OF THE ATS ANTARCTIC TOURISM REGIME

Level of acceptance

It was not difficult to achieve broad acceptance for such a solution among the Consultative Parties. Although a significant step forward since the 1992 Venice Consultative Meeting, the outcome of the 1994 Kyoto Consultative Meeting was not to pose any difficulty regarding acceptance. In fact, it is reducible to the following two statements:

1 the Consultative Parties have provided an interpretation of the already existing ATS rules pertaining to Antarctic tourism, now compiled in a single document; and
2 they have declared that visitors and tour organisers are bound by the national laws and regulations of each respective country, applicable to activities in the Antarctic.

This solution has been welcomed by Antarctic tour operators, since it relaxed their fears of their commercial activity in the Antarctic being over-regulated by the Consultative Parties. The main representative of the tourism industry (IAATO) expressed hopes that:

its voluntary Guidelines will be replaced by a comparable version as a result of the XVIII ATCM-Kyoto. The new version would be adopted for future use by IAATO members.[74]

---

[72] Russia was in particular hesitant to accept any such obligation.
[73] Recommendation XVIII-1, para. 2.
[74] *IAATO Report of Activities for XVIII ATCM-Kyoto*, doc. XVIII ATCM/INFO 96, 20 April 1994, p. 3.

Applicability of the existing tourism regime

The adaptation of the ATS to recent challenges posed by Antarctic tourism has not resulted in any substantial changes of its actual regulation within the ATS. No new regime has resulted as yet, and there are small chances that any new regime for Antarctic tourism will emerge soon: thus, we have to inquire into the existing body of rules within the ATS related to Antarctic tourism, and to estimate its applicability.

The *external* aspect of applicability of an Antarctic tourism regime has increased in recent years, with the inclusion of the two major tourism industry organisations in the consultative process. Previously, the self-regulation of these organisations might have been perceived as an external threat interfering with the Consultative Parties' monopoly to regulate all human activities in the Antarctic. However, these organisations unambiguously expressed their willingness to replace their own voluntary guidelines by an analogous instrument adopted within the ATS. This has meant that the ATS faces no threat of competing regimes in the matter of Antarctic tourism.

Regarding the *internal* aspect of applicability, the development of a single document on tourism at the 1994 Kyoto Consultative Meeting, interpreting existing ATS obligations for visitors and tour organisers, enhances the visibility of regulations. Also, consistency within the ATS context is high, since the document in no way questions either normative or structural sources of the ATS internal legitimacy. The three main principles of the ATS are fully recognised, along with the preservation of the pragmatic *modus vivendi* on sovereignty claims. Moreover, the Consultative Parties have retained their position as actors with special responsibility for Antarctic tourism, and kept the regulatory process within the framework of the consultative machinery. As such, the document adopted at Kyoto offers nothing more than a presentation of regulations on Antarctic tourism already existing within the ATS. What remains to be assessed in respect of such a tourism regime's internal applicability is how conducive it can be to solving the problem of regulation.

The Protocol and its Annexes apply indisputably to all activities in the Antarctic Treaty area, including tourist and other non-governmental activities. However, the Protocol has not yet entered into force. Even if the Protocol were already in force, its regulation of Antarctic tourism could face serious difficulties. One question still remains to be addressed more thoroughly: does the Protocol really offer an adequate legal regime for Antarctic tourism, applicable under the hypothesis that the Protocol is already in force? Is it really so simple to solve the problem of a tourism regime as New Zealand suggested at the XVII Consultative Meeting, by replacing the word 'activities' throughout the Protocol with the word 'tourism'? A concise answer has been offered by Pineschi:

The very fact that tourism is regulated by the same obligations preventing the environmental impact produced by other human activities on the Antarctic environment has not grasped the peculiarity of tourism and, therefore, has not given appropriate answers to the specific problems posed by this activity.[75]

There are several significant gaps in the coverage of Antarctic tourism under the Protocol caused by the peculiarities of Antarctic tourism.[76] For this reason:

Current regulations governing tourism under the Antarctic Treaty, though considerable, are inadequate and insufficiently integrated with other measures for regulating human access to Antarctica and use of its resources.[77]

There are a number of questions, related to liability and insurance,[78] jurisdiction, third-party activities and enforcement, to which answers are not found in the provisions of the Protocol. Furthermore, the rules of the Protocol in several instances offer only partial solutions, even when expressly related to tourism. The duty of prior environmental impact assessment (EIA), as provided for in Article 8 of the Protocol, may serve as an example: when the formulation from Article VII, paragraph 5 of the Antarctic Treaty is applied to an Antarctic tourist cruise, it is entirely unclear who will be responsible for the EIA.[79] Ships will often be flying a 'flag of convenience' and be owned by companies or individuals from different countries; and tour companies may be incorporated in one

[75] L. Pineschi, 'Tourist Activities and the Protection of the Antarctic Environment: Current Obligations and Possible Future Developments', in F. Francioni (ed.), *International Environmental Law for Antarctica* (Milano: Giuffrè Editore, 1992), p. 186.
[76] Norway's *Regulations Relating to Tourism and Other Travel in Svalbard*, issued by Royal Decree of 18 October 1991, offers a useful example of legal regulation dealing with the peculiarities of polar tourism.
[77] *Tourism in Antarctica*, doc. XVII ATCM/INFO 18, 11 November 1992 (submitted by IUCN).
[78] However, these two questions – liability and insurance – are currently being dealt with within the framework of an emerging liability regime, to be an additional annex to the Protocol.
[79] See B. S. Manheim, 'Gaps in Management of Antarctic Seaborne Tourism under the Protocol' (unpublished paper, delivered at the Informal Antarctic Treaty Meeting on Tourism, Venice, 9–10 November 1992), p. 6.

country, while organising trips in another country and proceeding to the Antarctic Treaty area from a third country.

A recent instance can illustrate these and other difficulties of applying the existing ATS regulation to Antarctic tourism.[80] In January 1994, a group of radio amateurs and tourists, aboard the Russian registered ice-breaker *Kaptain Khlebnikov* proceeded to the Antarctic from the Falklands/ Malvinas and approached a Norwegian-claimed territory, Peter I Øy. This group was led by a US national and was organised by *Quark Expeditions* (United States); expedition members were nationals of Antarctic Treaty parties (Belgium, Germany, the United Kingdom and the United States) and a non-Treaty party (Mexico). The group went ashore Peter I Øy, but the operation was soon stopped, as a fog bank built up and wind increased. If there had been an accident, or if environmental damage had resulted from the operation, where would the responsibility have lain? Here we should also recall that many ships visiting Antarctic waters fly flags of convenience; and this would make such questions even more complex.

CONCLUDING REMARKS

Comprehensive coverage of Antarctic tourism, within the parameters given by the ATS – as outlined in this chapter – does not appear at this stage to be a factor which would contribute to the legitimacy of ATS tourism regulation. On the contrary, wide acceptance was actually made possible only at considerable expense to the thorough regulation of Antarctic tourism in an ATS tourism regime. This has been the factor legitimising the most recent ATS regulatory solution on Antarctic tourism, as adopted at the 1994 Kyoto Consultative Meeting: and this is in fact not much more than a statement on already existing ATS regulation. This was the only solution acceptable to all the Consultative Parties and at the same time welcomed by interested Antarctic tour operators. To put it bluntly: at the end of the day everybody was content that no new regulation was adopted. On the one hand, this was made possible by the weakening of external pressure on the ATS concerning Antarctic tourism. On the other hand, it was conditioned by the persistent salience of possible internal conflict, should the regulation of Antarctic tourism be forced to

---

[80] The example cited is based on a report written by a staff member of that operation, Dr R. K. Headland, 'Note on Visit to Peter I Øy', prepared aboard the ship, printed and distributed in Cambridge, Scott Polar Research Institute, 31 January 1994.

its logical conclusion – i.e. to resolving the problem of jurisdiction in the Antarctic and thereby opening the entire sovereignty issue. Given that situation, the arrangement contained in the Kyoto guidance gained acceptance as legitimate. However, its implementation in practice will reveal to what extent the level of applicability of this arrangement will affect its legitimacy in the longer run.

PART V

===

Domestic politics and ATS change

Domestic politics and ATS change: introductory assessment

Olav Schram Stokke

We have seen in the preceding Parts that the effectiveness and legitimacy of the ATS has relied on its ability to *adapt* whenever new issues, like fisheries, minerals activities, or tourism, have reached sufficient magnitude to become contested, either among the Consultative Parties or in their relations to third parties. The typical response has been to hammer out new regimes in the ATS or to modify existing ones. In Part II, we investigated one set of reasons for this preparedness to adapt – the perceived need of the Consultative Parties for broad acceptance of ATS solutions among third parties. In Parts III and IV, changes in the ATS were explained at an issue-area level focusing on compatibility of views and the way certain solutions have permitted accommodation or adjustment of conflicting positions among the states involved. In the following chapters, ATS change is examined from a third perspective. By inspecting domestic politics and law in the Antarctic policy segments of four selected countries – Australia, Chile, Norway and the United States – we seek to bring out how sectional interest structures and decision-making processes affect the positions and roles of those states whenever controversial issues are decided upon in the ATS.

The interaction of domestic and international levels is a reciprocal one: sometimes, topics discussed in the ATS spill over into domestic debates and affect policy processes at that level. The clearest example of the latter, as shown in Chapter 6, is the issue of how to deal with the minerals question, which, once it reached maturity on the Antarctic agenda, had a tremendous effect on domestic interest and mobilisation in certain key countries, including the ones discussed more closely in this Part.

THE SAMPLE OF COUNTRIES

In the following country studies, special attention will be paid to how domestic politics and law, and changes therein, have affected the respective *positions* and *roles* assumed in the regime processes dealt with in this book. The configuration of those positions has determined the success or failure of various attempts to adapt ATS regimes to changing circumstances.

The sample is not randomly selected and we do not claim that it is representative of all Treaty parties – or even of the Consultative Parties; thus, we remain cautious about generalising findings beyond the sample. On the other hand, while all four states are original Consultative Parties, many of the other politically interesting categories in Antarctic politics are represented. The sample is drawn from four different continents; two of the states are located close to the Antarctic and have strong geopolitical ties to the Southern Continent, whereas the remaining two are strategically far more oriented towards the North. In terms of actual presence in the region, the United States, Australia and Chile have large Antarctic science programmes, while the Norwegian presence is relatively low. Of the four, one is a superpower and the rest are middle powers of varying size; they also differ substantially in terms of economic development.

Moreover, a primary purpose of Part V is to shed light on how features of domestic politics may affect the Antarctic policies of the states in question. And when dealing as we do with a small number of cases, random selection cannot ensure that cases are sufficiently different to allow causal discussion:[1] in particular, it is important that the states included vary in terms of positions and roles assumed in the four regime processes discussed in the book; and a crude initial assessment suggests that they do.[2] In the *minerals* case, treatment of the sovereignty issue was the most difficult divide, and the sample comprises a broad range of positions on this matter – from hard claimants, like Chile and Australia, over a moderate one, Norway, to the non-claimant United States. It also covers both sides of another important divide in the CRAMRA negotiations – that between industrialised and developing countries. In the *Environmental Protocol*, the minerals ban was clearly the most controversial element. Our sample includes both one of the original proponents of a ban, Australia, and a

---

[1] On the role of comparison and process-tracing in the substantiation of causal claims, see Chapter 1; see also G. King, R. O. Keohane and S. Verba, *Designing Social Inquiry: Scientific Inference in Qualitative Research* (Princeton University Press, 1994), in particular chapters 3 and 6.

[2] More in-depth accounts of the positions and roles of these states in the ATS are given in the subsequent chapters. On the need to ensure variance in the dependent variable when selecting cases for causal, rather than descriptive, analysis, see King *et al.*, *Designing Social Inquiry*, pp. 141–2.

leading recalcitrant, the United States. As for *tourism*, controversy has centred on whether or not this activity requires a separate instrument in addition to the Protocol: Chile and the United States have taken opposite positions on this matter, whereas Norway and especially Australia have assumed moderating roles. It is only regarding the *CCAMLR* case that the sample fails to represent the opposing camps on the most salient controversies, since it does not include countries which have resisted the growing stringency of this regime.[3]

INTERESTS AND PROCESSES

While there are significant contrasts between the countries studied in the following chapters, some common themes and patterns appear to stand out in the Antarctic politics segments of all of them. Let us review those themes briefly already at this stage.

National priorities in the Antarctic

It is not surprising that the key concerns pursued in Antarctic politics differ somewhat among the four states reviewed; this is especially true for the political salience of their positions on *sovereignty*. The territorial dimension is far more pronounced for Chile and Australia, than for Norway or the United States. This shows up in sharp differences in the political centrality of Antarctic affairs on the respective domestic policy agendas. Both Chile and Australia, geographically adjacent to the Antarctic, have taken great pains to demonstrate that they regard their Antarctic claimed areas as integral parts of their territories. Chile has placed administration of the claimed sector under the regional government in Punta Arenas, rather than directly under central authorities, and established an Antarctic municipality as well as family settlements in the Seventh Continent. These symbolic acts should be seen in light of the overlapping claims in the Antarctic Peninsula area and also the geographic proximity of the latter to the southern tip of South America. And Chapter 13 argues that the shift of bureaucratic responsibility for the Australian Antarctic Territory (AAT) from the Ministry of External Affairs to departments

---

[3] On the lack of efforts among fisheries industry organisations to become direct participants in the CCAMLR process, see Chapter 4; for an account of the industrial organisation of the ocean-going Japanese fishing industry, currently predominant in Antarctic waters, see O. S. Stokke, 'Transnational Fishing: Japan's Changing Strategy', *Marine Policy*, vol. 15, no. 4, 1991, pp. 231–43.

primarily concerned with internal affairs, occurred on similar grounds. Those concerns seem far less significant to Norway or the United States. And since the accommodation of sovereignty concerns is such a vital issue in all ATS regimes, differences like these are liable to have substantial bearing on the positions and roles assumed on matters pertinent to the effectiveness and legitimacy of the ATS.

While in the sealing and, later, the whaling period, *commercial* concerns loomed large among the goals pursued in the Antarctic, they are not salient today in any of the domestic policy arenas of countries dealt with in this volume. Tourism may prove an exception, but as yet it is relatively minor. And apart from Antarctic fisheries states like Japan and Russia, a quite low interest in commercial exploitation of the Antarctic is typical of the states active in Antarctic politics.[4] True, there are differences in the value which various states attribute to future economic activities, as reflected *inter alia* in their attitudes to a ban on minerals exploitation. Even in Australia, generally seen as the champion of the steadily more pervasive *environmental* concerns in the Antarctic, worries in the Treasury that CRAMRA would remove the basis for extracting fiscal revenues from possible future minerals activities in the AAT made it easier for opponents of that Convention to muster a decisive alliance against it. Still, in none of the states reviewed in this book did the mining industry mobilise forcefully in support of CRAMRA, even when the Convention became a major maverick for the environmental movement during the 1980s.

Science remains a major concern pursued in the Antarctic. In addition to providing knowledge less available elsewhere, scientific activities are also seen as a way to demonstrate an interest in the region: to most Consultative Parties, such activities are their major form of presence in the Antarctic. Original signatories, like those reviewed in this book, are not formally affected by the requirement in Article IX of the Antarctic Treaty that acceding parties must conduct substantial research activity in the region to acquire and retain consultative status. However, the latter requirement has strengthened the perception of a linkage in the ATS between scientific activity and political status. Thus, to some extent, the

---

[4] Chile has shown some interest in Antarctic fisheries in the past few years, and a dislocated United States pollock trawler previously operating in the Bering Sea has recently conducted a test fishery for crab. See *Report of the XIth Meeting of the Commission* (Hobart: Commission for the Conservation of Antarctic Marine Living Resources, 1992), pp. 28 and 20 respectively.

science concern is related to the sovereignty question and to aspirations to *influence* political developments in the Antarctic.

Segmented decision-making

As the following chapters will show, pervasive societal interest in Antarctic affairs is not the normal situation. Except during the 'green wave' of the 1980s and early 1990s, all four case studies portray a rather narrow, *bureaucracy-driven* policy segment which usually attracts only moderate interest from outside. In general, high-level political actors pay only sporadic attention to Antarctic affairs. Sometimes, because foreign policy is seen as the prerogative of the executive and sometimes because their electorates are indifferent to Antarctic issues, the legislative tends to take on a reactive and supportive role in these processes. The balance between those two reasons varies among the countries discussed here. In Chile, where parts of the wider public feel strongly involved with Antarctic matters, the constitutional situation has clearly favoured the executive side in foreign affairs. In contrast, while the Norwegian legislative traditionally plays a rather active role in foreign affairs, popular attention to the Antarctic has been very limited. Australia and the United States fall somewhere in between: in both cases, there is a latent societal interest for the Antarctic which, if activated, may produce ardent but rather episodic legislative attention to ATS affairs.

In this largely bureaucracy-driven segment, a country's ministry of foreign affairs tends to have a key coordinating role. In addition, the segment will typically include the ministry of defence, because of the logistical side of Antarctic operations, as well as ministries responsible for environmental and scientific affairs. It will also include representatives of the scientific organisations involved in the Antarctic, and often a scientific advisory group with evaluative functions. Other agencies may be involved as well, but normally on an *ad hoc* basis. A small, inter-agency mechanism allows policy coordination in the Antarctic segment as well as the inclusion of a wider range of bureaucratic or societal actors and advisors whenever needed.

While there may be disagreements about means, the Antarctic segments reviewed in this volume appear to be remarkably *consensual*: participants tend to share basic goals, values and problem understandings when dealing with Antarctic affairs. The segments are not marked by sharp articulation of interests, but rather, as noted about the United States process in Chapter 16, by 'the force of pure reason'. Support to the ATS structure is the most salient common denominator in these segments, and other goals are typically relegated to this. The Australian transition from support to rejection of CRAMRA, detailed in Chapter 13, illustrates this point well. When consensus on CRAMRA was destroyed among core participants in the domestic Antarctic segment, it was an amazingly rapid matter for a new national consensus to emerge on the very different but practicable notion of a comprehensive protection system.

In terms of *access and participation*, the Antarctic domestic processes tend to be quite narrow, but they have not been closed to outsiders desiring to influence policy formation. As noted, the usually passive role of the legislative and other parts of the state apparatus has been due to a high degree of consensus combined with the peripheral political status of most Antarctic issues. As for societal actors, both Australia and the United States have long traditions of gradually involving those wishing to con-tribute views or expertise – especially 'green' organisations but more recently industry as well – in the preparations for ATS meetings, or even in national delegations to them. With the democratisation in Chile in the late 1980s, societal organisations became increasingly involved in Antarc-tic affairs here as well. The lesser role of environmental organisations in the Norwegian case would seem to reflect lack of concern rather than lack of access. Thus, the relative harmony and consensus of the Antarctic policy segments reviewed in this book appears to have been open to chal-lenge by outside actors, as long as the latter possess enough knowledge about Antarctic affairs to provide relevant input.

As the following chapters will bring out, when the Antarctic resource management question caught the eye of the burgeoning green movement in the late 1970s, the level of *attention* and *conflict* increased in the dom-estic decision-making arenas. The controversy over minerals induced states to reassess their priorities in the Antarctic, especially the signifi-cance attributed to environmental considerations. Throughout the 1980s, the annual meetings of the Commission set up by CCAMLR and the protracted CRAMRA negotiations provided ample opportunity for the green movement to boost environmental consciousness and push for stricter international standards; this strategy was pursued in parallel at home and on international scenes. Unlike traditional participants in the Antarctic segments, some of those NGOs were unwilling to let their inclusion in the process prevent them from continued agitation against parts of the policies emerging within the ATS. Those organisations strove to attract wider public attention to Antarctic environmental problems by lobbying, offering expert advice and by calling informal meetings to rally support for preferred policies. As discussed in Chapter 4, this was not a one-sided affair. Increasingly sensitive to charges of exclusivism, the Consultative Parties have known very well that inclusion of green organisations at domestic levels and in ATS deliberations might be a powerful instrument to enhance the external acceptance of Treaty cooperation. In the domestic policy arenas reviewed here, the green organisations have never been seriously matched by industrial counterparts; so in this sense, the expansion of the Antarctic segments was clearly biased towards the green side of the use-versus-conservation dilemma.

The growing societal interest in Antarctic affairs in the late 1980s had a parallel at the state level. When Antarctic issues became closely linked to environmental values – a rising concern in the wider societal debates in the countries involved – the political stakes in this policy arena grew. This attracted the attention of political actors otherwise scarcely concerned with the Antarctic, including at times even heads of government. As discussed in Chapter 16, in the snowball process following the Franco-Australian rejection of CRAMRA, environmentally oriented Congressmen in the United States pushed eagerly for more restrictive legislation on Antarctic activities and moved to bind the President to certain positions on the minerals issue. In a similar vein, the Australian Parliament passed legislation banning minerals activity in the Australian Antarctic Territory. In Norway too, the greening of the ATS also implied wider executive participation by a steadily more active role on the part of the Ministry of Environment. Somewhat earlier, as discussed in Chapter 14, and as part of the wider reassessment of Chile's Antarctic policy in the light of growing UN criticism of the ATS, a broader range of academics and working groups became involved in the Antarctic deliberations of that country.

SUMMARY

Support of the ATS, environmental protection, science, the sovereignty issue and, to a lesser extent, commercial interests are recurrent themes in the Antarctic policies of the four countries reviewed in this book. For all of them, the sudden re-emergence of the minerals question, at a juncture when this matter was seen as settled, infused the domestic side of Antarctic decision-making with new concerns and much broader participation. An interesting question, therefore, is whether the adoption of the Environmental Protocol, which is widely perceived as putting this issue aside for the foreseeable future, may imply a return to a situation with less societal attention to ATS activities.

We have suggested that the patterns of domestic politics portrayed in the following chapters can be significant to the effectiveness and legitimacy of the ATS by affecting the collective ability of the Consultative Parties to adapt ATS regimes to new problems and challenges. This hypothesis has structured the country studies in Part V, which concentrate on three points:

1   the main interests and priorities pursued in the Antarctic and how they have changed over time;
2   the decision-making processes and fluctuations in participation and influence; and
3   how these interest and decision-making patterns link up to the positions and roles assumed by those states in the ATS deliberations reviewed in this book, on living resources, minerals, environmental protection and tourism.

13

ATS decision-making and change: the role of domestic politics in Australia

RICHARD A. HERR AND BRUCE W. DAVIS

INTRODUCTION

Domestic political processes have loomed rather larger in the Australian Antarctic policy-making process than is true for most of the other members of the Antarctic Treaty System (ATS).[1] There are two primary, and not unrelated, reasons for this circumstance. One is Australia's perception of its role internationally as a middle power; the other is the country's rich amalgam of historical and geographical involvement with the frozen south. As would be expected of a middle power, Australia's foreign policy has tended to define the country's place globally in terms of its capacity to influence regional events of importance to itself.[2] These two factors have combined broadly to promote a generally close agreement between elites and masses as to Australia's general international priorities. (Arguably, this has been true even at times when policy objectives were confused, as in the case of the Vietnam War.) Southeast Asia, Japan and the South Pacific have figured prominently as agreed areas of regional priority for most of the past generation of Australians. The same could be said for Antarctica – perhaps. Antarctica is undoubtedly a region of significance for Australians.[3] However, a key difference with other regional interests is that Antarctica has only been occasionally an area of dispute in the public consciousness over the last half-century. Thus, the public constituency has tended to be more a latent than an overt influence on Australia's Antarctic policy. Nevertheless this latent force is genuine –

---

[1] The authors would like to express their gratitude to Robert Hall, David Lyons and Pat Quilty for their helpful comments on earlier drafts of this chapter.

[2] G. Evans and B. Grant, *Australia's Foreign Relations in the World of the 1990s* (Melbourne University Press, 1991), pp. 322–6. For a classic definition of a 'middle power', see M. Wight, *Power Politics* (Harmondsworth: Penguin, 1979), pp. 63–4.

[3] For example, see Australia, Department of Defence, *The Defence of Australia* (Canberra: Australian Government Publishing Service, 1987), p. 19.

as was amply demonstrated by the Australian Commonwealth's decision in May 1989 not to sign the Convention on the Regulation of Antarctic Mineral Resource Activities (CRAMRA).

While the relevance of Antarctica to the general public is one feature which distinguishes Australian domestic policy-making from that of most other ATS members, it would be wrong to conclude that the Commonwealth's Antarctic policy is popularly driven. Rather, it has been, for the most part, very much a product of a bureaucracy-based policy process. The Westminster tradition, which leans toward elitism and tends to resist public participation, is a major strand in this bureaucratic process, but it is not an exclusive influence. Australia has incorporated such non-Westminster elements as an entrenched constitution, a partial separation of powers and federalism in its political process. These have profoundly influenced the general policy-making process in Australia, and, in recent years, have worked to make the political process more open than an unmodified Westminster system would suggest. The multiple derivations of its political heritage are becoming increasingly salient. While currently Australian policy-making may stand somewhat closer to that in the United Kingdom than in the United States in terms of the influence of public opinion on foreign policy, internal changes are operating in the direction of pluralism. The tension between these two approaches which characterises general policy-making also informs the specifics of the Antarctic policy process. Thus, by reviewing the domestic institutions and agencies which contribute to the making of Australian policy on Antarctica, this chapter seeks to show that this process has become more open in terms of public participation, and that the final policy product is framed with both domestic and foreign consumers in mind.

THE CHANGING FRAMEWORK OF AUSTRALIAN POLICY-MAKING

The domestic basis of any foreign policy-making process involves an interplay between the institutions with formal responsibility for policy-making and the contextual considerations which inform the actual operation of these institutions. While this chapter cannot outline in full the general framework within which Australian policy is made, it is necessary to have some understanding of this framework to appreciate the special features of the domestic Antarctic policy-making process. There are perhaps two key features of the general process which need to be canvassed here with regard to Antarctica. The first is that Australia's policy-making process has been in flux for some time. Thus changes in policy emphasis or direction may not be a result of the specific merits of a particular case but, rather, reflective of change in the fundamentals of the policy process itself. Second, Australia's approach to its regional environment has been undergoing change for nearly three decades. This general contextual influence on foreign policy has also had an influence on perceptions of the Antarctic.

The institutional framework for the making of Australian policy (including foreign policy) has been heavily influenced by changing interpretations of its hybrid political system – a blend of the British and the American which has been dubbed the 'Washminster mutation'.[4] Initially, the British (Westminster) strand was dominant, with the result that foreign policy was perceived to be an exclusive preserve of the executive branch of government. Ideally, this model presumed that the government of the day (the ministry) is a committee of the Parliament accountable to the people's representative assembly (primarily the House of Representatives) through such conventions as ministerial responsibility. Given the concentration of powers in the Parliament, it was assumed in theory that foreign policy would be as subject to popular will as any other aspect of policy-making. No special constitutional provisions were drafted to deal with such aspects of foreign policy-making as the appointment of ambassadors or the regulation of the treaty-making even though the founders of the Australian Constitution borrowed heavily from the US document in framing their own.

In practice, the Westminster model delivered Australian foreign policy-making into the hands of a bureaucratic elite protected from parliamentary oversight by party discipline – at least once Australia could develop its own professional service. The development of a specialist foreign service took some time, however. In the earliest years, the prime minister commonly acted as the foreign minister. Nevertheless, this aspect of government was often little regarded by the prime minister, largely because of the ambiguous relationship with the UK that persisted until well after the Statute of Westminster (1931) which allowed important foreign policy to be left to London. Until 1935 it was not uncommon for Australian governments to manage entirely without a separate department

---

[4] See D. Jaensch, *Getting Our Houses in Order: Australia's Parliament – How it Works and the Need for Reform* (Ringwood: Penguin, 1986), pp. 16–23; and H. Emy and O. Hughes, *Australian Politics: Realities in Conflict*, 2nd ed. (Melbourne: Macmillan, 1991).

for external relations.[5] A comprehensive department of foreign affairs (initially, the Department of External Affairs) headed by its own minister became the norm only from World War II, when Australia established its own missions in Ottawa, Tokyo and Washington, DC.[6] The elitist tendencies of this independent foreign policy process lasted barely a generation. In keeping with the pressures toward greater transparency and more public participation in foreign policy-making elsewhere during the second half of the twentieth century, Australian foreign policy has become more open in recent years. This general trend has been hastened by several specific events and processes which have worked against the earlier dominance of the Westminster strand in Australian politics.

Perhaps one of the more critical developments in promoting the separation of powers strand of the Australian Constitution was an electoral reform which reduced party dominance of the Senate. As a result, the Senate has developed an effective committee system with a capacity to oversee the executive's foreign policy and, through this mechanism, to influence executive action.[7] The confrontation between the government of the day and the vice-regal representative which resulted in the sacking of Prime Minister Gough Whitlam in November 1975 was another such event, but mainly because it dramatically drew attention to the separation of powers features of the Constitution which previously had been little appreciated. Similarly, the federal principle had scant relevance to foreign policy-making until the middle of the 1970s, when Prime Minister Malcolm Fraser included the states in the treaty-making process in a limited way.[8] Toward the end of the Fraser government, the High Court extended both the effects of treaties on Australia's domestic affairs and its own powers in the foreign policy arena through a decision which deter-

[5] Evans and Grant, *Australia's Foreign Relations*, p. 19; and D. J. McDougall *et al.*, *Australian Foreign Policy: Empire, Alliance and Region*, 2nd ed. (New York: Prentice Hall, 1987), pp. 25–6.

[6] *Ibid.*

[7] While the same cannot be said for House of Representative committees since these remain substantially under executive control via party discipline, joint committees do tend to exhibit the strength of the Senate system. For the effect of electoral reform on the policy role of the Senate, see G. S. Reid, 'The Trinitarian Struggle: Parliamentary–Executive Relationships', in H. Mayer and H. Nelson (eds.), *Australian Politics: A Third Reader* (Melbourne: Cheshire, 1973), pp. 523–4.

[8] R. A. Herr and B. W. Davis, 'The Impact of UNCLOS III on Australian Federalism', *International Journal*, vol. 41, Summer 1986, pp. 674–93.

mined that international treaties would prevail where they came into conflict with municipal (Commonwealth and State) law.[9]

Thus today the institutional framework of Australian foreign policy-making is much broader than at its origins, with the result that there are more points of access for domestic factors to influence policy outcomes. The Department of Foreign Affairs and Trade (DFAT) remains the central organ but its mandate has been diversified, as its name indicates, by the recent inclusion of a responsibility for international trade. Moreover, it has had to share its interests increasingly with other departments, including Prime Minister and Cabinet (PM&C), Defence, Attorney-General's, Treasury and the like. The increasing role of the PM&C has been a particularly significant development since it derives from a number of quite disparate influences. A major force has been the apparent transformation of the office of the Prime Minister into something more *primus* than *pares* (in terms of the conventional description of the Prime Minister as *primus inter pares*) so that its occupants expect to behave in a presidential manner.[10] Also important has been the Prime Minister's specific foreign policy role as in the direct and continuing responsibility of the Australian Prime Minister for South Pacific relations through the annual Heads of Government meetings of the South Pacific Forum. In addition, as noted above, other organs and levels of government which traditionally were not regarded as foreign policy actors have acquired noteworthy influence in recent years.

The context within which Australia's foreign policy has been formulated has played a significant, albeit somewhat changing, role in the shaping of domestic influence on external policy. Australia's size and location have constrained domestic perceptions of the foreign policy options available, in a number of important ways. The island continent is large – approximately the same size as the United States excluding Alaska and Hawaii. It is situated close to Southeast Asia, and its landmass helps to separate the Indian and South Pacific Oceans. These geographic givens, coupled with its relatively small population – about one-fifteenth that of the United States – and rich natural resources, have long made Australians anxious about the geopolitics of their foreign relations. In earlier decades this manifested itself in foreign policies intended to secure external pro-

---

[9] M. Crommelin, 'Federal–Provincial Cooperation on Natural Resources: A Comparative Discussion of Problems and Solutions, Intergovernmental Relations in Victoria Programme' (unpublished paper, Law School, University of Melbourne, 1985).

[10] M. Pusey, *Economic Relationalism in Canberra* (Melbourne: Cambridge University Press, 1991), pp. 59–64.

tection as a European island in an Asiatic sea (commonly expressed as 'the white Australia policy'); more latterly a consensus has emerged to make a virtue of geographic necessity by more fully engaging with Asia.[11] The emergence of Japan as Australia's major trading partner has forced a reassessment of the general relationship with Asia which today has made the whole of the Asia–Pacific area a region of high priority to Australia. The foreign policy effects of this change are being intensified by the more regionalist, more pragmatic, economic self-interest of the post-Cold War order.

Party ideology has at times proved a significant variable in the interpretation of Australia's role as an effective middle power in the region. The Australian Labor Party (ALP) from its origins was fearful of the threat of cheap imported labour that would undermine the strength of its industrial wing. It sought sufficient influence in its immediate neighbourhood to be able to minimise this threat. The ALP therefore has long advocated an activist regional foreign policy focused on the goal of regional security and autonomy. The anti-Labor parties (usually operating as a coalition whether in government or opposition) have tended to perceive Australia's responsibilities as a middle power more in terms of the global system. They have favoured a policy of acting as a loyal regional lieutenant to a protective global hegemon – described by Prime Minister Robert Menzies as 'great and powerful friends'.[12] Initially this was the United Kingdom, but more latterly has been the United States. It is a significant feature of the more pragmatic politics of the post-Cold War that today both sides of partisan politics in Australia have agreed that the country's appropriate posture internationally is that of a middle power with the concomitant regional focus that this stance requires.

ANTARCTICA AS A REGIONAL POLICY ARENA

Australia's long history of involvement in Antarctica and the Southern Ocean has given it a popular connection with the frozen continent second only to that of Chile and Argentina and on a par with fellow antipodean dominion New Zealand. This experience ranged from commercial whaling and sealing ventures in the early 1800s, through the 'heroic age' of

---

[11] T. B. Millar, 'Australia and the United States', in P. Dibb (ed.), *Australia's External Relations in the 1980s* (Canberra; Croom Helm, 1983), p. 155.

[12] Evans and Grant, *Australia's Foreign Relations*, p. 23.

Antarctic exploration prior to World War II, to foundation membership of the Antarctic Treaty System in 1959 and the more recent adumbrations of the ATS.[13] Ports in southern Australia such as Hobart served both as points of departure and as centres for resupply and recreation for the whaling and sealing fleets. Indeed, the ties were so close that Macquarie Island, a sub-Antarctic island, was permanently incorporated into the state of Tasmania largely for this connection. Public subscriptions helped to fund the 'heroic age' explorations which made Douglas Mawson a national hero, a knight, and more latterly a portrait on Australian currency. Mawson's explorations ultimately provided the basis for a territorial claim in the south (via British declarations) to two sectors now known as the Australian Antarctic Territory (AAT) that constitute approximately 42 per cent of the frozen continent.[14] More recently, the location of the headquarters of the Commission for the Conservation of Antarctic Marine Living Resources (CCAMLR) in Hobart was, at least in part, a symbolic reaffirmation of the importance of this city's historic ties with Antarctica for the country as a whole.[15]

The claim to sovereignty over a significant proportion of Antarctica due to the long period of direct involvement with the exploration and exploitation of Antarctica has been an important factor in Australian Antarctic policy. Two motivations impelled the desire for a territorial claim – security and economic gain.[16] The influence of this act lay primarily in confirming the regional significance of Antarctica to Australia. A Labor government, on regionalist grounds, openly resisted an attempt in the late 1940s to establish an Antarctic regime because it believed this would compromise Australia's claims to sovereignty. Later, a conservative coalition government, for ideological reasons, was uncertain of the emergent Antarctic Treaty because it feared this would give the Soviet Union access to the AAT.[17] The AAT has remained a formal preoccupation of all Aus-

---

[13] P. J. Beck, 'Australia's New Course in Antarctica', in W. Bateman and M. Ward (eds.), *Australia's Maritime Interests* (Canberra: Australian Centre for Maritime Studies, 1990), pp. 102–19; and R. A. Swan, *Australia in the Antarctic* (Melbourne University Press, 1961).

[14] G. D. Triggs, *International Law and Australian Sovereignty in Antarctica* (Sydney: Legal Books, 1986).

[15] CCAMLR is the only inter-governmental organisation headquartered in Australia.

[16] C. H. Grattan, *The Southwest Pacific Since 1900: A Modern History* (Ann Arbor, MI: University of Michigan, 1963), vol. II, pp. 614–17; and Swan, *Australia in the Antarctic*, p. 189.

[17] These observations are based on archival research reported in H. R. Hall, 'International Regime Formation and Leadership: The Origins of the Antarctic Treaty' (PhD, University of Tasmania, 1994).

tralian governments even after the freezing of the sovereignty issue by Article IV of the Antarctic Treaty. Intriguingly, bureaucratic responsibility for the AAT shifted from External Affairs a few years after the Antarctic Treaty came into force and has been lodged with a series of departments concerned with internal affairs since 1968. It is difficult to explain this shift at a time when the continent was being 'internationalised', except as an attempt to strengthen the symbolic claim to sovereignty over the AAT.[18] Indeed, the Australian government's stated objectives for being involved in Antarctica (which have changed remarkably little over time) routinely repeat the commitment to sovereignty. The most recent formulation, enunciated in the Australian Antarctic Division's current Corporate Plan, states Australia's principal aims as being:

> to enhance Australia's scientific environmental, political, strategic and economic interests (except mineral resource activity) in the Antarctic and, where relevant, the sub-Antarctic, and to preserve its sovereignty over the Australian Antarctic Territory.[19]

The degree to which Australia's historical experience has generated a regionalist perspective which serves as a basis for contemporary popular interest in the Antarctic is difficult to gauge. Anecdotal evidence suggests that there is a ready reservoir of interest which can be drawn upon by any policy actor – governmental or private – which wishes to engage public opinion on Antarctica. We believe it to be a significant, albeit often latent, factor in the domestic influence on Australia's Antarctic policy-making process. As demonstrated below, the perception among political elites that public awareness of Antarctica could convert either into a political resource or an electoral liability was telling in the CRAMRA debate.

MAKING AUSTRALIAN ANTARCTIC POLICY:
EXECUTIVE DOMINANCE

Due to its particularly close relationship with Antarctica, the general vicissitudes of foreign policy-making are only half the story for Australia as far as the Antarctic is concerned. Being a claimant state, the Commonwealth suffers a delicate schizophrenia in its approach to the specifics of

---

[18] The change could be justified on the grounds of a need to upgrade logistic support in the wake of increased demand in the post-IGY era, but logistics had not appeared to be a significant problem under External Affairs (interview with Phillip Law, 21 April 1994).

[19] Australia, Antarctic Division, *A Window on Antarctica* (Hobart: Antarctic Division, 1991), p. 22.

Antarctic policy, since the AAT makes Antarctic policy a domestic, as well as a foreign, policy issue. The making, funding and implementation of Australian Antarctic policy involves a considerable number of Commonwealth departments and ministerial portfolios; relevant professional interests from academic and scientific circles; national and international conservation organisations; and such sub-national instrumentalities as the Tasmanian Department of Environment and Land Management, which is responsible for administering the sub-Antarctic dependency of Macquarie Island. The range of interests is so disparate that reasonably not all these interests can have equal access to, or influence in, the Australian Antarctic policy process. There is a central or core policy process dominated by the key actors, and secondary process which deals with episodic or more marginal aspects of Antarctic issues.

The general features of the Westminster-based policy process in Australia ensure that all the key influences on core policy-making regarding Antarctica are located in the *executive* arm of government. Technically, the most influential single actor is the Prime Minister, followed closely by those ministers whose departments carry responsibility for core policy concerns and the Cabinet as the formal decision-making arena. And, in unusual circumstances such as the decision in May 1989 to refuse signature of the CRAMRA treaty, this nominal process is precisely what occurs in practice. However, Antarctic affairs rarely command the full attention of the executive arm of government. Routine policy is settled more conventionally at the ministerial and departmental levels.

In keeping with the Janus-like orientation of Australia's Antarctic interests, a domestic and an international policy department share the primary responsibility for formulating and articulating national priorities – the Australian Antarctic Division, which forms part of the Department of the Environment, Sport and Territories (DEST), and the Department of Foreign Affairs and Trade (DFAT). A third organ recognises the strong interests of the scientific community in contemporary Antarctic policy. The Antarctic Science Advisory Committee (ASAC), composed of senior policy-makers and researchers, provides direct and independent advice to the Minister for the Environment on scientific research needs and priorities. In terms of both routine and extraordinary decisions on Antarctic policy, these three bodies could be expected to have an early and significant voice, although it is not necessarily the case that each voice will carry equal weight on every issue.

The *Antarctic Division* is a rather complex and formally ambiguous policy organ to assess. The Division has always been the repository of

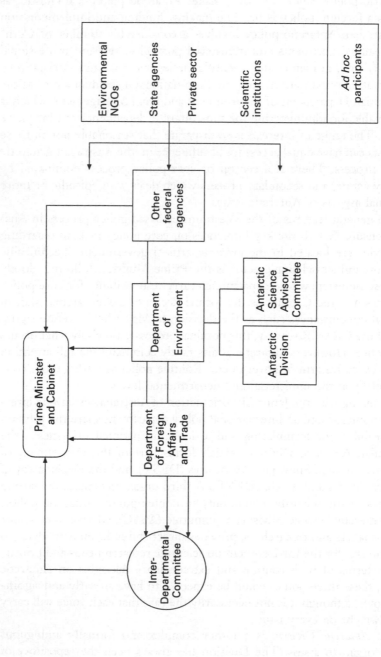

Figure 13.1 The Antarctic decision-making process in the Australian executive branch

substantive expertise on Antarctica due to such factors as its mandated responsibilities; its extensive operations on the frozen continent and the accumulation of staff with professional, logistical and scientific knowledge of Antarctica. Nevertheless, the Division has always only been just that – a division of a larger unit. This circumstance does not necessarily present a problem in itself but, from its inception in 1948, there have been confusing organisational signals as to its primary mission. As noted above, the Division has from time to time been transferred between the ministerial portfolios of External Affairs, through Supply and then Science, to its current lodgement with DEST – the last reflecting the increasing significance of the environment in Australia's approach to Antarctica as the Division was attached to the 'Environment' part of DEST.[20] Naturally each transfer somewhat altered the Division's mission to conform to the host department's ethos but, equally, each move also tended to carry some of the historical baggage of the previous activities. Thus, although focused essentially on the domestic aspects of Australia's Antarctic policy, its varied administrative past has given the Antarctic Division a much broader range of policy interests than might have been the case otherwise. Indeed, it would be difficult to find an area of Antarctic policy in which the Division does not have an interest. Division staff are routinely included in delegations to international meetings (ATS and other) as well as in domestic arenas dealing with the environment, science, logistics, general policy and the like.

The Division's extensive policy interests are reflected in an equally extensive range of responsibilities (although which is the cause and which is the effect is a 'chicken-and-egg' argument). The Antarctic Division not only provides the logistics support for Australian National Antarctic Research Expeditions (ANARE); it also bears primary responsibility, as the executive arm of ANARE, for the policies which maintain logistics and science support.[21] Predictably this requires presenting the case in the annual budgetary process for financial resources but it also involves, *inter alia*, setting the policy agenda for new equipment, infrastructure support, station and base maintenance, and alternative transport assessments. Similarly, the Division maintains a large internal scientific establishment and,

---

[20] B. W. Davis, 'Australia and Antarctica: Aspects of Policy Process', in S. Harris (ed.), *Australia's Antarctic Policy Options* (Canberra: Centre for Resource and Environmental Studies, Australian National University, 1984), pp. 339–53; and D. Lyons, 'Organisation and Funding of the Australian Antarctic Program', *Polar Record*, vol. 29, no. 170, 1993, p. 225.

[21] P. Law, *Antarctic Odyssey* (Melbourne: Heinemann, 1983), p. 196.

therefore, not only has a bureaucratic interest in science policy: it also carries a major portion of the obligations of raising the finances for achieving the objectives of Australia's Antarctic science policy. The Division also serves as the linchpin for implementing science policy. This it does in close connection with ASAC; a process which will be addressed in more detail below. Further, the Division's policy influence frequently extends into the international arena. Either as the responsible line agency or through its personnel by virtue of their expertise, the Antarctic Division often plays a prominent role in such international policy-making processes as those of the Antarctic Treaty Consultative Meetings (ATCMs), CCAMLR, the Council of Managers of National Antarctic Programs (COMNAP) and SCAR.

Extensive responsibilities, nonetheless, are no guarantee of a concomitant level of political influence. Generally, the bureaucratic and political status of the Antarctic Division has been a constraining factor on its capacity to meet its multifarious responsibilities. Because it has normally been either a relatively large part of a modest department or a relatively small part of a large department, the Division has had to compete for the attention of its minister with other sectors of its host department. The decision to locate the Antarctic Division in Hobart in the early 1980s has also proved a limiting factor on the Division's policy influence as its policy branch is removed from the routine of bureaucratic politics in Canberra. Partially offsetting these constraints, in recent years when two ministers have been assigned to its department, the Division normally has fallen under the responsibility of the senior portfolio minister.[22] In consequence, the Antarctic Division has routinely faced difficulties in securing what it deems appropriate funding levels although the high public salience of Antarctica from the middle of the 1980s did improve this situation for a few years. The Antarctic Division's bureaucratic circumstances have scarcely been accidental. The fact that Antarctica is regarded as an area of special interest to Australia has ensured that there is a specific agency designated for Antarctica, but its political importance has limited this commitment to the division level.

By comparison, the role of the *Department of Foreign Affairs and Trade*

[22] It should be noted that the arrangement for the sharing of ministerial responsibility within this multifaceted portfolio has the Antarctic Division under the senior minister since 'Environment' is normally held by this minister. The 'Territories' side of DEST, which might be a logical alternative in view of the claim to the AAT, is not regarded as appropriate since it is largely responsible for administering the people in dependent territories.

is relatively unambiguous: it has primary carriage of all diplomatic initiatives and foreign negotiations and DFAT heads all delegations at Antarctic Treaty meetings. Although DFAT has two ministers, there does not appear to be any equivocation with regard to responsibilities at this level. The second minister has a specific responsibility for 'Development Cooperation and Pacific Islands Affairs' and so does not figure directly in the Antarctic process. If there is an organisational problem for this department, it is that Antarctica generally has lower priority than that accorded dealings with North America, European nations and near neighbours of the Asia–Pacific region; thus, Antarctic policy must compete with more salient issue areas for the attention of senior policy-makers within DFAT. Moreover, at least in recent years, there has tended to be a fairly rapid turnover of staff within the Antarctic section of DFAT, which can create difficulties with continuity of experience.

DFAT has long maintained two strands of internal interest in Antarctic affairs. In addition to its Antarctic policy section, the legal office has had a significant involvement due to its responsibilities for international agreements and other legal affairs. It has been argued that, in recent years, an expansion of the legal office in keeping with Australia's more active role in promoting global environmental cooperation may have helped to offset the personnel difficulties of the Antarctic policy section over this period. Although normally the paramount bureaucratic actor in the foreign policy arena, DFAT does not always carry the day if PM&C or a combination of other departments intervene in an issue such as CRAMRA. Similarly, the general expertise of DFAT may well allow personalities in the department to extend their influence beyond the departmental arena.

Perhaps one of the key avenues by which DFAT influences the development of national policy is through its chairing of the *inter-departmental committee* (IDC) which serves as the arena for coordinating Antarctic policy across the executive arm of government. Foreign Affairs enjoys this role, for a variety of reasons which include DFAT's seniority in the bureaucratic hierarchy, its historical primacy in Antarctic policy and its responsibility as the recognised custodian of the national interest internationally. Like all policy IDCs, the Antarctic policy IDC is open to all interested agencies, although in practice few beyond the two departments with core policy responsibilities – DEST and DFAT – attend with regularity – Attorney-General's, Defence and Treasury normally. Other departments attend on an *ad hoc* basis, depending very much on their interest in a particular issue. The IDC is important because it keeps those within the executive arm with Antarctic interests in routine and regular contact with each other. It also provides the most important intersection between the core and secondary policy levels.[23] Anecdotal evidence suggests that chairing the Antarctic IDC gives DFAT some pre-eminence in this policy arena primarily through control of the meeting's agenda, although it is also noted that these meetings are relatively relaxed and tend to be focused on common interests.

The third principal organ of Australia's Antarctic policy process, the *Antarctic Science Advisory Committee* (ASAC), also falls within the executive arm of government due its function (to advise the minister) and its composition (appointment by the minister). Nevertheless, the ASAC membership is not drawn primarily from the bureaucracy, nor is its ethos necessarily that of subordination to the executive. Insofar as science is the basic currency of Antarctic politics,[24] the role and activities of ASAC could be interpreted as serving primarily to ensure that Australian policy is as effective as possible in the ATS. Yet ASAC's policy impact appears greater at the domestic level (albeit not directly on the administration of the AAT). The linkages between ASAC and the other two core agencies are much stronger with the Antarctic Division than with DFAT. The ASAC Grants Scheme, which provides the main dedicated Antarctic research assistance, is funded through the Antarctic Division's budget appropriation.[25] ASAC administers its grant system via the Antarctic Research Evaluation Group (AREG). Technically, AREG is a committee composed of the ASAC chair, some senior Division personnel and the chairs of each of the AREG specialist sub-committees which bear the primary responsibility for vetting research proposals submitted to ASAC. The AREG secretariat is located in, and staffed by, the Antarctic Division.

The close connection between ASAC and the Antarctic Division reveals the critical role of ASAC in the Australian Antarctic policy process. It is this management function in Antarctic science policy which has made

---

[23] For a fuller description of the secondary policy level and its interaction with the core actors, see Lyons, 'Organisation and Funding'.

[24] R. A. Herr and H. R. Hall, 'Science as Currency and the Currency of Science', in J. Handmer (ed.), *Antarctica: Policies and Policy Development* (Canberra: Centre for Resource and Environmental Studies, Australian National University, 1989).

[25] The recent establishment of the Antarctic Cooperative Research Centre somewhat qualifies this observation since its resources are substantial. However, the research available through the Antarctic CRC is not generally available through open, competitive grants. The Antarctic CRC is a consortium of research institutions the secretariat for which is provided by the Institute for Antarctic and Southern Ocean Studies at the University of Tasmania.

ASAC rather more domestic than international in its focus and in its policy impact. Both by its bureaucratic phylogeny and its current functioning, ASAC carries the onus not only for offering expert scientific advice to the responsible minister but also for serving as the premier lobby group for Antarctic science in Australia. And, perhaps predictably, this circumstance has over the years led to considerable political misgivings within the executive arm of Australian government as to the need for an independent source of advice on Antarctic science policy. The chequered history of ASAC's precursors demonstrates the uneasy place of such advice in Antarctic policy-making.

An ANARE Planning Committee was established in 1947 and operated until 1962 (although it met once in 1965 and twice in early 1966, but there mainly to conclude its work). Phillip Law, Director of the Antarctic Division throughout this period, argued that the Planning Committee was useful for policy orientation and short-term programming purposes but the hostility of its ministers and Antarctic policy bureaucrats left it to 'wither on the vine'.[26] The Advisory Committee on Antarctic Programmes (ACAP) followed in 1973, but as an *ad hoc* committee to offer advice on specific albeit wide-ranging sets of issues. Its green paper proposed several initiatives including programmes to rebuild the Antarctic stations and pursue marine science as well as planning for an Australian Antarctic ship.[27] An Antarctic Research Policy Advisory Committee (ARPAC) was established in May 1979, again to advise on the development of an effective and balanced programme of scientific and exploration activity in the Antarctic and sub-Antarctic. A series of reports made recommendations on science priorities as expected but, less helpfully from the bureaucracy's perspective, ARPAC also offered criticism of existing activities, funding, priorities and programmes.[28] Arguably, ARPAC simply became too vigorous an advocate for the domestic science community, regardless of its utility in other areas. The Antarctic Science Advisory Committee (ASAC) succeeded ARPAC in 1985. Its terms of reference

---

[26] Law, *Antarctic Odyssey*, pp. 196–7. In a telephone interview (21 April 1994) with Phillip Law to clarify the reasons for this lack of support, Law noted that the Planning Committee included such figures as Sir Douglas Mawson and John King Davis, whose opinions carried more political weight than the senior bureaucrats responsible for implementing the Committee's decisions. Thus, the bureaucracy gained influence by not referring issues to the Planning Committee.

[27] Advisory Committee on Antarctic Programmes, *Towards New Perspectives in Australian Scientific Research in Antarctica* (Canberra: Australian Government Printer, 1975).

[28] Lyons, 'Organisation and Funding'.

were to advise the Australian government through the relevant minister on:

1   the broad thrust of Australia's Antarctic programme, including scientific, exploration and support activities (including transport);
2   priority areas for scientific and technological research, having regard to Antarctica's resource potential and the need for sound environmental management; and
3   measures to ensure an effective Australian participation in international programmes involving the Antarctic.

The terms of reference were specially drawn to exclude matters directly related to the management of Antarctic Division, but they do permit ASAC to comment on aspects of transport and logistics that might affect research programmes.[29]

MAKING AUSTRALIAN ANTARCTIC POLICY:
THE LEGISLATIVE ROLE

The Parliament of Australia does not match the United States Congress as a counterpart actor in Antarctic policy-making either substantively or procedurally despite its relatively greater constitutional pre-eminence. Parliament does not have as central a role in foreign policy, nor is it as independent an actor in the finance appropriation process, as the US Congress. Nevertheless, the evolution of the Australian political system, with the traditional financial oversight role of the Parliament and the delicate schizophrenia noted previously regarding the internal–external character of Antarctic policy, have all served as factors in the increased legislative involvement, however modest, in Antarctic policy over recent years. The high public prominence of Antarctica during the 1980s undoubtedly encouraged the Parliament to use the traditional policy weapons in its limited armoury such as financial appropriation and accountability to carve out a limited, albeit perhaps temporary, policy niche for itself.

Whether these gains will be consolidated to ensure a routine involvement by the Parliament depends on two unresolved questions. Much of the Parliament's interest has derived from the high political salience of Antarctica in the public arena, not from an ongoing institutional responsibility. If public interest fades then it is likely that the parliamentary enthusiasm for matters Antarctic will wane as well. Second, the initiative

[29] *Ibid.*

for policy is jealously guarded by the executive arm of government in Westminster systems. The apparent sea change in institutional relations between the executive and the Parliament is real, but the scope for Parliament to challenge executive policy priorities remains essentially limited to reaction. This has been particularly evident from the decade of the 1980s, when the emergence of an independent committee system in the previous decade began to discover Antarctic policy as an area of interest. Parliament can scrutinise and criticise past or existing policies and practices, but it cannot propose future policies.

There have been four major parliamentary inquiries over the past decade. Significantly, the first was a Senate Standing Committee on National Resources which began a review of 'The Natural Resources of the Antarctic Territory' in 1985. Two inquiries have been pursued by joint committees of both houses – one was a specific investigation by the Joint Committee of Public Accounts (1989) into the 'Management of the Antarctic Division'; the other is a more or less continuous monitoring by the Joint Committee of Public Works of the ANARE stations rebuilding programme. In addition, there have been two inquiries by committees of the lower house – one by the House of Representatives' Standing Committee on Environment, Recreation and the Arts (1989) into 'Tourism in Antarctica' and the second by the House of Representatives' Standing Committee on Legal and Constitutional Affairs into the 'Legal Regimes of Australia's External Territories'.[30]

The generalisation that issues which pose more risks for the executive arm of government tend to be treated by parliamentary committees less controlled by the governing party is borne out for the most part by this experience. The Public Accounts Committee's review of the 'Management of the Antarctic Division' was a particularly serious episode in parliamentary oversight. An inquiry into the propriety of government expenditure by a committee not controlled by the government of the day exposes the teeth of a parliamentary process usually muzzled by party discipline. Despite the seriousness of the allegations that provoked the committee's interest, its hearings produced no evidence of impropriety. The upshot was not a recommendation for new policy, but the Public Accounts Committee's review did serve as a warning to the government's primary organ for implementing Antarctic policy that parliamentary accountability was a sanction not to be taken lightly.

The House Committee's inquiries into Antarctic tourism and the

---

[30] *Ibid.*

AAT's legal regimes, on the other hand, illustrate the significance of the AAT in Australian policy on Antarctica. Being controlled by the governing party, neither committee was likely to embarrass the government with unacceptable recommendations or findings. Nevertheless, the issues addressed were not immaterial to the government. In both these cases the parliamentary committee system enabled the government to open a politically agreeable opportunity for public participation in Antarctic policy-making. It is significant also that, in both cases, the committees were primarily concerned with the administration of the AAT rather than the regulation of Antarctica through the ATS. Indeed, given their formal mandates it would have been impossible for either committee to have opened their inquiries without the domestic issue at the core of their terms of reference. Nonetheless, both their *modus operandi* and their findings reinforced the domestic (i.e. territorial) aspects of Australia's Antarctic policy. The report of the Standing Committee on Environment, Recreation and the Arts was tabled in May 1989, the same month that the government announced its decision not to sign or ratify CRAMRA, and offered very specific recommendations on how tourism in the AAT should be regulated.[31] With even more force, the Committee on Legal and Constitutional Affairs made recommendations on how to apply more effectively Australian law to the AAT given a number of factors – only one of which was the Antarctic Treaty – which posed problems for the current administration of Australian municipal law in this territory.[32]

MAKING AUSTRALIAN ANTARCTIC POLICY: THE NGO ROLE

Non-governmental organisations have long provided a noteworthy avenue for domestic influence on Australia's Antarctic policy. This path

[31] Australia, House of Representatives, Standing Committee on Environment, Recreation and the Arts, *Tourism in Antarctica* (Canberra: Australian Government Publishing Service, May 1989). Although the timing of the Committee's report may now appear ironic, both were very much a product of their era. Anecdotal evidence suggests that the Committee was moved to address the issue of tourism in the AAT precisely because there were signs that Australian industry was planning to pursue development of tourism in the AAT and some senior Committee members were concerned that this would conflict with environmental values there. See R. A. Herr, 'Antarctic Tourism: Australia, Regulation and the Industry', in J. Handmer and M. Wilder (eds.), *Towards a Conservation Strategy for the Australian Antarctic Territory* (Canberra: Centre for Resource and Environmental Studies, Australian National University, 1993).
[32] Australia, House of Representatives, Standing Committee on Legal and Constitutional Affairs, *Australian Law in Antarctica* (Canberra: Australian Government Publishing Service, November 1991).

was not as broad initially as it is today and its growth has tended to diversify the domestic sources of national policy. The earliest NGO activity in the ATS period was almost exclusively confined to what might be described as the 'official' or 'professional' network established through the Scientific Committee on Antarctic Research (SCAR). The Australian National Committee for Antarctic Research (ANCAR), the national body corresponding to SCAR, served as a domestic influence on Antarctic policy on two levels. Through its involvement with SCAR, ANCAR directly helped to inscribe Australian science priorities onto the international agenda. More importantly, perhaps, ANCAR has operated at the national level to both aggregate and articulate the attentive scientific community's Antarctic priorities. Until the second wave of politicisation of the ATS in the late 1970s and early 1980s,[33] ANCAR enjoyed considerable, if informal, influence on domestic policy through its role in the formulation of Australian science priorities for Antarctica. The more political agenda of the 1980s suited ANCAR at the domestic level no more than it did SCAR internationally. Significantly, the re-emergence of a more science-led agenda in the wake of the Protocol on Environmental Protection to the Antarctic Treaty has revived the fortunes of ANCAR. The recent review of ASAC significantly extended ANCAR involvement with the Antarctic Division and in the ASAC decision-making processes particularly by including an ANCAR nominee on each of the AREG sub-committees.[34]

Returned expeditioner associations provided the second and much more informal source of domestic NGO advice on Antarctic policy. These associations primarily serve the social function of enabling expeditioners (retired and active) to keep in touch. However, the major body, the ANARE Club, publishes a newsletter, *Aurora*, which offers comment on general policy and specifics such as the operation of the Antarctic Division. Moreover, its membership tends to ensure that knowledge of current policy and implementation is relatively widespread among this attentive public which enables it to act with some authority as a 'ginger group' when public policy on Antarctica becomes contentious. With the

---

[33] The first wave of politicisation centred on the creation and early procedural development of the Antarctic Treaty, while the second is associated with the expansion of membership and the challenge of the UN which became public by the early 1980s.

[34] Australia, Department of the Arts, Sport, the Environment and Territories, ASAC, *Antarctic Science – The Way Forward* (Canberra: Australian Government Publishing Service, 1992). It should be noted that, if these recent trends do consolidate in favour of ANCAR, the primary points of access to domestic policy will be through the science policy avenues of the Antarctic Division and ASAC.

significant expansion of VIP and parliamentary fact-finding visits to the AAT in the 1980s, many of the individual ANARE Club branches around Australia now include MPs. It has been suggested the ANARE Club's annual Mid-Winter Feast in Canberra is a political asset for the Antarctic community. Regrettably no sustained research appears to have been pursued to date into policy effects of this NGO to enable an assessment of its influence.

In Australia as elsewhere, the network of NGOs concerned with Antarctic policy over the past fifteen years has been heavily weighted in the direction of those active in environmental protection.[35] Broadly, this orientation has not been a problem for Australia. Indeed, Australia was one of the first countries to include representatives of environmental NGOs in its delegations to ATCMs.[36] In part, the receptivity to environmental NGOs reflected the increasing openness of Australian policy-making discussed above. In part it was a prudential accommodation of a growing political force in the country. The Australian conservation movement grew rapidly in the 1960s and 1970s and, by the early 1980s, constituted a significant political force by virtue of its internal cohesion, its level of expertise and sympathetic public support.[37] Thus over more recent years the influence of NGOs, as one of the domestic sources of Australia's Antarctic policy, has been overwhelmingly dominated by the agenda and activities of the organised conservation movement in Australia.

The first substantial Australian environmental NGO to display an active interest in Antarctica was the Australian Conservation Foundation (ACF). From the early 1980s onwards, while Geoff Mosley was its Director, the ACF took a leading role in promoting the concept of Antarctica as a World Wilderness Park and attempting to educate the community about Antarctic issues.[38] In this, ACF was aided by well-produced television documentaries which promoted conservation values and depicted the frozen continent and its biota as one of the last great wilderness areas of

[35] This observation is developed more fully in Chapter 4 in this volume, on the roles of NGOs in Antarctic affairs.

[36] The Antarctic and Southern Ocean Coalition was included in the Australian delegation from 1983. See A. Bergin, 'The Politics of Antarctic Minerals: The Greening of White Australia', *Australian Journal of Political Science*, vol. 26, no. 2, 1991, p. 223.

[37] G. Holloway, 'The Wilderness Society: Transformation of a Social Movement Organization', Occasional Paper (Hobart: Department of Sociology, University of Tasmania, 1986), no. 4; and K. Walker (ed.), *Australian Environmental Policy* (Sydney: New South Wales University Press, 1992).

[38] J. G. Mosley, 'World Park for Antarctica: A Vision Within Our Reach', *Habitat*, vol. 17, October 1989, pp. 4–7.

the world. As a national umbrella organisation, ACF was able to mobilise a wide range of other environmental groups to spread its message into schools and communities at regional and national levels. There were also two direct means of lobbying legislators, the Cabinet and bureaucracy: ACF had a national liaison officer located in Canberra and with other peak conservation organisations such as the Worldwide Fund for Nature (formerly the World Wildlife Fund) enjoyed regular access to the Minister for the Environment and occasionally even the Prime Minister. The radical reputation of Greenpeace (due to its policy of direct action on such issues as whale and seal conservation and nuclear testing) adversely affected its relationship with Australian policy-makers for a time.[39] As with other groups, however, the individual expertise of some Greenpeace activists became an important factor in the increased acceptance of this NGO in Australian domestic politics and thus in the policy process.[40] The Antarctic and Southern Ocean Coalition (ASOC) has probably been the most influential of the NGO groups on Australian policy-making, for a variety of reasons. As a peak organisation with a specific focus on Antarctica, access to ASOC made it easy for officials to meet the political need for NGO consultation fairly 'cheaply'. It is an internationally recognised and accepted NGO (ASOC achieved observer status within CCAMLR as early as 1988) and the individual expertise of ASOC activists has been regarded generally as reliable and useful by official policy-makers.[41]

Although environmental NGOs have not been averse to using domestic policy mechanisms to achieve influence on Antarctic policy, essentially their interests have lain in the whole of Antarctica, and not merely in changing policy with regard to the AAT. Thus domestic policy arenas and agendas have tended to be perceived in instrumental terms – useful in gaining access to, and influence over, global Antarctic policy. Conservation NGOs have often advocated unilateralist acts by the Australian government – such as declaring the AAT an international park[42] – to put pressure on the ATS rather than as good national policy for Australia.[43]

---

[39] M. Brown and J. May, *The Greenpeace Story* (Morebank: Bantam Books, 1991).
[40] F. Pearce, *Green Warriors* (London: Bodley Head, 1991).
[41] As ASOC is an umbrella body, however, it should be noted that a number of these NGO activists may not distinguish significantly between their parent associations, e.g. Greenpeace, and ASOC.
[42] Mosley, 'World Park for Antarctica'.
[43] This is not to say that these NGOs believed that their proposals would be bad national policy. Rather, we are simply noting that the objective of the advice was to achieve systemic change in the ATS and the effect on the AAT was of lesser importance. Since the

Such proposals have not served to enhance the influence of these NGOs on 'mainstream' Antarctic policy within Australia – but then, neither was this their intention. The strength of the conservation NGOs' influence on the domestic policy-making process has rested on two pillars. One has been their capacity to mobilise politically significant public support on Antarctic issues. The second (which they share with other NGOs) centres on the expertise of key individual actors on topics of relevance to the Antarctic debate within policy-making circles. Both these resources could prove ephemeral in the longer term – public interest does change over time, and the Antarctic expertise of the Australian environmental NGOs has tended to be located in individuals rather than organisational structures.

THE POLICY PROCESS IN OPERATION: FROM CRAMRA TO THE MADRID PROTOCOL

Domestic influences on the Australian Antarctic policy-making process are uniquely illustrated by the decision to reject CRAMRA in favour of a comprehensive protocol to protect the Antarctic environment. Although atypical of routine policy-making, the progress of this issue drew all the domestic contributors to Antarctic policy into the arena and subjected them to the crucible of fundamental change. The CRAMRA–Protocol issue thus represents not the mainstream of Antarctic policy but policy at the extremes. Generally, traditional sources of policy have emerged with their influence intact but with some change in priorities, while new actors have exhibited a capacity to exert significant pressure at critical points. The appearance of novel actors in the domestic arena of Antarctic policy raises the methodological question of whether these will prove to have been merely contextual influences, concerned with specific issues, or whether they will become embedded in the core decision-making process.

Undeniably, the initiative for policy change on CRAMRA belonged to the environmental groups which opposed the agreement virtually from the outset. The NGOs, including some in Australia, were in the vanguard of this reaction, and their activities helped to set the Antarctic agenda both internationally and domestically.[44] The 1981 and 1982 meetings of the International Union for the Conservation of Nature (IUCN, now

---

systemic change was deemed to be desirable, it was presumed the local effect would be beneficial also in the longer run.

[44] J. N. Barnes, *Let's Save Antarctica* (Melbourne: Greenhouse Publications, 1982).

known as the World Conservation Union) passed resolutions on the need
to protect Antarctica which in turn gave further impetus to national lobbying within Australia. By 1983–4 a number of position papers had been
published and extensive lobbying of politicians was occurring, aided in
part by the ready access that key conservation organisations possessed to
the Minister for the Environment in Australia.[45] Nevertheless, changing
the Antarctic agenda proved a lengthy process fraught with many opportunities for failure. At some levels the environmental movement enjoyed
success. For example, ASOC managed to secure its inclusion on the
national delegations to ATCMs at this time. Yet, political acceptance in
this arena did little for the conservation NGOs in the frustrating process
toward the drafting and signing of the CRAMRA agreement. At the time,
the Department of Foreign Affairs and other core policy actors appeared
completely insulated from domestic lobbying pressure on this issue.

   The completion of the CRAMRA negotiating process in Wellington
in June 1988, however, had a significant effect on the issue. Immediately
the agreement was opened for signature, it no longer remained in the
hands of the managers of Australian foreign policy. Every element of the
executive arm of government which had a stake in the issue had a new
opportunity to assess the implications and value of this international
agreement. Although the signing of a treaty does not formally require the
involvement of the Parliament or any departments beyond those the
Prime Minister chooses to consult, in practice the realities of a collective
executive make it difficult to deny the interests of departments which
claim an interest. The process of signing, ratifying and implementing a
new treaty thus offered a new arena to dissident opinion. Awareness of
this new opportunity did not escape environmental groups such as the
Australian Conservation Foundation, Greenpeace and the Worldwide
Fund for Nature, which redoubled their efforts during 1988. It would be
inaccurate to say that Cabinet views were divided on the merits of
CRAMRA as a consequence of this 'last ditch' lobbying. There were
reasons other than the environment which motivated disquiet on
CRAMRA within the government and its bureaucratic advisers. The then
Treasurer, Paul Keating, expressed concern that Australia would have to
forego royalties to which it might be entitled and that CRAMRA would
undermine Australian territorial claims to the AAT, while the Resources

[45] B. W. Davis, 'Environmental Management', in B. Galligan, O. Hughes and C. Walsh
    (eds.), *Intergovernmental Relations and Public Policy* (Sydney: Allen and Unwin, 1991),
    pp. 146–62.

Minister, Peter Cook, believed CRAMRA could permit subsidised mining, to the detriment of Australian industry.[46] Nonetheless, whatever their origins, the divisions within the Cabinet did present exploitable avenues of access to the core decision-making process to interested NGOs and public alike.

Other contextual circumstances combined with the structural requirement of formally signing the CRAMRA Treaty to open further Australia's Antarctic policy process. One key factor was external. The Socialist government of Francois Mitterrand announced in April 1989 that it might not sign the CRAMRA Treaty because, on reflection, elements of it were found objectionable. This opened the door to a domestic argument that if Australia also objected it would not be acting alone. Other domestic factors began to emerge to undermine the government's resolve. On one side of the political spectrum, the Federal Opposition rejected CRAMRA, claiming that it would promote mining; on the other side, the Australian Democrats, who held the balance of power in the Senate, also opposed CRAMRA on environmental grounds.[47] Despite the arguments of proponents that CRAMRA was not a mining document,[48] the dismaying images in early 1989 of polar pollution resulting from the *Bahia Paraiso* and *Exxon Valdez* were widely circulated in media treatment of the CRAMRA debate and widely accepted as relevant projections of the Antarctic in a CRAMRA future. The Labor Party's 'numbers' people had a direct taste of the possible electoral strength of the environmentalist movement at a critical moment. A Tasmanian election in May 1989 gave five seats and the balance of power to a newly formed group of Green Independents. Labor was then able to form a government to oust the previous ruling Liberal Party. In the end, it was Prime Minister Bob Hawke who took the lead in Cabinet to defeat signature of CRAMRA. Essentially adopting a slightly modified version of the environmentalist NGOs' arguments, Hawke persuaded his colleagues that CRAMRA was incompatible with the comprehensive environmental protection of Ant-

---

[46] For a further discussion on the influence of sovereignty on Australia as an issue at this time see P. J. Beck, 'The Antarctic Resource Conventions Implemented', in A. Jørgensen-Dahl and W. Østreng (eds.), *The Antarctic Treaty System in World Politics* (London: Macmillan, 1991), pp. 252–5; and Bergin, 'The Politics of Antarctic Minerals', p. 225.

[47] Bergin, 'The Politics of Antarctic Minerals', pp. 226–7.

[48] J. A. Heap, 'Antarctic Sovereignty: A Source of Stress', in R. A. Herr, H. R. Hall and M. G. Haward, *Antarctica's Future: Continuity or Change?* (Hobart: Tasmanian Government Printer, 1990), p. 189; and R. T. Scully, 'The Antarctic Treaty as a System', in Herr *et al.*, *Antarctica's Future*, pp. 100–1.

arctica. Australia would not sign or ratify the CRAMRA Treaty, and it would pursue steps to ban all mineral exploration activities.[49]

Despite some international annoyance at the government's decision to refuse signature of CRAMRA, domestically, support for the minerals agreement disappeared virtually overnight. This development was scarcely surprising in the context of the CRAMRA signature and ratification process. There was virtually no public constituency of support for CRAMRA.[50] The mining industry itself had failed to mobilise actively and positively in favour of CRAMRA, although internally it was prepared to suggest somewhat belatedly that the measure ought to be supported.[51] Thus, whether politically motivated or not, Prime Minister Hawke had acted in the direction of the overwhelming flow of opinion of Australia's attentive public on Antarctic affairs. The domestic opposition to CRAMRA was visible, vocal and organised. The real support for CRAMRA within the Australian Antarctic policy process came from the core decision-making bureaucracy. Had CRAMRA remained a routine matter as it appeared to be through the Wellington signature ceremony, the strength of this support would undoubtedly have carried the day. CRAMRA did not, however, remain a routine policy issue because the NGOs and those in the penumbra around the core policy-making process were able to mobilise latent Australian public interest in Antarctica as a neighbouring region.

The *denouement* of CRAMRA policy debate within Australia may have been less in the subsequent negotiation of the Protocol on Environmental Protection than in the government's efforts to demonstrate to the public that CRAMRA was indeed dead. The negotiation of the Protocol did not rest entirely in the hands of the bureaucracies of DFAT and the Antarctic Division because their political masters took substantially more interest in this agreement than they had in the drafting of CRAMRA. Nevertheless, it would be fair to characterise this attention as more in the nature

---

[49] Australia, Department of Foreign Affairs and Trade and Department of Arts, Sport the Environment, Tourism and Territories, 'Protection of the Antarctic Environment', A Joint Statement, Canberra, 22 May 1989.

[50] There is a genuine problem of measurement on this issue. Some scientific and other support for CRAMRA was forthcoming but generally this was 'off the record' and therefore its extent is difficult to quantify. For one of the more prominent exceptions, see P. Law, 'The Antarctic Wilderness – A Wild Idea!', in Herr *et al.* (eds.), *Antarctica's Future*, pp. 71–80.

[51] See article by the Australian Mining Industry Council's Assistant Director, R. Knapp, 'The Antarctic Convention – Should We Sign?', *The Mining Review*, November 1989, pp. 11–12.

of a watching brief than in day-to-day involvement. Perhaps the one critical issue in the drafting of the Protocol was the means of conferring comprehensive environmental protection to Antarctica. On this, both the political and bureaucratic elements of the core decision-making process rediscovered their pre-CRAMRA consensus and so successfully opposed the NGOs' preferred solution – the world park concept. Once an internal agreement was reached on the world park proposal (an issue which did not distract Australia's Antarctic policy process long), the usual patterns of domestic decision-making reasserted themselves.

Rather than a change in international outcomes or practices as a result of the domestic crucible that tested CRAMRA and found it wanting, the *denouement* of CRAMRA in the Australian policy process was the rediscovery of the latent public interest in Antarctica. Foreign Minister Gareth Evans announced in August 1990 that Australia would use its sovereign powers to ban mining in the AAT by anyone and by Australians anywhere in Antarctica.[52] Naturally this gesture served to reinforce the government's position on CRAMRA, but it also played to the domestic public gallery to reassure doubters that the government was serious and was taking *all* steps to protect the Antarctic environment. Significantly, after the Protocol was drafted and signed, the government was careful not to risk popular support for the Protocol. Interested NGOs and individuals outside the core decision-makers were included in the preparation of a conservation strategy for the AAT.[53]

AUSTRALIA AND OTHER ATS ISSUES

The CRAMRA issue exposed and tested the essential duality of the Australian policy interests in Antarctica more than any other since the process leading to the Antarctic Treaty itself. Much more typically, Canberra has been inclined to view both Australia's interests as a claimant and its regional foreign policy interests as mutually reinforcing. Indeed, Australia has placed a premium on being a good corporate citizen within the ATS

---

[52] 'Green Australia Keeps the Antarctic Clean', *Australian Foreign Affairs and Trade: The Monthly Record*, vol. 61, August 1990, pp. 570–1.

[53] The draft strategy was prepared in October 1993 by the Australian Antarctic Foundation with the assistance of a consultancy firm, D. F. Michaels and Associates, which not only sought advice widely, but also organised a national conference – the 1993 Fenner Conference on the Environment – to ensure full and open involvement in this activity. The papers of the Fenner Conference are available as Handmer and Wilder (eds.), *Towards a Conservation Strategy*.

in large part because it has come to regard an effective and legitimate Antarctic Treaty System as the best protection for its domestic interests – including territorial claims.[54] This complementarity of interests can be seen in other issues affecting Canberra's policy-making for Antarctica.

The Australian government found no real domestic difficulties in serving as the ATS' public face at the United Nations when the 'Antarctic Question' was first inscribed on the agenda of the General Assembly. Despite a relatively strong anti-*apartheid* lobby and the growing support among Australian environmental NGOs for the world park concept, Australian representatives at the UN stoutly defended the legitimacy and effectiveness of the ATS against its international critics without serious embarrassment or contradiction at home.[55] The foreign policy objective of maintaining the Antarctic Treaty system clearly outweighed other considerations. Australia continues to support the Consultative Parties' position on the 'Antarctic Question' at the United Nations although it no longer has the lead responsibility on behalf of these states.

Australia's active role in the ATS over the years has acted almost as a positive feedback loop to reinforce the special place that Antarctica has in Australian policy. This effect can be seen in both the development of CCAMLR and in the progress of the tourism issue. Significantly, Australia is not a noteworthy player on the industry side of either of these issue areas, and it has played prominent roles in both issues. Australia hosted important negotiating sessions of the CCAMLR process, and this prominence (and the perception that it was a disinterested party in the development of Antarctic fisheries) greatly advanced Australia's offer to provide the Secretariat headquarters. This in turn led it to supply both the first Chairman and first Executive Secretary for CCAMLR. Nonetheless, the location of CCAMLR in Hobart (which more or less coincided with the decision to relocate the Antarctic Division to Hobart) was very much a product of Australia's internal politics. It was based in the then Liberal government's national programme of devolved federalism. Yet over the years, these developments have produced an important domestic constituency – both formal and informal – within Tasmania to support Australia's Antarctic efforts, including those of CCAMLR. The strong commitment within Australia's research community to CCAMLR-related

[54] J. Brook, 'Australia's Policies toward Antarctica', in Harris (ed.), *Australia's Antarctic Policy Options*, pp. 255–64.
[55] K. Suter, *Antarctica: Private Property or Public Heritage?* (London: Zed Books, 1991), pp. 81–5.

objectives such as CEMP and introduction of the 'precautionary principle' provides ample evidence of the value of this local and supportive constituency.[56]

A similar story has emerged with regard to Antarctic tourism. As is detailed in Chapters 4 and 8 in this volume, Australia has played a significant role in the progress toward an ATS sub-regime on tourism. While it may appear surprising, *prima facie*, that a substantial part of this contribution was the catalytic influence of an Australia-based industry association – PATA – this circumstance is not all that unexpected in the light of the argument of this chapter. The domestic influences that led Australia to take the lead in overturning CRAMRA and proposing an environmental protection regime were real. The community was aware of these issues, and it was reasonable for an industry association like PATA to want to play a role in the tourism issue as it emerged during the Protocol process. The close relationship that has developed in recent years between Australia's Antarctic policy-makers and interested domestic groups has promoted a dynamic adaptiveness in the current period of change in the ATS. This is certainly true of the tourism issue, where the core decision-makers encouraged considerable dialogue within Australia on tourism – a process which led the Australian delegation at the Kyoto ATCM to offer an apparently successful alternative to the Protocol annex on tourism. If, as appears likely, this less formal approach to the regulation of Antarctic tourism (which omitted the concept of the 'overseeing state' included in its Venice proposal) is acceptable to the ATS, the conservation movement and the tourism industry, then it will be due in large measure to the intelligent involvement of domestic interests in the decision-making process.

CONCLUDING REMARKS

Australia's domestic Antarctic policy-making process is significantly different today from what it was nearly a half-century ago. In part, these modifications stem from systemic changes – both international and national. The establishment of the ATS naturally compelled Australia's policy-makers to shift their focus from the AAT to the entire regional canvas of Antarctica. Indeed, at times it appeared that this refocusing was so complete that international obligations entirely overshadowed terri-

---

[56] See Chapters 5 and 9 in this volume.

torial policy. The ATS has itself evolved over the years, and these changes too have affected Australian domestic processes. The Protocol has elevated the priority of the environment both procedurally and substantively in the Australian process. Domestically, the continuing restructuring of the national policy-making process also has been a significant factor for change. The executive arm remains dominant but the political culture of Australia has moved towards a more participatory, pluralist style of policy-making. This shift has appeared in the Antarctic policy process through the involvement of the Parliament, NGOs and the public more fully than in the past.

Yet, for all the change, the contemporary policy process still would be recognisable to a policy-maker of the 1940s, the 1950s or the 1960s. Policy is still made by the executive arm of government. The Antarctic Division, Foreign Affairs and the science community are still the key bureaucratic and substantive actors. These agencies have been reorganised and their relationships redefined, but no new structures have arisen to challenge their centrality to the policy process. At one level, it is even arguable that their role as gatekeepers to the policy arena has been enhanced, since they are the responsible agencies for managing the incorporation of the Protocol-induced environmental changes into the domestic policy process. At another level, of course, the public interest in Antarctica, the government's political sensitivities to this interest, the emergence and institutionalisation of the conservation movement, the rediscovery of the AAT as a domestic policy responsibility and similar developments appear likely to prevent a return to 'business as usual'. Or, will they?

At least one significant imponderable looms over the Australian domestic Antarctic policy process as it stands on the threshold of the twenty-first century. Are the recent changes wholly contextual, or have they become entrenched in the permanent structure of policy-making? The evidence on this important issue is mixed. Clearly the recent period – from the abandonment of CRAMRA to the implementation of the Protocol – has been an extraordinary time for policy. Australia, in large part due to domestic public pressure, took a lead on an international issue which brought into play all the Antarctic policy-makers, even the most exalted. The Prime Minister and other senior ministers cannot be expected to exercise this degree of involvement in future when policy again becomes 'routine'. Similarly, when Antarctic issues no longer focus on the fundamentals of the global agenda, regime change and the consequences of these for Australian national interest, it seems unlikely that so many different interests will devote the time and effort to influence domestically the making of Australia's Antarctic policy.

Nevertheless, a die has been cast; even if it has not come completely to rest, it does seem likely that some recent changes will persist. The recognition that Australia is a claimant state, and a shift towards a territorial policy on the AAT, are likely to figure more prominently in Australian Antarctic policy than was true of the period to the middle of the 1980s. Also, the strong domestic commitment to environmental protection which appeared in the CRAMRA debate has imbued not only international policy but has, through the Protocol, also been incorporated into the Australian domestic process. The development of an AAT conservation strategy and the inclusion of environmental protection objectives into national policy objectives suggests that these interests will remain central in Australia's Antarctic policy-making process, for the medium-term future at least.

14

Chilean Antarctic policy: the influence of domestic and foreign policy

MARÌA TERESA INFANTE

INTRODUCTION

This chapter falls into three main sections: (1) the definition of Chilean national interests in relation to Antarctica; (2) the main characteristics of the elaboration and conduct of Chilean foreign policy and the Antarctic; and (3) the evolution and trends in Chile's Antarctic foreign policy making in the past decade, with particular emphasis on the four issue areas focused on in this book: minerals, living resources, environmental protection and tourism.

In order to analyse these subjects we assume that Chilean Antarctic policy is the result of a combination of traditional territorial positions, Chile's participation in the Antarctic Treaty ever since 1959 and the search for practical and legal accommodation with third-country positions and interests, under the cover of the Treaty. Professional diplomacy and academic expertise have been central in shaping this policy. In this process, due account must be taken of the history of Chile's involvement in Antarctic affairs, domestically and internationally. Also overwhelmingly important are the issues of natural resources, environmental protection, and the geographical vicinity and the possibilities of human settlement in the Antarctic lands. Over the past two decades, national attention in Chile has been attracted by these issues, whether because of the need to channel domestic demands and diplomatic initiatives, or to respond to them.

In the long term, Antarctic policy has remained more closely linked to foreign policy requirements and goals, than to the changing patterns of Chile's domestic politics – even after the democratic crisis of the 1970s and gradual transition to democracy in the late 1980s. In general, Antarctic policy orientations have not dramatically changed with the ideological patterns of the governments in power. Of course, there has also been an impact from the new issues emerging within the Antarctic Treaty System (ATS) in relation to the exploration and exploitation of natural resources, as well as the increase in number of Treaty parties and the UN debate, among other elements.[1] All this has contributed to a wider discussion of Antarctic issues in domestic fora; but all the same, the issue of Antárctica still belongs more to the domain of foreign policy than to the domestic scenario.

In this internal context the new issues mentioned above have fostered a scientific and academic contribution seeking to anticipate and enlighten the foreign policy-making process. Nevertheless, Chile's scientific community has not played a significant role as a consultative body in that process, in part due to the insufficiencies of the institutions and the lack of national or comprehensive research programmes.

In recent years, mainly in 1989–91, interest organisations and non-governmental groups have attempted to participate in defining Chile's Antarctic agenda, or to galvanise public opinion for change, especially in regard to the issue of mineral resources. At the regional level in Magallanes, these efforts have also been directed at criticising the nature of the activities undertaken by the Chilean government in the Antarctic territory – including the stations, tourism and human settlements. These elements will be discussed below.

CHILE'S NATIONAL INTERESTS IN RELATION TO ANTARCTICA

Chilean national interests in Antarctica are based upon three main elements: the territorial position, aiming at the claim of titles to the territory; the support of the Antarctic cooperative framework spelled out by the Antarctic Treaty; and the protection of the Antarctic environment as well as dependent and associated ecosystems.

With regard to the *territorial* claim, the Chilean position must be analysed in a balanced way. Until the negotiation of the Antarctic Treaty, this position was characterised by Chile's historical experience as a southern hemisphere country, often competing with colonial – especially British – power in the area. At the same time, this policy has applied the prevailing theories of international law concerning the acquisition of uninhabited territories.[2] In line with this, a territorial claim would be the most appro-

---

[1] See Chapter 2.
[2] Chilean Ministry of Foreign Affairs, 'Derechos Indiscutibles de Chile sobre la Antártica Chilena', *Revista Geográfica de Chile*, 1948, no. 1, pp. 155–64.

priate form to show a legitimate and direct interest in Antarctica, in circumstances of keen competition with foreign powers seeking to settle there either for exploitation purposes or for geopolitical imperatives. The year 1940 marked the officialisation of a national doctrine[3] which is in fact curiously related to a United States initiative to counter a possible German presence in the area.[4]

Strategic interests gradually became more apparent in Antarctica. This situation provided new arguments to justify an active role for Antarctica in Chilean foreign policy. An expression of this interest can be found in the strategic and geopolitical thought of R. Cañas Montalva (later Commander-in-Chief of the Army), aimed at strengthening the geographical factors of Chile's presence on the continent. Writing in the 1950s, he emphasised the geographical continuity and contiguity of the Magellan region and the Antarctic territories.[5] Chile's official negotiations with Argentina in 1906–8 and the fundamental agreements of 1941 and 1948 in favour of a common position with respect to the South American Antarctica (25° and 90°W)[6] are a further expression of this interest. In 1907, the geographer Luis Risopatrón had stressed the idea of an 'American Antarctica' to underline the geographical factors of the Chilean position.[7] Recent geopolitical studies have depicted this factor as fundamental for the Chilean interests.[8] A similar proposal emerges from the conclusions adopted at an official seminar convened by the Ministries of Foreign Affairs and Defence.[9]

The discussion of an agreed framework for settling positions and claims

[3] J. Berguño, 'Cincuenta años de política antártica', *Anales, Medio Siglo de Política Antártica (1940–1990)*, Academia Diplomatíca de Chile, 1991, p. 27.

[4] E. Gajardo Villarroel, 'Antecedentes de la negociación diplomática previa al Tratado de 1959 y la posición de Chile', in F. Orrego Vicuña *et al.* (eds.), *Política Antártica de Chile* (Santiago: Instituto de Estudios Internacionales, Universidad de Chile, 1984), pp. 81–2.

[5] R. Cañas Montalva, 'Chile, el más antártico de los países del orbe y su responsabilidad continental en el Sur-Pacífico', *Revista Geográfica de Chile*, no. 4, 1950, pp. 23–40; and 'El valor geopolítico de la posición antártica de Chile', *Revista Geográfica de Chile*, no. 9, 1953, pp. 11–16.

[6] O. Pinochet de la Barra, 'Antecedentes históricos de la política internacional de Chile en la Antártica: Negociaciones chileno-argentinas de 1906, 1906, 1907 y 1908', in Orrego *et al.* (eds.), *Política Antártica de Chile*, pp. 72–80.

[7] L. Risopatrón, *La Antártida Americana* (Santiago: Imprenta Cervantes, 1908).

[8] R. Riesco, 'Fronteras y temas geopolíticos chilenos en el Oceáno Pacífico Sur y en el continente antártico', *Revista Chilena de Geopolítica*, no. 2, 1985, pp. 17–27.

[9] The seminar, *Antártica: Un compromiso nacional*, was held 17–18 August 1993. Proceedings are unpublished. Some of these ideas were introduced by Captain C. de Toro, at the Practitioners' Session of the IARP Workshop, held in Santiago, 12 November 1993.

that led to the negotiation of the *1959 Antarctic Treaty*, constitutes the second main issue at stake in the national Antarctic policy that still characterises Chile's Antarctic involvement. Here, the national view can be described as firmly committed to the establishment of a scheme of cooperation such as that reflected in the Treaty – one which assigns the main responsibilities to the states parties rather than to international bodies. Some of the basic elements of the Treaty have been positively evaluated in the Chilean foreign policy-making process – that is to say, within the Ministry of Foreign Affairs, the armed forces and advisory bodies. The inclusion of the so-called hard claimants (Argentina, Australia and Chile), together with other states identified by their direct interests in Antarctica, whether claimants or not, and the consolidation of common rules of conduct, shared values or continued practice in the continent,[10] can explain much of the Chilean allegiance to this instrument.

Here we should note that Chile, under centre-left governments from 1938 until the emergence of a nationalist President in 1952, refused to support any initiative that would lead to internationalising Antarctica, directly or indirectly. In 1948, Chile introduced the concept of a moratorium or *modus vivendi* in relation to the sovereignty issue, for a reasonable period of time, requesting guarantees for the free conduct of scientific research and scientific international cooperation.[11] The Chilean perception at the time was that the United States had decided not to press its own territorial claim in Antarctica, so as to avoid any similar decision from the Soviet Union.

In the following years, the establishment and functioning of an Antarctic Treaty System derived from the 1959 Antarctic Treaty, as referred to in an article by Ambassador F. Zegers in 1978[12] using the expression put forward by Argentinian R. Guyer,[13] which had considerable impact in shaping a comprehensive Chilean Antarctic policy. This approach combined a territorialist position with international elements arising out of the 1959 Antarctic Treaty, which could eventually and only in specific

---

[10] J. Berguño, 'Operatividad del Sistema Antártico', *Primer Seminario Nacional sobre la Antártica*, Chilean Ministry of Foreign Affairs, Department of Special Policy, June 1986, p. 123.

[11] E. Gajardo Villarroel, 'Antecedentes de la negociación diplomática previa al Tratado de 1959 y la posición de Chile', in Orrego *et al.* (eds.), *Política Antártica de Chile*, pp. 84–5.

[12] F. Zegers, 'El Sistema Antártico y la utilización de los recursos', *University of Miami Law Review*, vol. 33, no. 2, 1978, pp. 432–64.

[13] R. Guyer, 'The Antarctic System', *Recueil des Cours*, vol. 139-II, 1973, pp. 149–226. See also the discussion in Chapter 2.

contexts lead to the establishment of institutions. The approach gained acceptance as the basis for a national Antarctic policy: ever since 1983, the Chilean position at the United Nations has stressed this point. In the Report submitted in accordance with Resolution 38/77 of the thirty-eighth UN General Assembly, Chile noted that the consolidation and effectiveness of the System have not been easily achieved, and to return to an earlier stage might endanger all the achievements beneficial not only to parties, but also to the international community as a whole.[14]

Until recently in the domestic debate in Chile, other areas of concern – such as the type and quality of the contribution to scientific research and related activities – have appeared to attract less attention from policy-makers. Instead, in the national political context most of the responsibilities implied by membership in the ATS have been seen in light of diplomatic priorities. Indicative here is the initiative launched in 1981, which concentrated on such fundamental aspects of the ATS as (1) efficiency and internal coordination within the System; (2) a broader and more efficient diffusion of the System and its accomplishments; and (3) better relations with third states, international organisations and entities which show a qualified interest in Antarctica.[15] According to the same source, Chile's sovereign interest and the fundamental security values attached to the zone of peace in Antarctica are directly related to the support given to the operation of the ATS.[16] Full membership in the Antarctic community implies the right to participate in the decision-making process concerning collective questions, which is one of the highest national policy priorities.

It is interesting to observe that these definitions were adopted at a time when the Law of the Sea (LOS) negotiations within the United Nations were coming to an end. The appraisal of the situation presented by this case and the experience of being a country deeply involved in the LOS process and UN negotiations, led to Chile's making a clear distinction between what should be achieved in a global context, and which strategy might apply to the case of Antarctica – where a special regime already existed.

Judging the origin of the *environmental* aspect of Chile's national position is more difficult. On the one hand, environmental concerns have been fundamental in negotiations over establishment of special regimes

---

[14] Cuestión de la Antártida: Estudio solicitado en la Resolución 38/77 de la Asamblea General, *Informe del Secretario General*, UN doc. A/39/583/ (Part II), 2 November 1984, p. 18.
[15] J. Berguño, 'Operatividad del Sistema Antártico', p. 137.
[16] *Ibid.*, pp. 147–8.

for natural resources or other uses of Antarctica.[17] On the other hand, the emphasis on environmental concerns is also in line with a genuine *national* position set forward at the time of the Treaty negotiation. Chile tried to introduce a provision to Article IX of the Treaty (VIII in the draft) referring to protection and conservation of natural resources in general.[18] To understand the Chilean attitude to this respect, account should be taken of the influence of whaling and marine living resources protection in the adoption of the 200 miles marine policy in 1947 and the further establishment of Southeast Pacific cooperation instruments to protect the maritime zone of 200 miles that preceded the Antarctic Treaty negotiations.

With respect to Antarctica, Chile has generally taken a basically conservationist position. This might have been inspired by considerations imposed by its claimant status, but has mainly served to justify and support cooperative undertakings within the ATS, especially towards third countries or organisations wishing to intervene in the Antarctic Treaty area.

CHILEAN FOREIGN POLICY-MAKING AND ANTARCTICA

Chile's Antarctic policy has not been unaffected by the general features of that country's foreign policy. The latter has been characterised by strong governmental supremacy in a presidential regime, based upon the constitutional rules of 1925 and the new Charter of 1980. According to the latter, the Executive Power, or more precisely the President, is to conduct foreign policy and negotiate and conclude treaties. Congress has powers only in relation to those international treaties subject to ratification,[19] while the Chamber of Deputies (Representatives) may control the political responsibilities of the Executive and the Central Administration.

[17] 'Chile nace en la Antártica: Contralmirante Le May, Jefe del Estado Mayor de la Armada', *El Mercurio*, Santiago, 21 November 1976, p. 33; 'Relación del ecosistema chileno con el antártico: Posición de Chile en Londres', *El Mercurio*, Santiago, 10 October 1977.

[18] Conferencia de la Antártida, *Confidencial de la Conferencia*, doc. COM.II/SR/6 (Final), 7 November 1959, p. 3.

[19] The Executive Power negotiates and ratifies all international treaties (Art. 32, para. 17 of the Constitution). Before ratifying a treaty, the Executive must seek the approval of Congress, in which case the Senate and the Chamber of Deputies are called to decide separately. A treaty follows the same stages as legislation. Treaties subject to this procedure are those which must meet the status of law according to the Constitution or do not fall under the special competence of the Executive Power.

Following the regionalisation process that started in 1974, the Chilean Antarctic Territory falls within the administrative authority of the *Regional Government* of the XIIth Region, based in Punta Arenas, Magallanes.[20] There has been an Antarctic *comuna* since 1979[21] with Puerto Covadonga as its capital (O'Higgins Base). As concerns maritime affairs, they are under the responsibility of the naval port authorities.[22]

Nevertheless, the role of the *Executive* is essential in Chilean Antarctic affairs, both regarding planning, coordination and decision-making. Moreover, some of Chile's major decisions adopted in relation to Antarctica show the President's personal involvement. Such was the case in 1940, when President Aguirre Cerda played a key role in approving the Act which determined the boundaries of the territorial claim.[23] This document defined the official position which has been followed in Chile's Antarctic policy ever since.[24]

The linkage between Chile's central administration and Antarctic affairs also has a practical explanation. Relevant here are the ability to conduct expeditions and organise major logistic operations; the participation of the armed forces in permanent Antarctic activities, especially the operation of stations and transport facilities, and the need to provide an administrative framework to lead and coordinate various groups and agencies that participate in those activities.

From an institutional perspective, too, the role of the Executive is highlighted. Two major councils, established by the organic law of the Ministry of Foreign Affairs,[25] are made up of high-ranking administration officials. The *Antarctic Policy Council*, which constitutes the main authority in Antarctic affairs, is presided over by the Minister of Foreign Affairs, whereas two other ministers have permanent seats – the Minister of Defence and the Minister of Finance. One former Minister of Foreign Affairs is appointed to the Council by his colleague in office. The Execu-

---

[20] Since 1955, the claimed sector had been administratively dependent on the provincial government in Punta Arenas: see Law no. 11,846, *Diario Oficial*, 21 June 1955; the Antarctic Statute was issued in 1956 by the Ministry of Foreign Affairs, Decree no. 298: see *Diario Oficial*, 3 October 1956.

[21] Decree Law No. 2,868: see *Diario Oficial*, no. 30,499, 26 October 1979.

[22] Law no. 18,629: see *Diario Oficial*, no. 32,822, 17 July 1987.

[23] On Chilean foreign policy, see M. Wilhelmy, 'Política, Burocracia y Diplomacia en Chile', *Estudios Sociales*, no. 35, 1983, pp. 123–59.

[24] M. Ruiz Solar, 'El Decreto de límites en la Antártica', *Anales, Medio Siglo de Política Antártica (1940–1990)*, Academia Diplomatica de Chile, 1991, pp. 7–10.

[25] Law no. 161, 1978: see *Diario Oficial*, no. 30,026, 31 March 1978. See in particular Art. 13, para. 5.

tive Secretary of this Council is the Director of the Special Policy Department. The Minister has the power to invite, for specific matters, other representatives of the public sector and prominent personalities. It has fundamental decision-making power in terms of policies, economics, science and law applicable to the Chilean Antarctic Territory and Antarctica as a whole. See Figure 14.1. A second institution is the Council of Foreign Policy, which enjoys permanent consultative status under the same legal framework. It is composed of former Ministers of Foreign Affairs, professors of international law and other personalities selected by the Minister of Foreign Affairs.

In part due to its composition, the Antarctic Policy Council concentrates on budgetary questions and accommodation among its bureaucratic components, rather than with operative aspects or Antarctic planning. Theoretically, the Council may examine and elaborate policy issues. In fact, this task is conducted by the permanent staff of the Ministry of Foreign Affairs through the Special Policy Department, by an advisory working group depending on the Council, and by the Chilean Antarctic Institute. This situation gives to the directors of these key agencies considerable power to influence the decision-making process – even on subjects like the issue of conservation of marine living resources, which also falls under the competence of the Fisheries Vice-Minister within the Ministry of Finance.

The *Chilean Antarctic Institute* (INACH) is an agency under the Ministry of Foreign Affairs and is aimed at planning, coordinating and controlling scientific and technological activities in Antarctica. It is funded over the annual budget, approved by the Congress, and administers funds for scientific research in Antarctica. Historically, the Institute was created to respond to the demands of growing international and financial commitments for scientific research in Antarctica, which no university could afford alone at the time (1964).[26] Its role in this field has been fulfilled basically independently of political authorities, depending on the circumstances the country has faced and the ability, knowledge or preference of its leaders towards scientific and technical aspects of Antarctic activities.

The extent to which these entities seek the advice or opinion of *independent bodies* or specialists, is largely a question of personal preference or inclination of those in charge. During the 1980s, for example, the Air Force emerged as an interested institution providing an additional source

[26] O. González Ferrán, 'La ciencia en la Antártica', *Anales, Medio Siglo de Política Antártica (1940–1990)*, Academia Diplomatica de Chile, 1991, p. 44.

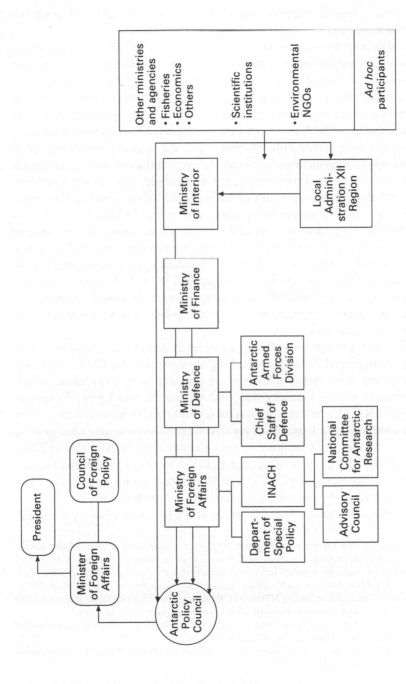

Figure 14.1 The Antarctic decision-making process in the Chilean executive branch

of contact, logistic support and financing for scientists and academic studies in general.

In addition, the subject of natural resources, specially minerals negotiations and the subsequent moratorium issue, had led to a more intense movement in favour of permanent exchange of opinion between academics and officials – but not at the level of permanent bodies, although there have been some consultative working groups operated under the chairmanship of the Ministry of Foreign Affairs.[27] Such groups were convened by the Antarctic Policy Council in order to study the international legal basis for negotiating a minerals regime and the constitutional aspects of the same subject. Interestingly, the first subject was already examined at length during the approval of Resolution XI-I that launched the corresponding negotiation, yet full support within the diplomatic sphere was not forthcoming until very late in the 1980s. Furthermore, these concerns were mainly raised by civilians within the bureaucracy, rather than by the armed forces – which were consulted constantly. As a demonstration of the need to seek a consensual diplomacy, in 1986 the Ministry of Foreign Affairs organised a seminar to discuss the current course of Antarctic affairs and possible alternatives for Chilean policy. The moment was considered a crucial one.[28]

The question of marine living resources in Antarctica has given rise to some institutional development along similar lines. In 1982 a National Section was organised to advise the government on matters related to the Convention on the Conservation of Antarctic Marine Living Resources (CCAMLR). This Section comprises representatives from industry, from the universities and from the Navy. Its composition was amended in 1992 so as to transfer the Executive Secretary position to the Ministry of Foreign Affairs, Department of Special Policy.[29] In practice, the main orientations of Chile's position in CCAMLR meetings are planned by the Ministry of Foreign Affairs with the advice of the other sectors.

In 1991, the Chilean Antarctic Institute set up a new advisory Council[30]

---

[27] Two confidential reports were prepared, one by a commission of political studies for the negotiation of a regime to explore and exploit Antarctic minerals; the second, by a commission to study the internal legal implications of such a regime, 1985. *Anales, Medio Siglo de Política Antártica (1940–1990)*, Academia Diplomatica de Chile, 1991, p 28

[28] 'Discurso Inaugural del Señor Ministro de Relaciones Exteriores de Chile Jaime del Valle Alliende', *Primer Seminario Nacional sobre la Antáritca*, June 1986, pp. 11–17.

[29] Decree no. 1679, Ministry of Foreign Affairs and Ministry of Economics, 12 December 1991: see *Diario Oficial*, no. 34,247, 20 April 1992.

[30] Decree no. 266, Ministry of Foreign Affairs, 6 March 1991: see *Boletín Antártico Chileno*, vol. 11, no. 1, 1992, pp. 29–30.

to permit wider participation of official operators in Antarctica and to include representatives of the University of Chile and, under special invitation, other important persons, from public or private entities. For example, INACH experts in consultation with the diplomatic and operative sectors have dealt with such a key subject as tourism and its implications under the 1991 Environmental Protocol, including the liability aspects. The National Committee for Antarctic Research was reorganised in 1990,[31] as an autonomous entity linked to the Ministry of Foreign Affairs through INACH, but not dependent on it. The Chilean representative to the Scientific Committee on Antarctic Research (SCAR) presides over the National Committee, a position held by the President of the National Scientific Commission.

This type of body, including also representatives from the industrial and academic sectors, may provide a new framework in dealing with Antarctic questions, although it is too early to draw definite conclusions on its impact upon the policy process. The main issues facing these bodies are directing, coordinating and fund-allocating for scientific programmes and projects, as well as real participation in components of the ATS.

Domestic sources clearly indicate that Chile's policy has been basically dominated by *foreign policy makers* and the requirements they have established. The now classic work, *La Antártica Chilena* (1944),[32] written by O. Pinochet de la Barra, dedicated to the study of the territorial titles, is clear evidence of this situation. Martinic introduces us to the work of diplomats and internationalists before 1940,[33] who wanted to strengthen the links between continental Chile, specially Magallanes, and the Antarctic lands, in order to narrow the distance to polar territories.

This is not to deny the importance of support given by domestic political forces in the adoption of major decisions before and after the 1959 Antarctic Treaty. As an example, the parliamentary hearings held in order to approve this Treaty before ratification show the existence of a common shared perception between government and opposition parties concerning the protection of national interests by this instrument. On that occasion, the socialist senator A. Rodríguez pointed out that the fundamental national interests such as peaceful co-existence, international cooperation

---

[31] Decree no. 641, Ministry of Foreign Affairs: see *Diario Oficial*, no. 33,755, 27 August 1990.

[32] This work has had four editions up to now.

[33] M. Martinic, 'Interés, Preocupación y Presencia Antárticos de Chile: Visión Sinóptica, 1494–1940', in F. Orrego Vicuña and A. Salinas (eds.), *El Desarrollo de la Antártica* (Santiago: Instituto de Estudios Internacionales, Universidad de Chile, 1984), pp. 67–80.

and Chilean sovereignty were well protected by the Treaty.[34] More recently, a group of twenty congressmen led by the Presidents of the two Chambers made a declaration during a visit to Antarctica in the spring of 1991, reaffirming their political commitment with the claimant position as well as their support for the Antarctic Treaty System and the new Environmental Protocol adopted in Madrid the same year.[35]

As a matter mainly subject to diplomatic evaluation as well as requiring peculiar logistic support and technical skills, ATS participation places high demands on institutional leadership and coordination. This is so not only at the level of policy-making, but also in relation to the execution of programmes and scientific research activities. Some of the main problems have been examined frankly after the adoption of the Madrid Protocol, and preliminary measures have been adopted during the past few years, such as the establishment of an Antarctic Coordinating Council in Punta Arenas, Magallanes, formed by public entities involved in current Antarctic activities; the creation of an Antarctic Centre sponsored by the University of Magallanes (Punta Arenas) and development programmes to promote interdisciplinary Antarctic studies at some universities, mainly the University of Chile.

ANTARCTIC POLICY, NATIONAL POSITIONS AND DOMESTIC FACTORS

Determining whether the main interests of Chile's Antarctic policy are fully integrated in official statements, documents and initiatives, is a complex question. The evolving situation of the 1970s, marked by the accession of new states to the Antarctic Treaty, the official opening of discussions to establish regimes for marine living and mineral resources as well as the need for a diplomatic strategy to discourage initiatives for the establishment of a UN machinery for Antarctica – all these factors have made it more difficult to define a coherent and clear national policy comprising the aforementioned international and foreign elements at stake.

The evolution of the ATS at the international level and discussions in external fora about its legitimacy and effectiveness, especially during the

---

[34] A. Rodríguez, *Diario de Sesiones del Senado*, Sesión 34, 5 April 1961, Santiago 1961, pp. 1,984–8.
[35] 'Nuestra presencia reafirma la soberanía de Chile en la Antártida', *El Mercurio*, Santiago, 6 November 1991.

1980s, did not present any major challenge to the principles underlying Chilean diplomacy until the minerals negotiations officially got underway.

Minerals regime and environmental protection

In no area have the dilemmas of the Antarctic policy been more apparent than in the case of the minerals resources negotiations which started in 1981. The only existing official document on the subject is classified,[36] and spells out very general principles which seemed to search for accommodation of aims and good feelings in a loosely integrated Antarctic community.

The search for both sovereignty consolidation in Antarctica, which is the main explicit goal of the national policy, and the establishment of clear rules for mineral activities, required additional efforts of policy-making and conceptual development. This proved to be the most controversial political task encountered by Chilean Antarctic diplomacy until then. During most of the 1970s, the predominant opinion had been that mineral activities would involve legal and political problems, especially concerning the Peninsula area, as well as pollution risks, and that anticipatory regulations could be needed to avoid confrontation. A more critical view was held by constitutional experts with a strict interpretation of the sovereignty claim, focusing on property rights and the legal nature of the state's rights to hydrocarbons and energy resources, and arguing that such rights could not be guaranteed by the type of arrangement foreseen for Antarctica.

During the negotiation of CRAMRA, and emphasising other dimensions than the economic significance that minerals activities may represent for Chile,[37] certain diplomatic sectors, former diplomats and even some media commentators[38] raised legal defence of the sovereignty paradigm or pointed to constitutional obstacles associated with minerals activities in the claimed sector of Antarctica. These opinions were for-

---

[36] Ministry of Foreign Affairs, 1983, manuscript, undated and unpublished.
[37] O. Pinochet, 'La Antártica chilena y sus implicancias diplomáticas', in W. Sanchez and T. Pereira (eds.), *Cientocincuenta Años de Política Exterior Chilena* (Santiago: Editorial Universitaria, 1977), pp. 262–3; also O. Pinochet, 'Bases para el desarrollo económico de la Antártica en una perspectiva político-jurídica', in Orrego and Salinas (ds.), *El Desarrollo de la Antártica*, pp. 365–6.
[38] F. Gamboa, 'Hacia una redefinición de nuestra soberanía antártica', *El Mercurio*, Santiago, 7 June 1986, p. A2; R. Ruiz Piracés, 'Antártida, tareas para un próximo decenio', *El Mercurio*, Santiago, 24 October 1989, p. A2.

warded with the intent to provoke a change in Chile's position on the minerals issue in a direction not clearly defined. After exhaustive analysis, however, those efforts proved fruitless, and in 1989 the Executive approved the signing of CRAMRA.[39]

In the meantime, Chile's academic sector and Air Force officers had viewed the definition of national interest differently, highlighting the need to make domestic use of the scientific, technical and logistic opportunities provided by Antarctic activities, and adapting to the new situation concerning natural resources, tourism and related activities. Rather than seeking to substitute the prevailing official position, these opinions suggested an enlargement or a redefinition of objectives in order to enhance Chilean influence in Antarctic affairs.[40] Part of this new trend to broaden national perspectives in Antarctica can be explained by the growing emphasis on practical matters, like communications, logistics, infrastructure and flight services, apparently rendering Chile's claimant position insufficient as a basis for influence in Antarctic affairs.[41] All these ideas suggested a need to exploit opportunities of national development and accommodate them with recent trends in international relations – rather than to discuss the traditional notions of Chilean geopolitics and the natural linkage between Magallanes and the Antarctic Peninsula.

A more comprehensive analysis of the *domestic setting* will reveal the importance of a variety of emerging elements which influenced the policy-making process at odds with traditional patterns. Some of these new elements were related to the democratic transition process. The post-1988 plebiscite period[42] encouraged a more participative discussion of foreign policy issues and some changes in diplomatic leadership within the Chilean Antarctic policy-making process.

A linkage can be drawn between this process and the gradual change

---

[39] 'Chile firmó la Convenión Antártica con Nueva Zelanda', *El Mercurio*, Santiago, 18 March 1989. The article quotes an official declaration by the Ministry of Foreign Affairs on the occasion of signing the Convention.

[40] F. Orrego Vicuña, 'Evaluación del aporte de las Universidades chilenas al desarrollo y conocimiento antártico', *Primer Seminario Nacional sobre la Antártica*, June 1986, pp. 67–81; J. Lopetegui, *Antártica Un Desafío Perentorio*(Santiago: Instituto Geopolítico de Chile, 1986), p. 106.

[41] Lopetegui, *Antártica Un Desafío Perentorio*, pp. 125–30.

[42] In accordance with transitional provisions of the 1980 Constitution, a plebiscite was convened to accept or reject a proposed candidate for the Presidency. If the official candidate was not accepted by the absolute majority, free competitive elections were to be held in the course of a year. Following the results, elections took place in December 1989.

in the tactical conduct of the emergent issue of Antarctic environmental protection which led up to the Environmental Protocol, including a smooth shift in the role played by Chile regarding the minerals issue in the ATS. Since 1989, Chile has been very active in promoting comprehensive measures to protect the environment, following the accidents of *Bahìa Paraìso* off Anvers Island and *Exxon Valdez* in Alaska. In order to promote a comprehensive approach to environmental protection in the ATS, Chile started out from those measures already in force within the ATS, as well as from CRAMRA, which served as a model for spelling out environmental principles.

In studying this period, we must distinguish between the academic perspectives that have contributed to define alternatives and foundations for a national Antarctic policy, and the involvement of *non-governmental organisations* committed to a model of Antarctic institutionalisation not always in accordance with existing instruments. The latter is directly related to the lobbying strategies preferred by certain international coalitions or movements; these have differed in the degree or nature of their political commitment or issue involvement. In Chile, non-governmental organisations did not become active in Antarctic affairs until very late in the 1980s although they had been important in other fields, such as the environment, during the years previous to the 1988 plebiscite. Their activism in the Chilean Antarctic context coincided with the opening of international discussions on the future of CRAMRA after its adoption in Wellington in 1988, and the proposal to establish an Antarctic wilderness park as a concept distinct from a natural conservation area. This domestic discussion was fuelled both by the questions raised internationally about the prospective effectiveness of CRAMRA as an environmental protection instrument, in conjunction with more subtle tactics geared to provoking a major change in Chile's official position, taking into account possible adjustments of the diplomatic negotiating team in 1990. To understand the involvement of the various non-official groups in the analysis and shaping of national Antarctic policy or in the decision-making process, we shall classify these groups in three categories, according to their characteristics.

The academic sector

The academic sector has played a key role in disseminating ATS principles and institutions, providing a critical view when necessary in relation to the needs and shortcomings of the Antarctic foreign and domestic policy. The Institute of International Studies (IEI) of the University of

Chile organised two important conferences in the 1970s and 1980s. At the first, held in Punta Arenas in 1977, the real problems facing the Antarctic scenario were discussed. The second was held on King George Island in 1982 at a time when negotiations on mineral resources had just started and no one else in Chile was discussing the legitimacy of the subject from a purely domestic perspective.[43] These conferences gathered specialists from Chile and foreign countries, participating in their personal capacity. People directly involved in Antarctic affairs in the Chilean private and public sector, regional personalities and members of the political opposition at the time were invited to take part.

A working group has operated under the direction of the IEI, to contribute to a more comprehensive discussion of issues facing the ATS, such as the threat posed by the Malaysian UN initiative from 1983 and the implications of the current minerals negotiations. One result of the group's efforts was the publication of the book, *Política Antarctica de Chile*, which covers a wide range of interest areas for a country like Chile.[44]

Working groups specially organised to deal with Antarctic politics

Within the framework of foreign policy studies or in relation to special problems arising from Antarctic negotiations, such groups have contributed to enrich the domestic policy-making process. Here we should mention the document elaborated in 1988 for a project on the future Chilean foreign policy,[45] sponsored by the Latin American Institute of Transnational Studies (ILET). This was the result of consultations with specialists from political sectors and the academic sector, some of whom were more inclined towards an 'internationalisation' of global issues as a future aim of the next government. At that time, many of the participants in the group did not have a clear view of the role of the ATS in the international context, or of the implications of an eventual revision of the Treaty after 1991. Curiously, CRAMRA, which had just been adopted, was not subjected to any criticism. Likewise, some contributions concerning foreign policy in a democratic context[46] went in the same direction.

---

[43] The conference was held at the Presidente Frei Base (formerly Teniente Marsh Base); see F. Orrego Vicuña (ed.), *Antarctic Resources Policy: Scientific, Legal and Political Issues* (Cambridge University Press, 1983).

[44] See Orrego *et al.* (eds.), *Política Antártica de Chile*. Contributors included renowned Chilean diplomats such as J. Berguño, O. Pinochet and F. Zegers.

[45] M. T. Infante, *Asuntos Especiales y Política Exterior* (Instituto Latinomaericano de Estudios Transnacionales, 1988).

[46] F. Orrego Vicuña, 'La consolidación de la política antárctica', in H. Muñoz (ed.), *Chile: Política Exterior para la Democracia* (Santiago: Pehuén, 1989), p. 88.

Once the dispute concerning the role of minerals within the ATS became known worldwide and a Special Consultative Meeting, to be held in 1990, had been convened, a working group was established in 1990 under the sponsorship of the Chilean Council of Foreign Relations.[47] At this stage, with a fully democratic government in place and with increasing tension between positions in relation to CRAMRA and its political linkages with the environmental protection initiatives, the working group provided the elements needed to clarify the options open to Chile and the main challenges facing its national policy in the 1990s.[48] The group indorsed a constructive approach towards the future of CRAMRA and a mining moratorium related to achieving a comprehensive regime to protect the Antarctic environment without banning peaceful human activities. Tourism was specifically identified as an important activity to be encouraged.

Although in 1989, Chile officially proposed the establishment of comprehensive measures in order to protect the Antarctic environment, a year later there was no agreement on how to produce legal and political linkages between this proposal and the future of CRAMRA. This situation created serious problems within the ATS. It was not until late 1990 during the Viña del Mar meeting, or even after the Madrid meeting in June 1991, that a final decision could be adopted in favour of the clause contained in Article 25 of the Environmental Protocol, which differs substantially from the previous moratorium clause rejected by the United States. Underlying this decision was the influence of neutral specialists through personal contacts with Foreign Ministry officials who were not in favour of a permanent ban on mining, and the moderating role played by some members of non-governmental entities associated with the Antarctic and Southern Ocean Coalition (ASOC).

Non-governmental organisations

The involvement in Chilean Antarctic affairs, as distinct from the academic and policy-oriented working groups, of NGOs is a more recent phenomenon in Chilean Antarctic history. The appearance of organised non-academic groups is related to the growing importance of environmental questions as such within the political debate. The possible adop-

---

[47] The Council was presided over by F. Orrego Vicuña and is totally independent of any official body or agency.

[48] *Una Política para 1991 y el Porvenir*, prepared under the direction of M. T. Infante (Santiago: Consejo Chileno para las Relaciones Internacionales, 1990).

tion of a general framework law to protect the environment, which began to be studied within government and by independent groups in 1990, and presented before the National Congress, provides the political background to this interest.

Most influential in terms of public opinion and media presence, as well as in their capability to appeal to official and academic sectors, have been the Antarctic Commission of the National Committee for the Defence of Flora and Fauna (CODEFF), supported by the World Wildlife Fund (WWF) and the Institute of Political Ecology. CODEFF convened a Latin American NGOs workshop in September 1990[49] which stressed the idea of undertaking new steps within the ATS to protect the environment while supporting a permanent ban on mining. However, the project, directed by M. Eugenia Zañartu, never indorsed Greenpeace's more radical approach concerning a world park, although it certainly contributed to increasing public awareness of new international issues affecting the ATS.[50]

The Institute of Political Ecology, on the other hand, is more related to politically committed transnational groups, and seeks to impact public opinion on ecological security. It has denounced sport, tourism and other human activities on the Antarctic continent and the surrounding seas.[51] In accordance with its views, Chile should reconsider the gradualist approach towards environmental protection and adopt a different stand in relation to mining and other economic activities, as well as declaring the Antarctic continent a world park. Moreover, this organisation has severely criticised the existence of the Antarctic Treaty.

Although public opinion sectors in Chile involved in Antarctic affairs seem to have been more attentive to CODEFF's project, it is interesting to note that at the regional level, particularly in Punta Arenas, alternative ideas put forward by other NGOs have also attained some degree of influence. One example is the case of Antarctic Conferences sponsored since 1989 by the Foundation for the Development of the XII Magallanes Region (FIDE XII), linked to the local Catholic Church; here Greenpeace values and orientations have received wide support from the beginning.[52] As an organisation with a local socio-political background, FIDE XII has directed its criticisms at the type and size of Chilean Antarctic invest-

---

[49] 'Declaración de Pichidangui', *Primer Taller Latinoaméricano de Organizaciones No Gubernamentales sobre Conservación Antártica* (Santiago: CODEFF, 1990), p. 57.
[50] An Antarctic NGO *Bulletin* was issued by CODEFF in 1990 and 1991.
[51] M. Baquedano, 'Ecología y Antártida', *La Epoca*, Santiago, 5 December 1990.
[52] *IIs Jornadas Antárticas: Las Jornadas del Medio Ambiente* (Punta Arenas: FIDE XII, 1990).

ments, especially the involvement of the armed forces and the economic and technological implications of national settlement on the continent. These ideas have obviously encountered opposition among local authorities and other influential sectors, but members of CODEFF and FIDE XII have been invited to participate in official delegations to the Antarctic Treaty Consultative Meetings since 1990.

Recently, NGO presence in the media and in organising colloquia has decreased somewhat in intensity. One explanation for this might be the adoption of the 1991 Madrid Protocol and the Rio UNCED Conference in 1992, events which for a while shifted the interest of transnational movements towards other global issues. Another explanation can be found in the fact that the Antarctic foreign policy of Chile's democratic government, after a short period under pressure of ecological activism, now seems more oriented toward putting the Madrid Protocol into force and to building up a national capacity to cope with its requirements, rather than joining countries with a restrictive view on Antarctic activities. The direct involvement of Chilean diplomats in drafting the rules applicable to the Committee for Environmental Protection is one indication of this.

The living resources issue

Less dramatic than the question of minerals and the adoption of the Madrid Protocol, the issue of living resources gave the occasion for defining some key elements of a more general natural resources approach in Chilean Antarctic policy in the 1970s. Curiously, it has given rise to few discussions; most of the time, it has only served to strengthen the idea that the decision to adopt a convention based upon an ecosystem approach was correct.

Protecting Antarctic flora and fauna has been at the core of the Chilean position in all the negotiations with the Treaty parties, as well as underlying the mention of living resources in Article IX of the Treaty and the outright support given to the adoption of the Agreed Measures for the Conservation of Antarctic Fauna and Flora in 1964. Chile has always favoured comprehensive measures within the Treaty framework rather than separate legal instruments,[53] so as to show that the Treaty does cover the issue and to minimise the risks of internationalisation of Antarctic affairs.

---

[53] R. Cabezas, 'Conservación de los recursos marinos vivos antárcticos', *Primer Seminario Nacional sobre la Antártica*, p. 100.

We can distinguish three interrelated concerns in the Chilean position concerning the Convention on the Conservation of Antarctic Marine Living Resources (CCAMLR). A first concern has been to make clear that it is with the Consultative Parties that the primary responsibility lies for protecting the Antarctic ecosystem, including the adoption of relevant regulations in the Southern Ocean. This approach sustained the efforts to stop the UN Food and Agricultural Organisation initiative to set up a project to deal with the resources of this ocean in the 1970s.[54]

Second, Chile has sought to confirm the understanding that the Antarctic Treaty also concerns maritime spaces and that there are law of the sea questions to be addressed by any future instrument to be adopted by the Consultative Parties. This point has a legal meaning not only as a way to satisfy national expectations with regard to the existence of an Exclusive Economic Zone, but also to give substance to the thesis that the Antarctic Treaty applies to the seas south of 60°S latitude, complemented by the ecosystem approach. A third concern has been the development interest derived from Chile's being a fishing nation.[55] Studies and efforts have been devoted to krill resources and most recently towards the harvesting of Patagonian cod (*dissostichus eleginoides*), where distant-waters fishing vessels have been active. From exploratory activity towards a clearly economic activity, applying the most developed fishing technology, Chile has become an important player in Antarctic fishing exploitation. While during the first eight years of CCAMLR Chile adopted a rather passive attitude towards the Convention, since 1991 the situation has changed dramatically. Chile now favours a more articulated position in terms of the scientific, economic, political and legal questions involved and the need to coordinate scientific, political, economic and legal efforts.

The latter process can be seen as anticipatory of the sorts of problems that the country will have to face if a definitive high seas fisheries strategy is adopted. One example here could be legal issues such as the competence of the flag state to exercise jurisdiction over ships registered in Chile while conducting activities in the high seas, which gave rise to an unexpected controversy during the past few years. Companies trying to play outside the official rules set up under CCAMLR defied the official view and argued that domestic courts do not have jurisdiction to apply national

---

[54] F. Zegers, 'El sistema antártico y la cuestión del aprovechamiento de los recursos en el área', *Estudios Internacionales*, vol. 47, 1979, pp. 312–13. See also Chapters 5 and 9.

[55] R. Cabezas, 'Alternativas de política para la utilización de los recursos vivos marinos antárcticos', Orrego *et al.* (eds.), *Política Antártica de Chile*, pp. 244–6.

enforcement measures within the Convention's area and beyond 200 miles. This issue has been ruled on by Chile's Supreme Court against the opinion of these companies[56] giving more support to the conservationist approach that Chile seeks to emphasise in the CCAMLR framework. As the Convention is the sole ATS instrument to combine scientific, economic and political interests in an operative multilateral way, fishing has become a real test in the search for a coherent domestic and international Antarctic policy for Chile.

Tourism

Tourism too shows a clear linkage with the environmental protection discussion in Chilean Antarctic diplomacy. Two factors give some insights to understand this relation. First, the intention to make it clear that a future Protocol to protect the environment will not hinder the freedom to conduct tourist activities, which could have been subject either to a ban or stringent regulations under a 'wilderness park' approach. Second, the recognition that tourism has provided a political factor to cooperate with countries promoting a restrictive environmental protection instrument, in particular France and Italy. Originally, the initiative was intended to include Argentina in the group.

A third aspect explaining the importance attached to the issue of tourism is the question of liability arising from accidents caused by tourist activities, especially the obligation to clean up, restore, repair and reimburse the related costs. Although this issue could be resolved through the liability discussions undertaken by the Consultative Parties, its bearing on the tourism question is of great importance for the Chilean position and represents a substantive element for giving political support to the Protocol.

While the first aspect helps to explain the explicit mention of tourism in some provisions of the Protocol,[57] the second aspect has led Chile to promote the adoption of an annex on tourism and non-governmental activities, explaining the support to a draft presented to the XVIIth Consultative Meeting in Venice in 1992. The advancement of technical and logistic studies and agreements within some components of the ATS, such as COMNAP and SCALOP, seems to have shifted the emphasis in Chile's efforts towards more systematic and operational regulations and

---

[56] *La Prensa Austral*, Punta Arenas, 10 November 1993, p. 5.
[57] For instance, Art. 3, para. 4, and Art. 8, para. 2.

less political involvement in the decision-making process related to tourism and human settlement.[58]

An important underlying factor here has been the enhancement of
Chilean interests in terms of port and ground facilities, air transportation,
navigational aids, etc., as well as the need for progress in enforcing marine
environmental control regulations including reimbursement of the costs
of emergency actions.

IMPLICATIONS FOR THE FUTURE

Chilean Antarctic policy will face three new main areas of concern that
might mean new development in Antarctic domestic politics. The first
challenge is internal coordination of political, scientific and logistic efforts
in accordance with the principles and rules of the 1991 *Environmental
Protocol* and participation in other components of the Antarctic Treaty
System. This urgent need derives not only from the various obligations
arising out of the Protocol, such as marine pollution control, environmental impact assessment, etc., but also – and importantly – as a way to
manage more efficiently the budget allocated to Antarctic activities for
logistic and scientific purposes and to obtain a bigger share. Here we may
note that at the seminar held by the two main bodies in charge of Antarctic programmes in August 1993,[59] two major priorities for scientific
research were articulated: research associated with economic uses of Antarctica (fisheries, ice and tourism); and environmental protection studies,
including pollution prevention and control. In a decentralised scientific
research system like that of Chile, this means the need for further coordination of the public entities, and regulated competition to allocate
resources to the best projects.

Second, the establishment of a *Secretariat* of the Treaty and the *Committee for Environmental Protection* based in one of the Consultative Parties'
territories, will call for new foreign policy efforts. In the period after
adoption of the Protocol and prior to its entry into force, this issue has
proved to be one of the most controversial in Antarctic diplomacy. Chile,
it will be recalled, has always been reluctant about the establishment of a
Secretariat. Now, the Argentinian candidacy for hosting it – after

---

[58] O. Pinochet, 'Turismo en Antártica: Posición de Chile' (unpublished paper, presented
at the symposium *Turismo en Areas Polares*, Colmar, France, 21 April 1992). See also
Chapters 8 and 12.

[59] *Antártica: Un compromiso nacional*, Ministerio de Relaciones Exteriores – Ministerio de
Defensa, 17–18 August 1993; proceedings not published. See also Chapters 8 and 12.

Argentina had long shared the same negative view with Chile – has created an even more complex and critical situation. The key issue here remains the linkage between the establishment of the Secretariat and the Committee as legally separate bodies, in order to make them function in harmony.

And finally, there is the evolution and regulation of *economic interests* in Antarctica and its maritime spaces, in particular the issues of fishing and tourism. While fishing implies an opportunity to put forward a sustained conservationist position, based on scientific evidence, tourism still remains an open issue in diplomatic and legal terms.

15

The making of Norwegian Antarctic policy

OLAV SCHRAM STOKKE

INTRODUCTION

What is the intensity and the kind of concerns found in the societal debate over Norway's policy in Antarctic affairs? To what extent is this debate reflected in the domestic policy-making process? And how do these interests and decision-making patterns affect Norway's positions and role in the four regime projects dealt with in this volume? These are the questions pursued in this chapter.

NATIONAL AND SECTIONAL CONCERNS IN THE ANTARCTIC

Norway is the only state to claim sovereignty over territory in both the Arctic and the Antarctic. Four major concerns underlie its policies in the south. In the early stage, during the whaling era, economic interests were predominant; and to a lesser and more derived extent, also sovereignty. With the dwindling of whaling in the middle of the 1960s, the foreign policy *visibility and prestige* associated with the status as one of the Antarctic stewards assumed more of an independent role, and Norwegian policy-makers have tended to portray their capacity in Antarctic politics as that of moderator and mediator. The significance of *environmental* concerns was fuelled by the national and international attention given to environmental issues in general, first in the 1970s and then during the second green wave in the late 1980s. Hence, although sovereignty claims have been a stable theme in Norway's Antarctic policy, they have usually been argued in instrumental terms: they are claims maintained to support other goals, first economic use and later political access and environmental protection. As we shall see, much the same holds true for Norwegian scientific investigations in the Antarctic, the continuity of which is seen as necessary for the ability to play a substantive and constructive role in the ATS process.

Commercial concerns

The whaling industry was the original occasion for Norway's Antarctic presence. Along with the British, Norwegians had a leading role in this industry, from the time of C. A. Larsen's 1892 Jason expedition until the middle of the 1930s, when Japanese, Soviet and German industries began to catch up. Today, commercial interests are insignificant as a cause for taking part in Antarctic political affairs. While occasional plans surface, Norway's long-distance *fishing* companies have so far decided against sending vessels in any significant numbers into the Southern Ocean, as e.g. the Russians and Japanese do. The finfish resources in the Southern Ocean are generally seen as too marginal to justify the costs of an expedition; and Norway has scant industrial experience with commercial krill operations. As regards the much-discussed Antarctic *mineral resources*, indifference has prevailed in the Norwegian mining and petroleum industry: there is little to suggest that the Antarctic resources have ever been considered as even a long-term option, despite Norway's technological edge in offshore operations under rough climatic conditions. In 1974, after the informal discussion of a minerals regime had begun, the Foreign Minister stated to the Storting[1] that economic exploitation must not be allowed to disturb scientific activities or the vulnerable environment, and that in Norway's view, economic activities should be avoided until the legal situation had been settled.[2] Hence, right from the start of ATS deliberations on resource management, economic concerns were subordinated to other principal Antarctic policy themes. This line was confirmed in 1982, when formal negotiations on CRAMRA had just started, in a government report to the Storting which noted that while there might be interesting resources in the area, Norway favoured a pre-emptive regulation regime only because a prohibition on minerals activity appeared impossible.[3]

---

[1] The *Storting* is Norway's Parliament.

[2] Foreign Minister Knut Frydenlund in the Storting: see *Forhandlinger i Stortinget* (Oslo: The Norwegian Storting), no. 343, 27 March 1974, pp. 2,680–1.

[3] See the Report to the Storting, *St.meld. 26 (1982–83), Miljøvern, kartlegging og forskning i polarområdene* (Environmental Protection, Charting and Research in the Polar Regions) (Oslo: Norwegian Ministry of Environment), p. 47.

This is not to say that Norwegian companies have no commercial interests in the Antarctic. Considerable amounts of equipment and shipping services are sold to various foreign Antarctic expeditions.[4] And while they have not so far played any considerable role in the Antarctic *tourism* industry, this might be an activity of future interest for Norwegian companies. As the market for adventure tourism is expected to expand, Norwegian companies may benefit from a prominent market position in the global cruise industry as well as from the substantial polar experience accumulated by many Norwegians both in the Arctic and the Antarctic. Still, Antarctic tourism will remain a specialised niche of only moderate economic significance. Moreover, like the provision of shipping services to scientific expeditions, this activity is hardly affected by a political presence in the area and does not in itself amount to a reason for taking part in the international deliberations over the Antarctic.

Sovereignty concern: from defensive claim to ticket-to-ride

With the inclusion under Norwegian sovereignty in 1928 and 1931 of two small islands, Bouvetøya and Peter I Øy,[5] and in 1939 the huge landmass named Dronning Maud Land, stretching from 20°W to 45°E,[6] Norway joined the claimants' group in Antarctic politics. The formal basis for the mainland claim was the unique exploration and mapping of these areas conducted by Norwegians. Ever since, the maintenance of this sovereignty claim has been a stable component of Norway's Antarctic policy. In reassessing this policy in late 1968, the government decided in favour of upholding the territorial claim and indeed intensifying the Norwegian presence in the area in order to strengthen that claim.[7] In a recent report to the Storting on Norwegian research activity, the government noted

---

[4] See *St.meld. 42 (1992–93), Norsk Polarforskning* (Norwegian Polar Research) (Oslo: Norwegian Ministry of Environment), p. 28.

[5] See Royal Decree of 23 January 1928, approving a proposal of the Ministry of Foreign Affairs that Bouvetøya be placed under Norwegian sovereignty; by an amendment of 24 March 1933, Peter I Øy was included in the Dependencies Act of 27 February 1930. These documents are reproduced and translated into English in W. M. Bush (ed.), *Antarctica and International Law: A Collection of Inter-State and National Documents* (London: Oceana, 1988), vol. III, pp. 115–37.

[6] See Royal Decree of 14 January 1939, reproduced and translated into English in Bush, *Antarctica and International Law*, vol. III, pp. 143–6.

[7] See O. G. Skagestad, *Norsk polarpolitikk: Hovedtrekk og utviklingslinjer 1905–1974* (Norwegian Polar Policy: Main Features and Developments 1905–1974) (Oslo: Dreyer, 1975), p. 96.

that research was more or less the only kind of presence Norway could mount in the Antarctic, and should for that reason be promoted.[8]

On the other hand, Norway has always been a fairly *dispassionate* claimant. The government was rather reluctant to put forward a claim in the first place, and, since then, a quite low posture has been maintained. It was a courteous Norwegian request in 1906 about the status of certain sub-Antarctic islands which gave rise to the first British sovereignty claim in the area.[9] Likewise, there was no move on the part of the Norwegian government to take territorial advantage of Amundsen's expedition to the Pole, which had included the exploration of considerable areas on the Antarctic plateau. With the implicit position that discovery alone forms an insufficient basis for sovereignty, a general open-door policy was pursued.[10] The Norwegian mainland claim is also unique in several ways. First, unlike other Antarctic claims, it makes explicit mention only of the coastal areas, defining neither a southern nor a northern limit. Second, the Royal Decree establishing the claim explicitly states that it does not seek to exclude non-Norwegians from operating in the adjacent sea area. And third, the Decree avoids reference to the sector theory which to a varying extent is applied by other states in order to support an extension of their claims southwards towards the Pole.

The historic roots of this restraint regarding sovereignty are to a large extent found in the territorial disputes in which Norway has been involved in the *Arctic*. A conservative view on the definition of effective occupation was consistent with Norway's rejection of the Danish claim to Eastern Greenland.[11] And the sector theory was unattractive because it was applied by the Soviet Union when claiming sovereignty over Franz Josef Land.[12] Even today Norway considers the sector theory untenable,

[8] See *St.meld. 28 (1988–89), Om forskning* (On Scientific Research) (Oslo: Norwegian Ministry of Cultural and Scientific Affairs), p. 46.

[9] See P. J. Beck, 'British Antarctic Policy in the Early 20th Century', *Polar Record*, vol. 21, no. 134, 1983, pp. 476–7.

[10] See Skagestad, *Norsk polarpolitikk*, p. 123.

[11] Partly because of the medieval Norse settlements in the western parts of the island, even Eastern Greenland commanded strong nationalist sentiments in Norway in the 1920s. From the 1880s, Norwegian hunters had occasionally spent the winter in Eastern Greenland. This activity intensified in the 1920s, and in 1931 a group of Norwegians laid claim to the area which was later confirmed by the government. This was followed up with considerable scientific activity during the Second Polar Year. In 1933, Norway yielded to a ruling by the Permanent Court of International Justice that Denmark had sovereignty over the entire territory of Greenland (See *Eastern Greenland Case (Denmark v. Norway) Judgment, 1933*, Permanent Court of International Justice Series A-B, no. 53).

[12] The sector principle was also applied by Canada when claiming the Sverdrup Islands.

because it is among the special circumstances cited by Russia in arguing for a deviation from the median line in the protracted negotiations over delimitation in the Barents Sea.[13]

Another signal that Norway's claim is a moderate one is the fact that it is expressed in the Dependencies Act, implying that parts of Norwegian legislation and administrative ordinances do not cover the Antarctic unless explicitly stated. Hence, unlike the Chilean position,[14] and unlike its own policy in the Arctic case of Svalbard, Norway does not emphasise that Antarctic areas have a status similar to the territorial core of the state. On the contrary, when presenting the Antarctic Treaty before the Storting, the government noted that Norway had been prepared to accept deviations from orthodox ideas about sovereignty in order to ensure non-militarisation of the Seventh Continent.[15]

Even in the 1930s, when the Norwegian sense of having a polar destiny was far more pronounced and pervasive than it is today, as shown especially in the Eastern Greenland affair, the Southern Ocean claims were largely of a *preventive* nature. The islands, claimed during the *Norvegia* expeditions in the late 1920s, were brought under Norwegian sovereignty primarily to avoid the risk that Norwegian whalers could be excluded from the Southern Ocean by the accumulation of British claims, further accentuated by the expansionist signals at the fifteenth Imperial Conference in 1926.[16] Bouvetøya is located north of 60°S, and this claim is not disputed by other states.[17] Likewise, while claimed already in 1933, Dronning Maud Land was not placed under Norwegian sovereignty until 1939, when Germany, at that time pursuing a quite expansionist policy, was believed to harbour territorial ambitions in the

---

[13] For an account of these and other northern boundary disputes, see D. Donders, A. Jørgensen-Dahl and O. S. Stokke, *Northern and Arctic Boundary Disputes* (Lysaker: Fridtjof Nansen Institute, 1989).

[14] See Chapter 14.

[15] See the Proposition to the Storting, *St.prp. 83 (1959–60)* (Oslo: The Norwegian Storting), p. 2.

[16] See M. J. Peterson, *Managing the Frozen South: The Creation and Evolution of the Antarctic Treaty System* (Berkeley: University of California Press, 1988), p. 34. On the change in British Antarctic policy in the post-war years towards a more consciously expansive one, especially from 1919, see Beck, 'British Antarctic Policy'.

[17] Initial opposition from the United Kingdom was withdrawn after Norway had pledged not to put forward claims in the quite extensive list of continental areas mentioned at the Imperial Conference: see Skagestad, *Norsk polarpolitikk*, p. 47; and Bush, *Antarctica and International Law*, vol. III, p. 119.

area.[18] The waters adjacent to Dronning Maud Land were of considerable significance for Norwegian whalers.

This is not to say that its claim to sovereignty is insignificant to Norway: only that it has never been pressed for its own sake. Indeed, it is fair to say that the Antarctic dependencies have never occupied a central place in the hearts and souls of most Norwegians. Today, the significance of the mainland claim is primarily that it supports political access to and even a certain prominence for Norway in Antarctic deliberations. Indeed, the claim can be seen as a top card which generally strengthens Norway's hand in Antarctic politics and allows other goals to be pursued: Norway's claim is retained and sometimes even emphasised because it serves as a ticket to ride first class on the ATS policy vessel.

Foreign policy prestige: Norway the mediator

A significant national concern pursued in the Antarctic is closely related to the symbolic efficiency of the Seventh Continent: namely the commitment to a self-image that Norway, despite its limited size and wealth, has an important role to play in international affairs. In particular, it is seen as well placed to promote peace and cooperation by helping other states to reach agreement on various issues. This *mediating* aspiration has been a stable theme in Norway's foreign policy in the post-war period, first in the East–West and later the North–South context. During the UNCTAD negotiations on the so-called New International Economic Order in the 1970s, Norway assumed a 'like-minded' role,[19] seeking to bridge the gap between the main contending interests. Likewise, during the UNCLOS III negotiations, the Norwegian delegation leader played a crucial role in

---

[18] See Recommendation of the Ministry of Foreign Affairs, approved by Royal Decree of 14 January 1939, in support of bringing part of Antarctica under Norwegian sovereignty; see also Recommendation of the Ministry of Foreign Affairs, approved by Royal Decree of 10 November 1933, authorising the *Thorshavn* expedition of 1933–4 to claim certain territory for Norway. Both documents are reproduced and translated into English in Bush, *Antarctica and International Law*, vol. III, pp. 138–46. Between 1933 and 1939, the boundaries of the Norwegian claim had been adjusted.

[19] The term, which referred to, *inter alia*, the Scandinavian and Benelux countries, suggests that while belonging to the OECD (Organization for Economic Cooperation and Development) countries, the like-minded countries were sympathetic, at least in principle, with many of the demands put forth by the Third World. It was a part of this like-mindedness that these countries provided the highest development aid contributions in the world, as measured in percentage of the Gross National Product.

organising informal meetings which hammered out compromises on some of the most controversial issues.[20] A recent illustration of this phenomenon is the so-called 'Oslo Channel' in the successful peace negotiations between Israel and the Palestinian Liberation Organization.[21]

In the Antarctic context, this focus on influence through mediation is blended with the wider and long-standing goal of promoting cooperative solutions to controversial issues in world affairs. The *peaceful use* clause of the Antarctic Treaty, making the Seventh Continent a breather in the East–West rivalry, and the fact that the Treaty was designed to avoid escalation of the sovereignty conflict, were cited as the main virtues by both government and opposition when the Treaty passed the Storting.[22] Since then, in the Norwegian Antarctic discourse, promotion of peaceful cooperation in the Antarctic has been operationalised as support for Treaty cooperation,[23] even when this has competed with other foreign policy positions like the support of political and cultural isolation of the *apartheid* regime in South Africa or Third World demands for a greater say in international institutions.

The pursuance of this mediating role has been facilitated by the fact that Norwegian delegates from the very beginning have belonged to the informal core group of *old hands* in Antarctic politics. Nigel Bonner has noted that in the early 1960s, when meetings concentrated on the Agreed Measures, a small group of countries took the lead: the United Kingdom, New Zealand, Norway and the United States.[24] Although the composition of this core group may have varied somewhat over the years, the

[20] The Group of Legal Experts, widely known as the Evensen Group, named after Jens Evensen, operated informally in the UNCLOS III negotiations right from the first (organisational) session in New York in December 1973. The group played a significant role, *inter alia*, by drafting negotiating texts.
[21] See J. Corbin, *Gaza First: The Secret Norway Channel to Peace between Israel and the PLO* (London: Bloomsbury, 1994).
[22] See the Recommendation of the Standing Committee on Foreign Affairs and the Constitution, *Innst.S. 128 (1959–60)* (Oslo: The Norwegian Storting); and *Forhandlinger i Stortinget*, no. 293, 17 March 1960, pp. 2,339–40.
[23] As discussed below, Treaty loyalty was an issue in the early years of UN criticism of the ATS. In this period, the role of Treaty cooperation in curbing international conflict is emphasised in *St.meld. 26 (1982–83)*, p. 48, in the associated Recommendation to the Storting of the Standing Committee on Local Government and Environmental Affairs, *Innst.S. 146 (1984–85)*, p. 11; and in the Statement of the Foreign Minister to the Storting (see *Forhandlinger i Stortinget*, no. 111, 5 December 1984, pp. 1,642–9, at p. 1,646).
[24] See N. Bonner, 'Development of the Science/Politics Interface in the Antarctic Treaty and the Role of Scientific Advice', in A. Elzinga (ed.), *Changing Trends in Antarctic Research* (Dordrecht: Kluwer, 1993), p. 37.

impression that informal networks among a small group of diplomats is especially influential in Antarctic politics is quite pervasive: critics have argued that in the CCAMLR negotiations, for instance, the real discussions were soon moved out of the formal sessions and into informal 'friends-of-the-Chairman' meetings.[25] Similarly, while emphasising that all delegations were represented in them 'one time or another', Arthur Watts notes the significance of such smaller, informal Chairman meetings during the CRAMRA negotiations.[26] This phenomenon is a quite general one in international diplomacy, but it is especially pronounced in the ATS because of the limited number of participants and the distinctive nature of the issues under discussion. In consequence, skill and experience in Antarctic affairs is concentrated within a quite thin layer of bureaucrats and experts. This also accounts for the stability of their assignment to Antarctic affairs, and in turn, the significance of personal relationships. The point here is that the Norwegian delegates, partly because of personal qualities and partly because of Norway's traditional foreign policy orientation towards the leading Antarctic states – the United Kingdom and increasingly the United States – have usually been included in this circle of old Antarctic hands.

Environmental protection

The environmental concerns pursued in the Antarctic are of three kinds, partly intertwined. First, remote and pristine areas like Antarctica, sufficiently majestic to capture our attention, are often ascribed a particularly high *intrinsic value*. As discussed in the Introduction to this volume, a part of the intrinsic value of the Antarctic environment stems from its symbolic role of representing other areas on the globe with similar qualities. Second, while it would be cynical to argue that the frequent official statements about the need to protect the Antarctic environment have no relation whatsoever to genuine concerns, we should not be blind to the fact that this symbolic efficiency of Antarctica also generates *instrumental* goals. In many domestic scenes, acting 'green' in Antarctica is an effective and usually inexpensive way to demonstrate a general attitude towards

---

[25] See K. Ramakrishna, 'A Critique of the Convention on the Conservation of Antarctic Marine Living Resources', in R. C. Sharma (ed.), *Growing Focus on Antarctica* (New Delhi: Rajesh, 1986), p. 182.

[26] See A. D. Watts, 'Lessons to the Learned from the Mineral Resources Negotiations', in R. Wolfrum (ed.), *Antarctic Challenge III: Conflicting Interests, Cooperation, Environmental Protection, Economic Development* (Berlin: Duncker & Humblot, 1988), p. 324.

environmental goals, and this observation does not apply solely to policy-makers. Its symbolic efficiency has also rendered Antarctica an attractive arena for political mobilisation for environmental organisations in their efforts to stimulate membership and raise funds. A third environmental concern pursued in the Antarctic is also instrumental: namely to safeguard certain functions related to global *environmental monitoring*. While un-likely in the foreseeable future, certain types of economic activity such as petroleum production do involve the danger of accidents which might jeopardise the role of Antarctica as a low-pollution reference in this context.

As mentioned above, Norway does not have significant commercial interests in the Antarctic, and the sovereignty concern is quite moderate. The only significant constraint upon Norwegian delegates when partici-pating in environmental debates in the ATS is their ambition to be able to mediate between contending parties and hence, a general reluctance to assume extreme positions. Otherwise, support for preservationist meas-ures in the Antarctic has hardly been costly for Norway. This is one of the reasons why, unlike the situation in many other countries, the environmental discourse in Norway has failed to produce any strong societal mobilisation for the protection of the Antarctic environment: on the few occasions when this issue has surfaced in the domestic debate, the government has been able to show that its own policy is consistently and reliably green.[27] Norway ratified the Environmental Protocol in 1993 and passed implementing legislation in the spring of 1995.

Derived policy

These four underlying concerns, and the balance between them, have produced three fairly stable operational goals in Norway's Antarctic policy: *sufficient scientific presence* in the Antarctic to gain adequate knowl-edge and expertise to ensure effective participation in Antarctic decision-making; responsible *management* of the Antarctic resources and environ-ment; and the strengthening of international cooperation and low tension in the area, operationalised to strong support of the *Antarctic Treaty System*.[28] The extent to which these policy goals are implemented in prac-tical action varies somewhat, as we shall see below.

[27] On the non-role of the Norwegian green movement in Antarctic politics, see pp. 403–4 below.

[28] For expression of these operational goals, see the statements in the most recent report to the Storting on polar research, *St.meld. 42 (1992–93)*, p. 35, as well as the foregoing ones: *St.meld. 28 (1988–89)*, p. 46, and *St.meld. 26 (1982–83)*, p. 48.

STRUCTURE AND PROCESS OF NORWEGIAN DECISION-MAKING
ON THE ANTARCTIC

In Norway, societal interest in Antarctic affairs has been moderate at most. Since Antarctic economic concerns are a thing of the past and the sovereignty claims have gradually been disentangled from the discourse of national pride, there are few attempts to question or challenge the Antarctic priorities made by the foreign policy elite in Norway. Indeed, of the four themes noted above, only Antarctic environmental protection links up to a domestic discourse with significant political energy, and the relative insignificance of economic resources in the Antarctic allows the government to sidestep the traditional dilemma between environmental and commercial concerns.

In Norway, as in many other countries, foreign affairs are generally seen as the prerogative of the government. As the government must have the support and confidence of the Storting to remain in power, however, there is formally nothing to stop the latter from guiding government behaviour even in foreign affairs and the Storting has become steadily more active in this respect. Parliamentary interest in Antarctic affairs has remained very moderate. There are at least three reasons for this, the most important being the relative insignificance of the Antarctic to the central issues in Norway's societal debate. As a consequence, parliamentarians have neither the incentive nor, as a rule, the expertise to raise and discuss Antarctic matters. Second, there is a strong tradition in Norway of emphasising unity and avoiding dissent where foreign policy issues are concerned – especially when most agree that, by and large, the government is handling national interests in a satisfactory manner. Third, only rarely do Antarctic issues require new legislation, which means that the Storting is seldom a required partner in decision-making; the recommendations of Antarctic Treaty Consultative Meetings are generally implemented administratively. Indeed, the only regular opportunity the Storting has to speak its mind on Antarctic affairs is in connection with the budget of the Norwegian Polar Institute; and usually, apart from encouraging the launching of expeditions to the Antarctic, the Storting expends little energy on this item. Hence, the Storting is little involved in Antarctic affairs, and when it is, this happens at a very late stage in the process.[29] With few exceptions, Antarctic politics is a government or even a bureaucratic business in Norway. Let us look more closely

---

[29] This pattern is stressed also in Skagestad, *Norsk polarpolitikk*, pp. 161–2.

at the way the concerns sketched above are aggregated in the Norwegian decision-making system.

The executive: in search of an integrated polar policy

When analysing the Norwegian polar administration in the early 1970s, Skagestad emphasised three features:[30] polar issues were dealt with by a number of bureaucratic units; all of them were oriented primarily towards other and more general topics, so that in dealing with polar issues, officials were drawn out of their respective hierarchies; and polar issues remained quite peripheral to each official handling them. In general, he argued, this situation led to an issue-specific, reactive and *status quo*-oriented approach to polar affairs.[31] This is compatible with the view expressed by certain outside observers that Norway along with Australia and the United States has appeared to lack clearly structured guidelines for its Antarctic policy.[32] In the Norwegian context, the *integrative ability* of the polar administration has been seen as too weak, and has been scruti-nised by three public committees in the 1960s and 1970s.[33] The prevailing view is nevertheless that although polar issues are special, a division of labour between several ministries is the best administrative solution. The idea of an all-embracing polar ministry has been rejected on two grounds:[34] it would involve considerable duplication of work and expert-ise; and, equally significant, it would seem to suggest that Norway's Arctic archipelago, Svalbard, is in significant ways administratively different from the rest of the country, which is exactly the opposite of the official view. Proposals for a specialised polar directorate have been declined on similar grounds, with the additional argument that the political sensitivity of the polar regions enhances the need for political governance and con-trol, making a directorate inappropriate.[35]

Instead, institutional responses to integrative needs have been of three

---

[30] *Ibid.*, p. 202.

[31] *Ibid.*, pp. 206–7.

[32] Such views are referred to in P. J. Beck, *The International Politics of Antarctica* (London: Croom Helm, 1986), p. 317.

[33] See P. G. Roness, *Forvaltningspolitikk gjennom organisasjonsprosessar* (Administrative Poli-tics Through Organizational Processes) (Bergen: Senter for Ledelse og Styring, Univer-sity of Bergen, 1992).

[34] *Ibid.*, p. 174.

[35] See the Norwegian Official Report, *NOU 5 (1977), Behandlingen av svalbardsaker og andre polarsaker i sentraladministrasjonen* (Handling of Svalbard Issues and Other Polar Issues in the State Administration) (Oslo: Norwegian Ministry of Justice), pp. 14–16.

kinds: an inter-ministerial Polar Committee;[36] the establishment of a Polar Department in the Ministry of Justice; and the strengthening of specialised polar sections in the other core ministries, the Ministry of Foreign Affairs and the Ministry of Environment. In addition, a series of preparatory meetings are held prior to ATS meetings involving representatives of relevant institutions. While ensuring more focused attention, the specialised units are quite small, heavily loaded and oriented predominantly towards the Arctic. At any rate, they do not eliminate the need for internal coordination between various sections within each ministry.

In *international deliberations* on Antarctica, the Polar Advisor of the Ministry of Foreign Affairs as head of delegation is traditionally the key Norwegian player. This was definitely so in the early period of the ATS, when the relative significance of the sovereignty claim was higher and the regulative efforts of the Consultative Parties were quite modest. The growing significance of the ATS as an arena for demonstration of more general attitudes in the foreign policy area has meant that Foreign Affairs has considered this leading role as quite natural. While, as noted above, the Norwegian delegation head has traditionally been part of the informal 'old hand' network of the ATS, the increasingly specialised and technical nature of the issues discussed at the meetings throughout the 1980s rendered other ministries increasingly relevant both in the preparatory phase and during Consultative Meetings.

In principle, the Ministry of Justice also occupies a central position in Antarctic affairs. Its Polar Department, however, is sparsely staffed and has a heavy workload with tasks associated with Arctic legislation and management, especially the Svalbard budget. Nevertheless, its legal expertise is often drawn upon in the delegations. The former Ministry of Petroleum and Energy had a significant role during the CRAMRA negotiations;[37] with the shelving of that Convention, this role has gradually been phased out. Due to the significance of environmental considerations in the CRAMRA deliberations, the Ministry of Environment has

---

[36] The inter-ministerial Svalbard Committee was established in 1965: see *St.meld. 40 (1969–70) Om opprettelse av et polarråd og et stedlig svalbardråd m.v* (On the Establishment of a Polar Council and a Local Svalbard Council) (Oslo: Norwegian Ministry of Justice), pp. 1–3. Six years later, Antarctic issues were added to its agenda and its name was changed accordingly: see Minister of Justice Oddvar Berrefjord's statement to the Storting (*Forhandlinger i Stortinget*, no. 41, 20 October 1971, p. 326). Today, the Ministries of Justice, Foreign Affairs, Environment and Industry as well as the Director of the Norwegian Polar Institute have permanent seats on the Committee.

[37] Its portfolio is today with the broader Ministry of Industry.

increasingly been called upon in the preparatory phase. Like the other ministries, however, its polar section has a very thin bureaucratic layer of Antarctic expertise and interest. Since 1979, the Ministry of Environment has been the chief unit and funding source of the Norwegian Polar Institute, along with several other relevant research institutions such as the Norwegian Pollution Control Authority, which means that it will remain a source of technical expertise on salient ATS issues.

Regarding the planning and funding of Antarctic *research*, the latest report to the Storting on polar research upgrades the role of the Polar Committee. Based on annual reports of a new National Committee for Polar Research under the Norwegian Research Council,[38] the inter-ministerial Committee is to discuss the status and profile of Norway's efforts in this area and relate it both to the priorities established in long-term plans and the financial constraints set by the state budget.[39] Hence, there is an effort to increase the *attention* of the various ministries to research activities in polar regions with a keen eye to better *coordination* of priorities and activities.

In summary then, there are rather few governmental players involved in the development of Norway's Antarctic policy, and Antarctic issues are generally quite peripheral to all of them. Both the specialised ministerial bodies and the inter-ministerial Polar Committee focus essentially on Arctic issues, especially Svalbard. Institutional reforms to enhance the integration of Norway's polar policy have been motivated largely by the salience of Arctic affairs. In Antarctic research, the Ministry of Environment carries prime responsibility, but the issue is on its way up on the agenda of the broader-based Polar Committee. Regarding Norway's positions in ATS deliberations, the Ministry of Foreign Affairs is the key player, though it relies heavily on the expertise of other specialised ministries.

The legislative: benign neglect

When the various *Conventions* of the ATS have been put before Norway's legislative assembly, the Storting has been moderately interested and largely quite content with government proposals.

---

[38] This new Committee will assimilate two other committees and hence join the *internal* functions of research planning and coordination so far conducted by the National Committee on Antarctic Research and the *external* functions, such as participation in SCAR, hitherto filled by a committee on polar research under the Norwegian Academy of Sciences: see *St.meld. 42 (1992–3)*, p. 93.

[39] *Ibid.*, p. 91.

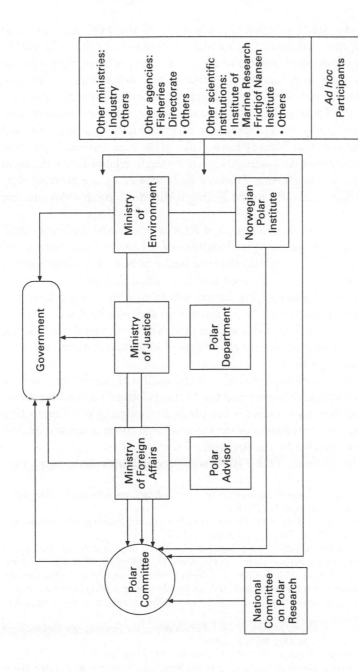

Figure 15.1 The Antarctic decision-making process in the Norwegian executive branch

1   When the Storting indorsed ratification of the 1991 *Environmental Protocol*, this took place in an amiably detached manner. The parliamentary committee noted the existence of Norwegian claims in the area and the importance of environmental protection, commented that research activities should be stepped up in the Antarctic, and welcomed the Protocol;[40] in the plenary debate, only one speaker took the floor, partly to tell about his recent visit to the Antarctic and partly to note that Norway has a claim in the area.[41] Apart from these generally supportive comments, rather weakly related to the Protocol itself, the Environmental Protocol had surfaced in the Storting only in two short questions to the Foreign Minister, one in 1990 and one in 1991.[42]

2   Similarly, the ratification of *CCAMLR* was indorsed with very little debate in 1983; indeed, it is illustrative of the level of information and involvement of the Storting that the leader of Norway's Liberal Party, which has a distinctively green and internationalist profile, in a question to the Minister of the Environment in May 1979, referred to reports from the British NGO EarthScan and asked if it was true that a convention on krill had been adopted, and if so, could the Storting please be informed about the contents of such deliberations and Norway's policy in them.[43]

3   The *Seals Convention*, likewise, was indorsed without debate;[44] noting that the Fisheries Ministry and the Sealing Council had no objections, the parliamentary committee was pleased to welcome this Convention as a practical consequence of the international cooperation and demilitarisation ensured by the Antarctic Treaty.[45]

4   Even the *Antarctic Treaty* itself was received with little more than

[40] See the Recommendation to the Storting of the Standing Committee on Foreign Affairs and the Constitution, *Innst.S. 91 (1992–93)*.

[41] Representative Jan P. Syse of the Conservative Party to the Storting: see *Forhandlinger i Stortinget*, no. 178, 11 February 1993, pp. 2,716–7.

[42] Representative Paul Chaffey of the Socialist Left Party, in a directed question to the Foreign Minister: see *Forhandlinger i Stortinget*, no. 13, 17 October 1990, pp. 202–3 and *ibid.*, no. 207, 17 April 1991, p. 3,043. The first of these was somewhat sharper than the second, arguing that if the government did not openly support a permanent ban on minerals activities, it would soon find itself in an unpleasant role as a green laggard in Antarctica.

[43] Representative Odd Einar Dørum of the Liberal Party in the Storting: see *Forhandlinger i Stortinget*, no. 228, 16 May 1979, p. 3,499.

[44] See *Forhandlinger i Stortinget*, no. 290, 23 March 1973, pp. 2,280–1.

[45] See the Recommendation to the Storting of the Standing Committee on Foreign Affairs and the Constitution, *Innst.S. 186 (1972–73)*.

moderately interested applause by the Storting. The amendments to the Dependency Act required to ratify that Treaty – specifically the granting of immunity and access to observers and the prohibition of nuclear explosions and nuclear waste in the Antarctic[46] – passed the Storting with no comment or debate whatsoever.[47] Ratification of the Treaty itself was also quite uneventful: stressing the non-militarisation set forth in the Treaty, the parliamentary committee praised it as a model for international cooperation,[48] and the Storting indorsed the Treaty unanimously after a brief exchange of views between the Foreign Minister and two representatives concerned about the extent to which it would protect the Norwegian sovereignty claim.[49] Apart from this, the sovereignty issue also surfaced on a few occasions in the 1970s when individual representatives raised questions about the adequacy of government action in support of the Norwegian claim.[50]

Indeed, there are only two Antarctic issues which appear to have aroused any degree of parliamentary concern: the level of Norwegian *research activity* in the Antarctic, and the role of the United Nations in Antarctic deliberations. Of these, only the former involves anything akin to criticism or efforts to affect Norwegian Antarctic policy. Over the past two decades, there has been a very stable concern for the Storting to promote a Norwegian presence in the Antarctic, usually rooted in the Norwegian claim and the management obligations stemming from it. In connection with the budget of the Norwegian Polar Institute, it has been a regular feature for the relevant Standing Committee of the Storting to

[46] Arts. VII and V of the Treaty respectively. Regarding the latter, Norwegian legislation goes farther than required by the Antarctic Treaty by prohibiting also the use of nuclear reactors, and by including Bouvetøya, which is located outside the Treaty Area, in the prohibition: see Bush, *Antarctica and International Law*, vol. III, pp. 173–4.

[47] See the Proposition to the Odelsting, *Ot.prp. 72 (1959–60)* (Oslo: The Norwegian Storting) and the Recommendation to the Odelsting of the Standing Committee on Foreign Affairs and the Constitution, *Innst.O. 165 (1959–60)*; and *Forhandlinger i Odelstinget* (Oslo: The Norwegian Storting), no. 60, 27 May 1960, pp. 473–4.

[48] See the Recommendation to the Storting of the Standing Committee on Foreign Affairs and the Constitution, *Innst.S. 128 and 129, 1959–60*.

[49] See *Forhandlinger i Stortinget*, no. 293, 17 March 1960, pp. 2,339–40.

[50] Representative Erik Gjems-Onstad of the Progress Party to the Foreign Minister and the Prime Minister respectively: see *Forhandlinger i Stortinget*, no. 7, 9 October 1974, pp. 50–1; and *ibid.*, no. 565, 28 May 1975, p. 4,393. In 1980, Anders Talleraas of the Conservative Party was critical of the decision not to support Norwegian participation in BIOMASS, given the sovereignty claims and the possible resource wealth: see *Forhandlinger i Stortinget*, no. 204, 21 May 1980, pp. 3,152–5.

comment disparagingly upon the absence of scientific expeditions in the coming year; or more rarely, praise the fact that such expeditions are planned.[51] This theme of Norwegian presence is almost ritually reiterated when reports to the Storting on polar research are up for discussion.[52]

The second Antarctic issue to trigger some parliamentary interest is Norway's attitude to the demands for a *greater role for the United Nations* in the ATS.[53] This issue links up to Norway's 'like-minded' position in the North–South divide, and the government has been treading softly on the issue. In 1983, the Foreign Minister emphasised the ambition to play a role as mediator, but nevertheless concluded that his administration fully accorded with the ATS group in that it would be regrettable indeed were Antarctica to be raised as a conflictual issue in the UN.[54] A year later, the UN Report on Antarctica was praised by the Foreign Minister as an important means of increasing general knowledge about Antarctic affairs, but support of the Treaty and avoidance of confrontation over it was the main Norwegian concern.[55] This policy was warmly received by the Storting. The Standing Committee on Foreign Affairs and the Constitution, in its deliberations on a report to the Storting on polar research, commented that while they in principle agreed with many of the arguments forwarded by critics in the UN, on balance Treaty cooperation must be supported, as otherwise stability in the region might be jeopardised.[56] In the subsequent plenary debate, all speakers save the representative of the Socialist Left Party supported the government policy.[57]

In summary, neither the minor budgetary comments, the scattered questions about the extent of Norway's presence in the Antarctic, nor the slight debate stirred by the United Nations issue can support a claim that the Storting has been any significant force in the shaping of Norwegian Antarctic policy. While formally its legislative and budgetary roles give

[51] Critical comments on the lack of expedition plans have been voiced in several Budgetary Recommendations to the Storting of the Standing Committee on Local Government and Environmental Affairs: see *Budsj.-innst.S. 3 (1986–87)* (Oslo: The Norwegian Storting), p. 42; *Budsj.-innst.S. 3 (1985–86)*, p. 40; *Budsj.-innst.S. 3 (1979–80)*, p. 13; and *Budsj.-innst.S. 3 (1977–78)*, p. 11.
[52] For a particularly clear statement, see *Innst.S. 146 (1984–85)*.
[53] See Chapter 2.
[54] Foreign Minister Svenn Stray to the Storting: see *Forhandlinger i Stortinget*, no. 46, 10 November 1983, pp. 691–2.
[55] Foreign Minister Svenn Stray in his Foreign Policy Statement to the Storting: see *Forhandlinger i Stortinget*, no. 111, 5 December 1984, p. 1,646.
[56] See *Innst.S. 146 (1984–85)*, p. 11.
[57] See *Forhandlinger i Stortinget*, no. 212, 11 April 1985, p. 3,158.

the Storting ample opportunity to influence policy, in practice the contrary is true: attention to Antarctic issues is low and the level of information generally modest. All in all, the Storting plays a passive and supportive role in this issue area.

Scientific organisations: stressing sovereignty and presence

Of the Norwegian scientific organisations with research interest in the Antarctic,[58] the Norwegian Polar Institute (NPI) is by far the most influential. Administratively subordinated to the Ministry of Environment, the NPI has traditionally enjoyed considerable autonomy. The substantial Antarctic experience accumulated in the NPI, also regarding the political process, makes it a valued participant in discussions on all aspects of Norway's Antarctic policy.[59] It is a permanent member of the inter-ministerial Polar Committee where all budgetary and legislative issues are discussed. Also, the institute was represented in the now defunct Polar Council, which will be dealt with below.[60] Through membership in various committees preparing official reports on the organisation of the polar administration, the NPI has definitely been well positioned to influence these processes. Of course, there are limits to such influence. In the groundwork for the establishment of the Polar Department in the Ministry of Justice, for instance, the NPI unsuccessfully promoted a solution where polar issues would be placed directly under the Prime Minister;[61] and the Institute's fierce and protracted opposition to being moved from Oslo to Tromsø in the northern part of Norway, finally failed in the summer of 1993. Regarding Norway's positions in ATS meetings, the Institute is always represented in the delegations to such meetings and takes active part in preparations. For obvious reasons, the role of the NPI is especially significant where the direction of *Antarctic research* is concerned. While several other research institutions participate as well, the NPI bears the logistical responsibility for Norwegian Antarctic expeditions. It has been a natural member of the committee which drew up the long-term plan

---

[58] For a presentation of the Antarctic research foci of the most relevant Norwegian scientific organisations, see *Perspektiver for norsk forskning i Antarktis* (Perspectives for Norwegian Research in the Antarctic) (Oslo: The National Committee for Environmental Research, the Norwegian Research Council, 1992).

[59] See *NOU 5 (1977)*, p. 12.

[60] *Ibid.*, p. 9.

[61] See Roness, *Forvaltningspolitikk*, p. 176.

for Norwegian Antarctic research in the early 1990s and also in the new National Committee for Polar Research.

In the social science field of Antarctic research, the Fridtjof Nansen Institute is traditionally the most central institution in Norway.[62] In 1973, this institute convened a first informal meeting of Antarctic experts to consider the emerging issue of minerals activity in the Antarctic.[63] It was central to the initiation of the process which culminated with the latest report to the Storting on polar research, involving a full reassessment of the sector;[64] and in recent years a researcher from the Fridtjof Nansen Institute has been part of the Norwegian delegation to various ATS meetings.

It is not surprising that while the foreign policy elite has been quite tempered on the issue, some scientific organisations have tended to emphasise the significance of the sovereignty claim and, especially, the research needs stemming from it. In a 1973 Perspective Analysis, the Norwegian Polar Institute pointed out that Norway's activity was at an extremely low ebb and argued that, in the long run, such an effort would not be sufficient for Norway to retain its position as an Antarctic power.[65] Formally, of course, Article IX of the Antarctic Treaty does not stipulate any such requirements for original signatories, but the parliamentary debates referred to above clearly reveal a sense that the weight of Norway's opinion depends upon a certain degree of activity in the Antarctic. As shown also in the new long-term plan for Antarctic research, this linkage is often mentioned by the scientists themselves.[66]

From examining the *funds* set aside by the NPI for Antarctic activities, including, *inter alia*, participation at SCAR meetings and the launching of expeditions, we may note three features. First, on average, the overall sums are quite small. The major reason for this is the substantial costs of launching expeditions to the Antarctic, as funds available for polar research are strictly limited; and also the fact that NPI has always given clear priority to its Arctic activities, especially Svalbard.[67] The share of

[62] See *St.meld. 42 (1992–93)*, p. 62; and *Innst.S. 146 (1984–85)*, p. 11.
[63] See A. D. Brown, 'The Design of CRAMRA: How Appropriate for the Protection of the Environment?', in A. Jørgensen-Dahl and W. Østreng (eds.), *The Antarctic Treaty System in World Politics* (London: Macmillan, 1991).
[64] I.e., *St.meld. 42 (1992–93)*.
[65] See Skagestad, *Norsk polarpolitikk*, p. 95.
[66] See *Perspektiver for norsk forskning*, p. 6.
[67] Indeed, it is instructed to place primary emphasis on the Arctic: *St.meld. 26 (1982–83)*, p. 48, notes that the costs of a full-year presence in the Antarctic are too great and that an expedition every three years is sufficient.

Antarctic activities of the total NPI budget varies between 20 per cent in years of Antarctic expeditions and roughly 1 per cent in years without such expeditions.[68] Second, however, since 1976, when the NPI launched its first independent expedition in a decade and a half, such expeditions have been regular events, roughly every three years. And third, in the 1990s there has been a marked step-up of Norwegian scientific activities in the Antarctic, partly with the construction of the Troll base some 200 kilometres off the coast of Dronning Maud Land, and partly by the fact that this was followed by the launching of the 'Nordic model' of Antarctic research: since 1991, Norway, Sweden and Finland have organised annually joint expeditions with the logistic responsibility rotating between them. This is meant to improve the continuity of Norwegian investigations in the Antarctic and permit sustained environmental monitoring, for which previous Norwegian expeditions had been too sporadic.[69]

Business and green NGOs: radical indifference

In the middle of the 1960s, when both government and Storting were eagerly trying to improve the integration of Norway's polar policy, it seemed only natural to create a body which could serve as a channel of information and priorities between the authorities and various private groups interested in polar affairs. Indeed, this idea was so ripe that when the government proposed the establishment of what is now the inter-ministerial Polar Committee, this was enthusiastically misunderstood by many in the Storting as one for a broader-based corporative body.[70] While some ministries questioned the need for such a body, no parts of the executive had any strong objections, except that it should be bipolar and stay away from foreign policy issues;[71] the government was later concerned about keeping the size moderate in order to save costs. The Storting had high hopes for the role of this new *Polar Council*, which was set up in 1972 with the Secretariat in the Ministry of Justice:[72] it was supposed to play an active advisory role in the drawing up of guidelines for Norwegian polar policy, in commercial, environmental and scientific priority ques-

---

[68] See *NOU 9 (1989), Norsk Polarforskning* (Norwegian Polar Research) (Oslo: Norwegian Ministry of Environment), p. 31.

[69] See *St.meld. 42 (1992–93)*, p. 66.

[70] See Roness, *Forvaltningspolitikk*, pp. 156 and 162.

[71] See *St.meld. 40 (1969–70)*, pp. 6–8.

[72] See the Recommendation to the Storting of the Standing Committee on Foreign Affairs and the Constitution, *Innst.S. 206 (1969–70)*.

tions.[73] From the beginning, the Polar Council was made up of sixteen individuals, largely from private business and various research organisations, including the NPI. After its establishment, however, little was heard from this body until it was silently terminated in 1986.[74] In theory, this could reflect a reluctance on the part of the executive to allow such a Council a significant say in the making of Norwegian polar policies. However, the fact that none of the few debates or questions in the Storting on Antarctic issues ever explicitly referred to information or views of the Polar Council, suggests that its role was always quite passive.

The latent interest of Norway's otherwise influential anti-*apartheid* lobby was never activated in the case of Antarctic politics, partly because of the marginality of the Antarctic part of that issue and partly because the ATS has enjoyed such wide acceptance in Norway. Similarly, and unlike the situation in the United States and Australia,[75] the Norwegian *green movement* has never shown much interest in Antarctic policy processes. In general, it is fair to say that the Antarctic remains a blind spot to most Norwegians, even those environmentally inclined. In a survey of the biggest Norwegian environmental organisations, only Greenpeace reported that they were interested in or actually working on Antarctic issues.[76] In Norway, this organisation is strongly associated with its global anti-whaling campaign, which has few supporters among Norwegians:[77] accordingly, Greenpeace is not as significant in the Norwegian green movement as in many other countries, and other environmental groups either lack global attachments or are linked to transnational organisations without any marked interest in the Antarctic.

IMPLICATIONS: NORWAY IN THE ATS

Given this interest structure and decision-making process, there are few surprises when narrowing in on the specific positions Norway has taken

---

[73] Representative Otto Lyng in the Storting: see *Forhandlinger i Stortinget*, no. 339, 15 May 1970, pp. 2,710–12.
[74] See Roness, *Forvaltningspolitikk*, p. 181. Nine years earlier, a Norwegian Official Report on the polar administration had noted briefly that the Council appeared to be functioning as intended: see *NOU 5 (1977)*, p. 13.
[75] See Chapters 13 and 16.
[76] See A. V. Hjukse, *Hva forklarer miljøorganisasjonenes saksprioritering in polarområdene?* (What Can Account for the Issue Priorities of Environmental Organisations in the Polar Regions?) (Lysaker: Fridtjof Nansen Institute, 1991), p. 52.
[77] In this country, anti-whaling campaigns are widely written off as cynical fund-raising efforts on the part of some NGOs, feeding on pervasive ignorance, especially among

regarding the emergence of international regulations within the ATS. Norway's general role in ATS politics is that of a consensus-oriented mediator with a basic loyalty to Treaty cooperation. This is evidenced in all four regime processes discussed in this volume.

Regarding marine living resources, the key Norwegian scientific institution taking part in *CCAMLR* is the Institute of Marine Research, which in northern waters has cooperated closely with scientists from the traditionally biggest Antarctic fishing nation, the Soviet Union.[78] Hence, in that process Norwegian participants can hardly be dismissed as idealists without knowledge of the dilemmas involved in fisheries management. At the same time, by having practically no commercial stakes in the Treaty area, Norway has been able to back conservationist proposals without significant costs. James Barnes, who participated in the negotiation of CCAMLR, has noted that Norway consistently sided with the conservationists on the most controversial issues: the ecosystemic standard, the decision-making procedure and the inspection system.[79]

This role can be juxtaposed to Norway's position regarding the management of Antarctic *whales*, which is conducted not in the ATS but in the International Whaling Commission (IWC).[80] Here too Norway favours conservation; but because in this process the real policy alternative is not weaker management measures but preservation, Norway's role is perceived by many as very different from that in CCAMLR. The main Norwegian concern in the IWC is to achieve international acceptance for closely managed and sustainable coastal whaling in the north. Hence, the whaling sanctuary around the Antarctic continent established by the IWC in 1994 does not directly affect Norwegian commercial interests. However, since the principle underlying Norway's position is that whales are natural resources which can be legitimately exploited as long as this is

---

urban dwellers, about both the multitude of whale species and the generally cruel realities of food production.

[78] For an account of the current Russo-Norwegian fisheries cooperation in the Barents Sea, see for instance A. H. Hoel, 'The Barents Sea: Fisheries Resources for Europe and Russia', in O. S. Stokke and O. Tunander (eds.), *The Barents Region: Cooperation in Arctic Europe* (London: Sage, 1994), pp. 115–30.

[79] See J. B. Barnes, 'The Emerging Convention on the Conservation of Antarctic Marine Living Resources: An Attempt to Meet the New Realities of Resource Exploitation in the Southern Ocean', in J. I. Charney (ed.), *The New Nationalism and the Use of Common Spaces: Issues in Marine Pollution and the Exploitation of Antarctica* (Totowa, NJ: Allanheld, Osmun and Co., 1982). See also Chapters 5 and 9 of this volume.

[80] Until late 1993, Norway was represented by the same commissioner to IWC and CCAMLR.

carried out at sustainable levels, a permanent sanctuary not based on scientific assessments of the needs of the stocks in question is highly problematic to Norway.[81]

During the *CRAMRA* negotiations, Norway belonged to the claimant group, but as indicated above, was not one to let such concerns block cooperative solutions. When the negotiations started, the Norwegian government summed up its position by stating that since it would probably be impossible to stop exploitation should viable resources be discovered, the primary goal would be to get adequate regulations in place before such exploitation could get started.[82] Unlike most other claimants, Norway responded favourably to the way claimant interests had been taken care of even in the first draft proposal for a convention.[83] According to the head of the Norwegian delegation during the CRAMRA process, Norway's rather sober-minded attitude towards the Antarctic dependencies enabled its delegation to play a constructive and moderating role;[84] members of the delegation saw it as their task to soften the proposals of the most radical claimants.[85] As an advanced offshore petroleum nation, Norway was also quite active in producing background documents on technological and environmental matters in this area and chaired a number of working groups. As noted above, from the informal preparatory talks in the early 1970s and throughout the negotiations, Norway tended to emphasise environmental imperatives far more strongly than commercial ones when presenting its policy at home as well as abroad. Even when CRAMRA was dying, after being stabbed by Australia and France, the Norwegian Foreign Minister staunchly defended it in the Storting, arguing that it provided satisfactory environmental safeguards and that it could be retained as a safety net in case the moratorium should be removed.[86]

---

[81] In a strong statement of this, Norway did not participate when the sanctuary was up for vote in the IWC in May 1994.

[82] See *St.meld. 26 (1982–83)*, p. 47.

[83] See B. Mørkved, *Veien til CRAMRA: en studie av forhandlingene om opprettelsen av et mineralregime i Antarktis* (The Road to CRAMRA: A Study of the Negotiations of a Minerals Regime for the Antarctic) (Lysaker: Fridtjof Nansen Institute, 1990), p. 88. This was the so-called Beeby I text, named after the leader of New Zealand's delegation, Deputy-Secretary Christopher Beeby, who chaired the eleven sessions of the Fourth Special Consultative Meeting on mineral resources. See also Chapters 6 and 10 of this volume.

[84] See R. T. Andersen, *Ressurser og storpolitikk: Norske interesser i Antarktis* (Resources and High Politics: Norwegian Interests in the Antarctic) (Oslo: The Norwegian Atlantic Committee, 1984), p. 22.

[85] See Mørkved, *Veien til CRAMRA*, p. 117.

[86] Foreign Minister Kjell Magne Bondevik to the Storting: see *Forhandlinger i Stortinget*, no. 13, 17 October 1990, pp. 202–3.

In the transition from CRAMRA to the *Environmental Protocol*, the so-called Andersen text, named after the Norwegian delegation leader who drafted it on the basis of discussions at the 1990 Special Consultative Meeting in Viña del Mar, is an obvious example showing that Norway is often seen as a useful sponsor of compromise solutions. As usual, this mediating role was not incompatible with a clear preference for solutions espoused by the United States and the United Kingdom: at the Viña del Mar meeting, Norway, together with those two states as well as Argentina and Uruguay, co-sponsored the draft which countered more radical proposals put forward by Australia, France, Belgium and Italy.[87] When queried about Norway's position on the moratorium, the Foreign Minister, quite in line with the interest structure presented above, told the Storting that the primary concern was cohesion among the Treaty parties – and that while Norway would prefer a permanent ban, the delegation was eager to serve as a mediator between the competing positions.[88]

The same characterises Norway's position in discussions on how to regulate Antarctic *tourism*. Drawing on the experience from tourism in the Arctic archipelago of Svalbard, Norway has leaned towards a mediating position: rather than new legal obligations, the increase in Antarctic tourism suggests a need for clearer explication and explanation of existing regulation.[89]

CONCLUDING REMARKS

A recurrent theme in this chapter has been the low intensity of various national and sectional concerns activated in Norway's Antarctic politics. Since the middle of the 1960s, a shift has occurred from economic to environmental and more general foreign policy concerns, seeking a role as a visible and productive mediator in Antarctic affairs. Sovereignty has been a stable but always derived component, rather soberly expressed. Interest in Antarctic affairs remains very low, so those involved at the bureaucratic level are rarely subjected to scrutiny in the societal debate. The only Antarctic issues which attract some attention are the ones which link up to North–South issues and more recently, but also more moderately, environmental ones. So far, Norwegian environmentalists do not appear eager to capitalise on the symbolic value of the Antarctic. The

---

[87] R. T. Scully, 'The Eleventh Antarctic Treaty Special Consultative Meeting', *International Challenges*, vol. 11, no. 1, 1991, p. 77.

[88] Foreign Minister Thorvald Stoltenberg to the Storting: see *Forhandlinger i Stortinget*, no. 207, 17 April 1991, p. 3,043.

[89] *Cf.* Chapters 8 and 12 of this volume.

very low level of societal interest in the Antarctic makes it hard to determine whether the access structure is open or closed. The establishment
of the now defunct Polar Council suggests that the decision-making
system is at least in principle open to interested societal organisations,
but also that it requires political energy to make use of this openness.

This moderate societal attention goes a long way in explaining why
the making of Norwegian Antarctic politics is largely the business of the
executive level, with the Storting as well as NGOs showing little interest
and moderate competence in Antarctic affairs. Within the executive, the
Ministry of Foreign Affairs has a central role, along with the Ministry
of Justice and the Ministry of Environment, the latter having primary
responsibility for Antarctic research activities. Since the late 1970s, the
key polar ministries have strengthened their specialised polar units, but
these are quite overloaded and generally focus on Arctic issues. The major
coordinative mechanisms are the inter-ministerial Polar Committee and
the preparatory delegation meetings, both of which also include the
Norwegian Polar Institute. Because of its locational expertise and political
experience, this Institute is centrally placed in all processes relevant to
Norwegian Antarctic policy. Funding has been insufficient to permit a
permanent Norwegian presence in the Antarctic throughout the Treaty
period. Since 1991, however, Nordic logistic cooperation has allowed
annual expeditions. In general, the Norwegian Antarctic decision-making
system is marked by only a small number of active participants; and
among these, there is a strong degree of consensus on major goals and
priorities.

We find a clear consistency between this low level of political loading
and participation and the positions Norway has taken on regulation issues
in the Antarctic Treaty System. Whether the issue is living resources,
minerals, the comprehensive Environmental Protocol or tourism,
Norwegian delegations have deliberately opted for positions which place
them in a mediating, consensus-oriented role. In terms of substance,
Norway has been moderate in articulating its concerns as a claimant and,
to the extent this is compatible with a mediating role, has been generally
supportive of strict regulative measures in the management of Antarctic
resources and the environment.

16

The role of domestic politics in making United States Antarctic policy

CHRISTOPHER C. JOYNER

INTRODUCTION

The foreign policy of the United States today is generally characterised more by change than continuity. That may be the inevitable consequence of living in an international situation governed by growing global interdependence and environmental complexities. Clearly, the multifaceted issue of Antarctica as a foreign policy concern has increasingly confronted US government decision-makers with these difficulties in recent years.

THE CONCEPTUAL FRAMEWORK FOR DOMESTIC POLICY SOURCES

US foreign policy towards Antarctica is variously shaped: by domestic needs and political demands from the US political system; by the processes through which US foreign policy is formulated; and by the persons who manage and direct them. To examine the domestic sources of US foreign policy is to examine conditions within the United States, not merely factors outside of it. To consider that domestic factors are relevant and influence US Antarctic policy is to acknowledge that forces within US society contribute to the quality and substance of foreign behaviour. In short, domestic stimuli are sources of US foreign policy and serve as links between internal conditions and external behaviour.[1]

Domestic influences act as conditioning factors that collectively shape the decision-making process. Foreign policy represents the goals that US decision-makers strive to realise internationally, the values and norms that

---

[1] Interrelationships between domestic politics and foreign policies are discussed in Chapter 1. For a comprehensive and insightful treatment of US foreign policy, see C. W. Kegley, Jr, and E. R. Wittkopf, *American Foreign Policy: Pattern and Process*, 5th ed. (New York: St Martins, 1996).

evoke those goals, and the means or instruments through which they are pursued. The myriad domestic influences on US Antarctic policy can be grouped into three broad categories: (1) the societal milieux of the United States; (2) the institutional setting of the government; and (3) individual traits and characteristics of US decision-makers and the policy positions that they occupy. Examination of these categories of internal sources of foreign policy supplies insights into how domestic political factors in the United States can influence the making of government policy on Antarctic issues.

The broadest, most diffuse level of influence on foreign policy-making is that formed by the *societal environment*. This refers to the political culture of the United States – the array of fundamental values, beliefs and self-images generally shared by Americans about their political system – and how it impacts on the formulation of foreign policy. One can discern these general beliefs in the ideological values and political institutions that US policy-makers have sought to export to other peoples since World War II, especially in the pronounced preference for democracy over totalitarianism, and for capitalism over socialism.

A second level of domestic sources for US foreign policy is the *institutional milieux*. Here are found the branches of US government and the departments and agencies assigned responsibility for decision-making and policy formulation. This category also includes those properties of the United States government that restrict or enhance foreign policy choices by decision-makers and condition how those choices are implemented. Critical to appreciating the institutional setting is the fundamental assumption that a genuine relationship exists between the substance of policy and the process through which it is made.

Responsibility and authority under the US Constitution for foreign policy is divided between the President and a bicameral Congress.[2] The basic belief here is that political power in foreign affairs is best controlled when fragmented by a system of checks and balances. There thus exists a separation of powers between the legislative and the executive branch that works to divide authority and responsibility for making and executing foreign policy affecting Antarctica.

Within the institutional context, domestic influences on US policy-making on Antarctic issues is not confined to the legislative and executive. US foreign policy is formulated through the activities of executive branch departments and agencies, which have tended to proliferate in size and

---

[2] See US Constitution, Art. I, section 8 and Art. II, section 2.

number as interdependence has grown between the United States and the global political economy. With this growth has come concomitant fragmentation in authority over policy-making, with various (often overlapping) roles assumed by the White House and National Security Council staffs, the Department of State, the Defense Department, the Treasury Department and the Central Intelligence Agency.[3] This proliferation and fragmentation of responsibility within the executive branch has also affected the formulation and implementation of Antarctic policies in recent decades.

The organisation of the US government is hierarchical, with distinct levels of authority to facilitate the efficacy and control of decision-making. Not surprisingly, government agencies are prone to adopt policies that promote stability, which in turn fosters maximisation of standard operating procedures. The US government as an organisation also prefers secrecy because this maximises power and minimises embarrassment.[4]

Beyond governmental institutions, a third level of domestic influence on US Antarctic policy is made up of the people who directly formulate and execute those policies. Here the focus falls on *decision-makers* and their respective policy positions. On this level of the influence model, the underlying presumption is that personalities, psychological traits, perceptions and role responsibilities of decision-makers affect attitudes toward and outcomes of US Antarctic policy formulation. In this regard, the individual US decision-maker becomes the ultimate source of influence on US Antarctic policy. Perhaps if even in only an incremental fashion, the individual policy-maker is viewed as effectively supplying the conduit that links US political culture and institutional performance with policy outcome.[5]

A popular notion suggests that foreign policy decision-makers are rational political actors who make decisions according to the perceived lowest short-term costs.[6] For this to occur, however, there must be specified goals, clearly defined national interests, and accurate and comprehensive information available to the decision-maker to assess opportunities and liabilities. Rarely are any, much less all, of these fundamental prerequisites present. In addition, rational actors apparently tend to dismiss

---

[3] See Kegley and Wittkopf, *American Foreign Policy*, pp. 378–419.

[4] For example, see generally B. Rubin, *Secrets of State: The State Department and the Struggle over US Foreign Policy* (New York: Oxford University Press, 1985).

[5] See Kegley and Wittkopf, *American Foreign Policy*, pp. 463–501.

[6] See generally G. T. Allison, *Essence of Decision: Explaining the Cuban Missile Crisis* (Boston, MA: Little, Brown and Co., 1971).

future developments from the calculation of available options. Often choices are selected as preferred because they defer costs into the future or assume that technological advances will mitigate undesirable future consequences of a decision made today.

Personality factors also help to explain how policy-makers manage the conduct of foreign affairs. Decision-makers are human beings, so various considerations of psychology, perceptions and the social context of behaviour must be taken into account. The personal goals of decision-makers may be dependent on the individual policy-maker's own personality and social background. Moreover, a decision-maker's psychological approach to information processing (cognitive style), his predisposition toward conflict or negotiation, and his sense of political effectiveness all contribute to understanding how he will deal with policy issues and other negotiators. Personality may well count as a significant source of domestic influence on the making of US Antarctic policy.[7]

Another factor to be considered is the official position occupied by the decision-maker. It may well be that role expectations, rather than psychological predilections, motivate certain behaviour. The official position of a policy-maker may give rise to certain policy predispositions, more so than psychological idiosyncracies. Institutional roles can constrain or channel the influence of particular policy-makers, though admittedly individuals can variously interpret their roles. Where the United States eventually stands on an Antarctic policy issue can depend on who and where some individual policy-maker – the President, Secretary of State, Under-Secretary of State, or head of delegation – sits. The relationship between an official and his governmental position, as well as that between the impact of decision-makers and their roles on policy outcomes, can produce important implications for American foreign policy. Accordingly, they can act as notable domestic sources of influence on US Antarctic policy.[8]

THE POLITICAL PROCESS OF MAKING US ANTARCTIC POLICY

To appreciate domestic political influences on US Antarctic policy, one must understand how that policy is formulated. This requires setting out

---

[7] Kegley and Wittkopf, *American Foreign Policy*, pp. 502–35; L. S. Etheredge, *A World of Men: The Private Sources of American Foreign Policy* (Cambridge, MA: MIT Press, 1978).
[8] See J. Q. Wilson, *Bureaucracy: What Government Agencies Do and Why They Do It* (New York: Basic Books, 1989).

the organisational structure of, as well as the most influential actors in, the US government that are responsible for formulating and implementing policy goals and objectives.

At this juncture, a caveat on methodology is in order. As noted, US Antarctic policy is highly dependent on the personalities of decision-makers. Since Antarctic affairs entail only a relatively narrow and discrete issue area in the broad scheme of US foreign policy, a few very informed individuals are able to exercise considerable power and influence in the crafting of US Antarctic foreign policy positions. Policy attitudes and resultant positions are determined in large measure by those few individuals. This in turn means that the personalities and perceptions of those few individuals matter substantially.

This study of Antarctic policy-making within the US government is original research. No official documentation, government reports or secondary studies are available that depict and analyse the institutional structure and bureaucratic linkages involved in formulating US Antarctic policy. As a consequence, the treatment here relies substantially upon interviews with several key decision-makers. There is, of course, the inherent possibility of bureaucratic bias on their parts, and the predictable risk that responses to queries were motivated by tendencies to protect bureaucratic turf. This risk was unavoidable. Even so, a type of control was applied. All government officials from various agencies were asked the same set of open-ended queries about US Antarctic policy-making. What became especially interesting was the manner in which every response from the interviewees tended to dovetail along similar lines to produce a uniform explanation and portrait of US Antarctic decision-making. That like responses on each question were obtained from different persons in different governmental agencies would seem to suggest that these responses contained accurate depictions of the ways and means through which decisions are formulated in the US executive branch. The study now turns to elaborate the findings of that consideration.

The executive branch

The executive branch determines the US Antarctic policy agenda. Clearly the most critical institutions are the White House, Department of State and the National Science Foundation. The most influential actors – the chief policy-makers – are the President, top advisors at the National Security Council, the Department of State and the Director of the

National Science Foundation, and, to a lesser extent, the Departments of
Defense, Commerce and Interior.[9]

The US governmental structure formally designated for determining, coordinating and managing Antarctic policy since 1965 has been the
Antarctic Policy Group (APG). Important to note, the Bush Administration in its National Security Decision 1 of 4 February 1989 revised
the APG into the 'Policy Coordinating Committee for Oceans, Environments, and Science' and designated that it should officially meet at the
Assistant Secretary level. Even so, this *Policy Coordinating Committee*
(PCC) functions basically the same as the APG did. The Committee consists of the heads of the three lead agencies: the Department of State
(who acts as chair), Department of Defense (DOD), and the National
Science Foundation (NSF). The PCC reports on Antarctic matters to the
Secretary of State and through him to the President. Some twenty other
departments and agencies, including Commerce, Interior, Transportation, the National Oceanic and Atmospheric Administration (NOAA),
Environmental Protection Agency (EPA) and Marine Mammal Commission (MMC), are *ad hoc* members and participate in working groups
set up to deal with particular Antarctic issues.[10] See Figure 16.1.

The Department of State nonetheless retains primary responsibility.
As chairman of the PCC and lead negotiator on Antarctic policy issues,
the Department of State represents the United States at all Antarctic
Treaty Consultative Meetings (ATCMs) and carries out diplomatic
relations with other participating governments. This includes legal matters concerning interpretation and implementation of the Antarctic
Treaty and its family of instruments.

The PCC reviews US activities in Antarctica each year on a schedule
coordinated with budget decisions, in order to evaluate the current programme as well as proposals for future US Antarctic activities. The PCC
also has responsibility for considering ATCM recommendations and
other related legally binding decisions. If acceptable to the PCC, these
are then submitted to the Secretary of State for approval. The PCC meets

---

[9] Interview with R. Tucker Scully, Director, Office of Oceans and Polar Affairs, Depart-
ment of State, 30 April 1992; interview with Raymond Arnaudo, Chief, Division of Polar
Affairs, Department of State, 30 April 1992; interview with Thomas Laughlin, Chief,
International Liaison Staff, Department of Commerce/NOAA, 1 May 1992.

[10] Other *ad hoc* participants are the Arms Control and Disarmament Agency (ACDA), the
Office of Science and Technology (OST) and the Office of Management and Budget
(OMB).

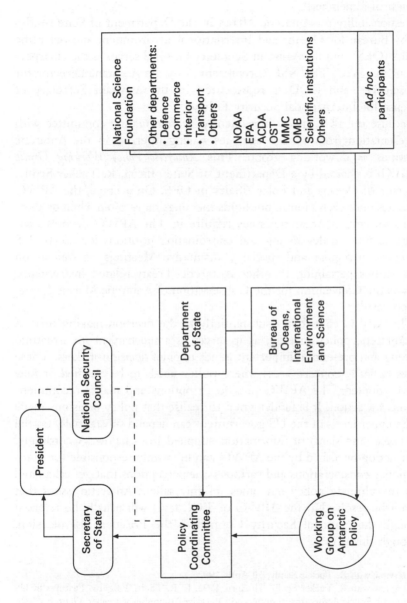

Figure 16.1 The Antarctic decision-making process in the US executive branch

as circumstances dictate, usually at the call of the chairman or the specific request of a member.[11]

Responsibility for Antarctic Affairs in the Department of State resides in the Bureau for Oceans and International Environment and Scientific Affairs (OES), and the Assistant Secretary for OES serves as the chairperson of the PCC. The NSF is represented by the Assistant Director for Geosciences, and DOD is represented by the Assistant Secretary of Defense for International Security Policy.[12]

Because the PCC meets infrequently, a coordinating committee with representation from various agencies having interests in the Antarctic functions as a working group. This *Antarctic Policy Working Group* (APWG) is chaired by a Department of State official, R. Tucker Scully, Director of Oceans and Polar Affairs in OES. On average, the APWG convenes once each month, but holds meetings more often when deliberations on certain Antarctic issues require it. The APWG devotes considerable time to developing and coordinating positions for use by US delegates to regular and special Consultative Meetings, as well as on negotiations pertaining to other Antarctic Treaty-related instruments, such as the Convention for the Conservation of Antarctic Marine Living Resources.[13]

The APWG contributes substantially to the decision-making process on Antarctic policy matters, as it serves as a mechanism for isolating, refining and presenting important issues to chief decision-makers. These issues typically concern areas where policy needs to be clarified or new policy adopted. The APWG puts forth options and makes recommendations for action. It is fundamental to realise that policy decisions made at the upper levels of the US government can depend substantially on the substance (and slant) of information supplied from below. Accordingly, information furnished by the APWG can be mainly responsible for shaping policy considerations and various issue perceptions that get calculated into the ultimate policy outcomes. Highly salient Antarctic issues that cannot be resolved at the APWG or PCC level will usually be referred through the National Security Council to the President for decision, although this is rare.[14]

[11] Interview with R. Tucker Scully, 30 April 1992.
[12] Interview with R. Tucker Scully, 30 April 1992; E. R. Theis, 'Essential Features of US Antarctic Policy: Actors, Institutions, and Objectives' (unpublished paper, George Washington University, April 1991), p. 35.
[13] Interview with Ray Arnaudo, 30 April 1992; Theis, 'Essential Features', p. 36.
[14] Interview with R. Tucker Scully, 30 April 1992.

Decision-making on Antarctic issues in the US government is a relatively consistent process. The APWG is a standing working group of
the PCC whose membership composition is determined by the particular
issue.[15] Policy decisions on Antarctica originate largely in the APWG.[16]
Decisions are by consensus. This is important to bear in mind. Not only
is US Antarctic policy reached through the same decision-making format
as the Antarctic Treaty itself, but it is arrived at through holistic agreement, rather than majority vote.

Policy questions can also originate from individual policy-makers in
OES involved with Antarctic issues, or they can arise from informal contacts with other individuals in the inter-agency process. Sometimes a foreign country makes a suggestion or wants the US to support a particular
measure, which in turn prompts a US policy initiative. US policy can
also originate from concerns and deliberations in the National Science
Foundation.[17]

While the Department of State is the lead agency on Antarctic policy,
the focus for US Antarctic operations 'on the ice', including management
of the US Antarctic Research Program, is the National Science Foundation. With its pre-eminent role in operations on the continent and,
more importantly, its control over the budget of US Antarctic research,
NSF maintains a prominent role in Antarctic affairs.[18]

US Antarctic policy appears to be generally formulated in an adaptive
fashion, although the essential elements of that policy have been laid out,
are agreed upon and have been constant for thirty years now.[19] To the
extent that incremental changes have occurred, they have come from the
extension of that Antarctic policy abroad. US Antarctic policy is well considered, debated and discussed; moreover, it is constructed upon decisions
taken or discussed in previous meetings. Thus, US Antarctic policy may
be modified incrementally, but the process of policy formulation is an
inter-agency process that proceeds through consensus and consensus-
building.[20]

---

[15] Interview with Ray Arnaudo, 30 April 1992.
[16] Interview with R. Tucker Scully, 30 April 1992.
[17] Interview with Ray Arnaudo, 30 April 1992; interview with Thomas Laughlin, 1 May
1992.
[18] Interview with John B. Talmadge, Head, Polar Coordinator and Information Section,
Polar Programs, National Science Foundation, 14 May 1992.
[19] Interview with R. Tucker Scully, 30 April 1992.
[20] Interview with R. Tucker Scully, 30 April 1992; interview with Thomas Laughlin, 1 May
1992.

During the decision-making process in the US government, turf battles over inter-agency interests naturally occur, though they are usually confined to the APWG. Personalities also become intertwined in issue positions, as might be expected in an inter-agency process of debate and deliberation. But issues have not become acutely emotional or made public. People involved in the APWG who work on Antarctic questions are genuinely interested in the subject area. This commitment generally outweighs bureaucratic concerns and tends to mitigate turf battles. Antarctic issues thus can be dealt with in a reasonable way, without becoming highly charged from bureaucratic infighting or from conflicting inter-agency political loyalties.[21]

Congress

Congress is obviously another important actor in US Antarctic policy formulation. Congress authorises appropriations and passes legislation to effect US Antarctic policy and implement programmes. The Senate Foreign Relations Committee supplies advice and consent for treaties that have been signed by the executive. Moreover, Congressional committees hold hearings on the oversight of Antarctic matters. These formal gatherings serve as occasional fora for public discussion of Antarctic issues and at times play an important role in Antarctic affairs. On balance, however, the impact of Congress on the formulation of US Antarctic policy is relatively modest. Antarctic issues are regularly not salient to most Congressmen, much less the American voter. As a consequence, chief US decision-makers on Antarctic questions retain a reasonably insulated position in designing and setting Antarctic-related policy.

The domestic political influence of Congress on US Antarctic policy was, however, activated during 1990 by its handling of the Antarctic minerals issue. Wielding the instruments of its institutional influence – joint resolutions, public hearings, public statements by congressmen and adopted legislation – the 101st Congress became a salient political force in shaping the course of US foreign policy on the minerals question for Antarctica.

The 101st Congress actually assumed an unusually active role in exerting its authority to effect Antarctic policy.[22] During 1989–90, Congress

---

[21] Interview with R. Tucker Scully, 30 April 1992.

[22] An insightful treatment of these Congressional actions is provided in J. Bondareff, 'The Congress Acts to Protect Antarctica', *Territorial Sea Journal*, vol. 1, no. 2, 1991, pp. 223–44, on which portions of the following analysis rely.

took decisive action to protect the continent from potentially adverse effects of mining and began to examine the environmental practices of federal agencies in Antarctica. Unlike the previous Congress when no bills pertaining to Antarctica were offered, during the 101st Congress, five bills and four resolutions were introduced on the subject of Antarctica. Why this sudden surge of interest in the remote, desolate frozen south polar region? Several answers are apparent.

In the first place, public attention in the United States had been focused on Antarctica since the early 1980s. No doubt one reason for this public prominence had been detection since 1985 of the existence each spring of an 'ozone hole' above Antarctica, i.e. re-occurring depletion of portions of the ozone layer over the continent. Clearly another reason for public interest in Antarctica has been the growing awareness of environmental interdependence in the world. In the United States during 1990, some major periodicals featured cover stories on Antarctica, which contributed to focusing public attention on environmental problems affecting the continent. Highlighted prominently among these concerns was the prospect that mining for Antarctic minerals and hydrocarbons might become a serious consideration. This notion was propelled by successful negotiation among the Antarctic Treaty Consultative Parties in 1988 of the Convention on the Regulation of Antarctic Mineral Resource Activities (CRAMRA), also known as the Wellington Convention.

The critical decisions by Australia and France in May and June 1989, respectively, not to support CRAMRA triggered action in the US Congress. On 26 September 1989, then Senator Albert Gore introduced Senate Resolution 206, which called for the United States to encourage immediate negotiations for a new agreement among Consultative Parties for the full protection of Antarctica as a global ecological commons.[23] The resolution called upon the US President to negotiate a new agreement that would close Antarctica for an indefinite period to commercial minerals development and related activities. On 5 October 1989, House Joint Resolution 418, a companion to the Gore Resolution, was introduced in the House of Representatives by Congressman Wayne Owens.[24] Like the Gore motion, the Owens Resolution recommended that the President not present CRAMRA to the Senate for its advice and consent pending negotiation and entry into force of a new agreement among the

[23] Senate Joint Resolution, 101st Congress, 2nd Session, 136 *Congressional Record* (1990) S 180043.

[24] House of Representatives Joint Resolution 418, 101st Congress, 2nd Session (1990), 135 *Congressional Record* (1989), p. 46,746.

Consultative Parties that would ensure the full protection of Antarctica as a global ecological commons.

Introduction of joint resolutions concerning a pending international question is a device that has been used by Congress to influence US policy for Antarctica. The US Constitution authorises the President to negotiate treaties and later transmit them to the Senate for its advice and consent.[25] Nevertheless, members of Congress often furnish advice to the President during the negotiation process by issuing statements, introducing bills and resolutions, and actually participating as members of delegations.[26] The point here is clear: reporting out of a joint resolution by the Senate Foreign Relations Committee that condemns a treaty negotiated by the State Department should give pause to the President in considering whether that instrument should be submitted to the Senate for its advice and consent. That is precisely the political signal sent about the CRAMRA agreement by the Gore–Owens Resolution in late 1989.

To bolster legal credibility for the resolutions, special bills were introduced in both houses of Congress that would make the policies of these resolutions binding upon US citizens. On 7 February 1990 Representative Silvio Conte introduced HR 3,977, the 'Antarctic Protection and Conservation Act of 1990'.[27] This bill would prohibit any US citizen from engaging in, financing, or knowingly providing assistance to any mineral resource activity in Antarctica. The Under-Secretary of Commerce for Oceans and Atmosphere (i.e., the Administrator of the National Oceanic and Atmospheric Administration) was authorised to assess civil and criminal penalties to enforce these prohibitions.[28] On the Senate side a companion bill was introduced by Senator John Kerry on 3 May 1990.[29] The Kerry bill, entitled the 'Antarctica Protection Act of 1990', would prohibit US citizens from mining in Antarctica, and called on the Secretary of State to negotiate with other Consultative Parties a new international agreement that would ban mineral resource activities by all countries.[30]

In a strong indication of their position against mining in Antarctica, the House of Representatives on 1 October 1990 passed the Owens Res-

---

[25] US Constitution, Art. II, section 2, clause 2.

[26] See Congressional Research Service, *Treaties and Other International Agreements: The Role of the United States Senate*, A Study Prepared for the Committee on Foreign Relations, United States Senate, 98th Congress, 2nd Session (1984), p. 10.

[27] House of Representatives 3977, 101st Congress, 2nd Session, section 4 (1990).

[28] *Ibid.*, sections 9–110.

[29] Senate 2575, 101st Congress, 2nd Session (1990).

[30] *Ibid.*, sections 4–5.

olution by a vote of 398–11. The resolution called on the President not to submit CRAMRA to the Senate for its advice and consent until a new agreement could be negotiated that would ensure the full protection of Antarctica as a global ecological commons, and closed Antarctica to minerals development for an 'indefinite period'.

On 4 October, the Senate passed the Gore Resolution. Over the next three weeks negotiations among the House, Senate and Department of State produced agreement on the text of a single resolution, passed by the House on 23 October and the Senate on 24 October. The Congress then sent the resolution to the President for signature. The Gore–Owens Resolution was signed into law by the President on 16 November 1990.[31]

Negotiations over the Conte and Kerry bills were more protracted. The bills passed on 15 and 16 October 1990 in the House and Senate respectively, but substantial differences in their provisions still had to be reconciled. For one, the Conte version in the House contained a provision that would apply the National Environmental Policy Act of 1969 (NEPA)[32] to federal actions in Antarctica. The Kerry bill recommended that the Secretary of State should negotiate a new agreement that would 'prohibit or indefinitely ban' Antarctic mineral resource activities. The Administration strongly opposed extension of NEPA beyond the boundaries of the United States, and wanted to retain negotiating flexibility in subsequent international negotiations by not being bound to either a permanent moratorium or an indefinite ban on mining. Consequently, the NEPA provisions in the Conte Bill were dropped from the final version of the text. Congress also was persuaded to compromise further by agreeing to urge the President to negotiate one or more international agreements that would 'prohibit *or* ban indefinitely' Antarctic mineral resource activities. The compromise Conte Bill was passed by the Senate on 24 October 1990, by the House two days later, and sent to the President for signature. On 16 November 1990 President Bush signed into US law the Antarctic Protection Act of 1990.[33]

Other concerns about the Antarctic environment pricked Congressional interest in 1990. Of particular concern was the problem of waste management practices at US bases in Antarctica, as well as marine pollution, garbage disposal practices of US ships visiting Antarctica, and

[31] Antarctica Treaty – Global Ecological Commons, Public Law no. 101-620, 104 Statutes 3,340 (1990).
[32] 42 United States Code sections 4,321–47 (1985).
[33] Antarctic Protection Act of 1990, Public Law no. 101-594, 104 Statutes 2,975 (1990).

the application of NEPA to federal activities in Antarctica. As a consequence, legislation was introduced by Congressman Walter Jones in the House in an effort to compel the National Science Foundation to clean up its act.[34] In the Senate a companion bill was introduced by Senator Gore.[35] While the environmental questions in these bills were acknowledged as important, Congress also realised that there would be opportunities in the future to deal with them. It appeared that the Consultative Parties would soon be undertaking major efforts to adopt environmental protection measures for the Antarctic Treaty System, and a more appropriate occasion would likely come thereafter. For now, critical concern turned on the minerals issue, and Congressional action on both these environmental bills was deferred.

General assessment

Congress does not assume the lead role in developing US Antarctic policy. The Congressional approach to foreign affairs in general, as well as Antarctic affairs in particular, is strongly influenced by personal, local, or special interest considerations. Efforts to treat the broad range of US interests in Antarctica take on far less significance. Two considerations appear especially decisive for explaining the lack of sustained influence by Congress on Antarctic policy-making.

The first factor is the episodic character of Congressional interest in Antarctic affairs. Involvement by Congress in Antarctic policy formulation tends to be cyclical, *ad hoc*, short-lived and strongly influenced by the level of public or group interest in a particular Antarctic-related issue. As Antarctica gains prominence in the news or gets more vigorously pressed as a concern by various interest groups, the interest of Congress in Antarctica tends to rise accordingly. Antarctic issues that are highly salient for powerful interest groups offer incentives for Congressmen to seek participation in policy formulation and engage in oversight activities. Indeed, the salience of an Antarctic issue and the intensity of support for a solution advocated by influential interest groups can often raise the prominence of an issue on the Congressional agenda. Periodic interest in Antarctic affairs and pursuing actions to mollify public interest groups and attain short-term gains, nevertheless, undercut the ability of Congress

---

[34] House Resolution 4,210, 101st Congress, 2nd Session (1990).
[35] Senate Bill 2,571, 101st Congress, 2nd Session (1990).

to assume a more influential role in sustaining a coherent and comprehensive long-term policy calculus for the Antarctic.

The second principal limitation concerns the decentralised character of the institution. The committee system, rendered more fragmented by the increasing proliferation of sub-committees, tends to disperse responsibility and foster jurisdictional overlap and duplication. Several disparate topics crosscut the jurisdiction of a number of Congressional committees. And no committee in either the Senate or the House functions as a focus point for Antarctic affairs. Antarctica is viewed as yet another amorphous foreign policy issue affecting United States interests abroad.

Nevertheless, the number of Congressional committees and sub-committees that have been involved in Antarctic matters in recent years is quite impressive. Since 1980, at least twenty public hearings have been convened by House committees and eight others have been held by the Senate. These public hearings, which are punctuated with expert and official testimony, promote public awareness about Antarctica and can generate political debate, albeit often unfocused, over US policies toward the Antarctic.

INTEREST GROUPS AND NON-GOVERNMENTAL ORGANISATIONS

A familiar theme in US politics is that powerful interest groups can and often do influence the formation of distinct government policies. The pluralist view of foreign policy suggests that national interest is not always the overriding determinant in national policy. Rather, decision-making is affected by the tug and tangle of competing groups as they vie for influence in the domestic political process. Presumably, then, the outcome of the policy process can reflect policies and programmes that benefit specific groups rather than the state as a whole.

This has, however, not been the general case with US Antarctic policy. Environmental interest groups have clearly become a force to be reckoned with in the domestic decision-making process, if for no other reason than the public political pressure they can apply.[36] Congressmen have been compelled to take positions on Antarctic environmental issues, and US decision-makers have increasingly sought to work with, rather than against, environmental interest groups in the formulation of US Antarctic

---

[36] Interview with Susan Sabella, Antarctic Campaigner, Greenpeace, 26 May 1992; interview with Ray Arnaudo, 30 April 1992; interview with Thomas Laughlin, 1 May 1992.

policy.[37] At most, however, these groups have swayed government policy-makers in certain directions on Antarctic policy; their activities have not produced major deviations from the pursuit of the full range of US national interest in Antarctica.

Interest groups have played *multiple roles* in the US Antarctic policy-making process.[38] They can influence the formulation of law and policy as government agencies prepare for law-making fora. Interest groups can also influence the implementation of law and policy as national laws are enacted, or in the legislative review and in enforcement of Antarctic-related international agreements.

Interest groups stimulate public awareness, foster development of public opinion and further educate the public on Antarctic issues. Interest groups may seek to stimulate public awareness in order to mobilise public opinion, which is often a necessary foundation for being able to affect policy formation and implementation. Environmental activists with a large membership or constituency are usually most effective in this latter strategy. Large-membership interest groups can communicate to their constituencies through newsletters, annual meetings, local chapter meeting and the like to explain issues and bring them to the attention of the media.[39]

To influence US Antarctic policy and law-making more directly, interest groups in the United States have employed several *tactics*. First, there is lobbying.[40] This process entails efforts to convince policy-makers that a certain policy or objective should be adopted. Lobbying involves compelling and single-minded pursuit of one's objectives through whatever suasion might be suitable for a particular audience. Coordinating members to write letters, send faxes, or make phone calls to public officials and law-makers are approaches commonly employed.

A second tactic used by Antarctic interest groups is to provide factual information and expert advice. Supplying factual data and expert analyses for government representatives is vital to garnering support for those init-

---

[37] In fact, since 1977 a membership slot on the US Antarctic delegation has been explicitly 'reserved' for a non-governmental organisation representative.
[38] For an insightful treatment of the national and international activities of Antarctic interest groups, see L. A. Kimball, 'The Role of Non-Governmental Organizations in Antarctic Affairs', in C. C. Joyner and S. K. Chopra (eds.), *The Antarctic Legal Regime* (Dordrecht: Martinus Nijhoff, 1988), pp. 33–63; see Chapter 4 of this volume.
[39] Interview with Susan Sabella, 26 May 1992. For a general discussion of NGOs in the Antarctic context, see Chapter 4 of this volume.
[40] Interview with R. Tucker Scully, 30 April 1992.

iatives.[41] During the 1980s, Antarctic-related interest groups in the United States contributed yeoman's work in furnishing information about Antarctica to public groups, the media, other governments and scholars, as well as US officials and Congressional representatives.

Third, interest groups may serve a catalytic function in the formulation of Antarctic policy. They can work to galvanise national agreement over Antarctic issues by sponsoring informal meetings among officials with opposing views so that these officials may exchange views more frankly than is possible in formal conference settings. The goal here is to find common ground acceptable to all sides. Interest-group fora also permit government officials to interact with various outside experts whose views probably would not have been otherwise solicited.[42]

As a fourth tactic, Antarctic interest groups have sought to create an international alliance of like-minded organisations around the world. Perhaps the best known of these is the Antarctic and Southern Ocean Coalition (ASOC), a network of more than 200 groups in 45 countries, all dedicated to the protection and conservation of the Antarctic wilderness.[43] By pursuing Antarctic conservation issues in such concerted arrangements, interest groups are better able to coordinate their educational activities and public pressure tactics worldwide without substantial overlap, unnecessary duplication, or wasted efforts.

Interest groups in the United States have different *channels* of access to the policy process, both formally and informally, through the different branches of government. In the executive branch, interest groups may attend meetings of and present their views to the Antarctic Advisory Committee. The intent here is for groups to set out for policy-makers their views on US Antarctic policy as it is being developed and implemented. Frequent contact with US policy-makers in different US government agencies may allow interest-group members further opportunities to comment on and offer friendly advice on Antarctic policy issues.

In the legislative branch, interest groups have turned to the Congressional committees responsible for funding, law-making and review of Antarctic policy as a main vehicle for influencing policy. Interest groups often are invited to testify before these committees, and they often consult

[41] Interview with Thomas Laughlin, 1 May 1992.
[42] Kimball, 'NGOs in Antarctic Affairs', pp. 49–50.
[43] See 'Statement of James Barnes', in *Antarctic Treaty Protocol on Environmental Protection: Hearings before the Committee on Merchant Marine and Fisheries*, US House of Representatives, 102nd Congress, 2nd session (30 June 1992) p. 164.

with committee staff members on Antarctic issues as these are being considered and formulated. In addition, interest groups may play a role in the convening and planning of hearings. Interest groups can also exert political influence by urging Congress to impose stronger enforcement of Antarctic-related agreements. This opportunity can be particularly effective during the process of getting passed the implementing legislation necessary to make an instrument operative under US law.

Finally, there is the judiciary branch. In the United States, environmental groups especially have increasingly sought to use the courts to halt perceived environmental threats, to delay commercial development, and to test whether national laws have been violated by various policies. Antarctica has not been the subject of great juridical attention in the past, mainly because other efforts through the US executive and legislative branches have largely succeeded, thus making widespread recourse to courts unnecessary.[44]

Several *environmental* interest groups have worked to influence US Antarctic policy in recent years. Perhaps foremost among these has been the Antarctica Project (and the Antarctic and Southern Ocean Coalition) and Greenpeace. Others include the Environmental Defense Fund, the Wilderness Society and the former International Institute for Environment and Development. Groups in the scientific community have also been influential, among them the Polar Research Board and BIOMASS, particularly during the CCAMLR negotiations in the late 1970s.[45]

The most effective strategy used by environmental interest groups on US policy-makers is 'the force of pure reason'.[46] The ability to understand Antarctic issues and discuss them in a reasoned, intelligent manner has sway with policy-makers.[47] Interest-group attempts to intensify pressure by creating a highly charged political climate have only limited impacts, and often those are negative.

That the *media* play a prominent role in shaping public opinion and hence foreign policy formulation is often presumed. Interestingly, according to some US Antarctic policy-makers, the most influential media force pertaining to Antarctic policy in recent years has been *The National Geo-*

---

[44] Kimball, 'The Role of NGOs', pp. 51–2.
[45] Interview with R. Tucker Scully, 30 April 1992; interview with Ray Arnaudo, 30 April 1992.
[46] Interview with Ray Arnaudo, 30 April 1992.
[47] Interview with Thomas Laughlin, 1 May 1992.

graphic magazine.[48] Other US policy-makers give little credit to the daily press or media in general for positively influencing US Antarctic policy. For example, press coverage of the minerals issue in the United States has been described as 'atrocious' and driven by sensationalism rather than accurate reporting. As perceived by US policy-makers, such slanted misrepresentation of political or geophysical facts tends to alienate respect for the media's influence, not enhance it.[49]

Interest groups have more direct influence than the media on policy formulation. Though environmental interest groups certainly exert domestic political influence on the formulation of US Antarctic policies, they have been less than successful in forcing those policies to fully meet their espoused environmental objectives – perhaps because the US government maintains a well-articulated Antarctic policy that relates US goals in the region to a wide range of interests. This approach clashes with that of environmental pressure groups which assert a narrower perspective and focus mostly on a single interest. Environmental groups tend to put a high value on environmental protection, while exhibiting a willingness to depreciate other interests for the sake of preserving the natural Antarctic environment.

Another significant force in Antarctic affairs is the *polar scientific community*.[50] Though less strident and less cohesive than organised interest groups, scientists may be among the most politically influential interest groups in the formulation of US Antarctic policy. Membership on the Advisory Committee for Polar Programs permits the scientific community to exert special leverage over US Antarctic affairs. This committee, established by the National Science Foundation in 1977, today consists of twelve polar scientists from each of the five scientific disciplines in which the Division of Polar Affairs supports research. The committee's principal purpose is to provide oversight of management and programme balance in the Division's Arctic and Antarctic programmes.[51]

---

[48] Interview with Ray Arnaudo, 30 April 1992. Interview with Thomas Laughlin, 1 May 1992.

[49] Interview with R. Tucker Scully, 30 April 1992. Not surprisingly, interest groups that use a media strategy to develop constituencies among both the public and the press on Antarctic issues tend to be blamed for slanted media coverage. Interview with Susan Sabella, 26 May 1992.

[50] Interview with John B. Talmadge, 14 May 1992; interview with R. Tucker Scully, 30 April 1992; interview with Thomas Laughlin, 1 May 1992.

[51] Interview with John B. Talmadge, 14 May 1992.

ASSESSMENT

The central thrusts of American Antarctic policy have shifted according to how changes in the international system have been perceived by policy-makers as affecting US national interests. During the 1950s, US policy toward the Antarctic was motivated by a strategic desire to counter the Soviet Union's mounting influence in the region, as well as by the hope to maintain the region as a preserve for scientific research. During the 1960s and 1970s, emphasis was placed on the need to conserve flora and fauna on the continent, as well as the need to protect and conserve living marine resources. During the 1980s, the pre-eminent policy theme concerned the need for and negotiation of a regime to regulate the possible development of mineral resources that might be discovered on or around the continent. In the 1990s, the direction of US policy once again shifted, this time toward a course supporting the broad protection and preservation of wilderness values, as well as the conservation of living and non-living resources throughout the Antarctic.

The domestic sources of political influence that impact most on the making of US Antarctic policy are the government, environmental interest groups, the Congress and the academic scientific community.[52] The US government clearly retains primary influence in the policy-making process. Since there is no Antarctic Department *per se*, all governmental agencies with interests in the Antarctic have policy-making input through the APWG inter-agency process. This process is important, as it balances, brokers and mitigates bureaucratic interests and facilitates cooperative interaction to produce meaningful policy. The inter-agency process refines the US position substantively and makes choices set by others within broader policy frameworks.[53]

The White House plays neither a pivotal nor important role in the routine formulation or framing of US Antarctic policy. However, when a highly salient issue cannot be resolved at the lower levels of government – as in the case of CRAMRA or the Environmental Protocol – then the National Security Council, Office of Management and Budget, and White House staff may become involved.

Congress does have certain powers that can impact upon US Antarctic policy: namely the powers of oversight, legislation, appropriation and to conduct hearings. But the impact of Congress in the making of US Ant-

---

[52] Interview with John B. Talmadge, 14 May 1992.
[53] Interview with Thomas Laughlin, 1 May 1992.

arctic policy is only intermittent, when an Antarctic issue becomes publicly visible. While certain individual Congressmen may have great personal interest in Antarctic matters, little substantial interest in Antarctica resides institution-wide.

THE BALANCE SHEET: IMPLICATIONS FOR US ANTARCTIC POLICY

The preceding analysis leads to some general conclusions on the nature of formulating US Antarctic policy and political influences encountered in doing so.

Antarctic policy issues are generally formulated and defined through the US government in a cyclical fashion. At least three stages can be discerned through which Antarctic policy initiatives pass in order to advance to policy outcomes. First, there is *agenda setting*. Here an Antarctic item is put up for serious consideration before policy-makers. For an item to become a public policy concern, it must be an issue that policy-makers are interested in addressing. Further, interested parties and representatives in Congress must be able to reach agreement on a policy and some governmental agency – e.g., the State Department – must have the incentives and resources necessary to carry out that policy. Failure at any point during these stages in policy-making process can impair that policy from being effectively realised.

The second stage is that of *actual policy-making*, when various actions are taken by decision-makers on the policy item. In the United States government, the focus of foreign policy-making falls mainly on the executive branch, especially the President, the National Security Council, the Departments of State, Defense and Commerce, and the Central Intelligence Agency. On Antarctic matters, the greatest weight for formulating policy generally falls on the Department of State and specifically on its Antarctic Policy Working Group.

The US government makes Antarctic policy adaptively, in a slowly evolving, accumulative fashion. Both practical and political reasons explain why this is so often the case. Practically, it is impossible to consider all the alternatives to a decision and their conceivable ramifications. To be sure, the character of American pluralist society, the numerous parties involved in the policy-making process, and the inherent limitations on being able authoritatively to analyse and assess all the implications of foreign policy options strongly suggests that incremental policy-making may be inevitable. Politically, adaptation permits participants in the policy struggle to work from past agreements, with shared assumptions for possible policy outcomes. Likewise, policy-making inherently involves trade-offs, bargaining and compromise. Adaptive decision-making fosters outcomes that do not differ radically from past decisions on like issues. In this manner, the process of Antarctic policy formulation can proceed with realistic expectations of what might be accomplished.[54]

The third stage in making US Antarctic policy is *implementation*, which entails carrying out a given policy decision. It is important to realise that *de facto* policy-making on Antarctica may occur in any of the three branches of US government. Even inaction – continuation of the *status quo* – is a form of decision-making leading to policy formation. A critical point here is that resources must be available for influencing the course of implementing US Antarctic policy. Resources most useful in this regard are the traditional ones of money, political support, information and expertise that foster productive inter-agency action.

CCAMLR

US foreign policy has been firm and consistent on the need for a regime to conserve Antarctic marine living resources. Since the late 1970s, the United States has strongly supported the need within the Antarctic Treaty System for a special regime to design and set conservation policies in the Antarctic. US policymakers have been forceful advocates of the critical need to implement scientific assessments and monitoring of living resource levels and their distribution throughout the Southern Ocean. US domestic legislation has been especially formulated to ensure that these international laws are made to pertain to US nationals.

CRAMRA

The United States was among the strongest proponents in the ATCP group during the 1980s which advocated negotiation and implementation of a minerals regime for the Antarctic. US decision-makers perceived the critical need to retain access to possible deposits of hydrocarbons and strategic hard minerals on or around the continent. They also recognised the need to preserve and protect the Antarctic environment. Consequently, the regime that eventually emerged contained an intricate voting system with checks and balances among Consultative Parties and required

---

[54] Interview with Thomas Laughlin, 1 May 1992.

consensus among all Consultative Parties for an area to be opened for minerals exploration and development.[55] The United States assumed a leading role in negotiating this regime, which collapsed under international pressure from environmentalists in 1989. When the demise of the minerals regime became perceived as inevitable, US officials shifted policy in 1991 toward a position more closely aligned with conservation, and worked to support negotiation of the Madrid Environmental Protocol.

Tourism

The United States formulated and has maintained a firm position on the issue of tourism throughout 1992–4. In the US view, the Madrid Protocol comprehensively applies to all activities by all Consultative Parties in the Antarctic, which meant there was no need for any new special instrument to regulate tourism. A special tourism annex might imply either the inadequacy of the Protocol, or unnecessarily duplicate its authority. Significantly, the US view was to prevail in the debate over the need for a special tourism annex. There will not be such an annex, at least for the foreseeable future. The Environmental Protocol will suffice for setting guidelines for tour organisers who sponsor visits to the Antarctic.

CONCLUDING REMARKS

The United States is a pluralist democracy. Public policy is determined in large part through bargaining, compromise and negotiation among various groups in society. This group activity emerges as a salient domestic political variable in influencing the public policy process. Interestingly, and perhaps not paradoxically, much the same can be concluded about domestic political forces on the making of Antarctic policy in the US government. The making of Antarctic policy largely through consensus-building in the American government – particularly in the Antarctic Policy Working Group, but also through Congress and the activities of domestic environmental interest groups – goes far toward capturing the essence of that domestic pluralistic political experience.

[55] See also Chapters 6 and 10.

Conclusions

OLAV SCHRAM STOKKE AND DAVOR VIDAS

This book has examined the effectiveness and legitimacy of the Antarctic Treaty System by analysis carried out at three levels. In Part II, we scrutinised the international setting of Treaty cooperation, highlighting tensions and compatibility between the ATS and the wider international community regarding salient norms and decision-making structures. A domestic counterpart to this was provided in Part V, through in-depth case studies of the interest and decision-making patterns of four Consultative Parties to the Antarctic Treaty. And in Parts III and IV, we have tried to bring out how these wider international and domestic settings influence the effectiveness and legitimacy of individual ATS regimes. The purpose of this final chapter is to draw these threads together.

THE INTERNATIONAL COMMUNITY AND CHANGES IN THE ATS

While the ATS started out as a governance system involving only a dozen states, gradually it became a matter of global concern. We have seen in Part II of this book that external challenges to the system were first voiced by the environmental lobby in the 1970s, when resource management surfaced on the ATS agenda. The challenge grew more severe in the early 1980s, when a group of mainly developing countries in the UN General Assembly attempted to link the Antarctic discourse to the wider North–South debate; and it was fuelled further by the new environmental wave later in that decade.

Over the years, however, as shown in Chapter 2, the arrow point of external critique has become increasingly blunt. The challenge from developing countries has softened considerably since consensus on the 'Question of Antarctica' in the UN was shattered in 1985. As noted in the Introduction, the most recent General Assembly resolution[1] re-

---

[1] UN General Assembly resolution 49/80, of 15 December 1994.

432

established consensus on the 'Question of Antarctica' in the UN, and focused instead on the positive achievements of the ATS, going a long way towards encouraging the Consultative Parties of the Antarctic Treaty to continue along the avenue chosen. And while they still tend to remain critical, the most salient environmental NGOs have moved from vehement attacks on the ATS to overall support and cooperation.

The main reason for this development is that – beginning back in the 1970s but accelerating during the past decade – the ATS has changed significantly. On the *normative* side, environmental protection has become a steadily more weighty element alongside the two original principles of the Treaty: peaceful purposes and scientific research. This process culminated in the adoption of the 1991 Environmental Protocol. With the ATS turning increasingly preservationist, it becomes more difficult to file charges of excessive resource orientation – and this change also undermines the argument that the Treaty cooperation is an instrument of wealthy states bent on reaping exclusive benefits from economic activity in the region. Simultaneously, a change has occurred in the decision-making *structure* of the ATS: participation has widened, transparency grown, and the Consultative Parties have moved to introduce permanent institutions with legal personality. Also, with the demise of the *apartheid* regime in South Africa, the role of that state as a Consultative Party is no longer a target of external criticism of the ATS.

These adaptations notwithstanding, certain features of the ATS have remained fixed. These include, on the normative side, the pragmatic *modus vivendi* on the sovereignty issue; and on the structural side, the privileged position of the Consultative Parties and the unique consultative mechanism. Hence, faced with pressure from the international community, the Consultative Parties have reacted with a blend of flexibility and persistence. But before delving into how this pressure from 'above' has influenced the effectiveness and legitimacy of the ATS, let us consider how ATS deliberations are also influenced from 'below', by discussing the impact of domestic politics and law in member states.

DOMESTIC POLITICS AND CHANGES IN THE ATS

Part V of this book showed that despite considerable differences between the states reviewed in this volume – Australia, Chile, Norway and the United States – quite similar decision-making patterns have emerged regarding Antarctic affairs. While the small sample dictates cautiousness regarding generalisation, this may suggest that the pattern revealed here is typical of participants in the ATS consultative process. All four domestic arenas are generally marked by a high degree of *consensus*, especially on the overriding goal of sustaining the ATS cooperation. The arenas tend to involve a rather *narrow* group of bureaucrats and scientists: coordinated by the foreign ministries, Antarctic matters usually receive only moderate attention from other parts of the state apparatus – or from societal organisations. For the United States as well as for Norway, this pattern reflects the rather peripheral position of Antarctic affairs on the policy agenda: economic stakes in the Antarctic are not overwhelming, and the emphasis on sovereignty is tempered. For Australia and Chile, however, the latter aspect carries more weight.

The *minerals* question had a marked impact on the domestic decision-making segments in the 1980s: especially in Australia and the United States, environmental organisations became heavily involved in Antarctic issues, and those issues climbed higher up on the political agenda. There are indications that the subsequent adoption of the Environmental Protocol, with its ban on minerals activity, might imply a *return* to less politicised domestic processes. In the Antarctic discourse, the minerals question has predominated for many years, and it may prove difficult for environmental organisations to generate a similar degree of popular attention to the issues which remain. In general, reduced normative tension between the ATS and the wider world community supports this development by rendering ATS governments less vulnerable to domestic criticism as well. While there are signs of somewhat reduced attention to Antarctic affairs from environmental organisations, we have also seen that in some countries, tourism operators are taking an increasing interest in the ATS. Together, these developments may shift the balance between industrial and green participation in domestic decision-making processes on the Antarctic.

Not surprisingly, nuances between the four states regarding intensity of concerns or societal interest appear to be borne out in the positions and roles they assume in international deliberations. As we have seen, Norwegian diplomats, with only moderate stakes in the Antarctic and scant interference from the domestic environmental movement, enjoy substantial leeway when elaborating national positions. This is probably conducive to the *mediator* role aspired to by this state: neither CRAMRA nor the transition from that Convention to the Protocol aroused controversy in the Norwegian political debate. Australia in many ways exemplifies the opposite situation: it has far stronger geopolitical ties to the Antarctic and a very active green movement targeting the frozen continent. There is little doubt that this has narrowed considerably the range of ATS solutions which would be domestically acceptable to that country. This is part of the reason why Australia, unlike Norway, especially in connection with the Protocol but in CCAMLR as well, has assumed a *leadership* role in pressing for certain clearly defined solutions, notwithstanding the international controversy aroused by them. Those solutions, incidentally, appear to accommodate both sovereignty concerns and demands from environmental groups active on the Australian domestic scene.[2]

Such differences should not be exaggerated, however: the four domestic-politics studies in this volume all portray largely consensual processes which normally tend to allow participants considerable *flexibility* when hammering out international arrangements for the Antarctic. And here we have the crucial linkage between domestic interest and decision-making patterns revealed in this volume and the effectiveness and legitimacy of ATS regimes. In combination with external pressures on the ATS, as we shall see, those domestic patterns are largely conducive to adaptation of national political positions whenever this is necessary to restore consensus or improve relations with the wider international community.

ADAPTATION AND IMPACT OF ATS REGIMES

We argued in Chapter 1 that the legitimacy of international regimes, or their persuasive force, is determined by whether provisions are applicable to the subject matter addressed and accepted by members as well as third parties. Over time, legitimacy is conditioned by the ability of a regime to *adapt* when applicability or acceptance is challenged by changing circumstances or actors, whether parties to the regime or thirds. This provides a bridge to the effectiveness of international regimes, or their impact on solving the problems which motivated their formation. In the Introduction to Part III, we showed that all the regimes discussed in this book address four basic problems: they must accommodate various external challenges to the ATS in the international community; uphold the ATS compromise on sovereignty; protect Antarctic science from inappropriate disturbances from other activities; and balance resource-utilisation concerns with those of conservation and preservation.

For each of those four problems, we will draw together the legitimacy and effectiveness argument by highlighting two aspects of the regimes

---

[2] See also pp. 440–3 below.

under scrutiny: (1) the degree of normative and structural *adaptation* to meet those challenges affecting the legitimacy of these regimes; and (2) the extent and mode in which the regimes have actually helped in *solving* the problems, which amounts to their effectiveness.

Accommodating external challenges

In all the regimes reviewed in this book, the problem of accommodating criticism from non-Treaty states, especially in the UN, has been prominent. And if, as one commentator observed, 'environmental groups cut their teeth'[3] on CCAMLR, then they staged the real hunt when the minerals negotiations got started early in the 1980s. As noted, outside challenges have focused as much on normative features of the ATS, such as principles for distribution of benefits from Antarctic activities or the balance between utilisation and preservation, as on structural features like participation rights and access to information.

By embodying a sharpening focus on environmental protection, the four regimes discussed here are cited by the Consultative Parties as significant evidence that the ATS works to the benefit of the world community as a whole. As shown in Chapters 5 and 9, *CCAMLR* filled a regulatory vacuum which, given rising commercial interest in krill, was perceived as potentially dangerous to the stability of Southern Ocean ecosystems. Hence, the very formation of this regime within the ATS was an accommodation not only of internal needs, but of external expectations as well. Certain normative features of the Convention were designed to enhance this effect, like the provision for management concepts enjoying wide support in the environmental community, especially the principle that large marine ecosystems should be managed as a whole. Later on, the emergence of a precautionary approach to regulations exemplified the same. These adaptations strengthened both the applicability and external acceptance of CCAMLR, thus enhancing the legitimacy of the regime.

This normative adaptation has a structural counterpart as well. We have seen how the Commission gradually granted observer status to the main actual or potential challengers to the regime, most notably to the UN Food and Agricultural Organization (FAO), the Antarctic and Southern Ocean Coalition (ASOC) and the International Union for the

---

[3] W. M. Bush, 'The Antarctic Treaty System: A Framework for Evolution', in R. A. Herr, H. R. Hall and M. G. Haward (eds.), *Antarctica's Future: Continuity or Change?* (Hobart: Tasmanian Government Printer, 1990); see also Chapter 4.

Conservation of Nature and Natural Resources (IUCN).[4] The Convention provides for open accession;[5] and any among the acceding parties may become a member of the Commission and participate in decision-making as long as it is engaged in research or harvesting activities in relation to Antarctic marine living resources.[6] At the same time, however, the Consultative Parties have not relinquished their privileged position in the regime.[7] Unlike original signatories, new parties to CCAMLR will retain Commission membership only as long as they satisfy the above activity criterion. Moreover, we have seen that the institutions set up by CCAMLR are closely linked to the Consultative Meetings, and the Convention acknowledges the special obligations and responsibilities of the Consultative Parties.[8] Hence, a fine balance has been established between the quest for external legitimacy and the determination to retain decision-making within the ambit of the ATS, thus legitimising the regime also internally.

CCAMLR has proven rather effective in stemming the tide of external challenges. No effort has materialised to establish a management arrangement outside the ambit of the ATS, and harvesting states active in the Southern Ocean have acceded to the Convention. While Chapter 5 argued that this is also due to other factors than the regime itself, especially the financial and political power of the Consultative Parties, CCAMLR has nevertheless facilitated the outcome. As indicated above, the mechanism applied by the Consultative Parties was mainly cooptation – or more generally, they made sure that potential challengers acquired a certain stake in the success of the regime, thus making them less prone to jeopardise it.

The Consultative Parties took great pains to accommodate external challenges also when moving to the controversial minerals area. During the protracted negotiation of *CRAMRA*, draft texts had been heavily criticised in the UN by developing countries and also by vociferous environmental organisations. While in the end the regime adaptations proved insufficient to curtail external criticism, the relative stringency of the normative safeguards in CRAMRA should not be overlooked. In particular,

---

[4] Of these, the FAO is mentioned explicitly in the Convention: see Art. XXIII, para. 2.
[5] CCAMLR, Art. XXIX.
[6] *Ibid.*, Art. VII, para. 2(b).
[7] Out of twenty-eight states parties to the Convention (as of 7 May 1995), only four were not Consultative Parties (Bulgaria, Canada, Greece and the Ukraine).
[8] See CCAMLR, Art. IX, para. 5; Art. V, para. 1; and Art. XXIII, para. 1. For a fuller discussion, see Chapters 5 and 9.

the emphasis on adequate prior information before initiating minerals activities was an early embodiment of the precautionary principle. Similarly, sensitive to the worries expressed by developing countries in the UN, the delineation of the Convention Area was conducted in a bifocal manner so as neither to recognise nor to contradict directly Part XI of the 1982 UN Law of the Sea Convention and the principle set forth in it, that the seabed beyond the limits of national jurisdiction and its resources should be seen as a common heritage of mankind.[9]

As to structural adaptation, CRAMRA contained even more explicit and extensive provisions for outside participation and access to information than those found in CCAMLR. CRAMRA provided explicitly for cooperation with the IUCN and other relevant NGOs, and for the possibility of according these organisations observer status in the Commission itself as well as in the Advisory Committee.[10] Clearly an attempt to accommodate the demands of certain developing countries, CRAMRA's formula of 'adequate and equitable representation of developing country members of the Commission' in Regulatory Committees[11] was negotiated in a period when the criticism of the ATS in the UN was at its peak. Even here, however, the privileged place of the Consultative Parties is confirmed, because the developing country members referred to in this provision were in practice those which simultaneously acceded to the Antarctic Treaty and gained Consultative Status.[12]

Despite these efforts, CRAMRA did not help the Consultative Parties to mitigate decisively the problem of external criticism, so in this respect it proved largely ineffective. As shown in Chapter 6, its final adoption coincided with several conspicuous marine accidents in polar waters and simultaneous shifts in the general national mood in a few key countries;

---

[9] See Art. 136 of the LOS Convention; Chapter 3 treats this problematic in more detail.

[10] CRAMRA, Art. 34, paras. 3 and 4; and Art. 25, para. 3.

[11] *Ibid.*, Art. 29, para. 3(b).

[12] See *ibid.*, Art. 18, para. 2. The provision of Art. 29 referred to 'developing country members of the Commission'. In accordance with its Art. 61, para. 2, CRAMRA was open to accession by states parties to the Antarctic Treaty. In order for a party to CRAMRA to become a member of the Commission, it would have either to be an ATCP (Art. 18, para. 2(a)) or to satisfy an activity criterion, as formulated in Art. 18, para. 2(b) and (c). Hence, 'developing country members' were actually limited to a small group of developing countries that were parties to the Antarctic Treaty capable of fulfilling the requirements of that provision – and these in practice already enjoyed consultative status under the Antarctic Treaty. This interpretation is supported by the Final Act of the Fourth Special Antarctic Treaty Consultative Meeting on Antarctic Mineral Resources, which states that Art. 29 'reflected the balance between developed and developing Consultative Parties at the date of the adoption of the Convention'.

and this enabled critics of this regime, both within the ATS and outside, to break the carefully forged consensus on minerals and dismiss the regime more rapidly than anyone had thought possible.[13]

Therefore, the *Environmental Protocol* is a far clearer example of effective external accommodation, at least in the short term. The ban on minerals activity removed the paramount target of external criticism. More generally, the codification and development of a comprehensive environmental protection system met a long-standing demand of the non-governmental environmental community, which in the preceding years had been voiced in the UN by developing countries as well.

On the structural side, the Protocol takes the cue of the ATS resource conventions, providing for the establishment of a Committee for Environmental Protection (CEP) and the possibility of granting observer status to relevant inter-governmental organisations and NGOs.[14] On the other hand, as in the preceding conventions, there are limits to the willingness of the Consultative Parties to accommodate external critics. The Committee is closely tied to the consultative machinery: it grants membership to all the twenty-six Consultative Parties;[15] and whereas the main function of the Committee is to supply the Consultative Meetings with scientific and technical advice, decision-making remains in the latter forum.[16]

Concerning effectiveness, we noted above that the Protocol has been highly successful in taking the heat off outside pressure on the ATS. The UN critique has softened markedly, and leading critics among the environmental NGOs, like ASOC, now regularly attend Consultative Meetings. While the Protocol supersedes CRAMRA, Chapter 6 shows that to a large extent it has simply adopted the environmental safeguards of that Convention. And since the Protocol at present enjoys a high degree of external acceptance, this could be portrayed as 'CRAMRA's legacy of legitimacy'.[17] However, we should also note that Chapter 7 questions the stability of this effectiveness, because the implementation of the Protocol as well as future developments in the ATS may fail to meet the high expectations stimulated by the Environmental Protocol.

It may yet be too early to make firm judgments as to normative adaptations in the *tourism regime* envisaged in the ATS, since this regime is

---

[13] See also pp. 448–9 below.
[14] Protocol, Art. 11, para. 4. See Chapter 11.
[15] *Ibid.*, Art. 11, para. 2, in conjunction with Art. 23, para. 1.
[16] *Ibid.*, Arts. 10 and 12.
[17] See Chapter 10.

still an evolving one. Chapters 8 and 12 have, however, demonstrated a gradual shift from an initial emphasis on protection of scientists from various disturbances to a more explicit concern with environmental aspects. To some extent, this shift may have been softened by the fact that recently a new external challenge has appeared, namely the self-regulation of certain tourism industry associations. Hence, in addition to protection of science and the environment, the Consultative Parties now must take into account the concerns of an established industry. However, unlike the environmental NGOs, these associations have neither deliberately questioned the competence of the Consultative Parties in regulating tourism nor actually criticised ATS solutions.

While no particular structural provisions are envisaged in the ATS tourism regime, at least at this stage, the approach taken by the Consultative Parties towards the tourism industry closely parallels that previously taken towards the UN specialised agencies and the environmental NGOs. The two relevant industry organisations – the International Association of Antarctic Tour Operators and the Pacific Asia Travel Association – were recently invited to attend Consultative Meetings, albeit without decision-making power.

In terms of effectiveness, this strategy of coopting selected external challengers by involving them in the consultative process appears just as successful here as it proved to be with environmental NGOs in the past. Tourism industry associations are currently highly cooperative with the Consultative Parties and support their efforts to develop appropriate provisions for a tourism regime within the ambit of the ATS.

The sovereignty problem

Like external accommodation, the sovereignty issue is a persistent problem in Antarctic regimes. In order to be internally acceptable, the legal positions of both claimants and non-claimants must remain intact – or as frozen as they are in Article IV of the Antarctic Treaty. When the Consultative Parties moved from decisions to prohibit or postpone commercial resource use, as in the Agreed Measures and the Seals Convention, to actual *management* of resources, this problem became increasingly difficult. Because resource management involves recurrent decisions about allocation and distribution, often requiring inspection and enforcement of rules, explicit exercise of authority cannot be avoided. This in turn has a large potential to activate the highly contested sovereignty issue.

We have seen in Chapters 5 and 9 that the main normative adaptation embodied in *CCAMLR* regarding this problem is the so-called bifocalism: certain formulations in the Convention on existing positions on the sovereignty situation which are productively ambiguous,[18] allowing claimants, when implementing CCAMLR regulations on their nationals, to rely on the principle of territoriality, and non-claimants that of nationality. This bifocalism is implicitly supported by structural adaptation as well. The consensus required for all decisions taken by the Commission on matters of substance ensures that no regulative measure can be established without the consent of the claimants – or for that matter, non-claimants. Even if choosing not to block such measures, all Commission members can avoid being bound by conservation measures they do not agree to.[19]

The bifocalism and the consensus rule of CCAMLR have enabled the Consultative Parties to conduct resource management in the Southern Ocean with minimal impact on their competing positions on the jurisdictional claims: regarding the sovereignty problem, the regime has been highly effective. The main mechanism is diversion of the problem by introducing deliberate unclarity about the agent of authority, thus decoupling the conflictual sovereignty aspect from the actual exercise of fisheries management; and as demonstrated in Chapter 5, this would have been difficult to achieve on an *ad hoc* basis.

In *CRAMRA*, the freeze Article was brought over from the Antarctic Treaty; but, very much due to the fixity of the resources addressed, this regime faced a more complex sovereignty problem than did CCAMLR. In terms of structural adaptation, the composition and voting rules in the Regulatory Committees were the first provisions adopted in the ATS which explicitly grant a special position to claimants.[20] When coupled with certain other provisions of CRAMRA, in particular the fact that the Commission may not overrule a Regulatory Committee's decision,[21] this feature raised fears among non-claimants that the overall balance on the sovereignty issue might be jeopardised.[22] As shown in Chapters 6 and 10,

---

[18] CCAMLR, Art. IV.
[19] *Ibid.*, Art. IX, para. 6(c) and (d); Art. XII, para. 1.
[20] CRAMRA, Art. 32 in conjunction with Art. 29.
[21] On this feature of CRAMRA institutional structure and decision-making balance, see Chapter 5.
[22] In addition, some other provisions of CRAMRA may be seen as fuelling such fears among non-claimants: the direct reference to submarine regimes 'as defined in accordance with international law' (i.e. continental shelf and the deep seabed beyond it) in Art. 5, para. 3, as well as the explicit mention of 'coastal state jurisdiction' in Art. 9(b) – especially when interpreted in conjunction with Art. 5, para. 1, on the CRAMRA Area which corresponds to the Antarctic Treaty Area.

these privileges were compensated in other solutions of the Convention, particularly in that claimants had to forego any aspirations to issue licences directly for mineral activities, impose taxes, collect royalties, or enforce national laws in the territories they claimed. This network of privileges and compensations in the sphere of sovereignty rendered consensus on the Convention highly fragile. Indeed, as we have seen, the failure of CRAMRA was closely related to the inability of the Consultative Parties to address the sovereignty problem in the minerals context as effectively as they did in the marine living resources context of CCAMLR.

For its part, the *Environmental Protocol* can be seen as an effort to *avoid* the sovereignty problem altogether by banning activities which require allocative and distributive regulations: the preservation approach introduced by the Protocol in the minerals area touches far more lightly on the sovereignty problem. We saw in Chapter 7 that this may have been crucial for the internal acceptance of the Protocol. On the structural side, it should be noted that all seven claimant countries must be members of the Committee for Environmental Protection for the Protocol to enter into force.[23] At the same time, the role of the Consultative Parties in the implementation of the Protocol ensures veto power to both claimants and non-claimants, thereby upholding the balance struck in the Antarctic Treaty.

Because it prohibits the kind of activity which had posed the greatest threat to the careful balance between claimants and non-claimants, the Environmental Protocol has been more successful than CRAMRA in meeting the sovereignty problem in Antarctic politics. The effectiveness of the Protocol in this respect demonstrates that the Antarctic is one of the few places in the world where concerns to protect competing views on sovereignty can be credibly presented as environmental awareness, thereby allowing states to be parochial and green at the same time.[24]

This diversionary approach is taken in the sphere of *tourism* as well. As shown in Chapter 12, the Consultative Parties have de-linked those issues most likely to activate jurisdictional questions, like liability and insurance, from the regulative process by the agreement to tackle them

---

[23] Each party to the Protocol shall be entitled to be a member of the CEP (Art. 11, para. 2); since the Protocol requires the ratification of all the twenty-six states which were Consultative Parties at the date of its adoption (Art. 23, para. 1), all claimant states will have to ratify the Protocol, in order for it to enter into force, and will hence become members of the CEP.

[24] See O. S. Stokke, 'Protecting the Frozen South', *Green Globe Yearbook 1992* (Oxford University Press, 1992), p. 139.

through the parallel and more general process of a working group to draft the liability annex to the Protocol.[25]

In summary, as they have moved hesitantly to manage economic activity in the Antarctic, the Consultative Parties have been able to *decouple* essential tasks of management from the difficult problem of sovereignty. This has been achieved by either shrouding or avoiding the exercise of authority through bifocal formulas supported by decision-making procedures which allow states to interpret the situation in ways congruent with their respective views. The nesting of each new regime in the broader ATS experience has been significant in this respect. When comparing the ways in which the sovereignty issue has been dealt with in the four regimes, we may note that a measure of learning seems to have taken place. Key solutions from previous agreements, including the Treaty itself, the Agreed Measures and the Seals Convention, have been carried over and recombined in increasingly adaptive ways as the sovereignty question reappeared in new and more difficult forms in subsequent ATS regimes.

The protection of science

Scientific investigations remain the most prolific activity in the region, and in order to be internally acceptable among the Consultative Parties, new ATS arrangements cannot severely disturb Antarctic science.[26] Physical disturbances are not too difficult to deal with: except in cases of emergencies or accidents, it is generally a matter of coordination to avoid needless interference with scientific measurements or logistical operations when elaborating, e.g., guidelines for Antarctic visitors. Financial and regulative disturbances are more salient. Even in the less politicised atmosphere of post-CRAMRA Antarctica, the environmental pillar of the ATS will remain prominent, also because it is becoming increasingly vital for the external standing of the system. Hence, close scrutiny of the environmental impacts of scientific operations will continue to be the rule of the day, and there will be rising pressure to channel scientific budgets to purposes connected with the growing resource management and environmental protection tasks of the ATS.

[25] The Group of Legal Experts on Liability for Environmental Damages in Antarctica.
[26] For a demonstration of the awareness of Antarctic decision-makers on this problem, see for instance R. T. Scully, 'Resource Management and the Changing Profile of Science in Antarctica: A Growing Pressure for Relevance?', *International Challenges*, vol. 10, no. 1, 1990, pp. 38–42.

Normative recognition of scientific research is among the basic principles of all four regimes.[27] and is further elaborated in each of them. The ecosystem management objective set forth in CCAMLR[28] places high demands on scientific knowledge. And in fulfilling its tasks, the Scientific Committee is urged to pay due regard to the work of other scientific activities conducted within the ATS framework.[29] Similar provisions are found in CRAMRA.[30] Most importantly, however, scientific research is exempted from the restrictions set forth in the Convention,[31] and prospecting is not allowed to interfere with scientific research.[32] The Protocol, for its part, provides that the value of the Antarctic for the conduct of scientific research shall be among the fundamental considerations when planning and conducting activity in the region;[33] and scientific research is the only exemption to the Protocol's ban on mineral activities.[34] At the same time, there are limits to the preparedness to protect Antarctic science from the rising tide of environmental concerns, as environmental impact procedures pertain also to these activities. For the evolving tourism regime too, protection of scientific research in the Antarctic is one of the main purposes: as discussed in Chapter 12, the provisions comprised in the recommendations on tourism until the 1980s were in significant part oriented towards reminding Treaty parties of their primary obligations to shield scientific investigations from any negative impacts of increased activity in this area. Also, their scattered and unsystematic nature suggests that such disturbances were, for a long period, not seen as too much of a problem and thus not in need of more than marginal attention.

On the *structural* side, all four regimes attribute high significance to science as the central advisory element in decision-making. In CCAMLR, this role is obvious in the composition and functions of the Scientific Committee, especially its relationship to decision-making in the Commission, which 'shall take full account of the recommendations and advice

---

[27] See CCAMLR, paras. 5 and 11 of Preamble, and Art. II(3)(c) ('Objective'); CRAMRA, paras. 3, 8 and especially 11 of Preamble, and Art. 3(d) ('Objectives and General Principles'); the Protocol, para. 6 of Preamble, and Art. 2 ('Objective and Designation'); Recommendation XVIII-1, para. 1 of Preamble.
[28] CCAMLR, Art. II, para. 3.
[29] *Ibid.*, Art. XV, para. 3.
[30] CRAMRA, Art. 2, para. 3(c) and (d); and Art. 15, para. 1(a) and (b).
[31] *Ibid.*, Art. 1, para. 7.
[32] *Ibid.*, Art. 37, para. 7(e).
[33] Protocol, Arts. 1 and 3.
[34] *Ibid.*, Art. 7.

of the Scientific Committee'.[35] Likewise, in CRAMRA, the position of Antarctic science is borne out in the composition and advisory functions of the Scientific, Technical and Environmental Advisory Committee.[36] Scientific advice is also among the main assignments of the Committee for Environmental Protection,[37] relevant for tourism activities as well; and if the Consultative Parties agree, the Committee may invite relevant scientific organisations to attend its sessions as observers. Both the President of SCAR and the Chairman of CCAMLR's Scientific Committee enjoy permanent observer status granted by the Protocol.[38]

Thus, the need to protect and promote Antarctic science is clearly reflected in the norms and structures of the four regimes discussed in this book, and this is important both for their applicability and acceptance. It is also important for their effectiveness. The central advisory role of scientific organisations in the regimes, as well as in domestic preparations, enhances the ability of the Consultative Parties to minimise *physical* disturbances to Antarctic investigations from other activities, such as tourism. As to *financial* disturbances, we have seen that one of the impacts of the resource and environmental regimes in the ATS has been to shift the focus of Antarctic science from basic to applied research, with a rising emphasis on various forms of environmental monitoring.[39] The first convenor of the SCAR Group of Specialists on Environmental Affairs and Conservation has related what he perceives as the declining role of SCAR to the growing significance of applied investigations within CCAMLR.[40] Chapter 5 argues that this regime, by assigning scientists to advisory roles, by stipulating the ecosystem principle which calls for very ambitious scientific investigations, and by facilitating cooperation and lowering costs of such activities, has served to support the generation of funds for applied science in the Southern Ocean. By the same token, had CRAMRA entered into force, the information requirements of such a regime before

---

[35] CCAMLR, Art. IX, para. 4.
[36] CRAMRA, Arts. 23 to 27 (and especially Art. 26, para. 1, for the advice to the Commission and Regulatory Committees).
[37] Protocol, Art. 12, para. 1.
[38] *Ibid.*, Art. 11, para. 4.
[39] See especially Chapters 5 and 6, on CCAMLR and CRAMRA respectively; see also A. Elzinga and I. Bohlin, 'The Politics of Science in Polar Regions', in A. Elzinga (ed.), *Changing Trends in Antarctic Research* (Dordrecht: Kluwer, 1993), pp. 7–30.
[40] See N. Bonner, 'Development of the Science/Politics Interface in the Antarctic Treaty and the Role of Scientific Advice', in Elzinga (ed.), *Changing Trends in Antarctic Research*, p. 38.

an operator could be allowed to explore and develop Antarctic minerals would have boosted the need for applied scientific research.

As to *regulative* disturbances of science, there were some worries that an extensive definition of prospecting in CRAMRA would impede applied geological science in the Antarctic. We have seen, however, that the primary impact of this Convention has been rather indirect, in that it served to pave the way for the Environmental Protocol. Although it might be too early to say whether the new regulations provided in the Protocol will imply severe disturbances to Antarctic science, since it depends on how they are implemented, the analysis in Chapter 7 suggests that they will not. As to the requirements for environmental impact assessment, the Council of Managers of National Antarctic Programs (COMNAP) has already reacted positively to them by preparing practical guidelines as to how they should be understood; and in several cases, national assessment procedures are more elaborate than those set forth in the Protocol. Also, many of the new waste management provisions, another source of worry for some in the science community, have been shown to be rather vague and full of loopholes. And importantly, enforcement of all these measures tends to be discretionary.

In summary, the science protection problem has not been too difficult to handle for the Consultative Parties: to a large extent, the relationship between scientific investigations and the evolving ATS regimes discussed here is symbiotic. The mechanisms at work are very similar from one regime to another. The insider position of Antarctic scientists at both domestic and international levels enhances the ability of the latter to influence the elaboration of operational rules, whether for tourism or for the running of scientific programmes, in order to minimise additional logistical costs. By establishing scientifically demanding management goals, and by giving the scientific community instrumental roles in decision-making processes, the resource regimes especially have served to safeguard the financial basis of Antarctic science. Quite possibly, these new regimes may even offer additional reasons for the Consultative Parties to invest in Antarctic applied science: today, contributions to global environmental monitoring and scientifically based resource management are essential for the external standing of Treaty cooperation.

Balancing utilisation and conservation

In the Introduction to Part III, we distinguished three basic tasks in the search for a balance between economic use of the Antarctic and the need to conserve regional ecosystems: generation of adequate knowledge to enable well-founded decisions; production of appropriate regulations to govern activities in the region; and ensuring proper enforcement of those regulations. Let us take a closer look at these three.

The provision of applied *scientific information* relevant to economic use of Antarctic resources has clearly been stimulated by the establishment of scientific advisory bodies in CCAMLR, CRAMRA and the Environmental Protocol. As we have seen, the fact that scientists are regularly called upon to offer informed opinions about the advisability of increased harvesting activities, has enhanced the effectiveness of CCAMLR, especially by rendering the flow of technical and scientific information steadily better tailored to the needs of decision-makers. Also, the growing transparency of all the ATS regimes implies that failure to provide sufficient information to assess environmental impacts can be spotted and criticised by outside observers or even fellow Consultative Parties. We have also seen that, for instance in the development of an ecosystemic monitoring programme under CCAMLR, scientific needs defined by regulative fora can give specific form and direction to the national programmes of states interested in contributing positively to the ATS and at the same time acquiring external or domestic credit for this.

On the *regulative* side, the legitimacy and effectiveness of ATS regimes hinge on whether they help the Consultative Parties cut through differences of opinion and provide a means to realise the objectives and principles set forth in them. Two trends are visible regarding these objectives. First, there is a tendency to emphasise a more *comprehensive* approach to regulation of human activities in the Antarctic. This is shown especially in the ecosystem principle of CCAMLR, but also, as substantiated in Chapter 10, in the fact that detailed environmental safeguards originally elaborated for minerals activities were subsequently extended through the Protocol to all types of Antarctic activities. Second, there is a trend towards a more *precautionary* approach in the guidelines for Antarctic regulations, in the sense that Antarctic engagements increasingly must await evidence that they will not be harmful to the natural environment. Requirements for prior information when planning activities in the Antarctic have been gradually strengthened in the four ATS regimes discussed here: they were introduced already in CCAMLR, but became far more explicit and detailed when elaborated for mineral resource activities under CRAMRA, later incorporated into the Protocol provisions for environmental impact assessment. As shown in Chapter 5, since 1991 precautionary catch quotas have been set for both krill and finfish in the management of Antarctic marine living resources; and the fifty-year ban on minerals activities set forth by the Protocol exemplifies the same.

Regarding the effectiveness of these regimes in helping the Consultative Parties to provide regulative means for such objectives, an important factor is growing *transparency*, which adds a measure of urgency to the meticulous consensus-building process so typical of the ATS. In CCAMLR, for instance, a high level of scientific uncertainty, combined with conflictual national interests, for several years rendered fisheries management immune to the accommodating atmosphere which has otherwise tended to mark ATS deliberations. As explained in Chapter 5, the transformation to more effective rule-making was achieved in a characteristic, incremental way. By using scientific uncertainty as a forceful argument for stronger information requirements, especially regarding the scale and frequency of catch reports, the basis was laid for a more realistic discussion of conservation measures. Moreover, the improved flow of scientific results and the gradual familiarisation with concepts like scientific observance and precautionary regulation reduced the level of conflict in the Commission and facilitated the introduction of such measures.

The transition from CRAMRA to the Protocol demonstrates another way in which these regimes affect regulative efforts among the Consultative Parties. In this case, the transparency of ATS decision-making combined with traditional conflict lines among the Consultative Parties, and deeply affected *domestic alignment* patterns in certain key countries. While CRAMRA failed as a basis for a regime governing minerals activity, Chapter 6 demonstrated its significance for the formation of an environmental protection regime, thus realising at least one of its purposes. This transition was due to the perceived shortcomings of CRAMRA, but we should avoid *post hoc* rationalisation when enumerating them: each feature criticised was the result of protracted negotiations and complex accommodations. As noted, when the Convention was finally adopted in 1988, it was the overall balance of a range of concerns which made the entire package acceptable to all Consultative Parties. The fragility of this package was such that even among those who adopted it, many remained rather dissatisfied with the compromise. Some disliked the Convention because the sovereignty safeguards did not go far enough, others because they went too far; some felt that the environmental restrictions were too vague, and yet others were frustrated that the Convention remained a maverick in the UN General Assembly.

Thus, the chief mechanism at work was that the very adoption of

CRAMRA implied a new opportunity for those critical of the Convention to assess it in detail, draw attention to specific weaknesses and rally support for a wider mobilisation against it. The finalisation of the Convention, together with certain external events like the grounding of the *Bahia Paraiso* and the political strengthening of green organisations in France and Australia, shifted domestic alignment patterns in these countries, and subsequently in the United States as well.[41] Thus, strongly urged by environmental organisations and temporarily alert legislatures, the diplomats found themselves unable to handle the minerals issue in a manner compatible with commercial interests. This forced them to opt out of that contentious issue, which rendered the negotiation of the Protocol an exceptionally rapid affair.

The full impact of the Environmental Protocol on the regulative ability of the Consultative Parties remains to be seen, since it was only recently adopted and the institutional apparatus envisaged is yet to be established. As noted, its stricter requirements for environmental impact assessment have stimulated COMNAP to draw up common guidelines to shape the operations of national programmes. Importantly, many of the new provisions – such as the new version of the Agreed Measures, the simplified area protection system and the applicability of both to marine areas – were already well underway in the regular consultative mechanism of the ATS, independently of the Protocol itself. Also, it may be questioned whether one of the major purposes of the Protocol, to put aside the minerals issue, has really been achieved. Chapter 6 argues that the onesidedness of the Protocol as compared to CRAMRA, in the sense that interests of potential operators are not reflected in the Protocol, may prove a decisive weakness if a serious interest in Antarctic minerals should emerge.

Here we may discern a parallel to the emerging regime for Antarctic tourism: until the late 1980s, this activity was addressed in a far more limited way than were fisheries and minerals. Chapters 8 and 12 argue that by not identifying and addressing the industrial needs of this sector, the incomplete ATS tourism regime stimulated self-regulation in the industry. In both the gateway countries and the United States – home of most of the firms involved – vested interest in Antarctic tourism was allowed to emerge without being conditioned by the ATS process. And this relative slowness in taking responsibility for tourism is part of the reason why it has been hard for the Consultative Parties to reach consen-

---

[41] These domestic policy processes are discussed in particular in Chapters 6, 13 and 16.

sus on how to proceed when they finally chose to address this matter in a more comprehensive manner in the early 1990s.

Partly because it is close to the core of sovereignty and partly because of the operational costs involved, the matter of coordinated *enforcement* practices is a relatively weak spot of Treaty cooperation. In all of the regimes discussed in this book, crucial parts of the enforcement tasks still remain with each contracting party, implying that whenever a state is out of tune with the balance struck between utilisation and environmental goals in the ATS, non-compliance will not necessarily be too costly.

Nevertheless, two normative processes in ATS regimes qualify this statement. First, we have seen that the obligation to give detailed reports on Antarctic activities to ATS institutions has been strengthened and made more precise over time. The reporting provisions of CCAMLR and CRAMRA, the latter to a large extent carried over into the Environmental Protocol and thus relevant to tourism as well,[42] are significant in this respect. Second, by drawing upon and adapting the general inspection system of the Antarctic Treaty,[43] an inspection arrangement has gradually emerged in the CCAMLR Area, although it is not yet in widespread use because of the costs of inspections. Again, there are limits to this adaptation: when drawing up the Environmental Protocol, the Consultative Parties did not yield to the demands of the environmental movement to establish a strong institutional machinery to monitor compliance with the Protocol provisions.

We have seen in the effectiveness studies in this book that these enforcement practices have been facilitated by the regimes under scrutiny. In particular, the nesting of new regimes within the broader ATS has allowed familiarisation with the inherent jurisdictional problems associated with inspection and thus helped to develop the decoupling techniques reviewed above.

The significance of ATS regimes for the ability of the Consultative Parties to cope with the dilemmas of use and conservation has been enhanced by three features borne out strongly in the country studies in Part V of this book. First, unlike the normal situation for regimes governing resource use, membership in the regimes discussed here is not confined to states actually involved in exploitation; on the contrary, such states are clearly outnumbered by non-user states. Second, the economic

---

[42] But see also the 1994 Recommendation XVIII-1, on Tourism and Non-Governmental Activities, and the Guidances attached to it.

[43] See Art. VII of the Antarctic Treaty.

stakes in the activities addressed have proved very moderate, at least within a reasonably long timeframe – and this is clearly perceived among participants. Third, and related to this, even in Australia and the United States where mining concerns are politically salient, industry organisations have not mobilised strongly, either at international or domestic levels, to protect whatever interests they hold in Antarctic resources.[44] Hence, in these influential countries, there has been a lack of strong countervailing forces to the environmental interests in the domestic segments. And precisely because commercial concerns have not been strongly articulated, the Antarctic has been very well suited for symbolic acts on the part of these states, especially the demonstration of environmental consciousness in a region where costs are moderate.

THE EFFECTIVENESS AND LEGITIMACY OF THE ATS

After thirty-five years, the Antarctic Treaty System is alive and kicking – although the latter half of this period has been characterised by considerable turbulence. Previously the domain of a narrow circle of scientists and diplomats, Antarctic affairs have been politicised both domestically and internationally: they have been drawn into much wider debates generated by the demands of developing countries for a New International Economic Order and by the global mobilisation of environmental concerns. We have seen that these debates cut right across traditional conflict lines in Antarctic politics, such as those separating claimants from non-claimants and resource-oriented states from those who remain sceptical to economic activities in the region. As noted, early speculations about tremendous amounts of commercially valuable Antarctic minerals and marine living resources added to these conflicts.

It seems rather impressive, therefore, that the ATS today stands forth as more effective and legitimate than ever before. Without disrupting consensus among themselves, the Consultative Parties have been able to accommodate much of the external criticism and adopt increasingly conducive and specific provisions for the governance of human activities in the Antarctic. True, part of the explanation for this robustness is the fact that the Consultative Parties count the most powerful states of the world, and that more than two-thirds of the world population lives in states parties to the Antarctic Treaty. Also, the fact noted above that economically viable resources have so far proved considerably scarcer than orig-

---

[44] See Chapters 13 and 16.

inally expected has facilitated an environmentalist turn in Treaty cooperation; and that shift has reduced both internal and external threats to the ATS. But while external conditions have been favourable, the growing effectiveness and legitimacy of the ATS is also a result of certain features of this governance system itself. This is true both for regimes which are based in conventions in force, like CCAMLR, and evolving regimes like the one set forth by the Environmental Protocol or the ATS measures addressing tourism. It is time to sum up the effectiveness and legitimacy *mechanisms* of the Antarctic Treaty System.

The *effectiveness* of international regimes can only be appraised relative to specific problems, and we have seen marked differences between the four ATS regimes discussed here in terms of which problems they have been instrumental in solving. For instance, CCAMLR has been far more successful in safeguarding the sovereignty balance and ensuring external acceptance for ATS solutions than in coping with the difficulties of resource management – although even the latter has improved markedly over time. Likewise, while the adoption of CRAMRA has not resulted in an effective regime for regulating Antarctic minerals activities, it was highly instrumental to the negotiation of a comprehensive and fairly advanced environmental protection system. And while the adequacy of the Protocol in balancing conservation and economic use depends on its implementation, it has already succeeded, at least for the time being, in taking the heat off external criticism of the ATS as well as internal worries about the sovereignty impacts of minerals activities. For its part, the incipient ATS tourism regime has been scattered and lacking in focus; this has promoted self-regulation within the industry, subsequently indorsed and confirmed by the Consultative Parties. Thus, a ranking of these regimes in terms of effectiveness would differ, depending on which of the problems is emphasised.

As to *how* the Treaty cooperation has affected the solution of these problems, five mechanisms, or intermediate processes, have been salient in our analysis of ATS regimes. They are in fact ATS-specific versions of the more general effectiveness mechanisms outlined in Chapter 1. Thus, just like the comments on legitimacy below, the processes reported here reflect back on the wider scholarly debate on the effectiveness and legitimacy of international regimes.

A first specific mechanism of the ATS, vital for the ability to overcome differences and reach consensual solutions, is that of generating a *productive deadlock phobia* among the Consultative Parties when addressing politically sensitive matters. Underlying that mechanism is the interplay of external pressure on the ATS and the continued salience of the sovereignty problem. A recurring theme in the domestic case studies in this book is the determination to support and further develop Treaty cooperation, especially when challenged from the outside. While they vary considerably in their emphasis on the sovereignty matter, these states share a belief that their respective positions are better protected by the ATS framework, carefully developed over time to circumscribe this problem, than by other possible arrangements for the region. Thus, previous successes are jeopardised whenever the Consultative Parties fail to address topical political challenges in a credible manner. This productive deadlock phobia is another instance where the interrelatedness of various ATS components enhances their effectiveness. It is channelled into the narrow, specialised and consensus-oriented domestic segments, and forms a fundamental condition for the flexibility which marks these segments, even when the issue at stake may affect core interests like the status of territorial claims. Similarly, as we have seen detailed in the case studies of Australia and the United States in particular, deadlock phobia is important in explaining why the rejection of CRAMRA, rather than destroying loyalty to the Treaty cooperation, created a domino effect among key ATS states which laid the basis for the Environmental Protocol.

A second recurrent mechanism is the ATS serving to *decouple* mutually beneficial cooperative practices from conflictual matters which otherwise would impede them. This has proved important for the ability of the Consultative Parties to cope with the sovereignty problem in Antarctic politics. Certain features of the regimes – like the 'freeze Article' in the Antarctic Treaty, the bifocalism of CCAMLR, the institutional balance in CRAMRA, or the very avoidance of resource management in the Protocol – have had the effect of shrouding the agent of authority when decisions are made, thus enabling states to overcome jealousy over sovereignty and achieve desired cooperation.

A third ATS mechanism, crucial for its ability to accommodate external criticism, is to provide means for *cooptation*. While decoupling involves removing certain costs of interaction, cooptation is the deliberate introduction of benefits for those who support the regimes. The ecosystem principle in CCAMLR has served this purpose. Also, the relative openness of the ATS, expressed in the evolving criteria for acquiring consultative status and the growing readiness of the Consultative Parties to grant observer status to interested parties, implies that there are substantial gains to be reaped for those who acknowledge the role of the ATS in Antarctic affairs. The operation of this mechanism is shown in the widening participation at Consultative Meetings and CCAMLR, in the increasingly permissive participation rules in the subsequent regimes envisaged by CRAMRA and the Protocol, as well as in the openness to tour operators in the elaboration of a tourism regime in the ATS.

A fourth ATS mechanism, important for its ability to protect scientific activities in the Antarctic and also for balancing utilisation and conservation in the region, is to *elevate science* as an instrument by which to achieve collective decisions on various uses of the Antarctic. This is shown both in the norms promulgated by ATS regimes and in the now-routinised practice of Antarctic states to resort to scientific advice whenever faced with controversy. Hence, through the ATS, the Consultative Parties are making deliberate use of the authority, or legitimising force, of science; and in so doing, they confirm and strengthen this authority. Chapter 7 notes that the wider interest in Antarctic affairs, especially by environmental organisations, has served to contain the influence of Antarctic scientists in the political deliberations on the region. We have seen, however, that the adoption of the Protocol renders the Antarctic less of a magnet to societal organisations, and this may again enhance the position of traditional participants in the ATS – diplomats and scientists. And whatever the political role of researchers, the elevation of science as an instrument for environmental management supports the generation of funds for future investigations in the Antarctic.

A fifth specific mechanism of the ATS is that it provides a *pool of acceptable solutions* to difficult political puzzles in the Antarctic. This way, the systemic nature of the ATS, as portrayed in Chapter 2, enhances the effectiveness of Treaty cooperation. When the Consultative Parties enter into new issue areas, such solutions are adaptively imitated in the emerging regimes: the ATS facilitates social learning and gradual familiarisation with norms and procedures relating to matters of conflict. The freeze Article of the Antarctic Treaty is clearly within this pool of solutions, as is the bifocal approach first applied in the Agreed Measures. Yet another example of this mechanism is the emergence of an inspection system within CCAMLR, largely modelled on the arrangement developed in the Antarctic Treaty.

These five specific effectiveness mechanisms of the ATS are also closely related to the *legitimacy* of Treaty cooperation and the regimes created within it. They have helped the Consultative Parties to develop regimes which are gradually becoming more conducive to solving the problems addressed, thus enhancing their applicability and acceptance. With a focus on normative and structural components of the ATS, we have identified both internal and external aspects of this. Our aim has not been to conclude sweepingly that the ATS is – or is not – legitimate: like effectiveness, legitimacy is a matter of degree. Rather, we have tried to bring out the legitimising process by showing how the Consultative Parties have constantly sought to adapt to internal as well as external pressures on the system. Throughout this book, we have seen that the emergence of environmental protection as a principal *norm* has been important for the acceptance of the ATS. Internally, the minerals ban now prohibits an activity which threatened internal cohesion among the Consultative Parties. Externally, the three normative pillars of the ATS appear to take turns: while during the Cold War, the pillar of peaceful use carried most of the external criticism of the ATS, we have seen that today this task is left primarily to the principle of environmental protection.

Similarly, regarding decision-making *structures*, the ATS has widened in participation, both regarding number and type of actors and their influence. The veil of secrecy which used to shroud the consultative process has gradually been swept aside, and today these deliberations are more transparent than what is common for international management fora. Also, the evolving institutionalisation of the ATS provides outside actors with additional contact points, further enhancing the external legitimacy of the system.

The legitimacy studies in this book have also shown that adaptation of the ATS has always remained within certain *stable limits*, defined by what is internally acceptable among the Consultative Parties themselves. Compatibility with the three principles of the ATS is one such stable feature of internally acceptable solutions. A second is the requirement of conformity with Article IV of the Antarctic Treaty, preserving the *modus vivendi* on the sovereignty issue in Antarctic politics. And as we have seen in all the regimes, a third internal constant is the maintenance and strengthening of the consultative mechanism and hence the preservation of the privileged position of the Consultative Parties. As discussed in Chapter 2, the latter have largely succeeded in consolidating their position, despite procedural concessions to external demands for transparency and participation.

This is how the systemic nature of the ATS influences the legitimacy of individual ATS regimes: if the Consultative Parties, in order to accommodate outside criticism, were to derogate from these three constants, it would severely weaken the internal legitimacy of the entire system. Hence, the legitimacy of the ATS is upheld by a sensitive balance between, on the one hand, adaptation to external challenges, and, on the other, the imperatives of retaining its core internal normative and structural elements.

Despite recent achievements, even today the Consultative Parties face a number of challenges to the effectiveness and legitimacy of Treaty cooperation. The consensually adopted UN resolution on the 'Question of Antarctica' of December 1994, leaves uncertain the future of the General Assembly involvement in Antarctic issues, and is likely to result in a shift of the emphasis to how the ATS shall relate to other international organisations – in particular the United Nations Environment Programme, the International Sea-Bed Authority and the International Maritime Organisation. Implementation of the Protocol is apt to bring to the forefront tensions between environmental protection and the value of scientific freedom in the Antarctic. The question of a secretariat, which has been put on hold due to the fact that most political energy in recent years has been geared to the Protocol, will now reappear. And it is currently unclear how stringent and explicit the Consultative Parties will be in their regulation of the one Antarctic activity currently on the rise, tourism. For this activity to be adequately governed, they may have to move further on more general matters such as liability and insurance, and this is very difficult to do without touching on the sovereignty issue. At the same time, there is little doubt that if the Protocol is not followed up or tourism is perceived as being poorly regulated, external criticism of the ATS may again arise as a serious problem.

In this situation, it is worth noting that the need to balance internal and external accommodation is no novelty to the Consultative Parties: and the political mechanisms we have identified and analysed in this book will remain crucial for their ability to elaborate an effective and legitimate Antarctic Treaty System.

Index

457